INTERNATIONAL
TRAVEL GUIDE

Publishing Director: Cécile Masse
Texts: Dominique Brunet
Translation: Käthe Roth
Art Director: Steve Louis
Production: Studio Lézard
Graphic Artist: Judith Weissmann
Production Assistant: Louise Chabalier

Cover Design:
Pierre Nadeau inc.
Cover Photography :
Réflexion Photothèque (Mauritius/Rossenbach, Mauritius/Vidler, SDP/Jonathan, Volvox, T. Bognar)

Legal deposit: 4th quarter 1995
ISBN 2-89111-651-8

1221 St. Hubert Street, Suite 200
Montréal, Québec H2L 3Y8
Tel.: (514) 286-9747
Fax: (514) 843-7678

INTERNATIONAL TRAVEL GUIDE

TABLE OF CONTENTS

INTRODUCTION

This guide is divided into ten, easy-to-identify sections highlighted with coloured markers. In each section, countries and destinations are presented in geographical order: West to East, starting in the North. This volume answers the Canadian traveller's questions in a simple, straightforward manner. It includes over 275 countries and destinations. In the back of the guide is a useful listing of foreign embassies, consulates and tourist offices in Canada. *The International Travel Guide* can also be used for locating a Canadian consulate or embassy when travelling abroad.

• ***The map:***

A comprehensive map of each country accompanies the text, highlighting the main attractions, making it easy for the reader to pinpoint the destination.

• ***The table:***

A general overview of each destination listing language, land area, the capital, airports, population, religion, visa requirements, driving, cost of living, etc. Continuously up-dated information.

- Where applicable, the Canada Direct™ access code is given, to call abroad *from Canada*, or to call *to Canada* from abroad.
- The stars given to accommodation, restaurants and transportation are subjective and indicate the norms and standards peculiar to each country.
- The tokens represent the cost of living for a Canadian travelling in a given country; low, moderate or high cost of living.
- The best months to visit the country are recommended in terms of the climate and the activities that might interest the Canadian traveller.
- A list indicates the main public holidays of each country.

• ***The text on WHAT TO DO and WHAT TO BUY:***

For each destination, the first part of the text highlights the main cities, the special attractions, the museums, the wildlife reserves and the most interesting sites to be visited. The second part suggests the best buys to be made. Crafts, food, literature, music and paintings are often mentioned to give an overview of the country.

• **Photos** illustrate the culture, geography, wildlife or people of each country.

• A pictogram indicates the **time difference** between Canadian regions and the various destinations.

• Each description includes a **weather chart.**

• Each country is represented by its **flag.**

NOTE :

The information listed in the table applies to Canadian citizens. Passport holders from other countries are advised to check their own requirements.

For a few countries and destinations, some of the information in the table is not available.

HOW TO USE THIS GUIDE

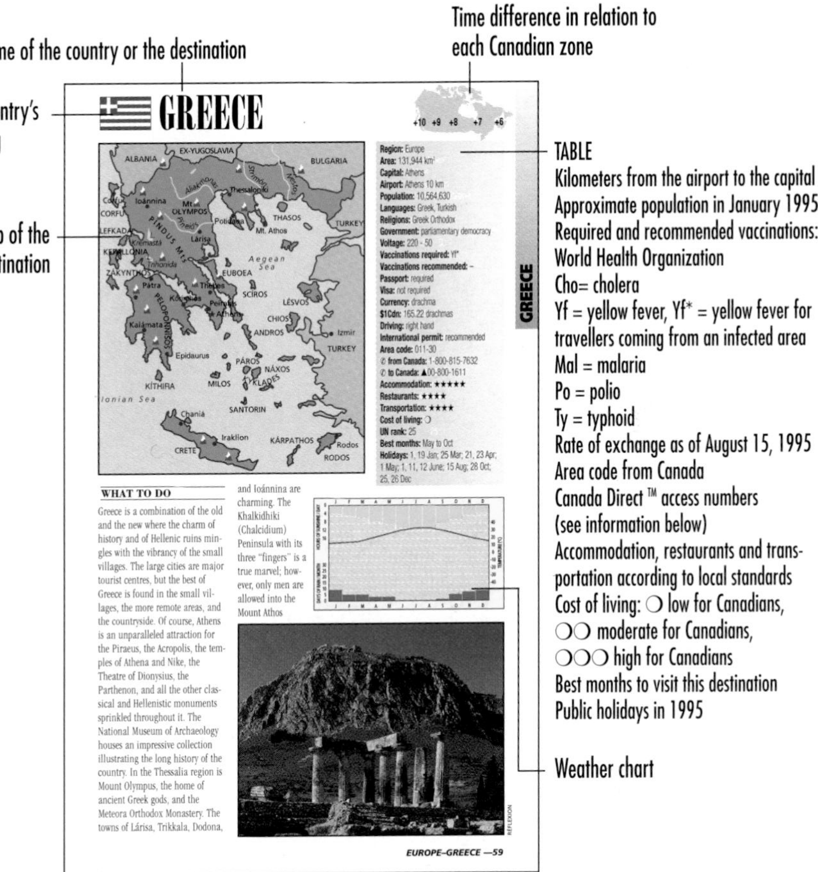

Canada Direct™

Canada Direct™ is a service, available in certain countries, that connects you directly with a Canadian operator, thus avoiding waiting for a connection and language problems with a foreign operator. Simply follow these steps:

1. To call to Canada from abroad, dial the number for the country you are calling from, which follows the pictogram ✆ **to Canada**.
2. Inform the Canadian operator of your intention to either call collect or to charge it to your Calling Card™.
3. Give the operator the area code and telephone number you wish to reach in Canada.

Legend:

■ Service only available on public phones
▲ Public phones require deposit of coin or calling card
◆ Wait for a second dial tone

NOTE: Before leaving Canada, check the Canada Direct™ acces codes of the countries where you plan on going by dialing 1-800-561-8868.

"The most beautiful places
are those we imagine,
and the most charming people
are the ones who live in our dreams.
This is what we think
before seeing the world."

D.B.

J. HUARD

EUROPE

Europe is like a vast linguistic, cultural, and geographic jigsaw puzzle. Travellers can enjoy its many wonders, from Ireland's emerald hills to Greece's ancient ruins, from the splendour of cities like Prague, Amsterdam, Madrid, and Venice, to the natural magnificence of the towering Austrian Alps or the majestic fjords of Norway. Although Europe is the smallest continent, it is one of the most diversified. Tourists can admire the architectural and historical marvels of its many countries, discover different cultures and customs, taste delights such as French *pâté de foie gras* and Scandinavian smoked herring, and sip English tea or Portuguese *vinho verde*. Europe is the dream destination for lovers of art, scenery, and history, as well as for amateur linguists who can practise saying "thank you" in various languages : Bulgarian *(blagodarya)*, Greek *(efharisto)*, Icelandic *(tokk fyrir)*, Rumanian *(multumesc)*, and even Gaelic *(go raibh maith agat)*!

ITALIAN GOV'T TRAVEL OFF.

GREENLAND

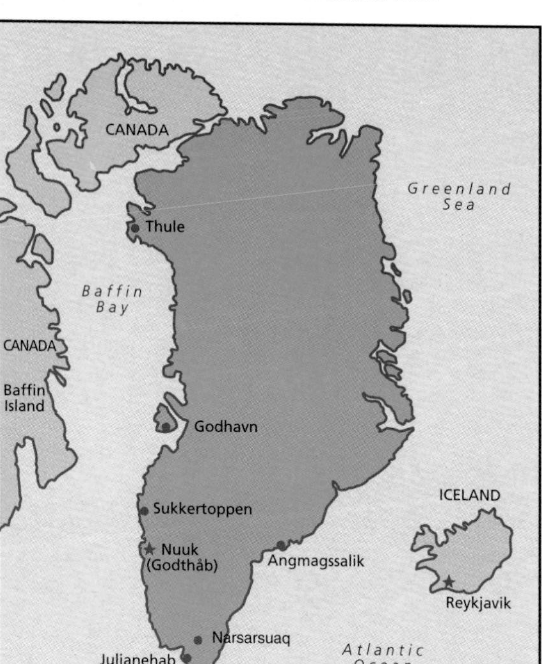

Region: Arctic Ocean
Area: 2,175,600 km²
Capital: Nuuk (Godthåb)
Airport: Nuuk
Population: 57,040
Languages: Danish, Greenlandic
Religion: Lutheran
Government: Danish territory
Voltage: 220 - 50
Vaccinations required: –
Vaccinations recommended: –
Passport: required
Visa: not required
Currency: Danish krone
$1Cdn: 3.97 kroner
Driving: right hand
International permit: recommended
Area code: 011-299
✆ from Canada: –
✆ to Canada: –
Accommodation: ★
Restaurants: ★★
Transportation: ★
Cost of living: ○○○
UN rank: -
Best months: June to Oct
Holidays: 1, 6 Jan; 13, 16, 17 Apr; 12, 25 May; 4, 5, 21 June; 24–26, 31 Dec

WHAT TO DO

Erik the Red discovered this ice-covered land in 985, and dubbed it *Gronland* ("green land" in Danish) to attract colonists. Today, the main attractions are mountain trails where one can study orography and geology, as well as meteorology and glaciology. Greenland is a dream destination for outdoor excursions such as the guided tours to Thule, the northernmost village on the planet. Just north of Thule is the impressive site of Etah, where lie the ruins of the first visits of Eric the Red. Nuuk (Godthåb), Sukkertoppen, and Julianehab are the largest cities. They are located on the southern coast, which is the most ice-free. Of course, in this arctic region, where from December to mid-January night never ends, one meets the warmest people! The magnificence of the midnight sun, which lights the Arctic Circle in the summer, is equalled only by that of the Northern Lights in September.

WHAT TO BUY

Reindeer and sheep farming is the basis of most crafts in Greenland. Wool and fur covers, harpoons and other traditional hunting objects, and soapstone animal sculptures are popular souvenirs. A good camera is nonetheless the best way to preserve the marvelous sights of dog sleds, vast icebergs, and Greenlanders' smiles.

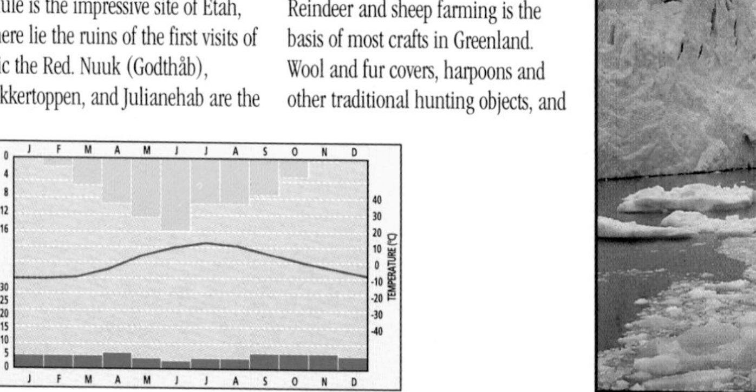

RÉFLEXION

ICELAND

+8 +7 +6 +5 +4

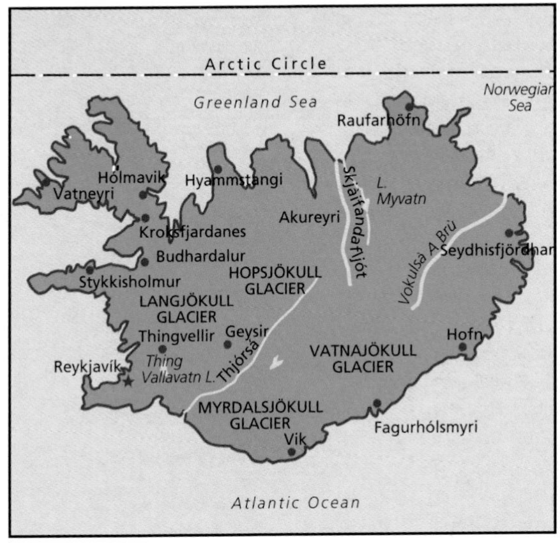

Region: Europe
Area: 103,000 km²
Capital: Reykjavik
Airport: Reykjavik 45 km
Population: 263,600
Language: Icelandic
Religion: Lutheran
Government: parliamentary democracy
Voltage: 220 - 50
Vaccinations required: –
Vaccinations recommended: –
Passport: required
Visa: not required
Currency: Icelandic krone
$1Cdn: 45.31 kroner
Driving: right hand
International permit: recommended
Area code: 011-354
© from Canada: 1-800-463-0085
© to Canada: ▲999-010
Accommodation: ★★★★
Restaurants: ★★★★
Transportation: ★★★★
Cost of living: OOO
UN rank: 14
Best months: June to Oct
Holidays: 1 Jan; 13–17, 20 Apr; 1, 25 May; 4, 5, 17 June; 7 Aug; 25, 26, 31 Dec

WHAT TO DO

Iceland was one of the first countries to establish a legal code: some laws dating from 930 are still in force! The waters of Lake Viti, in the crater of an ancient volcano, are still warm from an eruption that took place more than a century ago. Geysir is the best-known hot-water spring in the world, and the origin of the word "geyser." Iceland is, as its name implies, a country of ice, but it is also one of the warmest geothermic sites on the planet: volcanoes and thermal springs share the countryside with glaciers and grassy fields. The sea and the rivers are part of daily life, both in the city and in the country, to the delight of dedicated salmon fishers. Reykjavik, the northernmost capital in the world, offers many museums, including the Institute of Manuscripts, where works from medieval times are on display. The fjords of the northwest are majestic, and the narrow pass at Thingvellir is a not-to-be-missed wonder of nature. The midnight sun shines on part of the country in the summer, and rain sometimes falls horizontally: amazing natural phenomena!

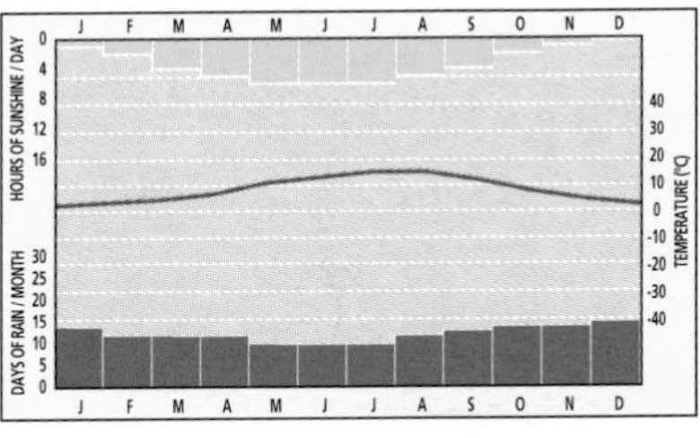

WHAT TO BUY

Brennivin, a schnapps-like drink, frequently accompanies dishes of fresh seafood and fish; shark, a favourite, is prepared in a variety of ways. The local cuisine features unusual flavour combinations, notably in a popular dish of fried soft cheese served with berry jam. Knitwear, sheepskins, and lava sculptures are Icelandic specialties. Visitors must be aware of the nature-protection laws; Icelanders have great respect for nature, and severe fines are levied against offenders.

S. NAIMAN / RÉFLEXION

NORWAY

+9 +8 +7 +6 +5

Region: Europe
Area: 324,220 km²
Capital: Oslo
Airport: Oslo 10 km
Population: 4,314,610
Language: Norwegian
Religion: Lutheran
Government: parliamentary monarchy
Voltage: 220 - 50
Vaccinations required: –
Vaccinations recommended: –
Passport: required
Visa: not required
Currency: Norwegian krone
$1Cdn: 4.51 kroner
Driving: right hand
International permit: required
Area code: 011-47
✆ from Canada: 1-800-363-4047
✆ to Canada: ▲800-19-111
Accommodation: ★★★★★
Restaurants: ★★★★
Transportation: ★★★★
Cost of living: ○○○
UN rank: 5
Best months: June to Oct
Holidays: 1 Jan; 14–17 Apr; 1, 17, 25 May; 4, 5 July; 25, 26, 31 Dec

WHAT TO DO

A country of jagged coasts punctuated with majestic fjords, tundra roamed by herds of shy reindeer, pristine mountains, and the midnight sun, Norway is an ideal country to tour on foot. Visitors need only good hiking boots to see the best of the countryside, from the town of Stavanger to the county of Finnmark. The capital, Oslo, though a large city, is imbued with respect for nature. Its attractions include the Town Hall; the Munch Museum, where Edvard Munch's famous painting *The Cry* is on display; the castle and fort at Akershus, built in 1300; the Viking Museum, with a collection of *drakkars;* and the Vigeland Museum, which displays Gustav Vigeland's sculptures. The southern end of the country is dotted with spa resorts. Some villages have preserved impressive Viking remains, among them Tönsberg, Tjøme, and Larvik. Bergen is one of the country's most beautiful towns; in winter it attracts enthusiastic skiers. Between Bergen and Maloy is the longest fjord in Europe, the Sognefjorden, with the town of Balestrand perched on its edge. The coast of Norway is indented with long, magnificent fjords; the prettiest towns from which to see them are undoubtedly Geiranger and Helleysylt. The Jotunheimen mountain range rises almost 2,000 m in altitude; Gjendesheim is a good stepping-off point for discovering this region. Hikers will especially enjoy the gentle slopes of the Dorve and Rondane national parks. Giske, near Ålesund, is well known for its old Viking chapel. The town of Ålesund offers a maze of small, pretty streets. Nearby, at Runde, is a bird sanctuary, where more than half a million birds nest each year. On the way to Finnmark, travellers pass through Trondheim, Bødo, the Lofoten Islands, and Vesterålen. This region is the Land of the Midnight Sun; farther north, the Northern Lights sparkle over Narvik, Tromsø, and Alta.

WHAT TO BUY

Norwegian cuisine is based on the sea: the *spekesild*, salted herring, and the salmon, fresh or smoked, are delicious. Jarlsberg cheese, *roomegrot* (a dessert made with rice), and reindeer steak are also specialties of the Norwegian menu. A quick hot-dog-like meal, *polse med lompe*, is often accompanied by blond beer. Alcohol is served only after 8:00 p.m. and never on Sundays. Lapp art, silverwork, furs, and knitwear make for lovely souvenirs. The cleanliness of the cities and natural sites is to be noted: let the traveller who dares to drop trash on the ground beware!

SWEDEN

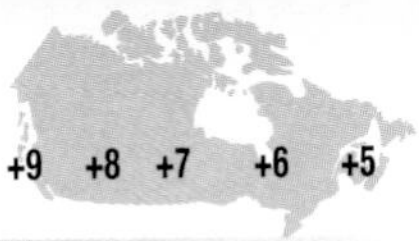

+9 +8 +7 +6 +5

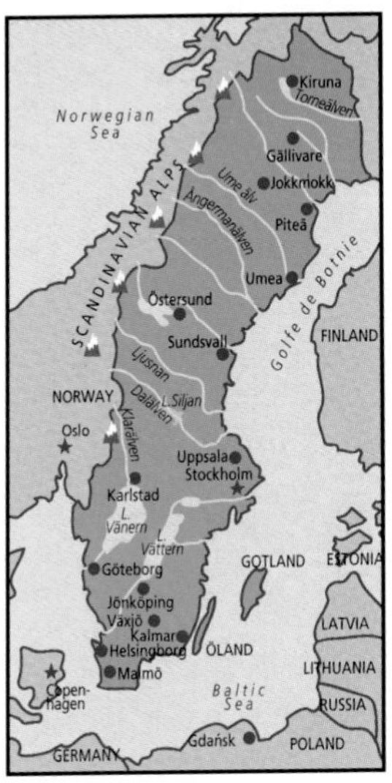

WHAT TO DO

Sweden is on the Scandinavian (Finnoscandia) Peninsula, a region rich in clear rivers and crystalline lakes. The beauty of its unspoiled environment is one of Sweden's major attractions; another is the charm of its people. If you can, visit the area around Dalarö with a Swedish person, who will explain the deeper meaning of *Smultronstallet* ("where wild strawberries grow"). In Göteborg, the *paddans* (waterbuses) tool the canals beneath the city's beautiful bridges. Its many parks and the Botanical Gardens are worth visiting, as are the museums, notably, the Fine Arts Museum. The islands around Kungälv, close to Göteborg, offer a fascinating side trip. Stockholm is built on 14 islands, so the city is steeped in maritime flavour. Gamla Stan, the old section, is definitely worth a visit, as are the Royal Palace; the Storkyrkan Church, which is more than 700 years old; the Riddarholms Kyrkan, where the kings of Sweden are buried; the Stadshuset, or city hall; the Riddarhuset (house of Lords); the many museums; and the National Library. Those who enjoy walking will want to visit some of the numerous islands surrounding the capital, in particular, Djursholm, for its beaches and Drottningholm, for its magnificent castle. Gotland and Öland, in the Baltic Sea, are favourite spots for Swedish vacationers, in part because of their many archaeological sites, including those at Visby, Bro, and Dalhem. Kalmar, in the southeast part of the peninsula, has a cathedral and a lovely twelfth-century castle. Malmö, the capital of the Skåne region, is known for its majestic fort, Gothic church, and superb theatre. Uppsala is a university city with more than 40,000 students. It is also Ingmar Bergman's home town—and a source of his inspiration! The Land of the Midnight Sun, at the northern tip of Sweden, extends from Piteå to Vännäs. Lapland is a unique destination with an unusual landscape: its great plains are dotted with pines and herds of reindeer grazing undisturbed except by the wind and curious tourists!

VOLVOX / RÉFLEXION

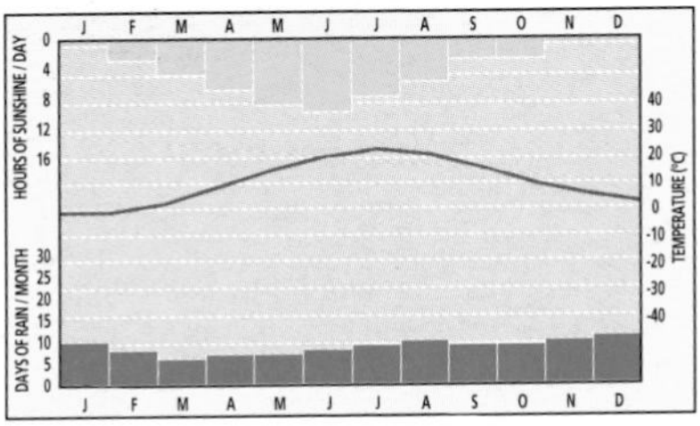

Region: Europe
Area: 449,964 km²
Capital: Stockholm
Airport: Arlanda Stockholm 41 km
Population: 8,778,470
Language: Swedish
Religion: Lutheran
Government: parliamentary monarchy
Voltage: 220 - 50
Vaccinations required: –
Vaccinations recommended: –
Passport: required
Visa: not required
Currency: Swedish krone
$1Cdn: 5.20 kroner
Driving: right hand
International permit: required
Area code: 011-46
✆ from Canada: 1-800-463-8129
✆ to Canada: ▲020-799-015
Accommodation: ★★★★★
Restaurants: ★★★★★
Transportation: ★★★★★
Cost of living: ○○○
UN rank: 4
Best months: June, July, Aug
Holidays: 1, 6 Jan; 14, 16, 17 Apr; 1, 25 May; 4–6, 24 June; 4 Nov; 25, 26 Dec

WHAT TO BUY

Gravlax (smoked salmon), reindeer meat, and smoked eel are typical Swedish foods, and *knackebrod*, a very dense bread, is a staple in the diet. *Akvavit* and schnapps are the most popular alcoholic beverages. The crafts of the Dalarö region, including *Dalahast* (hand-painted wooden horses), embroideries, and woven fabrics, are unique. The paintings of Carl Larsson, inspired by life in Dalarö, are famous and also pricey, but good reproductions are available.

FINLAND

+10 +9 +8 +7 +6

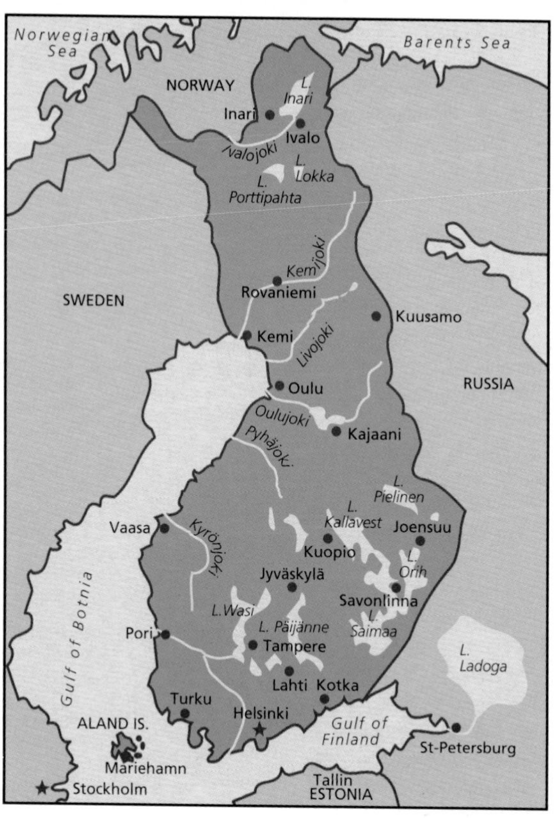

Region: Europe
Area: 337,032 km²
Capital: Helsinki
Airport: Helsinki 19 km
Population: 5,068,940
Languages: Finnish, Swedish
Religion: Lutheran
Government: parliamentary democracy
Voltage: 220 - 50
Vaccinations required: –
Vaccinations recommended: –
Passport: required
Visa: not required
Currency: Finnish mark
$1Cdn: 3.08 marks
Driving: right hand
International permit: required
Area code: 011-358
© from Canada: 1-800-363-4035
© to Canada: ▲9800-1-0011
Accommodation: ★★★★★
Restaurants: ★★★★★
Transportation: ★★★★
Cost of living: ○○○
UN rank: 16
Best months: June, July, Aug
Holidays: 1, 6 Jan; 14, 16, 17 Apr; 1, 25 May; 4, 5, 23 June; 4 Nov; 6, 24, 25 Dec

WHAT TO DO

Finland, one of the countries on the Scandinavian Peninsula (Finnoscandia), is a paradise of lakes, forests, and cities with a pure and simple architecture. Finland is one nation that can boast of keeping its fauna and flora intact. Helsinki, the capital, called the "white city of the North," provides a good example: the elegance of its neoclassical buildings and the order and harmony of its inhabitants quickly impress visitors. Respect for the environment is discernible in all things. Saunas, a Finnish invention, are found everywhere, especially in Lahti and Jyväskylä, on the shores of Lake Païjanne. In Jyväskylä, the Aalto Museum of Architecture is a prime attraction. An opera festival is held every July in Savonlinna. Kuopio is a lovely winter-sports resort with many charming painted-wood houses. The soap factory in Oulu is a curiosity, but this town is best known for its cross-country-ski race. On the island of Aland, the main form of transportation is the bicycle. Lapland is far to the north, but the beauty of its glaciers and its six-week-long mantle of darkness in winter enchant those who venture there.

WHAT TO BUY

Baaris are not bars, but little cafés that serve light meals like *kalakukko*, a fish pâté traditionally eaten with vodka or *lakka*, a cloudberry liqueur. Oulu soap, Helsinki porcelain, *ryijy* rugs, furs, and leather goods make good gifts. The crafts of Lapland, Lutheran religious art, and icons are also very popular.

P. HALLY

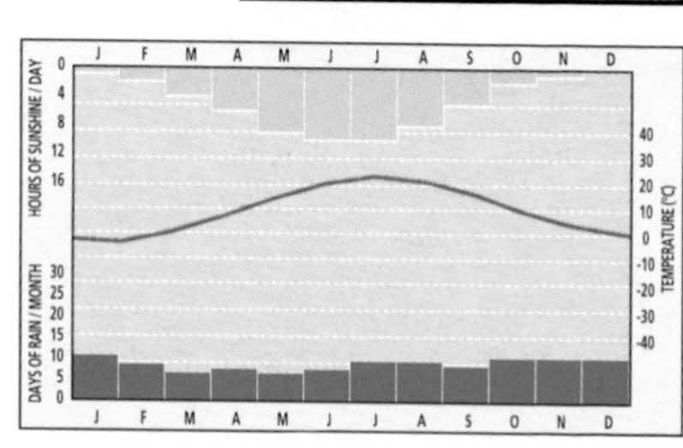

IRELAND

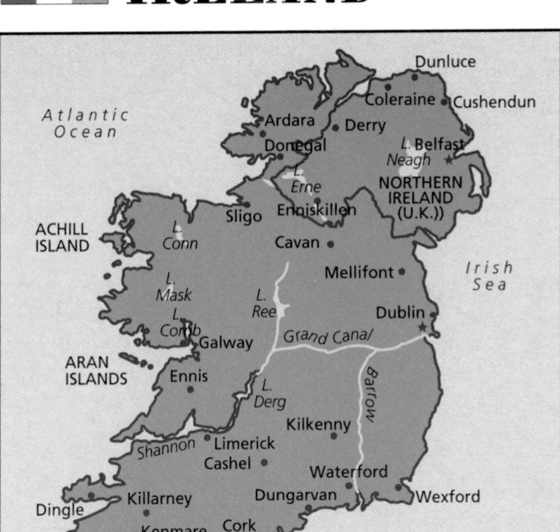

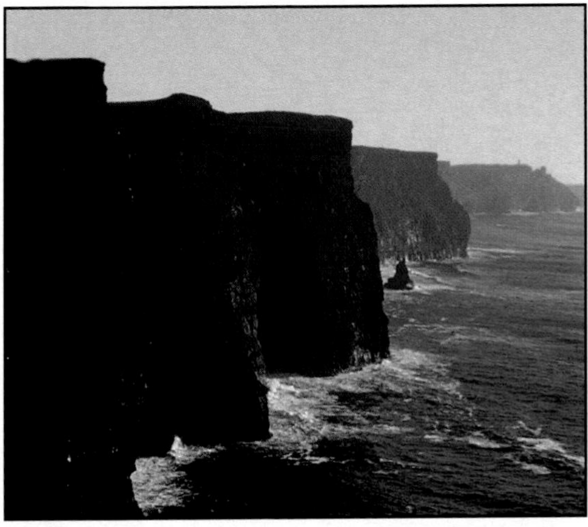

IRISH TOURIST BOARD

WHAT TO DO

The Eriann (the namesakes of Eire), the Celts, and the Gaels were all charmed by the green pastures and steep sea cliffs of Ireland. Today, visitors are still drawn to the splendour of the countryside, the tranquillity of fields of clover scattered with Celtic crosses, the baahing of thousands of sheep, and the rolling sea. The Republic of Ireland is divided into 26 counties, the most popular among tourists being the ones bordering the ocean. The capital, Dublin, is on the Bay of Dublin and at the mouth of the Liffey River. The city is known best for its university, Trinity College, the alma mater of Wilde, Moore, Burke, and Swift; the old library containing the very beautiful *Book of Kells*, one of the oldest existing manuscripts, dating from the eighth century; and the National Museum,

+8 +7 +6 +5 +4

IRELAND

Region: Europe
Area: 70,280 km²
Capital: Dublin
Airport: Dublin 9 km
Population: 3,539,300
Languages: Gaelic, English
Religion: Catholic
Government: parliamentary democracy
Voltage: 220 - 50
Vaccinations required: –
Vaccinations recommended: –
Passport: required
Visa: not required
Currency: Irish pound
$1Cdn: 0.45 pound
Driving: left hand
International permit: recommended
Area code: 011-353
✆ from Canada: 1-800-463-2050
✆ to Canada: 1-800-555001
Accommodation: ★★★★★
Restaurants: ★★★★★
Transportation: ★★★★★
Cost of living: ❍❍
UN rank: 21
Best months: May to Sept
Holidays: 1, 2 Jan; 17 Mar; 14, 16, 17 Apr; 5 June; 7 Aug; 30 Oct; 25, 26 Dec

NORTHERN IRELAND

Region: Europe
Area: 14,121 km²
Capital: Belfast
Airport: Dublin
Population: 1,601,200
Languages: Gaelic, English
Religions: Protestant, Catholic
Government: British possession
Voltage: 220 - 50
Vaccinations required: –
Vaccinations recommended: –
Passport: required
Visa: not required
Currency: pound sterling
$1Cdn: 0,46 pound
Driving: left hand
International permit: recommended
Area code: 011-232
✆ from Canada: 1-800-463-2050
✆ to Canada: 1-800-555001
Accommodation: ★★★★
Restaurants: ★★★★
Transportation: ★★★★
Cost of living: ❍❍
UN rank: 21
Best months: May to Sept
Holidays: 1 Jan; 13 Mar; 14, 16, 17 Apr; 1, 29 May; 10 June; 28 Aug; 25, 26 Dec

IRELAND

which offers a magnificent collection of Celtic artifacts. Cork is the second-largest city, famous for its Gothic cathedral St. Finbarr, and Blarney Castle, which is said to be inhabited by fairies. The jagged Munster Peninsula features archaeological sites, castles, beaches, and bays; Kenmare, Killarney, and Dingle are the main towns of the region. County Mayo is the least well known, yet the beauty of its Achill Island alone makes the trip to Ireland worthwhile. The famous Aran Islands and the Connemara and Cliffden coasts are stunning. For sandy beaches, travellers must visit County Waterford, particularly at Tramore and Dungarvan. The very pretty town of Kilkenny is home to the famous Smitswick Brewery. Cashel, in the heart of Tipperary, is one of the most important medieval sites in Ireland, with the Cross of St. Patrick and the country's first church, dating from the sixth century. NORTHERN IRELAND has received a lot of bad press, but it seems that the peace process between the I.R.A. and England is well under way. There have been only two incidents in the British province in recent months. All signs point to Ulster becoming a tourist attraction for those who like windswept moors and magnificent blue-tinted mountains. Belfast, the capital, is very lively, thanks in part to Queen's University. It is the Sperrin Mountains, veined with rushing streams, that give the towns of Strabane and Dungiven their special cachet. The islands on lakes Erne and Fermanagh are paradise for fishers. At Legananny, tourists can see the dolmens called the "Tomb of the Giants". In the north, the Giants' Causeway is a lunar landscape of rocks emerging from the ocean to scale the cliffs. The Dunluce Castle and the entire Derry region are also worth a visit.

WHAT TO BUY

Fleadhs are fairs where small orchestras, accompanied by the Irish *dodhran* (a large tambourine), play Irish tunes. The lyre, the country's emblem; the *Tara brooch*, a brooch with Celtic motifs; and Celtic crosses are very popular purchases. Irish engagement rings make original gifts. Ireland is synonymous with Guinness, a full-bodied dark beer brewed in Dublin, and Irish whisky (which is different from scotch). *Bannocks* and *barmbracks*, fruit-and-spice breads, are specialties of Northern Ireland. Beautiful hand-knit pullovers in off-white wool from the Aran Islands will always bring the Irish coast to mind.

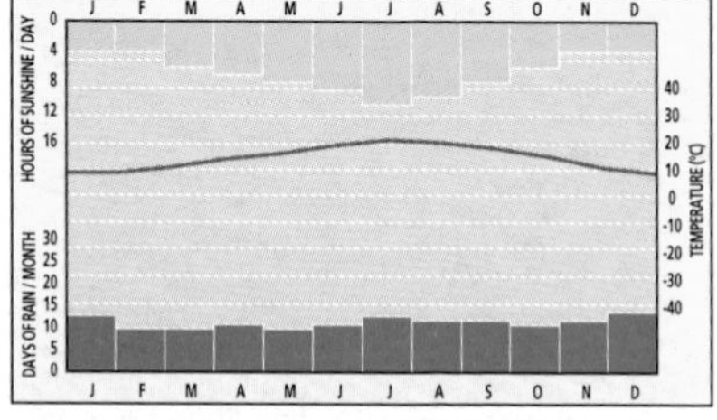

NORTH IRELAND TOURIST BOARD

GREAT BRITAIN

+8 +7 +6 +5 +4

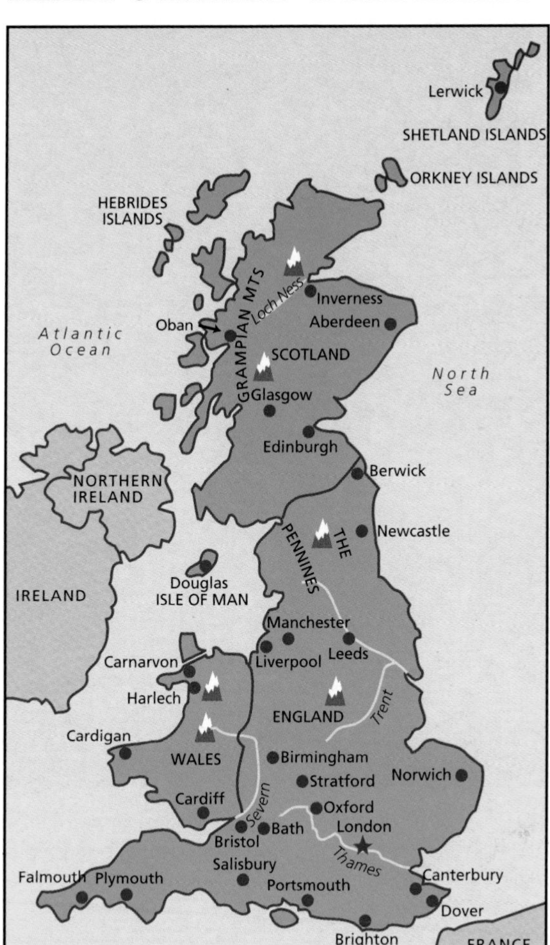

Region: Europe
Area: 231,295 km² (not including Ulster)
Capital: London
Airport: London Heathrow
Population: 58,135,110
Language: English
Religion: Protestant
Government: parliamentary monarchy
Voltage: 220 - 50
Vaccinations required: –
Vaccinations recommended: –
Passport: required
Visa: not required
Currency: pound sterling
$1Cdn: 0.46 pound
Driving: left hand
International permit: recommended
Area code: 011-44
✆ from Canada: 1-800-363-4144
✆ to Canada: 0-800-89-0016
Accommodation: ★★★★★
Restaurants: ★★★★★
Transportation: ★★★★★
Cost of living: ○○○
UN rank: 10
Best months: May to Oct
Holidays: 1 Jan; 13 Mar; 14, 16, 17 Apr; 1, 29 May; 10 June; 28 Aug; 25, 26 Dec

WHAT TO DO

Once inhabited by the Celts, the British Isles have remained independent, in part because of their separation from Continental Europe. It is this unique colour that thousands of tourists come to discover every year. Great Britain, which comprises England, Wales, Scotland, and Northern Ireland, is not a country stuck in the past; the English are always searching for novelty and often initiate the latest trends. A simple stroll through London proves this. Cheek by jowl with ladies sipping afternoon tea, one sees young people demonstrating for the right of homosexual couples to adopt children. And while some are enjoying a game of cricket, others are taking in Stephen Frears's latest film. This capital city features beautiful monuments and attractions, the most famous among them the Tower of London, the Tower Bridge, St. Paul's Cathedral, Westminster Palace and Abbey, Big Ben, Buckingham Palace, the Thames, the City, Fleet Street, the Templars' Church, the artsy districts of Soho and Chelsea, Piccadilly Circus, Trafalgar Square, and Hyde Park. An entire day or more is needed to take in the very beautiful Victoria and Albert Museum, as well as the National Gallery, the British Museum, the Tate Gallery, and the National

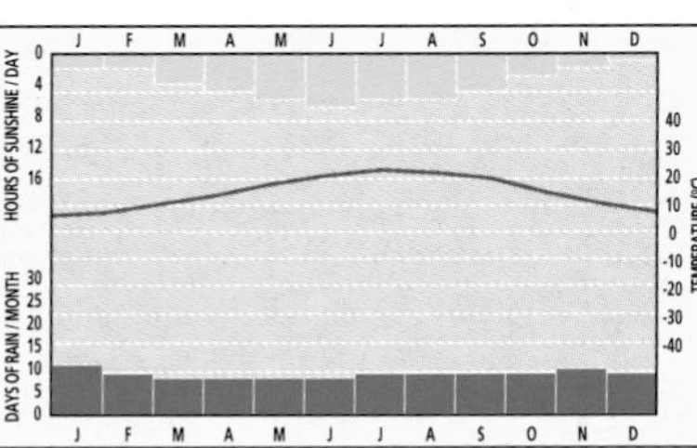

T. BOGNAR / RÉFLEXION

Portrait Gallery. Typical London sights are the double-decker buses; the tea rooms, especially the one in Brown's Hotel, which is often honoured with Queen Elizabeth's presence; the smoky pubs; and the great department stores. Just outside London, Windsor Castle and the remarkable St. George's Chapel are must-sees. Visiting Greenwich, on the International Date Line, is a unique experience. The reputation of the English countryside is well known: the delights of the green pastures and rolling hills are rivalled only by the splendid towns and charming villages along the way. Canterbury is home to the most impressive cathedral in the country. Rye is a typical little village with cobblestone streets. The pleasant Sussex coast has hiking trails at Eastbourne and Beachy Head, among other locations. Lovers of history and legends will want to visit the Wiltshire and Hampshire regions, where one finds Stonehenge, Wells, and Glastonbury, where, it is said, King Arthur and his wife Guinevere are buried, and the Bath region, where signs of extra-terrestrial visitors are said to have been found ... Cornwall, at the western tip of the peninsula, is worth a detour. The towns of Oxford and Cambridge are best known for their universities and the diploma ceremonies draw numerous spectators. Shakespeare lives on each year at Stratford-on-Avon during the theatre festival bearing his name. Chester, south of Liverpool, is a medieval town known also for its Tudor houses. The largest cathedral in the country is in York, a town nestled in the peaceful, green hills of the Yorkshire Dales. The Lake District, the Pennines, and Moors National Park are treats for nature-lovers. A major tourist stop is the ruins of Hadrian's Wall, built between the mouth of the Tyne and the Solway Firth. Wales is a country distinct from England by more than name alone: it is more mountainous, it has its own language, and Welsh customs are diametrically opposed to those of the English. The Welsh lan-

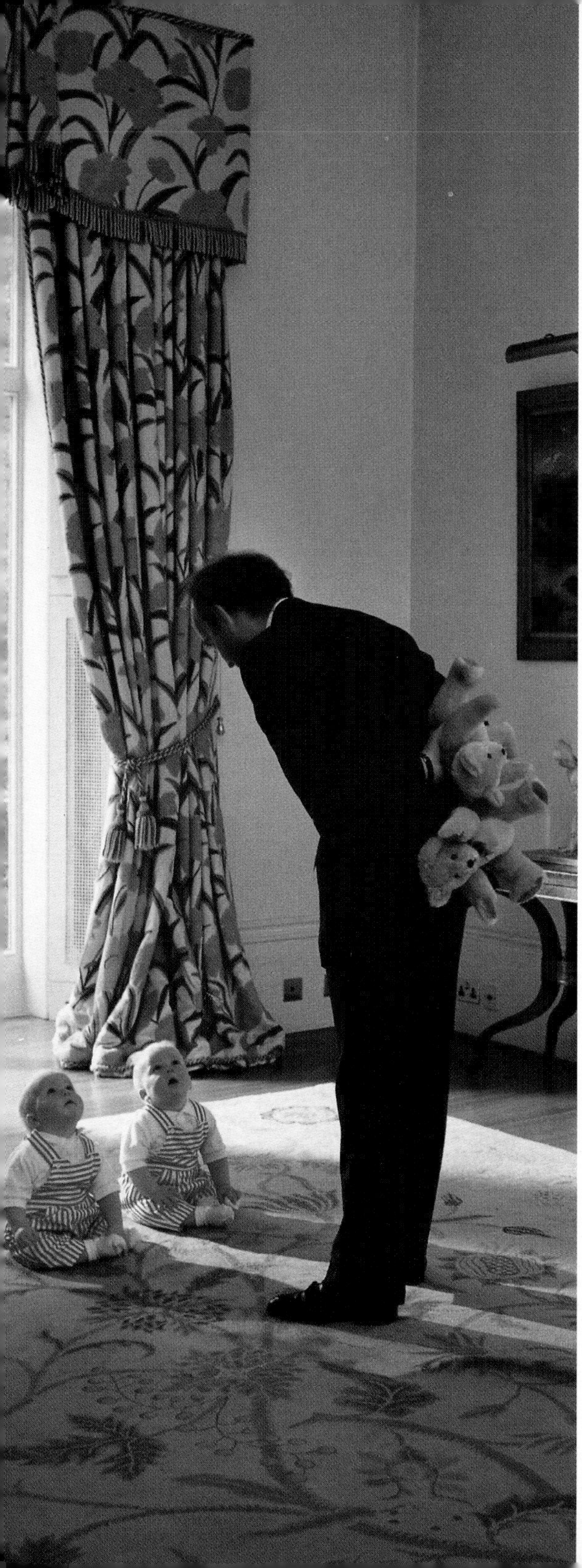

guage is heard more often these days, a result of rising nationalism, and so Aberystwyth is pronounced whistling the vowels through the teeth! (The word "Welsh" means "foreigner" in Old English.) Mount Snowdon, the castles at Carnarvon and Harlech, and the cities of Cardigan and Cardiff are stunning. The Wnion Valley and the town of Dolgelley are worth a visit, as is the Dee Valley, well known for the ruins of the Denbigh Fortress. Bangor is a seaside resort whose fine beaches are set against dramatic coastal cliffs. The Isle of Man is yet another special region, with its own language—Mannish, or Manx—and a pace of life from another era. In Scotland, nationalism is also present in everyday life. The clans would like to repossess this magnificent land, from the Lowlands to the Highlands. The medieval city of Edinburgh, the gateway to Scotland and home of Macbeth, is known for its fortified castle, its Gothic cathedral, and its numerous museums, notably the National Gallery. The Edinburgh Festival is a unique cultural event. Glasgow is a city brimming with interest and energy, if only because of its student population of 40,000. Inverness, the capital of the Highlands, is near the mysterious Loch Ness, and the drawbridge castles of the region are frequently shrouded in thick fog. Tourists to Scotland can get into the spirit of things by following the Whisky Trail, and stopping in at the nation's seven largest distilleries. Scotland's golf links are legendary, particularly the one at St. Andrews. Oban and the small holy island of Iona, where the Druids are said to have met for the last time, are also worth a visit. The Hebrides, Orkney Islands, and Shetland Islands enchant those ready to face a brisk climate to savour the breathtaking countryside.

WHAT TO BUY

One wag had it that if one wanted to eat well in Great Britain, one had to eat three breakfasts a day. This cynic surely had not tasted scones with Devonshire cream and jam, nor Stilton cheese steeped in port, not to mention *bara brith*, a Welsh fruit-and-nut bread, or the Scottish *haggis*, a mixture of meats and oatmeal. Then there are the beers, whiskies, marmalades, puddings, and teas. Knits, tweeds, cardigans, and jacquards are good buys. Scottish kilts, cricket sets, and brass rubbings (transferred from engraved copper plates) are popular souvenirs. Lewis Carroll's tales, nursery rhymes, *Guignol's Band* by L.-F. Céline, and *Memory of an English Village* by ethnologist Roland Blythe are all recommended reading.

J. HUARD

DENMARK

Region: Europe
Area: 43,070 km²
Capital: Copenhagen
Airport: Copenhagen
Population: 5,187,830
Language: Danish
Religion: Lutheran
Government: parliamentary monarchy
Voltage: 220 - 50
Vaccinations required: –
Vaccinations recommended: –
Passport: required
Visa: not required
Currency: Danish krone
$1Cdn: 3.96 kroner
Driving: right hand
International permit: recommended
Area code: 011-45
✆ from Canada: 1-800-363-4045
✆ to Canada: ▲80-01-00-11
Accommodation: ★★★★★
Restaurants: ★★★★★
Transportation: ★★★★★
Cost of living: ○○○
UN rank: 15
Best months: June, July, Aug
Holidays: 1 Jan; 13, 16, 17 Apr; 12, 25 May; 4, 5 June; 25, 26 Dec

WHAT TO DO

The Danes, descendants of the Vikings and heirs to a fondness for good living, treat their country with unequalled respect. Denmark's mosaic of 406 islands presents travellers with an infinite variety of countrysides, beaches, and coastal villages. Sjælland, the best-known island, is home to the nation's capital, Copenhagen. Touring the city by foot or bike, visitors will discover the famous statue of the Little Mermaid, inspired by a Hans Christian Andersen story, Rosenborg Castle, Radhuspladsen Square, and Amalienborg Palace. An evening at the Copenhagen Royal Ballet provides long-lasting memories. Farther north, Elsinor (Helsingør) is known for its fortress, where Shakespeare set the action of *Hamlet.* The towns of Hillerød and Roskilde have marvellous castles and cathedrals. Fyn (Fünen), known as the "Garden of Denmark," has some of the most beautiful castles in the country. Definite musts on any itinerary are Odense (the birthplace of Andersen), Nyborg, Valdemar, and Egeskov. The island of Bornholm, in the Baltic Sea, features the world-famous earthenware workshops and one of the oldest castles in northern Europe. Jylland (Jutland), the large peninsula in the northern part of the country, has many archaeological sites, including Ålborg and Århus. Anyone interested in the Vikings will want to put on lots of warm clothes and tour this large area, rich in the ruins and history of the "warriors of the sea." From Skagen, an old town at the northern tip of Denmark, one can see across the North Pole! The Faeroe Islands belong to Denmark, even though they are in the mid-Atlantic, more than 1,300 km from the capital. This archipelago comprises 17 islands, 50,000 inhabitants, and more than 70,000 sheep! It's worth visiting for the splendour of the countryside and the hospitality of the residents of Tórshavn, the capital, on the island of Strømø.

WHAT TO BUY

The light and tasty Danish beer is often quaffed with a *bakkebof*, a big, delicious sandwich. *Akavit*, a schnapps-like liquor, is served with the typically Danish *smorrebrod*. Danish design is known for its pure, simple lines: the cutlery, art objects, and jewelry are particularly lovely. The Royal Cophenhagen and Bing & Grondal porcelain manufacturers are famous worldwide. Furs, woollens, and the crafts of the Faeroe Islands are unusual. To get a taste of the country, movie-lovers can see *Babette's Feast*, based on a Karen Blixen story.

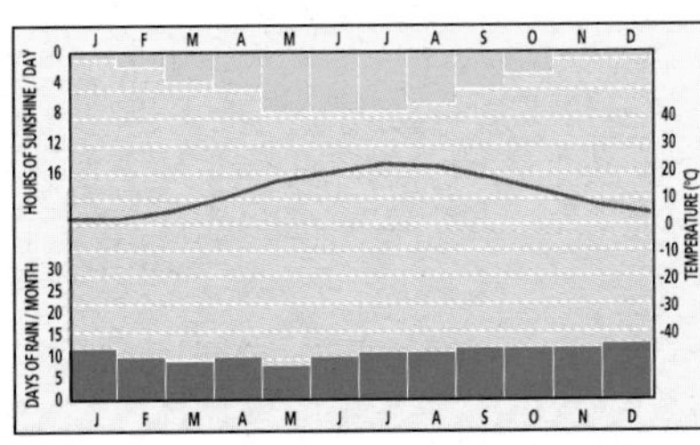

BELGIUM

+9 +8 +7 +6 +5

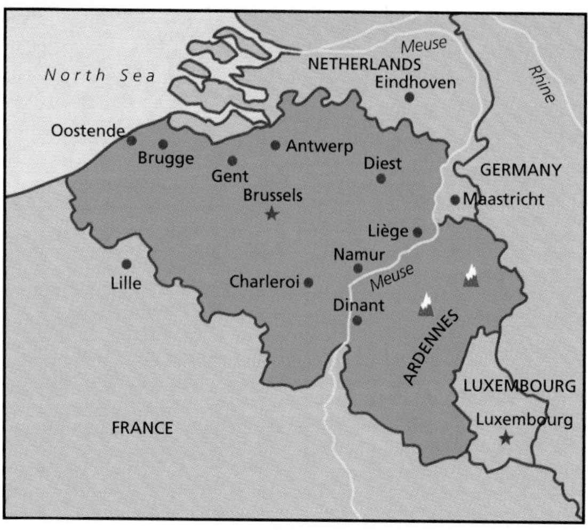

Region: Europe
Area: 30,507 km²
Capital: Brussels
Airport: Brussels 13 km
Population: 10,062,840
Languages: Flemish, French, German
Religion: Catholic
Government: parliamentary monarchy
Voltage: 220 - 50
Vaccinations required: –
Vaccinations recommended: –
Passport: required
Visa: not required
Currency: Belgian franc
$1Cdn: 20.25 francs
Driving: right hand
International permit: recommended
Area code: 011-32
✆ from Canada: 1-800-363-4032
✆ to Canada: ▲0-800-1-0019
Accommodation: ★★★★★
Restaurants: ★★★★★
Transportation: ★★★★★
Cost of living: ○○○
UN rank: 13
Best months: May to Sept
Holidays: 1, 2 Jan; 16, 17 Apr; 1, 25 May; 4, 5 June; 21 July; 15 Aug; 1, 13 Nov; 25, 26 Dec

WHAT TO DO

When King Baudouin I died in 1993, he left his country in deep mourning. Belgians, and especially residents of Brussels, are very attached to the monarchy, and Baudouin represented a link between traditional Belgium and the new Europe, as well as between the two Belgiums: Wallonia and Flanders. The language issue is increasingly delicate and must not be taken lightly: travellers should make sure to address residents in an appropriate language. But this should not keep them from appreciating the beauties of Belgium, especially its capital, Brussels, with its main square surrounded by gold-roofed

J. HUARD

Gothic buildings and the famous Manneken-Pis. Place Royale, the fifteenth-century city hall, and the old city's small, gabled houses rival the interest of the Béguin Church, the Museum of Art and History, and the Museum of Classic Art. Bruges, a very romantic city with its canals and Gothic architecture, is one of the most picturesque stops in Flanders. In Gent (Gand), tourists discover the splendours of the Renaissance, and Anvers is paradise for lovers of Rubens's work. The Ardennes region, whose name comes from the Celtic word *Ar-Denn*, meaning "the oaks," is laced through with moors and forests that are perfect for hiking. Flanders offers beautiful beaches at Oostende, Knokke-le-Zoute, and Zeebrugge. In Wallonia, the cities of Leuven (Louvain), Liège, and Tournai feature medieval churches, castles, and a variety of museums, while Dinant has a magnificent town hall and a prehistoric cave at Mount Fat. In Diest, the fifteenth-century houses have been beautifully preserved, and the fabric market testifies to the town's past as a trade centre.

WHAT TO BUY

Well known for the quality and variety of its beers (more than 355 brands!), Belgium also produces divine chocolate and serves up tasty waffles. The national dish, found on menus everywhere, is mussels and fries served with mayonnaise. Bruges lace, particularly Flanders point lace, is of unparalleled quality. Anvers crystal and diamonds are known throughout the world. Belgians have a great sense of humour, and visitors will appreciate the work of Belgian cartoonists as much as the natives do. Finally, no visitor to Belgium should come away without listening to the songs of the great Jacques Brel.

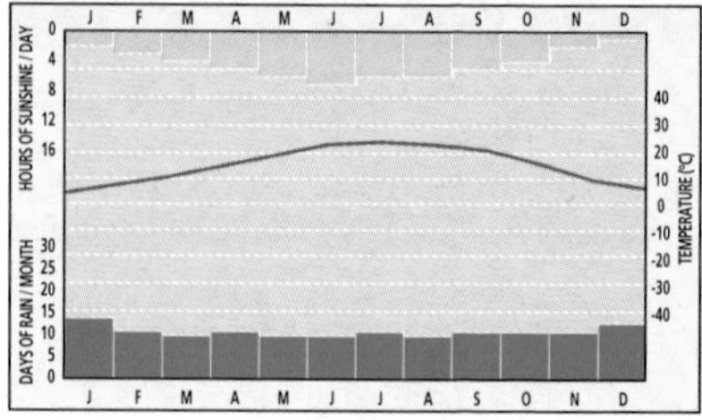

NETHERLANDS

+9 +8 +7 +6 +5

Region: Europe
Area: 41,548 km²
Capital: Amsterdam
Airport: Schipol 15 km
Population: 15,367,930
Language: Dutch
Religions: Catholic, Protestant
Government: constitutional monarchy
Voltage: 220 - 50
Vaccinations required: –
Vaccinations recommended: –
Passport: required
Visa: not required
Currency: guilders
$1Cdn: 1.15 guilders
Driving: right hand
International permit: recommended
Area code: 011-31
✆ from Canada: 1-800-363-4031
✆ to Canada: ▲06-022-9116
Accommodation: ★★★★★
Restaurants: ★★★★★
Transportation: ★★★★★
Cost of living: ❍❍❍
UN rank: 9
Best months: June to Oct
Holidays: 1, 2 Jan; 14, 16, 17, 30 Apr; 5, 25 May; 4, 5 June; 25, 26 Dec

WHAT TO DO

The Kingdom of the Netherlands is small, but the polders are reclaiming more and more land from the sea; they have already reclaimed almost half of the country. Thus, the dikes and dried-out marshes, the canals and the heaths, are as much part of the Dutch countryside as the windmills, tulip fields, and fishing ports. Completing the picture of the Netherlands is the contrast between medieval castles and modern cities.

The country's 12 provinces are all very scenic, and some seem to have stepped right out of a Dutch painting. Amsterdam, the capital, can be travelled by boat via its network of canals; on the list of prime attractions are the Royal Palace, the Munt Tower, the Tower of Tears, the Ancient Church (built in 1306), Anne Frank's house, the Rijksmuseum,

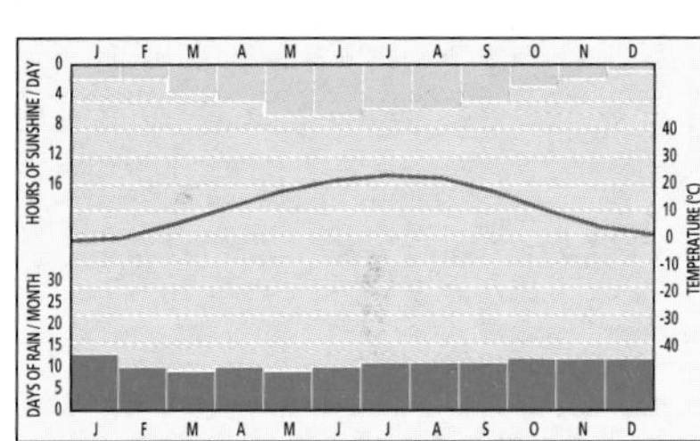

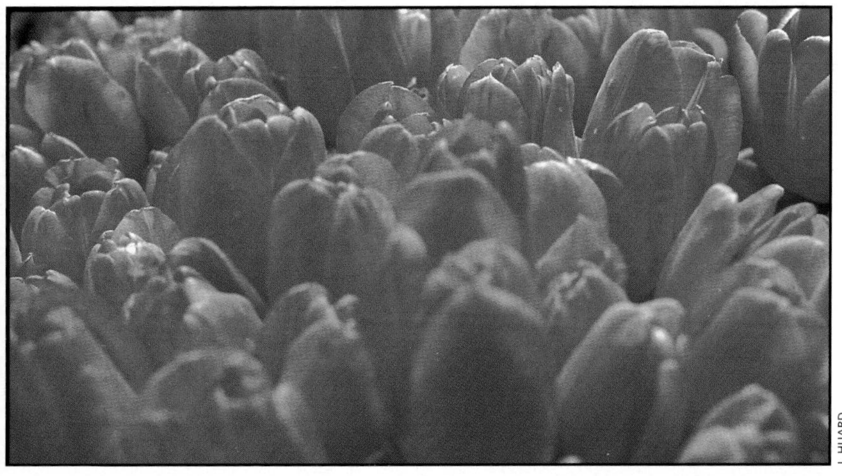
J. HUARD

J. HUARD

the Van Gogh Museum, and Rembrandt's house. The curious will want to venture into the Nieuwmarkt neighbourhood, near Oude Kerk, while others are best advised to avoid this area because of the pickpockets and prostitutes. The town of Aalsmeer is well known for its flowers, Alkmaar for its cheese market, Haarlem for its Frans Hals Museum, and Bergen and Egmond for their beaches. In southern Holland are Rotterdam and The Hague, two peaceful and very elegant cities; The Hague has the honour of being home to many consulates and the International Court of Justice. The tulip fields in Keukenhof Park are glorious from mid-April to mid-May.

Utrecht, in the heart of a spectacular forested region, has many attractions, among them the old canal, St. Michael's Cathedral, and the university. In the provinces of Zeland, North Brabant, and Holland, visitors will find small fishing ports, the very beautiful church in Den Bosh, and the catacombs at Valkenburg. Hoge Veluwe National Park, Arnhem's windmills, and the Van Gogh collection at the Kröller-Müller Museum are the main attractions of the Gelderland region. Prehistoric tombs have been found near Assen, a region tailor-made for bicycling. Friesland is a world apart, with its own language, Friesian; be sure to visit if you like water sports.

WHAT TO BUY

The delicious gouda and edam cheeses are just a couple of the many dairy products produced in the Netherlands. The black licorice popular among fishermen is typically Dutch. The beer and *Jenever*, a perfumed apéritif, are the most common alcoholic beverages. Delft china, Tilburg leather, figurines, and reproductions of works by the great masters such as Van Gogh, Rembrandt, and Vermeer are highly prized. Beware: very strict laws regulate the exportation of flower bulbs.

GERMANY

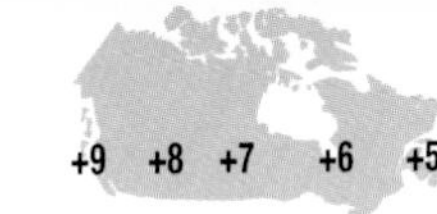

Region: Europe
Area: 357,325 km²
Capital: Berlin
Airport: Berlin 8 km, Frankfurt 12 km
Population: 81,087,500
Language: German
Religions: Protestant, Catholic
Government: parliamentary democracy
Voltage: 220 - 50
Vaccinations required: –
Vaccinations recommended: –
Passport: required
Visa: not required
Currency: mark
$1Cdn: 1.02 marks
Driving: right hand
International permit: recommended
Area code: 011-49, 37
✆ from Canada: 1-800-465-0049
✆ to Canada: ▲01-3000-14
Accommodation: ★★★★★
Restaurants: ★★★★★
Transportation: ★★★★★
Cost of living: ○○○
UN rank: 11
Best months: May to Oct
Holidays: 1, 6 Jan; 28 Feb; 1 Mar; 14, 16, 17 Apr; 1, 25 May; 4, 5 June; 15 Aug; 3, 31 Oct; 24–26 Dec

WHAT TO DO

The reunification of Germany has been widely celebrated as one of the most important events of recent decades, in spite of the many resulting socio-economic problems. Travellers can finally visit the marvels of the eastern part of the country without experiencing the disgrace of the "wall of shame." Berlin, once again Germany's capital, is experiencing a rebirth. The city has many attractions, including the Alexanderplatz; the Tiergarten; the Ku'Damm (the famous shopping street); the Brandenburg Gate; the Reichstag; the Charlottenburg Castle; the Pergame, Dahlem, and de Bode museums; the National Gallery; the Opera; and the many theatres, including the Bertolt Brecht Theatre. Many of the latest trends in fashion and the arts spring from Berlin's active and fertile night life. The very pretty medieval town of Goslar is the entranceway to the Harz, a rural region of forests and mountains perfect for outdoor sports. The Germany of the Brothers Grimm and Goethe is found among the castles of Wernigerode, Halle, Wittenberg,

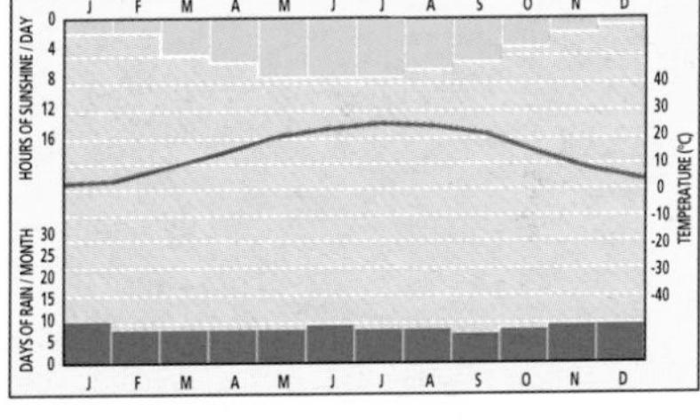

MAURITIUS / BECK / RÉFLEXION

J. HUARD

and Eisenach (the town where J.S. Bach was born). The "Romantic Road" through Bavaria, featuring castles along the way from Würzburg through Dinkelsbuhl to Nordlingen, can be followed to the music of Haydn, Mozart, Beethoven, Schumann, Mahler, and Brahms. Every year, Bayreuth hosts a Wagner festival. Munich, the capital of Bavaria, is the German city richest in museums and cultural sites, including the old *Pinakotek*, the National Museum of Bavaria, the Residenz Theatre, and the old Wittelsbach Palace—though it is best known for its *Oktoberfest*, when the barrels of delicious German beer overflow. Travellers can follow the Danube and the Rhine through a series of towns and villages with abundant charm. Include on the itinerary: Friburg im Breisgau in the Black Forest, the spa town of Baden-Baden, Lindau, and the very romantic Heidelberg. This town in the Neckar Valley is bathed in the sweet scent of vineyards. The large cities of Bonn, Koblenz, Köln (Cologne), and Düsseldorf offer many tourist attractions. Farther north, Hamburg is a must-see for its magnificent churches, the remains of the Hanse town, its harbour, lively Reeperbahn Street, and the museums of fine arts and decorative arts. In northern Germany, the Frisian Islands are known for their spas and hot springs—another aspect of the German countryside not to be missed.

WHAT TO BUY

The toys of Nuremberg are well known, as are the porcelain of Bayreuth, the eau de Cologne, the wines of the Rhine and Moselle valleys, and the Black Forest cakes. Among the gourmet delights are Hamburg's specialty, eel soup, and the four-o'clock *Kaffee und Kuchen* (coffee and cake). *Wurst* (sausages) and cold cuts are part of the German daily diet. Bavarian musical instruments and the famous Black Forest cuckoo clocks are unique. The crafts of the Bremen region include toys, hand-painted wooden objects, and magnificent traditional costumes. Recordings by the major German philharmonic orchestras are top quality.

POLAND

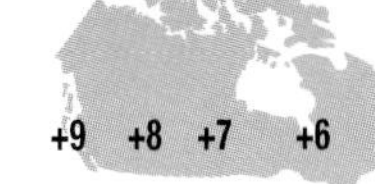

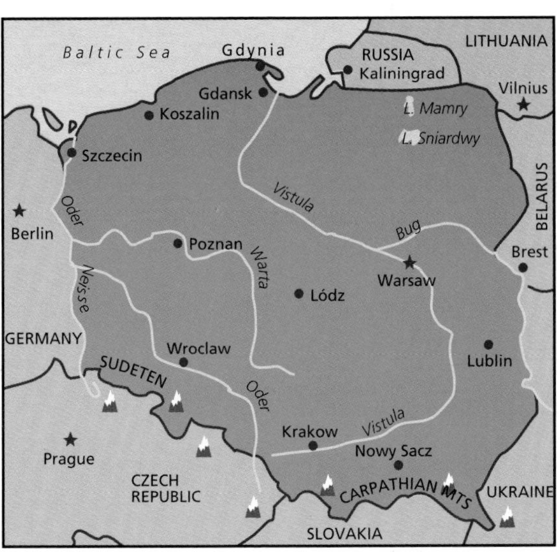

Region: Europe
Area: 312,683 km²
Capital: Warsaw
Airport: Warsaw 10 km
Population: 38,654,570
Language: Polish
Religion: Catholic
Government: parliamentary democracy
Voltage: 220 - 50
Vaccinations required: –
Vaccinations recommended: –
Passport: required
Visa: required
Currency: zloty
$1Cdn: 17,482.38 zlotys
Driving: right hand
International permit: required
Area code: 011-48
✆ from Canada: –
✆ to Canada: 00-104-800-118
Accommodation: ★★★★
Restaurants: ★★★★
Transportation: ★★★
Cost of living: ❍
UN rank: 49
Best months: May to Sept
Holidays: 1 Jan; 16, 17 Apr; 1, 3 May; 15 June; 15 Aug; 1, 11 Nov; 25, 26 Dec

POLAND

WHAT TO DO

Poland is paradise for music lovers. In addition to the Chopin Festival in Dszniki in August and the Warsaw Autumn Festival, there are 20 philharmonic orchestras, located throughout the country, jazz festivals, modern music performances, operas, and ballets. The Sculpture Gallery in Warsaw presents classical concerts every day, a practice that isn't unique to the capital. Warsaw (Warszawa) was completely rebuilt after the war, but the old town (*Stare Miasto*) has kept its soul intact. The Wilanow and Lazienkowski palaces, the Narodowe Museum, the Royal Palace, Chopin's house, and the Academy of Fine Arts are along the Royal Road, or *Trakt Krolewski*. The main attraction of the region around the town of Gdansk is the beaches on the Baltic Sea, while the towns of Sopot and Gdynia have very pleasant spa resorts. The Copernic Road leads to Malbork, where one can visit the castle of the Order of Teutonic Knights, dating from the fourteenth century. Krakow is a jewel of eastern Europe: its buildings miraculously escaped the destruction of the Second World War. The *Stare Miasto*, with its old market, is fascinating, and Jagiellonian University, founded in 1364, is one of the oldest in eastern Europe. The region also offers much less lighthearted stops, namely, the infamous Auschwitz and Birkenau concentration camps, which celebrated the fiftieth anniversary of liberation this year. From the town of Zakopane, tourists can discover the magnificent High Tatra region in the Carpathian Mountains.

WHAT TO BUY

Bigos (a stew of game and cabbage), *barszcz* (borscht), a beet soup, *pierogi* (potato or cheese dumplings), and flavoured vodka are Polish specialties. Notable among the numerous handicrafts available are beautiful hand-painted Easter eggs and woven shawls. The crafts of the Zakopane region, jewelry of Orneta, amber of the Baltic coast, and blown glass are the pride of Poland.

P. HALLY

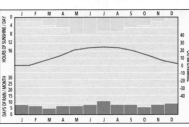

J F M A M J J A S O N D
HOURS OF SUNSHINE / DAY: 0 4 8 12 16
TEMPERATURE (°C): 40 30 20 10 0 -10 -20 -30 -40
DAYS OF RAIN / MONTH: 30 25 20 15 10 5 0
J F M A M J J A S O N D

CZECH REPUBLIC

+9 +8 +7 +6 +5

Region: Europe
Area: 78,864 km^2
Capital: Prague
Airport: Prague 16 km
Population: 10,408,280
Languages: Czech, German
Religions: Catholic, Protestant
Government: parliamentary democracy
Voltage: 220 - 50
Vaccinations required: –
Vaccinations recommended: –
Passport: required
Visa: not required for less than 30 days
Currency: Czech koruna
$1Cdn: 19.06 korunas
Driving: right hand
International permit: required
Area code: 011-42
✆ from Canada: 1-800-233-5612
✆ to Canada: 00-42-000-151
Accommodation: ★★★★
Restaurants: ★★★★
Transportation: ★★★★
Cost of living: ○○
UN rank: 27
Best months: May to Sept
Holidays: 1 Jan; 16, 17 Apr; 1, 9 May; 5, 6 July; 29 Aug; 28 Oct; 24–26 Dec

WHAT TO DO

The Czech Republic is dotted with picturesque towns, stately castles, and peaceful villages. Bohemia, Moravia, and Silesia, the country's main regions, each offer excursions to fortified castles, mountain paths that are great for hiking, and spa towns for relaxation; the Czech Republic is well known for its hot springs, especially those in Karlovy Vary, Frantiskovy Lázne, Podebrady, Mariánské Lázne (better known as Marienbad), and Luhacovice. The very beautiful Krkonosé National Park, in the Giant Mountains, is dominated by Mount Snezka, with an altitude of 1,602 m. The historic centres of Cesky Krumlov, Telc, and, of course, Prague attract travellers in search of turreted castles, creaking drawbridges, and lush gardens. Residents of Prague, the capital, are particularly proud of their city; some feel that it is even more beauti-

P. HALLY

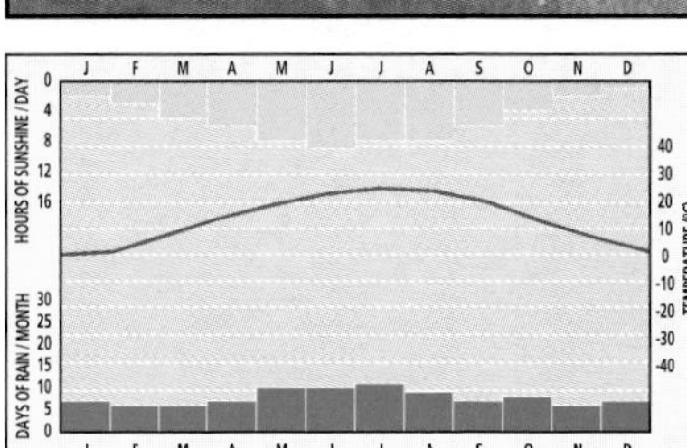

ful than Paris and Rome. It is overflowing with magnificent monuments: the Hradcany, the old royal palace; the Charles Bridge over the lovely Vltava River; St. Guy Cathedral; the "golden alley" where, it is said, alchemists met; Malá Strana, or the old town; Cernín Palace; the clock tower in the Old Town square; Franz Kafka's house; St. James Church, appreciated by Mozart for its fine acoustics; and the National Museum, which displays the works of the Great Masters. The music festival in the spring draws visitors from around the world, and the surrounding region is perfect for hiking. The Karlstein Castle, a few kilometres from Prague, has handsome Gothic murals. In Hradec Králove, the prime attractions are the musical-instrument factories and Saint-Esprit Cathedral. Plzen (or Pilsen) is well known for its brewery, and the walled town of Cesky for its lovely market square. Moravia has a unique culture, which can be appreciated both in the Moravian Museum in Brno and in the bistros of Ostrava. Olumouc, the historical capital of Moravia, has many ancient monuments that are worth a visit, like the stupendous cathedral dating from 1131, the archbishop's palace, and the Baroque churches. The vineyards of the Znojmo region are found in the deep Dyje Valley, one of the warmest parts of the country. In the summer, numerous orchestras give open-air concerts, performing the works of Czech composers, including Antonin Dvorák and Leos Janácek. With all these attractions, the Czech Republic has become a top-notch European tourist centre.

WHAT TO BUY

The Czech national dishes are *veprové*, grilled pork, and *knedlîky,* little patties stuffed with meat. Plzen's beer and *slivovice*, a plum liqueur, are delicious. The wine of South Moravia, especially from the cellars of Petrov, is worth a taste. Bohemian crystal and porcelain have a world-wide reputation. Embroidery from Moravia and musical instruments from Hradec Králové are also very popular. Milan Kundera's excellent novel *The Book of Laughter and Forgetting* transports readers to Bohemia. In July, tourists can enjoy the sight of Moravia's folk costumes, with their many streaming ribbons, at the Stráznice Folklore Festival.

SLOVAKIA

+9 +8 +7 +6 +5

SLOVAKIA

Region: Europe
Area: 49,036 km²
Capitals: Bratislava
Airport: Bratislava 12 km
Population: 5,403,510
Languages: Slovak, Hungarian
Religions: Catholic, Protestant
Government: parliamentary democracy
Voltage: 220 - 50
Vaccinations required: –
Vaccinations recommended: –
Passport: required
Visa: not required for less than 30 days
Currency: Slovak koruna
$1Cdn: 21.45 korunas
Driving: right hand
International permit: required
Area code: 011-42
✆ from Canada: –
✆ to Canada: –
Accommodation: ★★★
Restaurants: ★★★
Transportation: ★★★
Cost of living: ○○
UN rank: 27
Best months: May to Sept
Holidays: 1 Jan; 16, 17 Apr; 5, 6 July; 29 Aug; 1 Sep; 1 Nov; 24–26 Dec

J.HUARD

WHAT TO DO

Near the Austrian border and straddling the Danube, Slovakia's capital, Bratislava, is a charming city of churches, museums, and Gothic monuments. Founded in the tenth century, it has played an important part in the history and economy of Central Europe. Today, a prime attraction is the town hall, which has been transformed into a museum with an excellent collection of Slovak art. A music festival takes place every year in the magnificent castle called Bratislasvsky hrad. The Carpathian Mountains take up much of Slovakia's territory, and the countryside of deep valleys and mountain ranges is extremely beautiful. The highest point of the Lower Tatras Mountains, Mount Dumbier, at 2,043 m, is a great spot for hiking and skiing. Zilina is a good stepping-off point for visiting this region. Banská Bystrica and Kosice are charming cities. In the latter, make sure to visit St. Elizabeth Cathedral, built in the fourteenth century, St. Michael's Chapel, and the many old buildings. The spas of the Greater Tatras Mountains are attracting increasing numbers of visitors to take advantage of the curative waters and admire the superb mountainous countryside. History buffs will want to see the town of Komárno, with its Roman ruins and fortifications built in the sixteenth century, and the city of Nitra, for its old cathedral and many Baroque buildings.

WHAT TO BUY

Delicious plum liqueur is served at any opportunity. Bratislava's fabrics have a very good reputation. Slovak glass blowers and ceramicists have a perfect mastery of their respective arts. Marvellous evenings of Gypsy entertainment, to the tune of violins, will be your best memory.

CHANNEL ISLANDS

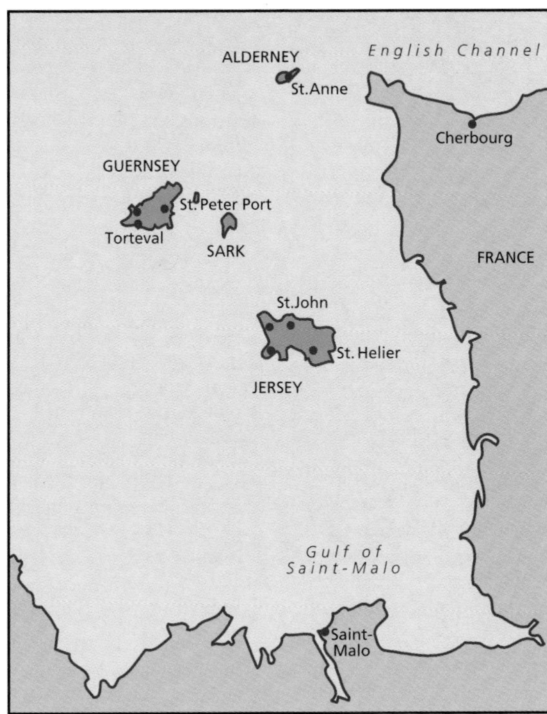

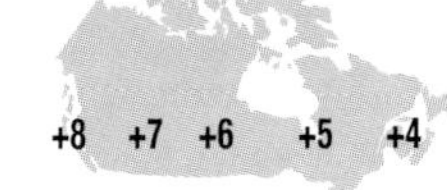

CHANNEL ISLANDS

Region: Europe
Area: 311 km²
Capital: –
Airport: Sark
Population: 250,000
Language: English
Religion: Anglican
Government: British dependencies
Voltage: 240 - 50
Vaccinations required: –
Vaccinations recommended: –
Passport: required
Visa: not required
Currency: Guernsey and Jersey pound
$1Cdn: 0,46 pound
Driving: left hand
International permit: recommended
Area code: 011-44
✆ **from Canada:** 1-800-363-4144
✆ **to Canada:** 0-800-89-0016
Accommodation: ★★★
Restaurants: ★★★
Transportation: ★★★
Cost of living: ○○○
UN rank: –
Best months: June to Oct
Holidays: 1 Jan; 13 Mar; 14, 16, 17 Apr; 1, 29 May; 10 June; 28 Aug; 25, 26 Dec

WHAT TO DO

The British Channel Islands (Les Normandes) are in the English Channel, closer to France than to

BRITISH TOURIST AUTHORITY

Great Britain. In spite of this proximity, English is the language used in Guernsey, Jersey, Alderney (Aurigny), and Sark (Sercq). Norman is still spoken, but it is on its way to extinction. Must-sees on Guernsey, are the house where Victor Hugo lived in St. Peter Port, and the Le Bouet and St. Sampson castles. Also worth a visit are the island's dolmens and prehistoric ruins, which can be reached by bicycle, the main form of transportation. On Jersey, the St. Aubin and St. Brelade beaches are known for their fine sand. The mysterious white menhir (stone monument) near St. Ouen and other archaeological sites will draw ancient-history lovers. The Elizabeth Castle and Regent Fort, in St. Helier, are other attractions on this island. Sark and Alderney, much smaller islands, also have interesting geological sites, notably, the Cut, a natural 91-km-long causeway on Sark.

WHAT TO BUY

Jerseys, cashmeres, and other knitwear are the main trade of Jersey. Blown glass and pottery, along with whisky and cider, also make very good souvenirs. Philatelists will appreciate the Channel Islands stamps, and numismatists will want to collect the currency struck on each island. The British pound sterling is also used on the islands.

FRANCE

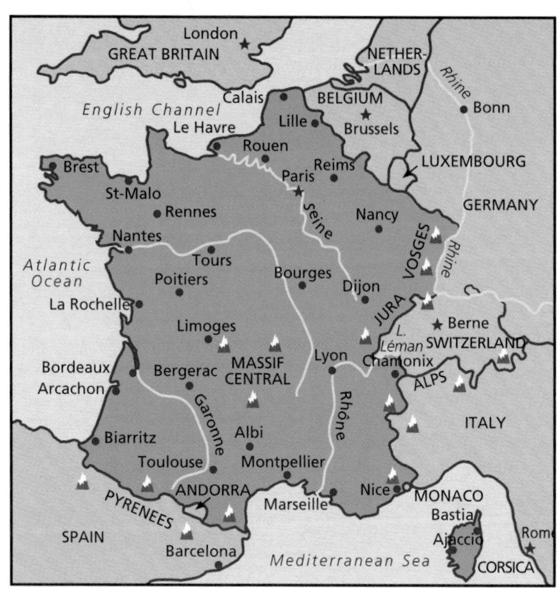

Region: Europe
Area: 547,030 km²
Capital: Paris
Airport: Roissy-C.DeGaulle 30 km, Orly 15 km
Population: 57,840,450
Language: French
Religion: Catholic
Government: parliamentary democracy
Voltage: 220 - 50
Vaccinations required: –
Vaccinations recommended: –
Passport: required
Visa: not required
Currency: French franc
$1Cdn: 3.52 francs
Driving: right hand
International permit: recommended
Area code: 011-33
✆ from Canada: 1-800-363-4033
✆ to Canada: ▲19◆00-16
Accommodation: ★★★★★
Restaurants: ★★★★★
Transportation: ★★★★★
Cost of living: ○○○
UN rank: 6
Best months: Apr to Nov
Holidays: 1 Jan; 16, 17 Apr; 1, 8, 25 May; 4,5 June; 14 July; 15 Aug; 1,11 Nov; 25 Dec

WHAT TO DO

From Île Saint-Louis in Paris, to the villages of Brittany and Provence, or to the Vosges and La Gironde, the beautiful country of France comprises 22 regions, each of which has attractions galore to bring tourists back year after year. The historic sites, museums, scenery, wines, and cheeses of these regions are quite simply unique. In other words, France is not just Paris, although the capital offers an incredible range of attractions, including Île de la Cité, Notre Dame Cathedral, the Louvre (one of the best museums in Europe, with da Vinci's *La Joconde* and *Venus de Milo*, among others), the Tuileries, the Marais, the Beaubourg Museum, Les Halles, the Arc de Triomphe, the Champs Élysées, Montmartre, the Sacré Cœur Basilica, and, of course, the Eiffel Tower. And then there are the smaller museums featuring the works of Renoir, Cézanne, and Monet; the tranquil avenues in the Père Lachaise Cemetery; the little stalls on rue Mouffetard; the many inviting quays, perfect to stroll along; and smoke-filled cafés where one sips

J. HUARD

J. HUARD

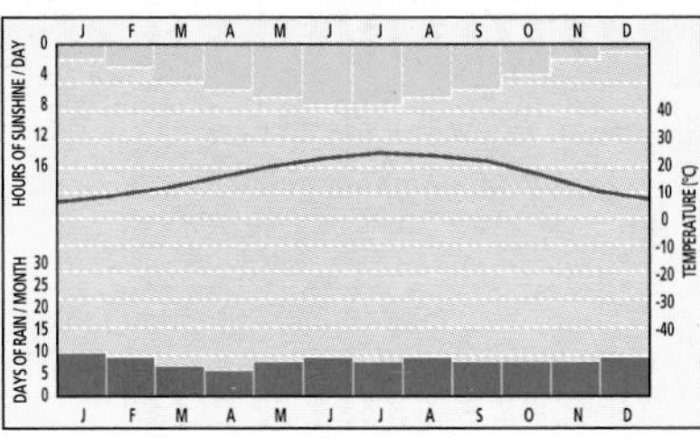

the traditional "demi" of beer. To know exactly what's going on in Paris, pick up *Pariscope* or *L'Officiel des spectacles*, where the most recent show at the Moulin Rouge is listed alongside schedules for local cinemas and tours of the Paris sewer system! Normandy and Brittany are dream destinations for amateur historians, with attractions ranging from the cloisters to the Jeanne d'Arc Tower in Rouen, to the battlefields of Dieppe and the megaliths at Carnac, to the Benedictine abbey in Mont Saint-Michel. The Loire Valley is a must-see for lovers of sumptuous castles: between Blois and Saumur, the castles in Amboise, Azay le Rideau, Chinon, Chambord, and Chenonceaux are particularly interesting. The cathedrals in Chartres and Bourges, along with the very beautiful Cistercian abbey in Noirlac, are the jewels of central France. All of France, from Champagne to the Rhône Valley, is heaven for the amateur oenophile, but the vineyards of the Bordeaux region are the most popular. In the city of Bordeaux, travellers should see the Tour Saint-Michel, Stock Market Square, and Place des Quinconces. Dordogne is known mostly for its prehistoric cave paintings at Lascaux, but Bergerac, Périgueux, and the *Landes* (sandy moors) around Arcachon are also worth seeing. In the Midi-Pyrénées, Toulouse, "La Ville Rose," is full of art; especially beautiful is the Romanesque basilica of Saint-Sernin. The tiny villages of Saint Cirq Lapopie and Figeac, the hillside town of Rocamadour, and Albi, with its famous Toulouse-Lautrec Museum, are also major tourist stops. The Cathar castles in Corbières, Carcassonne, Perpignan, Narbonne, and the mountainous Lozère region are as wonderful as the pretty city of Nîmes, with its arenas and the Roman Castellum. The main centre in Provence is Marseille, with its bustling port, but there are also Aix; Avignon, with its fabulous Palais des Papes; the Roman remains at Orange; Grasse, the city of perfumes; and the artists' town of Saint Paul de Vence. On the Côte d'Azur are Nice, Cannes, and Saint-Tropez (worth visiting in the winter for its dramatic skies). In the Rhône-Alps region, Lyon offers Roman ruins and the lovely basilica of Saint Martin d'Ainay. Grenoble and Roanne are also worth a visit. Food lovers be warned: Roanne is home to one of France's best restaurants. Skiers can head for the Alps, especially Mont-Blanc at Chamonix, where they can warm up after a day on the slopes with a Savoyard cheese fondue. The wine route in Burgundy winds through Meursault, Volnay, Beaune, and Nuits Saint George. The Fontenay Abbey, the Beaune Hospice, and the Cluny Museum are stunning. In Alsace are the Strasbourg Cathedral, the Rohan Castle, and the famous covered bridges leading to Lorraine, where visitors can admire the Metz windows of the Cathedral, designed by Marc Chagall. Then comes the gor-

M. JOLIBOIS

geous cathedral in Reims, in the Champagne region, where the eponymous nectar flows... In a "tour of Gaul," one must not forget the towns of Calvados, Rennes, and Saint-Malo, as well as the medieval town of Dinan and the island of Sein. Nantes, Angers, Tours, Poitiers, Cognac, and La Rochelle are popular destinations, as are the charming towns Cahors, Padirac, Bayonne, Montpellier, Clermont-Ferrand, Aurillac, Murat, Dijon with its famous Palais de Ducs, Vézelay with its Madeleine Basilica, Besançon, Arbois, and Vesoul. There are many parks and nature reserves in France, from the beautiful beaches of Biarritz to the forests of Jura, via the Dauphiné Mountains and the sheer sea cliffs of Finistère. France is also very interesting below the surface: spelunking is very popular in the Pyrenees, Provence, and Dordogne. The EuroDisneyland, near Reims, shows yet another facet of this fascinating country.

WHAT TO BUY

France is known the world over for its high-quality gastronomy—wines and liqueurs, cheeses and pastries—and every region has its specialty: Normandy camembert and calvados, Nantes muscadet, Bourges *forestines*, Cambray mint humbugs, the cognac of ... Cognac, Gers *foie gras*, Périgord prune brandy, Toulouse's violet candies, Roquefort cheese, Dijon mustard, Épernay champagne, Strasbourg sauerkraut, Lyon's cold cuts, Aix's marzipan lozenges, Marseille's bouillabaisse, Saint-Tropez's *tropézienne*, the Loire's Port-Salut, and much more. Some people even plan their trips as wine- or cheese-tasting tours! Cornouaille's fine china, Brittany's embroidery, Angers's tapestries, Angoulême's glassware, Limoges's porcelain, and Baccarat's crystal also make wonderful souvenirs. France, of course, also offers a wide choice of designer clothes, leather goods, and high-quality perfumes. French literature is bursting with novels, essays, and poems relating the exciting history of the country, but the masterpieces are undoubtedly *Les Rois maudits* by Maurice Druon and *Astérix and Obélix Tour Gaul*!

LIECHTENSTEIN

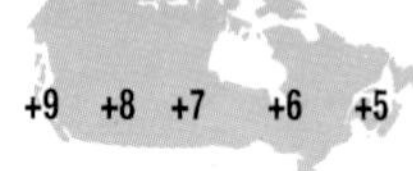

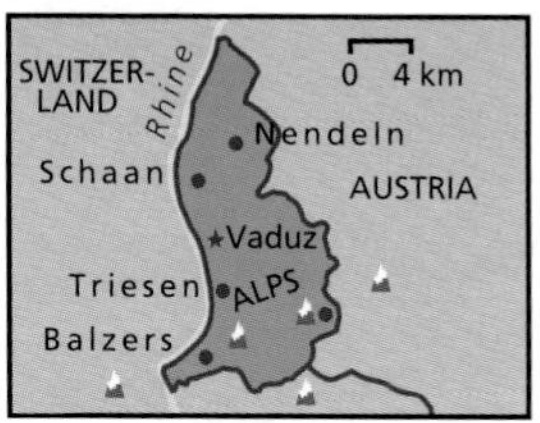

WHAT TO DO

Liechtenstein is one of the smallest countries in the world—but one of the richest; its capital, Vaduz, hosts the head offices of many international companies. Liechtensteiners are known for their respect for beauty, and their mountains and forests remain pristine. Vaduz, located on the right bank of the Rhine, is dominated by the impressive Liechtenstein Castle, home of the royal family. The National Museum and the Post Office Museum are worth seeing. The medieval castle in Balzers, the Neu Schellenberg Fort, and the very pretty chapel in the village of Bendern seem to be straight out of a fairy tale. The village of Triesenberg is a good stepping-off point for the ski resorts. In summer, skiing is replaced by hiking, rock climbing, and horseback riding as the main leisure activities in this sumptuous country.

WHAT TO BUY

Liechtenstein's postage stamps will enchant philatelists. The ceramics of Schaan and the wines of the Rhine Valley, as well as figurines, cuckoo clocks, and mechanical pieces such as music boxes, are Liechtensteinian specialties. Travellers are expected to respect the environment and the customs dictating restraint and discipline in public places.

Region: Europe
Area: 160 km²
Capital: Vaduz
Airport: Zürich (Switzerland) 100 km
Population: 30,290
Language: German
Religion: Catholic
Government: constitutional principality
Voltage: 220 - 50
Vaccinations required: –
Vaccinations recommended: –
Passport: required
Visa: not required
Currency: Swiss franc
$1Cdn: 0.85 franc
Driving: right hand
International permit: required
Area code: 011-41
✆ from Canada: –
✆ to Canada: ▲155-8330
Accommodation: ★★★★★
Restaurants: ★★★★★
Transportation: ★★★★★
Cost of living: ○○○
UN rank: –
Best months: May to Oct
Holidays: 1, 6 Jan; 2 Feb; 19, 25 Mar; 14, 16, 17 Apr; 1, 25 May; 4, 5, 15 June; 15 Aug; 1 Nov; 8, 25, 26, 31 Dec

LUXEMBOURG

+9 +8 +7 +6 +5

WHAT TO DO

Luxembourg has always had to protect its borders against invaders from both east and west, and so it abounds in mountainside fortresses and citadels. The country has beautiful forests and mountains, vineyards, romantic rivers, and flower-filled valleys. The capital of the duchy, the town of Luxembourg, has fascinating historic remains. Also worth a visit are the Casemates du Bouc, subterranean tunnels carved by hand out of rock in the eighteenth century. The Moselle Valley, the castles along the Esch River, the famous feudal castle in Clervaux, the Benedictine abbey in Echternach, and the spa in Mondorf-les-Bains are also worthwhile stops. Ettelbrück is a good stepping-off point for discovering the magnificent countryside of Luxembourg.

WHAT TO BUY

Tourists can buy luxury items, such as perfumes, furs, and jewelry, as well as arts and crafts, pottery, and porcelain. Moselle wine and blond beers often accompany elegant dishes such as fresh trout fished in Luxembourg's clear waters.

Region: Europe
Area: 2,586 km²
Capital: Luxembourg
Airport: Luxembourg
Population: 401,900
Languages: French, German
Religion: Catholic
Government: constitutional monarchy
Voltage: 220 - 50
Vaccinations required: –
Vaccinations recommended: –
Passport: required
Visa: not required
Currency: Luxembourg franc
$1Cdn: 20.95 francs
Driving: right hand
International permit: recommended
Area code: 011-352
✆ from Canada: 1-800-463-3780
✆ to Canada: 0-800-0119
Accommodation: ★★★★★
Restaurants: ★★★★★
Transportation: ★★★★★
Cost of living: ○○○
UN rank: 17
Best months: May to Sept
Holidays: 1, 2 Jan; 27 Feb; 16, 17 Apr; 1, 4, 5, 25 May; 23 June; 15 Aug; 1 Nov; 24–26, 31 Dec

SWITZERLAND

+9 +8 +7 +6 +5

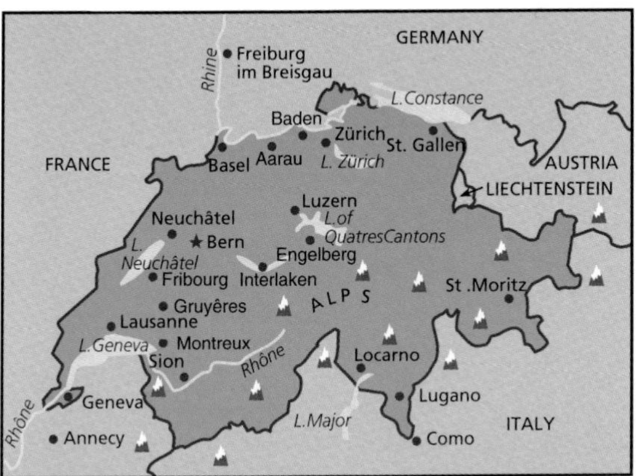

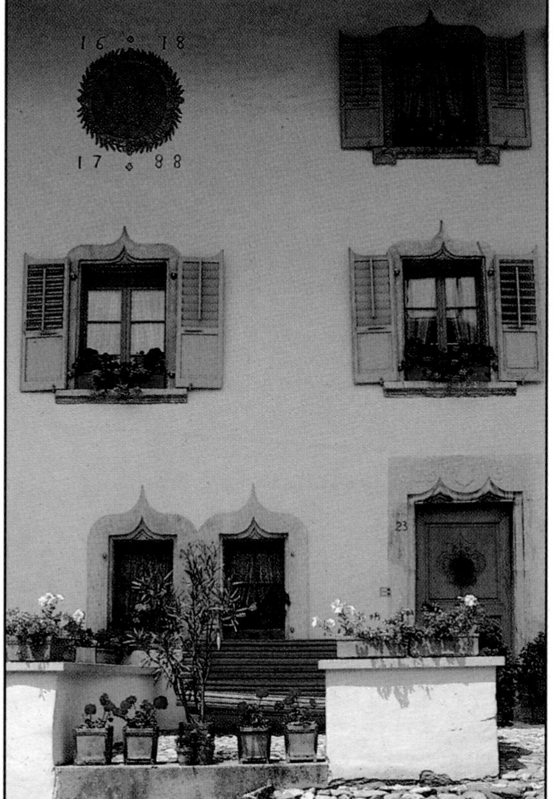

J. HUARD

Region: Europe
Area: 41,288 km²
Capital: Bern
Airport: Zürich 12 km, Geneva 4 km
Population: 7,040,120
Languages: German, French, Italian, Romanche
Religions: Catholic, Protestant
Government: parliamentary democracy
Voltage: 220 - 50
Vaccinations required: –
Vaccinations recommended: –
Passport: required
Visa: not required
Currency: Swiss franc
$1Cdn: 0.85 franc
Driving: right hand
International permit: required
Area code: 011-41
✆ from Canada: 1-800-244-8141
✆ to Canada: ▲155-8330
Accommodation: ★★★★★
Restaurants: ★★★★★
Transportation: ★★★★★
Cost of living: ❍❍❍
UN rank: 2
Best months: June to Oct
Holidays: 1,2,6 Jan; 19 Mar; 14,16 Apr; 1,25 May; 4,5 June; 1,15 Aug; 18 Sep; 1 Nov; 8, 25, 26 Dec

SWITZERLAND

WHAT TO DO

Helvetia, as poets have called it, is paradise for skiers and mountain-climbers: the resorts in the Berner Oberland region and the cantons of Grisons and Valais are among the most popular. The shores of Lake Geneva and the spa resorts of Loèche-les-Bains, Baden, and Scuol also offer a wide range of leisure activities. But Switzerland is more than a breathtaking landscape of snow-tipped mountains, it is also a nation of peace, neutrality, and technical expertise. Swiss cities exude comfort—and conformism. However, nothing can dull the beauty of their architecture, some of which goes back to the Middle Ages, and the wealth of the museums. Zürich is a typically serene Swiss city, with its old town (Altstadt); Fraumünster Cathedral, which features stained-glass windows by Chagall and Giacometti; Museum of Fine Arts, and major avenues, notably Bahnhofstrasse. Baden, Aarau, and Basel—regions that form a triangle between France, Germany, and Switzerland—are the centre of a lively tourist zone. Basel is a pretty medieval town, remarkable for its Markplatz (marketplace) and Rathaus (town

SWITZERLAND TOURIST OFFICE

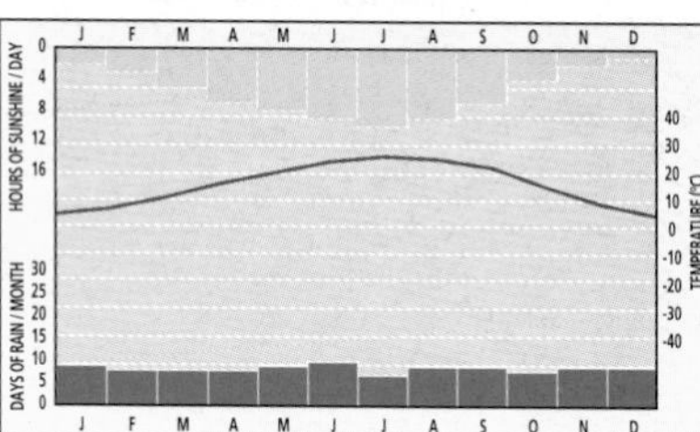

hall). Luzern (Lucerne) is a walled town with a health spa, covered bridges and interesting gardens; the Wine Market is a not-to-be-missed curiosity. Bern, the capital of Switzerland, is a remarkable cultural and historical centre; its very beautiful clock tower (with mechanical figurines) is a true marvel. In Bern, tourists can visit Albert Einstein's house and the Kunstmuseum, which has on display more than 2,000 works by Paul Klee. Interlaken, between lakes Thune and Brienz, and Engelberg are towns with a distinctly Swiss charm. Gruyères has a famous cheese factory; Lausanne, a major university. Geneva's attractions include the Cité district, the Art and History Museum, the famous fountain on the Eaux-Vives jetty, the headquarters of the United Nations, and a myriad of pretty parks. Near Lake Geneva, the Montreux Jazz Festival livens up summer evenings. Locarno, at the foot of the Alps, and Lugano, on the Italian border, are charming towns with distinct characters. The Alps need no introduction, but the Canton of Grisons is notable for its cultural specificity: there are just 200,000 Grisons, but most speak three languages, including Romanche, which has five dialects!

WHAT TO BUY

Swiss chocolate is among the best in the world. *Salsiz* (a dry sausage), wine, fondue, and raclette are the Grisons specialties. The gruyère and emmenthal cheeses go well with *kirsch* (cherry liqueur). Switzerland is also the place to buy high-precision items such as clocks and watches. The world-famous (ingenious) Swiss army knives are typical, as are Swiss ski equipment and musical instruments, especially horns.

J. HUARD

AUSTRIA

+9 +8 +7 +6 +5

Region: Europe
Area: 83,850 km²
Capital: Vienna
Airport: Vienna 18 km
Population: 7,995,000
Language: German
Religions: Catholic, Protestant
Government: parliamentary democracy
Voltage: 220 - 50
Vaccinations required: –
Vaccinations recommended: –
Passport: required
Visa: not required
Currency: schilling
$1Cdn: 7.15 schillings
Driving: right hand
International permit: recommended
Area code: 011-43
✆ from Canada: 1-800-463-6352
✆ to Canada: ▲022-903-013
Accommodation: ★★★★★
Restaurants: ★★★★★
Transportation: ★★★★★
Cost of living: ❍❍❍
UN rank: 12
Best months: May to Sept, Dec, Jan, Feb
Holidays: 1, 6 Jan; 16, 17 Apr; 1, 25 May; 4, 5, 15 June; 26 Oct; 1 Nov; 8, 25, 26 Dec

AUSTRIA

WHAT TO DO

Austria still seems to live under the spell of the Empress Sissi and Mozart; its rich ambience of history, music, art, and tradition is enchanting. The magnificent capital, Vienna, is chock-full of landmarks, among them the fourteenth-century church of the Minorates, the superb St. Stephen's Cathedral, and the Augustines' Gothic church. Most of the Habsburgs are at rest in the crypt of the Capuchin Church. The Hofburg, Lobkowitz, and Kinsky palaces are sumptuous, and the Schönbrunn Castle, once the Habsburgs' summer residence, is worth a trip. Of course, the History Museum and the exquisite Art Museum, among many others, are must-sees. The Opera, the Parliament, and the Burgtheater are located on the Ring, a circular boulevard in the heart of the city. Mozart, Brahms, Strauss, and Beethoven all lived in Vienna , this most musical of cities, at one time. Vienna could keep tourists busy for many weeks, but the rest of Austria shouldn't be missed. Salzburg, named for the beautiful Salzach River, which flows through it, is the city of Mozart, baroque churches, the Mirabell Castle and gardens, and the music festival that takes place at the Mozarteum. The *Kapitelschwemme* (horse trough) is a true marvel. Innsbruck, the capital of Tirol, is known for Maximilian's tomb, the "Little Gold Roof," and its spectacular snow-covered mountains. Graz, the capital of Steiermark and once an imperial city, has one of the oldest museums in the world, the Armoury. The superb Lipizzan stallions of the Spanish Riding School stand at the Piber stud, and Klagenfurt, the capital of Karnten, is famous for the shores of Lake Wörth. Upper and Lower Austria offer a wide variety of scenery, from mountains to clear lakes to spa resorts in fields of flowers.

WHAT TO BUY

In this very musical country, visitors should take in a concert by the Vienna Boy's Choir. All musical items, such as recordings by the great Austrian orchestras, make great souvenirs. Austrian knit goods are of unparalleled quality, and traditional Tirolian costumes are ever popular. With your delicious *sachertorte*, sip a famous Viennese coffee or some *Heuriger*, a young, fresh wine. *Pretzels* are another Austrian specialty. Arthur Schnitzler's novels, including *Vienna at Dusk*, paint a faithful picture of turn-of-the-century Austria.

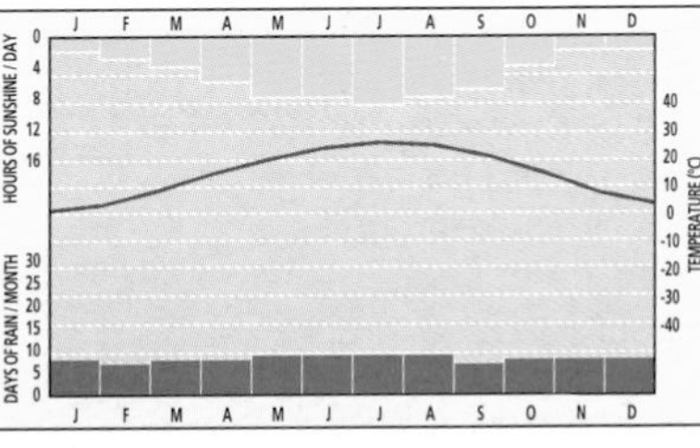

P. HALLY

HUNGARY

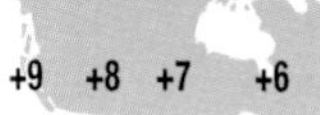

HUNGARY

Region: Europe
Area: 93,030 km²
Capital: Budapest
Airport: Budapest 16 km
Population: 10,319,120
Language: Hungarian
Religions: Catholic, Protestant
Government: parliamentary democracy
Voltage: 220 - 50
Vaccinations required: –
Vaccinations recommended: –
Passport: required
Visa: not required
Currency: forint
$1Cdn: 92.50 forints
Driving: right hand
International permit: required
Area code: 011-36
✆ from Canada: 1-800-463-8810
✆ to Canada: ▲00-800-01211
Accommodation: ★★★★★
Restaurants: ★★★★
Transportation: ★★★★
Cost of living: ○○
UN rank: 31
Best months: May to Oct
Holidays: 1 Jan; 15 Mar; 16, 17 Apr; 1 May; 4, 5 June; 20 Aug; 23 Oct; 25, 26 Dec

WHAT TO DO

Hungary is one of the countries in Central Europe that best fulfils the needs of tourists, with its beautiful scenery, wealth of history, sumptuous cities, and proverbially friendly citizens. The *Puszta*, or Great Plain, east of the River Tisza is among the most bucolic countrysides in Europe. Especially impressive are the paprika fields of Kalocsa, which must be seen in autumn, when they look like fields of fire. The capital, Budapest, is divided by the Danube: on one side is the old town Buda, dominated by the Fishermen's Bastion, the Royal Palace, and the Mathias Church; on the other side is Pest, which bustles with stores, theatres, and museums, including the National Museum, which has an impressive collection of Magyar art. Alongside the Danube are many public spas built around hot-water springs. Pécs and Eger are charming towns, and Esztergom, the medieval capital, is home to the most impressive basilica in Hungary. Lake Balaton has a famous resort, and the Hortobagy National Park preserves local fauna and flora.

WHAT TO BUY

Magyars are musicians: their ornamented musical instruments are works of art, and the gypsy rhythms they evoke are universally admired. Lace, the famous porcelain, and traditional costumes, especially men's hats, are typical. Among the culinary delights are *gulyas*, a beef soup seasoned with paprika; *porkolt*, a pork stew seasoned, of course, with paprika; and *retes,* a pastry that resembles apple strudel. The "blood of the bull" red wine, the *Tokaï* wines, and the apricot and pear liqueurs are excellent.

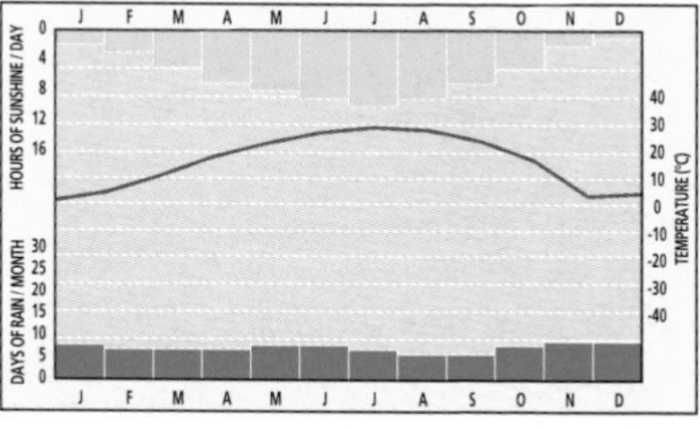

T. BOGNAR / RÉFLEXION

ROMANIA

+10 +9 +8 +7 +6

Region: Europe
Area: 237,500 km²
Capital: Bucharest
Airport: Bucharest 16 km
Population: 23,181,420
Language: Romanian
Religions: Romanian Orthodox, Catholic
Government: parliamentary democracy
Voltage: 220 - 50
Vaccinations required: –
Vaccinations recommended: –
Passport: required
Visa: required
Currency: leu
$1Cdn: 1467.93 lei
Driving: right hand
International permit: required
Area code: 011-40
✆ from Canada: –
✆ to Canada: 01-800-5000
Accommodation: ★★★
Restaurants: ★★★
Transportation: ★★★
Cost of living: ❍
UN rank: 72
Best months: May to Sept
Holidays: 1, 2 Jan; 16, 17 Apr; 1 May; 1, 25, 26 Dec

ROMANIA

WHAT TO DO

Long repressed by Ceaucescu and the Soviets, Romania is now enjoying its first years of freedom after the fall of communism. Happily, travellers no longer have to deal with long lines and mind-numbing bureaucracy. The country is not yet trouble-free, however, and tourists will still find people who will trade various services for a pack of cigarettes or a drink at the corner bistro. Bucharest lives up to its nickname, "Little Paris," with its many cafés and even an Arc de Triomphe; but it also features the Curtea Veche Church, the Art Museum, and the Museum of the Republic. Brave travellers will surely want to visit the Snagov Church (40 km from the capital), where, it is said, the blood-thirsty Count Dracula is buried. The Transylvanian Alps reach an altitude of 2,543 m, adding to the majestic beauty of the countryside. The main attractions of Cluj-Napoca, the capital of Transylvania, are St. Michael's Church, Mathias Corvin's house, Banffy Palace, and the ruins of the Tailors' Fort. Brasov is a medieval town that may, for some, evoke vampires. Sibiu and the border region of Moldavia are rich in monasteries and Roman ruins, notably, Trajan's Bridge in Drobeta-Turnu Severin. Poiana Brasov is a charming ski centre in the Carpathian Mountains, dominated by Mount Postavarul, 1,021 metres in altitude. The Romans left public baths and spas in the region, and a number of resorts offer various treatments in an enchanting ambience. Constantza and the bird sanctuary in the marshes of Dobruja are worth a detour, and the pretty town of Tulcea offers tourists vistas of the Danube Delta.

WHAT TO BUY

Ciorba, a sour-cream-based soup, and *tocana*, a spicy stew, are part of the traditional menu. Romanians also like pastries, ice cream, and coffee, not to mention *tzuica*, a strong plum liqueur, glasses of which are tossed back in one gulp! Romanians are of Latin origin, so women travellers can expect some special attention from local men, but a show of indifference should put an end to any advances. Poetry and music are as important to Romanians as religious art: the Orthodox icons are particularly beautiful. Sibiu's leatherwork is especially fine, and the traditional costumes are pretty and colourful. Rugs, embroideries, and pottery are sold in the markets.

J. HUARD

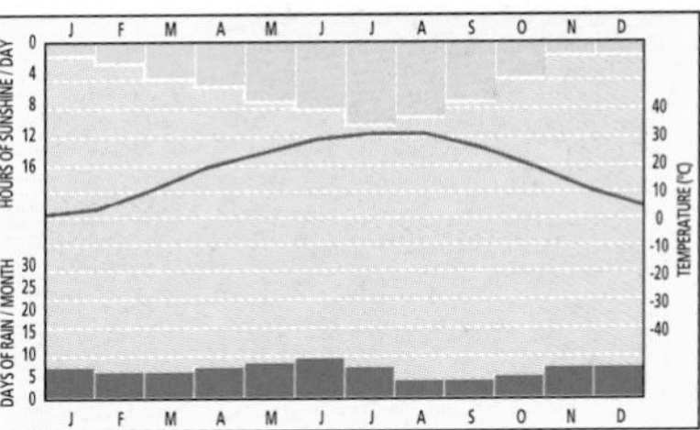

MONACO

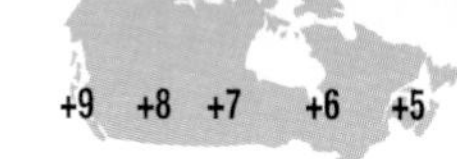

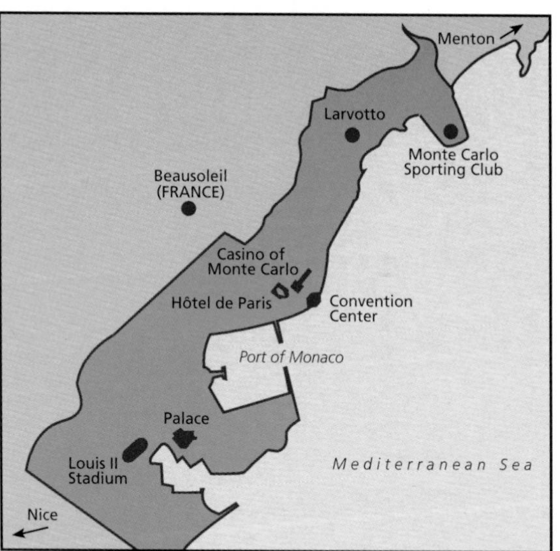

Region: Europe
Area: 1.5 km²
Capital: Monaco
Airport: Nice (France) 22 km
Population: 31,280
Language: French
Religion: Catholic
Government: constitutional principality
Voltage: 220 - 50
Vaccinations required: –
Vaccinations recommended: –
Passport: required
Visa: not required
Currency: French franc
$1Cdn: 3.52 francs
Driving: right hand
International permit: recommended
Area code: 011-33 (93)
✆ from Canada: –
✆ to Canada: ▲19◆00-16
Accommodation: ★★★★★
Restaurants: ★★★★★
Transportation: ★★★★★
Cost of living: ○○○
UN rank: –
Best months: June, July, Aug
Holidays: 1, 2, 27 Jan; 16, 17 Apr; 1, 25 May; 4, 5 June; 15 Aug; 1, 19 Nov; 8, 25 Dec

WHAT TO DO

The Principality of Monaco is one of the smallest countries in the world, and yet it takes more than a week to see all it has to offer. Within the walls of the city of Monaco are the Grimaldi Palace; the cathedral of St. Nicholas, where the princes of Monaco are buried; the Robot Museum; and the renowned Oceanographic Museum. The elegance of the citizens of Monaco is well known, and the casinos of Monte Carlo and the private clubs of Larvotto are the places to show off your river of diamonds and finest evening-wear.

WHAT TO BUY

Beauty products, high fashion, and luxury items are, of course, widely prized souvenirs of Monaco.

Monégasque postage stamps are appreciated by philatelists. The iconography related to the royal family is very popular with tourists.

P. HALLY

CORSICA

+9 +8 +7 +6 +5

Region: Europe
Area: 8,750 km²
Capitals: Bastia, Ajaccio
Airport: Ajaccio
Population: 250,000
Languages: Corsican, French
Religions: Catholic
Government: French department
Voltage: 220 - 50
Vaccinations required: –
Vaccinations recommended: –
Passport: required
Visa: not required
Currency: French franc
$1Cdn: 3.52 francs
Driving: right hand
International permit: recommended
Area code: 011-95
✆ from Canada: –
✆ to Canada: –
Accommodation: ★★★★
Restaurants: ★★★★
Transportation: ★★★★
Cost of living: ○○○
UN rank: –
Best months: Apr to Sept
Holidays: 1 Jan; 16, 17 Apr; 1, 8, 25 May; 4, 5 June; 14 July; 15 Aug; 1, 11 Nov; 25 Dec

WHAT TO DO

The Corsican seaside and mountains are famous for their beauty, as are the dense forests and the mysterious maquis (scrubland). Corsica is an island of the magic and the holy, fascinating for its stone giants and its proud and aristocratic residents. A sixteenth-century fort surrounds the mountainside town of Bonifacio. The Romanesque church of St. Mary the Greater and the church of St. Dominique are particularly beautiful. On the coast, between L'Île-Rousse and Calvi, La Balagne, or "garden of Corsica", is a favourite tourist site. In Ajaccio, the cathedral, the Fesch (uncle of Napoleon Bonaparte) Palace, the birthplace of Napoleon, and the bridge have a typically Corsican charm. At Bastia, St. Mary's Cathedral, the basilica of St. John the Baptist, the citadel, and the old town are lovely; as is Bastia Beach, a major tourist resort. Other interesting stops on the island are: Cap Corse in the far north, Brando, Canari, Nonza, Rogliano, and San Martino, to name a few. On the west coast, Porto is a choice destination. The ruins of the Porto-Vecchio Fort and the Filitosa archaeological site, near Propriano, are reminders of the island's long history. There are also ancient ruins at Aléria, at the mouth of the Tavignano River.

WHAT TO BUY

The markets offer all the delicacies of the island: wild boar, olives, chestnuts, rosé wines, cheeses, and figs. Corsican knives are famous, as are the garments knit from sheep and goat wool. The songs of Petru Guelfucci provide a taste of the musical talents of Corsicans, while the novel *Colomba*, by Mérimée, presents a very romantic image of Corsica.

M. JOLIBOIS

ITALY

Region: Europe
Area: 301,230 km²
Capital: Rome
Airport: Rome 32 km, Milan 7 km
Population: 58,138,400
Language: Italian
Religion: Catholic
Government: parliamentary democracy
Voltage: 220 - 50
Vaccinations required: –
Vaccinations recommended: –
Passport: required
Visa: not required
Currency: lira
$1Cdn: 1178.50 lire
Driving: right hand
International permit: recommended
Area code: 011-39
✆ from Canada: 1-800-363-4039
✆ to Canada: ▲172-1001
Accommodation: ★★★★★
Restaurants: ★★★★★
Transportation: ★★★★★
Cost of living: ○○○
UN rank: 22
Best months: Apr to Nov
Holidays: 1, 6 Jan; 17 Mar; 16, 17, 25 Apr; 1 May; 25 Aug; 1 Nov; 8, 25, 26 Dec

WHAT TO DO

It could be said that Italy is really a group of 20 small countries, each with its own dialect, traditions, wines, and landscapes. Each region has its own history and artistic heritage, as well, as shown by Firenze (Florence), with its Renaissance ambience, and Pompei, reminiscent of ancient Rome. From north to south, travellers pass through the Dolomite Mountains, studded with goats, to the beaches of Sicilia (Sicily), via Rome, city of archaeological treasures . In Lombardy, Milan, with its flair for high fashion, design, and the latest art, has a lot in common with Paris. The Dome, the second-largest cathedral in the world; the Santa Maria delle Grazie Church, famous for Leonardo da Vinci's fresco *The Last Supper;* La Scala, the world-renowned opera theatre; and the Brera Art Gallery are the city's main attractions. Torino (Turin) is a major trade centre, with beautiful Piedmontese buildings like the Duomo Giovanni Battista, a fifteenth-century

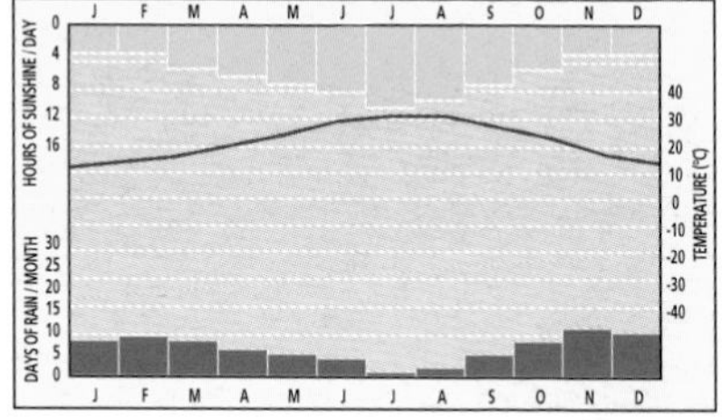

M. JOLIBOIS

ITALIAN GOV'T TRAVEL OFF.

marble cathedral where the Shroud of Christ (the "Turin Shroud") is preserved. The Dolomites are the Italian Alps, featuring high ski slopes, steep hiking trails, and lovely snowy peaks. Bolzano is a good stepping-off point for this region. The Italian Riviera begins at Ventimiglia, near the French border, and extends along the wooded coast to La Spezia. Venezia (Venice) could occupy any tourist for weeks, or even months, although the charm Thomas Mann wrote about has all but disappeared. Frantic tourism can mar the true pleasures of Venice, so it should be visited in the off-season, preferably in winter. The Doge's Palace, St. Mark's Square and Basilica, the 200 twisting canals, the 400 bridges, and the Clock Tower are stunning, as are the works of Venetian painters in the Academy Gallery. Padova (Padua), Vicenza, and Verona are also interesting. Bologna, Parma, and Ferrara are nestled in agricultural countryside, dotted with ruins from medieval times. Tuscany means, above all, Florence. Like Venice, this city could keep tourists busy for months. Art-lovers will be thrilled by its numerous Renaissance museums, filled with works, each of which seems better than the last. The Uffizi Gallery has one of the largest collections in the world, including works by Leonardo da Vinci, Michelangelo, Caravaccio, Titian, Botticelli, and many others. The Santa Maria del Fiore Cathedral, the Palazzo Vecchio, and the San Marco Museum, where Fra Angelico's frescoes adorn the cells of a monastery, are true marvels. Sienna, best known for its "terra Sienna" buildings, has preserved its medieval flavour. Twice a year, in July and August, during the feast of Palio delle Contrade, there is a great horse race on the Piazza del Campo. San Gimignano and Pisa are always attractive. In the Umbrian town of Assisi, Giotto painted frescoes on the walls of the Basilica di San Francesco, and in Orvieto, Fra Angelico decorated the cathedral. A visit to these two sites alone makes the trip to Italy worthwhile. Of course, there is also Rome. The capital should be visited on foot and at a leisurely pace. Avoid the summer months, when the tourists arrive, and the Romans themselves have left the city for the seaside. The monuments are still beautiful, but Rome loses its charm without its residents. The Coliseum, the Trevi Fountain, the Pantheon, the Sistine Chapel, the Forum, the Capitoline, the Palace of the Medici, the Vatican (see separate entry), the Catacombs, Villa

GUIDES VOIR
ROME
VISITES
SHOPPING
HÔTELS
ARCHITECTURE
PLANS
MONUMENTS
SITES

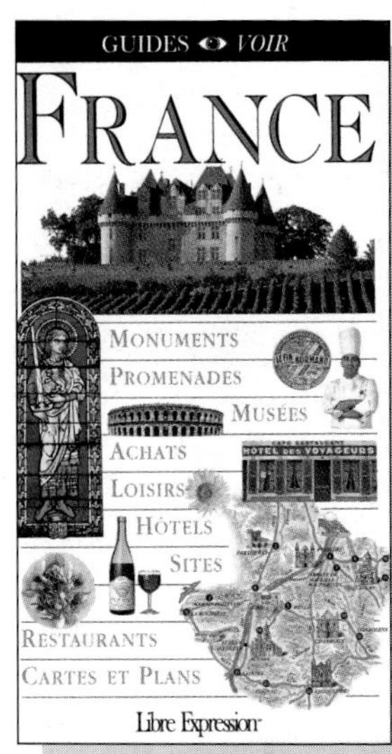
GUIDES VOIR
FRANCE
MONUMENTS
PROMENADES
MUSÉES
HOTEL DES VOYAGEURS
ACHATS
LOISIRS
HÔTELS
SITES
RESTAURANTS
CARTES ET PLANS
Libre Expression

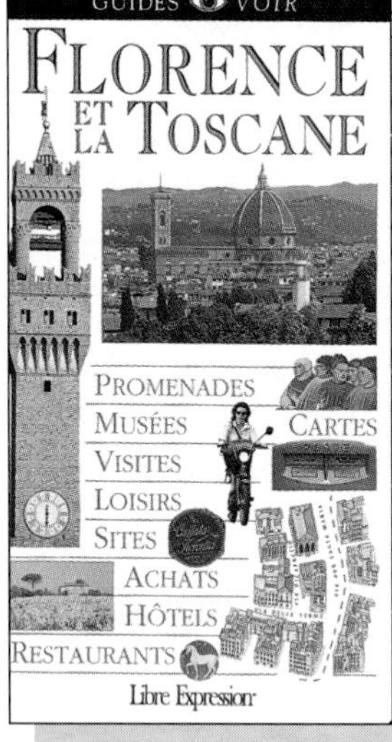
GUIDES VOIR
FLORENCE ET LA TOSCANE
PROMENADES
MUSÉES
CARTES
VISITES
LOISIRS
SITES
ACHATS
HÔTELS
RESTAURANTS
Libre Expression

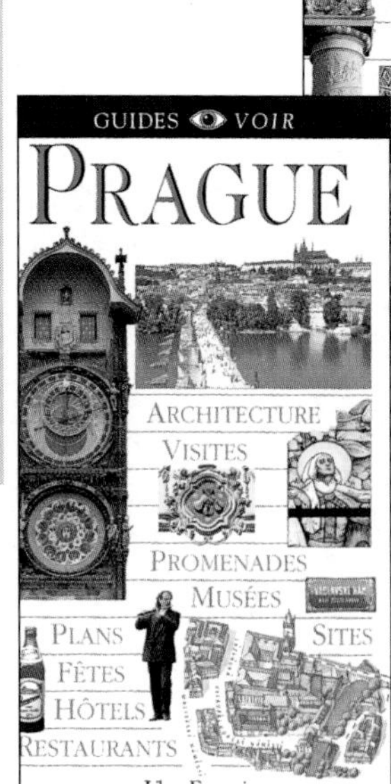
GUIDES VOIR
PRAGUE
ARCHITECTURE
VISITES
PROMENADES
MUSÉES
PLANS
SITES
FÊTES
HÔTELS
Libre Expression

GUIDES VOIR
VIENNE
ARCHITECTURE
PROMENADES
CAFÉS
PLANS
HÔTELS
MUSÉES
Libre Expression

Borghese, the temples and churches, the museums, the fountains, and the great avenues are fascinating, but visitors should save time for the vibrant neighbourhoods overshadowed by dripping clotheslines and shutters leaking streams of olive oil. Despite the bad reputation of the Mafia, Southern Italy holds many attractions for travellers. Napoli (Naples), like Rome, is perpetually crowded with traffic, but it offers tourists the magnificent mosaics of the National Museum of Archaeology and the superb villas on the slopes of Mount Vesuvius. Caserta has ruins dating from when it was the city of the kings of Naples. In Sicily, the mosaics at the Palatine Chapel in Palermo, the temples of Agrigento and Siracusa, and the volcanic landscape around Mount Etna are stunning. Sardonia is famous for the resorts on Costa Smeralda and the *nuraghi*, the well-preserved monolithic remains of the Bronze Age.

WHAT TO BUY

In Italy, everyone eats well. Each region has its specialties, both varied and tasty: *riso gallo* (saffron rice) and *cazzoeula* (pork and cabbage) in Milan; *panini* (little grilled sandwiches) in Venice; *crostini* in Florence; *spaghetti alle vongole* (seafood spaghetti), Napoli pizzas (cheese and mushrooms), *gnocchi, risotto, and saltimbocca* in Rome. Italian *gelati* (ice creams) are unique, as is the Sicilian marzipan; the minestrone; the mozzarella, gorgonzola, and parmigiano cheeses; the *pasticciata* (pastries), notably the *tiramisu*; and the excellent coffees, *espresso, cappucino*, and *caffelatte*. The reputation of Italian wines, both red and white, is excellent. Look for the wines of Piedmont, Tuscany, the Chiantis, Orvieto, Sangiovese, Soave, and Bardolino. *Campari*, an apéritif, and *grappa*, a liqueur, often accompany meals. If you don't go for the food, you'll love the opera, the fashionable leatherwear, shoes, and silk, and the marble and mosaics. Italian men have a reputation for being forward with women, so women should not be offended or shocked by simple gestures of gallantry, which are usually inoffensive: indifference discourages even the most eager. Beware of thieves: cars, purses, and baggage are the preferred booty. The holy places are not museums: restraint and discretion are required when visiting them. Women (and men) must always cover their shoulders and thighs, and men must not forget to take off their hats before entering.

ITALIAN GOV'T TRAVEL OFF.

VATICAN CITY

+9 +8 +7 +6 +5

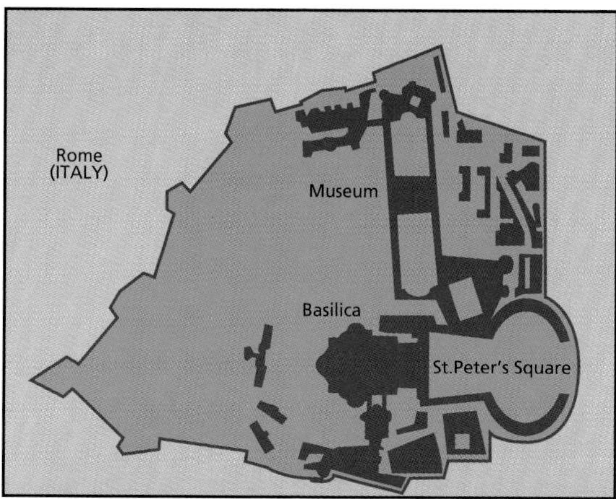

Region: Europe
Area: 0.44 km^2
Capital: Vatican City
Airport: Rome 32 km
Population: 820
Languages: Italian, Latin
Religion: Catholic
Government: sacerdotal monarchy
Voltage: 220 - 50
Vaccinations required: –
Vaccinations recommended: –
Passport: required
Visa: not required
Currency: Italian lira
$1Cdn: 1178.50 lire
Driving: right hand
International permit: recommended
Area code: 011-39
✆ from Canada: 1-800-363-4039
✆ to Canada: ▲172-1001
Accommodation: –
Restaurants: –
Transportation: –
Cost of living:
UN rank: –
Best months: May to Sept
Holidays: 1, 6 Jan; 17 Mar; 16, 17, 25 Apr; 1 May; 25 Aug; 22 Oct; 1 Nov; 8,25,26 Dec

VATICAN CITY

REFLEXION

WHAT TO DO

Vatican City is an enclave in the heart of Rome, encompassing the old gardens and Nero's Circus, where Christians were executed in the year 64. St. Peter was the first pope, and it is over his tomb that the basilica bearing his name was built. Today, the Holy See draws pilgrims from all over the world, as well as visitors who come to admire the tiny state's unique historical and artistic treasures. The Vatican's art collection is one of the largest in the world, and to see all of its masterpieces would require many days. A visit to St. Peter's Basilica alone is worth the trip, with its superb dome, the baldachin, the throne of St. Peter, and Michelangelo's exquisite *Pietà*. Other works by the grand masters are found in the Vatican's museums: Leonardo da Vinci's *St. Jerome*, Bellini's *Pietà*, and Raphael's *Transfiguration*. The splendour of the Borgia apartments, Raphael's rooms, the Sistine Chapel, the art gallery, and the Vatican Library, not to mention the Vatican Gardens, St. Peter's Square, and the thousands of architectural details, give this tiny state its well-deserved fame.

WHAT TO BUY

Reproductions of works by the grand masters, religious art, and Catholic cult objects are, of course, very popular. Beware of the many pickpockets at work in the area!

EX-YUGOSLAVIA

WHAT TO DO

War is still raging in the republics of ex-Yugoslavia. The international community has tried hard to impose peace by sending UN peacekeepers, but it seems that the Croats, Serbs, and Bosnians are not ready to live together. While the conflicts rage, tourism is nonexistent, and no one knows when it will resume. It is impossible to describe what can be visited in Bosnia and Serbia, for cities there have been ravaged and populations decimated. Macedonia, Montenegro, and Slovenia have not been as affected by the fighting, but travel to these regions is not advised unless with a humanitarian organization. It is to be hoped that the great natural riches of this area of Europe will be preserved, especially the Slovenian Alps, the islands of the Dalmacija (Dalmatia), in the Adriatic Sea, Montenegro's Mouths of Kotor, and the mountainous region of Projkletije, in Serbia.

V. PHILLIPS / RÉFLEXION

WHAT TO BUY

To keep their hearts warm, Yugoslavs drink *Slijvovica*, a strong plum liqueur. The war has put a stop to Solvenia's usually prolific wine production; the *tokaj* wine has a very good reputation. Crafts include carpets and copperware. In Macedonia, the hand-painted icons are worth their weight in gold.

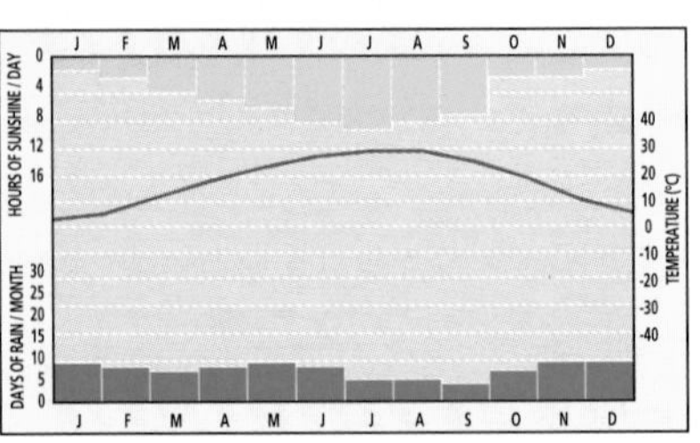

BOSNIA-HERZEGOVINA

Region: Europe
Area: 51,130 km²
Capital: Sarajevo
Population: 4,651,490
Language: Serbo-Croat
Currency: Bosnian dinar
$1Cdn: –

CROATIA

Region: Europe
Area: 56,538 km²
Capital: Zagreb
Population: 4,697,620
Languages: Croat, Hungarian
Currency: dinar
$1Cdn: 3.70 dinars

MACEDONIA

Region: Europe
Area: 25,714 km²
Capital: Skopje
Population: 2,033,970
Languages: Macedonian, Albanian
Currency: denar
$1Cdn: 22.24 denars

MONTENEGRO

Region: Europe
Area: 13,811 km²
Capital: Podgorica
Population: 655,590
Languages: Serb, Albanian
Currency: new dinar
$1Cdn: -

SERBIA

Region: Europe
Area: 55,968 km²
Capital: Belgrade
Population: 10,093,320
Languages: Serb, Albanian
Currency: new dinar
$1Cdn: -

SLOVENIA

Region: Europe
Area: 20,251 km²
Capital: Ljubljana
Population: 1,972,230
Languages: Slovenian, Hungarian
Currency: tolar
$1Cdn: 83.61 tolars

BULGARIA

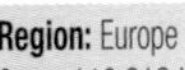

Region: Europe
Area: 110,912 km²
Capital: Sofia
Airport: Sofia 11 km
Population: 8,800,000
Language: Bulgarian
Religions: Orthodox, Islamic
Government: Parliamentary democracy
Voltage: 220 - 50
Vaccinations required: –
Vaccinations recommended: –
Passport: required
Visa: required
Currency: lev
$1Cdn: 48.97 levs
Driving: right hand
International permit: recommended
Area code: 011-359
✆ from Canada: –
✆ to Canada: –
Accommodation: ★★★★
Restaurants: ★★★★
Transportation: ★★★★
Cost of living: ❍
UN rank: 48
Best months: May to Sept
Holidays: 1, 2 Jan; 3 Mar; 23 April; 1, 24 May; 24, 25, 31 Dec

WHAT TO DO

Once the crossroad between the Byzantine Empire and the Slavic nations, Bulgaria has long been a stop-over for travellers voyaging eastward or westward. However, the country is worth a longer stay, even though tourism is not one of its main industries. In Sofia, the capital, a prime attraction is the crypt of the Alexander Nevsky Cathedral, where numerous icons and sacred objects are on display. The superb St. Sophia's Church dates from the sixth century, and the rotunda of St. George's Church is an excellent example of medieval architecture. In Rila, the thirteenth-century Orthodox monastery has been designated a World Heritage Site. Plovdiv boasts an old quarter with typical Bulgarian charm; also worth seeing is the historic town of Koprivshtitsa. But the main reason for visiting Bulgaria is the beautiful Black Sea coast, with its many winter resorts. The coast between Varna and Burgas is one of the most magnificent on the Black Sea. Skiers will appreciate the mountains around Borovets in the Rila Mountains and Pamporovo in the heart of the Rhodope Mountains. The Valley of the Roses, in central Bulgaria, is breathtaking, especially during the rose harvest in May and June.

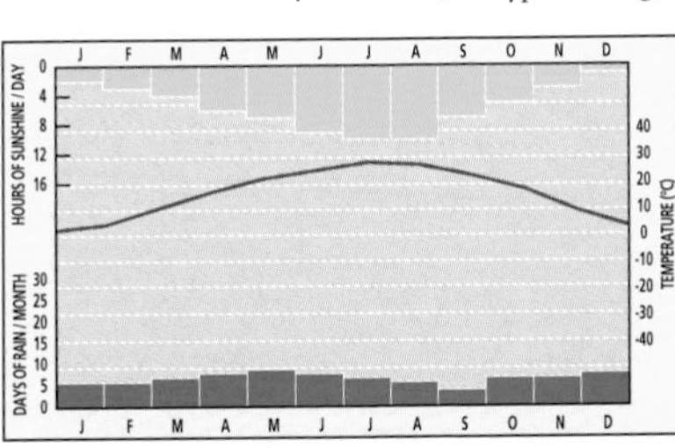

WHAT TO BUY

Bulgarian yogurt, made using a unique technique, is delicious, and the country is the world's foremost exporter of rose oil, which is used in perfumes. *Nadinitsa*, featuring sausages and vegetables, is a typical Bulgarian dish. The country is known for its ceramics and sculptures, as well as for its Cyrillic manuscripts (copies, of course!) that bear witness to its long history.

ALBANIA

+9 +8 +7 +6 +5

ALBANIA

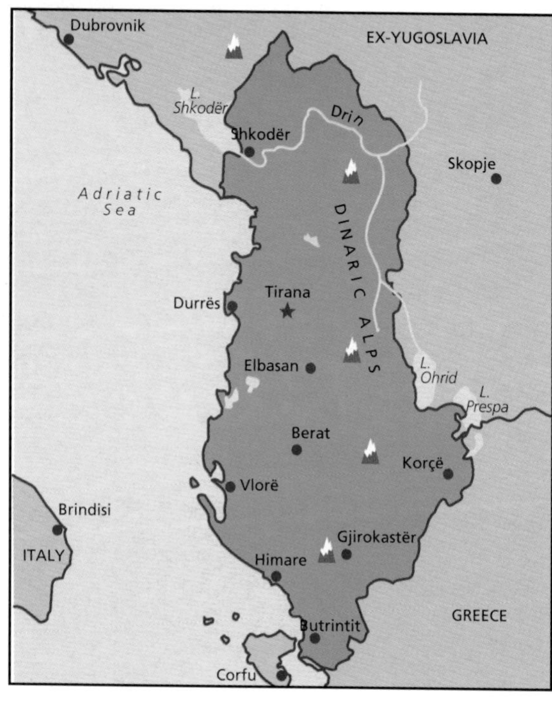

Region: Europe
Area: 28,748 km²
Capital: Tirana
Airport: Tirana 29 km
Population: 3,374,100
Language: Albanian
Religions: Islamic, Greek Orthodox
Government: parliamentary democracy
Voltage: 220 - 50
Vaccinations required: Yf*, Cho
Vaccinations recommended: -
Passport: required
Visa: required
Currency: lek
$1Cdn: 80.15 leks
Driving: forbidden to tourists
International permit: refused
Area code: 011-355
✆ from Canada: –
✆ to Canada: –
Accommodation: ★★
Restaurants: ★★
Transportation: ★
Cost of living: ❍
UN rank: 76
Best months: May, June, Sept
Holidays: 1, 19 Jan; 3 Feb; 4 Mar; 23 Apr; 1, 31 May; 10 June; 8 Aug; 28 Nov

WHAT TO DO

Albania is not very open to tourist traffic, and is still disputing its border with Greece. As well, it has some troubled neighbours: Macedonia, Serbia, and Montenegro. However, travellers will be delighted by its beautiful cities, resplendent with history going back to the time of the ancient Greeks. Must-sees include the capital, Tirana, as well as secondary towns like Butrintit, with its public Roman baths, the old city of Vlorë, and the ruins of Apollonia, dating from ca. 588 A.D. Durrës on the shores of the Adriatic Sea, has lovely beaches. Elbasan, in central Albania, and Korçë, near the Greek border, are worth visiting, as are the "museum-cities" of Berat and Gjirokastër. Lake Ohrid, once renowned for its beauty, should be avoided until the border conflicts are resolved.

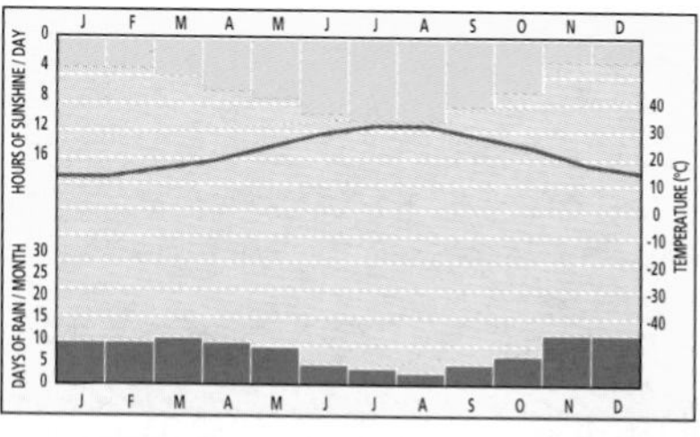

WHAT TO BUY

Albanians have mastered the craft of carpet weaving, and Korçë rugs are particularly beautiful. Berat is known for its fabrics. Copperwork and pottery can be found in all the markets, and some of the small villages produce unique silver jewelry.

J. HUARD

GREECE

+10 +9 +8 +7 +6

Region: Europe
Area: 131,944 km²
Capital: Athens
Airport: Athens 10 km
Population: 10,564,630
Languages: Greek, Turkish
Religions: Greek Orthodox
Government: parliamentary democracy
Voltage: 220 - 50
Vaccinations required: Yf*
Vaccinations recommended: –
Passport: required
Visa: not required
Currency: drachma
$1Cdn: 165.22 drachmas
Driving: right hand
International permit: recommended
Area code: 011-30
✆ from Canada: 1-800-815-7632
✆ to Canada: ▲00-800-1611
Accommodation: ★★★★★
Restaurants: ★★★★
Transportation: ★★★★
Cost of living: ❍
UN rank: 25
Best months: May to Oct
Holidays: 1, 19 Jan; 25 Mar; 21, 23 Apr; 1 May; 1, 11, 12 June; 15 Aug; 28 Oct; 25, 26 Dec

WHAT TO DO

Greece is a combination of the old and the new where the charm of history and of Hellenic ruins mingles with the vibrancy of the small villages. The large cities are major tourist centres, but the best of Greece is found in the small villages, the more remote areas, and the countryside. Of course, Athens is an unparalleled attraction for the Piraeus, the Acropolis, the temples of Athena and Nike, the Theatre of Dionysius, the Parthenon, and all the other classical and Hellenistic monuments sprinkled throughout it. The National Museum of Archaeology houses an impressive collection illustrating the long history of the country. In the Thessalia region is Mount Olympus, the home of ancient Greek gods, and the Meteora Orthodox Monastery. The towns of Lárisa, Trikkala, Dodona, and Ioánnina are charming. The Khalkidhiki (Chalcidium) Peninsula with its three "fingers" is a true marvel; however, only men are allowed into the Mount Athos

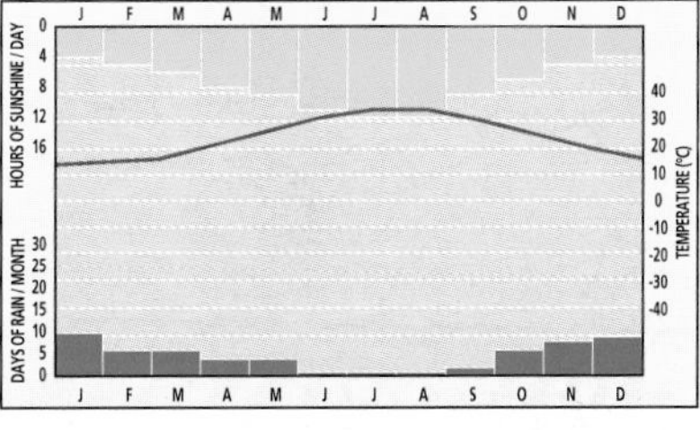

RÉFLEXION

RÉFLEXION

Monastery. The Peloponnisos Peninsula features magnificent wooded mountains, steep gorges, and deep caverns, along with the remains of ancient Korinthos (Corinth), the Temple of Apollo, and the Roman Odeon of Patras. Also worth seeing are Kalamata, Spartí (Sparta), and the famous theatre at Epidaurus. The wonderful Olympia archaeological site, with its Thermae, Palestra, Temple of Rhea, and *Heraion*, is stunning, as is the Lion Gate at Mycenae. The Ionian Islands, especially Corfu, have a charm all their own , thanks to their Byzantine heritage. Levkás; Itháki (Ithaca), the home of Ulysses; Kefallinia (Cephalonia); and the beautiful Kíthira, which is also called the Isle of Aphrodite, are less visited by tourists and are therefore more typical. This is true as well of the Cyclades: Thira (Santorini), Páros, Mikonos, with its windmills, and the prehistoric ruins at Mílos and Kéa (Kios) have lost none of their splendour over the years. The Sporades are still unspoiled and tranquil, and the Dodecanese Islands are a delight to history-lovers who will want to see the palace of the Grand Masters of the Knights of Rhodes. The islands of the Aegean Sea are a draw for the warm climate, especially the beaches of Lésvos (Lesbos) and the vineyards of Sámos. Kríti (Crete) is another popular destination; the south coast is much less well travelled than the large towns of Iráklion and Khania (Canea) on the north coast. Tourists to Greece who visit only the great monuments miss out on the country's greatest asset: the warmth of its citizens, although it should be noted that women travellers might have to deal with the forwardness of Greek men.

WHAT TO BUY

Canvas bags from Delphi, wooden sculptures from Tripolis, fabrics from Mykonos, jewelry from Epidaurus and Rodos (Rhodes), leather sandals from Spartí, marble from Páros, and ceramics and hats from Kríti are as well known as grapes from Korinthos and honey from Kíthira. Greek cuisine includes, among other famous dishes, *dolmades* (stuffed vine leaves), *moussaka*, *feta* cheese, *tzatziki* (yogurt, cucumber, and garlic), and *kourabiedes*, delicious almond cookies. The Orthodox religious art and *bouzouki* music also reflect the beauty and uniqueness of this country. The wonderful interpretations of songstress Irene Papas and *L'été grec* by Jacques Lacarrière are recommended for those wanting to get into the mood of Greece.

PORTUGAL

+8 +7 +6 +5 +4

Region: Europe
Area: 91,985 km²
Capital: Lisbon
Airport: Lisbon 7 km
Population: 10,524,210
Language: Portuguese
Religion: Catholic
Government: parliamentary democracy
Voltage: 220 - 50
Vaccinations required: –
Vaccinations recommended: –
Passport: required
Visa: not required
Currency: escudo
$1Cdn: 106.42 escudos
Driving: right hand
International permit: required
Area code: 011-351
✆ **from Canada:** 1-800-463-2776
✆ **to Canada:** 05-017-1226
Accommodation: ★★★★★
Restaurants: ★★★★★
Transportation: ★★★★
Cost of living: ❍
UN rank: 42
Best months: Apr to Oct
Holidays: 1 Jan; 28 Feb; 14, 16, 25 Apr; 1 May; 10, 15 June; 15 Aug; 5 Oct; 1 Nov; 1, 8, 25 Dec

WHAT TO DO

Historically, Portugal is best known for its great explorers of the fifteenth and sixteenth centuries: Bartolomeu Diaz reached the Cape of Good Hope, Vasco de Gama landed in India, Cabral touched ground in Brazil, and Magellan was the first to travel around the world by boat. To this day, shipping and trade are two of Portugal's main economic activities, and the port of Lisbon provides a prime example of their importance. The capital itself is worth the trip to Portugal: Lisbon, nicknamed "Queen of the Tagus" (for its river), is known for its old lower town (*Baixa*), the superb Sé Patriarcal Cathedral, the Sao Pedro Belvedere, the Belem Tower, the many Gothic churches, and the Manueline-style castles. The Classical Art and Fine Art museums are must-sees. North of Lisbon, at Sintra, are the old royal palace and the Pena Castle. Santarém is known for its bulls and its *touradas* (different from *corridas*), Tomar for the Templars' Castle, and Fatima for its pilgrimages. On the Costa de Prata are the picturesque ports of Nazaré and Figueira da Foz, where sea products, particularly cod and *caldeirada*, a Portuguese fish soup, are featured in the cuisine. With its magnificent Lagos and Sagres beaches, its many golf courses, and the scenery of Cap de São Vicente and Faro, the Algarve region is becoming increasingly popular. In the interior of the country, the town of Obidos, Batalha's Dominican abbey of Santa Maria, and Coimbra, with its Sé Vahla Cathedral and many Roman monuments, are major attractions, as are the mountain trails of the Beira Alta and Tras os Montes regions. Tourists should save the city of Porto (or Oporto) for the last and be sure to visit the Dos Clérigos Church with its high steeple, Cathedral Square, and especially the wine vaults, where the delicious Porto wine is stored. Farther north, the cities of Vila do Conde, Braga, and Vila Real, as well as the national park at Peneda-Geres are also very interesting.

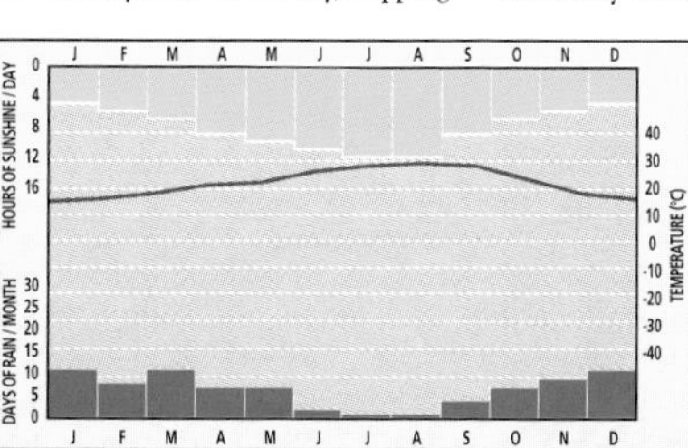

WHAT TO BUY

The "tawny" and "vintage" wines of Porto and the *vinho verde* of the Douro Valley are essential purchases. Portugal also offers pretty copper and pewter jewelry, ceramics, lace, pottery, and embroidery. Coimbra's leather goods are well known, as are the *azulejos*, squares of blue-and-white glazed earthenware. The languorous and dramatic *fado* (folk songs) are delightful. Portugal is a Latin country, where women are relatively subservient; however, women travellers won't have any problems if they show restraint.

SPAIN

+9 +8 +7 +6 +5

Region: Europe
Area: 504,748 km^2
Capital: Madrid
Airport: Barcelona 12 km, Madrid 15 km
Population: 39,302,670
Languages: Spanish, Basque, Catalan, Galician
Religion: Catholic
Government: constitutional monarchy
Voltage: 220 - 50
Vaccinations required: –
Vaccinations recommended: –
Passport: required
Visa: not required
Currency: peseta
$1Cdn: 87.55 pesetas
Driving: right hand
International permit: required
Area code: 011-34
© from Canada: 1-800-463-8255
© to Canada: ▲900-99-0015
Accommodation: ★★★★★
Restaurants: ★★★★★
Transportation: ★★★
Cost of living: ○○
UN rank: 23
Best months: May to Oct
Holidays: 1, 6 Jan; 13, 14, 16, Apr; 1, 2 May; 15 Aug; 12 Oct; 1 Nov; 6, 8, 25 Dec

WHAT TO DO

Spain, at the crossroads of Europe and Africa, was invaded many times over the centuries, and the cultures of these assailants have blended to produce a unique and proud people. The country's 12 regions are all unique geographically and culturally—worthy of chapters in themselves. Spain is the greenest in the Basque, with Bilbao, the beautiful beaches of San Sebastian (*Donostia* in Basque), and the cathedrals of Guernica and Vitoria. Cantabria is very popular for the famous prehistoric paintings in the Altamira caves, the Oviedo Cathedral in Asturia, and the magnificent Cantabrian Mountains. Galicia (*Finis Terrae*, the end of the world for the Romans), famous in the Middle Ages for the Santiago de Compostela Road, features rocky countryside and steep cliffs and has a distinct folklore and language. The glass-paned belvederes of the houses in La Coruña are very impressive, as are the Romanesque lighthouse and churches. One of the most beautiful cities in Spain is Santiago de Compostela, with its huge cathedral, the Archbishop's

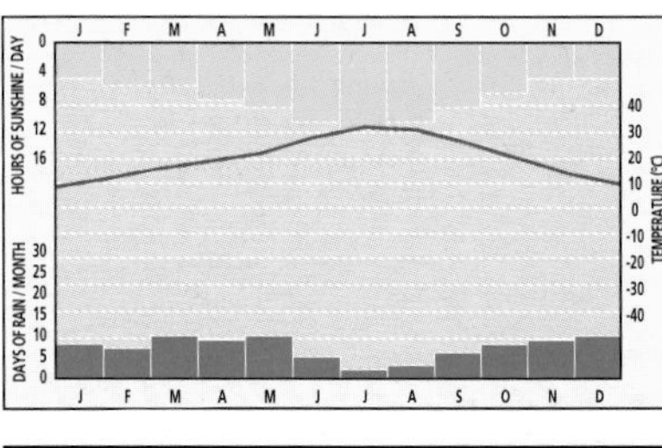

D. CARON / RÉFLEXION

Palace, the Royal Hospital, and numerous convents and monasteries. The towns of Lugo, Orense, Pontevedra, and Vigo retain their Romanesque ambience. A visit to Mediterranean Spain takes one to Catalonia, and especially to its capital, Barcelona, famous for the unfinished Sagrada Familia Church, Güell Park, and the Batllo and Mila houses. The Picasso Museum and the Miró Foundation are the best museums in the city. The citadel in Lérida, which sits atop the steep coast, leads to a superb fifteenth-century cathedral. The Costa Brava stretches along the entire coast of the province of Gerona; it features magnificent villas and charming seaside villages, such as Rosas, San Pedro, La Escala, and Blanes. The town of Gerona is known for its very old Jewish quarter and for the cathedral, built in 786. The Salvador Dali Museum at Figueras and the classical ruins in the town of Ampuero are not to be missed. The Costa Dorada is a long, tranquil beach stretching from Barcelona to Tarragona. In Tarragona is the superb Tomb of the Scipions. The Valencian region is world famous for its oranges, and its capital, Valencia, has one of the most colourful *Fallas* festivals. Tourist centres dot the Costa del Azahar (the orange-blossom coast): Vinaroz, Peñiscola, Beniscas, and the nearby Desierto de las Palmas Carmelite Monastery are special points of interest. Finally, the Costa Blanca, with its palm-tree-adorned beaches, is Spain's most popular tourist area. The Murcia

J. HUARD

region is noted for its ruins, dating from the Arab presence in the Middle Ages, among them the cathedral and university in the town of Murcia. Cartagena is an even older town, as its pre-Roman ruins testify. Southern Spain, and particularly Andalucia, is famous for its warm nights and its poets. Seville is home to attractions such as the Alcazar, an ancient Arab fortress, the Torre del Oro, and Casa de Pilatus. The Giralda Cathedral is the most impressive in Spain and makes the trip to Andalucia worthwhile. The Guadalquivir River runs through the town of Cordoba, which has a large mosque. In Grenada, Alhambra is famous for its patios and villas. Beach-goers will appreciate the Costa del Sol (sun coast), which bears out the promise of its name. The small towns of Mijas, Jaén, Almeria, and Ronda are typical for their charming whitewashed houses, rocky backdrops, and vast olive groves. The interior of Spain also has its treasures. La Rioja serves up its excellent and well-known wine, and the wine cellars of Haro are open all year round. The Castilla y Leon region, with Segovia, Avila (well known for the Santa Teresa Convent), and Burgos feature historic monuments from the old Castile kingdom. Salamanca is known for its university, one of the first in Europe, Plaza Mayor, and its two cathedrals, one Romanesque, the other Gothic. Toledo, El Greco's beloved town, has unique Mudejar monuments, and the museums feature the renowned painter's works. Ciudad Real, capital of La Mancha, is best known for Don Quixote's windmills. The suspended houses of Cuenca have a unique medieval charm, and the Arab town walls at Guadalajara are amazingly well preserved. Extremadura is relatively unknown among tourists, and yet the beautiful towns of Cáceres, Plasencia, and Mérida are well worth visiting. Pamplona, in Navarre, draws bull-fight fans, and Zaragoza (Saragosso), in Aragon, is the centre of the unique folklore of this Mediterranean region. Not to be overlooked are the splendours of Madrid: the Puerta del Sol, the Plaza Mayor, the Grand Square surrounded by arcades, the city hall, the Royal Palace and its gardens, the fabulous Prado Museum (one of the best in Europe), the Royal Theatre, and, of course, the many fountains. Famous throughout Spain are the *romerias*, colourful religious festivals. Each village places itself under the protection of a saint, whom villagers worship throughout the year. During the holy week, the processions and festivals are particularly beautiful, especially in Málaga.

WHAT TO BUY

The Madrilenian and Castilian cuisines are typical, but each Spanish region has its specialty: Valencia's *paella*, Andalucia's *gazpacho*, Alicante's *turron* (nougat), the north's eau de vie or *orjuo*, and Segovia's suckling pig, to name just a few. The wines are full-bodied, and the Jerez (xeres) wine is highly prized. Leather balls from *pelote*, an old Basque game, are rare souvenirs. Andalucia's flamenco and its traditional costumes, shawls, scarves, and castanets are unique to Spain. One can buy mosaics in Merida, pottery in Guadix, and ceramics and items relating to bullfighting in Valencia. Reproductions of works by many Spanish artists—among them Picasso, Goya, Miró, Dali, and Velazquez—are also available. Cervantes' *Don Quixote* must be read before a visit to Spain. Women travellers should not be offended by the *piropos*, the compliments that men address to women.

GIBRALTAR

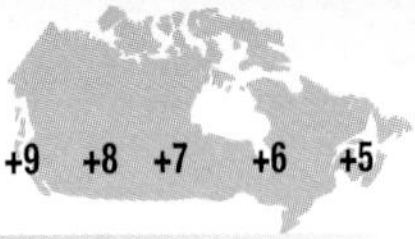

+9 +8 +7 +6 +5

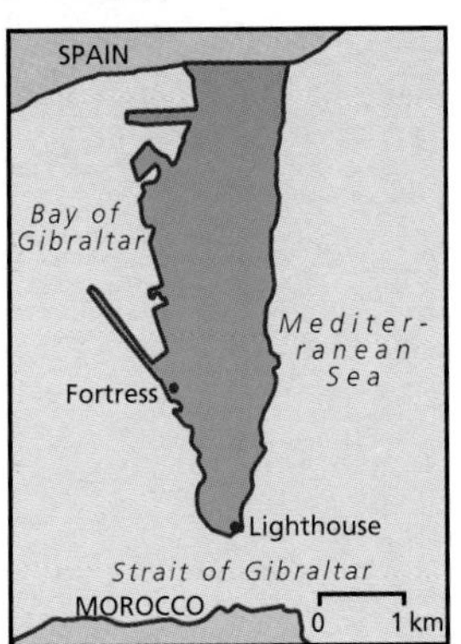

WHAT TO DO

From high on the Rock of Gibraltar, one can see two continents, Europe and Africa, separated by the Strait of Gibraltar, and two major bodies of water, the Mediterranean Sea and the Atlantic Ocean. Morocco and Spain are still fighting over this huge rock, which has been a British dependency since 1704. The various cultures that have gravitated to this site have left their marks: a European charm, an Arabic vitality, and an African grace. Spelunkers will want to visit the caverns and caves, some 425 m deep. Many prehistoric artifacts have been found in the region, and the Gibraltar Museum houses a fine collection of them. The Moorish remains, like the palace and the mosque, are worth seeing. The beaches on Gibraltar's east coast are great for water sports and underwater exploration, especially in Catalan Bay.

WHAT TO BUY

Prices in Gibraltar are among the lowest in Europe: perfumes, jewelry, wines and liquor, cigarettes, and electronic goods are sold tax-free. Because of the mix of cultures, a wide variety of products are available, among them English beer and the scotch whisky.

Region: Europe
Area: 6.5 km
Capital: Gibraltar
Airport: Gibraltar 2 km
Population: 31,690
Languages: English, Spanish
Religions: Catholic, Protestant
Government: British possession
Voltage: 240 - 50
Vaccinations required: –
Vaccinations recommended: –
Passport: required
Visa: not required
Currency: Gibraltar pound
$1Cdn: 0.46 pound
Driving: right hand
International permit: recommended
Area code: 011-350
✆ from Canada: –
✆ to Canada: –
Accommodation: ★★★★★
Restaurants: ★★★★
Transportation: ★★★★
Cost of living: ○○
UN rank: –
Best months: May, June, Sept, Oct
Holidays: 1 Jan; 13 Mar; 14, 16, 17 Apr; 1, 29 May; 28 Aug; 5 Oct; 25, 26 Dec

MAURITIUS / VIDLER / RÉFLEXION

ANDORRA

+9 +8 +7 +6 +5

ANDORRA

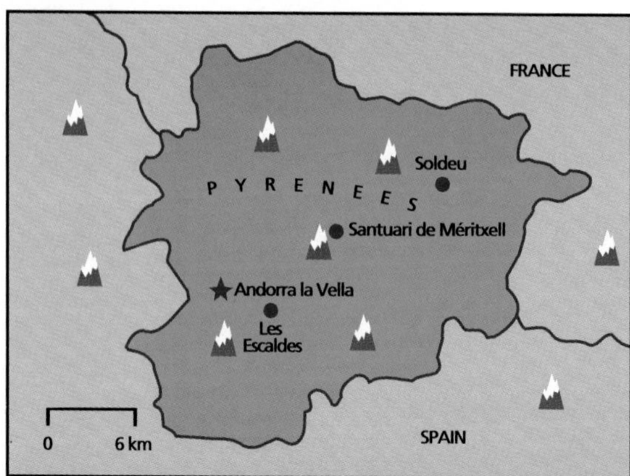

Region: Europe
Area: 453 km²
Capital: Andorra La Vella
Airport: –
Population: 63,930
Languages: Catalan, Spanish, French
Religion: Catholic
Government: new constitutional state
Voltage: 220/110 - 50
Vaccinations required: –
Vaccinations recommended: –
Passport: required
Visa: not required
Currency: peseta, franc
$1Cdn: 87.55 pesetas, 3.52 francs
Driving: right hand
International permit: recommended
Area code: 011-33
✆ from Canada: –
✆ to Canada: –
Accommodation: ★★★★★
Restaurants: ★★★★★
Transportation: ★★★
Cost of living: ❍❍
UN rank: –
Best months: June, July, Aug, Dec, Jan, Feb
Holidays: 1 Jan; 14–17 Apr; 12, 22 May; 15 Aug; 8 Sep; 1 Nov; 25 Dec

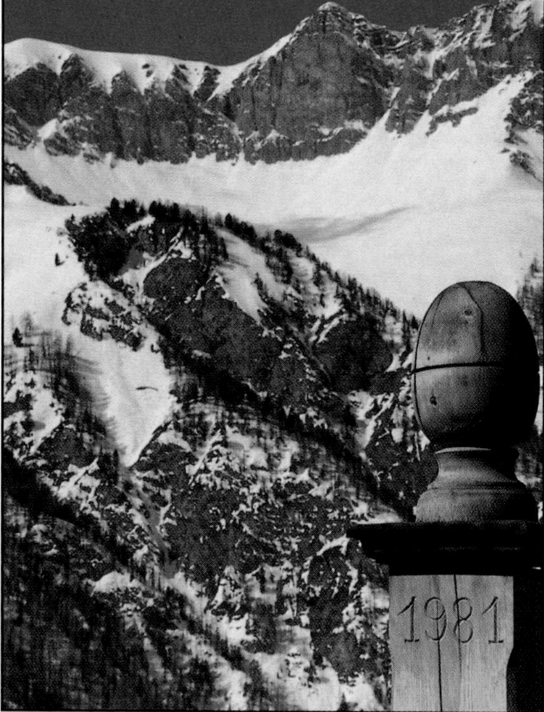

P. LESAGE

WHAT TO DO

For seven centuries, the Principality of Andorra was under the joint sovereignty of the head of State of France and the bishop of Urgel. Then, in 1993, with its first elections, Andorra became a sovereign state and member of the United Nations. This new status has not, of course, affected the beauty of the mountainous countryside popular among winter-sports enthusiasts, especially skiers. Although Soldeu is the largest ski resort, the mountain resorts from Portella Blanca to Arinsal are famous for their elevations and their twisting trails. The pleasant mixture of French and Spanish cultures is reflected in the architecture of the capital, Andorra La Vella, especially the superb Casa del Val Church. The Escaldes Spa, the Méritxell Shrine, and the Valira and Ordino valleys are all set against a backdrop of snowy mountains and, in summer, mirror-smooth lakes.

WHAT TO BUY

Andorra, a tax-free zone, is the place to buy tobacco, spirits, and the latest electronic gadgets at the best prices in Europe. The religious art of Andorra is unique; craftsmen sculpt and draw on *aïoses*, a type of slate found throughout the country.

AZORES

+7 +6 +5 +4 +3

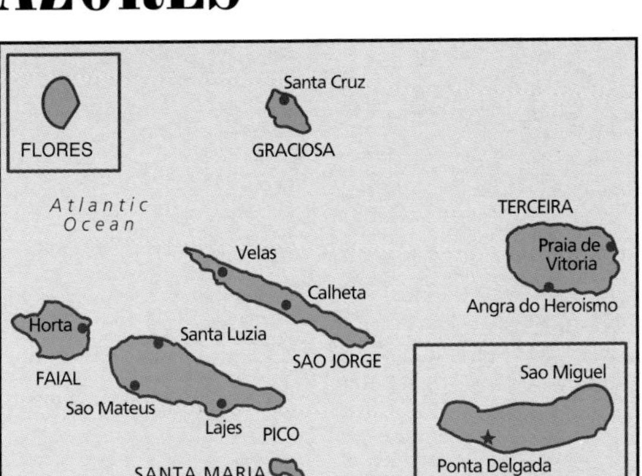

Region: Atlantic Ocean
Area: 2,247 km²
Capital: Ponta Delgada
Airport: Ponta Delgada
Population: 259,000
Language: Portuguese
Religion: Catholic
Government: Portuguese territory
Voltage: 220 - 50
Vaccinations required: Yf
Vaccinations recommended: –
Passport: required
Visa: not required
Currency: escudo
$1Cdn: 106.42 escudos
Driving: right hand
International permit: required
Area code: 011-351
✆ from Canada: –
✆ to Canada: 05-017-1226
Accommodation: ★★★
Restaurants: ★★★
Transportation: ★★★
Cost of living: ❍❍
UN rank: -
Best months: July, Aug, Sept
Holidays: 1 Jan; 28 Feb; 14, 16, 25 Apr; 1 May; 10, 13, 24 June; 15 Aug; 5 Oct; 1 Nov; 1, 8, 25 Dec

AZORES

WHAT TO DO

Legend has it that the nine volcanic islands of the Azores are the ruins of Atlantis. Located in the Atlantic Ocean more than 1,200 km from Portugal, these islands have unspoiled beauty, abundant vegetation, and a relaxed lifestyle. The old volcano craters are now beautiful azure lakes, including the two lakes in the Sete Cidades Crater on São Miguel, the largest island. Santa Maria is a sight-seers paradise featuring windmills, vineyards, deep caverns, and sandy beaches, while Pico is famous for its snowy summit rising to an altitude of 2,365 m. The gigantic grass-covered Caldeira Crater on Faial and the multicoloured hydrangeas on Flores are also must-sees.

WHAT TO BUY

Hand-painted ceramics are the specialty of Lagoa, on São Miguel. Woven goods, cotton fabrics, and embroideries make charming gifts, as do the pottery and wooden sculptures inspired by the maritime tradition of the Azores. The Pico wine is pleasantly fruity.

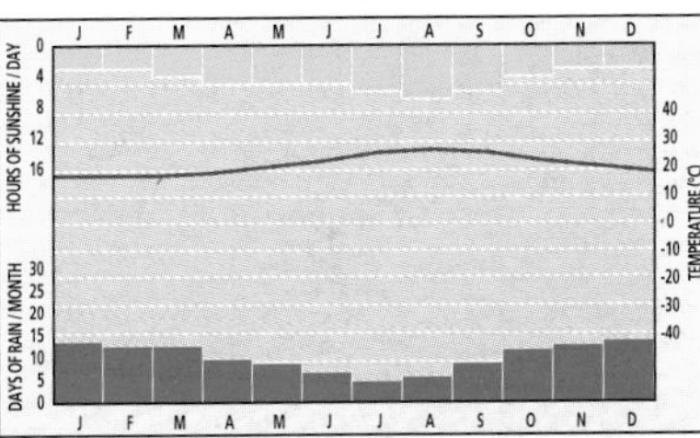

PORTUGESE TOURIST OFFICE

MADEIRA

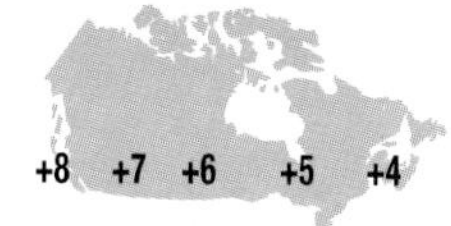

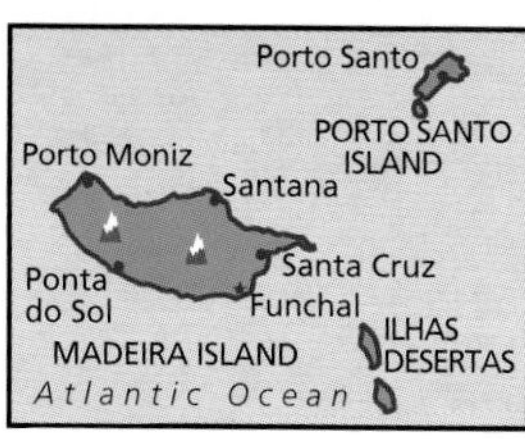

Region: Atlantic Ocean
Area: 794 km²
Capital: Funchal
Airport: Funchal 23 km
Population: 263,000
Language: Portuguese
Religion: Catholic
Government: Portuguese territory
Voltage: 220 - 50
Vaccinations required: –
Vaccinations recommended: –
Passport: required
Visa: not required
Currency: escudo
$1Cdn: 106.42 escudos
Driving: right hand
International permit: required
Area code: 011-351
✆ from Canada: –
✆ to Canada: 05-017-1226
Accommodation: ★★★★★
Restaurants: ★★★★★
Transportation: ★★★★
Cost of living: ❍❍
UN rank: –
Best months: June to Oct
Holidays: 1 Jan; 28 Feb; 14, 16, 25 Apr; 1 May; 10, 15 June; 15 Aug; 5 Oct; 1 Nov; 1, 8, 25 Dec

WHAT TO DO

The islands of Madeira are often referred to as "a floating garden", because of their profusion of flowers and fruits. In the capital, Funchal, cobble-stone streets wind their way through the lower town. Prime attractions are the Manueline Sé Cathedral and the Museum of Sacred Art. Vineyards, *levadas* (aqueducts that irrigate the farmland), and terraces on the slopes of the mountains shape Madeira's countryside. The small fishing port of Porto Moniz, and the very pretty village of Santana are not to be missed. In the centre of the island rises Pico Ruivo, with an altitude of 1,860 m; the panoramic view from its peak is breathtaking.

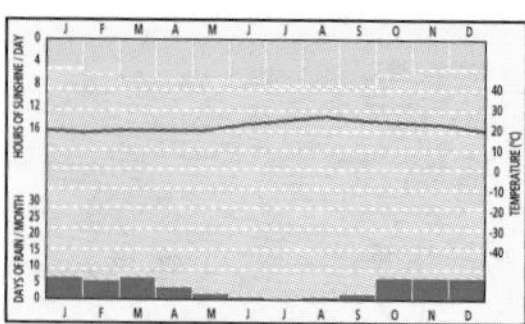

WHAT TO BUY

The August grape harvest provides an opportunity for festivals that finish, of course, with tastings of Madeira's excellent wine. The women of Madeira make delicate lace, pretty embroideries, and magnificent tapestries. Madeira is the natural habitat for brilliant orange *strelitzias* (birds of paradise) and enormous mauve jacarandas; it is strictly forbidden to pick these or any other flowers.

MALTA

+8 +7 +6 +5 +4

Region: Europe
Area: 316 km²
Capital: Valletta
Airport: Luqa 8 km
Population: 366,770
Languages: Maltese, English, Italian
Religion: Catholic
Government: parliamentary democracy
Voltage: 220 - 50
Vaccinations required: Yf*, Cho
Vaccinations recommended: –
Passport: required
Visa: not required
Currency: Maltese pound
$1Cdn: 0.26 pound
Driving: left hand
International permit: required
Area code: 011-356
✆ from Canada: –
✆ to Canada: 0-800-890-150
Accommodation: ★★★★
Restaurants: ★★★★
Transportation: ★★★★
Cost of living: ❍❍
UN rank: 41
Best months: June, July, Aug
Holidays: 1 Jan; 10 Feb; 19, 31 Mar; 14, 16, Apr; 1 May; 7, 29 June; 15 Aug; 8, 21 Sept; 8, 13, 25 Dec

WHAT TO DO

People go to Malta primarily for the wonderful white-sand beaches, but one cannot ignore the historical importance of this little archipelago. The National Museum of Fine Art in Valletta offers a good collection of the treasures of the Knights of Malta. The Grand Master's Palace and St. John's Cathedral are prime attractions for anyone interested in religious history. The National Museum of Archaeology explores through its displays Malta's long past. Archaeological sites and historic ruins are sprinkled throughout the islands, notably the Ghar Dalam Cavern at Birzebbuga, where one finds fossils from the Ice Age, and the *medina* (old city) of Rabat. Ghaudes (Gozo), believed to be the legendary island where Ulysses met Calypso, and Comino are each studded with Arabic ruins and surrounded by fishing ports and tranquil beaches.

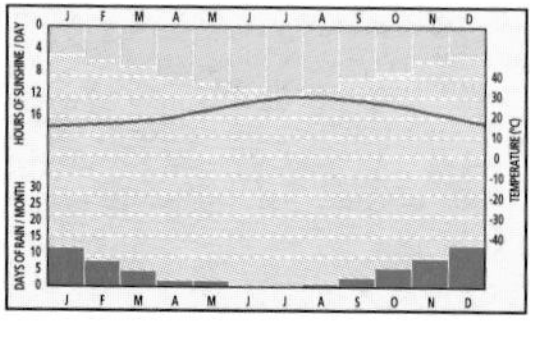

WHAT TO BUY

Gozo lace is world famous for its delicacy. Malta's silver and copper jewelry, ceramics, and pottery are also highly praised. Maltese wine has a fine, distinctive taste, and goes well with *bragiolo*, a typical beef dish. Reproductions of the Cross of the Maltese Knights are, of course, unique souvenirs.

CANARY ISLANDS

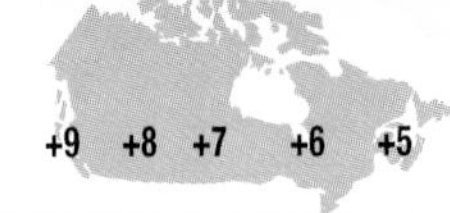

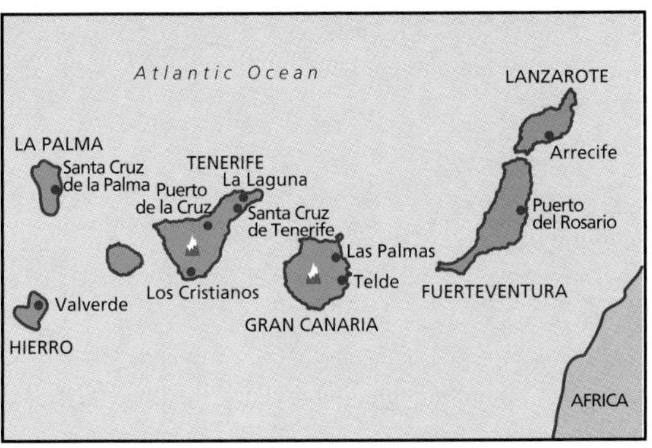

Region: Atlantic Ocean
Area: 7,273 km²
Capitals: Santa Cruz de Tenerife, Las Palmas
Airports: Tenerife 15 km, Las Palmas 20 km
Population: 1,602,000
Language: Spanish
Religion: Catholic
Government: Spanish dependency
Voltage: 220 - 50
Vaccinations required: –
Vaccinations recommended: –
Passport: required
Visa: not required
Currency: peseta
$1Cdn: 87.55 pesetas
Driving: right hand
International permit: required
Area code: 011-22 Santa Cruz, -28 Las Palmas
✆ from Canada: –
✆ to Canada: ▲900-99-0015
Accommodation: ★★★★
Restaurants: ★★★★
Transportation: ★★★
Cost of living: ○○○
UN rank: –
Best months: Apr, May, June
Holidays: 1, 6 Jan; 13, 14, 16 Apr; 1, 2 May; 15 Aug; 12 Oct; 1 Nov; 6, 8, 25 Dec

CANARY ISLANDS

WHAT TO DO

The Canary Islands (Islas Canarias) are divided into two provinces, Las Palmas and Santa Cruz de Tenerife. Canarians have long called their home the "Fortunate Islands," because of the mild climate; the temperature never drops below 18°C. The ancient dracena trees of Tenerife testify to the age of this volcanic archipelago, and on Gran Canaria are found the remains of an extinct indigenous population, the Guanches. The historic towns of Galdar and Agaete are particularly interesting. Christopher Columbus once lived on Gran Canaria and on Gomera. The Hermigua Valley, on Gomera, is a paradise of banana and palm plantations surrounding hamlets of white houses nestled at the foot of the sea cliffs. Lanzarote offers unique geological sites, with caverns, craters, and lagoons, notably at Salines de Janubio and Papagayo Point. The other major islands, Hierro and Fuerteventura, are also worth visiting for their beaches, their sculpted countryside, notably the boulders at Salmor, and the easy-going Canarian way of life.

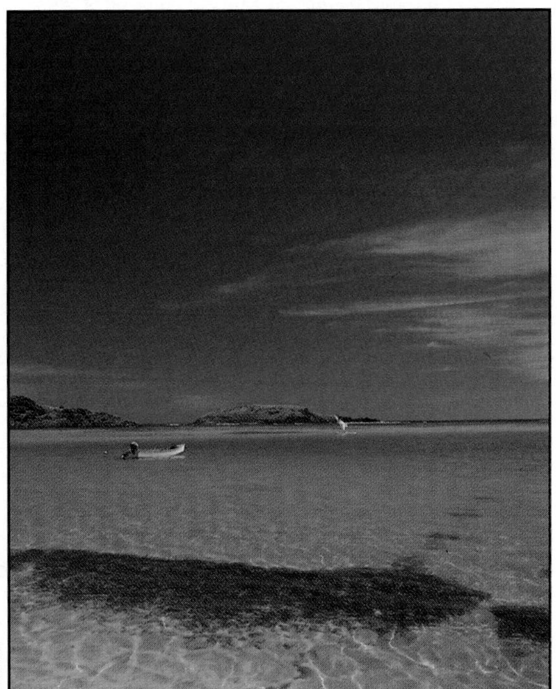
P. LESAGE

WHAT TO BUY

Crafts include embroidery, pottery, and plaiting. The Hierro wines are delicious. Las Palmas grows tobacco, and its tobacco products are of the best quality. A long tourism tradition makes the Canary Islands a favourite stop for travellers. The cuisine is based essentially on fish. Watch out for the *mojo picon*, a typical hot sauce.

EX-U.S.S.R.

V. PHILLIPS / RÉFLEXION

The Community of Independent States (C.I.S.) has a population of more than 300 million, made up of Russians, Georgians, Latvians, and Uzbeks, to name just a few of its ethnic groups. Each republic has its own culture, language, religion, history, and traditions. Some regions are known for their beautiful scenery, others for their magnificent historic monuments. Still others have been in the spotlight for the civil wars or international conflicts raging there. Unquestionably, what the republics of the C.I.S. have in common is faith in a brighter future. Travellers can help increase the pace of economic recovery by taking a greater interest in this part of the world, which has so much to offer the adventurous tourist.

RUSSIA

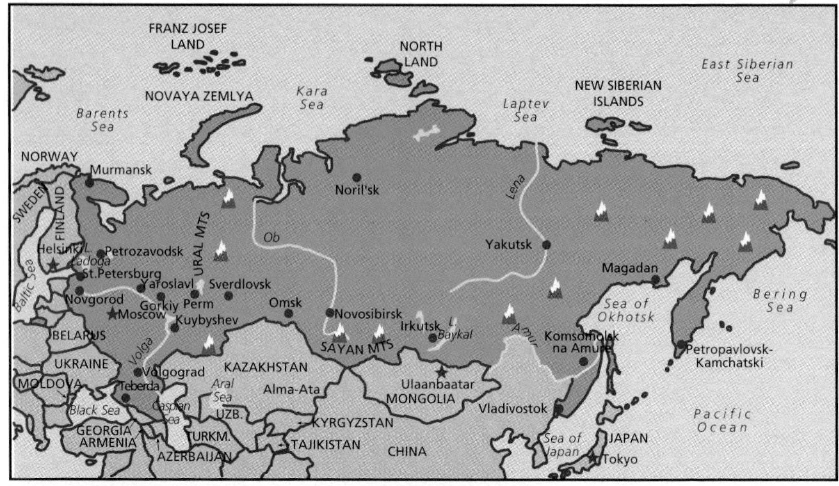

RUSSIA

T. BOGNAR / RTÉFLEXION

Region: ex-U.S.S.R.
Area: 17,075,200 km²
Capital: Moscow
Airport: Moscow 28 km, St. Petersburg 17 km
Population: 149,608,960
Language: Russian
Religion: Russian Orthodox
Government: parliamentary democracy
Voltage: 220 - 50
Vaccinations required: –
Vaccinations recommended: –
Passport: required
Visa: required
Currency: rouble
$1Cdn: 3346.31 roubles
Driving: right hand
International permit: required
Area code: 011-7095
✆ from Canada: –
✆ to Canada: 8-10-800-497-7233
Accommodation: ★★★★
Restaurants: ★★★★
Transportation: ★★★★
Cost of living: ○○
UN rank: 34
Best months: May to Sept
Holidays: 1, 2 Jan; 8 Mar; 1, 9 May; 12 June; 7 Nov; 25 Dec

WHAT TO DO

The Russian Federation has experienced disruptions and tensions over the past few years, notably, its problems with Chechnya, which is claiming independence, and the conflict between the Ossetian Republic and Checheno-Ingush in the northern Caucasus Mountains. Thus, Russia's difficult situation has deteriorated even further. Despite the falterings of its new economic policy, Russia is still the major tourist centre in the ex-U.S.S.R. and St. Petersburg is its star attraction. The City of the Tsars is on the Neva River. Its many canals and bridges lead variously to the Nevski Prospekt, the Winter Palace, the golden spire of the Old Admiralty, the Fort of Peter and Paul, St. Isaac's Cathedral with its marvellous dome, and the Hermitage, the old residence of the tsars, containing one of the largest picture galleries in the world. The collection of icons at the Russian Museum is also worth seeing. Moscow is, of

V. PHILLIPS / REFLEXION

RUSSIA

course, the best-known city in Russia. Among its artistic riches are Red Square, the Kremlin, Lenin's Tomb, St. Basil's Cathedral, the Church of St. Nicholas of the Weavers, the theatres, the Bolshoi Ballet Theatre, and the beautiful subway stations. For a tour of the museum-towns of Holy Russia—Sergiyev Posad, Yaroslavl', Kostroma, Suzdal, Vladimir, and Novgorod—travellers can follow the Golden Circle route. The many Orthodox churches along the way, each as beautiful as the next, hold treasures of Russian religious art. The name Siberia evokes images of ice and snow, but a summertime visit to the shores of the deep Lake Baikal and the pretty town of Irkutsk will change anyone's mind. Jules Verne's novel *Michael Strogoff* gives a very romantic picture of the Russia of yore. Kareliya, at the extreme northwest of Russia, near Finland, is best known for the beauty of Onega Lake.

WHAT TO BUY

Its cuisine is not one of Russia's major attractions. Nevertheless, tourists should taste *blinis*, little pancakes served with sour cream, and *zakuski*, salmon and sturgeon appetizers. Russian vodka is particularly good; try also the *pivo* (beer) and *kvass*, a very strong drink made with fermented rye bread. Chocolate, tea (and samovars), nested dolls, wooden toys, *balalaikas*, hand-embroidered shirts, icons, and traditional costumes have a place of honour in the markets. Russian men are good drinkers, and a glass too many can whet their appetite for feminine conquest: a woman's *nyet* will usually cool their ardour.

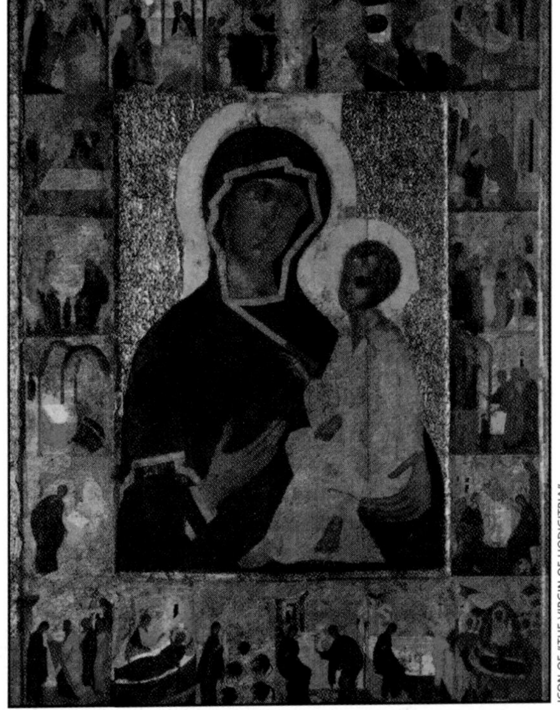

ICON OF "THE VIRGIN OF HODIGITRIA"

ESTONIA

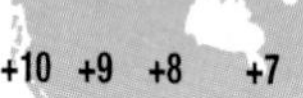

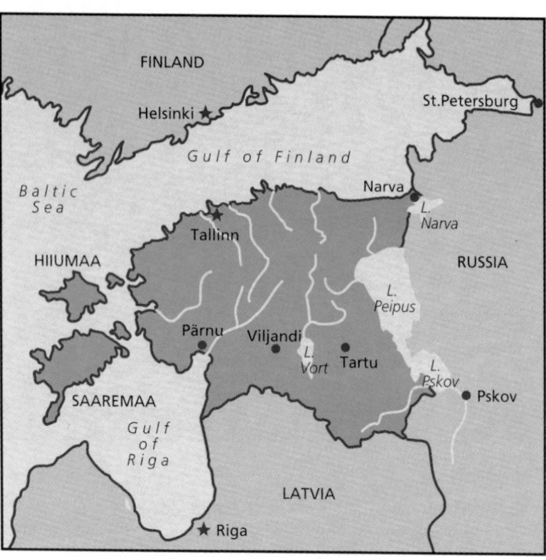

Region: ex-U.S.S.R.
Area: 45,100 km²
Capital: Tallinn
Airport: Tallinn
Population: 1,616,890
Languages: Estonian, Russian
Religion: Protestant
Government: parliamentary democracy
Voltage: 220 - 50
Vaccinations required: –
Vaccinations recommended: –
Passport: required
Visa: required
Currency: Estonian kroon
$1Cdn: 8.18 kroons
Driving: right hand
International permit: required
Area code: 011-7-0142
✆ from Canada: –
✆ to Canada: –
Accommodation: ★★★
Restaurants: ★★★
Transportation: ★★★
Cost of living: ❍❍
UN rank: 29
Best months: Mayto Sept
Holidays: 1 Jan; 24 Feb; 14,16 Apr; 1 May; 4, 23 June; 16 Nov; 25, 26 Dec

WHAT TO DO

The Baltic republics are distinct from the rest of the C.I.S., no doubt because of the Baltic Sea. Inland from its shores is a gentle countryside dotted with sparkling lakes and rivers, such as Narva Bay and Lake Peipus. Pärnu is a popular spa resort that enjoys the mild climate of the Gulf of Riga. Tallinn, the capital, is a museum-city. Its walled Toopera Fort and lower town, which still has a medieval charm, are especially interesting. The city hall's spire, dating from the fifteenth century, is one of the oldest in northern Europe. The home of Peter the Great and the Kadriorg Palace, which now houses the Fine Arts Museum, are must-sees. Tartu is a major university town, known for its cultural vitality. Narva, on the border with the Russian Federation, bears numerous vestiges of the passage of Peter the Great and Ivan the Terrible.

WHAT TO BUY

Located on the shores of the Baltic Sea, Estonia is a good place to buy products such as caviar and seafood. The *sovkhozes* (state fish farms) are very popular with anglers. Coloured fabrics and sculpted wooden objects are sold in all the markets.

J. FONTEIN

LATVIA

+10 +9 +8 +7 +6

Region: ex-U.S.S.R.
Area: 64,500 km^2
Capital: Riga
Airport: Riga
Population: 2,749,220
Languages: Latvian, Russian
Religion: Catholic
Government: parliamentary democracy
Voltage: 220 - 50
Vaccinations required: –
Vaccinations recommended: –
Passport: required
Visa: required
Currency: lat
$1Cdn: .38 lat
Driving: right hand
International permit: required
Area code: 011-7-0132
✆ from Canada: –
✆ to Canada: –
Accommodation: ★★★★
Restaurants: ★★★★
Transportation: ★★★★
Cost of living: ○○
UN rank: 30
Best months: May to Sept
Holidays: 1 Jan; 14, 16 Apr; 7 May; 14, 23, 24 June; 11,18 Nov; 24–26 Dec

LATVIA

WHAT TO DO

Spa resorts and curative-water health centres are very popular in Latvia, whose Baltic seashore and many water and mineral-mud springs are perfectly suited to this type of facility. The Gulf of Riga enjoys a mild climate and the beaches are, at Jurmala and elsewhere, particularly peaceful. Riga, the capital, is a very lively historic and cultural city: founded in 1201 by the bishop of Livonia, Albert de Buxhörden, the city has more than 200 monuments dating from the thirteenth to fifteenth centuries. The Dome, the marvellous cathedral in the old town, St. Peter's Church, and the City's medieval houses are must-sees. Ligatne is a jumping-off point for the Gauja National Park, which features large areas of original forest. Cesis (once called the Pearl of the Vidzeme region) and Rundale will please aficionados of history and architecture: the Rundale Palace Museum houses a collection of Latvian art and Eastern European crafts that should not be missed.

WHAT TO BUY

From the sea come fresh fish and shellfish, which the Latvians prepare with a flourish. Latvian art is still very influenced by the traditions of the Livians, their ancestors. In Riga, tourists can find very beautiful traditional costumes, embroidered fabrics, and silver crafts.

LITHUANIA

+10 +9 +8 +7 +6

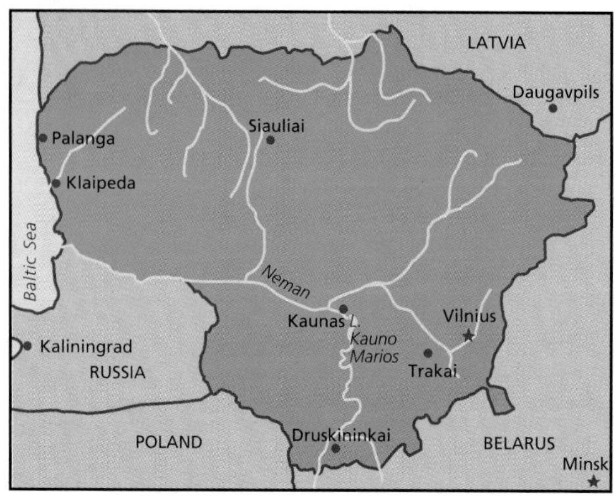

Region: ex-U.S.S.R.
Area: 65,200 km²
Capital: Vilnius
Airport: Vilnius
Population: 3,848,390
Languages: Lithuanian, Russian
Religions: Catholic, Orthodox
Government: parliamentary democracy
Voltage: 110/220 - 50
Vaccinations required: –
Vaccinations recommended: –
Passport: required
Visa: required
Currency: litas
$1Cdn: 2.94 litas
Driving: right hand
International permit: required
Area code: 011-7-0122
✆ from Canada: –
✆ to Canada: –
Accommodation: ★★★★
Restaurants: ★★★★
Transportation: ★★★★
Cost of living: ○○
UN rank: 28
Best months: May to Sept
Holidays: 1, 6 Jan; 16 Feb; 16 Apr; 24 June; 6 July; 15 Aug; 1 Nov; 25, 26 Dec

WHAT TO DO

The Russian enclave of Kaliningrad lies within the Republic of Lithuania. Its existence has provoked tensions between Lithuania and its giant neighbour, Russia: Lithuanian's borders do not seem to exist for Russians who want to go to Kaliningrad. This conflict, however, should not keep travellers from the country's tranquil beaches, with their twinkling pearls of amber, on the shores of the Baltic Sea. Inland lakes and rivers, notably, the Neman River, flow through beautiful forests, and the small villages have a distinctive charm that dates from the Middle Ages. Vilnius, the capital, is a lively, university town, while Trakai, the old capital, has preserved its important medieval monuments. Music is part of the Lithuanian tradition: there are music festivals and choral performances all over the country.

WHAT TO BUY

Lithuanian dairy products are well known for their quality, especially the cheese, which is aged for several years. Everywhere is found jewelry and crafts made of amber as well as beautiful shawls made of linen and other fine fabrics. Lithuanian music and poetry are very popular.

I. HUARD

BELORUSSIA

+10 +9 +8 +7 +6

E.A. ZAITSEV / ED. BELARUS

Region: ex-U.S.S.R.
Area: 207,600 km²
Capital: Minsk
Airport: Minsk
Population: 10,404,870
Languages: Belorussian, Russian
Religions: Russian Orthodox
Government: parliamentary democracy
Voltage: 220 - 50
Vaccinations required: –
Vaccinations recommended: –
Passport: required
Visa: required
Currency: dollar
$1Cdn: .74 dollar
Driving: right hand
International permit: required
Area code: 011-72
✆ from Canada: –
✆ to Canada: –
Accommodation: ★★★
Restaurants: ★★★
Transportation: ★★★
Cost of living: ❍❍
UN rank: 40
Best months: May to Sept
Holidays: 1 Jan; 8 Mar; 9 May; 27 July

BELORUSSIA

WHAT TO DO

After fighting to win its independence, the new republic of Belorussia (Belarus) has had to turn to Russia for assistance. Belorussians have little to build on apart from their vast historic and cultural resources. Minsk, the capital, has many such attractions: the opera, the theatre, the university, the ballet, and the square at the train station, almost completely destroyed during the last war. The region along the Polish border, from Hrodna to Brest, has a long history of turmoil. In Brest, the Heroes' Fort reminds tourists that the town once belonged to Poland.

WHAT TO BUY

Belorussian painters are particularly prolific; their works are inspired as much by the past as by the present, providing an excellent introduction to the country's history. Two major crafts are weaving and embroidery. Belorussian tobacco products are of very high quality, and traditional samovars are still used throughout the country.

UKRAINE

+11 +10 +9 +8 +7

Region: ex-U.S.S.R.
Area: 603,700 km²
Capital: Kiev
Airport: Kiev
Population: 51,846,960
Languages: Ukrainian, Russian
Religions: Russian Orthodox, Catholic
Government: parliamentary democracy
Voltage: 110/220 - 50
Vaccinations required: –
Vaccinations recommended: –
Passport: required
Visa: required
Currency: karbovanets
$1Cdn: 106032.26 karbovanets
Driving: right hand
International permit: required
Area code: 011-7-044
✆ from Canada: –
✆ to Canada: 8-10-0-17
Accommodation: ★★★★
Restaurants: ★★★★
Transportation: ★★★★
Cost of living: ○○
UN rank: 45
Best months: May to Sept
Holidays: 1, 6, 7 Jan; 8 Mar; 23 Apr; 1, 9 May; 24 Aug

N. MELIKOFF

WHAT TO DO

Ukraine is situated on a vast plain traversed by the Dnieper River. The country's few mountains are clustered in Crimea and along its extreme western end, at the foot of the Carpathian Mountains. The beauty of the countryside is incomparable, but Ukraine is most appreciated by tourists for its wonderful capital, Kiev. The "golden city" rises on the shores of the Dnieper, and water-buses are a good way to discover its marvels: St. Sophia Cathedral, famous for its frescoes and mosaics, and classified a World heritage Site by UNESCO; St. Andrew's Church; the cathedral of St. Michael's Monastery; the ruins of the Golden Gate, built in 1037; and St. Vladimir's Cathedral. Near Kiev is the oldest monastery in the ex-U.S.S.R., Kievo-Petcherskaya Lavra. The Museum of Ukrainian Art in L'viv (Lvov) is a must-see. Odessa, an important resort on the Black Sea, is situated in a region that enjoys a mild Mediterranean climate. Crimea is claiming independence, and the resulting tensions could tarnish the reputation of the many spa resorts in the region, such as those at Yalta and Sevastopol'. Simferopol', the capital of Crimea, still has nuclear capability. The contamination from Chernobyl, unfortunately, has closed the northeast region of the country to visitors.

WHAT TO BUY

Ukrainian cuisine is particularly tasty: garlic *bortch*, sour-cream *galushki*, and horseradish *kvas* are real treats. *Pysankas*, hand-painted Easter eggs, are true works of art, as are Ukranian icons. Traditional Ukrainian costumes, richly coloured fabrics, and finely worked leather goods also make fine gifts and souvenirs.

MOLDOVA

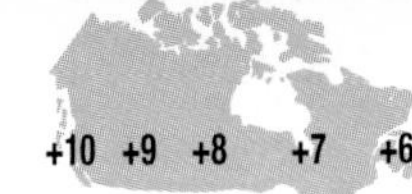

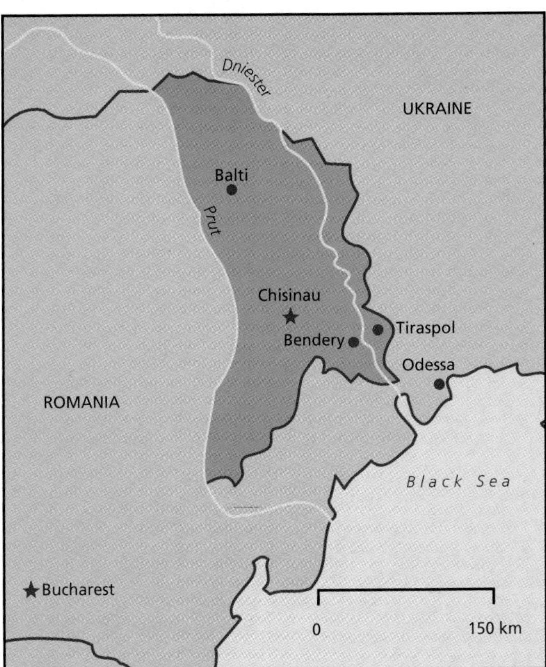

Region: ex-U.S.S.R.
Area: 33,700 km²
Capital: Chisinau
Airport: –
Population: 4,473,040
Languages: Romanian, Russian, Ukrainian
Religion: Orthodox
Government: parliamentary democracy
Voltage: 220 - 50
Vaccinations required: –
Vaccinations recommended: –
Passport: required
Visa: required
Currency: leu
$1Cdn: 3.33 leus
Driving: right hand
International permit: required
Area code: 011-7
✆ from Canada: –
✆ to Canada: –
Accommodation: ★★★
Restaurants: ★★★
Transportation: ★★★
Cost of living: ○○
UN rank: 75
Best months: May to Sept
Holidays: 1 Jan; 8 Mar; 9 May; 27 Aug

WHAT TO DO

Negotiations on the issue of annexing Transdniestr, the new self-proclaimed republic around Tiraspol, to Romania have resulted in minor disruptions in this normally peaceful country. In the capital, Chisinau (Kichinev), the Opera Theatre and the philharmonic orchestra remind travellers of the true passion of Moldovans: music. The Chisinau music and folk-dancing festival, in March, provides a good opportunity to sample this country's cultural wealth, while a sail down the Dniester River is a good way to discover the lush countryside and see interesting historic sites. The town of Bendery has preserved buildings dating from the twelfth century as well as a wonderful eight-towered citadel.

WHAT TO BUY

The Moldovans are very warm and welcoming: it is not uncommon for travellers to be invited to taste the local wine or the Moldovan "champagnes" to the tune of a gypsy melody. Tobacco products, liqueurs, embroidery, and very pretty hats are the pride of the country.

N. MELIKOFF

GEORGIA

+12 +11 +10 +9 +8

Region: ex-U.S.S.R.
Area: 69,700 km²
Capital: Tblisi
Airport: Tblisi
Population: 5,681,030
Languages: Georgian, Russian, Abkhazi
Religions: Christian, Islamic
Government: presidential democracy
Voltage: 220 - 50
Vaccinations required: –
Vaccinations recommended: –
Passport: required
Visa: required
Currency: rouble
$1Cdn: 3346.31 roubles
Driving: right hand
International permit: required
Area code: 011-7-8831
✆ from Canada: –
✆ to Canada: –
Accommodation: ★★★
Restaurants: ★★★
Transportation: ★★★
Cost of living: ○○
UN rank: 66
Best months: May to Sept
Holidays: 1 Jan; 8 Mar; 9 Apr; 9 May

GEORGIA

WHAT TO DO

Abkhazia and Georgia have signed a peace accord: the Enguri River now marks the southern border of the republic of Abkhazia, which covers more than 12 per cent of Georgia's territory, including a large part of the sandy coast on the Black Sea. The Transcaucasus republics have undergone changes in the last few years, but the beauty of the Black Sea has remained intact. The spa resorts at Bat'umi, Kobuleti, P'ot'i, and Sochi are particularly pretty. The capital, Tblisi, on the banks of the Kura River, is among the most beautiful cities of the ex-U.S.S.R. The sixth-century Zion Cathedral, the fortified castle, and the ruins of the citadel make old Tblisi a fascinating tourist site. The Grishahvili History and Ethnography Museum mounts displays on the history of the region, which goes back to the Neolithic Age. The old capital, Mtskheta, and the grape-growing region around T'elavi are prime tourist attractions. The sanatorium in Borzhomi is famous for its curative waters.

WHAT TO BUY

In Georgia, tourists can buy Abkhazian tobacco products, wine from Telavi, tea, and sea products. Georgian cuisine is tasty, particularly the pilaf rice and the *shashliks*, meat kebabs. The Georgians love poetry, and men's choirs frequently perform outdoors in town parks and squares, to the pleasure of everyone within earshot.

T. BOGNAR / RÉFLEXION

ARMENIA

+12 +11 +10 +9 +8

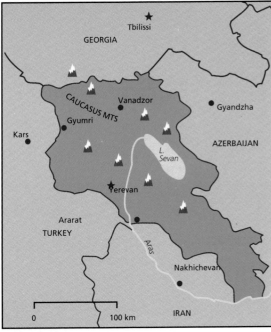

Region: ex-U.S.S.R.
Area: 29,800 km²
Capital: Yerevan
Airport: Yerevan
Population: 3,521,520
Language: Armenian
Religion: Christian
Government: parliamentary democracy
Voltage: 220 - 50
Vaccinations required: –
Vaccinations recommended: –
Passport: required
Visa: required
Currency: dram
$1Cdn: 300.22 drams
Driving: right hand
International permit: required
Area code: 011-7
✆ from Canada: –
✆ to Canada: –
Accommodation: ★★
Restaurants: ★★
Transportation: ★★
Cost of living: ❍❍
UN rank: 53
Best months: May, to Sept
Holidays: 1 Jan; 8 Mar; 2, 28 May; 21 Sept; 25 Dec

N. MELIKOFF

WHAT TO DO

The republics of the Transcaucasus have yet to blossom from the advent of their independent status: Armenia is currently at war with Azerbaijan for control of Upper Karabakh, an enclave with an Armenian majority. The civil war in Georgia and the tensions with Turkey, which is accusing Armenia of harbouring Kurdish independence fighters, have plunged the country into deeper chaos, to the point that Armenians are leaving their country en masse, particularly for Russia. Tourism is not being encouraged at the moment. This is unfortunate for travellers seeking cities of fantasy: Yerevan has been in existence for more than 3,000 years, making it one of the oldest towns in the world, and a very important cultural and historical centre. Beautiful Lake Sevan and the Caucasus Mountains, in particular Mount Ararat (on the border with Turkey), where, according to the Bible, Noah's ark came to rest after the flood, are spectacular in spite of the conflicts in the area.

WHAT TO BUY

Grape vines and fruit trees flourish in Armenia's gentle climate and the country is a major producer of liqueurs and wines.

AZERBAIJAN

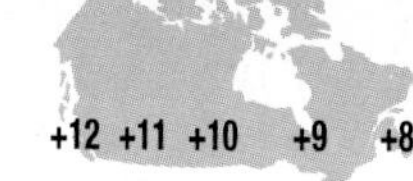

Region: ex-U.S.S.R.
Area: 86,600 km²
Capital: Baku
Airport: Baku
Population: 7,684,460
Languages: Azeri, Turkish, Russian
Religion: Islamic
Government: parliamentary democracy
Voltage: 220 - 50
Vaccinations required: –
Vaccinations recommended: –
Passport: required
Visa: required
Currency: manat
$1Cdn: 3235.1 manats
Driving: right hand
International permit: required
Area code: 011-7-8922
✆ from Canada: –
✆ to Canada: –
Accommodation: ★★
Restaurants: ★★
Transportation: ★★
Cost of living: ○○
UN rank: 71
Best months: May to Sept
Holidays: 1 Jan; 21, 22 Mar; 9 May

WHAT TO DO

Upper Karabakh is the most dangerous region of this country: Armenia and Azerbaijan are fighting over this territory, populated by a majority of Armenians. The Iranian border, along the Aras River, is also a region of frequent conflicts. Fortunately, the capital, Baku, is at the other end of the country, on the shore of the Caspian Sea. A historic city, founded before the second century, it is an important intellectual centre, largely because of its university. Kirov Park; the minarets; the very beautiful Primorsky Boulevard, which runs along the sea shore; and the Museum of Folklore are the city's main attractions. In nearby Kobu, amateur archaeologists will find prehistoric cave paintings, while Khachmas features Roman ruins.

WHAT TO BUY

In Samaxi, at the foot of the Greater Caucasus Mountains, silk goods, copperware, and pottery can be purchased. The Azerbaijani carpets are renowned, while the wines of Khachmas, the tea, and the *shekerbur*, a nut cake, are delicious. *The Prisoner of the Caucasus*, by the famous Russian novelist Leo Tolstoy, is set in Azerbaijan.

J. HUARD

KAZAKHSTAN

+14 +13 +12 +11 +10

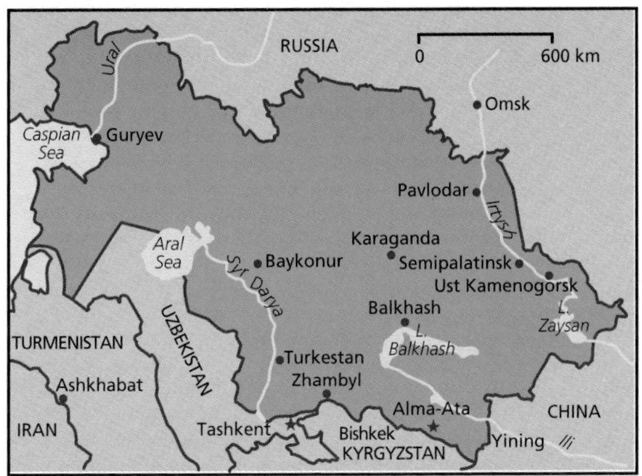

Region: ex-U.S.S.R.
Area: 2,717,300 km²
Capital: Alma-Ata
Airport: Alma-Ata
Population: 17,267,560
Languages: Kazakh, Russian
Religions: Russian Orthodox, Islamic
Government: parliamentary democracy
Voltage: 220 - 50
Vaccinations required: –
Vaccinations recommended: –
Passport: required
Visa: required
Currency: tenge
$1Cdn: –
Driving: right hand
International permit: required
Area code: 011-7-3272
✆ from Canada: –
✆ to Canada: –
Accommodation: ★★
Restaurants: ★★
Transportation: ★★
Cost of living: ❍❍
UN rank: 61
Best months: May to Sept
Holidays: 1 Jan; 8, 22 Mar; 9 May; 16 Dec

KAZAKHSTAN

WHAT TO DO

More than 2,000 years ago, Kazakhstan was a stop on the Silk Road for caravans filled with precious cargoes of Chinese silk goods. In fact, Kazakhstan and China are separated only by the very beautiful Tien Shan Mountains. Alma-Ata, the capital, is located at the foot of Mount Kok-Tyubek, which gives it a very special ambience. The Art Museum and Archaeology Museum are worth seeing, as is the cathedral, one of the largest wooden buildings in the world. *Yurts*, the magnificent skin tents once used by Kazakh nomads, are on exhibit at the tourist complex of Kazakh Aul, near Alma-Ata. The era of the *khans*, or Mongolian rulers, seems to live again in the town of Turkestan, another important stop on the Silk Road. The Mashat Pass near Shymkent, on the Uzbekistan border, is a beautiful natural site. Other areas of the Kazakh countryside are, unfortunately, marred by nuclear power stations.

WHAT TO BUY

Alma-ata means "father of apples" in Kazakh; cider and other apple products are thus very popular in this country. Musical instruments, wooden sculptures, leather goods, and copper and pewter objects are always beautifully crafted. Gold and silver jewelry are also finely worked.

J. HUARD

TURKMENISTAN

+13 +12 +11 +10 +9

TURKMENISTAN

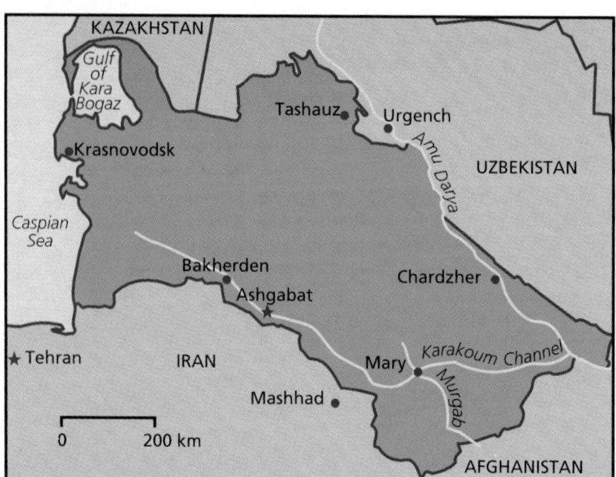

Region: ex-U.S.S.R.
Area: 488,100 km²
Capital: Ashgabat
Airport: Ashgabat
Population: 3,995,130
Languages: Turkmen, Russian
Religion: Islamic
Government: parliamentary democracy
Voltage: 220 - 50
Vaccinations required: –
Vaccinations recommended: –
Passport: required
Visa: required
Currency: rouble
$1Cdn: 3346.31 roubles
Driving: right hand
International permit: required
Area code: 011-7
✆ from Canada: –
✆ to Canada: –
Accommodation: ★★
Restaurants: ★★★
Transportation: ★★
Cost of living: ○○
UN rank: 80
Best months: May to Sept
Holidays: 1 Jan; 8, 22 Mar; 9 May; 27 Oct

WHAT TO DO

Squeezed between Russia and Iran, Turkmenistan has nonetheless managed to maintain its economic and cultural independence. Unlike most other republics in the C.I.S., Turkmenistan is almost ethnically homogeneous; this has enabled it to maintain a calmer political climate. Ashgabat, which means "city of love" in Turkmen, is a relatively young capital city, because the Turkmen were a nomadic people until relatively recently. The city's History Museum documents their customs well. Magnificent Turkmen rugs, the pride of the country, are on display at the Fine Arts Museum. Travellers should be sure to visit the Akhal Tekke stables, home to the famous Thoroughbred horses, exported throughout the world, notably, to the Queen of England. At Annau, archaeologists have discovered vestiges of a town from 3,000 years before Christ. Inside the cavern at Bakherden is an underground lake renowned for its curative waters.

WHAT TO BUY

Turkmen rugs, wrongly called "Bukhara rugs" (for the Uzbek city where they are sold), are definitely worth buying, even though the prices are sometimes very high. Silk goods and the large astrakhan hats worn by Turkmen men are typical of the country.

N. MELIKOFF

UZBEKISTAN

+13 +12 +11 +10 +9

Region: ex-U.S.S.R.
Area: 447,400 km²
Capital: Tashkent
Airport: Tashkent
Population: 21,608,870
Languages: Uzbek, Russian, Tajik
Religion: Islamic
Government: parliamentary democracy
Voltage: 220 - 50
Vaccinations required: –
Vaccinations recommended: –
Passport: required
Visa: required
Currency: rouble
$1Cdn: 3346.31 roubles
Driving: right hand
International permit: required
Area code: 011-7-3712
✆ from Canada: –
✆ to Canada: –
Accommodation: ★★
Restaurants: ★★
Transportation: ★★
Cost of living: ❍❍
UN rank: 91
Best months: May to Sept
Holidays: 1 Jan; 8 Mar; 9 May; 1 Sept

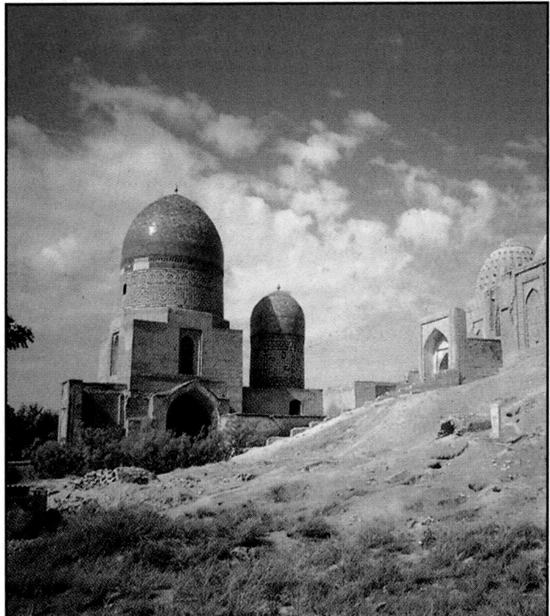
N. MELIKOFF

WHAT TO DO

This Central Asian republic was occupied many times by the Turks and attacked by the armies of Ghengis Khan and Alexander the Great. A thousand years before Christ, empires arose and fell in this region. The very pretty Samarkand, one of the oldest towns in the world, provides the best example of this tumultuous history. Rich in historic sites, this town alone is worth the trip to Uzbekistan. Must-sees include Reghistan Square, dating from the fifteenth century; the Chakh-Zind mausoleum and mosque; the Gur-Emir mausoleums; and the fourteenth-century Ichrat-Khan. Bukhara, with its 140 monuments and its minaret, is also worth a visit. The town of Shakhrisabz is known for its fifteenth-century baths, while Fergana features fabulous gardens. Unfortunately, pollution in the Aral Sea has turned the once beautiful northern part of the country into a desert.

WHAT TO BUY

Uzbekistan's astrakhan coats, leather goods, and cotton are as famous as its silk. Craftsmen weave beautiful carpets and fashion fine copper objects. Amin Maalouf's novel *Samarkand* is essential reading for those wanting to become familiar with the country.

KYRGYZSTAN

+14 +13 +12 +11 +10

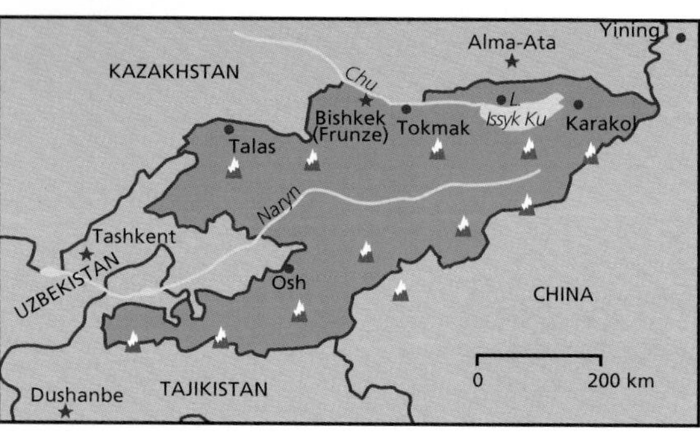

Region: ex-U.S.S.R.
Area: 198,500 km²
Capital: Bishkek
Airport: –
Population: 4,698,110
Languages: Kyrgyz, Russian
Religion: Islamic
Government: parliamentary democracy
Voltage: 220 - 50
Vaccinations required: –
Vaccinations recommended: –
Passport: required
Visa: required
Currency: rouble
$1Cdn: 3346.31 roubles
Driving: right hand
International permit: required
Area code: 011-7
✆ from Canada: –
✆ to Canada: –
Accommodation: ★★
Restaurants: ★★
Transportation: ★★
Cost of living: ○○
UN rank: 82
Best months: May to Sept
Holidays: 1 Jan; 8 Mar; 9 May; 23, 31 Aug; 2 Dec

WHAT TO DO

Conquered by the Mongols in the thirteenth century, the Kyrgyz have always maintained a link with the nomadic tradition of their ancestors. Cave paintings and prehistoric artifacts have been found around Bishkek, the capital. The Fine Art Museum and History Museum retrace the history of the region. Bishkek is a city of greenery that enjoys a pleasant climate. The countryside is very beautiful, especially near the Ala-Artcha Pass, from which one can view steep rocky hills, juniper forests, and cascading waterfalls. Pik Pobedy, with its snowy summit, in the Tien Shan Mountains, is a prime attraction for mountain climbers.

WHAT TO BUY

Tobacco, leather, embroideries, and woollens are Kyrgyzstan's main products, along with perfumes drawn from the many fragrant plants of the Fergana Valley.

N. MELIKOFF

TAJIKISTAN

+13 +12 +11 +10 +9

Region: ex-U.S.S.R.
Area: 143,100 km²
Capital: Dushanbe
Airport: –
Population: 5,995,470
Languages: Tajik, Uzbek
Religion: Islamic
Government: parliamentary democracy
Voltage: 220 - 50
Vaccinations required: –
Vaccinations recommended: –
Passport: required
Visa: required
Currency: rouble
$1Cdn: 3346,31 roubles
Driving: right hand
International permit: required
Area code: 011-7
✆ from Canada: –
✆ to Canada: –
Accommodation: ★
Restaurants: ★
Transportation: ★
Cost of living: ○○
UN rank: 97
Best months: May to Sept
Holidays: 1 Jan; 8 Mar; 9 May; 9 Sep

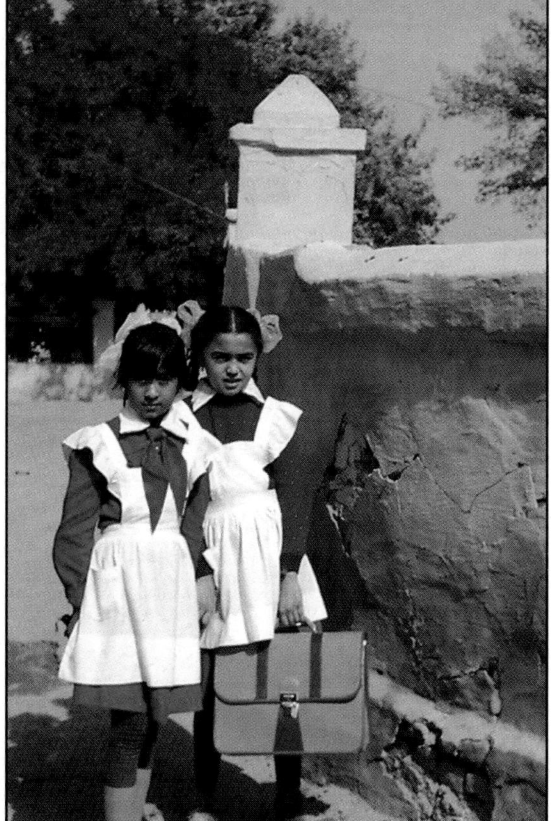

N. MELINKOFF

WHAT TO DO

Tajikistan is at war with fundamentalist Islamic Afghanistan, which wants to submit the new republic to its religious values. The entire southern border of Tajikistan is thus considered a powderkeg, at risk of blowing up any time. This war has already killed more than 50,000 Tajik. Tajikistan provides a good example of what some call "Soviet-remodelled Islam". Dushanbe, the capital, is not, unfortunately, beyond the range of Afghani guns. One cannot help but be pessimistic with regard to the future of this part of Central Asia. Nonetheless, the country has many historical attractions, such as the archaeological site at old Pendzhikent and the fort at Gissar. There are many natural wonders as well, including the gorges at Varzob and Pik Lenin.

WHAT TO BUY

The cultivation of geraniums and roses provides raw materials for Tajikistan's perfume industry. Tajik astrakhan coats, cotton, embroidery, and silk have a very good reputation. The country's weavers produce excellent rugs.

MIDDLE EAST

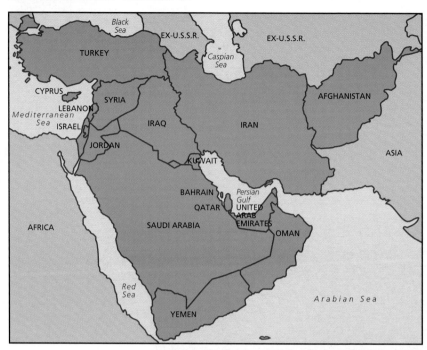

The Middle East is a part of the world where the confluence of religious, ethnic, and cultural influences can be positively explosive. "Middle East" usually designates the region between the eastern shores of the Mediterranean Sea and the north shore of the Indian Ocean (or the Gulf of Oman), where Asia starts. Christianity, Judaism, and Islam were all born in this region; religion is thus an essential aspect of daily life. Travellers should be well acquainted with each country's allegiances so that they don't offend anyone or get into difficult situations: the

BOB BURCH / RÉFLEXION

emerging new values are a concern for all tourists. The rich archaeological sites and other reminders of the fascinating history of the Middle Eastern countries make this region a choice destination for lovers of lost cities and mysterious deserts.

TURKEY

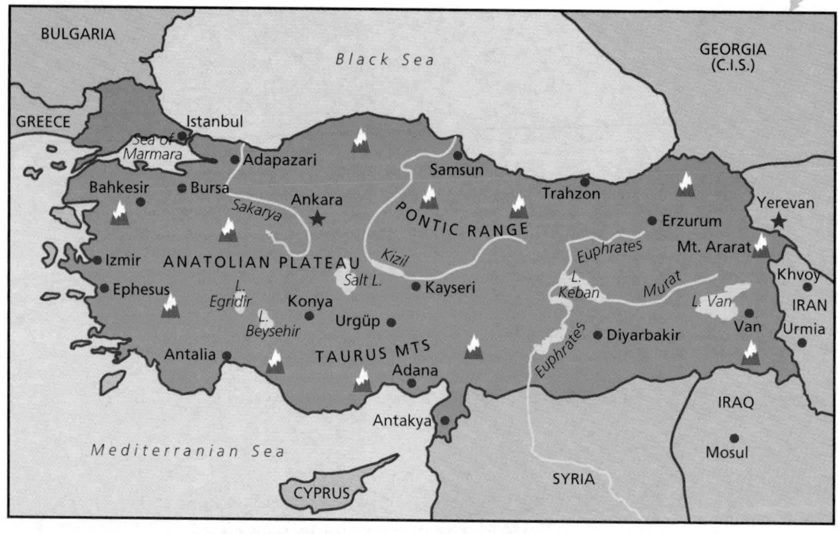

TURKEY

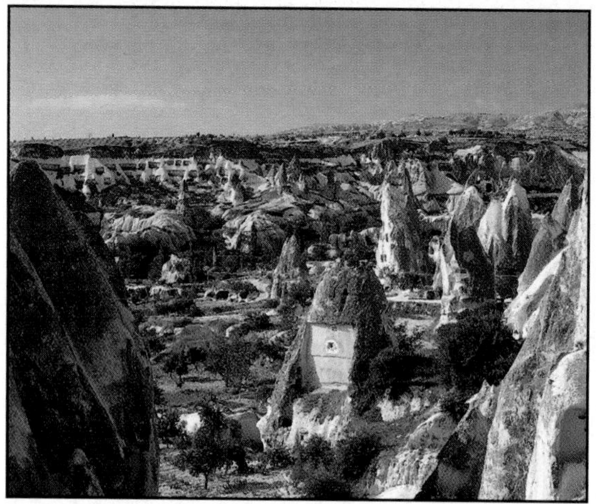
RÉFLEXION

Region: Middle East
Area: 780,580 km²
Capital: Ankara
Airport: Ankara 35 km, Istanbul 24 km
Population: 62,153,898
Languages: Turkish, Kurdish
Religion: Islamic
Government: parliamentary democracy
Voltage: 220 - 50
Vaccinations required: –
" recommended: Cho, Ty, Po, Mal
Passport: required
Visa: not required
Currency: Turkish lira
$1Cdn: 33119.35 liras
Driving: right hand
International permit: required
Area code: 011-90
✆ from Canada: 1-800-463-9433
✆ to Canada: ▲00-800-16677
Accommodation: ★★★★
Restaurants: ★★★★
Transportation: ★★★★
Cost of living: ❍
UN rank: 68
Best months: June, July, Aug
Holidays: 1 Jan; 4 Mar; 23 Apr; 11, 19 May; 30 Aug; 29 Oct

WHAT TO DO

Turkey is synonymous with Istanbul, a city that has borne the magical names Constantinople and Byzantium, and long been a gateway to Europe, to the west, and Asia, to the east. The Byzantine and Ottoman districts contain the most beautiful historical monuments in the city, including the St. Sophia Basilica, the foundations of which date from the year 425; the 450-year-old Suleymaniye Mosque; and the pride of the city, the exquisite Blue Mosque. The Kahriye Camii, the Topkapi Sarayi (imperial residence), the ruins of the Hippodrome, and the many museums, including the Ancient Orient and Antiquities museums, must be seen. The Kapali Carsi (great bazaar) is one of the largest covered markets in the world and is in itself worth the trip to Turkey—but beware of pickpockets! The shores of the Karadeniz Bogazi (Bosporus) are dotted with palaces and magnificent gardens that are most easily viewed from the deck of a boat. The towns of Bursa and Ephesus are home to ruins from the Ottoman era, and Ankara, the capital, is considered

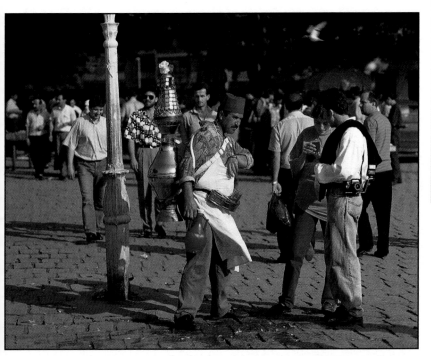

a museum-city because of its many Roman ruins. The Hittite Museum and the Ankara Museum of Archaeology have mounted insightful displays on the history of the region. Cappadocia's geological wonder is unique to Turkey; there, volcanic, chimney-like formations of white rock have created a lunar landscape on the floor of a rocky valley. In the Ürgüp region are fascinating cave (troglodytic) dwellings. Konya is known for its monastery of whirling dervishes, members of a religious order with rituals that are as fantastic as they are strange. Aqri Dagi (Mount Ararat), where, it is said, Noah came to rest after the flood, is too dangerous to visit because the region surrounding it is involved in armed conflicts. At the other end of the country, the Aegean and Mediterranean seas offer superb beaches and resorts. The Kurdish conflict has somewhat slowed the Turkish tourism industry; however, visitors will not be affected by the conflict if they remain within well-trod tourist areas.

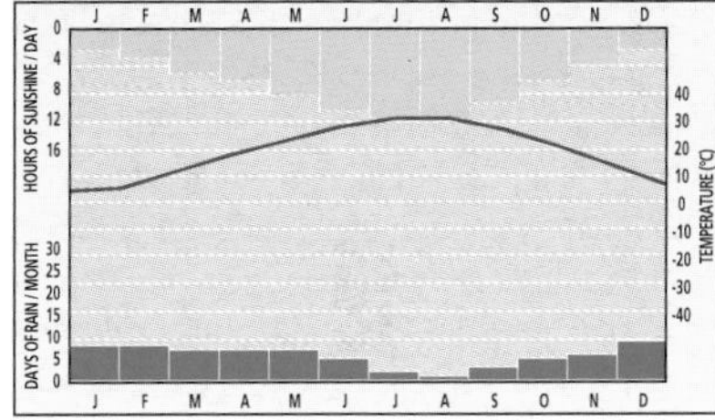

WHAT TO BUY

Turkish cuisine is tasty; among the best dishes are *tarhana corbasi*, a tomato-and-yogurt soup; *zeytin*, olives; and *kofte*, spicy meatballs. *Raki*, an anise-flavoured liquor, is the national drink. The vineyards of Thrace and Anatolia produce a delicious wine. The cotton, wool, mohair, and silk from Adana, Izmir, and Bursa are famous. Turkish carpets have been known for their quality since the Ottoman period, and the copper objects are also meticulously worked. The water pipes, *hookahs*, may seem like good buys, but don't give in to the temptation: anything connected with drugs (remotely or otherwise) is strictly forbidden in Turkey, especially for tourists. Outside of the major cities, the women are veiled; women travellers should thus be as discreet as possible. In fact, it is inadvisable for women to travel alone to some central and eastern parts of the country. Always find out where the closest police station is. If you want to experience the *hammams*, Turkish baths, be sure to respect the rules.

CYPRUS

+10 +9 +8 +7 +6

Region: Middle East
Area: 9,251 km²
Capital: Nicosia
Airport: Larnaka
Population: 730,084
Languages: Greek, Turkish, English
Religions: Greek Orthodox, Islamic
Government: parliamentary democracy
Voltage: 240 - 50
Vaccinations required: –
Vaccinations recommended: Ty, Po
Passport: required
Visa: not required
Currency: Cyprus pound
$1Cdn: .32 pound
Driving: left hand
International permit: recommended
Area code: 011-357
✆ from Canada: 1-800-463-3053
✆ to Canada: ▲080-900-12
Accommodation: ★★★★
Restaurants: ★★★★
Transportation: ★★
Cost of living: ❍
UN rank: 26
Best months: May to Oct
Holidays: 1, 19 Jan; 25 Mar; 1, 21–24 Apr; 1 May; 15 Aug; 1, 20 Oct; 15 Nov; 25 Dec

WHAT TO DO

The island of Cyprus remains divided: the north is claimed by Turkey, the south by Greece, and the two countries are still fighting over this beautiful territory. , The conflict does not, however, keep tourists from enjoying the magnificent beaches, the beauty of the Cypriot monasteries, and the historical attractions, such as the Templars' Castle in the town of Limassol, which is also known for its beaches. In the Troodos (Troghodhos) Mountains there are small villages, monasteries perched on hillsides, and forest hiking trails. Platres is a good stepping-off point for visiting the region. In Nicosia, the capital, the border between the Greek and Turkish sections is reminiscent of the Berlin Wall, but the city is well worth visiting for the immense Byzantine palace of the archdeacon of Cyprus and for the Cyprus Museum, which has a fascinating collection of artifacts from the Neolithic Age. The Turkish district of Nicosia boasts the ancient St. Sophia Cathedral, now converted into the Selimiye Mosque. Girne (Kyrenia) has a fabulous medieval castle and a picturesque old town.

WHAT TO BUY

The best buys in Cyprus are Limassol's perfumes, Lefkara's laces, and Paphos's carpets, along with *ouzo*, an anise-flavoured liquor, and Cypriot wine.

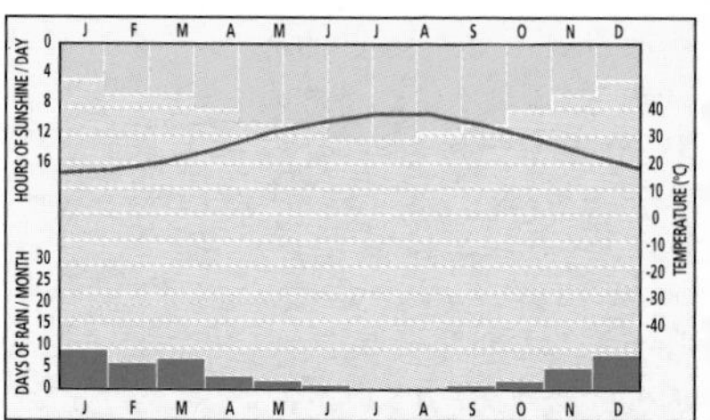

GREEK NATIONAL TOURIST OFFICE

SYRIA

+10 +9 +8 +7 +6

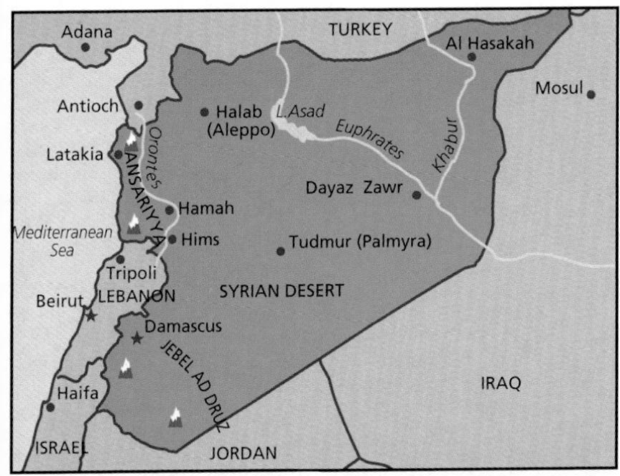

Region: Middle East
Area: 185,180 km²
Capital: Damascus
Airport: Damascus 30 km
Population: 14,886,672
Language: Arabic
Religion: Islamic
Government: presidency
Voltage: 220 - 50
Vaccinations required: Yf*
Vaccinations recommended: Cho, Ty, Po, Mal
Passport: required
Visa: required
Currency: Syrian pound
$1Cdn: 31.65 pounds
Driving: right hand
International permit: required
Area code: 011-963
✆ from Canada: –
✆ to Canada: –
Accommodation: ★★★★
Restaurants: ★★★★
Transportation: ★★★
Cost of living: ○○
UN rank: 73
Best months: Apr, May, Oct
Holidays: 1 Jan; 4, 8, 21, 22 Mar; 16, 17

SYRIA

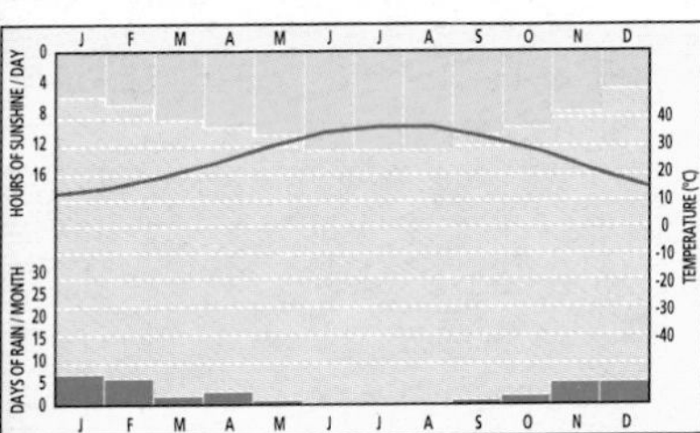

WHAT TO DO

Among Middle Eastern countries, Syria is unique when it comes to tourism: in Damascus, the capital, mixed crowds of men and women, Christians and Muslims, fill the nightclubs and the busy streets. Its tolerance and cultural diversity make this country a choice destination for travellers seeking the flavour of the Middle East. Damascus is also a good stepping-off point for visiting the country: historical remains like the Anani Chapel and the beautiful Umayyades Mosque are worth a visit, as are the souks and alleys in the old part of the city. In Tudmur (Palmyra), a desert oasis, must-sees include the Bêl Sanctuary, the arcades, and the burial vaults dating from the second century. Halab (Aleppo) is known for its magnificent citadel and its covered bazaar of stores and mosques, some dating from the sixteenth century. The Mediterranean shore, mainly near Al Ladhiqiyah (Latakia), draws enthusiasts of water sports and sunbathing alike.

WHAT TO BUY

The rose jelly of Damascus, the tobacco from Halab, and items made from olive wood are Syrian specialties. The souks offer products from all parts of the country, especially pistachio candies, pine nuts, and almonds, which are served with delicious mint tea.

IRAQ

+11 +10 +9 +8 +7

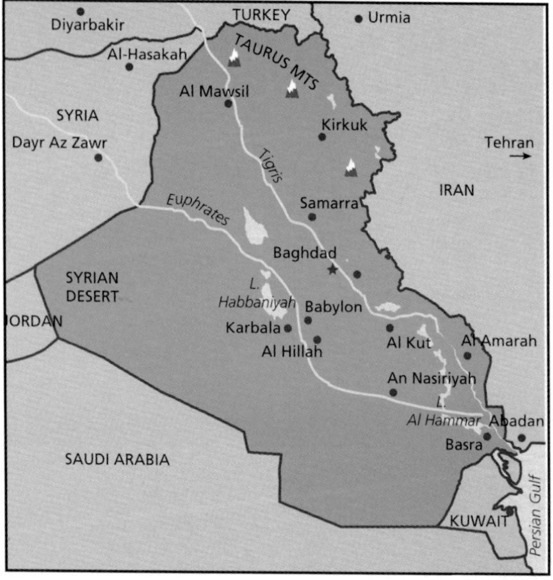

Region: Middle East
Area: 437,072 km²
Capital: Baghdad
Airport: Baghdad 17 km
Population: 19,889,666
Languages: Arabic, Kurdish
Religions: Islamic (Shiite)
Government: military rule
Voltage: 220 - 50
Vaccinations required: Yf*, Cho*
Vaccinations recommended: Ty, Po, Mal
Passport: required
Visa: required
Currency: Iraqi dinar
$1Cdn: .44 dinar
Driving: right hand
International permit: required
Area code: 011-964
✆ from Canada: –
✆ to Canada: –
Accommodation: ★★
Restaurants: ★★
Transportation: ★★
Cost of living: ○○
UN rank: 100
Best months: Apr, Oct
Holidays: 1, 6 Jan; 8 Feb; 4, 21 Mar; 1, 11, 31 May; 10 Jun; 14, 17 Jul; 8 Aug

WHAT TO DO

For some, the names Baghdad and Babylon evoke magic carpets and beautiful princesses veiled in gold-embroidered silk. For others, Iraq, under Saddam Hussein's rule, is responsible for tensions with Kurdistan and Iran, and even with Kuwait, Syria, and Turkey! The cradle of great historical eras and civilizations—Mesopotamia, the Assyrian Empire, and Babylonia—Iraq is rich in magnificent ruins, notably, in Basra in the south, and in Al Mawsil (Mosul), in the north. Samarra', Al Faw, and Al Nasiriyah have monuments dating from the time of the Abbassides Caliphs, between 750 and 1258 A.D. Unfortunately, Baghdad is still suffering the after-effects of the Gulf War.

WHAT TO BUY

Tinwork is an Iraqi specialty: the souks offer finely engraved everyday wares such as pots, vases, and plates. Carpets, sheepskin goods, and woollens are Baghdad specialties.

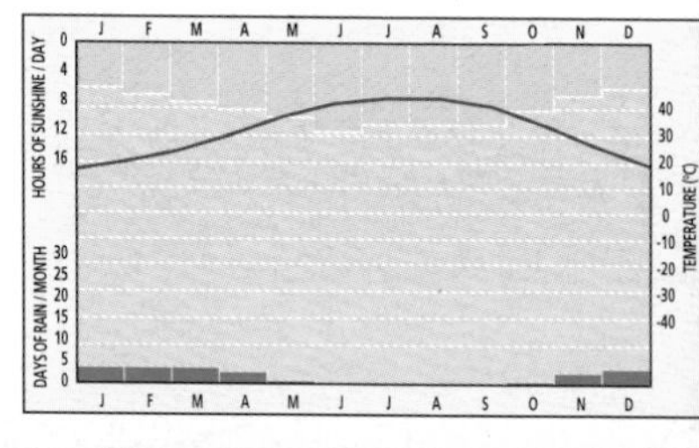

IRAN

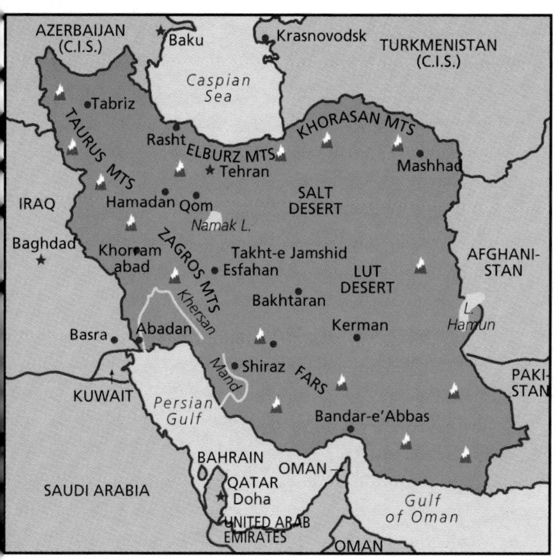

Region: Middle East
Area: 1,648,000 km²
Capital: Tehran
Airport: Tehran 11 km
Population: 65,615,474
Language: Farsi
Religion: Islamic
Government: Islamic republic
Voltage: 220 - 50
Vaccinations required: Yf*, Cho*
Vaccinations recommended: Ty, Po, Mal
Passport: required
Visa: required + visitor's permit
Currency: Iranian rial
$1Cdn: 2208.30 rials
Driving: right hand
Int'l permit: required + visitor's permit
Area code: 011-98
✆ from Canada: –
✆ to Canada: –
Accommodation: ★★
Restaurants: ★★
Transportation: ★★
Cost of living: ❍❍
UN rank: 86
Best months: Apr, Oct
Holidays: 11 Feb; 4, 20–24 Mar; 1, 2 Apr; 11, 24, 31 May; 4, 5, 10 Jun; 8 Aug

WHAT TO DO

There are still tensions between Iran and the international community: Islamic fundamentalism has brought tourism in this country to almost a complete standstill. Men with a visitor's visa can, however, visit the golden triangle of the ancient cities of Hamadan, Bakhtaran, and Khorram abad. Esfahan and Takht-e Jamshid are home to historical and archaeological marvels. In Tehran, the Shah Mosque, the Sepahsalar mosque, and its eight minarets, and the Archaeological Museum are must-sees. Aficionados of ancient art will be thrilled with the Museum of Decorative Art, with its magnificent works of Islamic art. The smaller towns of Rey, Varamin, and Shemshak have preserved their own special ambience.

WHAT TO BUY

Alcohol is not consumed in Iran, but the food is delicious: *shelo khoresh*, a rice-and-vegetable dish topped with a nut sauce, and *polo shirin*, a saffron-flavoured rice, are fine examples of local cuisine. Iranian carpet-makers and silk weavers still use traditional methods dating back to ancient Persia. The beauty of the wooden sculptures, as finely worked as lace, is equalled only by the engraved gold and silver jewelry. Ceramics and leather goods are also of top quality.

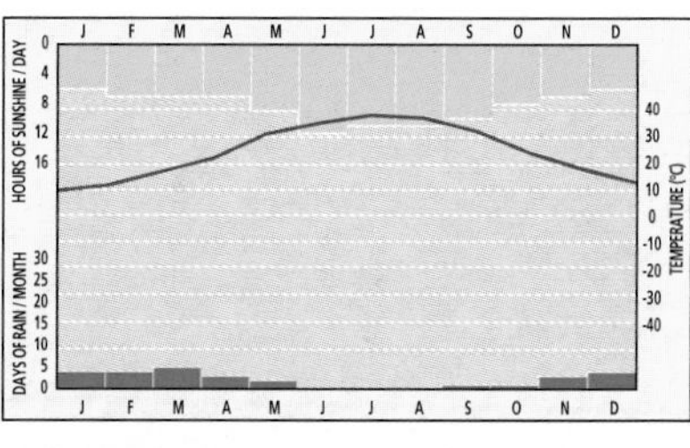

RÉFLEXION

AFGHANISTAN

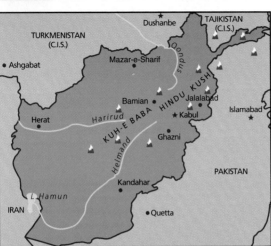

+12 +11 +10 +9 +8

AFGHANISTAN

Dushanbe
TAJIKISTAN (C.I.S.)
TURKMENISTAN (C.I.S.)
Ashgabat
Mazar-e-Sharif
Qondus
HINDU KUSH
KUH-E BABA
Bamian
Jalalabad
Islamabad
Herat
Harirud
Kabul
Ghazni
Helmand
PAKISTAN
Kandahar
L. Hamun
IRAN
Quetta

S.D.P / RÉFLEXION

Region: Middle East
Area: 647,500 km²
Capital: Kabul
Airport: Kabul 16 km
Population: 16,903,400
Languages: Persian, Pashtu
Religion: Islamic
Government: Islamic military rule
Voltage: 220 - 50
Vaccinations required: Yf*, Cho
Vaccinations recommended: Mal
Passport: required
Visa: required
Currency: Afghani
$1Cdn: 3549.67 Afghanis
Driving: right hand
International permit: required
Area code: limited service
✆ from Canada: –
✆ to Canada: –
Accommodation: ★
Restaurants: ★
Transportation: ★
Cost of living: ❍
UN rank: 171
Best months: May, October
Holidays: 4, 21 Mar; 28 Apr; 1, 4, 11 May; 10 June; 8, 19 Aug

Mazar-e-Sharif is the beautiful tomb of Caliph Ali. The ruins of Buddhist stupas and monasteries in the town of Hadda are adorned with Gandhara frescoes dating from the first and fifth centuries.

WHAT TO BUY

Afghanis produce a wide range of goods from processed sheepskin: the vests, hats, coats, and blankets are particularly prized. Their carpets, jewelry, and ceramics are also of top quality. The silk from Herat is still as fine as it was in the era of the Silk Road.

WHAT TO DO

Kabul, the capital, has been almost completely destroyed due to years of civil war. The war with Tajikistan and political tensions with Uzbekistan and Iran have plunged the country into a period of Islamic radicalization. Unfortunately, the breathtaking Hindu Kush Mountains, on the Pakistan border, are the site of the most violent battles, but Bamian is still the stepping-off point for excursions to their high peaks. The small towns of Kandahar and Herat are very charming. In Begram, visitors must see the superb ivory sculptures; in

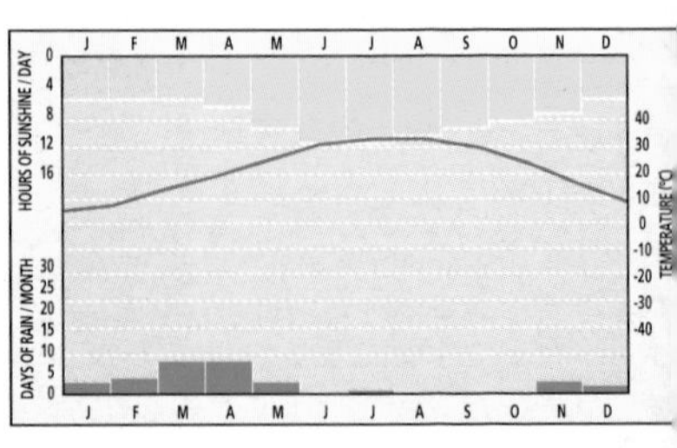

LEBANON

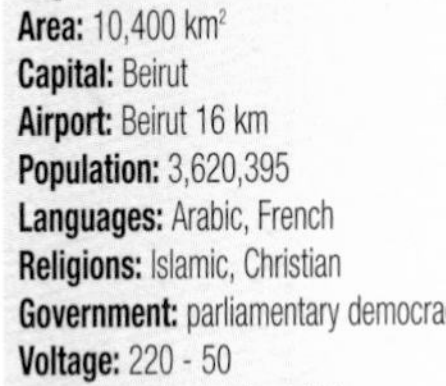

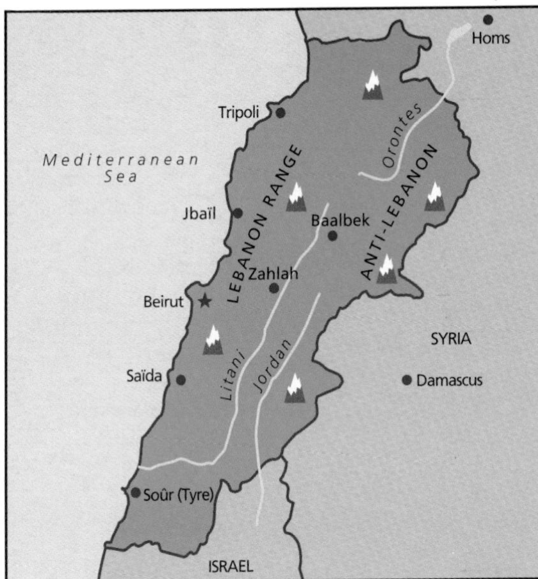

Region: Middle East
Area: 10,400 km²
Capital: Beirut
Airport: Beirut 16 km
Population: 3,620,395
Languages: Arabic, French
Religions: Islamic, Christian
Government: parliamentary democracy
Voltage: 220 - 50
Vaccinations required: Yf*
Vaccinations recommended: Cho, Ty, Po
Passport: required
Visa: required
Currency: Lebanese pound
$1Cdn: .1189.91 pounds
Driving: right hand
International permit: recommended
Area code: 011-961
✆ from Canada: –
✆ to Canada: –
Accommodation: ★★★
Restaurants: ★★★★
Transportation: ★★★
Cost of living: ○○
UN rank: 103
Best months: Mar, Apr, May
Holidays: 1 Jan; 9 Feb; 4 Mar; 14, 16, 17, 21–24 Apr; 1, 11, 31 May; 10 June; 8, 15 Aug; 1, 22 Nov; 25, 31 Dec

LEBANON

WHAT TO DO

Beirut and Tripoli are no longer the splendid cities they were before the civil war, but Lebanon is trying to recapture its reputation for being "the Switzerland of the Middle East." Travellers can easily forget the traces left by the ravages of war and concentrate instead on the rich history and beauty of the countryside. It is claimed that Jbaïl (Byblos) is the oldest city in the world: it was in existence by 3000 B.C. Today, it is a pretty port town. Soûr (Tyre) has preserved its ancient amphitheatre, and Saïda its fortifications. Lebanon's main attraction is its natural beauty: Mediterranean beaches, deep valleys, stretches of desert, and pine forests. Climbers can scale the mountains of the Galilee, the highest peaks of which, at Qornet es Saouda, rise to 3,090 m.

WHAT TO BUY

The cedar is Lebanon's emblem; unfortunately, there are few of these trees left in the country. The vineyards produce an excellent rosé wine that goes perfectly with the delicious Lebanese cuisine. *Tahini*, a sesame paste, and yogurt are the basis for a number of dishes. Fabrics, glassware, and tin objects make good gifts, as do finely worked silver and gold.

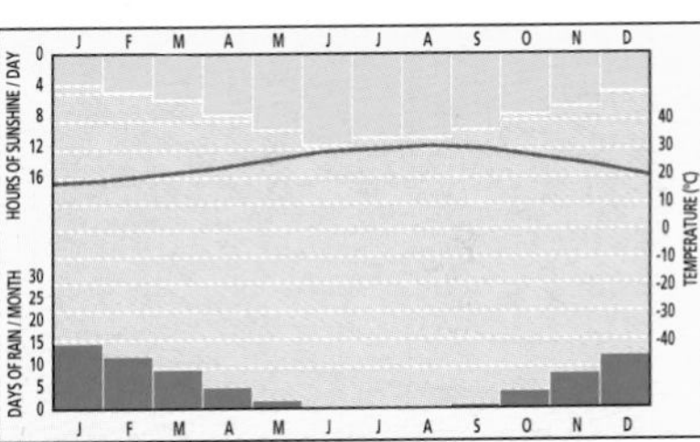

P. LESAGE

ISRAEL

+10 +9 +8 +7 +6

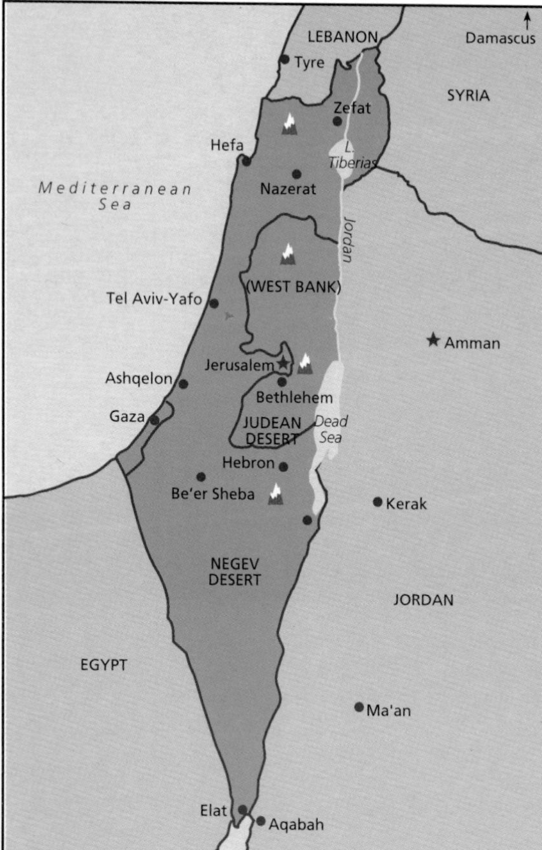

Region: Middle East
Area: 20,770 km²
Capital: Jerusalem
Airport: Tel Aviv 20 km
Population: 5,050,850
Languages: Hebrew, Arabic, English
Religions: Jewish, Islamic
Government: parliamentary democracy
Voltage: 220 - 50
Vaccinations required: –
Vaccinations recommended: Ty, Po
Passport: required
Visa: not required
Currency: shekel, american dollar
$1Cdn: .74 dollar
Driving: right hand
International permit: recommended
Area code: 011-972
✆ from Canada: 1-800-463-1148
✆ to Canada: 177-105-2727
Accommodation: ★★★★
Restaurants: ★★★★
Transportation: ★★★★
Cost of living: ○○
UN rank: 19
Best months: May, June, Sept, Oct
Holidays: 16 Mar; 15, 20, 29 Apr; 4, 5 June; 25, 26 Sept; 4, 9, 16, 17 Oct; 18–25 Dec

WHAT TO DO

The peace accord between Israel and the Palestinians won Israel's prime minister, Itzak Rabin, and the PLO's leader, Yasser Arafat, the 1994 Nobel Peace Prize. This event proved to be a major turning point in the history of the region, which has been deeply embroiled in conflict ever since the state of Israel was formed; in Hebrew, Jerusalem means "peace will come." The diversity of ethnic groups and religions living side by side give the Holy Land its character. Jews from all over the world, as well as Christians and Muslims, make pilgrimages to the country. The Wailing Wall, the stone dome, Christ's tomb, the Golgotha, the Via Dolorosa, and the mosque of Omar are Jerusalem's main attractions. For a historical tour of Israel, one can visit the towns with biblical names, from Bethlehem to Nazareth, via Sodom and Gemorrah. Hefa (Haifa) is a good stepping-off point for visiting the Galilee. Elat, at the northern tip of the Red Sea, has a wonderful coral reef that will attract diving fans. The Hanegev (Negev) region used to be a desert; orange and olive trees have transformed the area into a vast garden. No visit to Israel would be complete without a stop at one of the *kibbutzes*, agricultural co-operatives unique

RÉFLEXION

to this country.

WHAT TO BUY

Falafels, fried balls of ground-chickpeas, are sold everywhere. The wine and spirits are excellent. Diamonds, precious stones, and ceramics with religious themes are always available in the markets.

JORDAN

+10 +9 +8 +7 +6

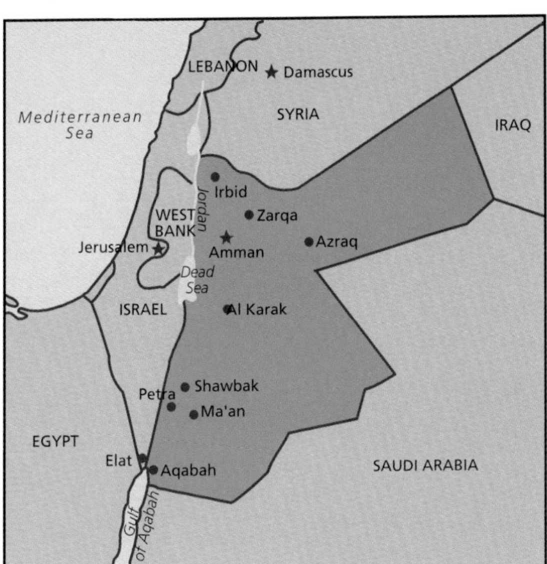

Region: Middle East
Area: 89,213 km²
Capital: Amman
Airport: Amman 32 km
Population: 3,961,194
Languages: Arabic, English
Religion: Islamic
Government: parliamentary monarchy
Voltage: 220 - 50
Vaccinations required: –
Vaccinations recommended: Cho, Ty, Po
Passport: required
Visa: required
Currency: Jordanian dinar
$1Cdn: .51 dinar
Driving: right hand
International permit: required
Area code: 011-962
✆ from Canada: 1-800-447-8481
✆ to Canada: 18-800-962
Accommodation: ★★★
Restaurants: ★★★
Transportation: ★★★
Cost of living: ○○
UN rank: 98
Best months: Dec to May
Holidays: 1 Jan; 4 Mar; 16 Apr; 1, 11, 25, 31 May; 10 June; 8, 11 Aug; 14 Nov; 25, 26, 31 Dec

WHAT TO DO

The Jordan River is one of the most historic rivers in the world: the Hebrews crossed its bed without wetting their feet, John the Baptist baptised Jesus in it, and generations of farmers have grown grapes and figs in the miraculously fertile valley surrounding it. Jordan abounds with historical and archaeological sites from a wide variety of civilizations: the Hebrews, Greeks, Romans, Byzantines, Arabs, and Ottomans left signs of their passage, as did the Crusaders. So Jordan has an openness to the rest of the world that makes it unique among Middle Eastern countries. In Amman, the capital, the Romans left a theatre dating from the second century, and the Umayyades, a sumptuous palace. The Archaeology Museum offers a fabulous collection of artifacts from sites on Jordanian soil. At Jarash, the temple of Artemis, the Arch of Triumph, the Hippodrome, and the Avenue of Columns are incomparable attractions. Near Petra, the old capital of the Nabateans, is the fascinating Khaznah, the Pharaohs' Treasure —a town carved out of rock in a quiet countryside of red and ochre canyons. Aqabah is known for the beauty of the coral reefs along the bed of its eponymous gulf.

WHAT TO BUY

The many everyday objects, made of olive wood, especially the very pretty backgammon boards (the game is popular in Jordan), are popular souvenirs. *Arak*, an anise-flavoured liquor, is available everywhere, as is mint tea served with pine nuts.

J. HUARD

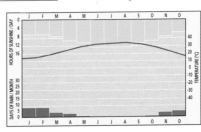

SAUDI ARABIA

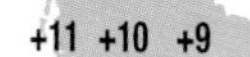

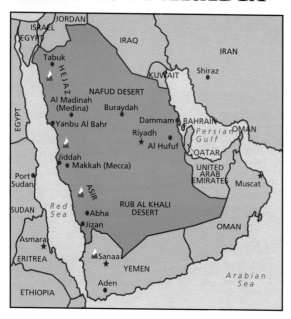

Region: Middle East
Area: 1,960,582 km²
Capital: Riyadh
Airport: Riyadh 35 km, Jiddah 17 km
Population: 18,196,783
Language: Arabic
Religion: Islamic (Shiite)
Government: monarchy
Voltage: 220 - 50
Vaccinations required: Yf*, Cho*
Vaccinations recommended: Ty, Po, Mal
Passport: required, Israeli stamp refused
Visa: required
Currency: Saudi riyal
$1Cdn: 2.76 riyals
Driving: right hand
International permit: required
Area code: 011-966
✆ from Canada: –
✆ to Canada: –
Accommodation: ★★★★
Restaurants: ★★★
Transportation: ★★★★
Cost of living: ○○○
UN rank: 67
Best months: Dec to May
Holidays: 4 Mar; 11, 31 May; 23 Sep

WHAT TO DO

The best-known destination in Saudi Arabia is Makkah (Mecca), the cradle of Islam, with its Great Mosque and the *Ka'ba*. This marvel of the history of the caliphs, where Mohammed delivered many of his sermons, is not, unfortunately, accessible to non-Muslims. Tourism is not encouraged in this country; however, businessmen who are guests of the major Saudi oil companies may visit Riyadh, the capital, the markets of Jiddah, and the coral coast of the Red Sea. Businesswomen are still not very well integrated into economic life in Saudi Arabia, and Saudi women do not appear in public.

WHAT TO BUY

Mutton and *kabsah*, a rice-and-meat dish, are usually served to guests: if you are not offered eating utensils, it is preferable to eat with only your right hand. The souks (markets) offer a very wide variety of goods, from gold to fresh figs to electronic gadgets, but beware: prices are exorbitant!

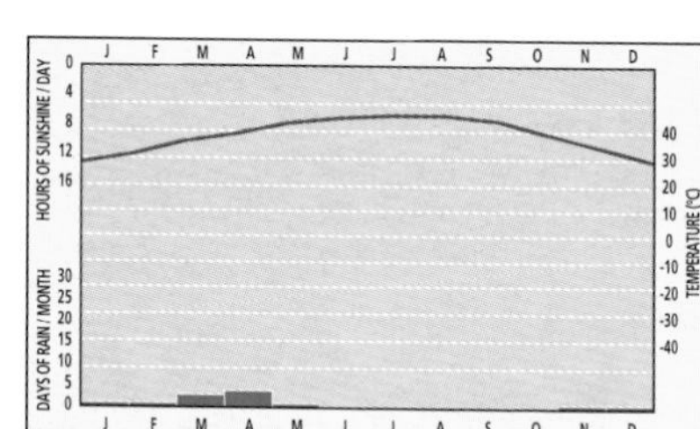

RÉFLEXION

KUWAIT

+11 +10 +9 +8 +7

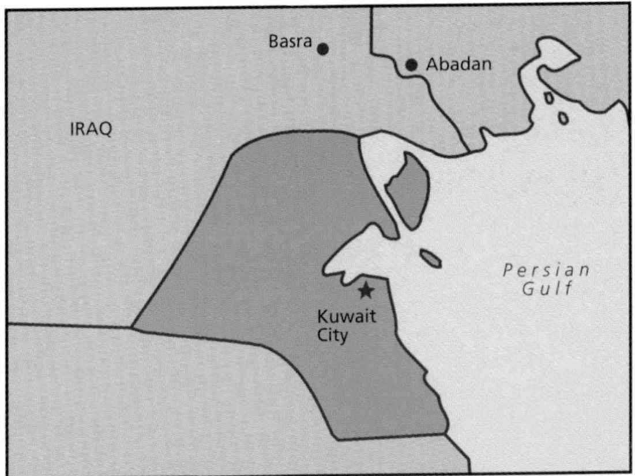

Region: Middle East
Area: 17,820 km²
Capital: Kuwait City
Airport: Kuwait City 16 km
Population: 1,819,322
Language: Arabic
Religion: Islamic
Government: monarchy
Voltage: 240 - 50
Vaccinations required: Yf*, Cho*
Vaccinations recommended: Ty, Po
Passport: required
Visa: required
Currency: Kuwaiti dinar
$1Cdn: .22 dinar
Driving: right hand
International permit: required
Area code: 011-965
✆ from Canada: –
✆ to Canada: –
Accommodation: ★★★★
Restaurants: ★★★★
Transportation: ★★★★
Cost of living: ○○○
UN rank: 51
Best months: Dec to May
Holidays: 19 Jan; 25 Feb; 1, 4 Mar; 11, 31 May; 10 June; 8 Aug; 31 Dec

KUWAIT

WHAT TO DO

Kuwait is now a familiar name, although it is a sad fact that war brought this country international attention. The most Westernized of the Gulf countries, it is also one of the most expensive in the world. Although it has oil reserves, it has little potable water; the sea-water desalinization plants are highly sophisticated and very interesting to visit. The latest in high technology and ancient traditions exist side by side in this country: visitors can see modern shipyards alongside with traditional fishing skiffs and mosques surrounded by sky-scrapers.

WHAT TO BUY

Sayyadiya, a fish and rice dish, is typical Kuwaiti fare. In downtown Kuwait City, travellers can find anything they want, from hand-woven Turkish carpets to German cameras; however, the prices are exorbitant. Kuwaiti women do not appear in public, and foreign women are not made to feel particularly welcome.

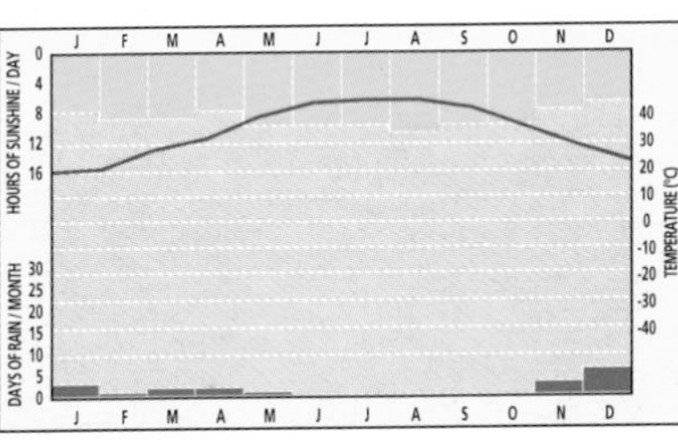

BAHRAIN

+11 +10 +9 +8 +7

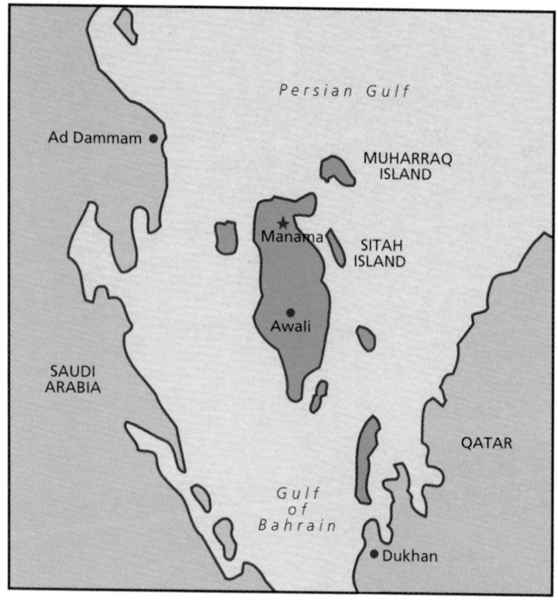

Region: Middle East
Area: 620 km²
Capital: Manama
Airport: Manama 6 km
Population: 585,683
Language: Arabic
Religion: Islamic (Shiite)
Government: monarchy
Voltage: 220 - 50
Vaccinations required: Yf*
" recommended: Cho, Ty, Po, Mal
Passport: required
Visa: required
Currency: Bahrain dinar
$1Cdn: .27 dinar
Driving: right hand
International permit: required
Area code: 011-973
© from Canada: 1-800-463-7396
© to Canada: 80-01-00
Accommodation: ★★★★
Restaurants: ★★★
Transportation: ★★★★
Cost of living: ○○○
UN rank: 58
Best months: Dec to May
Holidays: 1 Jan; 4 Mar; 11, 31 May; 10 June; 8 Aug; 16 Dec

WHAT TO DO

The tourism infrastructure in the Emirate of Bahrain is by far the best organized on the Arabian Peninsula: Western visitors are offered good hotels and restaurants, along with tours to the country's most interesting sites. The emirate has a cosmopolitan flavour, largely because of foreigners working in the oil industry. As in other Arabic countries, however, women do not appear in public. The old town of Bilas Al Qadir, just outside the capital, Manama, offers a curious contrast of ancient and modern: skyscrapers tower above souks and winding streets. The Siyadi house is a masterpiece of the notched-wood structures typical of the region. One also finds there beautiful examples of Islamic architecture, including the Shaikh Isa, a building dating from the nineteenth century. The climate in Bahrain is ideal for enjoying the sandy beaches, on the south end of the island, and for walking in the nature preserve at Al Areen, where a variety of desert flora and fauna can be observed.

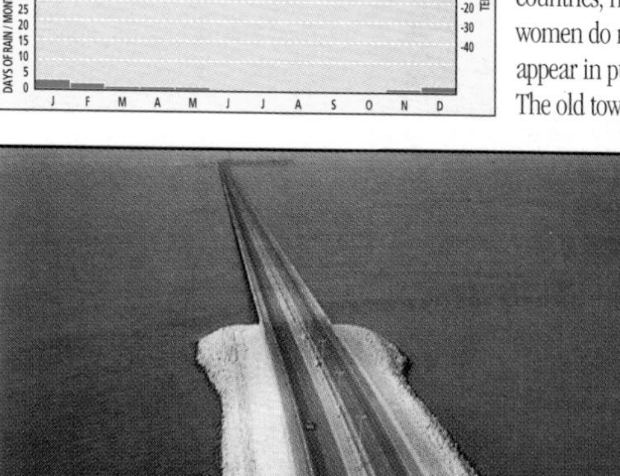
BAHRAIN TOURIST OFFICE

WHAT TO BUY

The production of cultured pearls is slowly replacing the emirate's traditional pearl-diving industry. The hand-woven goods and pottery from Ali are renowned. The hotels serve *arak*, a delicious anise-flavoured liquor.

QATAR

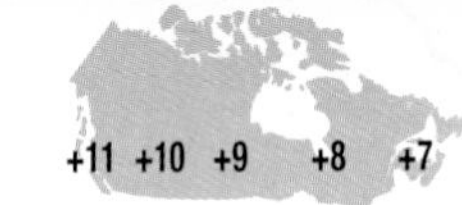

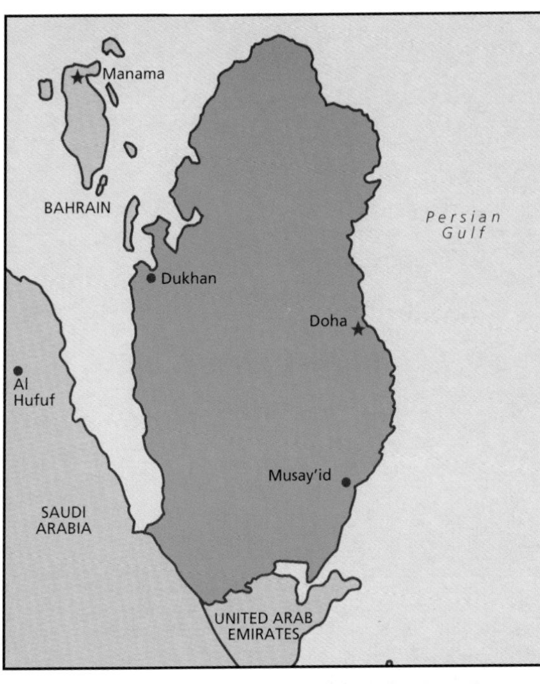

Region: Middle East
Area: 11,000 km²
Capital: Doha
Airport: Doha 8 km
Population: 512,779
Language: Arabic
Religion: Islamic (Sunni)
Government: emirate
Voltage: 220 - 50
Vaccinations required: Yf*,
Vaccinations recommended: Cho, Ty, Po
Passport: required
Visa: required
Currency: Qatari riyal
$1Cdn: 2.67 riyals
Driving: right hand
International permit: required
Area code: 011-974
✆ from Canada: –
✆ to Canada: –
Accommodation: ★★
Restaurants: ★★
Transportation: ★★
Cost of living: ○○○
UN rank: 56
Best months: Dec, Jan, Feb, Mâr, Apr
Holidays: 22 Feb; 4 Mar; 11 May; 3 Sep

WHAT TO DO

Wahhabite (Islamic fundamentalism) forbids the tourist industry; Qataris respect this state of affairs, even though more than 70 per cent of the country's workers are foreigners. A work permit is less difficult to obtain than a travel visa. Businessmen involved with the major Qatari oil companies can obtain a very short-term visa that allows them to visit the capital, Doha, an austere city where life revolves around the petroleum industry. The National Museum and the aquarium are the only leisure attractions.

WHAT TO BUY

In Qatar, one can find very beautiful pearls and miniatures of *dhaws*, the sailing ships found in the Gulf countries. Women are not allowed into the country, and Qatari women do not take part in public life.

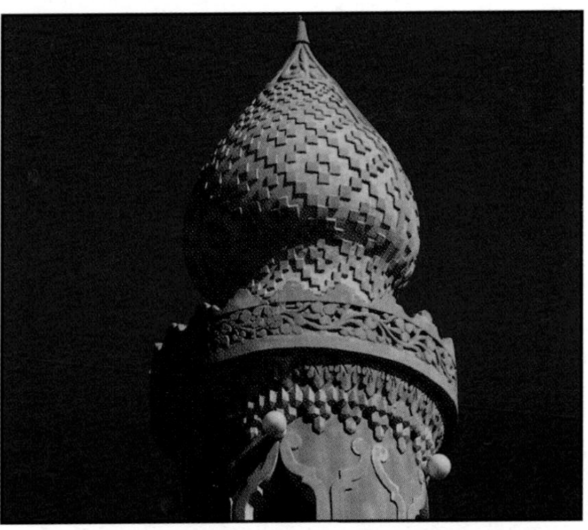

J. HUARD

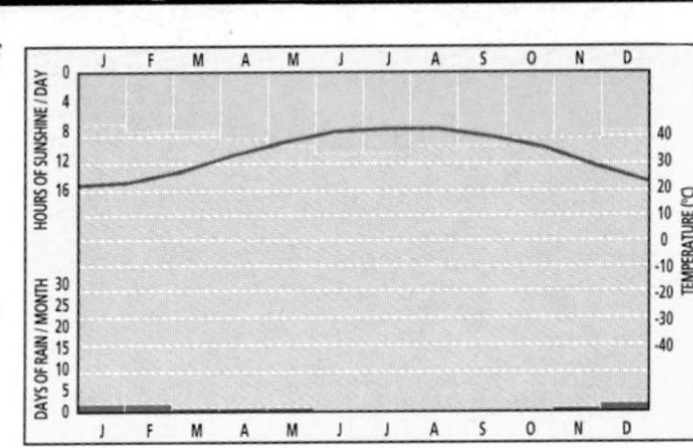

UNITED ARAB EMIRATES

+12 +11 +10 +9 +8

Region: Middle East
Area: 75,581 km²
Capital: Abu Dhabi
Airport: Abu Dhabi 37 km
Population: 2,791,141
Language: Arabic
Religion: Islamic
Government: emirate
Voltage: 220 - 50
Vaccinations required: Yf*, Cho*
Vaccinations recommended: Ty, Po, Mal
Passport: required
Visa: required
Currency: dirham
$1Cdn: 2.7 dirhams
Driving: right hand
International permit: required
Area code: 011-971
✆ from Canada: –
✆ to Canada: –
Accommodation: ★★★★
Restaurants: ★★★
Transportation: ★★★
Cost of living: ○○○
UN rank: 62
Best months: Dec to May
Holidays: 1 Jan; 4 Mar; 11, 31 May; 6–8 Aug; 2 Dec

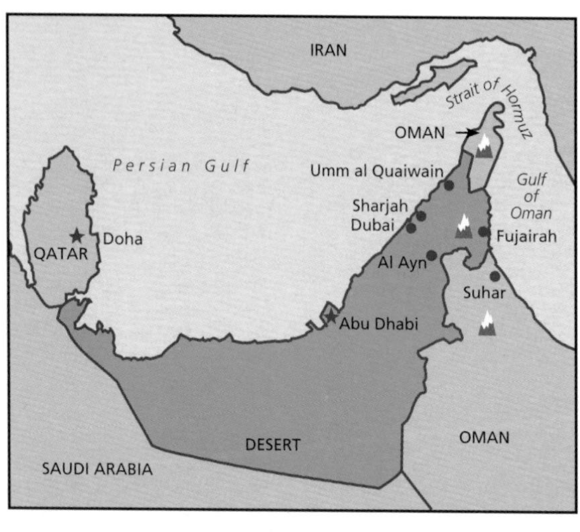

WHAT TO DO

This federation comprises seven independent emirates. Dubai is the only emirate open to tourism; the others are closed to all visitors but businessmen. Fortunately, Dubai is a pretty coastal city surrounded by red-sand dunes inhabited by Bedouins. The "Pirate Coast", as the British dubbed it, stretches along the Persian Gulf from Dubai to Abu Dhabi: the region's gold and sumptuous fabrics have long attracted privateers. Thousands of foreigners work in the emirates, giving some of the cities a multicultural ambience. Women are almost completely absent from public life, and it is unusual to see women travellers, even in Dubai.

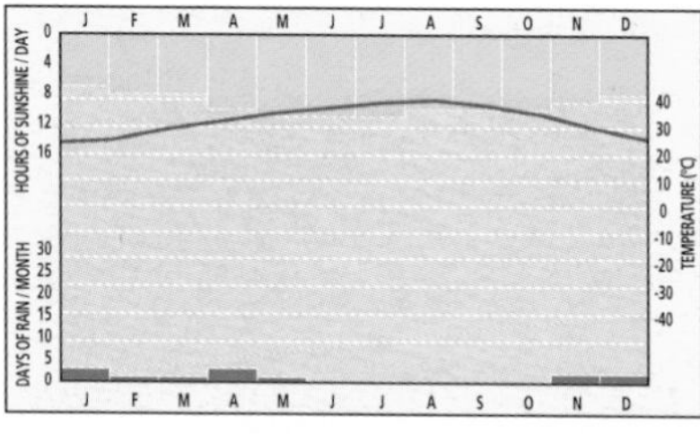

WHAT TO BUY

The souks offer all sorts of merchandise, from finely engraved copper objects to miniature reproductions of the famous *dhaws*, the country's typical sailing ships. The hotels in Dubai serve *arak*, an anise-based liquor, to visitors.

RÉFLEXION

OMAN

+12 +11 +10 +9 +8

Region: Middle East
Area: 212,460 km²
Capital: Muscat
Airport: Muscat 37 km
Population: 1,701,470
Language: Arabic
Religions: Ibadi, Islamic
Government: sultanate
Voltage: 220 - 50
Vaccinations required: Yf*
Vaccinations recommended: Cho, Ty, Po, Mal
Passport: required
Visa: required
Currency: Omani rial
$1Cdn: .28 rial
Driving: right hand
International permit: required
Area code: 011-968
✆ from Canada: –
✆ to Canada: –
Accommodation: ★★★
Restaurants: ★★★
Transportation: ★★★
Cost of living: ❍❍❍
UN rank: 92
Best months: Dec, Jan, Feb
Holidays: 19 Jan; 3 Feb; 1, 4 Mar; 11, 31 May; 10 June; 8 Aug; 18 Nov; 31 Dec

OMAN

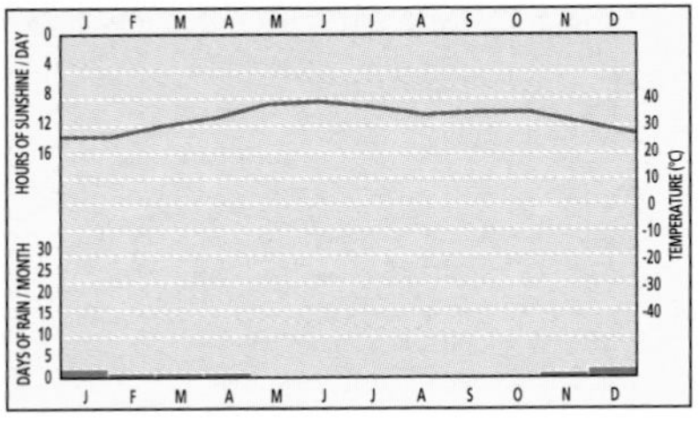

WHAT TO DO

The Sultanate of Oman is not open to tourists. However, businessmen who are guests of Omanis or oil companies can obtain visas and discover a country that is still populated by Bedouin tribes that roam from oasis to oasis. The desert is the country's greatest attraction, with its unimaginably beautiful flora and fauna. Date palms, orange trees, pomegranate trees, and grape vines grow in the fertile plains at the foot of rocky mountains. Muscat, the capital, is a modern city with a number of archaeological treasures, many of which can be found at the Museum of Culture, History, and Archaeology.

WHAT TO BUY

The souks, particularly the one in Matrah, offer a wide variety of products, from stuffed snakes (trade in which is not encouraged) to Omani daggers, famous for the quality of their blades. The fabrics and carpets are also of very high quality.

YEMEN

+11 +10 +9 +8 +7

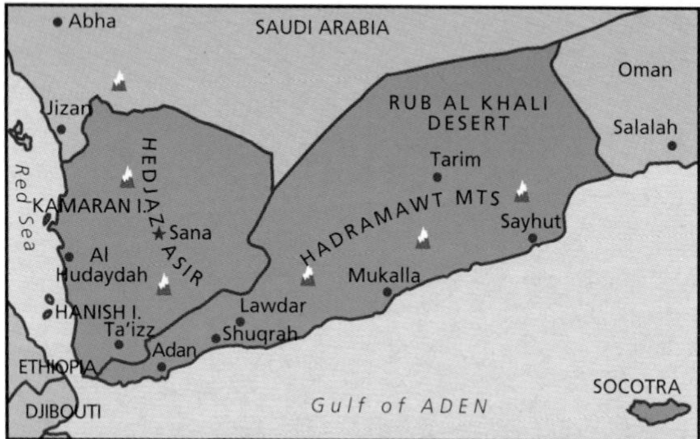

egion: Middle East
Area: 527,970 km²
Capital: Sana
Airport: Sana 3 km
Population: 11,105,202
Language: Arabic
Religion: Islamic
Government: multi-party democracy
Voltage: 220 - 50
Vaccinations required: Yf*
" recommended: Cho, Ty, Po, Mal
Passport: required
Visa: required
Currency: Yemeni rial, Yemeni dinar
$1Cdn: 8.84 rials
Driving: right hand
International permit: required
Area code: 011-967/969
✆ from Canada: –
✆ to Canada: –
Accommodation: ★★
Restaurants: ★★
Transportation: ★★
Cost of living: ○○
UN rank: 142
Best months: Mar, Apr, Sept, Oct
Holidays: 1 Jan; 4, 8 Mar; 1, 11, 22, 31 May; 10 June; 8 Aug; 26 Sept; 14 Oct; 30 Nov; 31 Dec

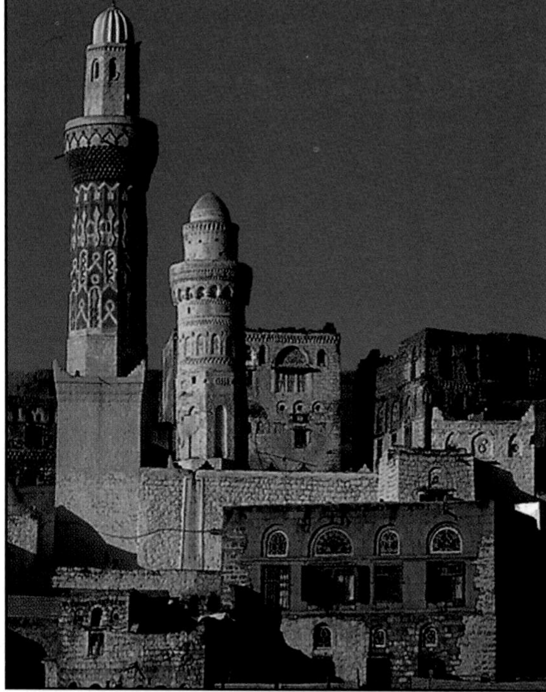

J. HUARD

WHAT TO DO

North Yemen has invaded South Yemen. This civil war has caused hundreds of casualties and destroyed entire towns. Sana was considered one of the most beautiful cities in the Middle East for its minarets, its houses with white turrets and stained-glass windows, and its mosques. Fortunately, the recent armed conflicts have not destroyed everything. Rawdha, a little north of Sana, is a garden city featuring vines heavy with grapes. In the town of Amran is a rampart that dates from pre-Islamic times. The beautiful mountains, deep valleys, and small villages perched on cliffs are not impervious to the conflict. However, visitors should try to visit Hajjah, nestled between Mounts Wadi Sherez and Kohlan, at an altitude of 2,400 m.

WHAT TO BUY

Cotton, tobacco, coffee, and *qat*, a drug that should definitely be avoided, are the main products of Yemen. Jewelry, pottery, leather goods, incense, amber, and spices are sold in the souks of both North and South Yemen.

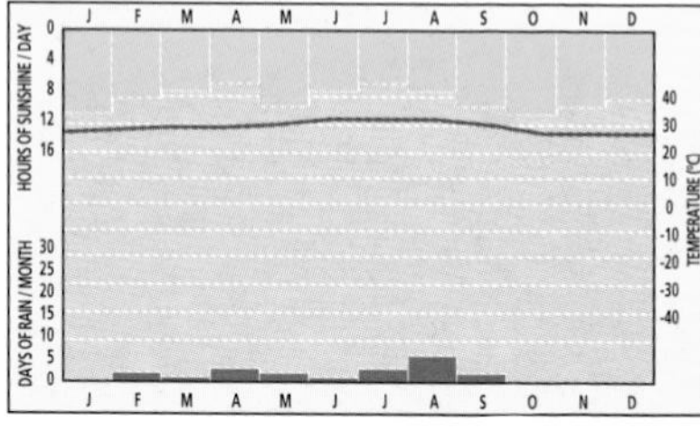

YEMEN

ASIA

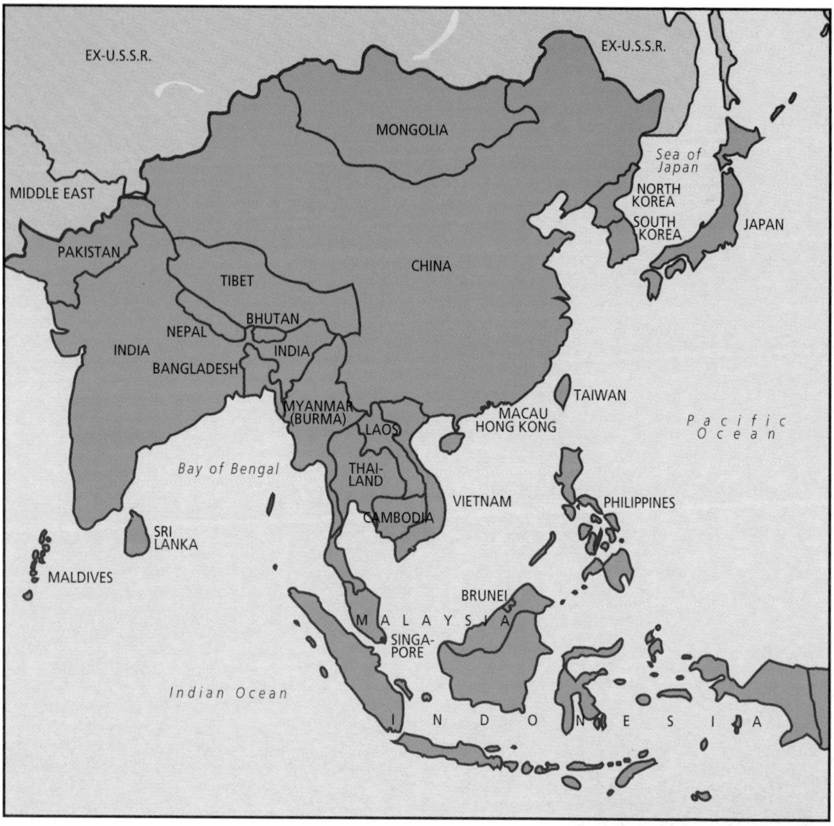

Asia, the largest continent, contains more than half of the planet's total population. India and China are Asia's largest—and most populous—countries, but several smaller countries play an important role in tourism development, especially Indonesia, with islands such as Java, and industrialized countries such as Malaysia and Japan. There is no lack of exotic destinations—Bhutan and Sri Lanka are just two examples. There are fabulous discoveries in store for those who want to explore in the company of local residents: seeing Seoul with a Korean or uncovering the secret spots of Manila with a Filipino is an unforgettable experience. To understand the diversity of Asian cultures, there is much that can be read and studied, but perhaps it is easier simply to venture into the floating markets of Thailand or the steppes of Mongolia and learn first hand.

J. HUARD

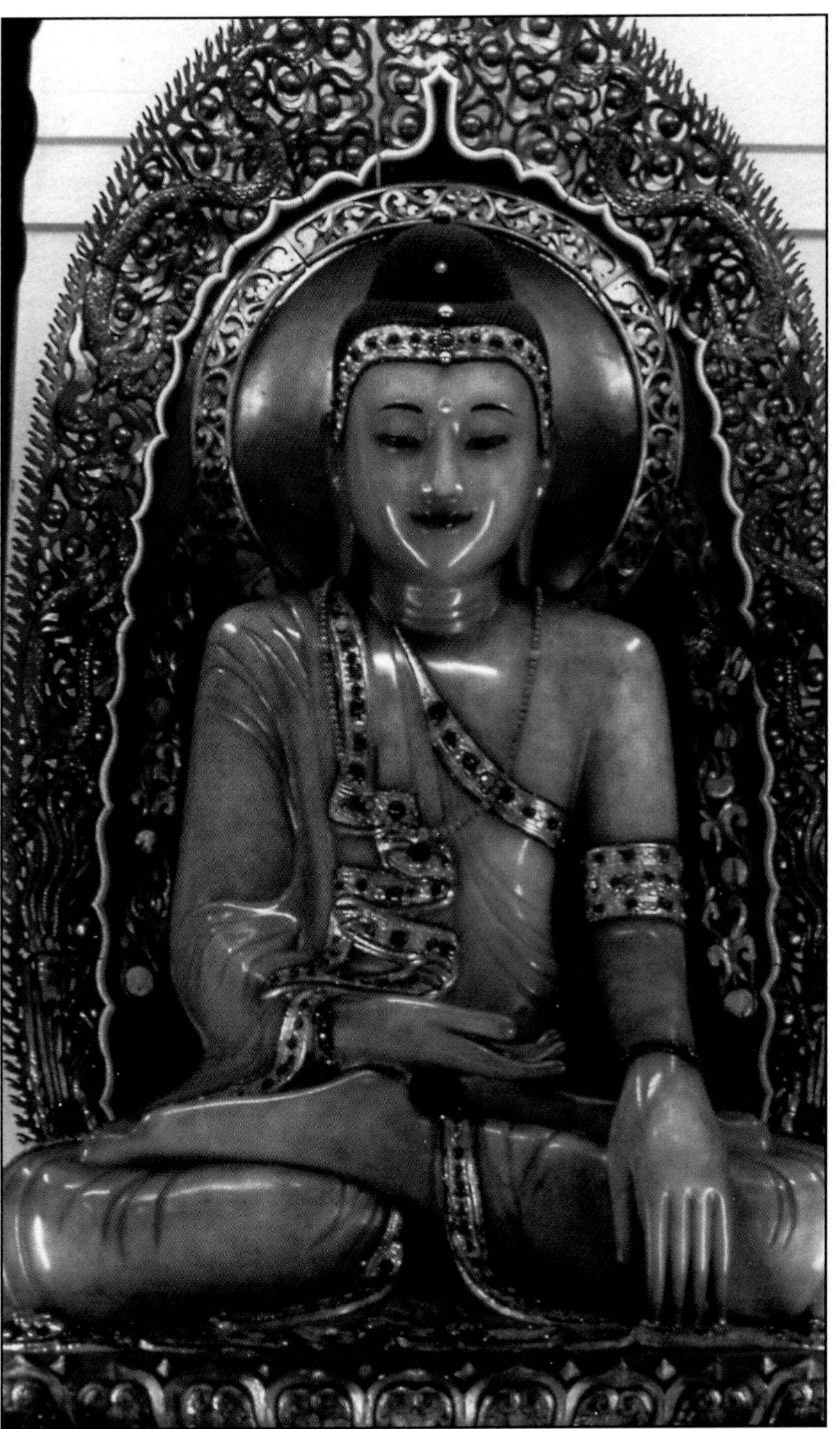

CHINESE EMBASSY

MALDIVES

+13 +12 +11 +10 +9

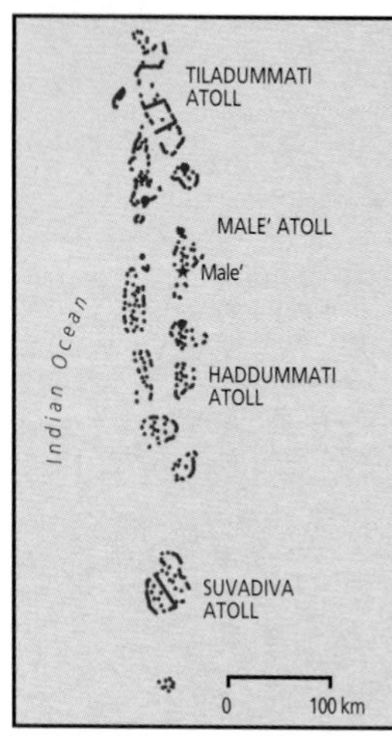

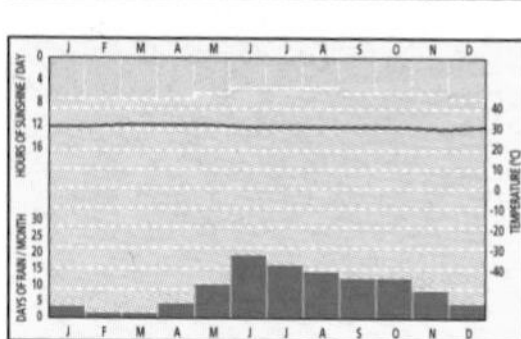

WHAT TO DO

The tourism industry developed in the Maldives thanks to the archipelago's mild climate and the great beauty of the underwater scenery. The coral, sea animals, and clear water make these islands a prime destination for divers. The capital, Male', offers many historical and cultural tourist attractions, including the beautiful gold-roofed mosque and the National Museum.

WHAT TO BUY

Seafood and fish are the basis for Maldivian cuisine. It is strictly forbidden to purchase coral other than in authorized stores. The jewelry decorated with coral is particularly popular.

Region: Indian Ocean
Area: 298 km²
Capital: Male'
Airport: Male' 2 km
Population: 252,080
Languages: Dhivehi, English
Religion: Islamic
Government: presidential democracy
Voltage: 220 - 50
Vaccinations required: Yf*
Vaccinations recommended: Cho, Ty, Po, Mal
Passport: required
Visa: required
Currency: rufiyaa
$1Cdn: 8.66 rufiyaas
Driving: –
International permit: –
Area code: 011-960
✆ from Canada: –
✆ to Canada: –
Accommodation: ★★★★
Restaurants: ★★★★
Transportation: ★★
Cost of living: ○○○
UN rank: 118
Best months: Jan, Feb, Mar
Holidays: 1 Jan; 15 Mar; 11, 21 June; 26 July; 9, 11, 21 Sept; 11, 12 Nov; 9 Dec

MONGOLIA

+16 +15 +14 +13 +12

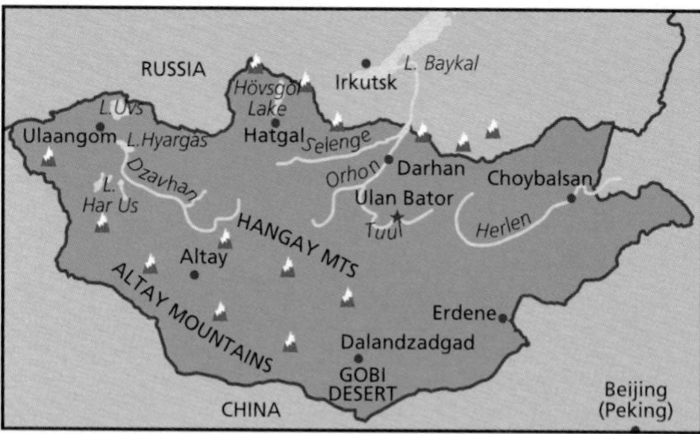

WHAT TO DO

Ulaanbaatur (Ulan Bator), the capital, is an important religious centre for Lamaism, and the monastery is a prime attraction of the city. The Trans-Mongolia Railway takes visitors to beyond the capital: Erdene, with its huge mosque, is worth the trip, as are Darhan and Hotol.

WHAT TO BUY

Mongolian chants, paintings, dance, and theatre have a style inherited from the khans. The beautiful film *Urga*, by Russian director Nikita Mikhalkof, presents an insightful view of everyday life in Mongolia.

Region: Asia
Area: 1,565,000 km²
Capital: Ulaanbaatur
Airport: Ulaanbattur
Population: 2,429,770
Language: Khalkha Mongolian
Religion: Buddhist
Government: parliamentary republic
Voltage: 220 - 50
Vaccinations required: Yf*
Vaccinations recommended: Ty, Po
Passport: required
Visa: required
Currency: tughrik
$1Cdn: 318.55 tughriks
Driving: right hand
Int'l permit: vehicles not available
Area code: limited service
✆ from Canada: –
✆ to Canada: –
Accommodation: ★★
Restaurants: ★★
Transportation: ★★
Cost of living: ○○○
UN rank: 102
Best months: July, Aug
Holidays: 1, 31 Jan; 8, 18 Mar; 11–13 July; 26 Nov

CHINA

+16 +15 +14 +13 +12

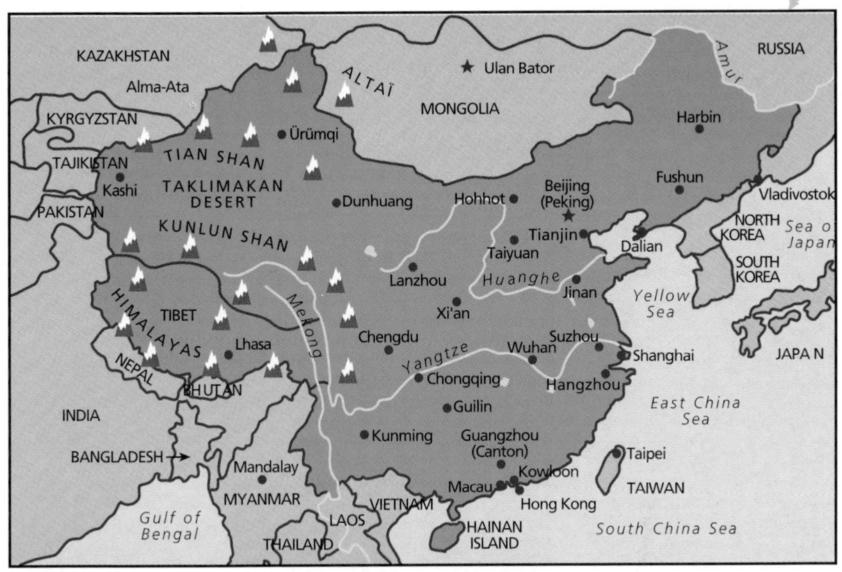

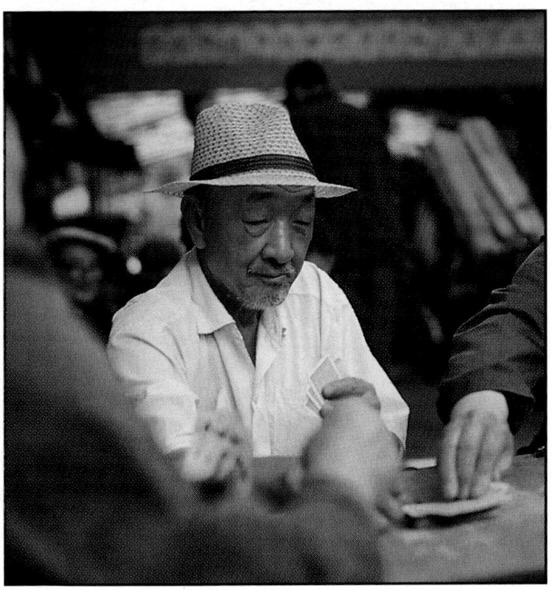

Region: Asia
Area: 9,596,960 km2
Capital: Beijing
Airport: Beijing
Population: 1,190,431,110
Languages: Mandarin, Cantonese Chinese
Religions: Buddhist, Taoist
Government: people's republic
Voltage: 220 - 50
Vaccinations required: Yf*
" recommended: Cho, Ty, Po, Mal
Passport: required
Visa: required
Currency: yuan
$1Cdn: 6.11 yuans
Driving: right hand
International permit: not available
Area code: 011-86
✆ from Canada: 1-800-663-4405
✆ to Canada: 108-186
Accommodation: ★★★
Restaurants: ★★★
Transportation: ★★
Cost of living: ❍
UN rank: 94
Best months: Oct, Nov, Dec
Holidays: 1, 2, 31 Jan; 8 Mar; 1, 4 May; 1, 13 June; 1 July; 1 Aug; 10 Sept; 1 Oct

WHAT TO DO

Insulated by deserts, the formidable plateaus of Tibet, and the ocean, China was long impermeable to other civilizations. After 30 years of the Cultural Revolution, the country has quietly begun to open up, and more and more travellers are visiting this huge country. Tourists will have to hurry to catch the last remnants of Marco Polo's China: the first Chinese music-halls have already sprung up at the foot of the Great Wall of China. Of course, China comprises a wide range of spectacular scenery, an immense cultural heritage, and an extravagant history, but it is, above all, its citizens: there are about 1.2 billion Chinese, approximately one

CHINA

CHINA

fifth of the world's population. To really appreciate China, one must get to know the people, and language is a major barrier. In the big cities, English can be used, but in the countryside and villages, you'll have to develop mime skills. The cultural heritage of Beijing is awesome. The Forbidden City, now open to visitors; the Imperial Palace; the Summer Palace; the Cambaluc (the khan's city, named by Marco Polo); the Three Seas Imperial Park, with its white pagoda; Mao Zedong's mausoleum; and the shopping streets are just some of the highlights. The city's many museums exhibit collections of bronzes, calligraphy, and the treasures of the Ming and Qing dynasties. The Beijing subway is a good way to visit the different districts of the city. The Great Wall is more than 5,000 km long, stretching from Shanhaiguan east to Jiayuguan, in the Gobi Desert, but it is in Badaling, 70 km north of Beijing, that travellers stop. At Guilin, the Cave of the Reed Flutes and the karstic countryside that have inspired so many Chinese artists are as breathtaking as ever. Guangzhou (Canton) is an important commercial centre: the porcelain factories and jade sculpture workshops are very impressive. The hot-water spas in the neighbouring mountains are well worth visiting. Shanghai is a commercial port, but the city's museums and historical monuments attest to its cultural importance. See especially the Shanghai Museum, the jade temple of Buddha, and the tomb of Lu Xun. Xi'an is a well-known destination: the 6,000 clay soldiers at the tomb of Qui Shi Huangdi and the Forest of Steles, comprising more than 1,000 pieces, are veritable treasures of humanity. China's major tourist sites are astonishing, but there are also the rice paddies, the small temples, the markets, and the villages... Here is where to take the pulse of real life in this nation.

SDP / RICHERE /RÉFLEXION

WHAT TO BUY

Rice, tofu, soup, and noodles are the main daily foods of the Chinese. However, travellers can sample the specialties of each region: Mandarin cuisine is spicy because it originates in the north, which is cold; in the port of Shanghai, seafood has place of honour on the menu; Szechuan cuisine is very spicy and features glazed duck; and Cantonese cuisine is known for its steamed dishes. Cat meat, dog meat, pig snout, monkey brain, rat embryos, and snake meat are found in the markets—and in the best restaurants! (*Wo chi su* means "I am a vegetarian" in Chinese...) Tea, beer, and *mao tai*, a sorghum (type of millet) liquor, are the national drinks. Some souvenirs to take home are porcelain objects, jade jewelry, silk goods, handmade paper, calligraphy, traditional clothes, and common household items, which are very different from our own. Travellers must be discreet, especially in the countryside, where local people aren't used to meeting foreigners. Open-toe sandals that leave the toes uncovered will draw a look of surprise, and women who are too talkative will make no friends among the Chinese. Opium dens may sound romantic, but the reality is quite different; drugs are strictly forbidden in China. Cameras are not allowed in holy sites and monasteries.

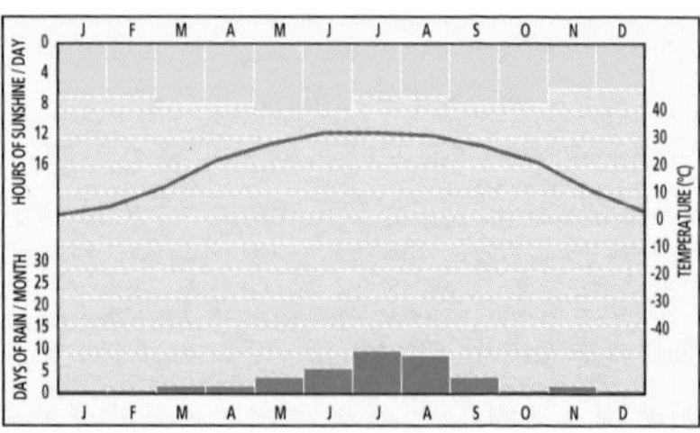

NORTH KOREA

+17 +16 +15 +14 +13

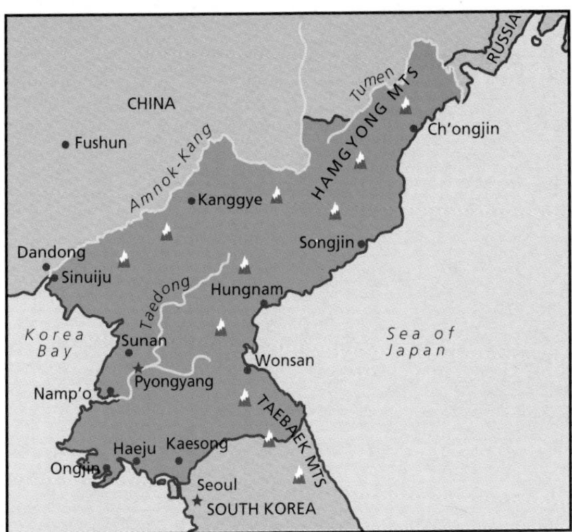

Region: Asia
Area: 120,540 km²
Capital: Pyongyang
Airport: Pyongyang 30 km
Population: 23,066,575
Language: Korean
Religions: Buddhist, Confucianist
Government: socialist republic
Voltage: 110/220 - 60
Vaccinations required: –
Vaccinations recommended: Cho, Ty, Po
Passport: required
Visa: required
Currency: won
$1Cdn: 1.61 wons
Driving: right hand
International permit: required
Area code: limited service
✆ from Canada: –
✆ to Canada: –
Accommodation: ★★
Restaurants: ★★
Transportation: ★★
Cost of living: OOO
UN rank: 101
Best months: Aug, Sept
Holidays: 1 Jan; 16 Feb; 15 Apr; 15 Aug; 9 Sept;10 Oct; 27 Dec

NORTH KOREA

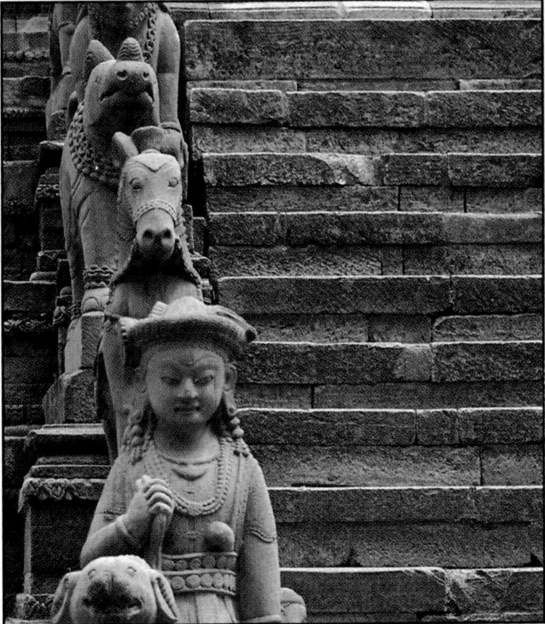
J. HUARD

WHAT TO DO

Recent negotiations opened the way for North Korea to allow an international consortium to build two electricity plants to replace the nuclear reactors that have been supplying electricity to the country for the last 40 years. This communist country is beginning to establish relations with the West, and so it might soon be open to tourism. When travellers can cross into North Korea, they will be astonished by the nation's capital, Pyongyang, with its superb city gates and Morangborg and Taesongsan parks. Kaesong is the old capital, where the treasures of the country's imperial past are preserved.

WHAT TO BUY

The ceramics, bronze hand-bells, and Korean tea services are particularly fine. North Korea is a major producer of rice and fish; the regional cuisine is inspired primarily by these two foods.

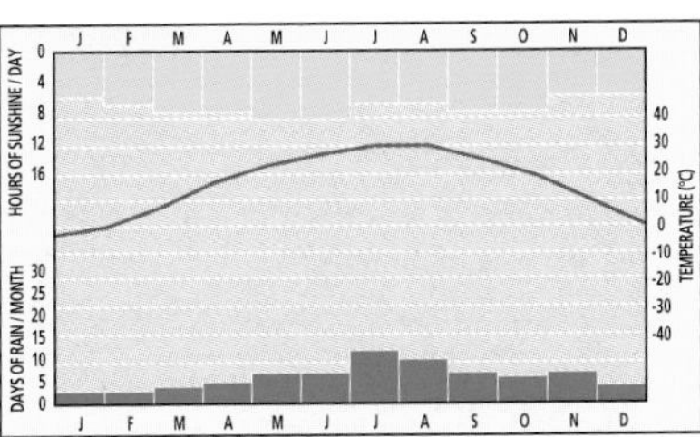

SOUTH KOREA

+17 +16 +15 +14 +13

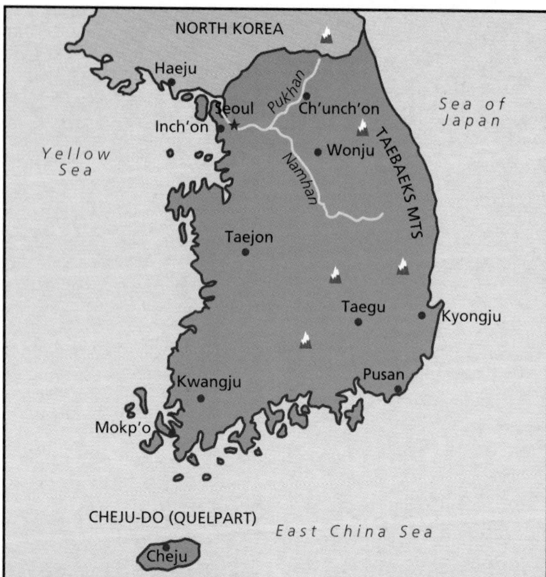

Region: Asia
Area: 98,480 km²
Capital: Seoul
Airport: Seoul 26 km
Population: 45,082,880
Language: Korean
Religions: Buddhist, Christian
Government: presidential democracy
Voltage: 110/220 - 60
Vaccinations required: –
Vaccinations recommended: Cho, Ty, Po
Passport: required
Visa: required
Currency: won
$1Cdn: 557.26 wons
Driving: right hand
International permit: required
Area code: 011-82
✆ from Canada: 1-800-663-9889
✆ to Canada: ▲009-0015
Accommodation: ★★★
Restaurants: ★★★
Transportation: ★★★
Cost of living: ○○○
UN rank: 32
Best months: Dec, Jan
Holidays: 1–3 Jan; 1 Mar; 5 Apr; 5 May; 6 June; 17 July; 15 Aug; 3 Oct; 25 Dec

RÉFLEXION

WHAT TO DO

South Korea's capital, Seoul, was heavily damaged during the 1950–53 war, but the ultramodern reconstructed city has preserved intact a few historic monuments such as the Chandokkung Palace, the gates to the city, the Kyongbok Palace, and the magnificent Secret Gardens (which are, of course, quite difficult to find). Kyongju, a few hours south of Seoul, has its own impressive historic monuments: the Pulguksa Temple, with its royal tombs dating from the year 742 A.D., and the giant Buddhas carved out of the granite walls of the Sokkuram Cave are fine examples. South Korea's shores on the Yellow Sea, the China Sea, and the Sea of Japan are edged with beaches and resorts, the most popular of which are at Inch'on, Mokp'o, and the island of Cheju-do. Soraksan National Park is a good stepping-off point for visits to the magnificent Taebaek Mountains, known for their natural beauty and important historical sites, such as the Kwangumsong Fort, which dates from the year 57 A.D., and the Sinhong-sa Temple.

WHAT TO BUY

Korean grilled foods are tasty, as is the *shabu-shabu*, which is mistakenly called "Chinese fondue". Korean cuisine is often heavily spiced with garlic. *Pulgogi*, marinated beef, is served with *makoli*, rice wine, or *sul*, a rice liquor. The ginseng liquor is a Korean specialty. In Cheju-do, women still dive for natural pearls, perpetuating a tradition hundreds of years old. Laquer, silk, amber, and jade are worked into furniture, scarves, jewelry, and other items. Koreans are much more outgoing than other Asian peoples; some say that they even have a little Latin blood!

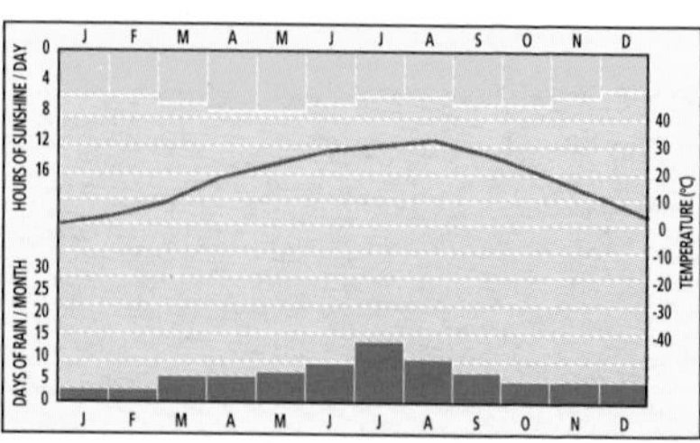

JAPAN

+17 +16 +15 +14 +13

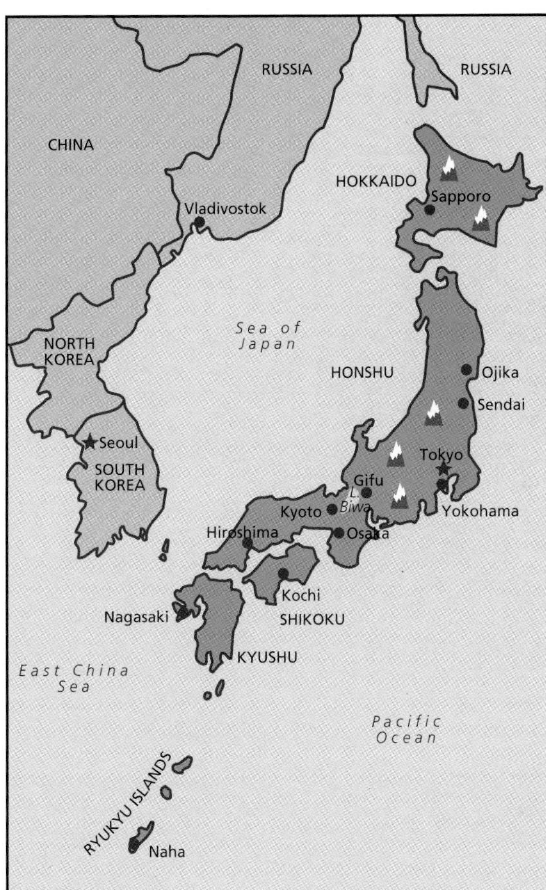

Region: Asia
Area: 377,835 km²
Capital: Tokyo
Airport: Tokyo 66 km
Population: 125,106,940
Language: Japanese
Religions: Shintoist, Buddhist
Government: parliamentary monarchy
Voltage: 110 - 50/60
Vaccinations required: –
Vaccinations recommended: Ty, Po
Passport: required
Visa: not required
Currency: yen
$1Cdn: 66.53 yen
Driving: left hand
International permit: required
Area code: 011-81
✆ from Canada: 1-800-663-0681
✆ to Canada: 0039-▲161
Accommodation: ★★★★★
Restaurants: ★★★★★
Transportation: ★★★★★
Cost of living: ○○○
UN rank: 3
Best months: May, June, Sept, Oct
Holidays: 1, 2, 16 Jan; 11 Feb; 21 Mar; 29 Apr; 3–5 May; 15, 23 Sept; 10 Oct; 3, 23 Nov; 23 Dec

WHAT TO DO

Legend has it that the tears of a goddess, falling into the Pacific Ocean, formed Japan's main islands of Kyushu, Honshu, Shikoku, and Hokkaido, as well as its 3,900 smaller islands. The beauty of the Japanese countryside is such that it's easy to believe this story: mountains, volcanoes, and indented coasts provide the backdrop to Japan's magnificent rice paddies, iris gardens, flowering cherry trees, and frost-flecked forests. Its cities, even megalopolises like Tokyo and Yokohama, have an elegance typical of Japanese culture. The Japanese are great masters of the art of living in modern times, following a code that goes back to the era of the shoguns. Tokyo is a good example of the mixture of these two worlds: ultramodern skyscrapers tower over small wooden houses and tiny temples, while businessmen in suits and old women in traditional kimonos share the sidewalks. Visitors should make a point of strolling through the Ginza, Shinjuku, and Shibuya districts and spending time at the Tokyo National Museum in the Ueno district, the Asakusa Kannon (or Sensoji Temple), and the Tsukiji fish market. But there is more to Japan than just Tokyo. Kamakura is host to a huge bronze Buddha and 65 Buddhist temples, 19 Shinto temples, and 5 Zen temples! An expedition to Mount Fuji, just a couple of hours from Tokyo, is a unique experience. Nikko is worth a visit, especially for the Toshogu Temple with its more than 5,000 sculptures: the Shinkyo, a very romantic sacred bridge; and Shogun Way, protected by a barrier of stone stat-

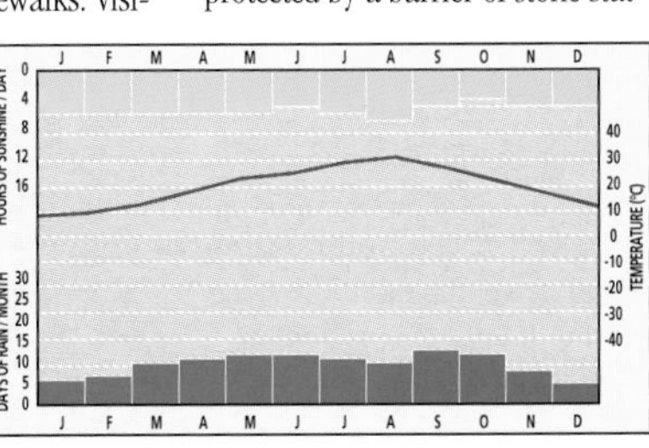

T. BOGNAR / RÉFLEXION

ues. Gifu is famous for its factories for making paper, an ancient art form in Japan. Travellers who have time to visit only one place in the country should see Kyoto and its surrounding area, where the attractions include the Ryoan ji Temple, famous for its gardens; the Golden Pagoda (Kinkaku ji) and Silver Pagoda (Ginkaku ji); the Nishi Honganji, built in 1591; the Higashi Honganji, built in 1602; the Nijo Palace and Imperial Palace; and, for those who haven't seen enough yet, the National Museum, which presents one of the most beautiful collections of Japanese art in the country. Nara is also a city of tremendous cultural wealth. Osaka is a large, modern city that has preserved vestiges of its glorious past, including a castle rebuilt after the Second World War. To see the effects of this war is, of course, the main reason to visit Hiroshima. Its excellent museum recalls the horrors that the atomic bomb visited on the city: some visitors may not be able to finish touring the displays. If possible, be in Hiroshima on August 6, when the Ceremony of Lanterns takes place: thousands of little candles are set floating in the river in memory of the 80,000 who died on that date in 1945.

Access to Miyajima (island of Temples) is via the magnificent *torii* (sacred gate). The island is a sanctuary where fawns roam freely among the pagodas and temples. Because Sapporo, on the island of Hokkaido, is surrounded by mountains, winter is the best season to visit. The island of Kyushu is less developed for tourism, but it is worth a visit for its beautiful beaches and mild climate.

WHAT TO BUY

Sushi and *sashimi* (raw fish), *soba* and *udon* (noodles), *dojo* (rice patties served with an egg), and *okonomiyaki* (a sort of pancake with eggs, beans, and sweet sauce—delicious!) are just a few typically Japanese dishes. Seafoods are a mainstay in Japanese cuisine, but there is more than fish and seaweed in Japan; Kobe beef is delicious and tender (the cattle are fed on beer), and the *yakitori* (grilled meat brochettes) are slightly spicy. Try *bentos*, boxed snacks available throughout the country. Cold *sake* is a Japanese specialty. Tea and items related to the tea ceremony, such as fans to cool the tea and superb cast-iron teapots, are highly prized souvenirs. Laquered objects, paper, calligraphy, kimonos and *yukata* (cotton kimonos, less expensive than silk ones), incense, and bronze bells are other popular souvenirs.

JAPANESE TOURIST OFFICE

PAKISTAN

+13 +12 +11 +10 +9

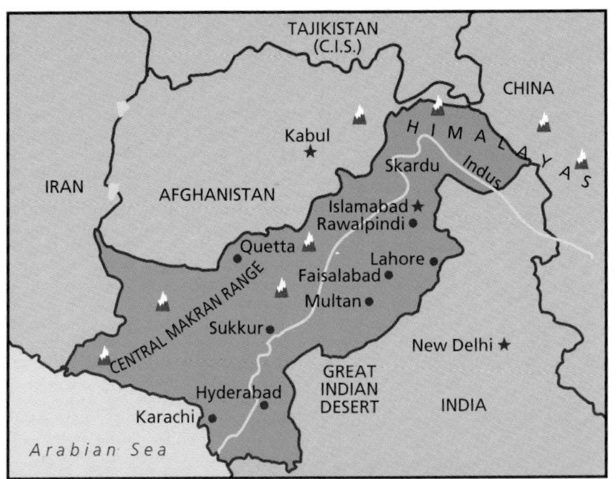

Region: Asia
Area: 803,940 km²
Capital: Islamabad
Airport: Karachi 16 km, Islamabad 8 km
Population: 128,855,970
Languages: Urdu (off.), English
Religion: Islamic
Government: presidential democracy
Voltage: 220 - 50
Vaccinations required: Yf*
Vaccinations recommended: Cho, Ty, Po, Mal
Passport: required
Visa: required
Currency: Pakistani rupee
$1Cdn: 22.94 rupees
Driving: left hand
International permit: required
Area code: 011-92
✆ from Canada: –
✆ to Canada: –
Accommodation: ★★
Restaurants: ★★
Transportation: ★★
Cost of living: ❍
UN rank: 132
Best months: June to Mar
Holidays: 4, 23 Mar; 1, 31 May; 10 June; 1 July; 8,14 Aug; 6,11 Sept; 9 Nov; 25,31 Dec

REFLEXION

WHAT TO DO

The Punjab, or "Country of Five Rivers", is the site of conflict among Muslims, Sikhs, and Hindus: living together has become impossible as the war in Kashmir has heated up. Travellers should stay away from these regions. However, the archaeological ruins at Mohenjo-Daro, near Sukkur, are very interesting, as are the historical monuments in Tatta, south of Hyderabad. The Buddhist ruins of Takht-e-Bahi and the Bahlol archaeological site are also worth seeing. The economic capital, Karachi, offers a superb white-marble mausoleum, the Quaiz-e-Azam. The port and vestiges of British colonization give the city a very special ambience. And one should not forget Lahore, a city of major historical importance, with its many Mogul-style monuments, its magnificent Shalimar Garden, and its huge mosque, the largest in Asia.

WHAT TO BUY

Chicken with red butter (chicken *tikka*) is a typically Pakistani dish served with *nan* (flat bread). The chicken curries (*peshaware* and *mussallam*) are also delicious. Alcohol is sold to foreigners only in hotel bars. ("Pakistan" means "country of the pure" in Urdu.) Glassware, pottery, and woollen goods from Kashmir are sold in all the bazaars. Camel skin is used to make pretty items. Anyone who wants to discover all the wealth and variety of Pakistani voices will want to pick up recordings of masters of the *qawwali* chant, the Sufi cult, and the great Nursat Fatheh Ali Khan. Women travellers must always be discreet in Pakistan.

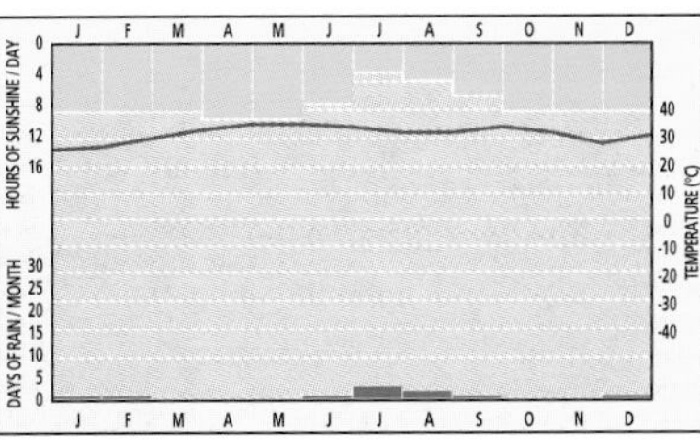

TIBET

+14 +13 +12 +11 +10

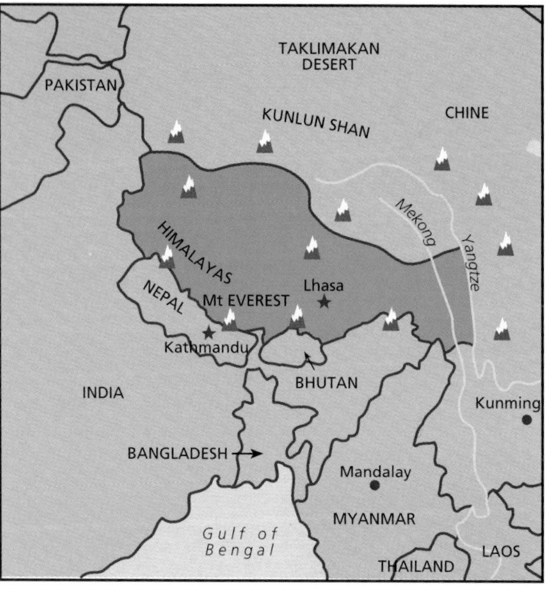

Region: Asia
Area: 1,228,400 km²
Capital: Lhasa
Airport: –
Population: 2,196,000
Languages: Tibetan, Chinese
Religion: Buddhist
Government: region of China
Voltage: 220 - 50
Vaccinations required: Yf*
" recommended: Cho, Ty, Po, Mal
Passport: required
Visa: required
Currency: yuan
$1Cdn: 6.11 yuans
Driving: right hand
Int'l permit: vehicles not available
Area code: 011-86
✆ from Canada: –
✆ to Canada: –
Accommodation: –
Restaurants: –
Transportation: –
Cost of living: ○○
UN rank: –
Best months: Aug, Sep, Oct
Holidays: 1 Jan; 1 Oct

WHAT TO DO

Tibet is a country of eternal snow and mountains, herds of yaks, cloistered temples, and smiling Buddhist and Lamaist monks. Tourism in Tibet is still not very well developed; however, organized excursions take expeditions to the high plateaus of the Himalayas, even though tensions with China have increased the isolation of this region. Lhasa, with its magnificient Jokhang Temple and the Potala Mountain Palace, is the point of departure for visiting Tibet. Norbulinka, the summer residence of the Dalai Lama, is an interesting architectural complex. Elsewhere in the country, the monasteries of Drepung, Ganden, and especially Sera (where one can admire the Ming frescoes) are also interesting. The *rlung-rta,* small banners flying from the roofs of the religious buildings, are pretty and bright. Visitors to Tibet will not want to miss seeing the plateaus of the high mountains—especially around the base of Mount Everest, with an altitude of 8,882 m—and the beauties of the countryside that loses itself in an endless sky.

WHAT TO BUY

Qingke, a barley-based alcoholic drink, and *koumis*, made with fermented milk, are specialties that you must taste. Yak butter is used to salt the tea, which is often accompanied by *momos*, small, tasty meat patties. Tibetan craftspeople are famous for their carpets and goldsmithery. The incense in Buddhist temples is particularly enchanting.

J. HUARD

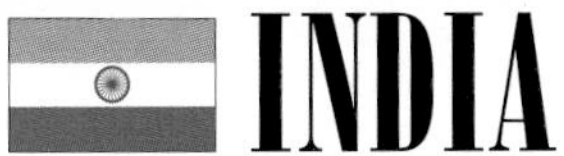

INDIA

+13½ +12½ +11½ +10½ +9½

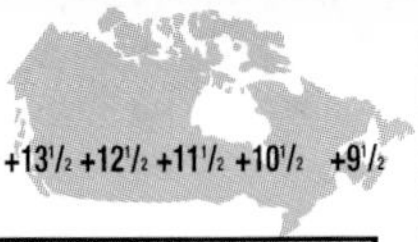

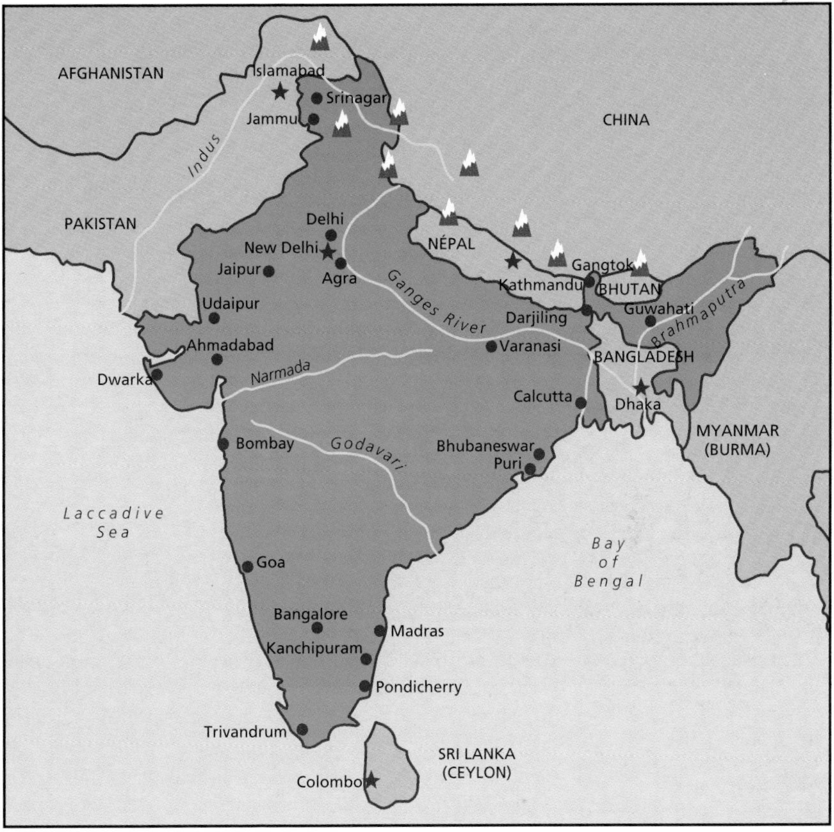

AFGHANISTAN
Islamabad
Srinagar
Jammu
CHINA
Indus
PAKISTAN
Delhi
New Delhi
Jaipur
Agra
NÉPAL
Kathmandu
Gangtok
BHUTAN
Ganges River
Darjiling
Guwahati
Brahmaputra
Udaipur
Ahmadabad
Varanasi
BANGLADESH
Dwarka
Narmada
Calcutta
Dhaka
MYANMAR
(BURMA)
Bombay
Godavari
Bhubaneswar
Puri
Laccadive
Sea
Bay
of
Bengal
Goa
Bangalore
Madras
Kanchipuram
Pondicherry
Trivandrum
SRI LANKA
(CEYLON)
Colombo

WHAT TO DO

India's ethnic diversity is the cause of much conflict: different religions, languages, economic forces, and cultural heritages live side by side in India, not always successfully. The civil war that is dragging on in Kashmir and the inter-ethnic conflict and Punjab nationalism in the Northeast States known as the "Seven Sisters", on the border with Burma, illustrate the impossible mission of making India a unified country. This will be very obvious to visitors who travel from New Delhi to Madras, or from Bombay to Calcutta. They should avoid the entire region on the border with Burma, as well as the region north of Delhi. Even leaving aside these regions, there is still an immense country to discover. With its extremes of wealth and poverty, India is not an "easy" country, but travellers seeking something truly different will have a unique experience there. To start, visit old Delhi, with its Red Fort, Chandni Chowk Market, Jama Masjid Mosque, and Laxminarayan Temple; the National Museum, where some artifacts are more than 7,000 years old; and the bustling streets crowded with shops. In New Delhi, the Qutb Minar Minaret and Humayun Mausoleum sit happily beside modern buildings. The Golden Triangle links Delhi; Agra, famous for the magnificent Taj Majal; and Jaipur, which has the Shich Mahal (Palace of Mirrors), the Temple of Kali, the Sukh Niwas (Room of Pleasures), and the Hawa Mahla (Palace of Winds). Some of the temples in Khajuraho,

J F M A M J J A S O N D
HOURS OF SUNSHINE / DAY
0
4
8
12
16
40
30
20
10
0
-10
-20
-30
-40
TEMPERATURE (°C)
DAYS OF RAIN / MONTH
30
25
20
15
10
5
0
J F M A M J J A S O N D

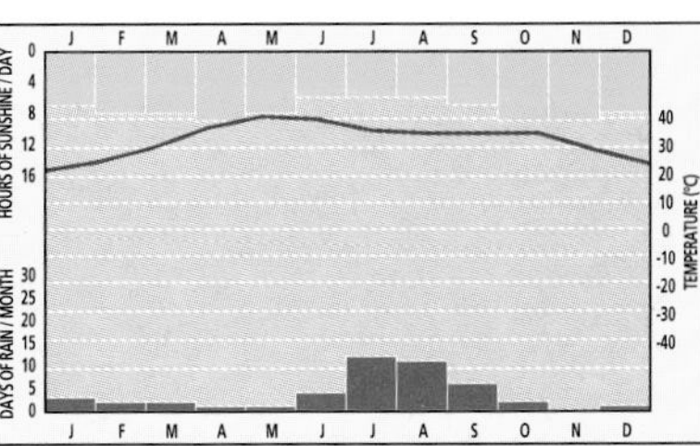

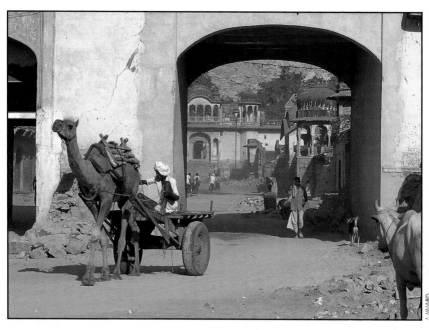

are famous for their erotic sculptures. The *ghats* (stone steps leading down to the Ganges River) of Varanasi are always packed with pilgrims who come to make their ablutions.The Bharatmata Temple, the Golden Temple, the Sacred Bull, and the Sarnath (where Buddha gave his first sermon) are breathtaking. The city of Calcutta is, unfortunately, often associated with the terrible poverty of its *bustees* (slums), and for good reason. But, Calcutta is also a dynamic cultural centre, where are found the very beautiful Indian Museum, Temple of Kali, Memorial Hall, and Maidan Park. Mother Teresa's clinic should not be approached as a tourist attraction; however, if you leave a cash donation, it will be put to good use. Madras is worth visiting, if only to stop at the stalls of its weavers; they who make the most beautiful fabrics in India. The coast from Madras to Pondicherry and in the state of Kerala, on the Sea of Oman, is very pleasant. Bombay is a large, modern city, where street people are becoming more and more numerous. In the surrounding region, Elephanta Island, the Ajanta Range, the hidden temples of Ellora, and the rock temple in Ahmadabad are must-sees. In Goa, a pretty town edged by white-sand beaches, the Portuguese influence is still visible: Largo da Igreja Square, with its Manuelin-style church, looks as if it might be in Portugal. The gate into the Lamaist Buddhist Centre is found

Region: Asia
Area: 3,287,590 km²
Capital: New Delhi
Airport: Delhi 21 km, Bombay 29 km
Population: 919,903,060
Languages: Hindi, English
Religions: Hindu, Islamic, Sikh
Government: parliamentary democracy
Voltage: 220 - 50
Vaccinations required: Yf*, Cho, Ty, Po
Vaccinations recommended: Mal
Passport: required
Visa: required
Currency: rupee
$1Cdn: 23.12 rupees
Driving: left hand
International permit: recommended
Area code: 011-91
✆ from Canada: –
✆ to Canada: 000167
Accommodation: ★★★★
Restaurants: ★★★★
Transportation: ★★★
Cost of living: ❍
UN rank: 135
Best months: Dec, Jan, Feb
Holidays: 26 Jan; 4 Mar; 14, 16 Apr; 11, 31 May; 8, 15 Aug; 2 Oct; 10 Nov; 25 Dec

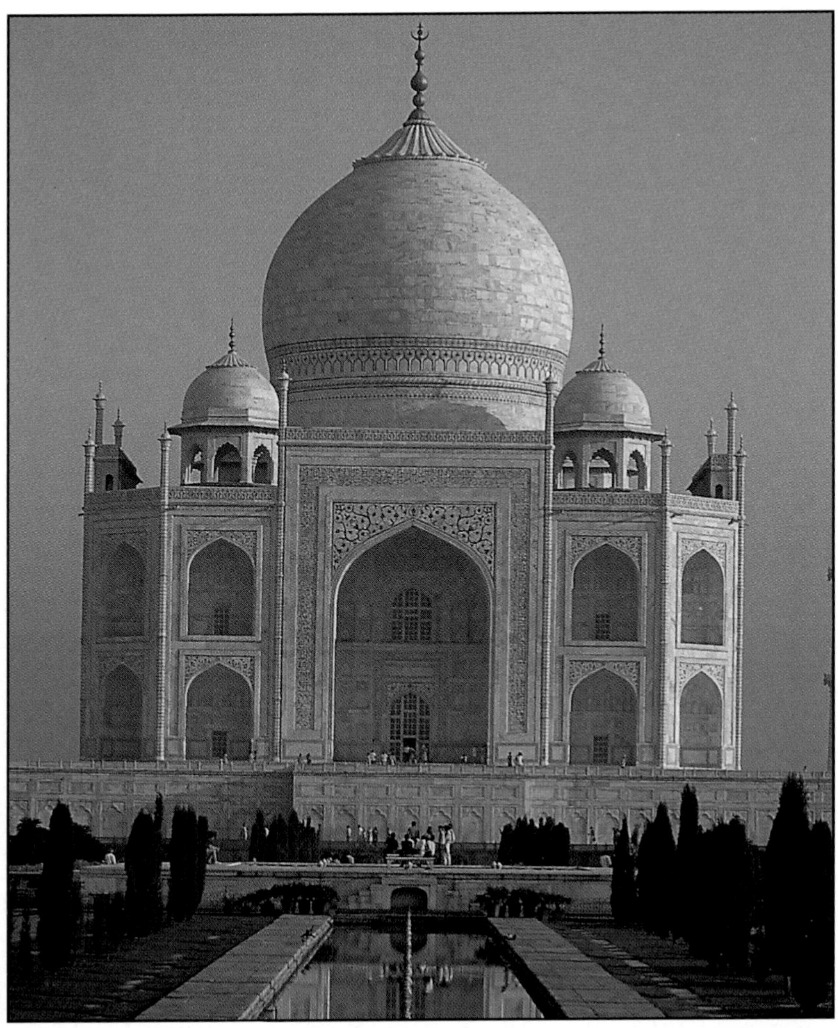

J. HUARD

in Gangtok, near Darjiling (well known by tea-lovers). Unfortunately, this region is part of the Seven Sisters territory mentioned above.

WHAT TO BUY

India is the biggest spice exporter in the world. This means that Indian cuisine is flavoured with cardamom, nutmeg, cloves, turmeric, saffron, anise, and ginger—not all at once! The *masalchis* (spice mixers) are the great masters of Indian cooking. The curries, yogurt *raita*, *basmati* rice, *nan* bread, and tea are all excellent. *Samosas* (small patties stuffed with vegetables), *lassi* (a yogurt drink), chutneys (condiments), *biryanis* (rice dishes), and *chapatis* (small breads) are part of any basic meal. *Tandoor* is a style of cooking, in a cylindrical oven, that is unique to India. Silk, cotton, fabrics shot with gold thread, and batiks are always of high quality. The *saris* worn by the women are often true works of art. The jewelry, sculpted wood, musical instruments such as the sitar, and, of course, Darjiling tea, make good souvenirs. Antonio Tabucchi's *Nocturne Indien* takes readers behind the scenes of the India that tourists see, and *The House and the World*, by the great Indian writer Tagore, must be read before a visit to India.

NEPAL

+13½ +12½ +11½ +10½ +9½

NEPAL

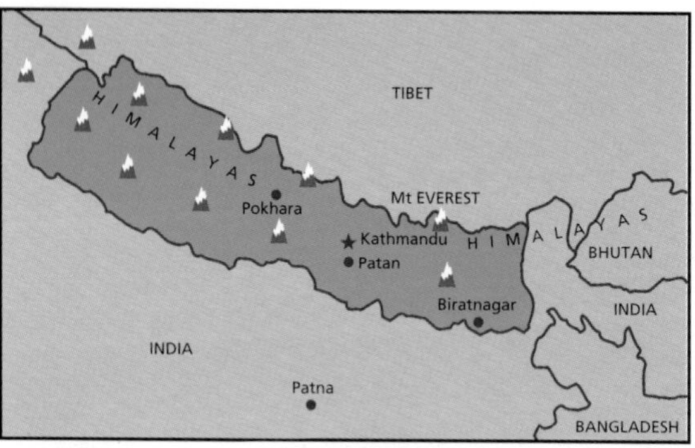

J. HUARD

Region: Asia
Area: 140,800 km²
Capital: Kathmandu
Airport: Kathmandu 6 km
Population: 21,041,530
Language: Nepali (off.)
Religion: Hindu
Government: parliamentary monarchy
Voltage: 220 - 50
Vaccinations required: Yf*
" recommended: Cho, Ty, Po, Mal
Passport: required
Visa: required
Currency: Nepalese rupee
$1Cdn: 37.32 rupees
Driving: left hand
International permit: required
Area code: 011-977
✆ from Canada: –
✆ to Canada: –
Accommodation: ★★★
Restaurants: ★★★
Transportation: ★★
Cost of living: ❍
UN rank: 149
Best months: Oct to Feb
Holidays: 19 Feb; 9 Nov; 28 Dec

WHAT TO DO

Nepal's nickname is the "Roof of the World", for this country, in the Himalayas, boasts the highest mountain on earth: magnificent Mount Everest, at 8,882 m altitude. Trekking to the Himalayan peaks is one of Nepal's main tourist attractions; the country's rich cultural heritage is another. The many Hindu and Buddhist monuments in the capital, Kathmandu, make this city a fascinating sanctuary. The sacred Pashupatinath Temple and the ancient Bodhnath group of buildings are particularly interesting. Farther south, Patan is a museum-city recognized as the "City of Beauty and the Arts". Pokhara is the starting-point for most expeditions to the mountains: organized excursions are, obviously, the safest way to journey into the mountains.

WHAT TO BUY

Nepalese cooking is always very tasty, especially the slowly cooked curries. *Jand*, very mild beer, often accompanies meals, but *chiya* tea is the favourite drink in Nepal. Carpets and sculpted wood and ivory are the specialties of Kathmandu. The copper statues from Jawalakhel and the *pashmins*, lambswool blankets, are great buys.

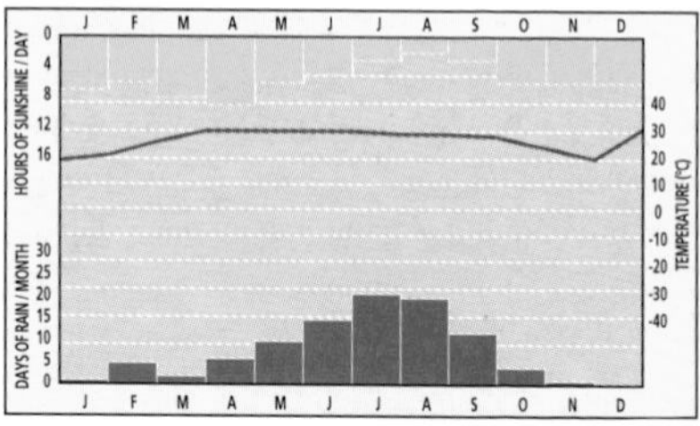

BHUTAN

+14 +13 +12 +11 +10

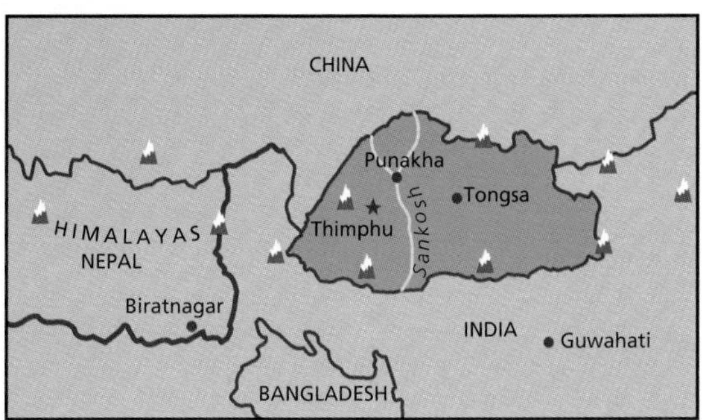

Region: Asia
Area: 47,000 km²
Capital: Thimphu
Airport: –
Population: 1,700,000
Languages: Dzhonkha, Nepali
Religions: Buddhist, Hindu
Government: constitutional monarchy
Voltage: 220 - 50
Vaccinations required: Yf*
: recommended: Cho, Ty, Po, Mal
Passport: required
Visa: required
Currency: ngultrum
$1Cdn: 23.12 ngultrums
Driving: right hand
International permit: required
Area code: limited service
✆ from Canada: –
✆ to Canada: –
Accommodation: ★
Restaurants: ★
Transportation: ★
Cost of living: ○○○
UN rank: 162
Best months: July, Aug, Sept
Holidays: 11 Nov; 17 Dec

BHUTAN

WHAT TO DO

Bhutan is a tranquil country where large herds of yaks graze in deep valleys over-shadowed by high Himalayan peaks. The 1,300 monasteries ensconced among the snow-topped mountains are protected by *dzongs* (fortified walls) that jealously guard the secrets of monastic life. It can be very difficult to enter a monastery, but the wait will be greatly rewarded. The monastery in Thimphu, the capital, is worth the trip to Bhutan. The Paro Valley is breathtaking, with its famous Tongsa Monastery perched precariously on the edge of a precipice more than 900 m high. It is in the guard tower of the Paro that one finds the National Museum of Bhutan, where the history of the country and its many battles against Chinese and Indian invaders is explained. The countryside is still wild, and the tourism industry is not well developed: for adventurers only! Bhutan limits entry to 4,000 visitors a year in order to preserve its culture.

WHAT TO BUY

Wood, cardamom, and products from yak-raising are the country's main wares. Woven bamboo and ruby-coloured fabrics are typically Bhutanese, and Bhutan's stamps make fine gifts for philatelists.

BANGLADESH

+14 +13 +12 +11 +10

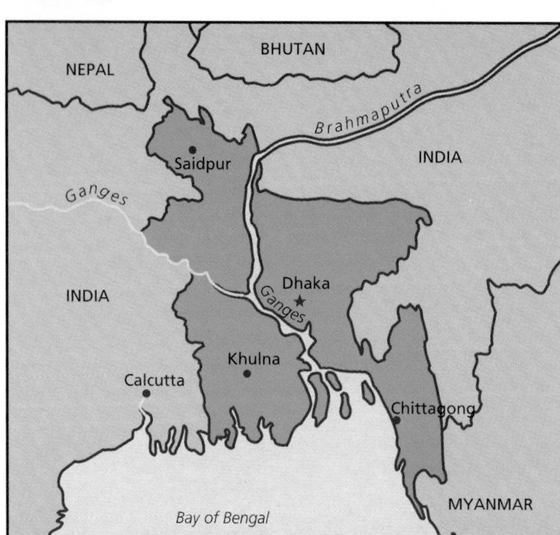

Region: Asia
Area: 143,998 km²
Capital: Dhaka
Airport: Dhaka 19 km
Population: 125,149,500
Languages: Bengali, Urdu, English
Religions: Islamic, Hindu
Government: parliamentary democracy
Voltage: 220 - 50
Vaccinations required: Yf*
" recommended: Cho, Ty, Po, Mal
Passport: required
Visa: required
Currency: taka
$1Cdn: 29.52 takas
Driving: left hand
International permit: recommended
Area code: 011-880
✆ from Canada: –
✆ to Canada: –
Accommodation: ★★
Restaurants: ★★
Transportation: ★★
Cost of living: ❍
UN rank: 146
Best months: Jan, Feb
Holidays: 19 Jan; 21 Feb; 1, 4, 26 Mar; 14 Apr; 1, 11, 31 May; 10 June; 8 Aug; 7 Nov; 16, 25 Dec

J. HUARD

WHAT TO DO

Bangladesh has always had the reputation of being an ideal destination for tourists in search of a completely new experience. The country, of course, is often in the news because of the typhoons, floods, and famines that sweep through it periodically, but Bangladesh has much wealth to offer travellers, especially a wealth of unique scenery, including rice paddies irrigated by the majestic Ganges and Brahmaputra rivers. Bangladeshis are proud of their capital, Dhaka, where the prime attractions are Banga Bhavan, the presidential palace; the Dhakeswari Temple; and the tomb of Bibi Peri. Chittagong is a more European city, but it nevertheless has a unique Asian cachet, and the villages of the Rajshahi region, in the northern part of the country, are rich in archaeological sites. Sundarbans National Park is famous for its Bengal tigers.

WHAT TO BUY

Bangladeshi tea is known the world over. The country's cuisine is based on rice, but meats like chicken and lamb are often on the menu. The traditional *sari*, the draped length of fabric worn by the women, the lace and muslin of Dhaka, and the pink pearls are good buys. Jute is another Bangladeshi product.

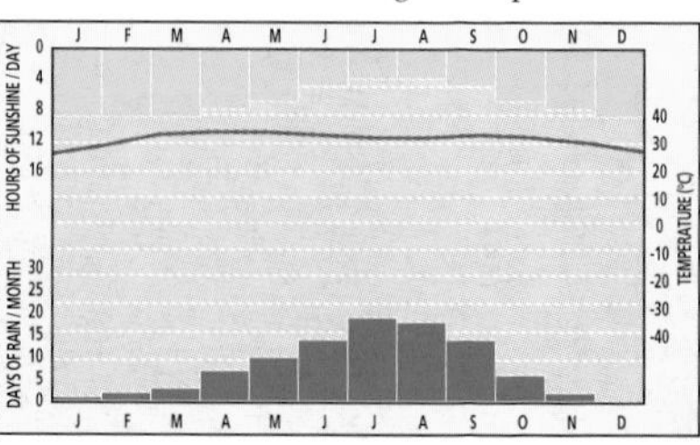

MYANMAR

+14½ +13½ +12½ +11½ +10½

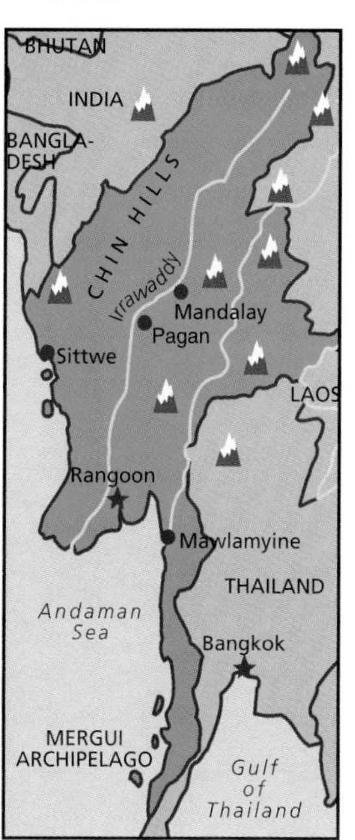

WHAT TO DO

Often associated with opium production, Myanmar (Burma) is now trying to attract visitors by publicizing the beauty of its scenery, especially among the mountains in the north of the country, and in Tenasserim, the tongue of land abutting Thailand. The Mergui Archipelago is a paradise for travellers seeking a timeless experience. Rangoon, the capital, has one of the largest Buddhist monuments in the world, the Schwedagon, with roofs of gold leaf and precious stones. Mandalay, with its pagoda and royal palace, is definitely worth seeing. Pagan is a sanctuary of over 2,000 Buddhist monuments.

Region: Asia
Area: 678,500 km2
Capital: Rangoon
Airport: Rangoon 19 km
Population: 44,277,020
Languages: Burmese, dialects
Religion: Buddhist
Government: military dictatorship
Voltage: 220 - 50
Vaccinations required: Yf*
" recommended: Cho, Ty, Po, Mal
Passport: required
Visa: required
Currency: kyat
$1Cdn: 3.98 kyats
Driving: left hand
International permit: required
Area code: 011-095
✆ from Canada: –
✆ to Canada: –
Accommodation: ★
Restaurants: ★
Transportation: ★★
Cost of living: ❍
UN rank: 130
Best months: Dec, Jan, Feb
Holidays: 4, 31 Jan; 12 Feb; 2, 4, 27 Mar; 13–16 Apr; 1, 11 May; 19 July; 8, 25 Dec

WHAT TO BUY

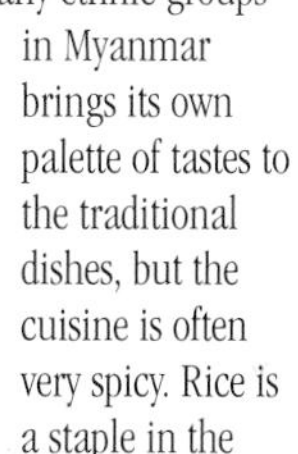

Each of the many ethnic groups in Myanmar brings its own palette of tastes to the traditional dishes, but the cuisine is often very spicy. Rice is a staple in the Burmese diet. The many pearl-oyster farms produce magnificent pearls. Teak, alabaster, and silk are crafted into a variety of fine souvenirs. Laquer objects from Pagan are very pretty.

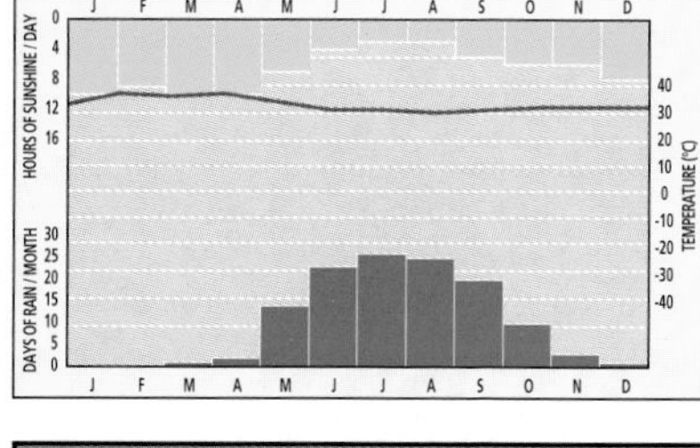

MYANMAR

LAOS

+15 +14 +13 +12 +11

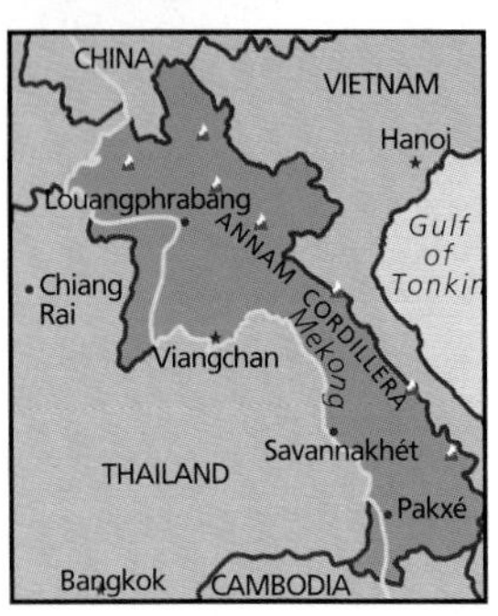

WHAT TO DO

Laos is slowly opening to tourism, an industry which saw little encouragement in the past. From the city of Louangphrabang, take the Mekong Highway to discover the countryside. Xientong Wat is an important historical site, and the entire country is dotted with Buddhist monuments. Viangchan (Vientiane), the capital, bears many vestiges of the country's past as a French colony.

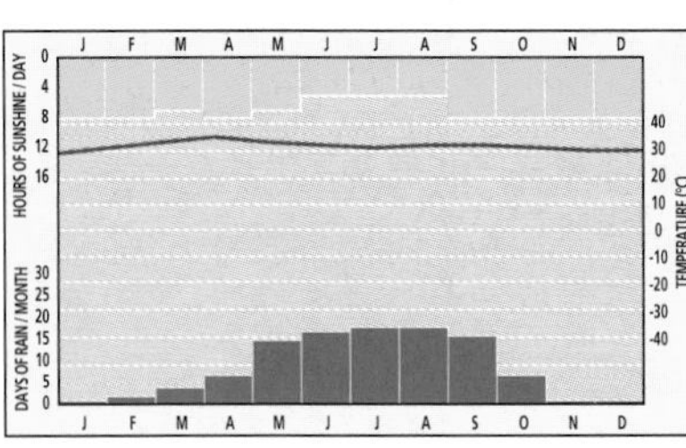

WHAT TO BUY

Laos's sericulture (silkworm-breeding) industry produces a wide variety of top-quality silks. Teak wood is used to manufacture finely worked everyday objects.

Region: Asia
Area: 236,800 km²
Capital: Viangchan
Airport: Viangchan 4 km
Population: 4,701,660
Languages: Lao (off.), French, English
Religion: Theravada Buddhist
Government: people's republic
Voltage: 220 - 50
Vaccinations required: Yf*
' recommended: Cho, Ty, Po, Mal
Passport: required
Visa: required
Currency: kip
$1Cdn: 536.62 kips
Driving: right hand
International permit: recommended
Area code: service via Bangkok (66)
✆ from Canada: –
✆ to Canada: –
Accommodation: ★★
Restaurants: ★★
Transportation: ★
Cost of living: ○
UN rank: 133
Best months: Dec to May
Holidays: 1 Jan; 2 Dec

MACAU

WHAT TO DO

This small Portuguese territory in Asia is well known for its gaming houses, hare and horse races, automobile races, and casinos, which draw millions of visitors each year. For those with other interests, Macau has an impressive number of Catholic churches decorated in the typically Portuguese *azulejos* style. Travellers arriving from China will find Macau quite different: the streets bear Portuguese names, the people speak Portuguese, and the architecture is firmly in the Manuelin style. On the island of Taipa is found a strange architectural mix of Buddhist temples and European buildings.

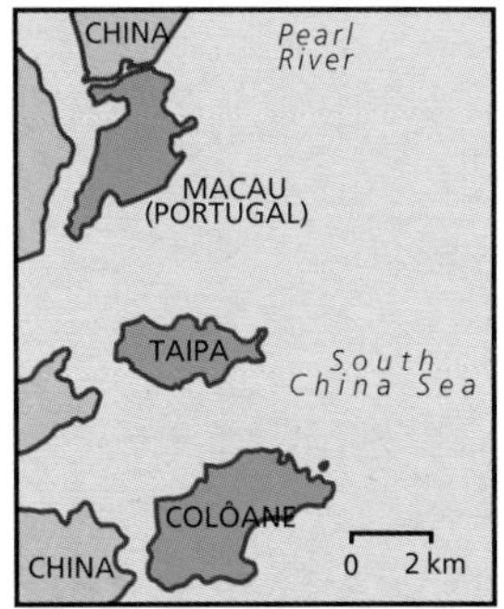

The Chinese character of Coloane complements the island's beautiful beaches.

WHAT TO BUY

Macau is a duty-free zone: electronic and high-precision equipment is well priced, as are gold and jewelry of all types. Typically Portuguese products such as porto and *azulejos* are available, along with incense, calligraphy, and silk goods from China.

Region: Asia
Area: 16 km²
Capital: Macau
Airport: —
Population: 484,560
Languages: Portuguese (off.), Cantonese
Religions: Buddhist, Christian
Government: special territory of Portugal
Voltage: 220 - 50
Vaccinations required: –
Vaccinations recommended: –
Passport: required
Visa: not required
Currency: pataca
$1Cdn: 5.88 patacas
Driving: left hand
International permit: required
Area code: 011-853
✆ from Canada: 1-800-463-0809
✆ to Canada: 0800-100
Accommodation: ★★★★
Restaurants: ★★★★
Transportation: ★★
Cost of living: ○○○
UN rank: –
Best months: Nov to April
Holidays: 1 Jan; 25 Apr; 10, 24 June; 15 Aug; 5 Oct; 1 Nov; 1, 8, 25 Dec

THAILAND

+15 +14 +13 +12 +11

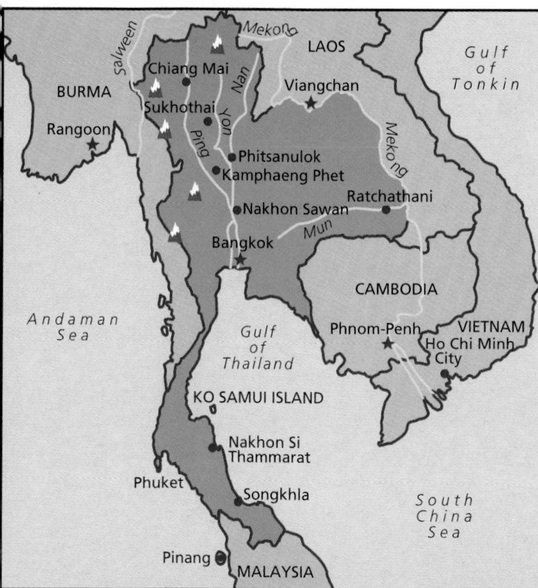

Region: Asia
Area: 514,400 km²
Capital: Bangkok
Airport: Bangkok 25 km
Population: 59,510,480
Languages: Thai, Chinese, English
Religion: Theravada Buddhist
Government: constitutional monarchy
Voltage: 220 - 50
Vaccinations required: Yf*
' recommended: Cho, Ty, Po, Mal
Passport: required
Visa: not required
Currency: baht
$1Cdn: 18.22 bahts
Driving: left hand
International permit: required
Area code: 011-66
✆ from Canada: 1-800-663-7174
✆ to Canada: 001-999-15-1000
Accommodation: ★★★★
Restaurants: ★★★★
Transportation: ★★★
Cost of living: ○○
UN rank: 54
Best months: Dec, Jan, Feb
Holidays: 1 Jan; 6, 13 Apr; 5, 14 May; 12 Aug; 23 Oct; 5, 10, 31 Dec

THAILAND

WHAT TO DO

Once the ancient kingdom of Siam, Thailand still has the aura of romance its rich culture acquired from Thai dynasties and European influences. The brilliant smiles and warm welcome of the Thai people make the country a destination of choice. Some travellers maintain that a trip to Asia should begin in Thailand. Bangkok, the "City of Angels," is best known for its exotic Thai architecture, including the Royal Palace and the Wat Phra Keo, which are covered with gold leaf and precious stones. In Thon Buri, visit some of the hundreds of Buddhist temples and the pretty floating market, then ferry across the Chao Phraya River to the smaller neighbourhoods of the city. A performance of classic Thai theatre is a must-see. North of Bangkok, the ancient capital of Ayuthya is known mainly for the Suan Pakkard Palace. The bronze Buddha of Phra Phutta Chinarat, in Phitsanulok, is definitely worth seeing. Chiang Rai is a small, tranquil town that enjoys a spring-like climate all year round, while Chiang Mai draws visitors for its elephant camps, orchid plantations, and craft centre, one of the largest in the country. The wildlife sanctuary of Thung Yai-Huai Kha Khaeng, in the northwest of the country, will attract those who enjoy high mountains covered with dense and majestic vegetation. The archaeological site of Ban Chin is worth a visit,

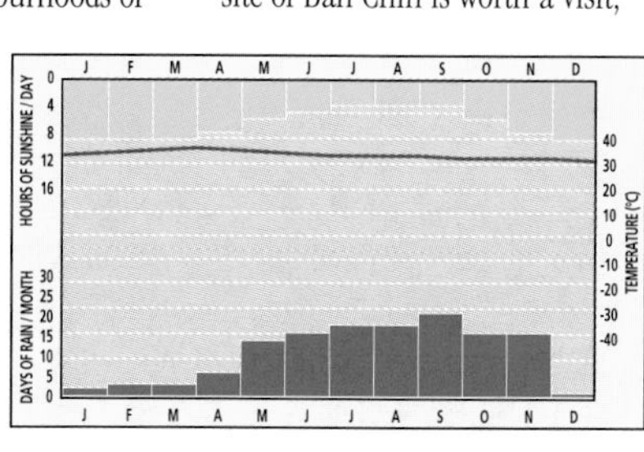

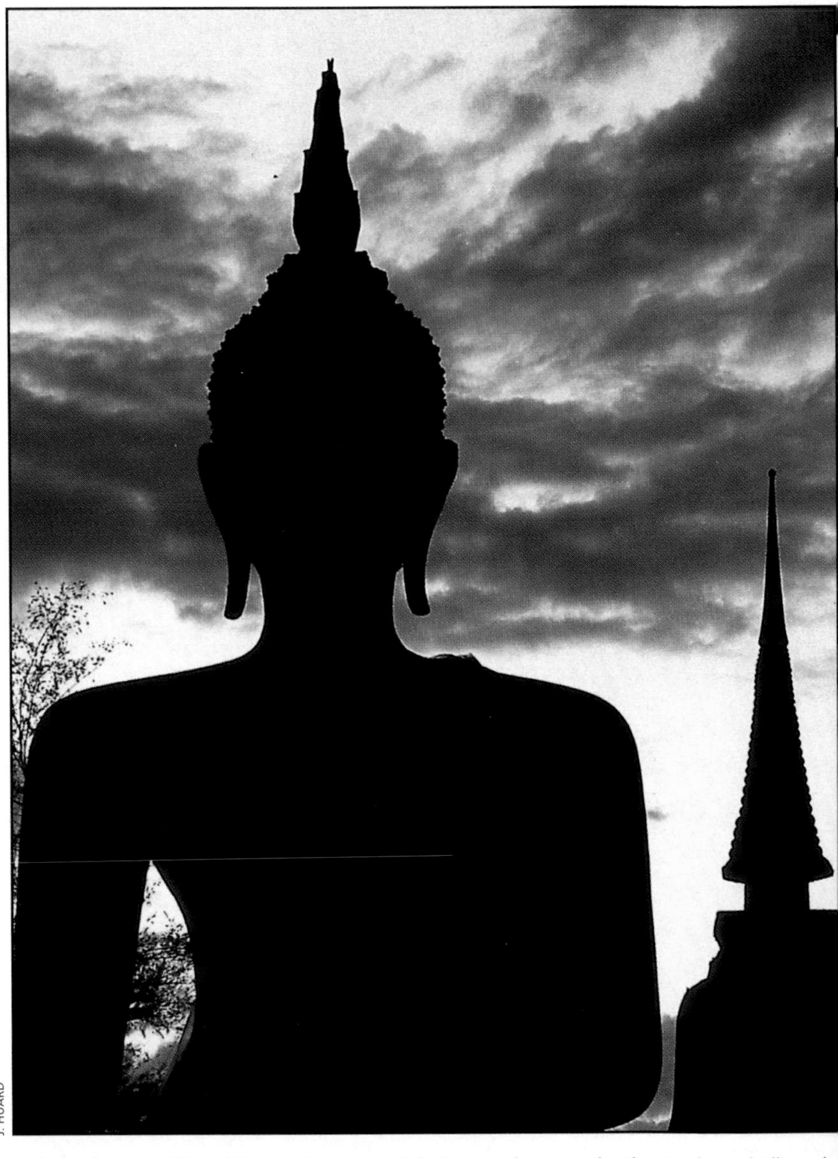

J. HUARD

while beach-lovers will head for the fine sand and calm seas of Phuket and the island of Ko Samui.

WHAT TO BUY

Thai cuisine is often very spicy: *pri-kee-noo* is a small, very strong pepper that is found in almost every dish. Fortunately, the rice (a world-renowned delicacy) cools the palate effectively. *Tom yam*, spicy soups, make excellent meals. At Chiang Mai, one can find products made by craftspeople from all over the country: wooden sculptures, lacquer goods, pottery, paper parasols, silver jewelry, and silk goods. Prostitution is a scourge into which are drawn many young Thais: the "sex tourism" network, unfortunately, attracts many travellers to this country. However, women who want to travel there on their own will have no problems.

CAMBODIA

+15 +14 +13 +12 +11

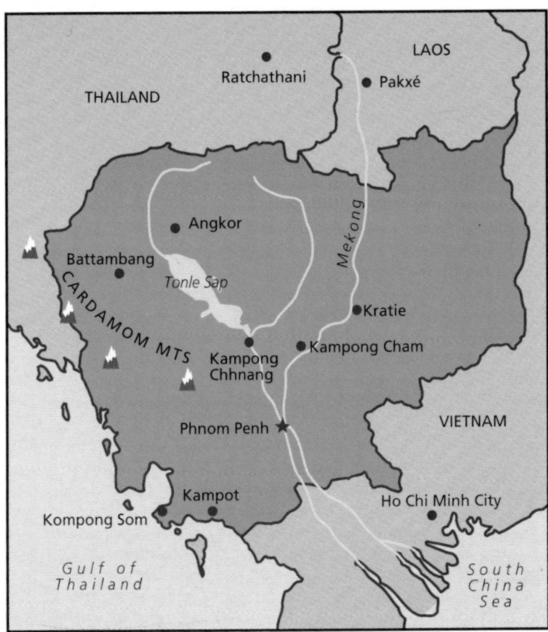

Region: Asia
Area: 181,040 km²
Capital: Phnom Penh
Airport: Phnom Penh 10 km
Population: 10,264,630
Languages: Khmer, French, English
Religion: Theravada Buddhist
Government: constitutional monarchy
Voltage: 220 - 50
Vaccinations required: Yf*
' recommended: Cho, Ty, Po, Mal
Passport: required
Visa: required
Currency: riel
$1Cdn: 1693.03 riels
Driving: forbidden to tourists
International permit: group visits
Area code: 011-7 (via Moscow)
✆ from Canada: –
✆ to Canada: –
Accommodation: ★
Restaurants: ★
Transportation: ★
Cost of living: ❍
UN rank: 147
Best months: Aug, Dec to Mar
Holidays: 7 Jan; 14 Apr; 1 May; 9 Nov

CAMBODIA

WHAT TO DO

When the prime minister of a country advises tourists to stay away, it means that the situation is indeed catastrophic. This is what is happening right now in Cambodia: tourists and aid workers have been the target of violence by the Khmer Rouge, who refuse to recognize the new, elected government. Until things get back to normal, travellers will have to forgo visiting the superb archaeological site at Angkor, one of the most beautiful groups of temples, monuments, statues, towers, and funerary steles ever discovered. Spread over more than 300 km², the site dates from the ninth to fifteenth centuries and features buildings made of finely worked sandstone and walls ornamented with splendid architectural details. The Bakong temple dates from the year 881; the one in Phnom Bakheng, from 900; and the most impressive and beautiful, Angkor Wat, dates from the twelfth century. Forgotten by the world for many centuries, Angkor is becoming one of the most important archaeological sites in the world.

MAURITIUS / BECK / RÉFLEXION

WHAT TO BUY

Cambodian rice is the best in Southeast Asia. The scent of spices, especially cardamom and pepper, wafts through the markets. Tobacco, cotton, and latex plantations provide the raw materials for the country's other products.

VIETNAM

+15 +14 +13 +12 +11

VIETNAM

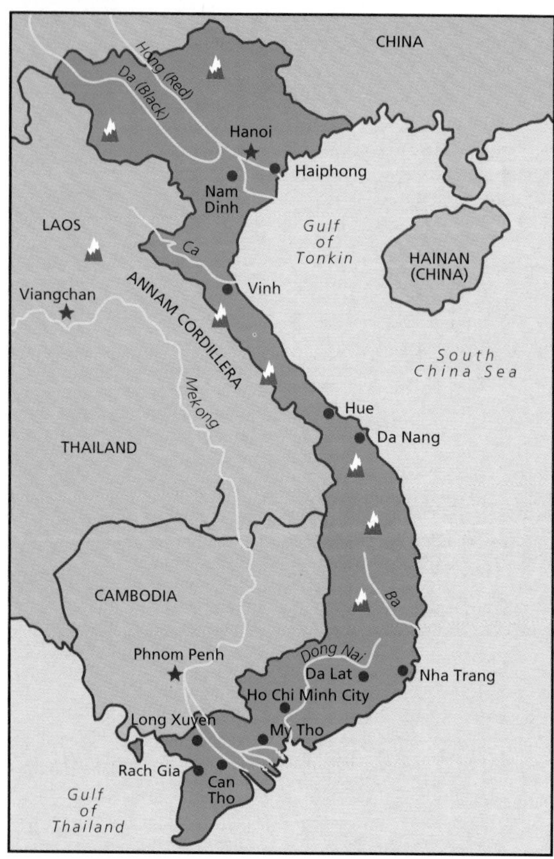

Region: Asia
Area: 329,560 km²
Capital: Hanoi
Airport: Hanoi 45 km
Population: 73,103,900
Languages: Vietnamese (off.), Khmer, Cham
Religions: Taoist, Hindu
Government: communist
Voltage: 240 - 50
Vaccinations required: Yf*
" recommended: Cho, Ty, Po, Mal
Passport: required
Visa: required
Currency: new dông
$1Cdn: 8121.39 dôngs
Driving: right hand
Int'l permit: vehicles not available
Area code: 011-84
✆ from Canada: –
✆ to Canada: –
Accommodation: ★★
Restaurants: ★★
Transportation: ★★
Cost of living: ❍❍
UN rank: 116
Best months: Dec to May
Holidays: 2 Sep

WHAT TO DO

For some, Vietnam is one of the most beautiful countries in Asia. The countryside provides a contrast between high, steep mountains and terraced plains of rice paddies. The coasts are indented with bays and capes gently washed by the South China Sea. Ho Chi Minh City (formerly Saigon) still bears marks of the war, but the Ben Thanh and Cholon markets illustrate the vitality of the Vietnamese people. Tây Ninh is a pleasant place to stop before moving into the Vietnamese countryside, to see the Caodaist ceremonies venerating Buddha, Jesus, Mohammed, Lao Tzu, Victor Hugo, and Flammarion! The underground city of Cu Chi is another curiosity. The Marble Mountain of Danang is pierced with enchanting caves. Make sure to visit the Cham Museum of Art for its collection of sculptures dating from the fourth and tenth centuries. At Hué, the Imperial City, the tomb of Minh Mang, and the Pagoda of the Celestial Lady are true works of art. Hanoi remains a charming city with many vestiges of its long colonial history. All the beaches on the Golf of Tonkin have the charm of places that time seems to have passed by. The caves at Hua Loc, near Hanoi, are true natural wonders, with their stalagmites and stalactites.

WHAT TO BUY

Vietnamese cuisine has the delicate aroma of carefully mixed herbs: the spring rolls, noodle soups, and delicious perfumed rice are now classics. Marble from Da Nang, the varnished urns from Thu Duc, and objects made of bamboo, such as the long traditional pipes, are the pride of Vietnamese craftspeople.

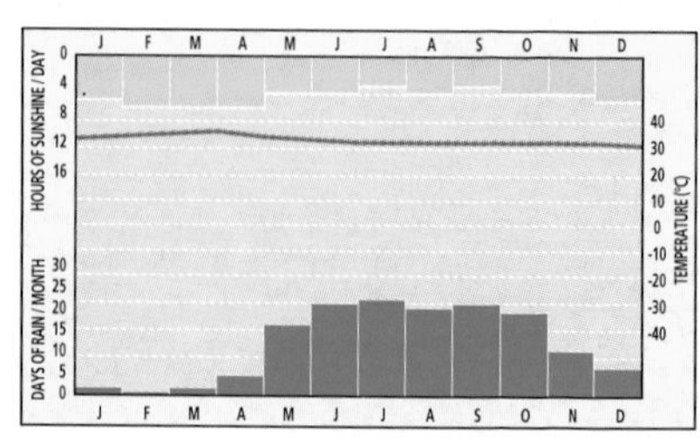

HONG KONG

+16 +15 +14 +13 +12

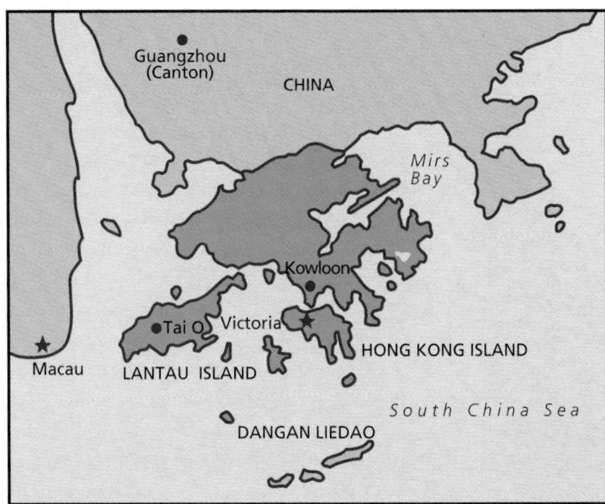

Region: Asia
Area: 1,040 km²
Capital: Victoria
Airport: Kai Tak 7.5 km
Population: 5,548,755
Languages: Cantonese, English
Religions: Buddhist, Confucianist, Taoist
Government: British Crown colony
Voltage: 220 - 50
Vaccinations required: –
Vaccinations recommended: Cho, Ty, Po
Passport: required
Visa: not required
Currency: Hong Kong dollar
$1Cdn: 5.70 dollars
Driving: left hand
International permit: recommended
Area code: 011-852
✆ from Canada: 1-800-663-0685
✆ to Canada: 800-1100
Accommodation: ★★★★★
Restaurants: ★★★★★
Transportation: ★★★★
Cost of living: ○○○
UN rank: 24
Best months: June to Sept
Holidays: 1, 30 Jan; 1, 2 Feb; 4, 14, 16, 17 Apr; 12 June; 26, 29 Aug; 25, 26 Dec

WHAT TO DO

Hong Kong will be returned to China on July 1, 1997. In the meantime, this British Crown colony is undergoing a phenomenal economic boom as its busy commercial arteries, crowded restaurants, and many tourists reveal. Hong Kong Island and the New Territories have an area of only 1,000 km², but the list of attractions is long: Mount Victoria; Repulse Bay; the port of Aberdeen, which is well known for its *sampans* (fishing boats); the bird market; Tiger Balm Garden; the Temple of Ten Thousand Buddhas; Temple Street, with its night market; the Kowloon Market, and the Miu Fat Monastery. Hong Kong is often used as a point of departure for China, but it is in itself a destination that can keep travellers busy for weeks.

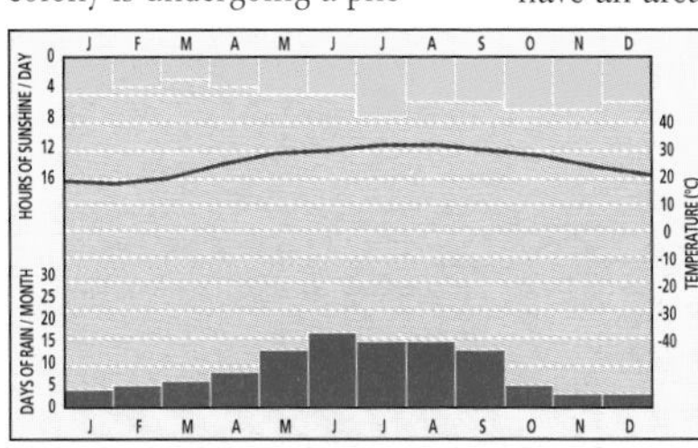

J. HUARD

WHAT TO BUY

Hong Kong, a duty-free zone, is a dynamic commercial centre where one can find almost anything, from knickknacks worth a quarter to high-end electronic equipment. Traditional Chinese art objects, silk goods, ivory, and jade are good buys. Hong Kong's restaurants are among the best in Asia: they feature specialties from every region of China and from all over the world.

TAIWAN

+16 +15 +14 +13 +12

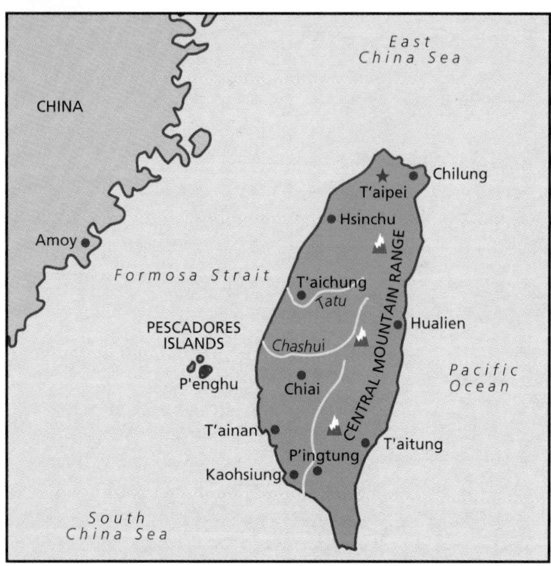

Region: Asia
Area: 35,980 km²
Capital: T'aipei
Airport: T'aipei 40 km
Population: 21,298,930
Languages: Chinese, Taiwanese
Religions: Buddhist, Taoist, Confucianist
Government: semi-presidential democracy
Voltage: 110 - 60
Vaccinations required: Yf*
Vaccinations recommended: Cho, Ty, Po
Passport: required
Visa: not required for under 2 weeks
Currency: New Taiwan dollar
$1Cdn: 19.48 dollars
Driving: right hand
International permit: required
Area code: 011-886
✆ from Canada: 1-800-663-0688
✆ to Canada: ▲0-801-20012
Accommodation: ★★★★★
Restaurants: ★★★★★
Transportation: ★★★★★
Cost of living: ❍❍❍
UN rank: –
Best months: Jan, Feb, Mar, May
Holidays: 1, 31 Jan; 29 Mar; 5 Apr; 28 Sept; 10, 25, 31 Oct; 12 Nov; 25 Dec

WHAT TO DO

Previously known as Formosa, which means "Beautiful Island" in Portuguese, Taiwan earns its name, even though it is often associated with plastic knicknacks labelled "Made in Taiwan". The island is very mountainous: the highest peak of the Central Mountain Range is Jade Mountain, with an altitude of 4,000 m, in Yushan National Park. Yangmingshan National Park must be seen in May, when its thousands of cherry trees are in bloom! The sandy coasts of the western part of the island are washed by the *kuroshio*, a warm current that moderates the country's climate. The capital, T'aipei, is a dynamic metropolis, where Chinese traditions still thrive: try to catch a glimpse of people practising their Tai Chi in city parks, in the shadow of the ultramodern skyscrapers. The T'aipei National Palace Museum offers the largest and most beautiful collection of Chinese art in the world: most of the works come from the treasure trove of the Forbidden City in Beijing. The traditional architecture of the smaller city of T'ai-nan, home to 200 Confucian temples, makes a trip to the other end of the island very worthwhile.

WHAT TO BUY

In Taiwan, one can sample all the regional dishes of China, from Szechuan to Cantonese. In the large restaurants you will find Western eating utensils, but everything tastes better when you use chopsticks! Hot sake often accompanies meals. Precious stones, lacquer items, finely worked jade curios, and ceramics are the pride of the Taiwanese craftspeople.

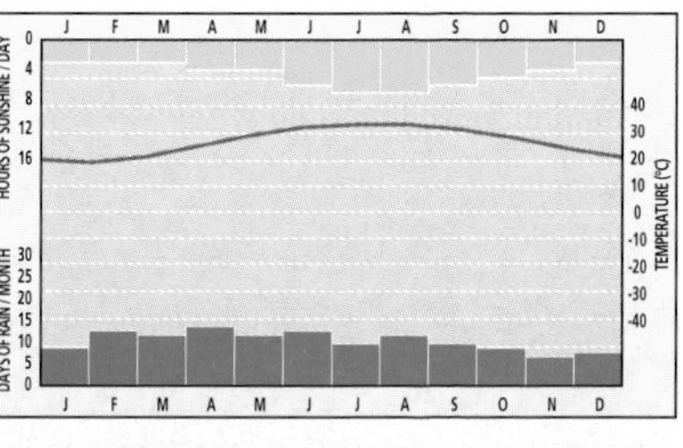

I. HUARD

PHILIPPINES

+16 +15 +14 +13 +12

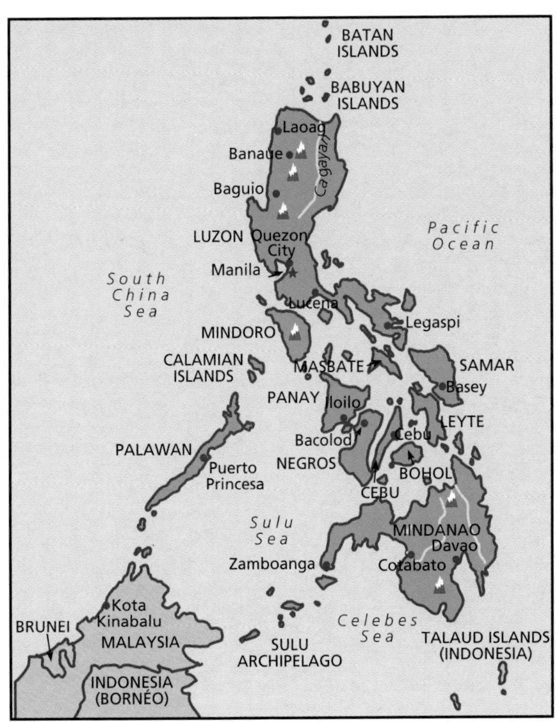

Region: Asia
Area: 300,000 km²
Capital: Manila
Airport: Manila 12 km
Population: 69,808,930
Languages: Filipino (Tagalog), English
Religion: Catholic
Government: parliamentary democracy
Voltage: 220 - 60
Vaccinations required: Yf*
Vaccinations recommended: Cho, Ty, Po, Mal
Passport: required
Visa: required
Currency: Philippine peso
$1Cdn: 18.87 pesos
Driving: right hand
International permit: required
Area code: 011-63
✆ from Canada: 1-800-565-7445
✆ to Canada: ▲105-10
Accommodation: ★★★★
Restaurants: ★★★★
Transportation: ★★★
Cost of living: ○
UN rank: 99
Best months: Dec, Jan, Feb
Holidays: 1,2 Jan; 10,13,14,16 Apr; 1 May; 12 June; 27 Aug; 1, 30 Nov; 25, 30 Dec

WHAT TO DO

The Philippines Archipelago is made up of five major zones, each of which has its own attractions: Luzon, the Visayan Islands, Mindanao, Palawan, and the Sulu Archipelago. The splendour of the scenery, especially of the famous terraced rice paddies, is the trademark of this country. For travellers, the first step into the Philippines should be Manila, on the island of Luzon—a city with a Latin ambience in a very Asian atmosphere. Manila still has vestiges of the Spanish and American eras. The *Intramuros*, the old part of the city, is particularly interesting, as is the National Museum in Rizal Park. Farther north on Luzon, at Banaue, the 2,000-year-old rice paddies are marvels of ingenuity. The Philippine volcanoes, some of which, like Mount Pinatubo, are still active, provide a graceful counterpoint to the otherwise flat countryside. The island of Mindanao is famous for its sandy coastline and profusion of flowers. Here is found Zamboanga, one of the most beautiful spots in the country, even though tourism is starting to take it over. The Muslim villages in the Sulu Islands are built on pilings, a style of building unique to this region. The Visayan Islands were conquered by the Spanish; Magellan erected a cross there in 1521 after discovering the island of Cebu. All of the islands are worth visiting, especially Bohol, for its strange geological formation called Chocolate Hill.

WHAT TO BUY

Sinigang is a fish soup unique to the Philippines. Pork is the basis of most dishes, notably, the delicious *lechon*, roast pig and *adobo*, pork seasoned with garlic. Beer, *tuba* (a palm-tree liquor), and *lambanog* (coconut wine) accompany the often rather spicy foods. Wooden objects, fabrics made from pineapple fibre and banana-tree bark, cotton, and virgin silk are very popular, as is the gold and silver jewelry from Mindanao.

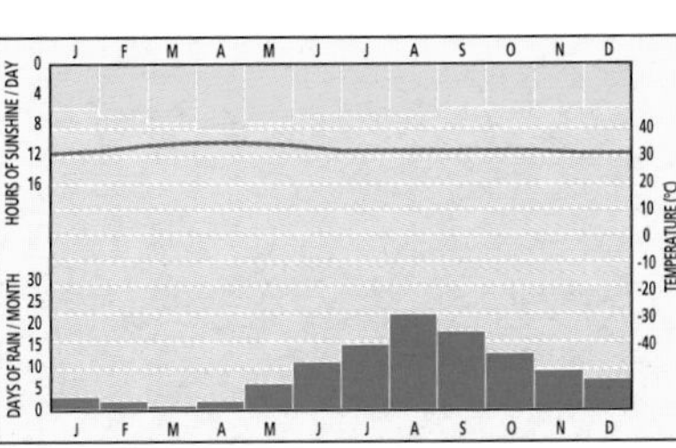

SRI LANKA

+13½ +12½ +11½ +10½ +9½

SRI LANKA

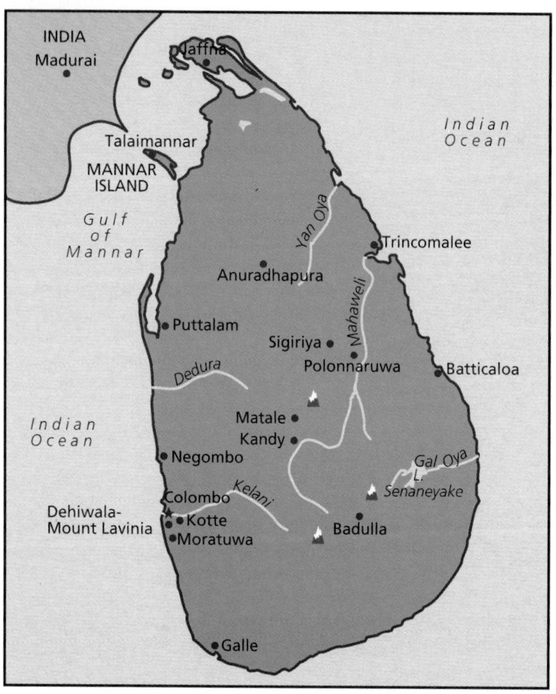

Region: Asia
Area: 65,610 km²
Capital: Colombo
Airport: Colombo 30 km
Population: 18,129,850
Languages: Sinhalese, Tamil, English
Religions: Buddhist, Hindu, Christian
Government: presidential democracy
Voltage: 220 - 50
Vaccinations required: Yf*
" recommended: Cho, Ty, Po, Mal
Passport: required
Visa: not required
Currency: Sri Lanka rupee
$1Cdn: 37.16 rupees
Driving: left hand
International permit: required
Area code: 011-94
✆ from Canada: 1-800-665-0062
✆ to Canada: 01-430077
Accommodation: ★★★
Restaurants: ★★★
Transportation: ★★★
Cost of living: ❍
UN rank: 90
Best months: Feb, Mar
Holidays: 4 Feb; 4 Mar; 14, 16 Apr; 1, 11, 22 May; 30 June; 8 Aug; 25 Dec

WHAT TO DO

The Tamil separatist rebellion in the north and east of the country has somewhat undermined Sri Lanka's good reputation as a tourist destination, but travellers who do not venture into those regions should not have any problems. Colombo, the capital, is rich with Buddhist temples, mosques, and monuments from the British colonial era. The ancient royal cities of Polonnarua, Kandy, and Sigiriya are sacred cities for Sinhalese Buddhists. In Kandy, they celebrate *Esala Perahera*, a 10-day procession in August that involves transporting a reliquary of Buddha on elephants wearing richly decorated harnesses. The beaches of Sri Lanka are very popular with divers.

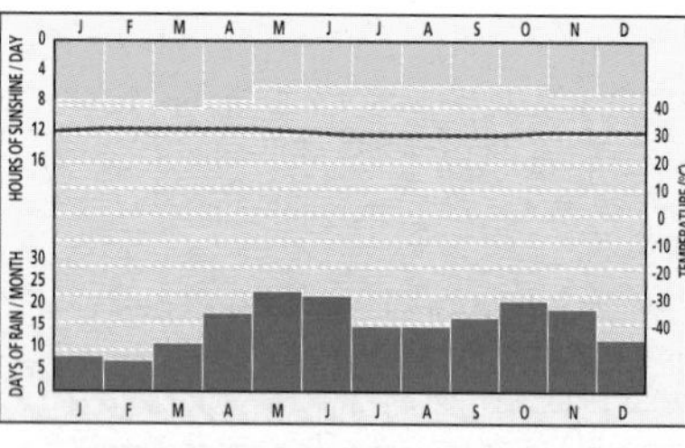

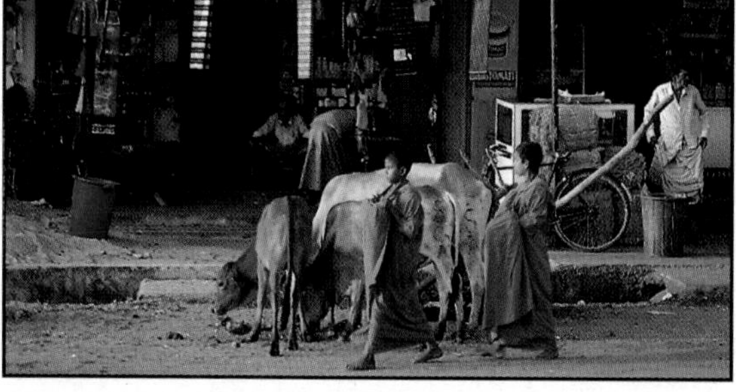

WHAT TO BUY

Sri Lankan cuisine is often very spicy, but the *lamprai*, a dish of rice cooked in banana skin, is a good antidote to hot foods. Coconut milk also douses the fiery spices. Tea, coffee, and rice are cultivated in the valleys and mountains in the southwest part of the island. The striking *saris* worn by the women and the beautiful batiks sold there make a visit to the market colourful and pleasant. Tortoise shell is protected by very strict laws: it is forbidden to purchase jewelry or other items decorated with tortoise shell, or ivory from elephant tusks.

RÉFLEXION

MALAYSIA

+16 +15 +14 +13 +12

Region: Asia
Area: 329,750 km²
Capital: Kuala Lumpur
Airport: Kuala Lumpur 22 km
Population: 19,283,160
Languages: Malaysian, Chinese, English
Religions: Islamic, Hindu, Buddhist
Government: constitutional monarchy
Voltage: 110/220 - 50
Vaccinations required: Yf*
" recommended: Cho, Ty, Po, Mal
Passport: required
Visa: not required
Currency: ringgit
$1Cdn: 1.81 ringgits
Driving: left hand
International permit: recommended
Area code: 011-60
✆ from Canada: 1-800-663-6817
✆ to Canada: ▲800-0017
Accommodation: ★★★★★
Restaurants: ★★★★★
Transportation: ★★★★★
Cost of living: ○○
UN rank: 57
Best months: June to Oct; Mar
Holidays: 1, 2, 31 Jan; 1, 2 Feb; 4 Mar; 1, 11, 31 May; 3 June; 8, 31 Aug; 25 Dec

WHAT TO DO

Malaysia is a dream destination for those who love lush countryside where the animal kingdom still rules. This is a country of impenetrable forests, jungles teeming with wildlife, orderly plantations, steep mountains, and tranquil beaches, as well as many national parks and reserves to protect these incomparable natural resources. Malaysia may be divided into three regions: to the west, Malaya on the Malay Peninsula, the state of Sarawak and the state of Sabah on the island of Borneo. Malaya is modern, while the provinces on Borneo are still relatively wild. Travellers can combine golfing in Malaya on one of the most beautiful networks of courses in Asia, with photo expeditions to Sarawak in search of sea turtles that lay their eggs on the beaches. In Kuala Lumpur, the capital, visit the National Mosque, the market, and the Buddhist caves at Batu. Malacca, with its Portuguese, Dutch, Chinese, and English influences, offers St. Paul's Cathedral, Santiago Fort, and the very beautiful Nyona Baba Museum. The island of Pinang, nicknamed the "Pearl of the Orient", offers magnificent beaches, typically Malaysian houses, and the Kek Lok Se Temple, with its 10,000 Buddhas. Kuching, the capital of Sarawak, is worth a visit, as is the jungle around the city, the nearby tea plantations, and the fascinating caves. Bako National Park is breathtaking, known especially for its famous carnivorous flowers. The caverns on the coast from Niah to Miri have existed for thousands of years. In the state of Sabah, Mount Kinabalu Park is a paradise for birdwatchers.

WHAT TO BUY

Satay, meat brochettes with peanut sauce; *rendang*, beef with ginger; and *panggang golek*, braised duck, are typically Malaysian dishes. Bird's-nest soup is a Bornean specialty. Coconut beer and coconut water (*ayer kelapa*) are served as apéritifs. *Makyong*, plays performed exclusively by women, and *menora*, plays performed by men, are part of Malaysia's cultural heritage. Malayan shadow-theatre puppets, *wayang kulit*, are unique pieces of art. Batiks from Pinang, *kain songket* (fabrics shot with gold thread), and pewter objects are among the many beautiful items to buy.

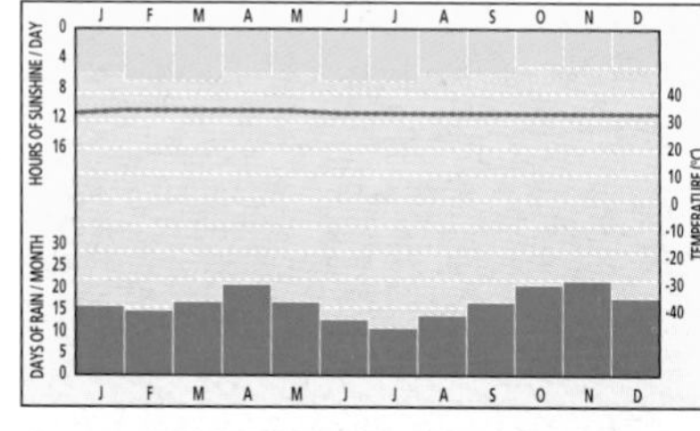

RÉFLEXION

SINGAPORE

+16 +15 +14 +13 +12

SINGAPORE

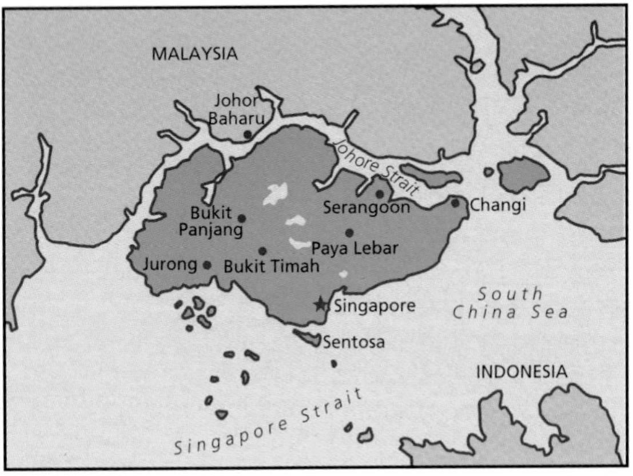

Region: Asia
Area: 632 km²
Capital: Singapore City
Airport: Singapore City 25 km
Population: 2,859,150
Languages: English, Chinese, Malay
Religions: Buddhist, Taoist
Government: parliamentary republic
Voltage: 220 - 50
Vaccinations required: Yf*
Vaccinations recommended: Cho, Ty
Passport: required
Visa: not required
Currency: Singapore dollar
$1Cdn: 1.02 dollars
Driving: left hand
International permit: required
Area code: 011-65
✆ from Canada: 1-800-665-6002
✆ to Canada: 8000-100-100
Accommodation: ★★★★★
Restaurants: ★★★★★
Transportation: ★★★★
Cost of living: ○○○
UN rank: 43
Best months: May to Sept
Holidays: 1, 31 Jan; 1 Feb; 4 Mar; 14, 16 Apr; 1, 11 May; 9 Aug; 25 Dec

WHAT TO DO

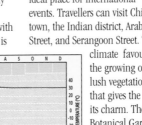

A city-state situated at the southern tip of the Malay Peninsula, Singapore (which means City of Lions) is a crossroad for tourism in Asia. The island is resolutely Asian, although it has a very Western ambience. Mixed in with the colonial-era monuments, is the ultramodern architecture of the buildings in the business and ethnic districts. Singapore's many luxury hotels , conference centres, and great restaurants make it an ideal place for international events. Travellers can visit Chinatown, the Indian district, Arab Street, and Serangoon Street. The climate favours the growing of the lush vegetation that gives the city its charm. The Botanical Gardens contain an exceptional variety of flowers, and Jurong Park is home to more than 3,000 species of birds. Singaporeans are very proud of Merlion Park and the Tiger Balm Gardens. The island of Sentosa has a distinctly "resort" feel, because of its many beaches and gardens.

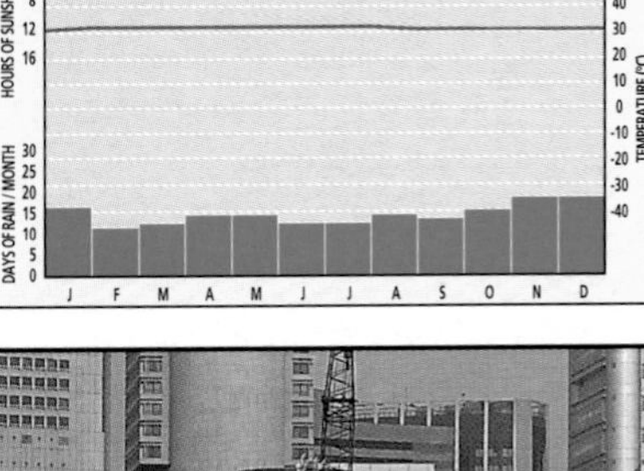

T. BOGNAR / RÉFLEXION

WHAT TO BUY

Singapore offers Chinese, Malaysian, Indian, and Indonesian cuisine: there's no lack of choice! Beer, coconut liquor, and the famous Singapore Sling are featured in all the bars. Batiks, jade figurines, Singaporean theatre puppets, and jewelry make for much better souvenirs than the crocodile- and snake-skin items offered by some vendors. Take care to obey Singapore's civic laws: transgressors are punished by beating with a bamboo cane!

BRUNEI

+16 +15 +14 +13 +12

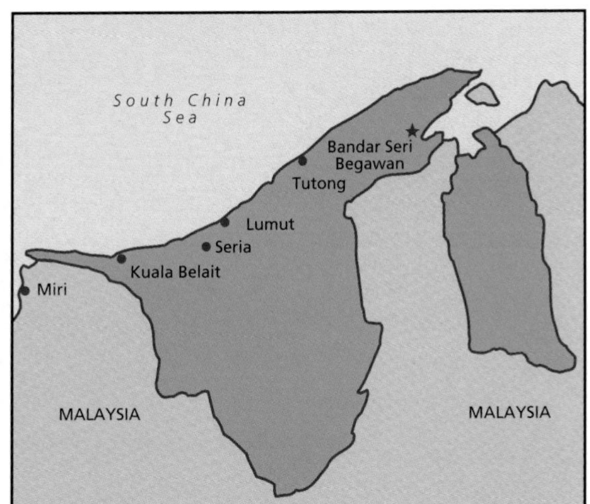

Region: Asia
Area: 5,765 km²
Capital: Bandar Seri Begawan
Airport: Bandar Seri Begawan 10 km
Population: 300,000
Languages: Malay, Chinese, English
Religions: Islamic, Buddhist
Government: monarchy
Voltage: 220 - 50
Vaccinations required: Yf*
Vaccinations recommended: Cho, Ty, Po
Passport: required
Visa: required
Currency: Brunei dollar
$1Cdn: 1.03 dollars
Driving: left hand
International permit: recommended
Area code: 011-673
✆ from Canada: –
✆ to Canada: –
Accommodation: ★★
Restaurants: ★★
Transportation: ★★
Cost of living: ○○○
UN rank: 44
Best months: Dec, Jan, Feb
Holidays: 1 Jan; 23 Feb; 3, 4 Apr; 1 May; 21 June; 15 July; 19 Aug; 25 Dec

BRUNEI

WHAT TO DO

Some would say that this country is a paradise: social services, housing, and transportation are free! The sultan of Brunei is one of the wealthiest men in the world, and his subjects enjoy a large number of advantages. Oil is the source of all this wealth. Brunei is accessible, however, only to businessmen who have dealings with the oil companies. Between meetings, they can discover the gold-roofed mosque of the capital, Bandar Seri Begawan, and the towns on the shores of the South China Sea, including Kuala Belait.

WHAT TO BUY

Brunei's fabrics and carpets are always very colourful. Silver, pewter, and bronze are used in the manufacture of everyday items and jewelry.

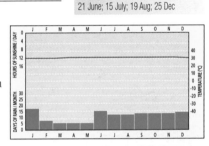

J F M A M J J A S O N D
HOURS OF SUNSHINE / DAY: 0 4 8 12 16
TEMPERATURE (°C): 40 30 20 10 0 -10 -20 -30 -40
DAYS OF RAIN / MONTH: 30 25 20 15 10 5 0
J F M A M J J A S O N D

P. LESAGE

INDONESIA

+15 +14 +13 +12 +11

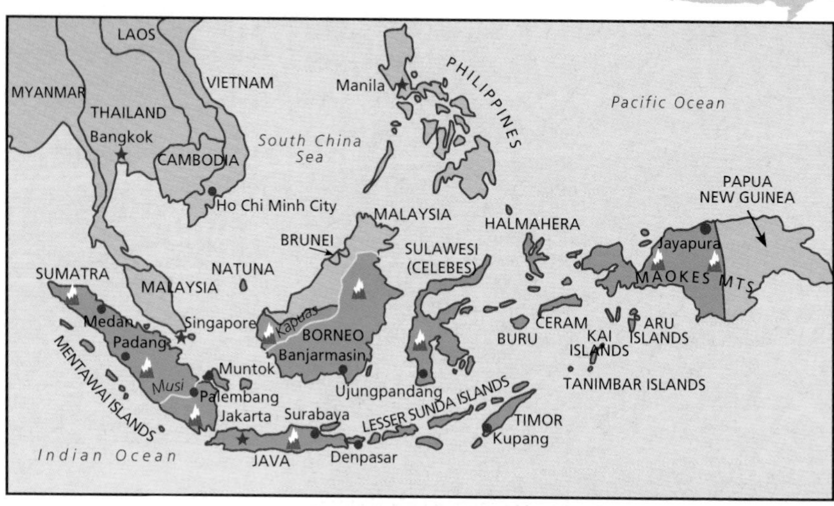

Region: Asia
Area: 1,919,440 km²
Capital: Jakarta
Airport: Jakarta 20 km
Population: 200,409,740
Language: Bahasa Indonesia (off.)
Religions: Islamic, Hindu, Christian
Government: authoritarian presidency
Voltage: 110/220 - 50
Vaccinations required: Yf*
" recommended: Cho, Ty, Po, Mal
Passport: required
Visa: not required
Currency: rupiah
$1Cdn: 1636.35 rupiahs
Driving: left hand
International permit: required
Area code: 011-62
✆ from Canada: 1-800-665-2596
✆ to Canada: ▲001-801-16
Accommodation: ★★★★
Restaurants: ★★★★
Transportation: ★★★
Cost of living: ❍
UN rank: 105
Best months: May, June, July, Oct, Nov
Holidays: 1 Jan; 4 Mar; 14, 16 Apr; 11, 25, 31 May; 8, 17 Aug; 25, 31 Dec

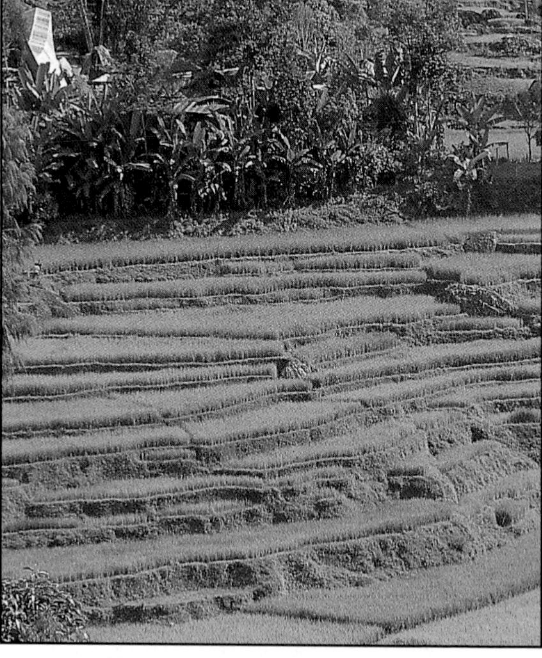

T. BOGNAR / RÉFLEXION

WHAT TO DO

East Timor is a small island south of the Sunda Islands that is fighting for independence from Indonesia. This conflict has brought to light serious human-rights problems in this region of the country. Travellers can visit Indonesia without being exposed to these internal conflicts; nevertheless, it would be wise to avoid the island of East Timor for the moment. There is a vast choice of other destinations in Indonesia, since it comprises an archipelago of 17,000 islands and islets. The regions of Mount Jaya, Sumatra, Kalimantan (on the island of Borneo), Sulawesi (Celebes), and Irian Jaya (on the island of

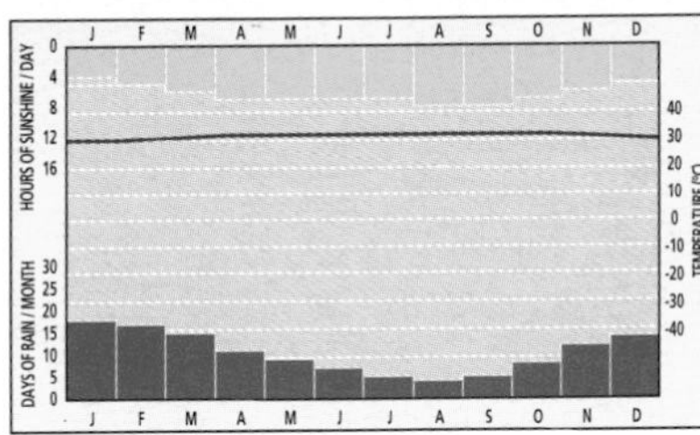

New Guinea) are the best known tourism centres. Bali is much smaller, but it is a hugely popular destination. Denpasar, the island's capital, is renowned for its Balinese theatre, dance, music, painting, and sculpture. The great attractions of the island are the Tanah Lot and Besakih temples, the Tampak Siring Palace, and Lake Batur. On the island of Sumatra, visit the cities of Medan, Padang, and Palembang, as well as the Batak villages. The island of Java is known best for its fabulous batik fabrics. In Jakarta, the Museum of Archaeology and Ethnography and the Borobudur Buddhist stupa, one of the largest in the world, are worth seeing. The very beautiful marionettes used in Indonesian theatre are made in Surakarta. The Lesser Sunda Islands, notably, Flores and Lombok, have lovely beaches and very interesting archaeological sites. Around the towns and villages in Kalimantan Province, on the almost untouched island of Borneo, are dense forests inhabited by the Dayaks, a people long associated with head hunters. The Bugis people on the island of Sulawesi are known for the beautiful sailboats that they build, and the Torajas for their houses with spired roofs. The scenery in the part of the country inhabited by the Toraja is extraordinarily beautiful.

WHAT TO BUY

Indonesian cuisine can be very spicy: *sate dengeng*, a meat dish with a hot sauce, is a traditional dish. *Gadogado*, a tasty mixture of vegetables and peanut sauce, and the Balinese *babi guling*, roast pork, are particularly delicious. Coconut milk is used in many Indonesian recipes. Art is in the soul of Indonesians: their sculptures, costumes, jewelry, musical instruments, and fabrics are particularly fine. Balinese marionettes, of course, are excellent purchases, as are the *kriss*, small Javanese knives with a curved blade. Javanese batiks make beautiful souvenirs. Indonesia is known for its warm welcome to tourists, but travellers should beware of pickpockets, who work in the main tourist centres. A woman travelling alone will encounter no problems if she dresses discreetly.

OCEANIA

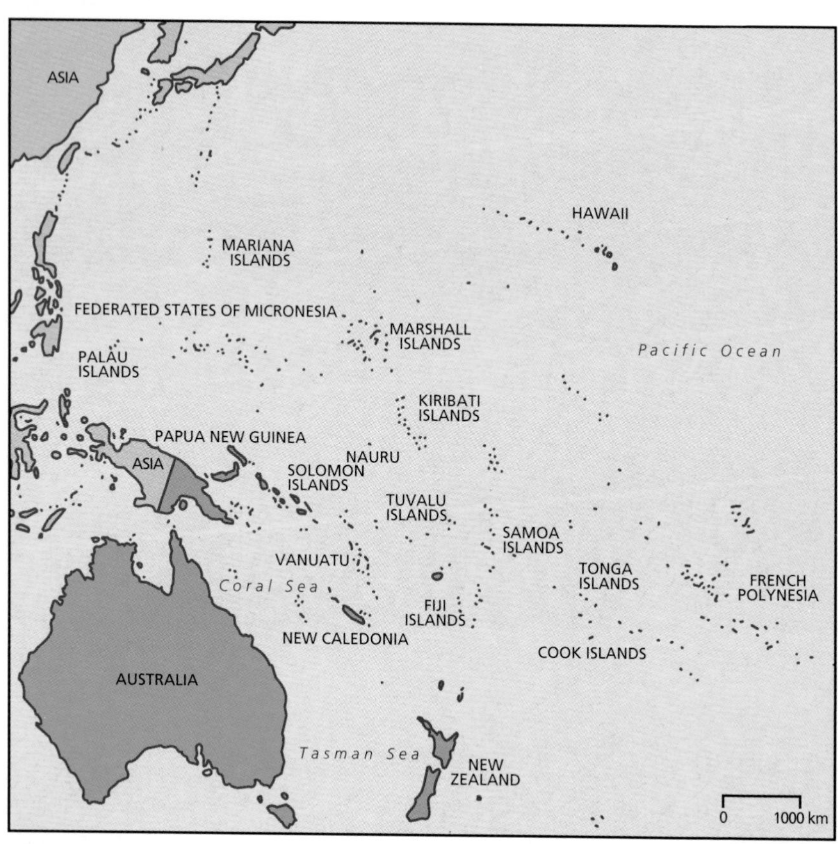

Oceania, one of the major regions of the world, comprises Micronesia, Polynesia, Melanesia, New Zealand, and Australia. Apart from the last two countries, most of the Pacific islands are tiny, but size belies the wealth of culture and splendour of scenery found among them. Many peoples of Oceania are still not well known; some groups speak forgotten languages and seem to have been left behind by the modern world. Students of anthropology, ornithology, vulcanology, botany, and oceanography will find countless subjects to study... and those who seek only warm, sandy beaches will not be disappointed!

COOK ISLANDS TOURISM OFFICE

COOK ISLANDS TOURISM OFFICE

MARIANA ARCHIPELAGO

MARIANA ARCHIPELAGO

+18 +17 +16 +15 +14

Region: Oceania
Area: 477 km²
Capital: Garapan (Saipan)
Airport: Garapan
Population: 49,800
Languages: English, Chamorro
Religion: Catholic
Government: U.S. territory
Voltage: 110 - 60
Vaccinations required: –
Vaccinations recommended: Ty, Po
Passport: required
Visa: not required
Currency: U.S. dollar
$1Cdn: .74 dollar
Driving: right hand
International permit: required
Area code: 011-670
✆ from Canada: –
✆ to Canada: –
Accommodation: ★★★
Restaurants: ★★★
Transportation: ★★★
Cost of living: ○○○
UN rank: –
Best months: Mar, Apr, May
Holidays: 1, 17 Jan; 14, 17 Apr; 4 July; 25 Dec

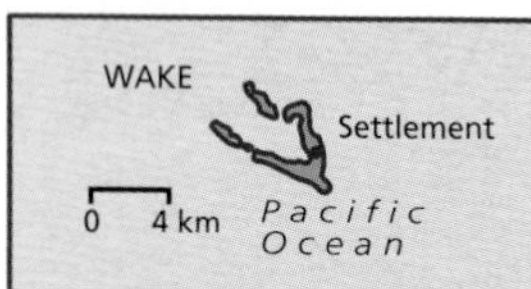

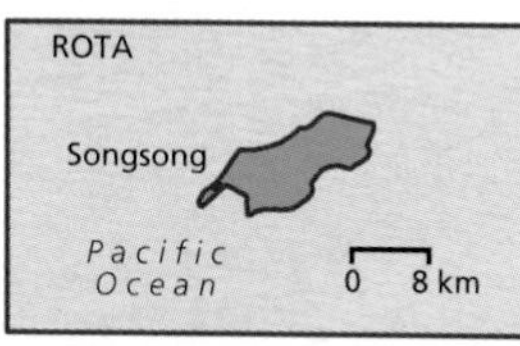

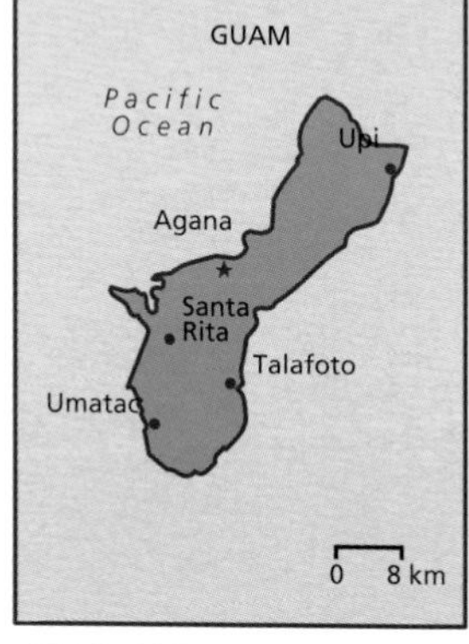

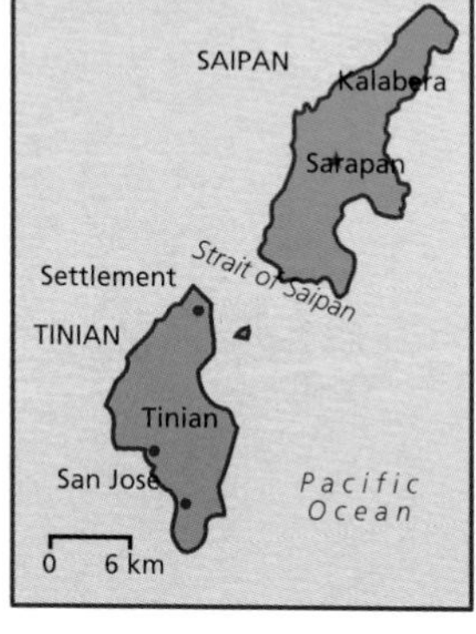

WHAT TO DO

Guam and the islands of the Mariana Archipelago are each as beautiful as the next. Magellan discovered them in 1521; travellers still seek out their warm and peaceful beaches and heavenly climate (except during typhoon season, in September and October). On Saipan, remains of the Second World War can be seen amidst the natural splendours. On the island of Rota, the Songsong Cavern, with its stalagmites and stalactites, is particularly interesting. Guam, with its rough, mountainous terrain, caverns, and volcanoes, is earthquake-prone. There are few of the Chamorro people left, but a fine collection of works from their culture can be seen in the Agana Museum.

WHAT TO BUY

A Spanish influence is present not only in the religious festivals but also in the cuisine: paella and full-bodied wines are often on the menu in Guam. Travellers can purchase works of art inspired by the Chamorro culture, including masks and dolls, as well as objects carved from coconut shell.

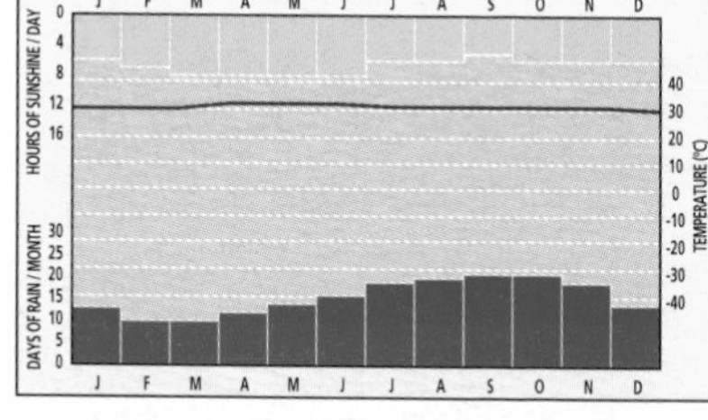

VOLVOX / RÉFLEXION

PALAU

+17 +16 +15 +14 +13

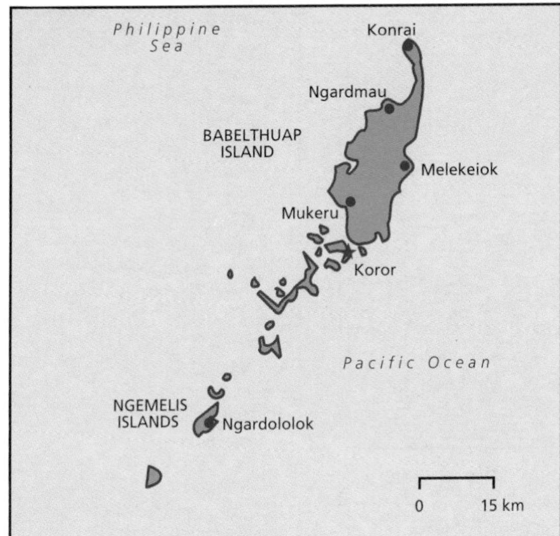

Region: Oceania
Area: 458 km²
Capital: Koror
Airport: Koror
Population: 15,000
Languages: English, dialects
Religions: Catholic, Adventist
Government: administered by the U.S.
Voltage: 110 - 60
Vaccinations required: –
Vaccinations recommended: Ty, Po
Passport: required
Visa: not required
Currency: U.S. dollar
$1Cdn: .74 dollar
Driving: right hand
International permit: required
Area code: 011-680
✆ from Canada: –
✆ to Canada: –
Accommodation: ★★★
Restaurants: ★★★
Transportation: ★★★
Cost of living: ○○○
UN rank: –
Best months: Feb to June
Holidays: 1, 17 Jan; 14, 17 Apr; 4 July; 25 Dec

WHAT TO DO

The State of Palau (Belau) is an archipelago in the Caroline Islands, well known for its role during the Second World War. The Americans left many signs of their presence, but the islands are best known for the immense coral reef surrounding them and for their clear sea water. Babelthuap is the largest island, but most people live on the smaller island of Koror. The national sport, of course, is diving: the best place to dive is Rock Island, popular for its unique underwater geography. Not to be missed are the marvellous waterfalls at Ngardmau, in the north part of Babelthuap, and the megaliths on the Ngarchelong Peninsula, still farther north.

WHAT TO BUY

Palauans like to tell legends about the early inhabitants of the islands, and to carve these stories into the bark of trees. The carvers of *dilukais*, sacred statuettes, take their inspiration from Modekngai ancestral beliefs that date back to the dawn of time. Shells and coral make beautiful jewelry, but it is not advised to encourage the sale of tortoise-shell objects.

A. GARDON / RÉFLEXION

MICRONESIA

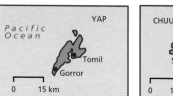

+20 +19 +18 +17 +16

YAP
Pacific Ocean
Tomil
Gorror
0 15 km

CHUUK
Moen
SHIKI ISLANDS
SHICHIYO ISLANDS
Pacific Ocean
0 15 km

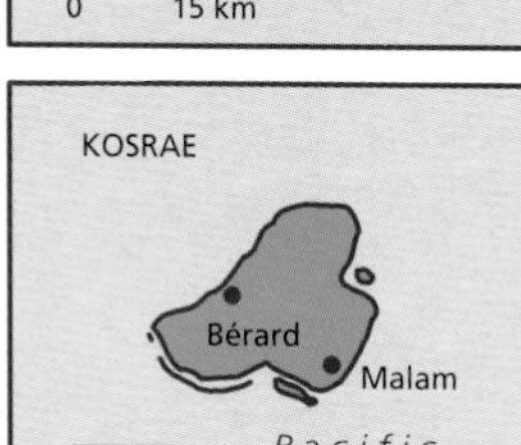

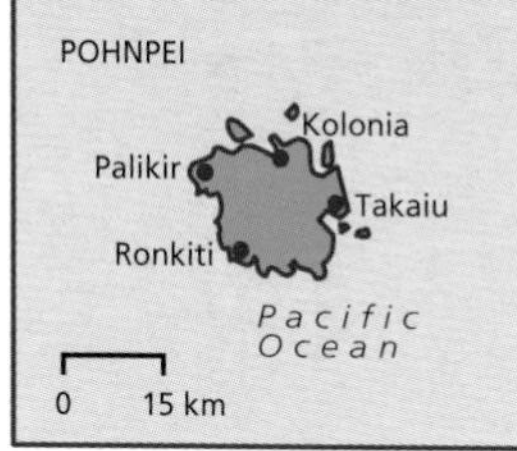

Region: Oceania
Area: 702 km²
Capital: Kolonia (Pohnpei)
Airport: Kolonia 1 km
Population: 120,340
Languages: English, dialects
Religions: Catholic, Protestant
Government: parliamentary democracy
Voltage: 110 - 60
Vaccinations required: –
Vaccinations recommended: Ty, Po
Passport: required
Visa: not required
Currency: U.S. dollar
$1Cdn: .74 dollar
Driving: right hand
International permit: required
Area code: 011-691
✆ from Canada: –
✆ to Canada: –
Accommodation: ★★★★
Restaurants: ★★★★
Transportation: ★★★
Cost of living: ○○○
UN rank: –
Best months: all year
Holidays: 1 Jan; 14, 17 Apr; 10 May; 4 July; 25 Dec

WHAT TO DO

Micronesia is made up of four main island cluster states: Kosrae, Pohnpei, Chuuk, and Yap. Its islands and atolls cover several thousand square kilometres, so the main means of transport is boat, and sailboats still ply these waters. On the islands, the vegetation is dense. The tropical forests and their flora attract nature-lovers. Of course, the coral reefs and underwater scenery are also spectacular, and in some places are found the wrecks of boats that sank during the Second World War. A main attraction is the ruins of Nan Madol on the island of Pohnpei.

WHAT TO BUY

Sakau is an alcoholic beverage made with the roots of a small shrub: don't drink too much of this powerful brew! Betel nuts, taro, coconut, and the fruit of the pandanus tree are the main ingredients of Micronesian cuisine. *Lava-lavas* are traditional skirts made from hibiscus bark.

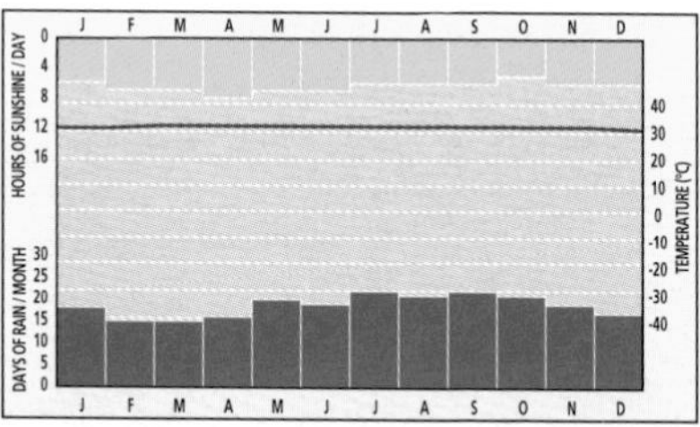

MICRONESIA TOURISM OFFICE

MARSHALL ISL.

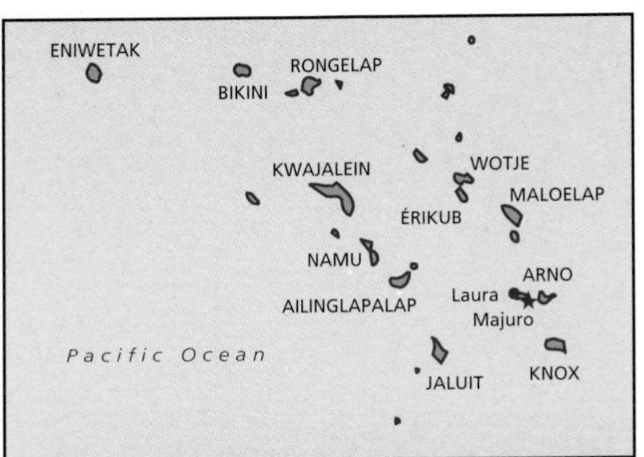

Region: Oceania
Area: 181 km²
Capital: Majuro
Airport: Majuro
Population: 54,040
Languages: English, dialects
Religion: Protestant
Government: parliamentary democracy
Voltage: 110 - 60
Vaccinations required: –
Vaccinations recommended: Ty, Po
Passport: required
Visa: not required
Currency: U.S. dollar
$1Cdn: .74 dollar
Driving: right hand
International permit: recommended
Area code: 011-692
✆ from Canada: –
✆ to Canada: –
Accommodation: ★★★
Restaurants: ★★★
Transportation: ★★
Cost of living: ○○○
UN rank: –
Best months: Feb to June
Holidays: 1, 17 Jan; 14, 17 Apr; 4 July; 25 Dec

P. LESAGE

WHAT TO DO

The Marshall Islands, comprising the Ratak (Rising Sun) Chain and the Ralik (Setting Sun) Chain, are among the most appealing of the Pacific islands for their kilometres and kilometres of beaches, the largest atoll in the world (Kwajalein, 120 km long), coral reefs, multicoloured fish, and citizens who know how to enjoy a sunset. Unfortunately, it is in this enchanting area, on the atoll of Bikini, that the Americans tested the atom bomb. Since the end of the Second World War, however, the atolls of Enewetak and Kwajalein have regained their peace and tranquillity.

WHAT TO BUY

Handicrafts on the Marshall Islands consist mainly of shell jewelry, objects of woven palm leaves, and coral. The *kili* is a handwoven bag typical of Bikini. As its name indicates, wearing a bikini is *de rigueur* on this atoll; however, it should be noted that monokinis are not tolerated.

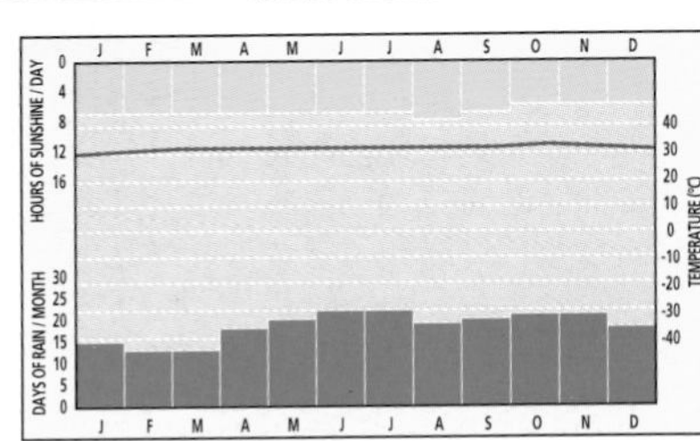

PAPUA NEW GUINEA

+18 +17 +16 +15 +14

egion: Oceania
Area: 461,690 km²
Capital: Port Moresby
Airport: Port Moresby 8 km
Population: 4,196,810
Languages: English, Pidjin, Motu
Religion: Catholic
Government: parliamentary democracy
Voltage: 240 - 50
Vaccinations required: Yf*
Vaccinations recommended: Cho, Ty, Po
Passport: required
Visa: required
Currency: kina
$1Cdn: .99 kina
Driving: left hand
International permit: recommended
Area code: 011-675
✆ from Canada: –
✆ to Canada: –
Accommodation: ★★★
Restaurants: ★★★
Transportation: ★★
Cost of living: ○○○
UN rank: 129
Best months: June to Oct
Holidays: 1, 2 Jan; 14, 16, 17 Apr; 12 June; 24 July; 16 Sept; 25, 26 Dec

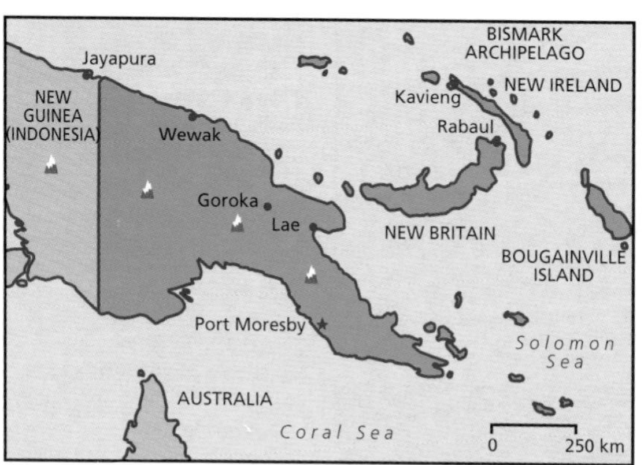

WHAT TO DO

Papuans have always fascinated travellers with their traditions and appearance. The word "Papua" comes from the Malaysian *pupuwa*, which means "woolly," for Papuans have the darkest skin of any Melanesians. Their elaborate costumes, colourful facial paint, and ancestral beliefs are sure to fascinate. The beauty of the Papuan countryside is also a major attraction. The indented coast is protected by a coral reef and deep submarine trenches, ideal for diving. The islands of the Bismarck Archipelago are covered with dense forests that shelter rare animals. The cities also have a special ambience. Port Moresby combines exoticism and modernity: its parliament buildings are decorated with primitive-art frescos, its National Museum has exhibits covering 50,000 years of art, and its Catholic cathedral was built in the Papuan style. In the town of Lae is the Wau Ecology Institute, featuring magnificent butterflies and birds of paradise along with rare varieties of rhododendrons. The Highlands region, especially around Goroka, is a dream come true for amateur anthropologists, who can attend *singsings*, Papuan gatherings featuring traditional chants and dances. Mount Wilhelm, with an altitude of 4,510 m, is at the centre of the province of Simbu, well known for its caves and caverns that have long served as sacred cemeteries. Travellers may visit this site only in organized tours.

WHAT TO BUY

Papuan traditional costumes, ornaments, and jewelry are the envy of all who see them. Wooden statuettes from villages along the Sepik River, tribal musical instruments, pottery from Madang, and woven baskets from the island of Buka are also very beautiful. Beware of laws regulating the exportation of butterflies and flowers, as well as those protecting Papuan heritage: the ceremonial spears and crocodile skins carved with stories from the Trobriand Islands are not for sale.

VIESTI / RÉFLEXION

SOLOMON ISLANDS

+19 +18 +17 +16 +15

Region: Oceania
Area: 28,450 km²
Capital: Honiara
Airport: Honiara 20 km
Population: 385,820
Languages: English, Bislama
Religions: Anglican, Catholic
Government: parliamentary democracy
Voltage: 240 - 50
Vaccinations required: Yf*
Vaccinations recommended: Ty, Po, Mal
Passport: required
Visa: not required
Currency: Solomon Islands dollar
$1Cdn: 2.20 dollars
Driving: left hand
International permit: recommended
Area code: 011-677
✆ from Canada: –
✆ to Canada: –
Accommodation: ★★
Restaurants: ★★
Transportation: ★★
Cost of living: ○○○
UN rank: 126
Best months: May, June
Holidays: 1 Jan; 14, 17 Apr; 7 July; 25 Dec

SOLOMON ISLANDS

WHAT TO DO

The prehistoric Lapita culture came to the Solomon Islands in the first thousand years A.D.; traces of this long-ago era are found in the museum in Honiara. The Second World War has left scars, especially on Guadalcanal. The main attraction of the Solomon Islands remains the diversity of the wildlife: exotic birds that are found nowhere else in the world, strange reptiles and marsupials, frogs, and colourful butterflies. Of course, photography is the only kind of shooting allowed on the islands; even fishing is strictly controlled.

WHAT TO BUY

Crafts from the island of Malaita are often inspired by ancient customs: the much sought-after bracelets, necklaces, and belts are made of polished shells that once served as currency between the tribes. Beware: it is against the law to buy jewelry made with the teeth of mammals. The ebony sculptures from the island of New Georgia are very beautiful.

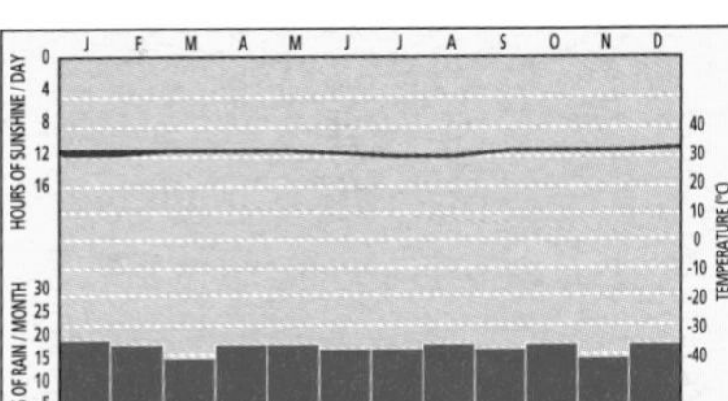

VOLVOX / RÉFLEXION

NAURU

+20 +19 +18 +17 +16

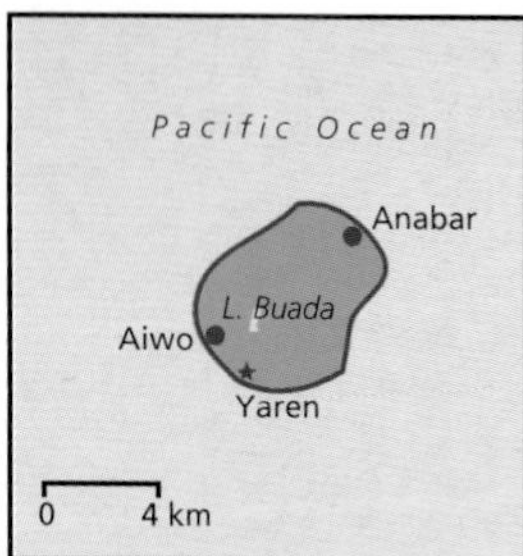

WHAT TO DO

Nauru is a tiny coral reef in the middle of the Pacific Ocean. This former British colony obtained its independence in 1968. The tourism industry is not well developed, with the result that the island has changed little over the centuries. The water is shallow off-shore, enabling divers to observe the abundant sea life. Farther out, the waters are apparently the deepest on the planet. The island is so small that rain clouds often miss it. Years may pass with no rain at all. The phosphate mines are the only place of interest in the interior of the island, and the pending exhaustion of this mineral resource threatens to plunge the charming island into obscurity. The Yaren, Aiwo, and Anabar beaches will nonetheless remain true paradises on earth.

WHAT TO BUY

Life is very simple in Nauru: fishing, diving, and gathering shells are the main activities. The cuisine is based on shellfish and fish, and craftsmen use the treasures of the sea to make jewelry and ornaments.

Region: Oceania
Area: 21 km^2
Capital: Yaren
Airport: Yaren
Population: 10,020
Languages: English, Nauruan
Religions: Protestant, Catholic
Government: parliamentary democracy
Voltage: 240 - 50
Vaccinations required: Yf*
Vaccinations recommended: Ty, Po
Passport: required
Visa: required
Currency: Australian dollar
$1Cdn: 1.00 dollar
Driving: left hand
International permit: recommended
Area code: 011-674
✆ from Canada: –
✆ to Canada: –
Accommodation: ★
Restaurants: ★
Transportation: ★
Cost of living: ○○○
UN rank: –
Best months: May to Oct
Holidays: 1, 2, 26, 31 Jan; 6, 13, 20 Mar; 14, 17, 25 Apr; 1 May; 12 June; 2 Oct; 25, 26 Dec

VOLVOX / RÉFLEXION

KIRIBATI

+20 +19 +18 +17 +16

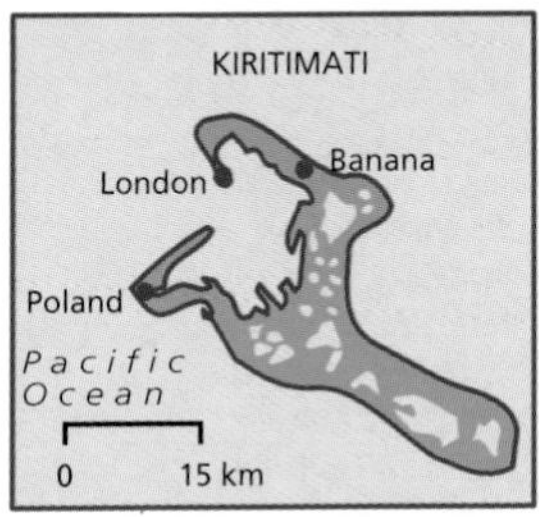

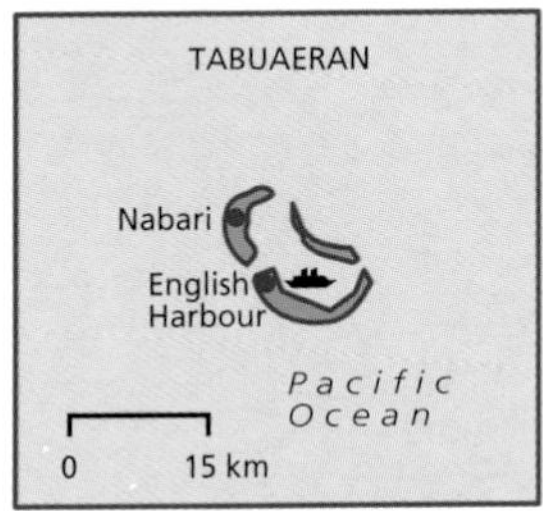

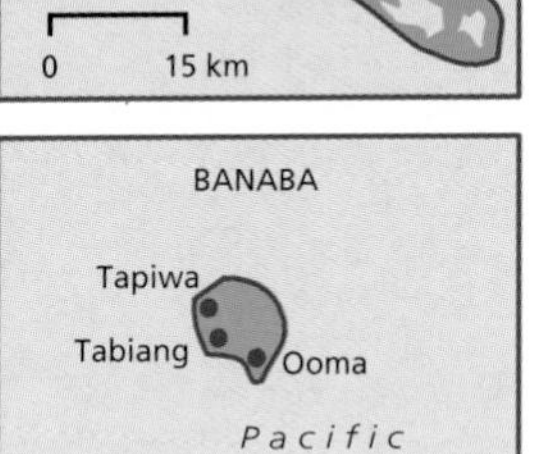

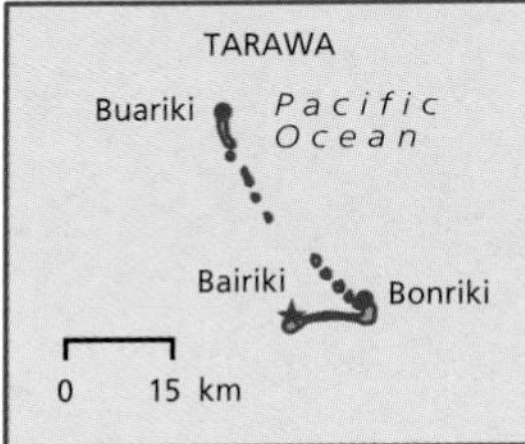

Region: Oceania
Area: 717 km²
Capital: Bairiki
Airport: Bairiki
Population: 77,860
Languages: English, Gilbertese
Religions: Catholic, Protestant
Government: parliamentary democracy
Voltage: 240 - 50
Vaccinations required: Yf*
Vaccinations recommended: Ty, Po
Passport: required
Visa: not required
Currency: Australian dollar
$1Cdn: 1.00 dollar
Driving: left hand
International permit: required
Area code: limited service
✆ from Canada: –
✆ to Canada: –
Accommodation: ★★
Restaurants: ★★
Transportation: ★★
Cost of living: ○○○
UN rank: –
Best months: Oct to Feb
Holidays: 1, 2 Jan; 14, 17 Apr; 13 June; 12 July; 25,26 Dec

KIRIBATI

WHAT TO DO

The inhabitants of the coral atolls that form the Republic of Kiribati still follow the rhythm of the waves that lap at these beautiful sandy beaches. The sea life in the waters around the islands is abundant and fascinating. Bird-watchers will have a chance to study rare species on the island of Kiritimati. To observe the traditional dances, travellers must head for the community of Maneaba, where the customs recall a long-ago era.

WHAT TO BUY

The specialty of Kiribati cuisine is *palu sami*, onions in coconut cream served on a taro leaf. The fruit from the pandanus palm tree, boiled in coconut milk, is also very popular. Coconut shell is fashioned into a variety of objects—necklaces, ornaments, utensils, and games—as are pandanus leaves and sea shells.

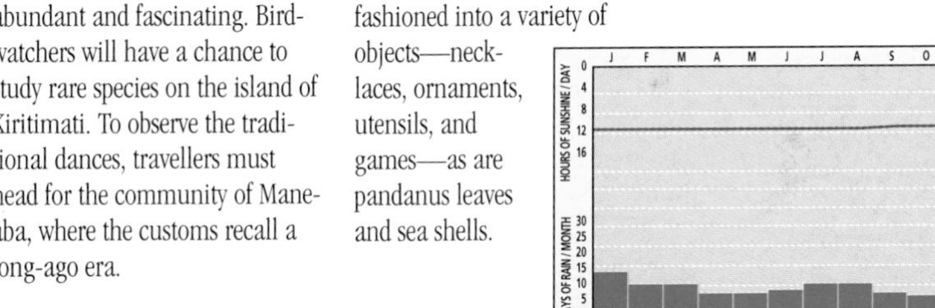

VOLVOX / RÉFLEXION

VANUATU

+19 +18 +17 +16 +15

VANUATU

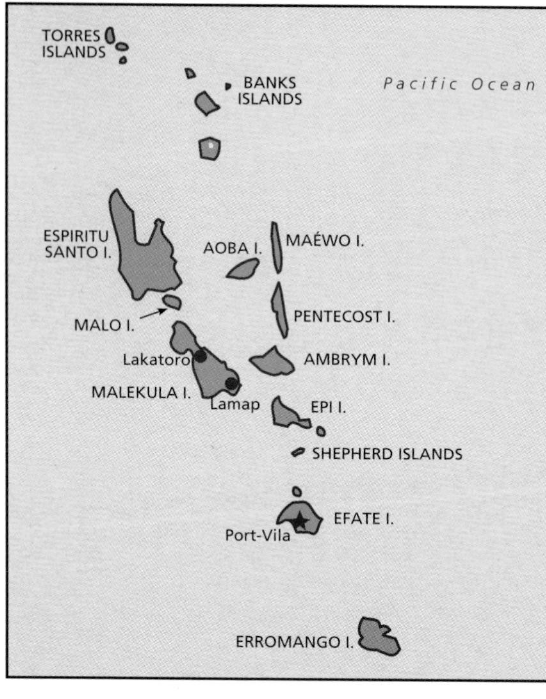

Region: Oceania
Area: 14,760 km²
Capital: Port-Vila
Airport: Port-Vila 35 km
Population: 169,780
Language (s): English, French, Bislama
Religion (s): Presbyterian, Anglican
Government: parliamentary democracy
Voltage: 240 - 50
Vaccinations required: –
Vaccinations recommended: Ty, Po
Passport: required
Visa: not required
Currency: vatu
$1Cdn: 81.66 vatus
Driving: left hand
International permit: recommended
Area code: 011-678
✆ from Canada: –
✆ to Canada: –
Accommodation: ★★★
Restaurants: ★★★
Transportation: ★★★
Cost of living: ○○○
UN rank: 119
Best months: May to Oct
Holidays: 1 Jan; 14, 17 Apr; 30 July; 25 Dec

WHAT TO DO

The climate in Vanuatu no doubt inspired its old colonial name, New Hebrides: the rain and fog are reminiscent of the coast of Scotland. However, travellers will forget this detail when they see the splendour of the volcanoes, some of which are still active. The most beautiful, and accessible, is the Yasur Volcano. The coconut plantations on the shores of the islands give Vanuatu a special ambience. The interior of most of the islands is covered with dense forest, where beautiful flowers grow and magnificent birds nest. Birdwatchers will want to visit during mating season, from September to January. Port-Vila, on the island of Éfaté, is the cultural centre of the country, and its National Museum contains a large collection of Melanesian art. On the island of Espiritu Santo, visitors can watch the famous "Gallic Leap": a man attached by the ankles to a carefully measured liana vine jumps from the top of a cliff, his fall stopped just centimetres from the ground. This practice is supposed to encourage good harvests!

WHAT TO BUY

A "Gallic Leap" vine makes an original souvenir, and ceremonial wooden masks, woven pandanus goods, and traditional costumes are very popular. Shell jewelry and grass skirts are typical of Vanuatu.

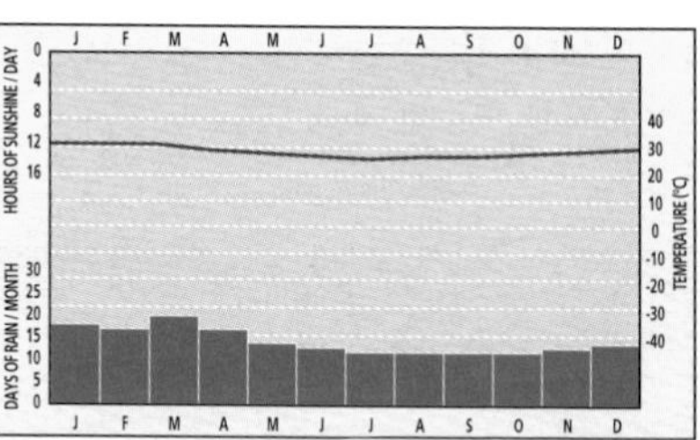

VOLVOX / RÉFLEXION

TUVALU

+20 +19 +18 +17 +16

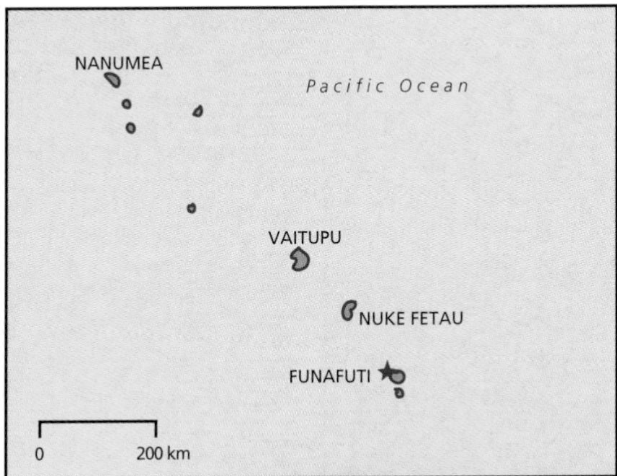

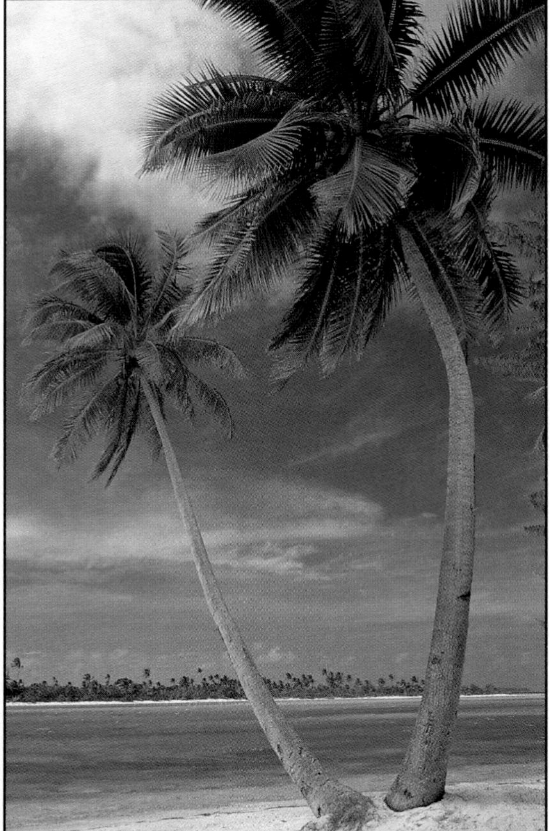

Region: Oceania
Area: 26 km²
Capital: Funafuti
Airport: Funafuti
Population: 9,900
Languages: English, Tuvaluan
Religion: Church of Tuvalu
Government: parliamentary democracy
Voltage: 240 - 50
Vaccinations required: Yf*
Vaccinations recommended: Ty, Po
Passport: required
Visa: not required
Currency: Tuvaluan dollar, Australian dollar
$1Cdn: 1.00 Australian dollar
Driving: left hand
International permit: recommended
Area code: limited service
✆ from Canada: –
✆ to Canada: –
Accommodation: ★
Restaurants: ★
Transportation: ★
Cost of living: ○○○
UN rank: –
Best months: all year
Holidays: 1, 2, 26 Jan; 6, 13, 20 Mar; 14, 17, 25 Apr; 1 May; 12 June; 1, 2 Oct; 25, 26 Dec

TUVALU

WHAT TO DO

Tuvalu was once called the Ellice Islands. Many of its atolls are still unexplored and covered with luxuriant forests of pandanuses, coconut palms, and breadfruit trees that lend their shade to the hot beaches. The coral reefs harbour an extraordinary variety of underwater flora and fauna, while the lagoons contain a treasure trove of shells and fish. Beware of sharks! The colonial past of this region is still visible in the capital, Funafuti.

WHAT TO BUY

Tuvalu is considered one of the most isolated nations in the world, and so Tuvaluan stamps are highly prized by philatelists. *Tulumas*, pretty wooden boxes used by fishermen, are typical of the islands. Life is very tranquil in Tuvalu, if not a little old-fashioned. Custom forbids the wearing of bikinis—a one-piece bathing suit is considered more proper attire for women—and alcoholic beverages are available only in bars.

WESTERN SAMOA

-3 -4 -5 -6 -7

Region: Oceania
Area: 2,860 km²
Capital: Apia
Airport: Apia 35 km
Population: 204,450
Languages: Samoan, English
Religions: Congregationalist, Catholic
Government: constitutional monarchy
Voltage: 240 - 50
Vaccinations required: Yf*
Vaccinations recommended: Ty, Po
Passport: required
Visa: not required
Currency: tala
$1Cdn: 1.77 talas
Driving: left hand
International permit: recommended (minimum age 25)
Area code: 011-685
✆ from Canada: –
✆ to Canada: –
Accommodation: ★★★★
Restaurants: ★★★★
Transportation: ★★★
Cost of living: ○○○
UN rank: 104
Best months: May to Sept
Holidays: 1 Jan; 14,17 Mar; 1 June; 25 Dec

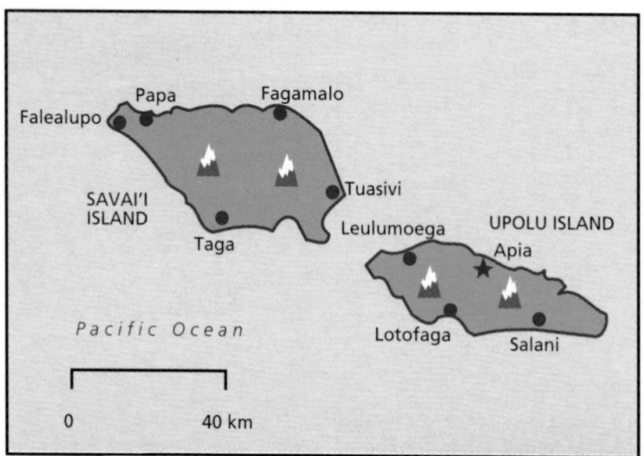

S. O'NEILL / RÉFLEXION

WHAT TO DO

Savai'i and Upolu are two islands formed by volcanoes, some of which are still active. Most people live on Upolu, where the lava flows left by repeated eruptions have been less devastating. On the east coast is a stunningly beautiful string of lagoons and reefs. The Aleipata region east of the town of Apia, is the prettiest part of the island, with its waterfalls, white-sand beaches, and small authentic villages.

WHAT TO BUY

Stamps from Western Samoa are highly prized by philatelists. *Kava* is the sacred drink served at ceremonies: drinking *kava* is an activity that must not be treated lightly. Hand-painted fabrics (*siapos*) are unique to Samoa. The hand-painted works on mulberry bark and the shell and coral jewelry are also very pretty.

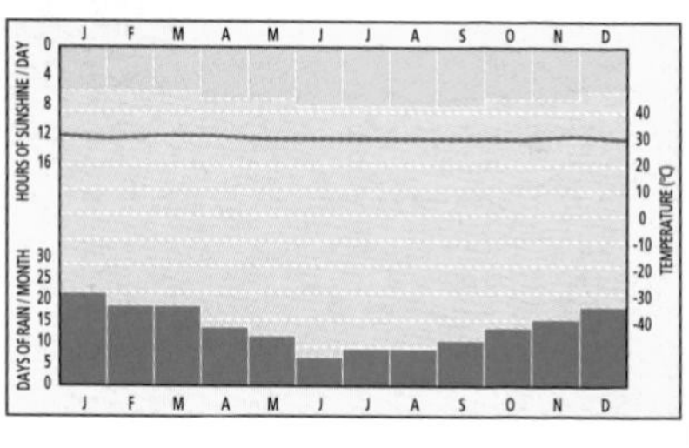

AMERICAN SAMOA

-3 -4 -5 -6 -7

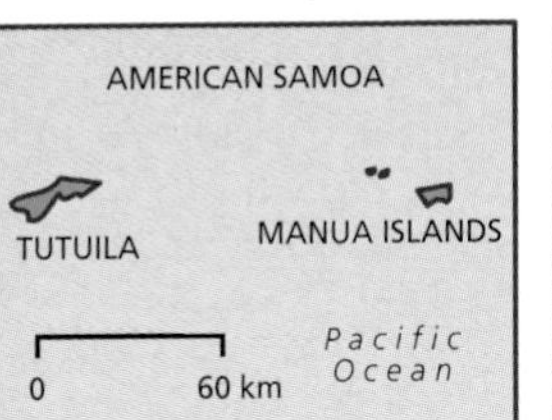

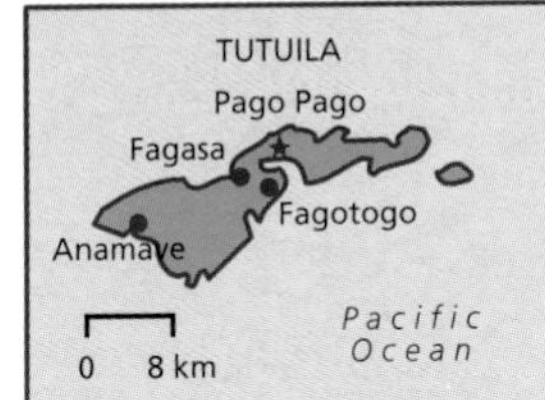

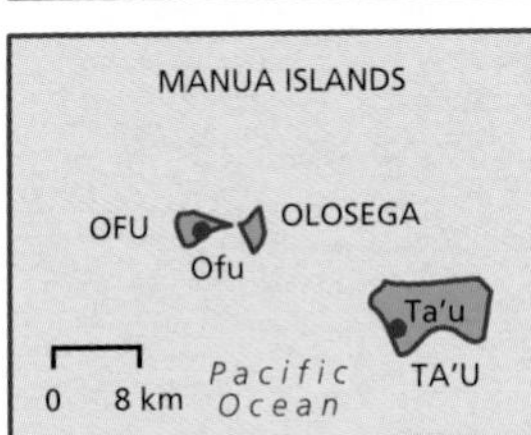

Region: Oceania
Area: 199 km^2
Capital: Pago Pago
Airport: Pago Pago 11 km
Population: 55,230
Languages: Polynesian, English
Religions: Congregationalist, Catholic
Government: unincorporated U.S. territory
Voltage: 110 - 60
Vaccinations required: Yf*
Vaccinations recommended: Ty, Po
Passport: required
Visa: not required
Currency: U.S. dollar
$1Cdn: 0.74 dollar
Driving: right hand
International permit: recommended (minimum age 25)
Area code: 011-684
✆ from Canada: –
✆ to Canada: –
Accommodation: ★★★★
Restaurants: ★★★★
Transportation: ★★★
Cost of living: ○○○
UN rank: –
Best months: May to Sept
Holidays: 1 Jan; 14,17 Apr; 4 July; 25 Dec

WHAT TO DO

The tourism infrastructure in American Samoa is among the best in Polynesia, and the standard of living is higher than elsewhere in the Pacific. On the main island of Tutuila, the prime attraction is Pago Pago, a port built on the slope of an extinct volcano. Fagasa, on the other side of the island, is a dream destination, with its Forbidden Bay, one of the most beautiful in the Pacific. The traditional Samoan villages on the east side of the island have been preserved intact and are well worth visiting. Visitors can take organized boat trips to discover the charms of the other islands and of their Samoan culture.

WHAT TO BUY

The best way to sample Samoan cuisine is to taste *fia fia*, a feast of fish, pork, and chicken served with coconut milk. *Kava* is the national drink, consumed during sacred ceremonies. *Kava* bowls are very beautiful and finely decorated. *Puletasis* (women's dresses) and *lavalavas* (men's sarongs) are the pride of the islands' weavers.

NEW CALEDONIA

+19 +18 +17 +16 +15

Poum
Hienghêne
OUVÉA ISLAND
LOYALTY ISLANDS
LIFOU ISLAND
Mou
NEW CALEDONIA ISLANDS
Tadine
Î. MARÉ
Thio
Bourail
Coral Sea
Païta
Yaté
Nouméa
OUEN ISLAND
ISLE OF PINES
0 80 km

Region: Oceania
Area: 19,060 km²
Capital: Nouméa
Airport: Nouméa 51 km
Population: 181,310
Languages: French, dialects
Religion: Catholic
Government: French territory
Voltage: 220 - 50
Vaccinations required: Yf*, Cho
Vaccinations recommended: Ty, Po
Passport: required
Visa: not required
Currency: XPF franc
$1Cdn: 64.72 francs
Driving: right hand
International permit: required
Area code: 011-687
✆ from Canada: –
✆ to Canada: –
Accommodation: ★★★★
Restaurants: ★★★
Transportation: ★★
Cost of living: ○○○
UN rank: –
Best months: Sept, Oct, Nov
Holidays: 1 Jan; 14, 17 Apr; 14 July; 25 Dec

P. LESAGE

WHAT TO DO

Grande Terre, the main island of New Caledonia, stretches over 400 km in length, offering fine beaches as well as mountains and tropical forest. The eastern side of the island is particularly luxuriant, with its coconut palms, liana vines, and shrubs bearing scarlet flowers. On the western coast is a plain covered with niaoulis, native shrubs. In Nouméa, the St. Joseph Cathedral and many colonial houses testify to the French influence. The city's aquarium is a prime attraction. Île des Pins is well known to spelunkers: its many caverns feature magnificent columns of stalagmites and stalactites. At one time, the island served as a penal colony for 3,000 prisoners. The Îles Loyauté (Maré, Lifou, and Ouvéa) are ideal for deep-sea diving.

WHAT TO BUY

Crabs, shrimp, crawfish, oysters, and exotic fish are part of the daily menu. Taste the *bougna*, meat grilled in banana skin. The coffee grown on Grande Terre is excellent. A typical souvenir is Kanaka painting, often done on naiouli bark. Artwork is also done on coconut shell, which also serves as a raw material for jewelry and other ornaments. Travellers should not encourage the trade in jewelry made with tortoise shell.

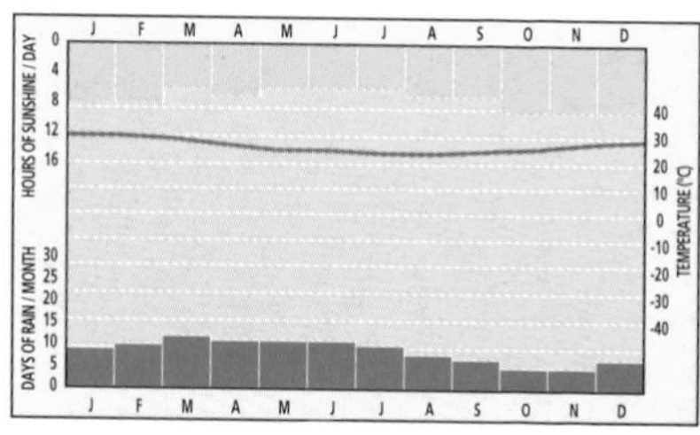

FIJI

+20 +19 +18 +17 +16

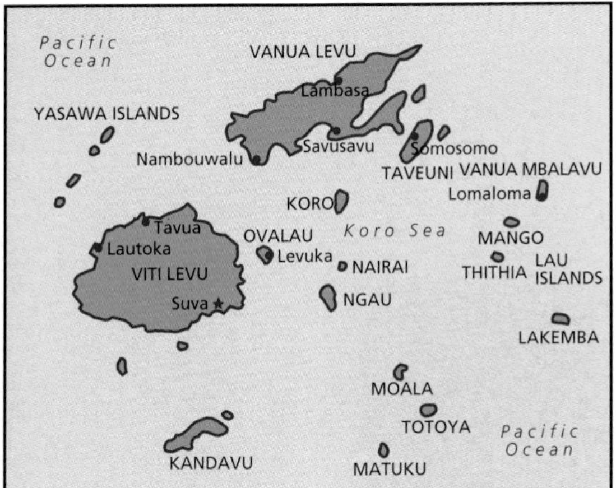

Region: Oceania
Area: 18,270 km²
Capital: Suva
Airport: Nadi 5 km, Suva 21 km
Population: 764,390
Languages: English, Fijian
Religions: Methodist, Hindu, Catholic
Government: parliamentary democracy
Voltage: 240 - 50
Vaccinations required: Yf*
Vaccinations recommended: Ty, Po
Passport: required
Visa: not required
Currency: Fijian dollar
$1Cdn: 1.02 dollars
Driving: left hand
International permit: recommended
Area code: 011-679
✆ from Canada: 1-800-665-0793
✆ to Canada: 004-890-1005
Accommodation: ★★★★
Restaurants: ★★★★
Transportation: ★★★
Cost of living: ○○○
UN rank: 59
Best months: June to Nov
Holidays: 1 Jan; 1, 3, 4 Apr; 6, 13 June; 1, 19 Aug; 10 Oct; 7, 14 Nov; 25–27 Dec

It is against the law to hunt animals or insects (especially butterflies) and to pick wild flowers.

WHAT TO DO

The breathtakingly beautiful islands of Fiji are synonymous with heaven on earth. Western audiences first learned of them in the marvellous accounts of explorers, who praised Fijians for their warm hospitality, a tradition that continues to this day. The main island, Viti Levu, has magnificent beaches and a stunning barrier reef on the south side. Suva, the capital, serves as a stepping-off point to the interior of the island, where the small villages, the Wairoro waterfalls, the trails on Mount Korobaba, and the caverns on the Rewa River will charm travellers. The traditional boats, made of bamboo cane, are probably the best way to discover the rivers of the island. The other islands, including Ovalau, Vanua Levu, Taveuni, and the Yasawa Group, are also worth visiting. Students of archaeology and anthropology will find Fijian historical sites fascinating, especially the megaliths on Taveuni and the sacred site of Naicobocobo, at the western tip of Vanua Levu.

WHAT TO BUY

Fijian cuisine is composed mainly of shellfish and fish cooked in *lolo*, or coconut milk. *Yaqona*, a drink made from pepper roots, is delicious. Coconut soap, *sulus* and *bulas*, colourful printed shirts, coral jewelry, and wooden sculptures are always very popular. Forks from cannibal rituals are a unique memento of Fiji. Objects made with whale teeth are sacred and cannot be exported: beware of people who want to sell you such objects.

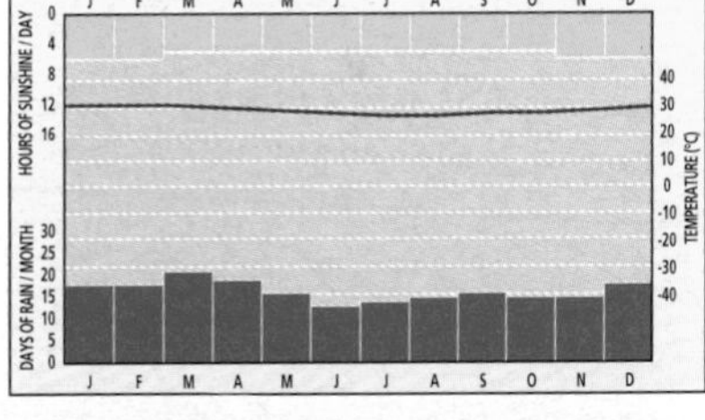

VOLVOX / RÉFLEXION

TONGA

+20 +19 +18 +17 +16

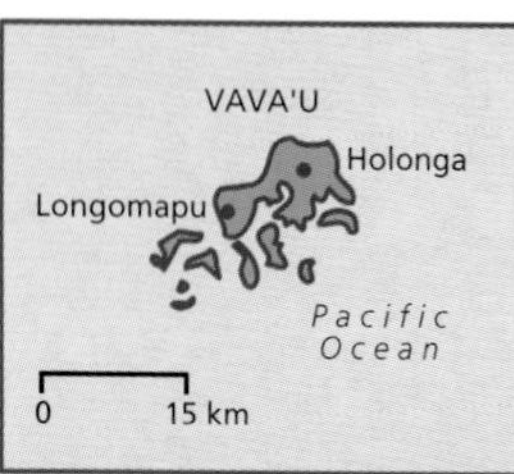

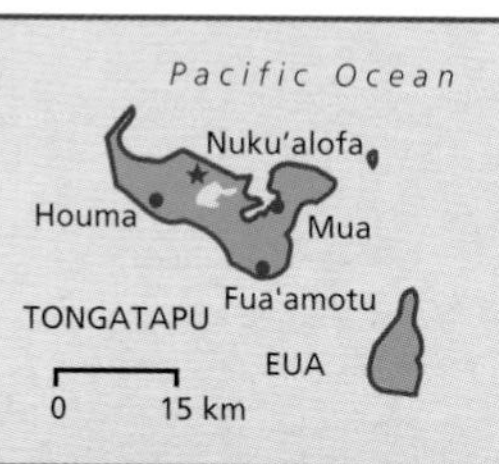

Region: Oceania
Area: 748 km²
Capital: Nuku'alofa
Airport: Nuku'alofa 21 km
Population: 104,800
Languages: English, Tongan
Religion: Catholic
Government: monarchy
Voltage: 240 - 50
Vaccinations required: Yf*
Vaccinations recommended: Ty, Po
Passport: required
Visa: not required
Currency: pa'anga
$1Cdn: 1.00 pa'anga
Driving: left hand
International permit: recommended
Area code: 011-676
✆ from Canada: –
✆ to Canada: –
Accommodation: ★★
Restaurants: ★★★
Transportation: ★★★
Cost of living: ○○○
UN rank: –
Best months: May to Nov
Holidays: 1 Jan; 14, 17 Apr; 4 June; 25 Dec

TONGA

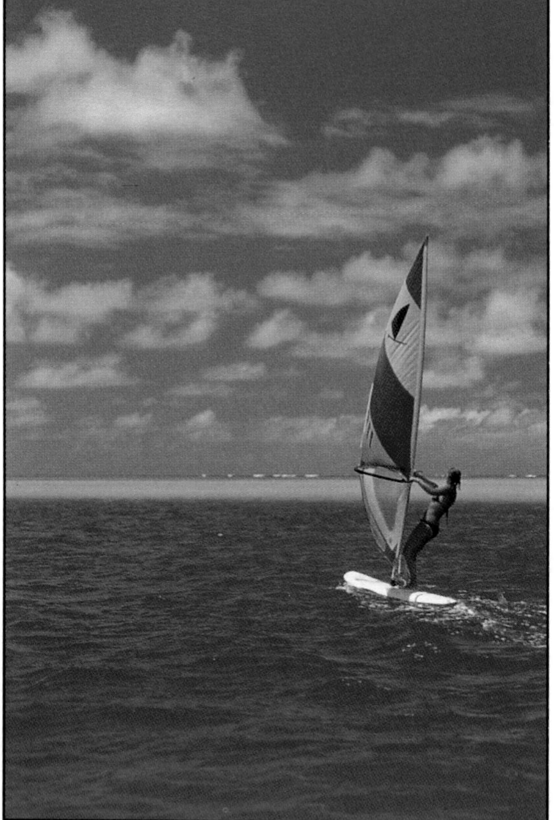

VOLVOX / RÉFLEXION

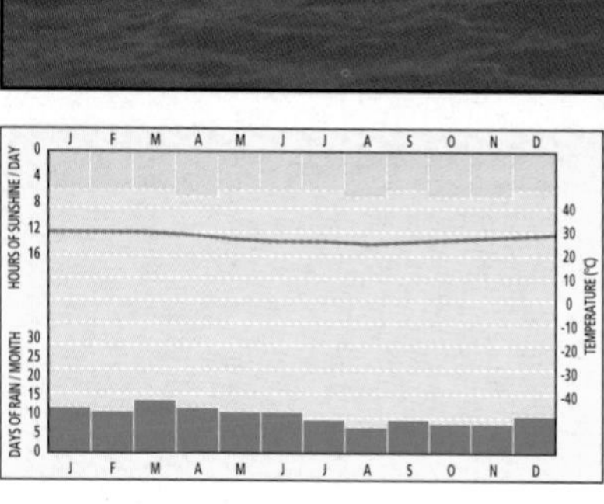

WHAT TO DO

The beauty of the islands and atolls that make up the "Friendly Islands" is well known. The 172 islands of Tonga, most of them inhabited, enjoy a pleasant climate that is a little cooler than that of the other Pacific islands. Most people live on Tongatapu, and the main tourist attractions are found near the capital, Naku'alofa: the royal palace, Mala'ekula (royal crypts), the crater at Houma, and the superb beaches at Ha'atafu and Monotapu. Ten minutes away by plane is the island of 'Eua, another exceptional spot. Essentially devoted to tourism, 'Eua is the habitat of thousands of exotic birds.

WHAT TO BUY

Lu pullu is typically Tongan, made of meat marinated in coconut milk and cooked in a taro leaf. The best way to taste all the specialties of Tonga is to try a *pola* (a long tray with a number of foods on it). Pandanus leaves are woven into beautiful mats and baskets, and shells are used to make necklaces and bracelets.

COOK ISLANDS

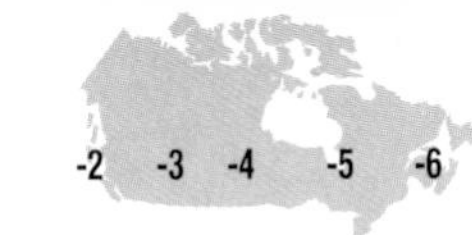

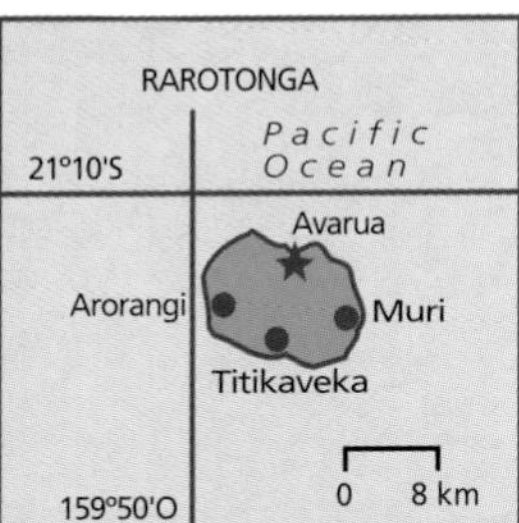

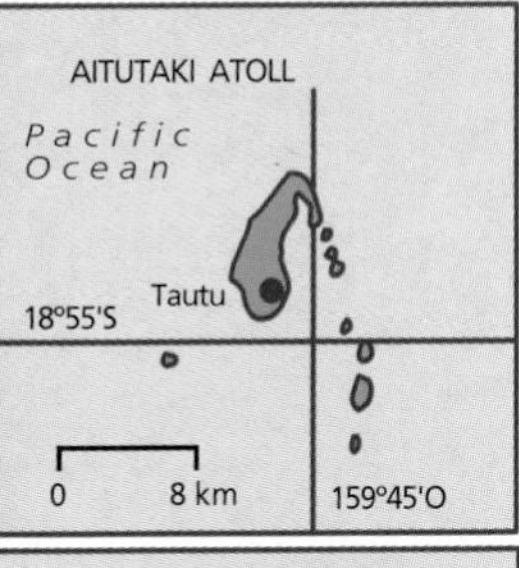

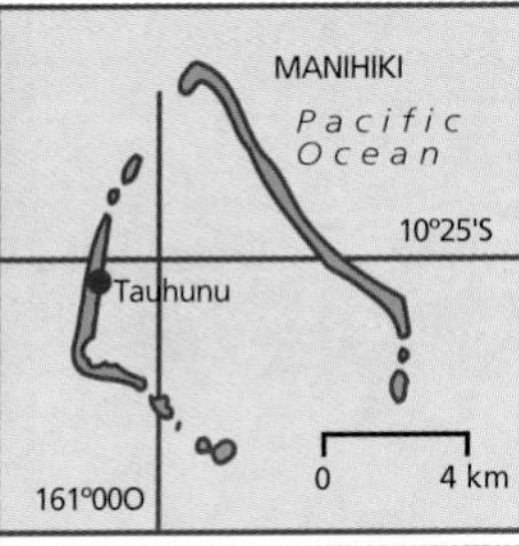

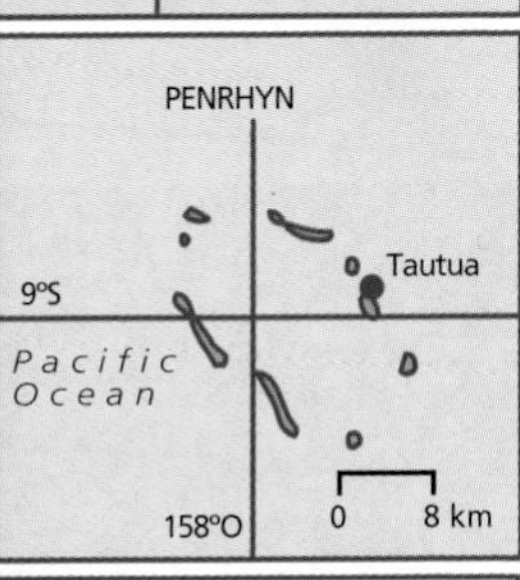

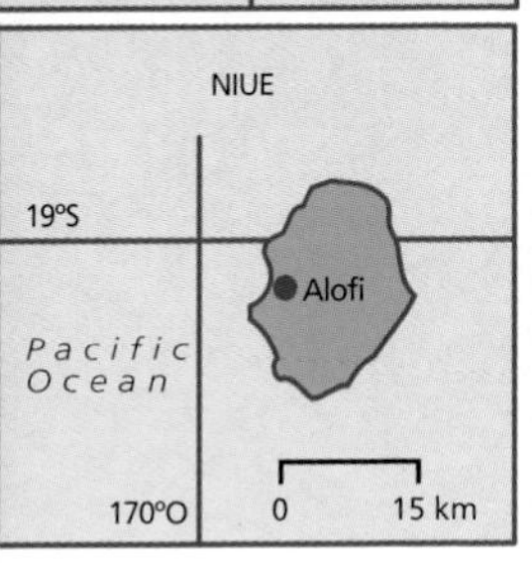

WHAT TO DO

Sprinkled over more than 2,200,000 km², the Cook Islands are divided into the Southern Cook Islands, formed from volcanoes, and the Northern Cook Islands, formed from coral atolls. Rarotonga is the largest and highest island, with its Te Manga peak rising to 650 m altitude. Its coral reef is well known to divers the world over. All the islands are covered with luxuriant vegetation and edged with beaches and lovely inlets. The best beaches are those on Aitutaki and Rarotonga. The remains left behind by Captain Cook are the main historical attraction.

Region: Oceania
Area: 240 km²
Capital: Avarua
Airport: Avarua
Population: 19,125
Languages: English, Maori
Religion: Catholic
Government: parliamentary democracy (New Zealand)
Voltage: 220 - 50
Vaccinations required: –
Vaccinations recommended: Ty, Po
Passport: required
Visa: not required
Currency: New Zealand dollar
$1Cdn: 1.09 dollars
Driving: left hand
International permit: recommended
Area code: 011-682
✆ from Canada: –
✆ to Canada: –
Accommodation: ★★★
Restaurants: ★★★
Transportation: ★★★
Cost of living: ❍❍
UN rank: –
Best months: June to Oct
Holidays: 1–3 Jan; 6 Feb; 14, 16, 17, 25 Apr; 5 June; 4 Aug; 23 Oct; 25, 26 Dec

WHAT TO BUY

Shellfish and fresh fish are the basis of the cuisine of the Cook Islands. Many tropical fruits are also featured on local menus. The fruit punches are very colourful and refreshing. Shells are used to make jewelry, while palm leaves are woven into baskets and mats of all shapes and sizes.

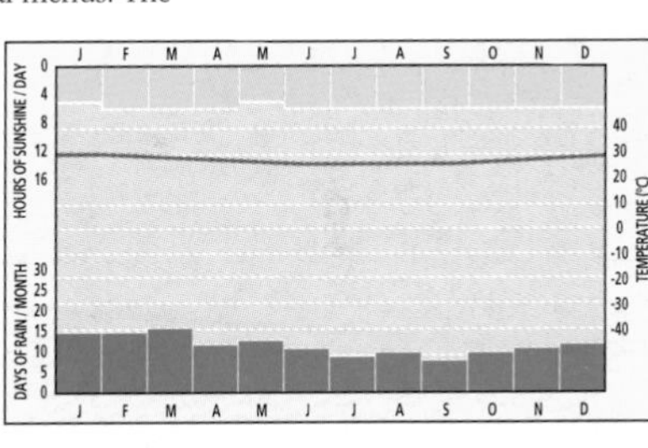

COOK ISLANDS TOURISM OFFICE

FRENCH POLYNESIA

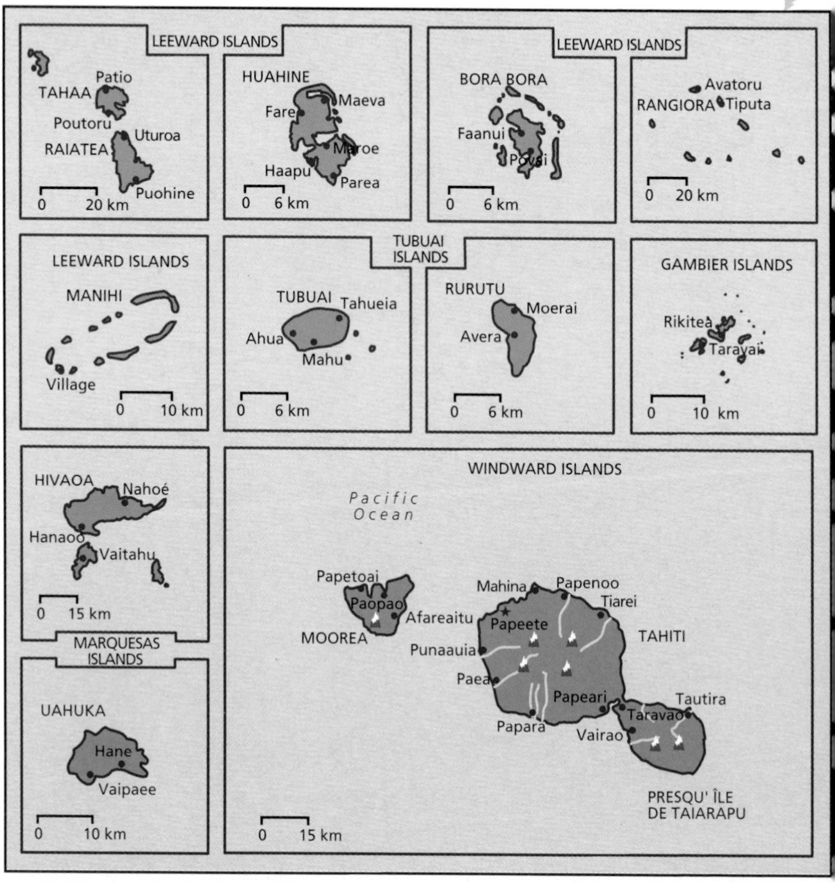

FRENCH POLYNESIA

LEEWARD ISLANDS

TAHAA
Patio
Poutoru
RAIATEA
Uturoa
Puohine
0 20 km

HUAHINE
Fare
Maeva
Maroe
Haapu
Parea
0 6 km

LEEWARD ISLANDS

BORA BORA
Faanui
Povai
0 6 km

RANGIORA
Avatoru
Tiputa
0 20 km

LEEWARD ISLANDS

MANIHI
Village
0 10 km

TUBUAI ISLANDS

TUBUAI
Tahueia
Ahua
Mahu
0 6 km

RURUTU
Moerai
Avera
0 6 km

GAMBIER ISLANDS

Rikitea
Tarayai
0 10 km

HIVAOA
Nahoé
Hanaoo
Vaitahu
0 15 km

MARQUESAS ISLANDS

UAHUKA
Hane
Vaipaee
0 10 km

WINDWARD ISLANDS

Pacific Ocean

Papetoai
Paopao
Afareaitu
MOOREA
Mahina
Papenoo
Tiarei
Papeete
TAHITI
Punaauia
Paea
Papeari
Papara
Tautira
Taravao
Vairao
PRESQU' ÎLE DE TAIARAPU
0 15 km

SDP / JONATHAN / RÉFLEXION

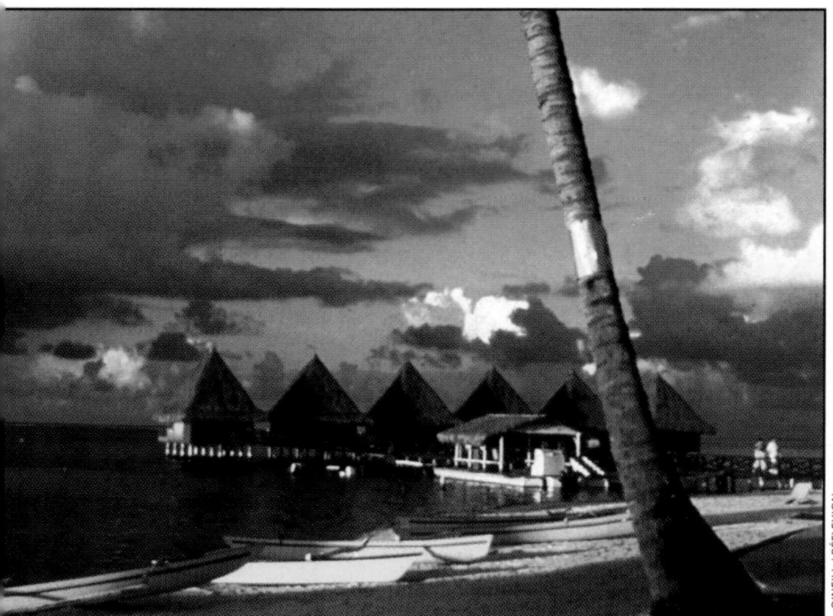

S. O'NEILL / RÉFLEXION

Region: Oceania
Area: 3,941 km²
Capital: Papeete
Airport: Papeete 6 km
Population: 215,130
Languages: French, dialects
Religions: Protestant, Catholic
Government: French overseas possession
Voltage: 240 - 60
Vaccinations required: Yf*
Vaccinations recommended: Ty, Po
Passport: required
Visa: not required
Currency: XPF franc
$1Cdn: 64.72 francs
Driving: right hand
International permit: recommended
Area code: 011-689
✆ from Canada: –
✆ to Canada: –
Accommodation: ★★★★★
Restaurants: ★★★★★
Transportation: ★★★
Cost of living: ○○○
UN rank: –
Best months: Aug, Sept
Holidays: 1 Jan; 16, 17 Apr; 1, 8, 25 May; 14 July; 15 Aug; 1, 11 Nov; 25 Dec

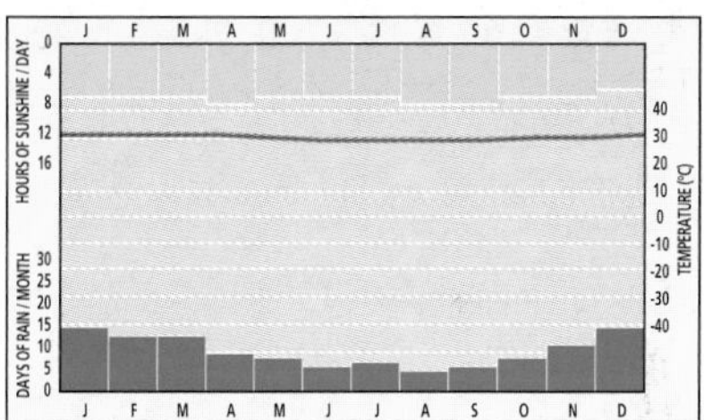

WHAT TO DO

ach a paradise of multicoloured flowers, sunny beaches, and crystalline seas, the islands of French Polynesia offer travellers the peaceful ambience captured in Paul Gauguin's paintings. The towns are truly exotic: Papeete, on the island of Tahiti, is not only the liveliest tourist centre in Polynesia, but also one of the most charming for its banana trees, lush gardens, and gentle slopes on Mount Orohena. The Gauguin Museum is a prime attraction. For a more tranquil setting, there's Mooréa with its lovely beaches and enticing lagoons (ideal for scuba diving). The monuments in Opunohu Valley are worth a trip. The other islands are spread over an area of more than 3,000 km², and the best way to get around is by boat. Bora Bora attracts travellers for its many temples and typical villages. The Îles Marquises and Îles Gambier are far away from Tahiti, but they are worth visiting, if only to discover the magnificent scenery that inspired Gauguin and Jacques Brel.

WHAT TO BUY

Coconut and vanilla are the basic flavours in most Polynesian foods. *Paréos* are loose-fitting loincloths typical of French Polynesia. Mother-of-pearl, pearls, seashells, and coconut shells are transformed into pretty jewelry. The sculptures from the Îles Marquises and the perfume from Tahiti, made from a base of coconut oil, are unique.

AUSTRALIA

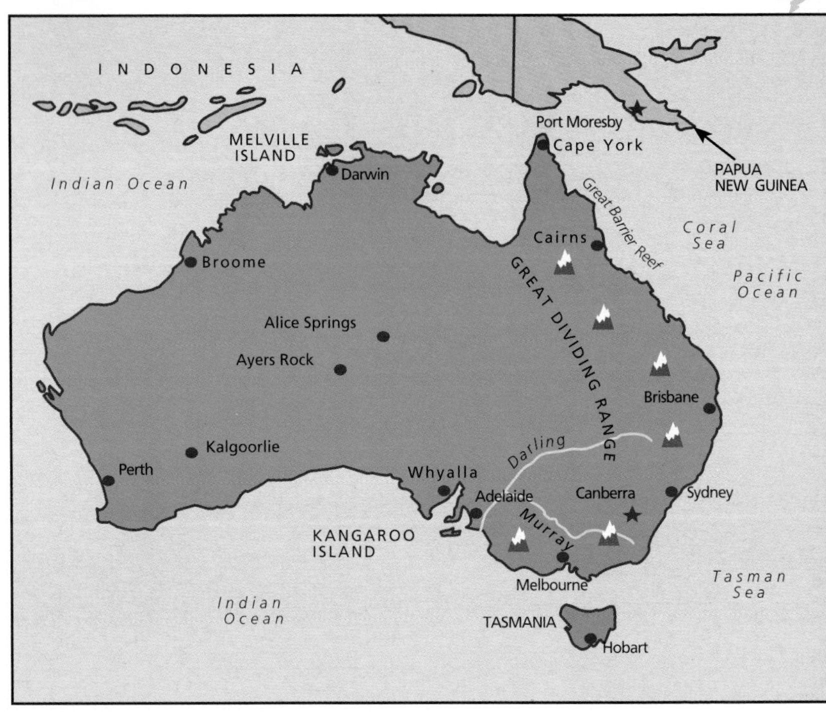

WHAT TO DO

According to legend, Australia was once a vast, flat, and drab land inhabited by giants. To find something to do, the giants decided to travel across the country, creating mountains, rivers, and boulders along the way. Aborigine culture is omnipresent in Australia, though visitors may visit the sacred territories only in organized tours. Other territories are also protected: Uluru National Park (containing Ayers Rock and the Olga Mountains) is home to peoples who have lived there for millennia; this area alone is worth the trip down under. Aborigine guides excel in the art of telling *tjukurrpa*, the myths that rule their lives. Nature-lovers and hikers will find unspoiled countryside from Sydney to the Great Barrier Reef, from Alice Springs to Tasmania. Sydney is the best-known Australian city, with its port on one of the prettiest bays in the world. The beaches at Bondi and Manly offer stretches of white sand against the backdrop of the vibrant city. The Art Gallery offers a fine collec-

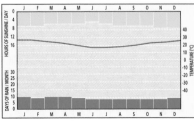

Region: Oceania
Area: 7,686,850 km^2
Capital: Canberra
Airport: Canberra 20 km, Sydney 12 km
Population: 18,077,420
Language: English
Religions: Anglican, Catholic
Government: parliamentary democracy
Voltage: 220 - 50
Vaccinations required: Yf*
Vaccinations recommended: –
Passport: required
Visa: required
Currency: Australian dollar
$1Cdn: .1.00 dollar
Driving: left hand
International permit: recommended
Area code: 011-61
✆ from Canada: 1-800-663-0683
✆ to Canada: 1-800-551-177
Accommodation: ★★★★★
Restaurants: ★★★★★
Transportation: ★★★★★
Cost of living: ○○○
UN rank: 7
Best months: Nov to Mar
Holidays: 1, 2, 26 Jan; 6, 13, 20 Mar; 14 17, 25 Apr; 1 May; 12 June; 2 Oct; 25, 26 Dec

tion, while the Australian Museum retraces the history of the Aborigines. The Sydney Opera House, a unique architectural complex, features performances by one of the best orchestras of the world, while the Rocks, a neighbourhood in old Sydney, has houses dating back to the first European colony. Outside of the city, the Blue Mountains feature small towns and national parks with waterfalls, spectacular rock formations, and gorgeous scenery. Hunter Valley is the oldest grape-growing region in Australia; be sure to see the operations at Lower Hunter Valley, outside of the pretty town of Cessnock. The Australian National Gallery in Canberra, the country's capital, has one of the best collections in the world (with more than 70,000 works) of Australian and Aborigine art. The Snowy Mountains are well known among skiers, who will head for Kosciusko National Park and the peaks of the Crackenback Range. The cosmopolitan city of Melbourne has some of the best restaurants in the southern hemisphere. It is also the stepping-off point for Gippsland, a region of dense forests and sparkling lakes. The cave paintings at Grampians must be seen. Wildlife lovers can find birds, koala bears, seals, and penguins on Phillip Island, 130 km southeast of Melbourne, and watch the penguins climb up the beaches to spend the night on land—an unforgettable sight. Tasmania offers splendid countryside, including unique

T. BOGNAR / RÉFLEXION

geological formations such as Tasman Arch and Devil's Kitchen. Hobart, the island's capital, is a quiet town that has preserved the aura of the colonial era. The vineyards of Barossa Valley, near Adelaide, are well known for the quality of their white Chardonnay wine. On Kangaroo Island wildlife is abundant; one finds koala bears, kangaroos, and emus (huge birds unique to Australia). The region around Perth is worth a visit; especially the desert-like countryside at the Pinnacles, in Nambung National Park. Darwin is the point of departure for the fantastic Kakadu National Park, with its more than 19,000 km^2 of rock formations, the habitat of little-known wildlife, and more than 1,000 sacred Aborigine sites which can only be visited with a guide. In the sea off the coast at Cairns is the Great Barrier Reef, one of the world's finest natural wonders with its more than 1,800 km of coral teeming with multicoloured fish, strangely beautiful sea animals, and incomparable sea plants: paradise for divers!

WHAT TO BUY

The reputation of Australian wines is excellent. Aborigine paintings, "bush"-style clothing, sheepskin products, and precious stones are available almost everywhere in the country. Tasmanian stamps make great gifts for philatelists. Beware of objects made of coral: very strict laws protect the reefs, and only authorized stores may sell coral products.

NEW ZEALAND

NEW ZEALAND

+20 +19 +18 +17 +16

Region: Oceania
Area: 268,680 km²
Capital: Wellington
Airport: Auckland 22 km, Wellington 8 km
Population: 3,388,740
Languages: English, Maori
Religion: Anglican
Government: parliamentary democracy
Voltage: 220 - 50
Vaccinations required: –
Vaccinations recommended: –
Passport: required
Visa: not required
Currency: New Zealand dollar
$1Cdn: 1.09 dollars
Driving: left hand
International permit: required
Area code: 011-64
✆ from Canada: 1-800-663-0684
✆ to Canada: 000919
Accommodation: ★★★★
Restaurants: ★★★★
Transportation: ★★★★
Cost of living: ○○○
UN rank: 18
Best months: Dec, Jan, Feb
Holidays: 1–3 Jan; 6 Feb; 14, 16, 17, 25 Apr; 5 June; 23 Oct; 25, 26 Dec

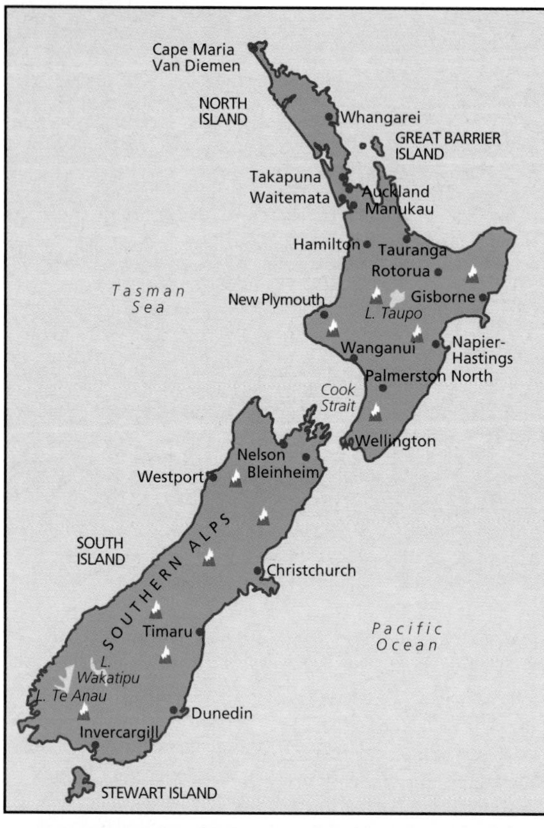

RÉFLEXION

WHAT TO DO

The Maori name for New Zealand is Aotearoa, "Land of the Long Cloud," no doubt because of the hot-water geysers on the islands, which often leave fog on the horizon. The volcanoes of North Island dot the landscape of snowy peaks and exceptionally beautiful bluffs. South Island (the "Jade Island") features a series of fertile plains dotted with outcroppings of the nephrite that gives this land its greenish colour. New Zealand prides itself on being on the cutting edge of ecological awareness; the towns, and even the major cities, are environmentally friendly. Auckland is a good example: this economic centre lies in the shadow of the magnificent Mount Eden and a series of volcanoes that have been set aside as a park island. The beaches of

NEW ZEALAND

J. O'NEILL / REFLEXION

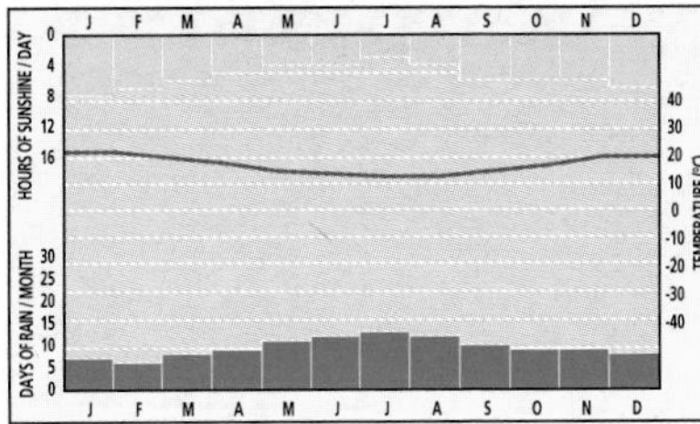

Takapuna, and the shores on the outskirts of the city are perfect for water sports. Wellington, the capital, has lovely cobblestone streets, museums filled with Maori art, and a very active port. The best-known attraction in New Zealand is Rotorua. The cradle of Maori culture, it also draws travellers for its geysers, boiling mudbaths, hot-water springs, and breathtaking mountainous terrain. The fluorescent cavern at Waitomo is unique. A trip up the northern peninsula to Cape Maria Van Diemen, renowned for its beautiful beaches and splendid countryside, is highly recommended. New Zealand's immense trees and giant ferns—and more than 72 varieties of orchids—are the joy of plant-lovers. The major city on South Island is Christchurch, which has preserved its neo-Gothic cathedral, Canterbury University, and a number of buildings that seem to have been transplanted directly from England. The rural areas are pristine and unspoiled: among the places to visit are the very beautiful Abel Tasman National Park and Fjordland National Park, home to many rare birds, and an abundance of flora, including the kiwi fruit. Queenstown has a popular ski centre, which in summer attracts hikers. With an altitude of more than 3,700 m, Mount Cook offers a unique view of New Zealand's lakes, forests, and bays.

WHAT TO BUY

There are more sheep (about 70 million head) in New Zealand than there are people: the cuisine understandably features mutton in stews, pastries, kebabs, salads, and burgers. Wool is used to make very attractive clothes, including shepherds' vests. Delicious kiwi fruit are served plain or with crème de Grand Marnier. *Pavlova* is a cake much favoured by New Zealanders. New Zealand wine is gaining a reputation for its subtle qualities. The Maori art, with its amulets, charms, and talismans, is highly prized. *Tiki* is the most popular amulet. The Maoris have adapted well to a European way of life, but their language and culture still flourish: *Kio Ora* means "hello" in Maori.

CANADA

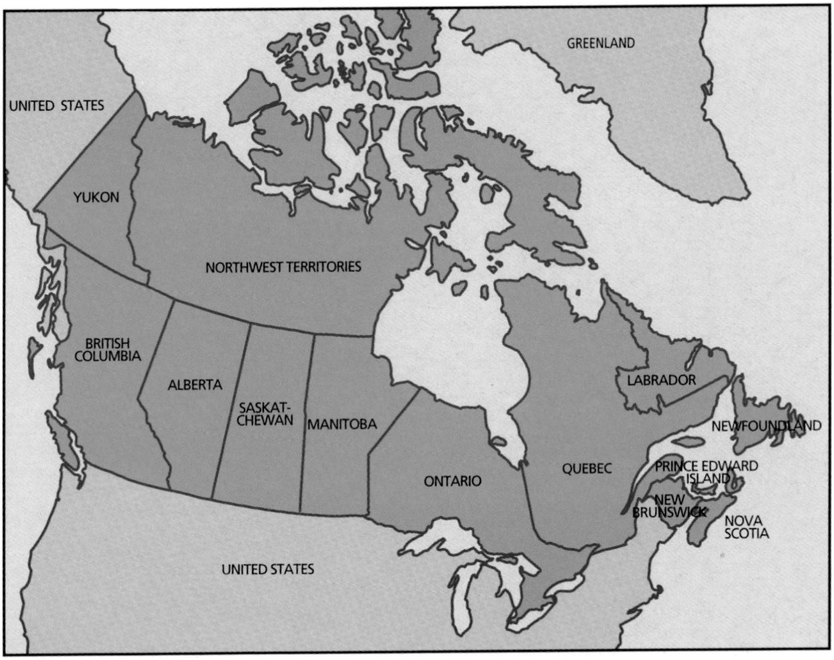

Region: North America
Area: 9,970,610 km²
Capital: Ottawa
Airport: Ottawa 17 km
Population: 27,402,100
Languages: English, French
Religions: Catholic, Protestant
Government: parliamentary democracy
Voltage: 110 - 60
Vaccinations required: –
Vaccinations recommended: –
Passport: –
Visa: –
Currency: Canadian dollar
$1Cdn: 1.00 dollar
Driving: right hand
International permit: –
Area code: different for each province
✆ from Canada: -
✆ to Canada: -
Accommodation: ★★★★★
Restaurants: ★★★★★
Transportation: ★★★★★
Cost of living: ❍❍
UN rank: 1
Best months: May to Oct
Holidays: 1 Jan; 14 Apr; 22 May; 1 July; 4 Sept; 9 Oct; 25, 26 Dec

Canada is a land of wide-open spaces, a festival of sweeping forests, soaring mountains, wind-swept tundra, sunny seasides, and meadows redolent with the fragrance of berries and flowers. Each region has its own distinctive personality: Manitoba with its wealth of wheat, the rugged natural beauty of Newfoundland, Alberta with its magnificent Rockies, the vigorous and unique culture of Quebec. Travellers who want to discover Canada from sea to sea should plan to spend months there: no one who spends only a few weeks can claim to have seen the country, for each province is so vast and offers such a multitude of unique activities and attractions.

S. O'NEILL / RÉFLEXION

J. KROENER / RÉFLEXION

NORTHERN CANADA

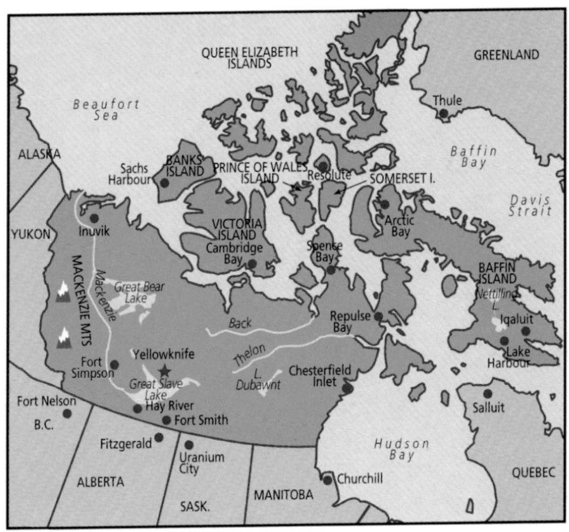

N.W. TERR.

-3 -2 -1 0 -1

Region: Canada
Area: 3,426,320 km²
Capital: Yellowknife
Airport: Yellowknife 1 km
Population: 56,500
Languages: English, native languages
Religion: Protestant
Area code: (403)
Best months: June to Oct
Holidays: 1 Jan; 14 Apr; 22 May; 1 July; 7 Aug; 4 Sept; 9 Oct; 25, 26 Dec

WHAT TO DO

The five territories of the NORTHWEST TERRITORIES (Fort Smith, Inuvik, Kitikmeot, Keewatin, and Baffin) comprise one third of Canada's total area.

This region of forests, lakes and rivers, tundra, and ice will enchant travellers seeking the rare beauties of the North. Wood Buffalo National Park is well known for its bison herds, and Nahanni National Park attracts

RÉFLEXION

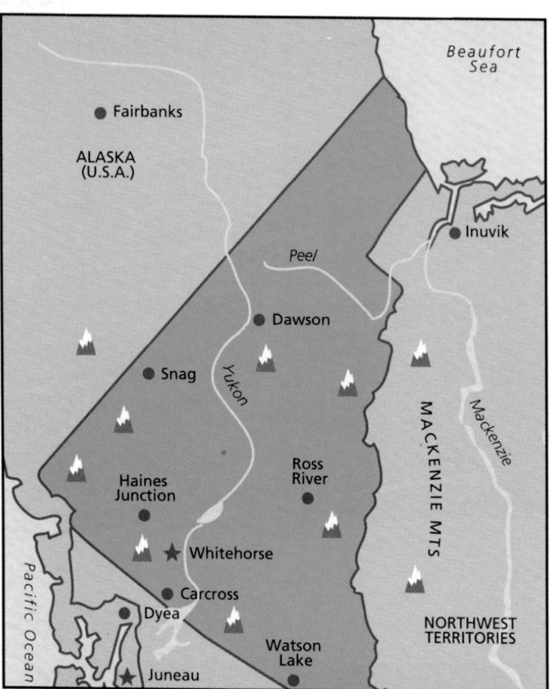

YUKON

Region: Canada
Area: 483,450 km²
Capital: Whitehorse
Airport: Whitehorse
Population: 27,900
Languages: English, native languages
Religion: Protestant
Government: legislative assembly
Area code: (403)
Best months: June, July
Holidays: 1 Jan; 14 Apr; 22 May; 1 July; 7 Aug; 4 Sept; 9 Oct; 25, 26 Dec

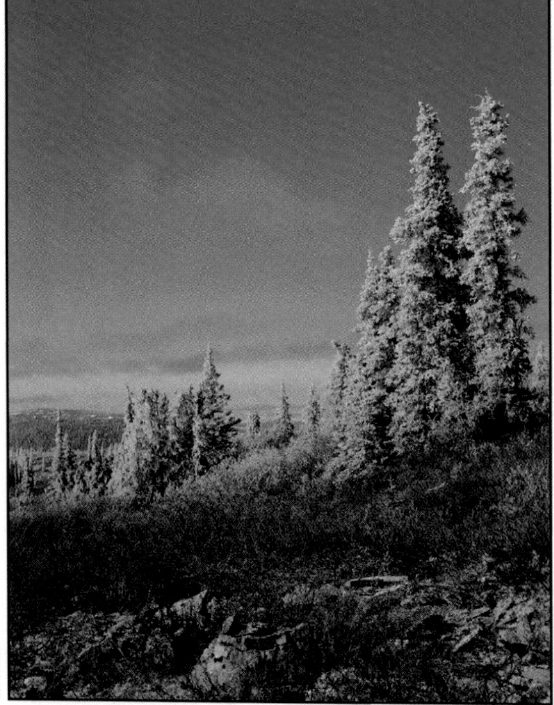
RÉFLEXION

adventurers who relish shooting rapids in canoes. The main population centre of the region is Yellowknife, but many villages dot the route north along the magnificent Mackenzie River to Inuvik. In the YUKON, visitors can find out for themselves how well plants and animals have adapted to some of the most rigorous climatic conditions on the planet. One way to discover the full glory of this region is to follow the gold-rush route from Dyea, Alaska, to the Klondike, near Dawson. Remains of the 1898 gold rush are still visible throughout this spectacular mountainous countryside, where Mount Logan rises to an altitude of almost 6,000 m.

WHAT TO BUY

Caribou meat and *muktuk* (whale meat soaked in its own oil) are specialties of the Northwest Territories. In the Yukon, visitors keen on culinary novelties can sample porcupine meat, a true delicacy. The Inuit culture offers a wide range of artworks and handicrafts often based on hunting and fishing.

WESTERN CANADA

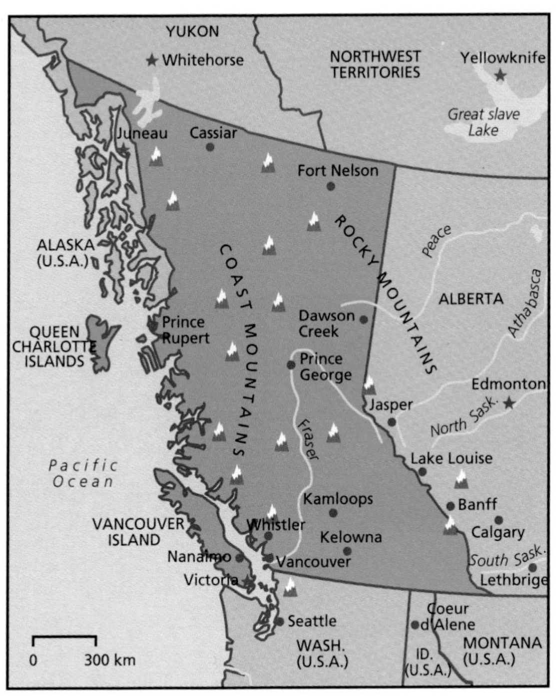

BRIT. COLUMBIA

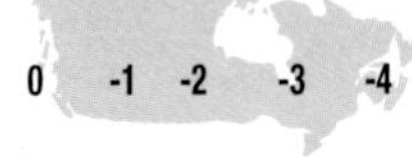

Region: Canada
Area: 947,800 km²
Capital: Victoria
Airport: Victoria, Vancouver
Population: 3,297,600
Language: English
Religion: Protestant
Area code: (604)
Best months: May to Oct
Holidays: 1 Jan; 14 Apr; 22 May; 1 July; 7 Aug; 4 Sept; 9 Oct; 25, 26 Dec

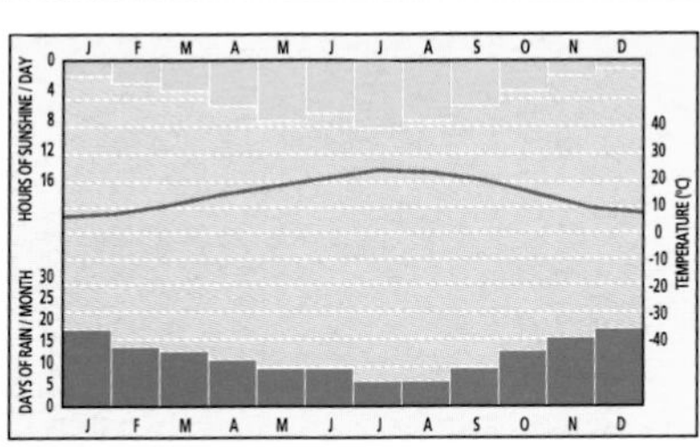

WHAT TO DO

The Canadian West is dominated by the majestic splendour of the Rockies. BRITISH COLUMBIA, on the Pacific coast, has an ideal climate blending the joys of winter and the warmth of spring almost throughout the year, as visitors to Vancouver will discover. The city's effervescence is due in large part to the many ethnic groups that have settled there and the lively cultural life. Among the many museums, the Centennial and Maritime museums are the most interesting. Stanley Park, right in the heart of the city, offers a spectacular view of the Pacific coast. Grouse Mountain is a popular ski centre close to the city, but Whistler Mountain gets higher marks from skiers. The provincial capital, Victoria, is famous for its stately Victorian architecture. The rest of the province is best known for its natural beauty; Pacific Rim Park, Tatshenshini-Alsek Park, and Glacier National Park are spectacular national parks. These and other parks make British Columbia a paradise for travellers who like wide-open spaces. The Okanagan Valley orchards, the Kimberley mines (the largest in Canada), and the Fraser Valley cattle herds testify to the economic vitality of the province.

ALBERTA is the gateway to the Rockies: the charming towns of Banff (with a major cultural centre), Lake Louise, and Jasper are nestled in the shadow of the snowy peaks along the eastern flank of the spectacular mountain range. In Edmonton, the capital, visitors can still find traces of the Klondike Gold Rush. The prime attraction for some is the West Edmonton Mall, the biggest shopping centre in the world, featuring theatres, restaurants, a swimming pool, and a golf course! The Edmonton Space Science Centre boasts the biggest planetarium in Canada. The Dinosaur Trail is an attraction unique to Alberta, featuring displays of the skeletons of gigantic prehistoric animals. Calgary, the largest city on the Prairies, is home to the world-famous Calgary Stampede.

WHAT TO BUY

Pacific smoked salmon, reproductions of Emily Carr's paintings, and Haida artworks are typical souvenirs of British Columbia, while Alberta is known for its rodeo accessories and leather goods. Of course, Western beef is of the highest quality, and it tastes great cooked over charcoal. The rivers of the West abound with fish—making this land paradise for those who like catching and eating them!

ALBERTA

+1 0 -1 -2 -3

Region: Canada
Area: 661,190 km²
Capital: Edmonton
Airport: Edmonton 30 km, Calgary 17 km
Population: 2,562,700
Language: English
Religion: Protestant
Area code: (403)
Best months: May to Sept
Holidays: 1 Jan; 20 Feb; 14 Apr; 22 May; 1 July; 7 Aug; 4 Sept; 9 Oct; 25, 26 Dec

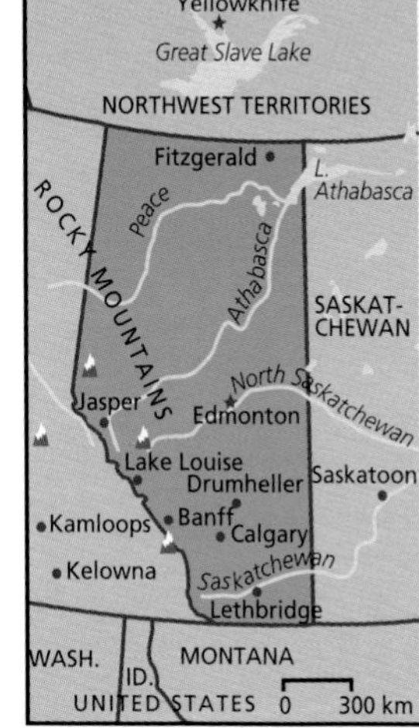

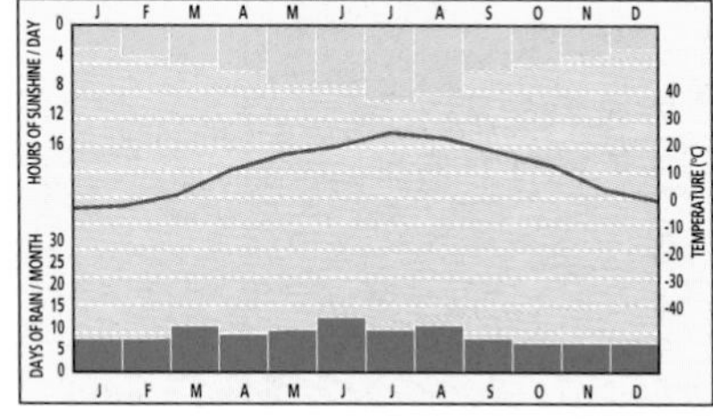

T. BOGNAR / RÉFLEXION

THE PRAIRIES

SASKATCHEWAN

+2 +1 0 -1 -2

Region: Canada
Area: 652,330 km²
Capital: Regina
Airport: Saskatoon 8 km, Regina 5 km
Population: 993,200
Language: English
Religion: Protestant
Area code: (306)
Best months: June, July, Aug
Holidays: 1 Jan; 14 Apr; 22 May; 1 July; 7 Aug; 4 Sept; 9 Oct; 25, 26 Dec

MANITOBA

+2 +1 0 -1 -2

Region: Canada
Area: 649,950 km²
Capital: Winnipeg
Airport: Winnipeg 6 km
Population: 1,096,800
Languages: English, French
Religions: Protestant, Catholic
Area code: (204)
Best months: June to Oct
Holidays: 1 Jan; 14 Apr; 22 May; 1 July; 7 Aug; 4 Sept; 9 Oct; 25, 26 Dec

WHAT TO DO

SASKATCHEWAN has two distinct types of scenery: in the north, crystalline lakes and virgin forests; in the south, vast stretches of prairie wheat fields, punctuated with herds of grazing cattle and small, pretty towns. Farther south, the Cypress Hills provide a little relief to the flatness of the prairie. Regina is the largest city in the province, and its main attractions are the Museum of Natural History and the Royal Canadian Mounted Police Museum. The many museums in Saskatoon are an indication of this city's cultural and artistic vitality. The Prince Albert and Batoche national parks are among the best known in the province; the latter is named in tribute to Louis Riel and the Métis. MANITOBA is also carved in the south by wheat fields; moving north one encounters beautiful, dense forests, thousands of lakes, and a coastal plain along Hudson

S. NAIMAN / RÉFLEXION

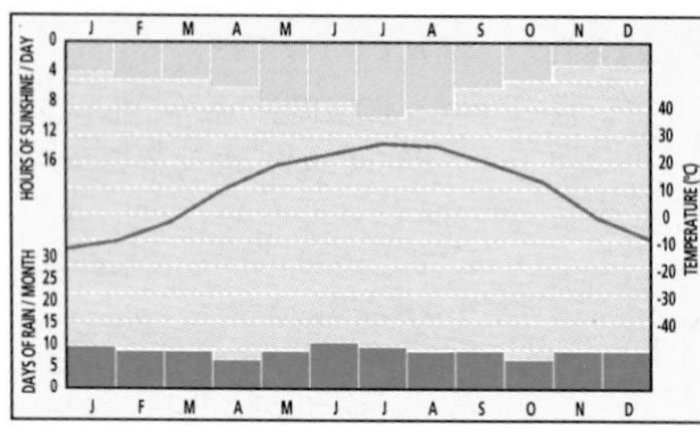

Bay. The provincial capital, Winnipeg, is one of the most interesting and dynamic cities in Canada, with its Royal Ballet, symphony orchestra, theatre centre, and several art galleries. Nearby Saint-Boniface, the birthplace of author Gabrielle Roy, is the heartland of Franco-Manitobans, who reveal a completely distinct facet of the province's culture. To see Manitoba at its most spectacular, take a ferry across the Red or Assiniboine rivers. In some places, the Red River runs very swift and rough! Lake Winnipeg is a paradise for water-sports fans, and cross-country skiers should head for Riding Mountain National Park. The area around the town of Flin Flon offers outstanding salmon fishing.

WHAT TO BUY

Handicrafts are inspired by the Métis and aboriginal culture: the woven goods, embroidery, and pottery are often decorated with their traditional motifs. At The Pas, in northern Manitoba, tourists will find leather moccasins, mittens, and coats decorated with intricate beadwork.

J. HUARD

ONTARIO

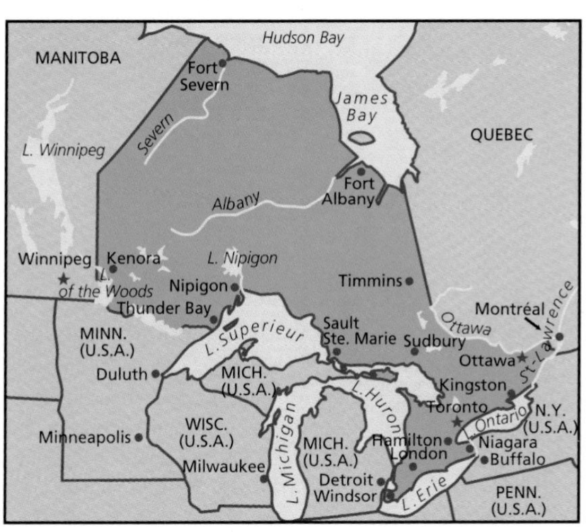

Region: Canada
Area: 1,068,580 km²
Capital: Toronto
Airport: Toronto 35 km
Population: 10,098,600
Languages: English, French
Religions: Protestant, Catholic
Area codes: (416),(519),(613),(705),(807),(905)
Best months: June to Oct
Holidays: 1 Jan; 14 Apr; 22 May; 1 July; 7 Aug; 4 Sept; 9 Oct; 25, 26 Dec

WHAT TO DO

Although the Province of Ontario is synonymous with its capital, Toronto, the province also offers sparkling lakes, dense forests, and gushing rivers. The shores of lakes Erie and Superior, as well as Georgian Bay, are favourite vacation spots, while the White River, which empties into Lake Superior, is very popular with white-water adventurers. Niagara Falls, the Thousand Islands, and the many national parks, notably Pukaskwa National Park, are the pride of the province. Toronto is well worth visiting; major attractions include the CN Tower, the zoo, the science centre, Chinatown, and its multitude of art galleries, museums and international events such as the Festival of Festivals (Toronto's film festival). There is a rich and vibrant cultural scene in the rest of Ontario, from the Franco-Ontario Festival in Ottawa, to the Summer Festival in Guelph. The theatre productions at Stratford draw large audiences every summer. The main attractions in Ottawa, the national capital, are the impressive Parliament buildings, the Museum of Civilization, and the National Art Gallery. In winter, visitors must try skating on the Rideau Canal, a unique experience. A number of smaller Ontario towns are worth a visit, including Windsor, with its very British ambience, and Thunder Bay, for its ski resorts. The region around Lake Nipigon features numerous sites that recall the First Nations, who once lived there, while the tourist attraction of Upper Canada Village provides a faithful picture of Canadian life in the nineteenth century.

WHAT TO BUY

Toronto galleries exhibit the wide range of work by Ontario artists. Their special cultural cachet is frequently eluded to in Robertson Davies's novels. The restaurants in Toronto and Ottawa offer the best of national and international cuisines, while Eaton Centre in Toronto is a mecca for shoppers. The Niagara Grape and Wine Festival, which takes place in the autumn, provides a taste of Ontario's very fine wines.

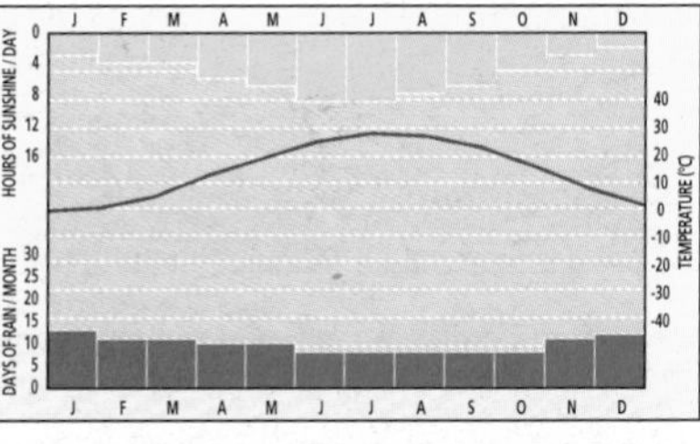

J. HUARD

QUEBEC

+3 +2 +1 0 -1

Region: Canada
Area: 1,540,680 km²
Capital: Quebec City
Airport: Mirabel 55 km, Dorval 22 km
Population: 6,925,200
Languages: French, English
Religions: Catholic, Protestant
Area codes: (514), (418), (819)
Best months: June to Nov
Holidays: 1 Jan; 14 Apr; 22 May; 24 June; 1 July; 4 Sept; 9 Oct; 25, 26 Dec

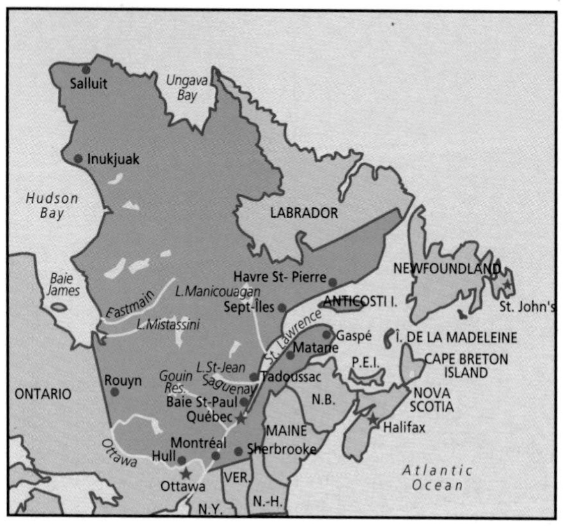

WHAT TO DO

"La Belle Province" is richly endowed with sparkling rivers and snowy mountains, lakes teeming with fish and forests alive with wildlife. The cities and towns, each with particular charms, follow the rhythm of the seasons. In summer, vacationers flock to the beaches, while in winter, they take to the woods for snowshoeing and skiing. Quebec also offers a wide range of unique cultural activities, from the Western Festival in Saint-Tite, the Carnaval in Quebec City, and the hot-air balloon festival in Saint-Jean-sur-Richelieu to the World Film Festival in Montreal—to name just a few. Montreal, the largest city, is the heart of tourism and culture in the province; major attractions include the famous Olympic Stadium, the Biodome, the Botanical Gardens, the cobble-stone streets of Old Montreal, the Fine Arts and Contemporary Art museums, the numerous art galleries, the shopping arteries, the distinct neighbourhoods (Plateau Mont-Royal and Outremont are good examples), and the downtown department stores—not to mention the magnificent green space in the centre of the city, Mount Royal. Quebec City, is a favourite destination for history-lovers: the Petit-Champlain neighbourhood (the oldest settlement in mainland North America), Place Royale, the very beautiful Notre-Dame-des-Victoires Church, Château Frontenac, the Citadel, and the walls of the old city testify to the historical importance of the provincial capital. The Musée du Séminaire, the National Assembly buildings, the Plains of Abraham (or National Battlefield Park), and the Musée de la Civilisation are also prime attractions. Nearby, Île d'Orléans is one of the most charming destinations in the province, with its century-old houses and historical churches. Opposite this island, a spectacular

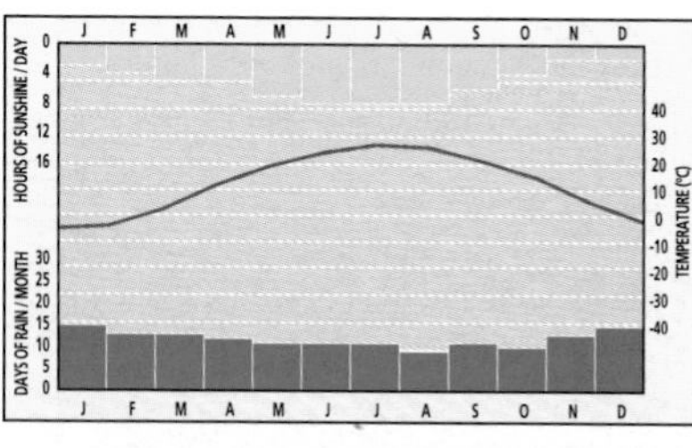

Y. TESSIER / RÉFLEXION

QUEBEC

J. HUARD

sight is Montmorency Falls (the highest in North America), breathtaking both summer and winter. Many other regions of Quebec are also worth a visit. Charlevoix attracts both nature and culture lovers to Haute-Gorges-de-la-rivière-Malbaie Park, the town of Baie-Saint-Paul with its art galleries, the picturesque Île aux Coudres, and the majestic mouth of the Saguenay River, where whales cavort in the deep waters. Gamblers should drop in at the new La Malbaie casino. Saguenay-Lac-Saint-Jean offers sumptuous scenery, especially the fjords, peaks, and capes along the Saguenay River, and the people living on the shores of beautiful Lac Saint-Jean are renowned for their friendliness. The Gaspé Peninsula is a famous tourist region with its superb Forillon Park, Gaspésie Park (one of the most magnificent in the country), and the majestic gulf of the St. Lawrence River, which widens out around Île Bonaventure, a seabird sanctuary. The towns and villages along the coast of the peninsula are truly charming. The North Shore of the Gulf of St. Lawrence is rugged and beautiful. Archipel-de-Mingan, the island of Anticosti, and the Îles de la Madeleine (Magdalen Islands) offer nature in all its splendour. The Eastern Townships boast great ski resorts and cosy villages known for their fine restaurants, especially North Hatley. In Montérégie, travellers will discover the history of the 1837 Patriotes, at Saint-Denis-sur-

RÉFLEXION

Richelieu, and lovely apple orchards, around Rougemont and Mont Saint-Hilaire. Lanaudière is well known for its international music festival and the beautiful Joliette Art Museum, but the region is also studded with rivers and forests—perfect hiking country. Snowmobilers are familiar with the charms of the forests in Saint-Michel-des-Saints. Skiers will head for the Laurentians, where there are major ski centres at Saint-Sauveur-des-Monts, Morin Heights, Mont-Laurier, and Mont-Tremblant. In summer, this region, with its variety of wildlife, is a favourite for hikers. The Outaouais region offers many touristic and natural attractions: Chateau Montebello, Papineau-Labelle Park, and Gatineau Park provide clear, trout-filled lakes and trails that hikers share with deer. The Abitibi features the dynamic towns of Val-d'Or, Amos, and Rouyn-Noranda, where the International Film Festival draws crowds of film-lovers. Northern Quebec can be explored through organized tours; dogsleds and snowmobiles are the favoured forms of winter transportation in this relatively inaccessible but stunningly beautiful region.

WHAT TO BUY

Quebec cuisine is not limited to meatball stew and *tourtière* (meat pie). Each region has its specialty: lobster in the Magdalen Islands, shrimp in Matane, blueberries in the Saguenay, apples—and cider!—in Rougemont, maple syrup in the Beauce, and cheese from Oka. It is in the *brasseries* (neighbourhood restaurants that serve beer) that one finds Quebec family cuisine at its best. Quebec beer, especially from the microbreweries, is delicious, and Quebec vineyards are beginning to gain a reputation, particularly the Orpailleur vineyard in Dunham. In Montreal, whose immigrants brought recipes from their countries of origin, restaurants offer cuisine from, for example, Madagascar, Korea, Switzerland, and Peru. There is also a multitude of fine French and Italian restaurants. The carvers in Saint-Jean-Port-Joli are well known for their wooden sculptures, but all tourist centres offer an impressive variety of handicrafts, especially knitted goods, pottery, and aboriginal crafts. The Crafts Exposition that is held every December in Montreal provides a unique opportunity to see crafts made in Quebec. Works by Quebec's artists (singers, painters, writers) also make for unforgettable souvenirs.

ATLANTIC CANADA

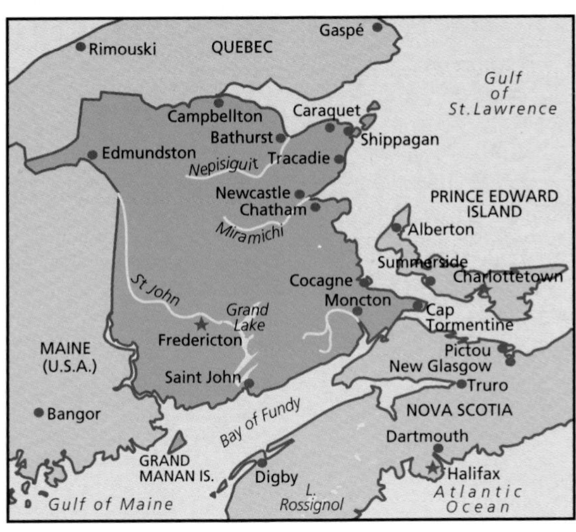

N. BRUNSWICK

+4 +3 +3 +1 0

Region: Canada
Area: 73,440 km²
Capital: Fredericton
Airport: Fredericton, Saint John
Population: 729,300
Languages: English, French
Religions: Protestant, Catholic
Area code: (506)
Best months: June, July, Aug
Holidays: 1 Jan; 14 Apr; 22 May; 1 July; 7 Aug; 4 Sept; 9 Oct; 25, 26 Dec

WHAT TO DO

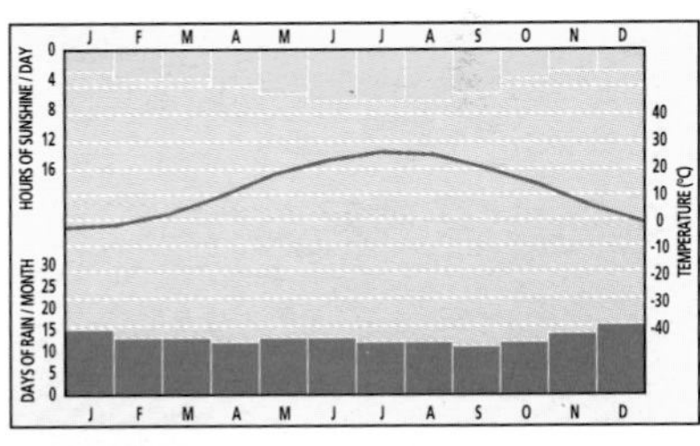

Eastern Canada's history is inextricably linked to the sea. From the sandy beaches of Prince Edward Island to the rocky shores of Nova Scotia, the Atlantic Ocean has shaped this land and its people. NEW BRUNSWICK is the largest province in the Maritimes. The majority of its inhabitants live along the Gulf of St. Lawrence and the Bay of Fundy. Fundy Park is one of the most spectacular natural sites in Atlantic Canada, although the bird sanctuary on Grand Manan Island runs a close second. The small towns of Acadia, including Caraquet, Shippagan, and Tracadie, have a special charm. Near Tracadie, Village Acadien recreates the life of eighteenth-century French colonists. The major cities of Fredericton, Saint John, and Moncton are modern and clean, but the pace of life is gentle, enabling residents and visitors alike to enjoy the beauties of this province. Travellers in search of sandy beaches will head for PRINCE EDWARD ISLAND, which will soon be

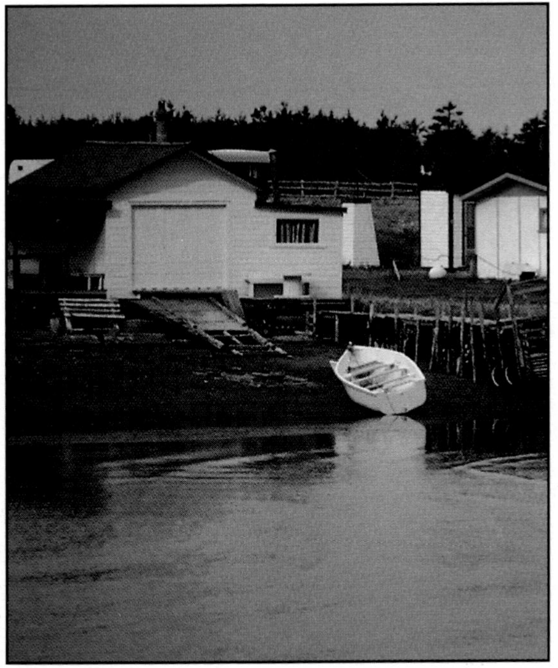

P. HALLY

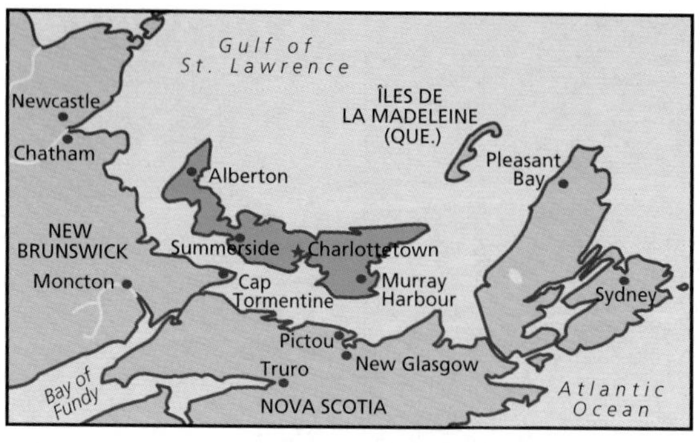

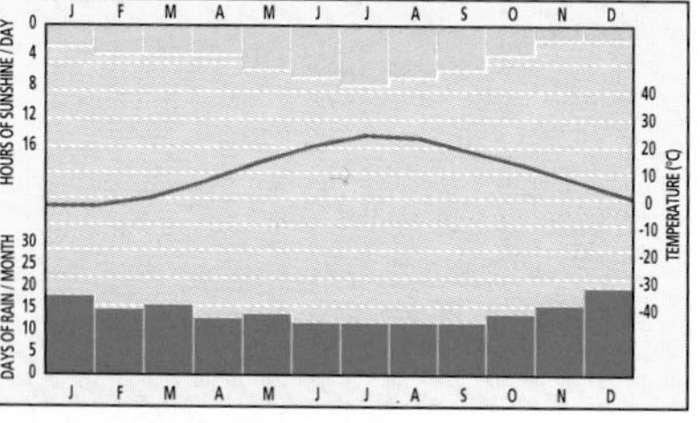

J. HUARD

PRINCE EDWARD ISLAND

+4 +3 +3 +1 0

Region: Canada
Area: 5,660 km²
Capital: Charlottetown
Airport: Charlottetown 8 km
Population: 130,500
Language: English
Religion: Protestant
Area code: (902)
Best months: June, July, Aug
Holidays: 1 Jan; 14 Apr; 22 May; 1 July; 7 Aug; 4 Sept; 9 Oct; 25, 26 Dec

linked to New Brunswick by a bridge. The north shore of the province is particularly beautiful, with its unique red-sand dunes. Charlottetown, the capital, is a charming town that has preserved its colonial architecture. The little fishing ports, the Acadian villages, and the tobacco fields in the centre of the island are other attractions of Canada's smallest province. Sea-swept, rugged NOVA SCOTIA has a climate that is reminiscent of its British namesake. Cape Breton Park, on Cape Breton Island, is a uniquely beautiful natural site, with its majestic countryside and breathtaking ocean views. The fort at Louisbourg testifies to the history of the French colonists, while the towns along Northumberland Strait still bear Scottish influences, and Acadian villages such as Grand Pré recall the deportation of the Acadians. Halifax, the capital, is a pleasant city, and the large towns of Truro and New Glasgow have preserved their nineteenth-century charm. The large island province of NEWFOUNDLAND is isolated from the rest of Canada, which gives it a certain cachet. Most Newfoundlanders live in the capital, St. John's, on the eastern side

ATLANTIC CANADA

NOVA SCOTIA

+4 +3 +3 +1 0

Region: Canada
Area: 55,490 km²
Capital: Halifax
Airport: Halifax 41 km
Population: 906,300
Language: English
Religion: Protestant
Area code: (902)
Best months: June, July, Aug
Holidays: 1 Jan; 14 Apr; 22 May; 1 July; 7 Aug; 4 Sept; 9 Oct; 25, 26 Dec

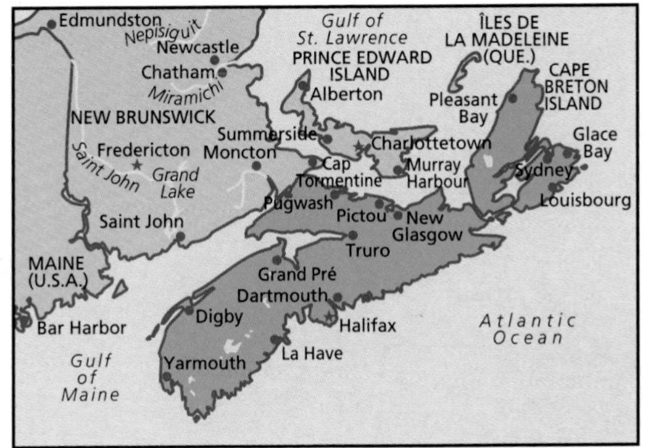

of the Avalon Peninsula, a coastline that knows the fury of the North Atlantic. The Trans-Canada Highway goes all the way around the island; starting in Port-aux-Basques, it passes through towns like Gander and South Brook. Much of the island, especially the peninsula stretching northwest, is stunningly beautiful. The remains of Viking villages dating back to the year 1000 have been found on the northern tip, at L'Anse aux Meadows. Labrador is just a few kilometres away from this point of land, across the Strait of Belle Isle. An almost unexplored land of ice, Labrador offers unequalled attractions for those who love wide-open spaces.

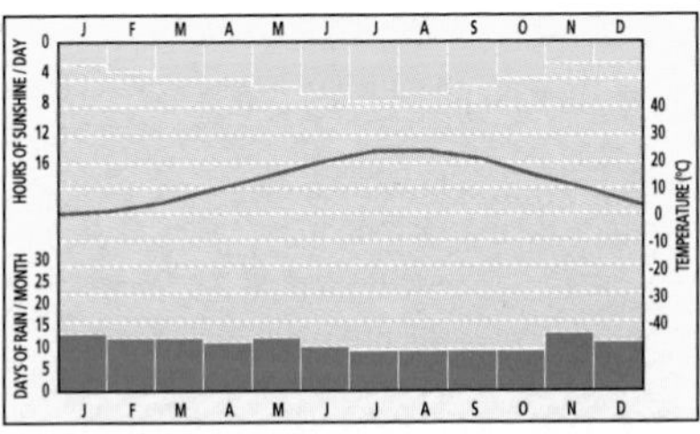

WHAT TO BUY

The cuisine of Atlantic Canada is based on seafood: oysters from Caraquet and Malpèque, lobster from Nova Scotia and New Brunswick and fresh fish cooked a thousand different ways. The handicrafts explore the maritime theme in sculpture and paint.

RÉFLEXION

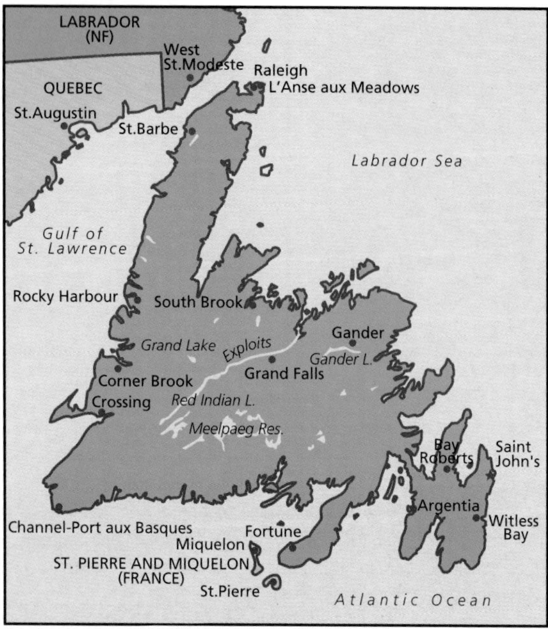

NEWFOUNDLAND & LABRADOR

+4 +3 +3 +1 0

Region: Canada
Area: 405,720 km²
Capital: St. John's
Airport: St. John's 9 km; Gander 3 km
Population: 577,500
Language: English
Religion: Protestant
Area code: (709)
Best months: June, July, Aug
Holidays: 1 Jan; 14 Apr; 22 May; 1 July; 4 Sept; 9 Oct; 25, 26 Dec

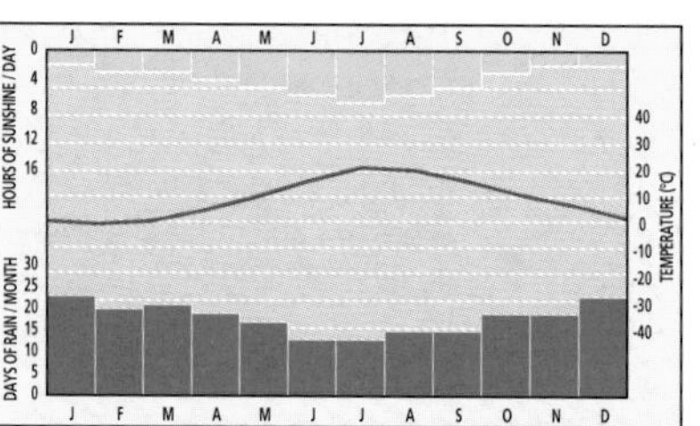

Tobacco products from Prince Edward Island are top quality. Acadian culture has produced fine singers, such as Édith Butler, and the stunning writing of Antonine Maillet. Hugh MacLennan, a famous Canadian novelist, was born in Atlantic Canada.

A. GARDON / RÉFLEXION

SAINT-PIERRE-ET-MIQUELON

+4 +3 +3 +1 0

Region: North America
Area: 242 km²
Capital: Saint-Pierre
Airport: Saint-Pierre
Population: 6,710
Language: French
Religion: Catholic
Government: French department
Voltage: 220 - 50
Vaccinations required: –
Vaccinations recommended: –
Passport: required
Visa: not required
Currency: French franc
$1Cdn: 3.52 francs
Driving: right hand
International permit: recommended
Area code: 011-508
✆ from Canada: –
✆ to Canada: –
Accommodation: ★★★
Restaurants: ★★★★
Transportation: ★★★
Cost of living: ○○
UN rank: –
Best months: July, Aug
Holidays: 1 Jan; 16, 17 Apr; 1, 8, 25 May; 4, 5 Jun; 14 July; 15 Aug; 1, 11 Nov; 25 Dec

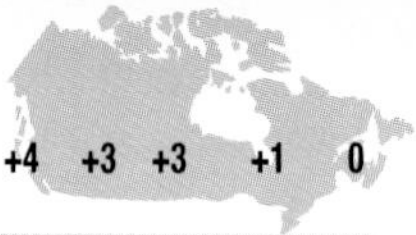

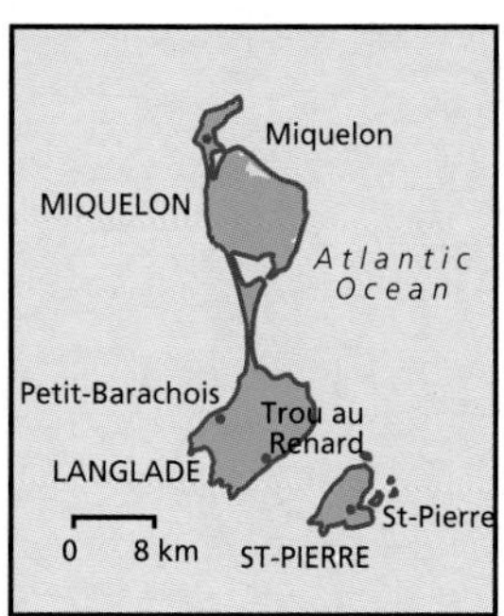

WHAT TO DO

The small islands of Saint-Pierre-et-Miquelon, south of Newfoundland, still belong to France, so they provide a bit of European ambience at Canada's door. Saint-Pierre features bakeries selling *baguettes* and croissants, bistros where patrons quaff good red wine and *pastis* (an anise-based liqueur), a French post office, and even a Place du Général-de-Gaulle. The islands of Langlade and Miquelon are natural wonders in themselves, with nesting sites for many types of seabirds, and horses running free on the sand dunes of L'Anse du Gouvernement.

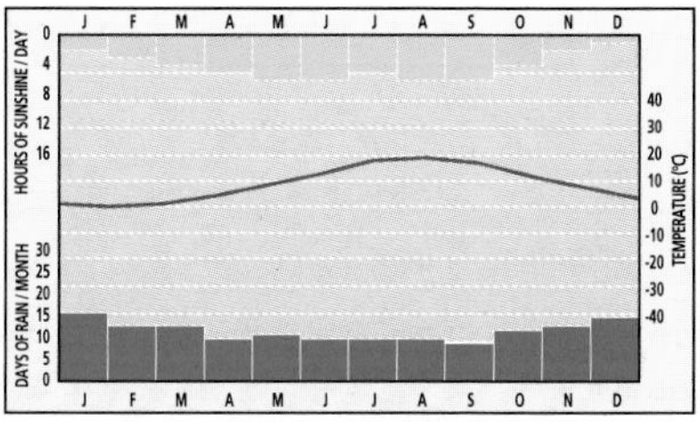

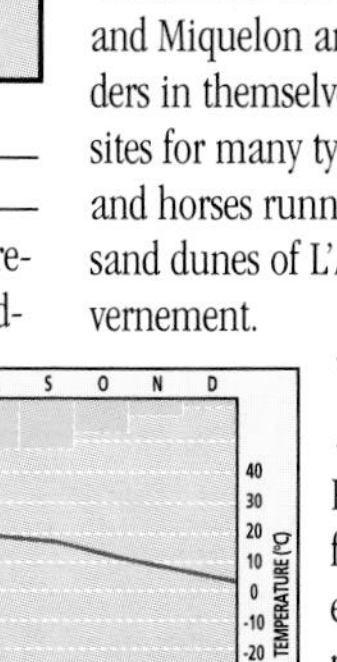

WHAT TO BUY

Postage stamps from Saint-Pierre-et-Miquelon are prized by philatelists. Local crafts, marine objects, woodcarvings and paintings are also very interesting.

UNITED STATES

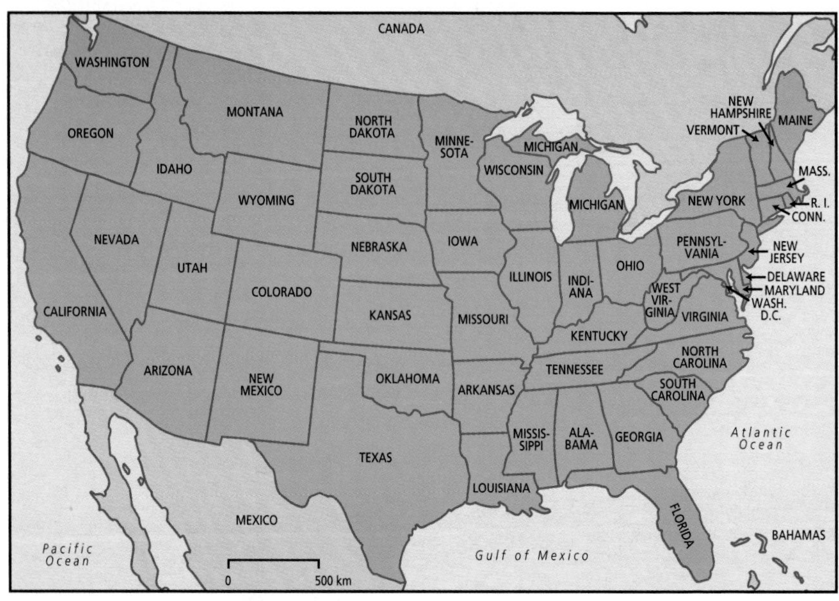

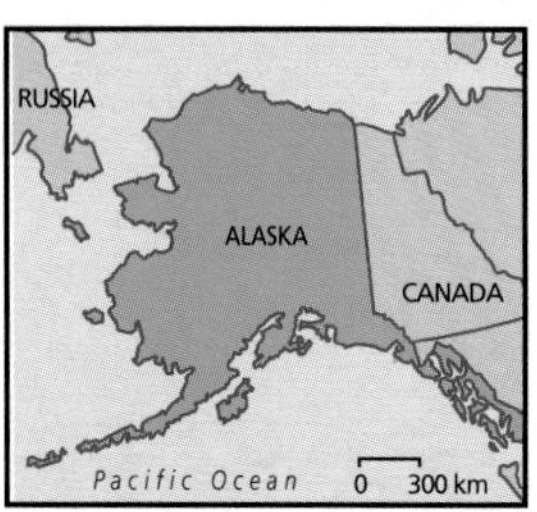

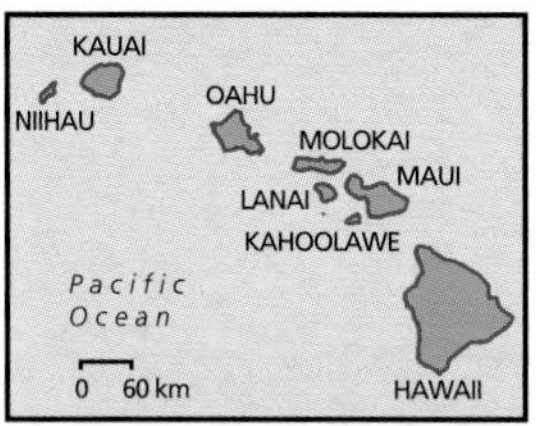

From its deep canyons to its golden beaches, from its skyscrapers to its colonial houses, the United States offers a panoply of countrysides and urban attractions that will appeal to everyone from mountain-climbers to wine-lovers. From playing the casinos of Nevada to diving expeditions in Maui to meeting grizzly bears in Yellowstone Park, travellers will discover not a homogeneous country but a variety of regions whose differences make up the rich fabric of this vast land.

Region: North America
Area: 9,372,610 km²
Capital: Washington, D.C.
Airport: Washington, D.C. 40 km
Population: 260,713,590
Languages: English, Spanish
Religions: Protestant, Catholic
Government: presidential democracy
Voltage: 110 - 60
Vaccinations required: –
Vaccinations recommended: –
Passport: proof of citizenship
Visa: –
Currency: American dollar
$1Cdn: .74 dollar
Driving: right hand
International permit: –
Area code: different for each state
✆ from Canada:
✆ to Canada:
Accommodation: ★★★★★
Restaurants: ★★★★★
Transportation: ★★★★★
Cost of living: ○○
UN rank: 8
Best months: different for each region
Holidays: 1, 16 Jan; 12, 20 Feb; 14, 16 Apr; 29 May; 4 July; 4 Sept; 9 Oct; 11, 23 Nov; 25, 26 Dec

P. HALLY

THE NORTHWEST

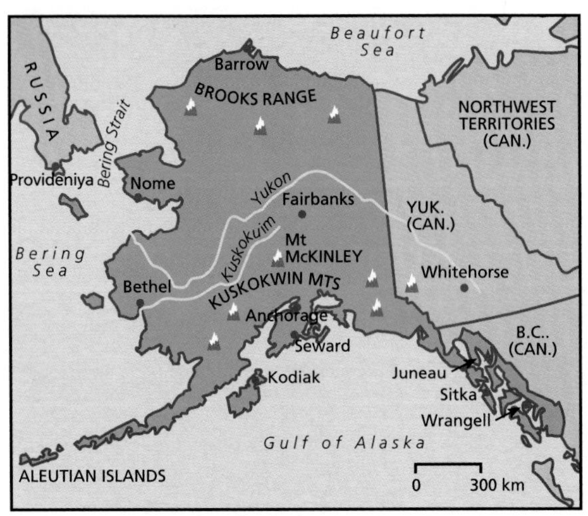

UNITED STATES TOURIST OFFICE

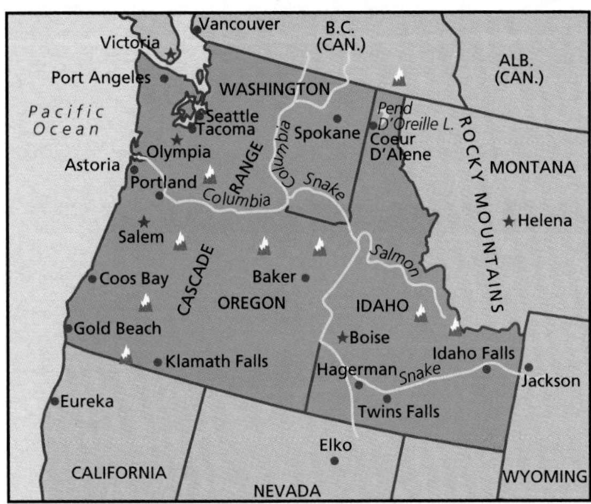

IDAHO

Region: United States
Area: 216,413 km²
Capital: Boise
Airport: Boise 11 km
Population: 1,007,000
Area code: (208)
Best months: June, July

ALASKA

Region: United States
Area: 1,518,740 km²
Capital: Juneau
Airport: Anchorage 10 km, Fairbanks 5 km
Population: 550,000
Area code: (907)
Best months: June, July

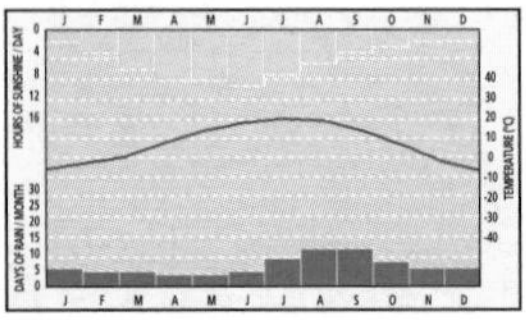

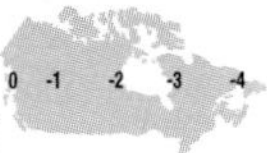

OREGON

Region: United States
Area: 248,281 km²
Capital: Salem
Airport: Portland 14 km
Population: 2,842,000
Area code: (503)
Best months: June, July

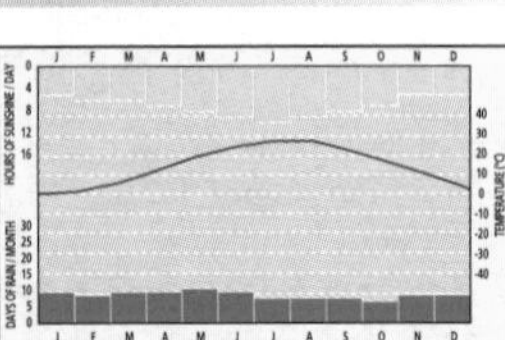

WASHINGTON

Region: United States
Area: 176,617 km²
Capital: Olympia
Airport: Seattle 22 km
Population: 4,867,000
Area codes: (206), (509)
Best months: June, July

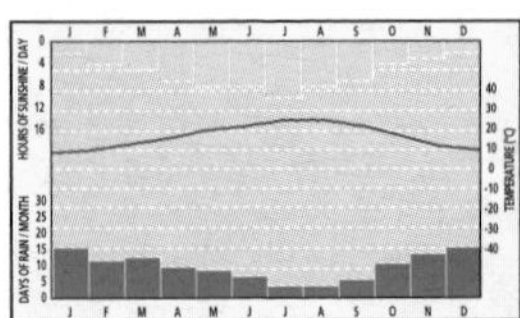

WHAT TO DO

ALASKA, the largest state, is also the least populated. Its glaciers, rivers, and fjords share the magnificent countryside with tundra and forests. Denali National Park, the ski centres, and Mount McKinley (which, at 6,194 m, is the highest mountain in North America) are the main attractions of this land of the nineteenth-century gold rush. IDAHO also has natural wonders, including Hell's Canyon, the deepest in North America, and the craters of the Moon National Monument. Skiers will want to visit the Sun Valley region, and hunters will head for the Chamberlain Basin. OREGON is best known for its section of Hell's Canyon, its 230 national parks, its protected forests, and its famous caves. Portland is a very pleasant city; its beautiful public gardens have earned it the nickname "City of Roses". WASHINGTON State is a mixture of large modern cities, like Seattle, and natural wonders; Olympic National Park, Mount Rainier National Park, and Mount St. Helens alone are worth the trip to this west coast state.

THE OLD WEST

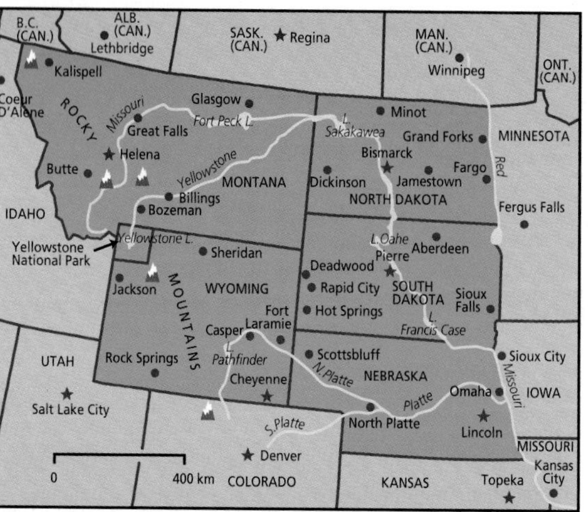

ZEPHYR / BUCHANAN / RÉFLEXION

WHAT TO DO

For lovers of westerns, NORTH DAKOTA is a fantasy come true: Fort Lincoln, Slant Indian Village, Colonel Custer's headquarters, and the many cattle ranches testify to the conquest of the West by armies of soldiers and colonists. In SOUTH DAKOTA is the famous Mount Rushmore, on which are sculpted the faces of four presidents. The Badlands is an area of fertile prairie land once crossed by pioneers, and the Black Hills is a region of forests, lakes, and caverns, much frequented by hikers. The Rockies and the Missouri River cross MONTANA, making it a landscape of mountains and buttes, lakes and waterfalls. Omaha is one of the main cities in NEBRASKA, along with Lincoln and Scottsbluff, but travellers should make a point of visiting Fort Robinson, Chimney Rock, and Buffalo Bill Historical Park. WYOMING is known for the splendour of Yellowstone Park, one of the most spectacular natural sites in the world, with canyons; geysers, including Old Faithful, which spouts every hour; and roaming wildlife, including bison, pumas, and grizzly bears, as well as a multitude of birds and small mammals.

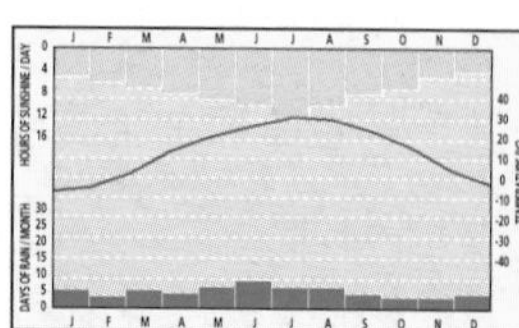

NORTH DAKOTA

Region: United States
Area: 183,022 km²
Capital: Bismarck
Airport: Bismarck, Fargo, Grand Forks
Population: 669,000
Area code: (701)
Best months: May to Oct

SOUTH DAKOTA

Region: United States
Area: 199,552 km²
Capital: Pierre
Airport: Pierre, Rapid City, Sioux Falls
Population: 715,000
Area code: (605)
Best months: May to Oct

MONTANA

Region: United States
Area: 381,087 km²
Capital: Helena
Airport: Helena, Butte, Great Falls
Population: 809,000
Area code: (406)
Best months: May to Oct

NEBRASKA

Region: United States
Area: 200,018 km²
Capital: Lincoln
Airport: Lincoln
Population: 1,605,000
Area codes: (308), (402)
Best months: May to Oct

WYOMING

Region: United States
Area: 253,597 km²
Capital: Cheyenne
Airport: Casper, Jackson
Population: 483,000
Area code: (307)
Best months: May to Oct

THE GREAT LAKES

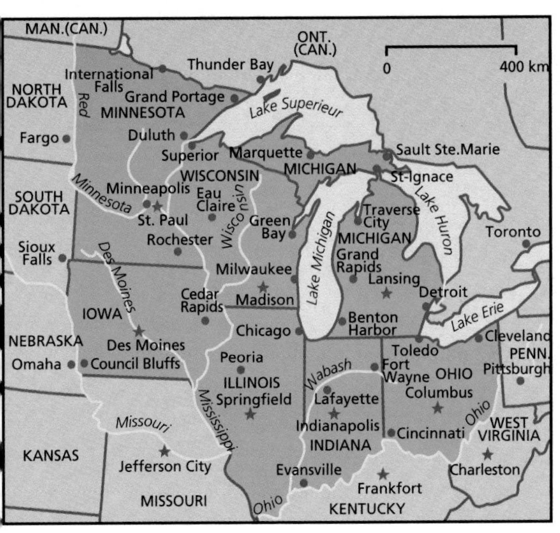

IOWA

Region: United States
Area: 145,791 km²
Capital: Des Moines
Airport: Des Moines
Population: 2,777,000
Area codes: (319), (515), 712)
Best months: June to Oct

MICHIGAN

Region: United States
Area: 150,779 km²
Capital: Lansing
Airport: Detroit 34 km
Population: 9,295,000
Area codes: (313), (517), (616), (906)
Best months: June to Oct

OHIO

Region: United States
Area: 106,289 km²
Capital: Columbus
Airport: Cincinnati 23 km, Cleveland 19 km
Population: 10,857,000
Area codes: (216), (419), (513), (614)
Best months: June to Oct

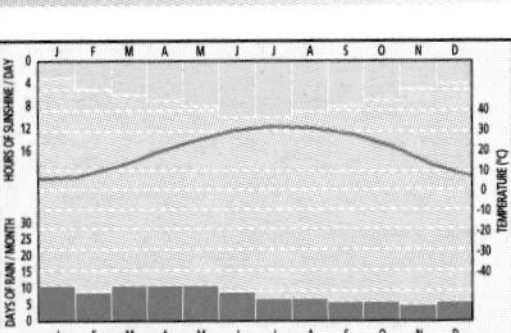

ILLINOIS

Region: United States
Area: 146,756 km²
Capital: Springfield
Airport: Chicago 27 km
Population: 11,630,000
Area codes: (312), (708)
Best months: June to Oct

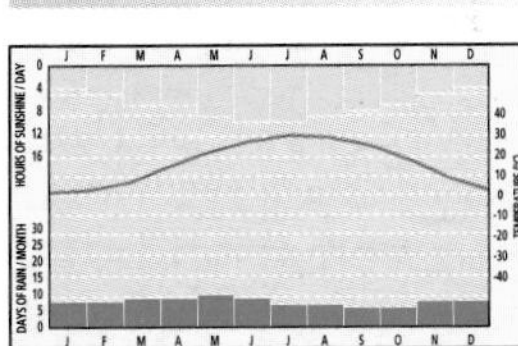

MINNESOTA

Region: United States
Area: 217,736 km²
Capital: St. Paul
Airport: Minneapolis, St. Paul
Population: 4,375,000
Area codes: (218), (507), 612)
Best months: June to Oct

INDIANA

Region: United States
Area: 94,153 km²
Capital: Indianapolis
Airport: Indianapolis 8 km
Population: 5,559,000
Area codes: (219), (307), (812)
Best months: June to Oct

WISCONSIN

Region: United States
Area: 145,439 km²
Capital: Madison
Airport: Milwaukee 9 km
Population: 4,892,000
Area codes: (414), (608), (715)
Best months: June to Oct

WHAT TO DO

The Great Lakes make the states that border them major centres for sailing and boating. Although its shoreline along Lake Michigan is not long, ILLINOIS offers a wide variety of water sports, and its ports are among the most active in the country. Chicago also features lovely beaches, although the city is better known for its skyscrapers and underworld. Its many museums and variety of cultural activities make Chicago a very dynamic city. The historical sites of Fort Crèvecoeur and New Salem State Park provide glimpses of the history of the region. In INDIANA, the beautiful Wabash River divides the state in half. The Dunes National Lake Shore on Lake Michigan is worth seeing, as is Fort Wayne, where a number of historic battles took place. Agriculture is the main activity in IOWA. Colonists from Germany, the Netherlands, Switzerland, and Alsace brought their traditions when they settled in this state, as visitors can see from the tulip fields reminiscent of Holland and the architecture in some of the towns. Water sports are high on the list of attractions in MICHIGAN, which borders on four Great Lakes. Pictured Rocks National Lakeshore and Isle Royale National Park are richly endowed with natural wonders: the immense boulders of Pictured Rock are especially interesting. Detroit's Institute of Art is one of the largest museums in the country, but it is only one of the many galleries and cultural centres that give this city an artistic atmosphere. In MINNESOTA, the charms of St. Paul and Minneapolis attract art and architecture fans alike. Beyond these centres, the state features more than 11,000 lakes, 64 national parks, and 55 protected forests. OHIO is perhaps best known for the gorgeous Cuyahoga Valley Park and the tranquil islands of Lake Erie. Near the city of Cleveland, on Lake Erie, are the pleasant beaches of Cedar Point. WISCONSIN also has long stretches of beautiful beaches. The Lake Michigan shoreline and the more than 15,000 lakes and rivers, as well as the state's large farms, provide tourists with many scenic vistas. The European influence is obvious in both large towns and small villages, and Milwaukee is one of the most charming cities in the United States.

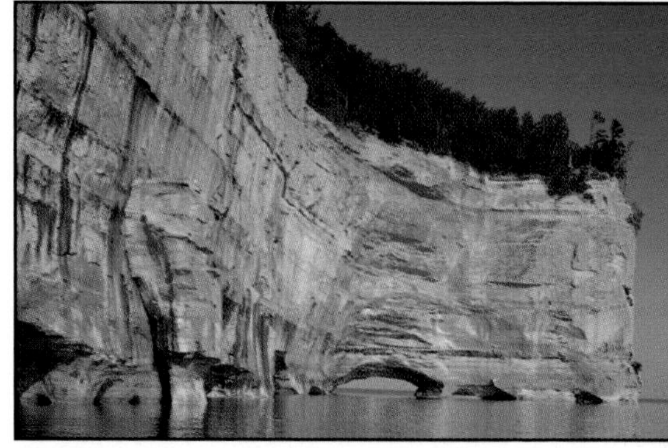

THE EAST COAST

NEW JERSEY

Region: United States
Area: 21,300 km²
Capital: Trenton
Airport: Newark 27 km
Population: 7,730,000
Area codes: (201), (609)
Best months: May to Oct

NEW YORK

Region: United States
Area: 127,433 km²
Capital: Albany
Airport: N.Y.C. (JFK 24 km, La Guardia 13 km)
Population: 17,990,000
Area codes: (212), (315), (518), (716)
Best months: May to Oct

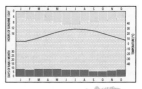

PENNSYLVANIA

Region: United States
Area: 117,413 km²
Capital: Harrisburg
Airport: Philadelphia 13 km
Population: 11,882,000
Area codes: (215), (412), (717)
Best months: May to Oct

WHAT TO DO

The east coast of the United States has much more to offer than just the major metropolis of New York. NEW JERSEY, with its long stretches of beautiful beaches and lively towns, is the envy of many states. Atlantic City is one of the oldest holiday resorts on the coast, along with Wildwood and Cape May. Trenton is a charming city replete with art galleries and historic sites, for in 1794 it was the capital of the country. The Skylands region, in the northwest part of the state, is considered to be one of the most beautiful spots on the east coast; in winter, the ski centres of Vernon Valley attract downhill aficionados, and in summer, hikers enjoy the views on the trails of the Great Gorge. The state of NEW YORK also has numerous natural wonders: the famous Niagara Falls, the Thousand Islands, and the Adirondacks. Lake George is a pretty resort town. And then, of course, there's New York City. The island of Manhattan is always fascinating, with its crowded streets, art galleries and museums (including the fabulous Metropolitan Museum of Art and the Museum of Modern Art); majestic skyscrapers, like the Chrysler Building and Rockefeller Center; the artists' district of Soho and the nightclubs of Greenwich Village; Central Park; Times Square; and the magnificent Lincoln Center. The department stores along Fifth Avenue and the best-known attractions, like the Statue of Liberty, the Empire State Building, and the World Trade Center, are all worth a visit. The Declaration of Independence was signed in Philadelphia, PENNSYLVANIA. This city offers a number of very important historical sites, including Franklin Court, the old city hall, and the Independence National Historical Park. Pittsburgh and the Pocono Mountains are other attractions in this state.

NEW ENGLAND

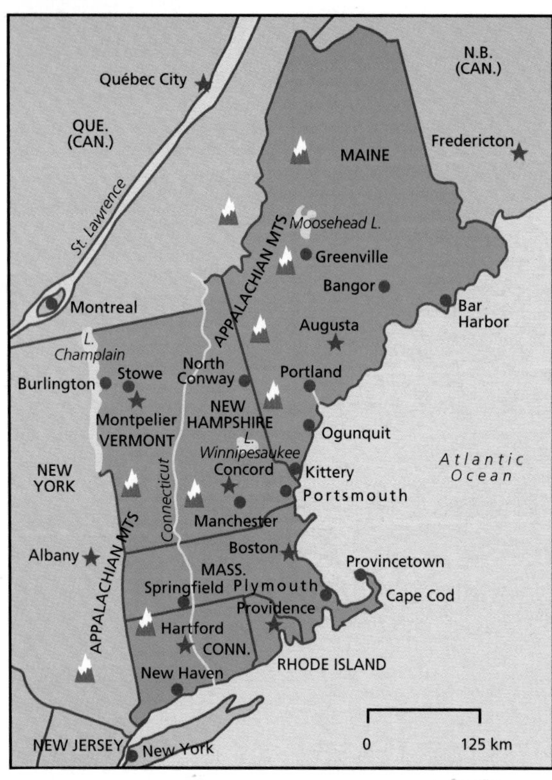

MAINE

Region: United States
Area: 86,027 km²
Capital: Augusta
Airport: Bangor, 6 km, Portland 5 km
Population: 1,228,000
Area code: (207)
Best months: May to Oct

MASSACHUSETTS

Region: United States
Area: 21,408 km²
Capital: Boston
Airport: Boston
Population: 6,016,000
Area codes: (413), (508), (617)
Best months: May to Oct

NEW HAMPSHIRE

Region: United States
Area: 24,192 km²
Capital: Concord
Airport: Manchester
Population: 1,109,000
Area code: (603)
Best months: May to Oct

RHODE ISLAND

Region: United States
Area: 3,233 km²
Capital: Providence
Airport: Warwick
Population: 1,003,000
Area code: (401)
Best months: May to Oct

CONNECTICUT

Region: United States
Area: 12,850 km²
Capital: Hartford
Airport: Hartford 19 km
Population: 3,287,000
Area code: (203)
Best months: May to Oct

VERMONT

Region: United States
Area: 24,887 km²
Capital: Montpelier
Airport: Burlington 5 km
Population: 563,000
Area code: (802)
Best months: May to Oct

WHAT TO DO

The New England States, one-time British colonies founded in the seventeenth century, have a typically "English" ambience, that makes them special. Like Oxford in Great Britain, CONNECTICUT is best known for Yale University in New Haven. But nature is another prime attraction: the states' stretches of beaches are dotted with little fishing ports and charming villages. MAINE is the perfect holiday destination: the coast, from Bar Harbor to Ogunquit, features beautiful beaches and pretty towns. Inland, more than 2,000 lakes are hidden among the state's forests and mountains. During the academic year, the massive inflow of students to Harvard and Cambridge universities in MASSACHUSETTS make this state's largest city, Boston, burst with vitality. One of the most beautiful cities in New England, Boston features distinctive red-brick Victorian buildings and cobble-stone streets. The Freedom Trail leads walkers along a tour of the city's his-

P. HALLY

oric sites. The Boston Art Museum often features unique xhibitions. Provincetown, Martha's Vineyard, and the Cape Cod National Seashore raw thousands of tourists to heir harbours and beaches. Mount Washington is the rime attraction in NEW HAMPSHIRE, where the White Mountains offer vistas of deep alleys, rolling hills, and snowy peaks. Franconia Notch is a spectacular gorge that is worth a visit. The beaches at Hampton and the pretty town of Laconia are sure to delight. RHODE ISLAND is the smallest state, but its friendly eighteenth-century towns, as well as its beaches and yacht clubs, make it a very popular destination. VERMONT does not lie along the Atlantic coast, but it has a lovely shoreline on huge Lake Champlain. Vacationers love the clear lakes, warm waters. Vermont is also known for its many ski resorts, hiking trails, and forests full of wildlife.

UNITED STATES TOURIST OFFICE

CALIFORNIA-NEVADA

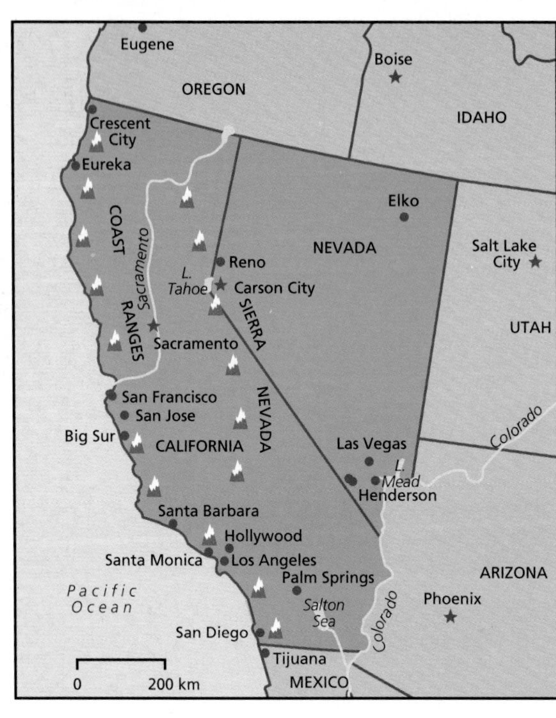

CALIFORNIA

Region: United States
Area: 411,012 km²
Capital: Sacramento
Airport: L.A. 24 km, San Francisco 21 km
Population: 30,000,000
Area codes: (213), (215), (619)
Best months: all year

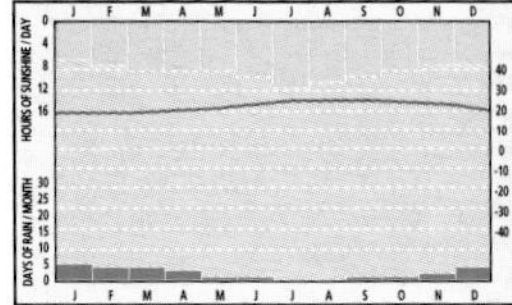

NEVADA

Region: United States
Area: 286,299 km²
Capital: Carson City
Airport: Las Vegas 13 km
Population: 1,202,000
Area code: (702)
Best months: all year

WHAT TO DO

Los Angeles, San Francisco, and Hollywood are the best-known cities in CALIFORNIA, but this state's reputation is based on its almost year-round sunshine. The Golden State is a land of mountains, beaches, deserts, forests, orchards, and vineyards. Cities with sunny names are dotted along the coast from San Diego to San Francisco, via Santa Barbara and Los Angeles. Joshua Tree National Park, the Sierra Nevada, and the very beautiful Yosemite Park offer incomparable natural marvels. The Napa Valley is a grape-growing region that attracts aficionados of California wines. In the middle of the NEVADA desert is Las Vegas, a city dedicated to gambling and fun, known for its casinos, nightclubs, and stage shows. But Las Vegas is not the only attraction in the state: Lake Mead; Mount Charles and its fabulous caverns; and Death Valley, offering an otherworldly landscape, must also be seen.

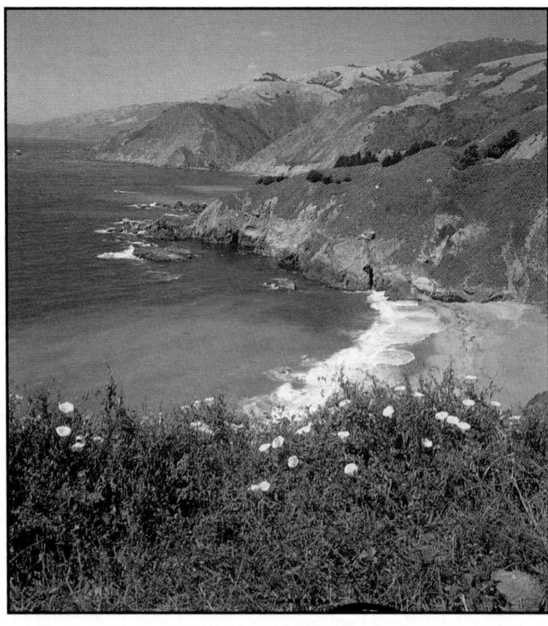

ZEPHYR / BUCHANAN / RÉFLEXION

THE ROCKIES

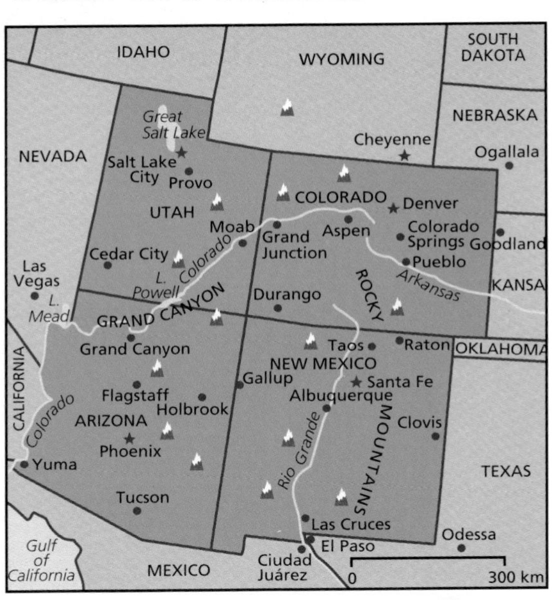

+1 0 -1 -2 -3

ARIZONA

Region: United States
Area: 295,014 km²
Capital: Phoenix
Airport: Phoenix 6 km
Population: 3,665,000
Area code: (602)
Best months: all year

+1 0 -1 -2 -3

COLORADO

Region: United States
Area: 270,000 km²
Capital: Denver
Airport: Denver 11 km
Population: 3,305,000
Area codes: (303), (719)
Best months: all year

+1 0 -1 -2 -3

NEW MEXICO

Region: United States
Area: 315,115 km²
Capital: Santa Fe
Airport: Albuquerque
Population: 1,515,000
Area code: (505)
Best months: all year

+1 0 -1 -2 -3

UTAH

Region: United States
Area: 219,932 km²
Capital: Salt Lake City
Airport: Salt Lake City 11 km
Population: 1,723,000
Area code: (801)
Best months: all year

WHAT TO DO

The best-known tourist attraction in the United States is no doubt the Grand Canyon, in ARIZONA. Travellers can visit this geological marvel in several different ways: by foot, plane, helicopter, or train. The rough, red and ochre rock and deep wind-carved valleys are incomparably beautiful. Monument Valley, home to the Navajo Indians, is a protected site. The museums in the city of Phoenix have excellent displays on the history of the Navajos and Hopis. Colorado Springs, COLORADO, in the heart of the Rocky Mountains, has earned a reputation as a first-class ski resort. The state also boasts many mineral-water springs which are very popular with vacationers. Other prime tourist attractions are the old troglodytic habitations in Mesa Verde National Park and the ghost towns that date from the gold rush. Half Spanish, half American, the state of NEW MEXICO blends its two cultures well:

P. HALLY

Santa Fe and Albuquerque have preserved many traces of the Spanish colonial era and erected monuments to the memory of the American conquest. The Rio Grande cuts the state in two and gives the countryside a unique ambience. UTAH is famous for its many national parks as well as for its Mormon populations, based in Salt Lake City, on the shores of Great Salt Lake. The parks at Canyonlands, Capitol Reef, Zion, and

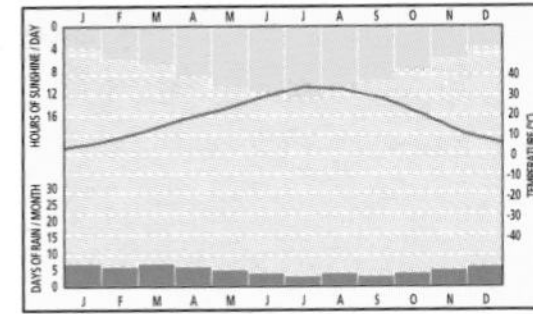

Glen Canyon are prime areas of natural beauty. The Dinosaur National Monument near Vernal is also a must-see.

MIDDLE AMERICA

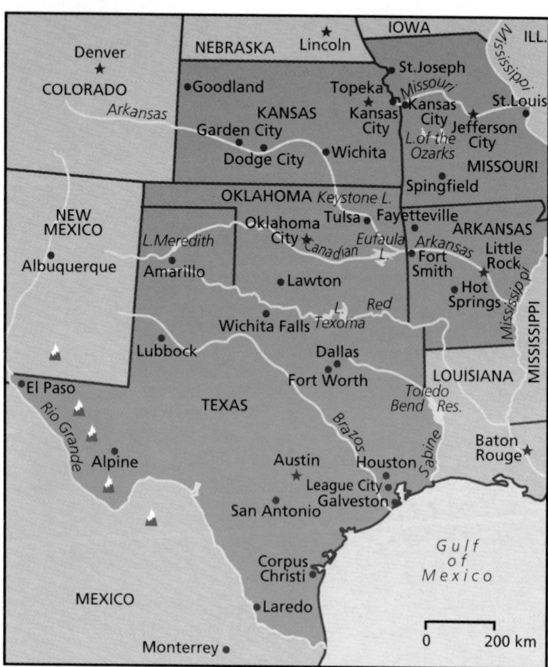

WHAT TO DO

There are many signs of the conquest of the West in ARKANSAS: Little Rock was one of the first sites settled by colonists. KANSAS, the geographical centre of the United States, is dominated by wheat fields. Dodge City recreates the ambience of the era of large ranches. The city of St. Louis, in MISSOURI, has preserved several reminders of its colonial past. The Ozark National Scenic Riverways is a major park and tourist attraction. OKLAHOMA is home to many Native tribes; tourists should not miss the Tulsa powwow in July or August. The second-largest state, after Alaska, TEXAS, nicknamed the Lone Star State, is a vast region of mountains, canyons, lakes, beaches, and ranches atop rich oil fields. El Paso is the gateway to the big canyons of Texas: Big Bend National Park, formed by the meanders of the Rio Grande, is worth a trip. The Guadalupe Mountains Park, a few kilometres east of El Paso, is a trekkers' paradise.

TEXAS

Region: United States
Area: 692,408 km²
Capital: Austin
Airport: Dallas 29 km, Houston 32 km
Population: 16,987,000
Area codes: (214), (713)
Best months: Feb, Mar, Apr, Oct

ARKANSAS

Region: United States
Area: 137,539 km²
Capital: Little Rock
Airport: Little Rock 7 km
Population: 2,399,000
Area code: (501)
Best months: Feb, Mar, Apr, Oct

KANSAS

Region: United States
Area: 213,095 km²
Capital: Topeka
Airport: Kansas City 29 km, Wichita 16 km
Population: 2,478,000
Area codes: (316), (913)
Best months: Feb, Mar, Apr, Oct

MISSOURI

Region: United States
Area: 180,456 km²
Capital: Jefferson City
Airport: St. Louis 16 km
Population: 5,117,000
Area codes: (314), (417), (816)
Best months: Feb, Mar, Apr, Oct

OKLAHOMA

Region: United States
Area: 181,090 km²
Capital: Oklahoma City
Airport: Oklahoma City
Population: 3,245,000
Area codes: (405), (918)
Best months: Feb, Mar, Apr, Oct

ZEPHYR / BUCHANAN / RÉFLEXION

SOUTHERN HEARTLAND

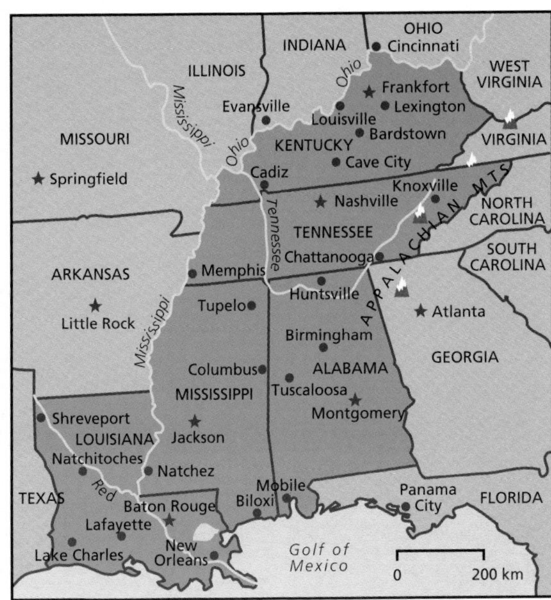

ALABAMA

Region: United States
Area: 105,145 km²
Capital: Montgomery
Airport: Montgomery, Birmingham
Population: 4,105,000
Area code: (205)
Best months: Feb, Mar, Apr, Oct

KENTUCKY

Region: United States
Area: 104,623 km²
Capital: Frankfort
Airport: Louisville 8 km
Population: 3,685,000
Area codes: (502), (606)
Best months: Feb, Mar, Apr, Oct

MISSISSIPPI

Region: United States
Area: 123,584 km²
Capital: Jackson
Airport: Jackson
Population: 2,573,000
Area code: (601)
Best months: Feb, Mar, Apr, Oct

WHAT TO DO

The South is synonymous with huge cotton plantations, Dixieland music, and bayous. In ALABAMA, it is, however, the beaches near Mobile and the Russel Cave National Monument that attract the most tourists. Beaches are also a big draw in KENTUCKY, a state best known for its thoroughbred horses, bourbon, and Fort Knox, where the U.S. government's gold is locked away. The full cultural and geographic charm of the South is revealed in Louisiana and Mississippi. In LOUISIANA, New Orleans is a prime destination: the French Quarter, with its colonial architecture, jazz, nightclubs, and sidewalk artists, makes the city one of a kind in North America. MISSISSIPPI dates from the era of the great cotton plantations, traces of which can be seen on a boat ride down the Mississippi River. The beaches on the Gulf of Mexico, especially those near Biloxi, are very popular. TENNESSEE, home of Nashville, paradise for country-music-lovers, and Graceland, Elvis Presley's home, have given this state its nickname of "The Music Capital". Smoky Mountain National Park is one of the most beautiful parks in the south, especially for travellers who relish dense forests.

TENNESSEE

Region: United States
Area: 109,412 km²
Capital: Nashville
Airport: Memphis 12 km
Population: 4,877,000
Area codes: (615), (901)
Best months: Feb, Mar, Apr, Oct

LOUISIANA

Region: United States
Area: 125,625 km²
Capital: Baton Rouge
Airport: New Orleans 18 km
Population: 4,220,000
Area codes: (318), (504)
Best months: Feb, Mar, Apr, Oct

ZEPHYR / BUCHANAN / RÉFLEXION

CRADLE OF THE U.S.A.

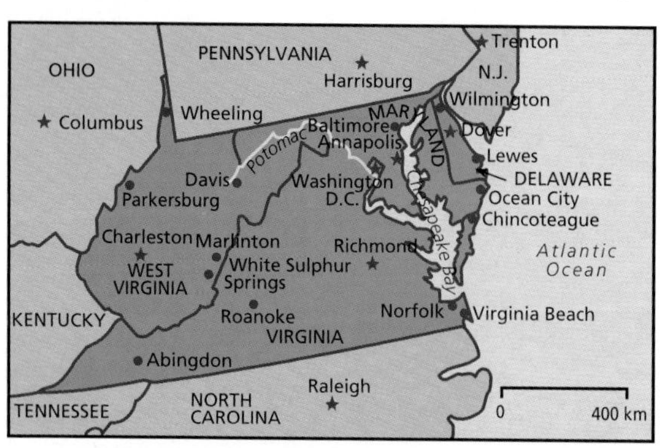

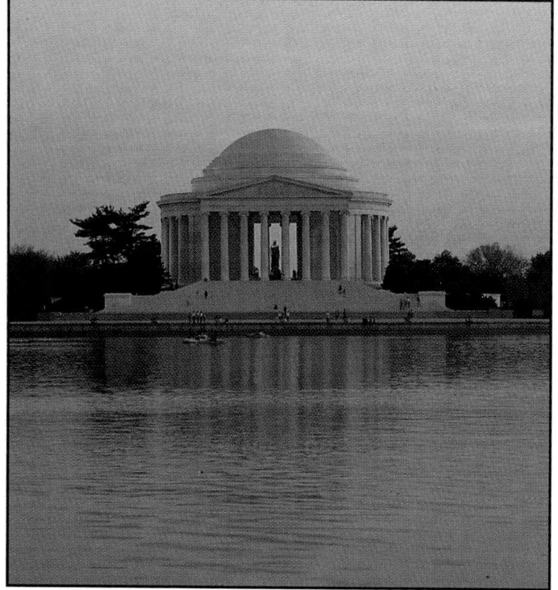

A. GARDON / RÉFLEXION

DELAWARE

Region: United States
Area: 6,138 km²
Capital: Dover
Airport: Wilmington
Population: 666,000
Area code: (302)
Best months: May to Oct

MARYLAND

Region: United States
Area: 31,296 km²
Capital: Annapolis
Airport: Baltimore 16 km
Population: 4,781,000
Area code: (301)
Best months: May to Oct

VIRGINIA

Region: United States
Area: 105,613 km²
Capital: Richmond
Airport: Richmond 10 km
Population: 6,187,000
Area codes: (703), (804)
Best months: May to Oct

WASHINGTON D.C.

Region: United States
Area: 163 km²
Capital: Washington
Airport: Washington-Dulles (Virginia) 40 km
Population: 607,000
Area code: (202)
Best months: May to Oct

WEST VIRGINIA

Region: United States
Area: 62,600 km²
Capital: Charleston
Airport: Charleston 6 km
Population: 1,793,000
Area code: (304)
Best months: May to Oct

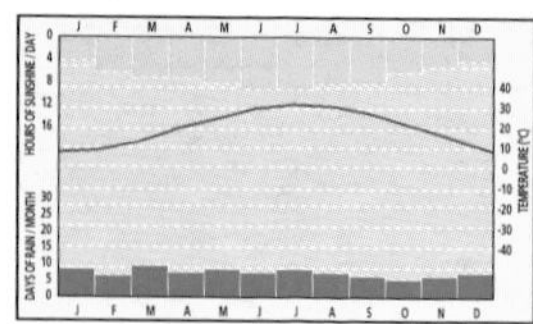

WHAT TO DO

The United States was conceived along this section of the east coast. Stories about George Washington, the first American president, are told throughout the region, wherever he set foot during the War of Independence. The main attraction in DELAWARE, however, is the Delaware Seashore State Park, famous for its beautiful beaches. In MARYLAND, the shores of Chesapeake Bay are a major draw for vacationers and water-sports lovers. The entire state rings this great bay. Ohio Canal National Park, the Assateague Island National Seashore, and Deep Creek Lake are all worth a visit. The city of Baltimore offers a variety of points of interest, including the Maryland Historical Museum and the lively old port. VIRGINIA contains the most sites related to the Civil War, notably in Richmond, Williamsburg, Yorktown, and Jamestown. Norfolk and Virginia Beach, on the Atlantic coast, are very popular holiday resorts. Running through WEST VIRGINIA are the Appalachian Mountains; this state features the Monongahela National Forest and several other beautiful national parks, including Bluestone and Pipestone. Mammoth Mound is an aboriginal holy sanctuary that draws the respect of visitors. In WASHINGTON, D.C., tourists flock to the White House, the Capitol, the Pentagon, and the superb Library of Congress. The American capital also has an impressive number of museums and art galleries; the National Gallery of Art is one of the city's most beautiful museums. Parks dot the lovely Potomac River, which winds scenically through the capital.

UNITED STATES TOURIST OFFICE

THE SOUTHEAST

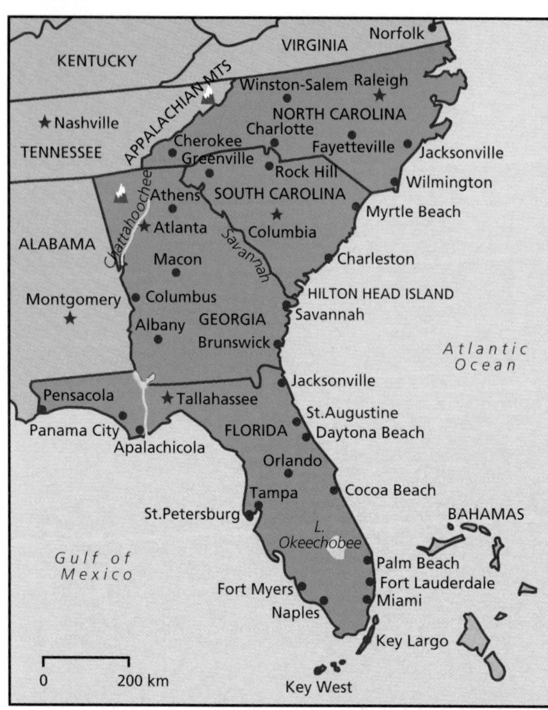

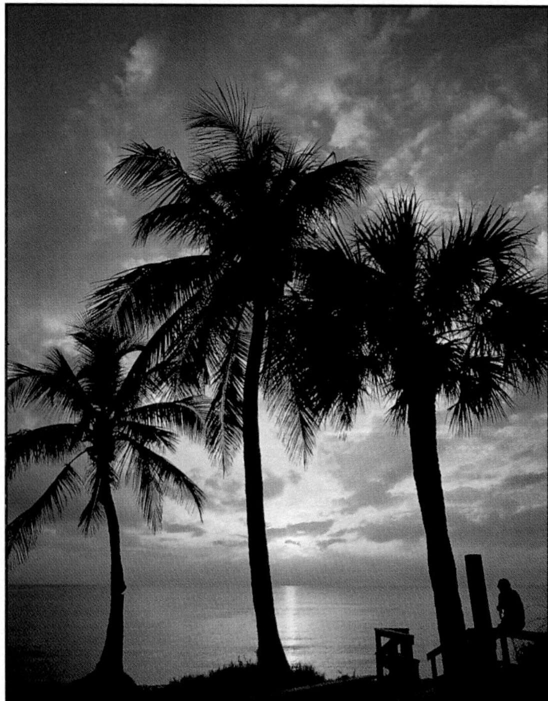

ZEPHYR / BUCHANAN / RÉFLEXION

NORTH CAROLINA

Region: United States
Area: 135,000 km²
Capital: Raleigh
Airport: Charlotte 11 km, Raleigh 23 km
Population: 6,629,000
Area codes: (704), (919)
Best months: Feb, Mar, Apr, Oct

SOUTH CAROLINA

Region: United States
Area: 79,176 km²
Capital: Columbia
Airport: Charleston 18 km
Population: 3,487,000
Area code: (803)
Best months: Feb, Mar, Apr, Oct

FLORIDA

Region: United States
Area: 151,940 km²
Capital: Tallahassee
Airport: Miami, Orlando, Tampa
Population: 12,938,000
Area codes: (305), (407), (813), (904)
Best months: Nov to Apr

GEORGIA

Region: United States
Area: 152,589 km²
Capital: Atlanta
Airport: Atlanta 14 km, Savannah 16 km
Population: 6,478,000
Area codes: (404), (912)
Best months: Dec to Apr

WHAT TO DO

The sun and pleasant climate are the top attractions in this part of the United States. The Southeast has thousands of kilometres of beaches, where the ocean can be calm and inviting or choppy and challenging. Swimmers, take your choice. NORTH CAROLINA is

well known for the beauty of Cape Hatteras National Seashore and the Outer Banks Islands. Inland, Great Smoky Mountains National Park provides a pleasant alternative to water sports. In SOUTH CAROLINA, the beaches from Myrtle Beach to Hilton Head Island deserve their reputations as the most beautiful on the eastern seaboard. A series of national parks protect the shoreline and a variety of other habitats; the Congaree Swamp National Park is especially interesting for its exotic fauna. FLORIDA, the Sunshine State, is known worldwide as a winter destination. Its golf courses and beaches are, of course, wonderful, but there is much more to this state: charming towns with a Spanish flavour such as St. Augustine; the Keys, including the famous Key West; the magnificent Everglades Park; Cape Canaveral; Universal Studios, where feature films are shot; and, of course, Walt Disney World, Epcot Center, and the Magic Kingdom. Golfers love the state for the quality and quantity of its courses. There are many amusement and theme parks; Büsch Garden offers a microcosm of American flora and fauna. The large cities of Miami, Orlando, and Tampa offer restaurants, museums, department stores, and theatres to please every taste. In GEORGIA, there are sunny coasts and windswept mountain peaks. The Blue Ridge Mountains run through the state to Okefenokee Swamp, a wildlife sanctuary. Atlanta and Savannah, Georgia's two largest cities, are worth a visit—Savannah for its typically Georgian architecture; Atlanta, for its vitality.

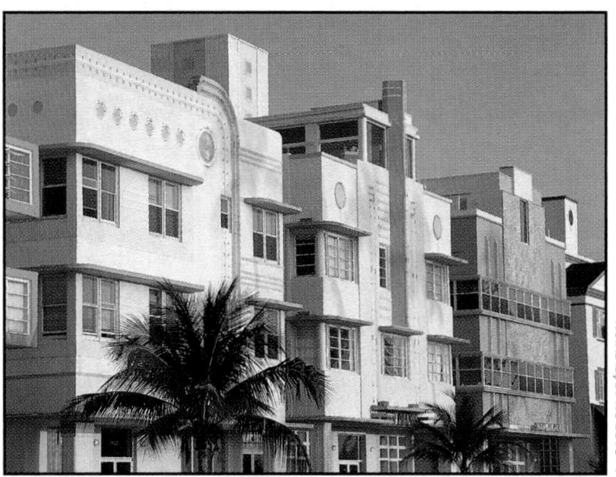

A. GARDON / RÉFLEXION

HAWAII

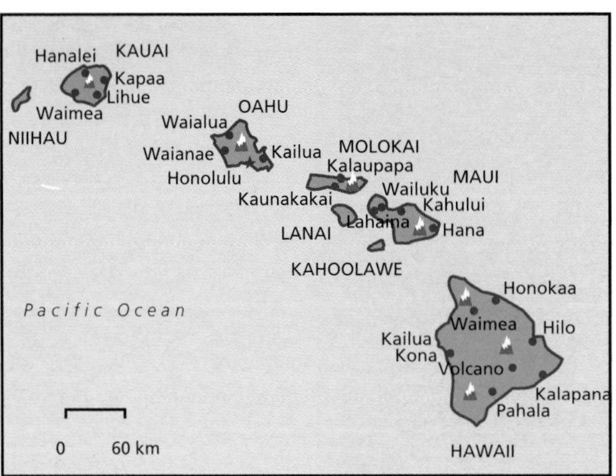

Region: Pacific Ocean
Area: 16,764 km²
Capital: Honolulu
Airport: Honolulu 14 km
Population: 1,108,000
Area code: (808)
Best months: May to Oct

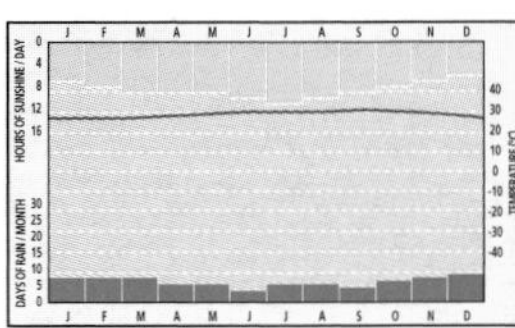

HAWAII

WHAT TO DO

Once populated by Polynesians, the islands of Hawaii became part of the United States in 1893 and gained statehood in 1959. Since Hawaii is separated from the mainland by the immense Pacific Ocean, it has not lost its Polynesian roots, evident in the names of the islands (Oahu, Maui, Kauai, and Molokai) and in the style in which residents enjoy the lovely climate. Travellers who go to Hawaii expect to see crystal waters, palm trees weighed down with coconuts, and smiling dancers in grass skirts. But there is more: magnificent waterfalls on Oahu, exotic fruit plantations on Hawaii, spectacular volcanoes on Maui, and fantastic sea life in the waters around each island. The city of Honolulu, on Oahu, is the stepping-off point for most tours of the islands. Sea Life Park, the Polynesian Cultural Center, the beach at Waikiki, and the solemn memorial at Pearl Harbor are all must-sees. Visitors can familiarize themselves with the history of the islands by visiting the city's many museums.

T. BOGNAR / RÉFLEXION

WEST INDIES

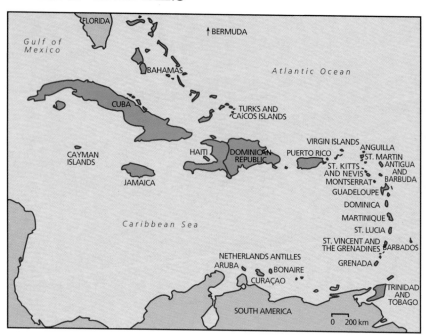

FLORIDA
BERMUDA
Gulf of Mexico
BAHAMAS
Atlantic Ocean
CUBA
TURKS AND CAICOS ISLANDS
VIRGIN ISLANDS
ANGUILLA
ST. MARTIN
ANTIGUA AND BARBUDA
CAYMAN ISLANDS
HAITI
DOMINICAN REPUBLIC
PUERTO RICO
ST. KITTS AND NEVIS
MONTSERRAT
JAMAICA
GUADELOUPE
DOMINICA
MARTINIQUE
Caribbean Sea
ST. LUCIA
ST. VINCENT AND THE GRENADINES
BARBADOS
NETHERLANDS ANTILLES
ARUBA
BONAIRE
CURAÇAO
GRENADA
TRINIDAD AND TOBAGO
SOUTH AMERICA
0 200 km

The first European explorers to reach the Caribbean islands thought that they had sailed around the world and landed in India, hence the region's name. Discovered by the Spanish, the West Indies were later colonized by the French, the English, and the Dutch, all of whom regarded the peaceful islands as heaven on earth. Travellers still escape to their crystalline waters and explore their lush, tropical forests. The warmth of the welcome extended by West Indians is equalled only by the passion with which they celebrate their islands, which feature a wealth of extraordinary landscapes and fascinating historical sites.

BERMUDA

BERMUDA

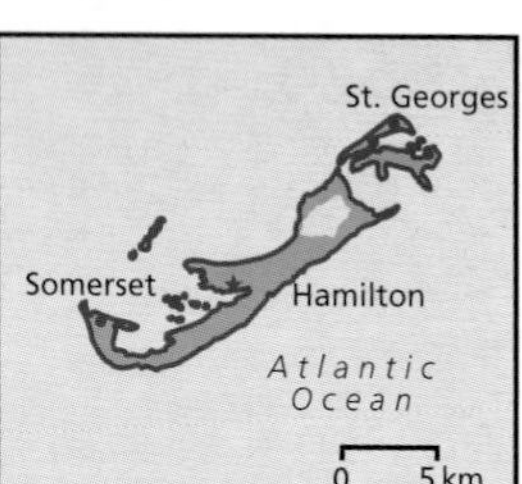

Region: North Atlantic
Area: 50 km²
Capital: Hamilton
Airport: Hamilton 19 km
Population: 61,160
Language: English
Religions: Anglican, Catholic
Government: British Crown colony
Voltage: 110 - 60
Vaccinations required: –
Vaccinations recommended: –
Passport: not required
Visa: not required
Currency: Bermudan dollar
$1Cdn: .74 dollar
Driving: left hand
International permit: recommended
Area code: 011-809
✆ from Canada: 1-800-363-4099
✆ to Canada: ■1-800-744-2580
Accommodation: ★★★★
Restaurants: ★★★★
Transportation: ★★★
Cost of living: ○○○
UN rank: –
Best months: June to Oct
Holidays: 1, 2 Jan; 14, 16 Apr; 22, 24 May; 19 June; 27, 28 July; 4 Sept; 13 Nov; 25, 26 Dec

WHAT TO DO

Bermudans are well known for their love affair with golf, and their courses are among the most famous in the world! But travellers who come here will also be enchanted by the pink-sand beaches, the caverns carved by the sea, the coral reefs, and charming little port towns. St. George and especially Hamilton, the capital, retain the style and ambience of the British colonial period; visitors will see not only typically English "bobbies" walking the beat, but also cricket matches. Forts dot the countryside of Bermuda Island: Fort Hamilton, St. Catherine Fort, and Gates Fort. Staying in bed-and-breakfasts is one of the best ways to discover the nooks and crannies of the island, and to encounter the warmth and friendliness of Bermudans.

WHAT TO BUY

Lobster is the most popular food in Bermuda. Outerbridge Sherry Pepper hot sauce is usually added to fish and seafood stews. Craftspeople make beautiful pottery, cedar sculptures, and printed fabrics.Painters find ample inspiration in the beauty of the scenery.

BERMUDA TOURIST OFFICE

BAHAMAS

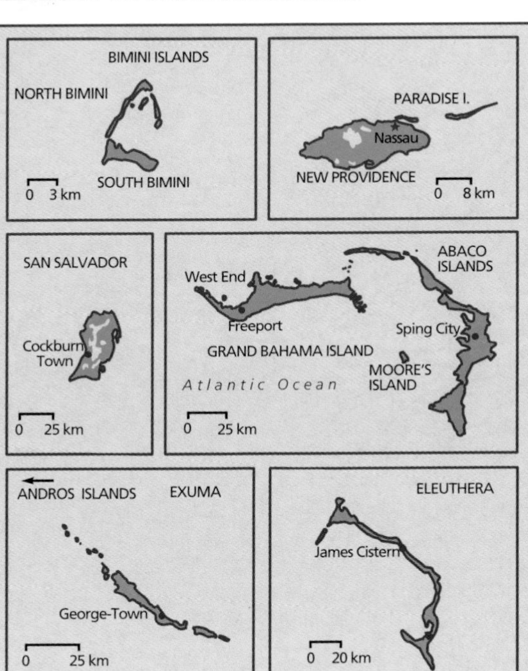

Region: West Indies
Area: 13,935 km²
Capital: Nassau
Airport: Nassau 16 km
Population: 273,060
Languages: English, Créole
Religions: Baptist, Anglican, Catholic
Government: parliamentary democracy
Voltage: 120 - 60
Vaccinations required: Yf*
Vaccinations recommended: –
Passport: not required
Visa: not required
Currency: Bahamian dollar
$1Cdn: .74 dollar
Driving: left hand
International permit: recommended
Area code: 011-809
✆ **from Canada:** 1-800-463-0585
✆ **to Canada:** 1-800-463-0501
Accommodation: ★★★★★
Restaurants: ★★★★★
Transportation: ★★★★
Cost of living: ○○○
UN rank: 36
Best months: Apr to Sept
Holidays: 1, 2 Jan; 14, 16, 17 Apr; 2, 4, 5 June; 10 July; 7 Aug; 25, 26 Dec

WHAT TO DO

Some historians believe that it was on the island of San Salvador that Christopher Columbus first set foot on North American soil, on October 12, 1492. The other 700 islands of the Bahamas also enjoyed a rich history, and vestiges of Spanish, English, and French occupations can be seen everywhere. But people go to the Bahamas for the beautiful beaches and the tranquil towns and villages. Nassau, the capital, is the perfect place to relax, and to explore the botanical gardens, the bazaars, and the casinos. The deep waters off the Andros and Bimini island chains offer superb fishing, while the bays and straits around the islands of Exuma are ideal for sailing. The national park of Exuma, with its exotic flora and fauna is a must-see for nature-lovers; the Abaco Islands are paradise for golfers; and Long Island is a favourite destination among surfers.

WHAT TO BUY

Rum is a specialty of the Bahamas.

Turtle stew is a very delicate dish, but some prefer to avoid it so as not to contribute further to the declining turtle populations.

Among the typically Bahamian crafts are woven baskets, pottery, wooden sculptures, and coral and shell jewelry.

J F M A M J J A S O N D
HOURS OF SUNSHINE / DAY: 0 4 8 12 16
TEMPERATURE (°C): 40 30 20 10 0 -10 -20 -30 -40
DAYS OF RAIN / MONTH: 30 25 20 15 10 5 0
J F M A M J J A S O N D

T. BOGNAR / RÉFLEXION

TURKS AND CAICOS

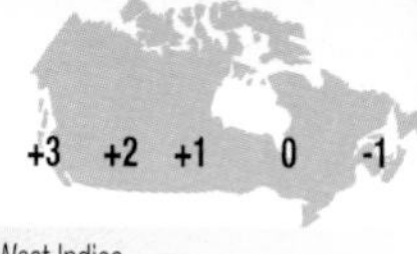

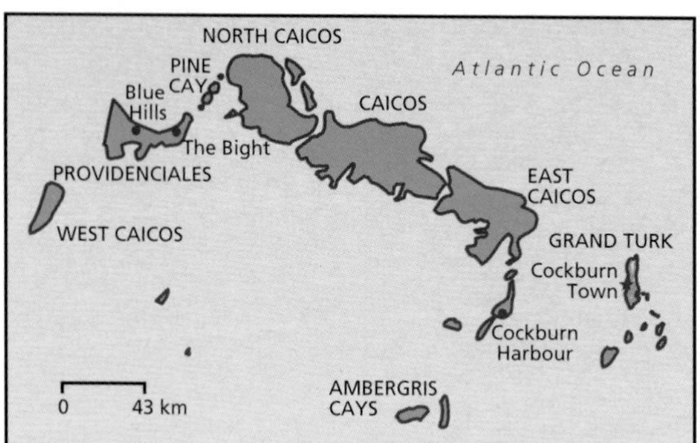

TURKS AND CAICOS

Region: West Indies
Area: 430 km²
Capital: Cockburn Town
Airport: Grand Turk
Population: 13,560
Language: English
Religions: Baptist, Anglican
Government: British dependent territory
Voltage: 220 - 50
Vaccinations required: Yf*
Vaccinations recommended: Ty, Po
Passport: not required
Visa: not required
Currency: U.S. dollar
$1Cdn: .74 dollar
Driving: left hand
International permit: recommended
Area code: 011-809
✆ from Canada: –
✆ to Canada: ■01-800-744-2580
Accommodation: ★★★★
Restaurants: ★★★★
Transportation: ★★★
Cost of living: ○○
UN rank: –
Best months: Feb, Mar, Apr
Holidays: 1, 2 Jan; 13 Mar; 14, 16, 17 Apr; 29 May; 12 June; 7, 30 Aug; 12, 23 Oct; 25, 26

WHAT TO DO

The tourism industry on the Turks and Caicos Islands has not spoiled the beauty of the beaches and villages. There are still places where residents offer visitors boat rides to admire secret caves and little-known but gorgeous bays. The Caicos Islands are the main destination, mostly because of Providenciales, the best-known tourist centre. The other Caicos Islands offer paradises of exotic birds and sandy beaches, and extremely beautiful underwater scenery. Magnificent fish spawn in the multicoloured coral reef in Caicos Cays National Underwater Park, on the shores of Pine Cay; of course, fishing is forbidden. The Turks Islands are smaller than the Caicos, but the splendour of the sea around them makes the trip worthwhile. Grand Turk Island, and especially lively Cockburn Town, draws not just divers but also those interested in colonial architecture.

WHAT TO BUY

The sea provides not just food for the islands' restaurants but also the raw materials—pearls, coral, and shells—with which craftspeople make jewelry and ornaments. A gift of stamps from the Turks and Caicos Islands will delight any philatelist.

J. HUARD

CUBA

+3 +2 +1 0 -1

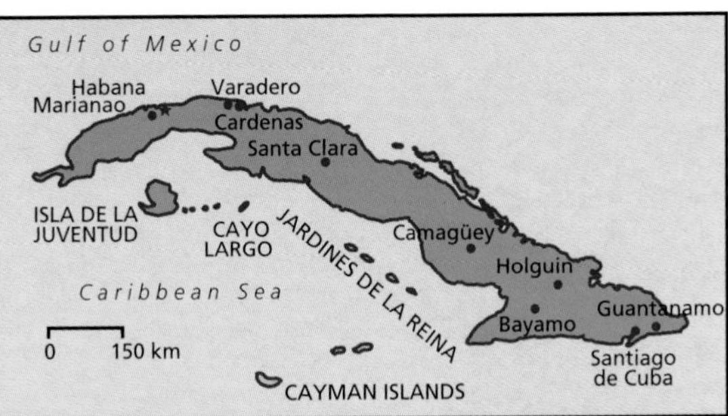

Region: West Indies
Area: 110,860 km²
Capital: Havana
Airport: Havana 18 km
Population: 11,064,350
Language: Spanish
Religion: Catholic (atheist country)
Government: single-party socialism
Voltage: 110/220 - 60
Vaccinations required: –
Vaccinations recommended: Ty, Po
Passport: required
Visa: required
Currency: Cuban peso
$1Cdn: .55 peso
Driving: right hand
International permit: recommended
Area code: 011-53
✆ from Canada: –
✆ to Canada: –
Accommodation: ★★★★
Restaurants: ★★★★
Transportation: ★★★
Cost of living: ❍❍
UN rank: 89
Best months: Dec to Apr
Holidays: 1 Jan; 1 May; 26 July; 10 Oct

CUBA

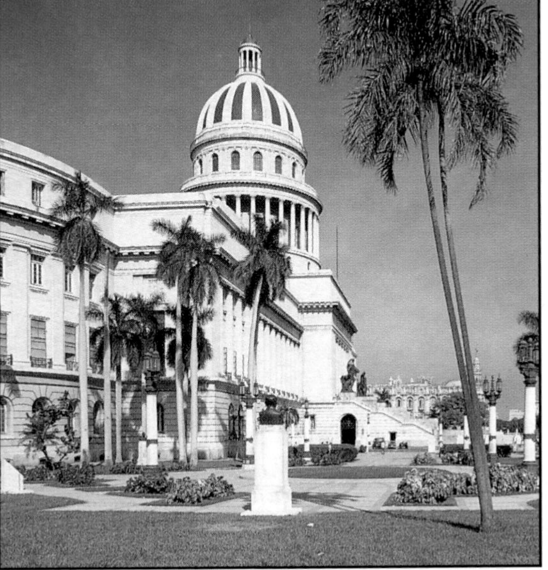

WHAT TO DO

Cuba, the largest island in the West Indies, is located a little less than 145 km from the southernmost point of Florida. A mountainous terrain of pine and mahogany forest covers more than a quarter of the island, making it an ideal habitat for birds. Cuba's beaches, wildlife, climate, and historical sites make it an excellent resort destination. More than 280 beaches are found on the island, the most beautiful of which are at Varadero, Cayo Largo, Playa Giron, and Maria del Portillo. Many exotic birds, including the *tocororo* (the national bird), live in the national park on the Península de Zapata. The inland marshes are also home to a wide variety of birds and *jicoteas*, small freshwater tortoises. La Habana (Havana) is known for its wealth of historical sites, especially the old town which offers many vestiges of the Spanish conquest. The caves at Bellamar, near Varadero, and Cienfuegos, a charming colonial town, are rivalled in interest by only Santiago de Cuba, a town best known for its carnival in July. The Vinales Valley produces some of the best tobacco in the world, and its *mogotes* (irregular buttes) make it a unique natural site.

WHAT TO BUY

Havana cigars are, without doubt, the best purchase in Cuba. Of course, the rum, the typical Cuban shirts (*guayaberas*), and the items made of mahogany are also popular purchases. *Tropicana* evenings are punctuated with the exotic beat of the Cuban drum, the *conga*.

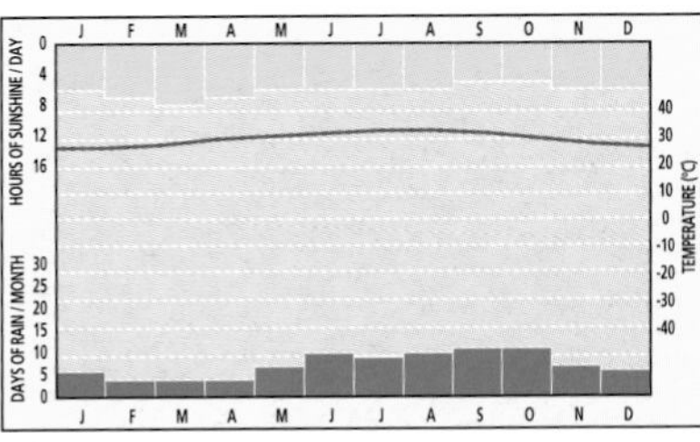

CAYMAN ISLANDS

+3 +2 +1 0 +1

CAYMAN ISLANDS

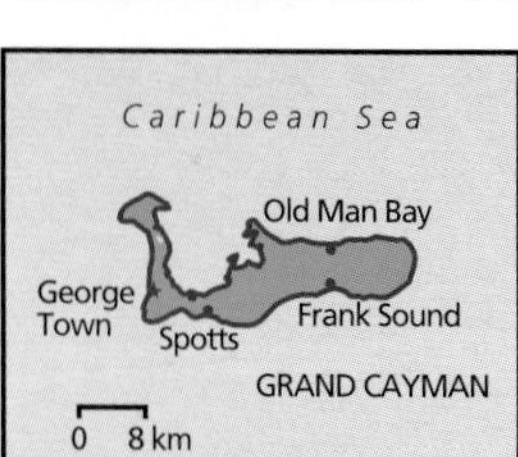

Region: West Indies
Area: 260 km²
Capital: George Town
Airport: George Town
Population: 31,800
Language: English
Religions: Presbyterian, Anglican
Government: British dependent territory
Voltage: 110 - 60
Vaccinations required: –
Vaccinations recommended: –
Passport: not required
Visa: not required
Currency: Cayman Islands dollar
$1Cdn: .61 dollar
Driving: left hand
International permit: required
Area code: 011-809
✆ from Canada: 1-800-263-6402
✆ to Canada: ■1-800-744-2580
Accommodation: ★★★★
Restaurants: ★★★★
Transportation: ★★★
Cost of living: ○○○
UN rank: –
Best months: Sept to Apr
Holidays: 1 Jan; 1 Mar; 14, 16, 17 Apr; 15 May; 19 June; 3 July; 6 Nov; 25, 26 Dec

WHAT TO DO

Some say that Seven Mile Beach, north of George Town, is the most beautiful stretch of shoreline in the West Indies: a coral reef protects the coast, and the Caribbean Sea is always warm and calm. The tourism industry has not destroyed the charm of the beaches and countryside, as has occurred in other places. In Bodden Town, visitors can see the "Chinese Wall" of Grand Cayman, an imposing stone structure erected in the seventeenth century to protect the inhabitants against pirates. The island's turtle farm is the only one of its kind in the world; it raises turtles for local consumption. Before eating turtle, make sure that it comes from the farm, since the wild turtles that live in the ocean depths near Grand Cayman, Little Cayman, and Brac are an endangered species. Divers come to the islands to discover underwater splendours such as the coral reef southwest of Grand Cayman. Splendid birds and iguanas live on Brac and Little Cayman.

WHAT TO BUY

Turtle steak, turtle soup, and seafood soups are specialties of the Cayman Islands. Again, make sure the turtle comes from the local farm before ordering. It is not recommended to encourage the trade in jewelry made of tortoise shell or any object produced from iguana skin. Local craftspeople do offer an abundance of shell jewelry and straw hats. The Caymans, known for being a tax haven, are a duty-free zone: luxury items such as perfumes or cameras can be purchased at low prices. But your best souvenirs will no doubt be the photographs you take.

JAMAICA

+3 +2 +1 0 -1

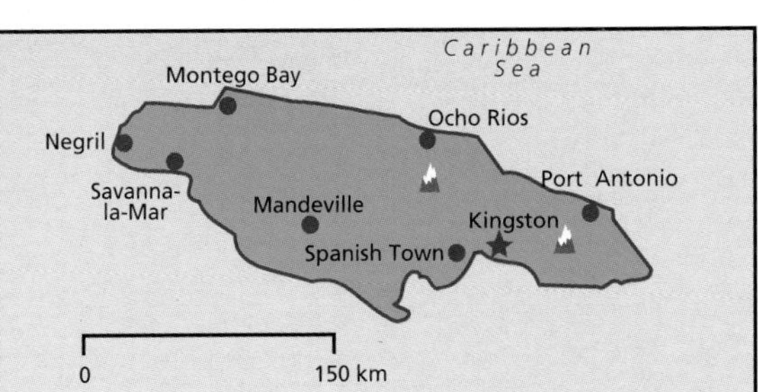

Region: West Indies
Area: 10,990 km²
Capital: Kingston
Airport: Kingston 17 km
Population: 2,555,070
Languages: English, Créole
Religion: Protestant
Government: parliamentary democracy
Voltage: 110/220 - 50
Vaccinations required: Yf*
Vaccinations recommended: Ty, Po
Passport: not required
Visa: not required
Currency: Jamaican dollar
$1Cdn: 25.36 dollars
Driving: left hand
International permit: required
Area code: 011-809
✆ from Canada: 1-800-463-2403
✆ to Canada: 800-222-0016
Accommodation: ★★★★
Restaurants: ★★★★
Transportation: ★★★
Cost of living: ○○
UN rank: 65
Best months: Dec to Apr
Holidays: 1, 2 Jan; 1 Mar; 14, 16, 17 Apr; 23 May; 7 Aug; 16 Oct; 25, 26 Dec

JAMAICA

WHAT TO DO

The name *Xamaica* comes from the Arawak language and means "country of springs and woods". One could easily add "country of mountains and steep ravines". The Blue Mountains rise to an altitude of 2,256 m, then stretch out into crevassed hills of cascading waterfalls and luxuriant vegetation. The mountains slope down to superb beaches, among the most beautiful in the West Indies. Montego Bay is well known for its clear water and view of the coral reefs that extend around the island. The beaches at Doctor's Cave and Cornwall are the most popular on the island. Birdwatchers will love Rockland Feeding Station, where they can observe the most colourful and exotic species in the West Indies. The villages along the north coast are renowned for their friendliness, especially Ocho Rios, which has become a popular resort town. Port Antonio draws visitors for its majestic estates dating back to the era of the great plantations, and for its rivers full of fish. Kingston, the capital, is the cultural centre of Jamaica. Its prime attractions include the National Gallery of Art and the White Marl Museum, which has a good exhibition on the history of the Arawak Indians. Golfers will love the courses outside of Kingston. Spanish Town and Mandeville are lively and interesting towns; the first for its Spanish ruins, the other for its numerous citrus groves.

WHAT TO BUY

Some of the best coffee in the world is grown on the slopes of the Blue Mountains, and Jamaican rum is of equally high quality. The cuisine is not for those who like their food bland—a sip of rum helps douse the flames of the spicy food. Tia Maria is a liqueur produced on the island, as is Rumona, a rum-based liqueur. The craft centre in the town of Negril offers a wide assortment of necklaces, bracelets, and embroidered caps. The reggae festival in July is a not-to-be-missed event. Beware: travellers are often offered drugs but their consumption is punishable by a jail sentence.

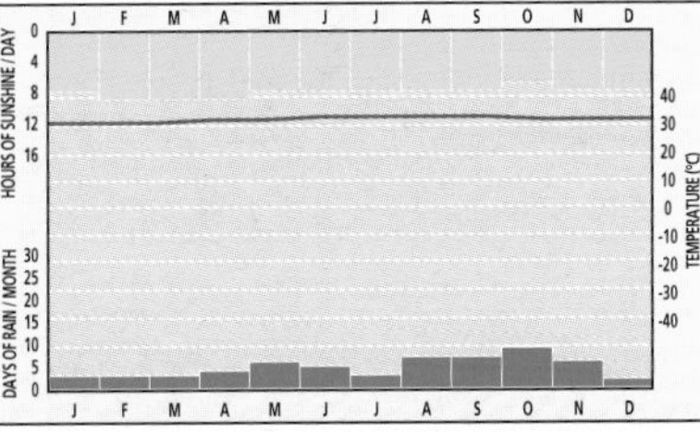

V. PHILLIPS / RÉFLEXION

HAITI

HAITI

+4 +3 +2 +1 0

Region: West Indies
Area: 27,750 km²
Capital: Port-au-Prince
Airport: Port-au-Prince 13 km
Population: 6,591,450
Languages: French, Créole
Religion: Catholic
Government: presidential
Voltage: 110 - 60
Vaccinations required: Yf*
Vaccinations recommended: Ty, Po, Mal
Passport: required
Visa: required
Currency: gourde
$1Cdn: 10.97 gourdes
Driving: right hand
International permit: recommended
Area code: 011-509
✆ from Canada: –
✆ to Canada: 001-800-522-1055
Accommodation: ★★
Restaurants: ★★
Transportation: ★
Cost of living: ○○
UN rank: 137
Best months: Dec to Apr
Holidays: 1, 2 Jan; 26 Feb; 14 Apr; 1, 18, 25 May; 15 June; 15 Aug; 17, 24 Oct; 1, 18 Nov; 5, 25 Dec

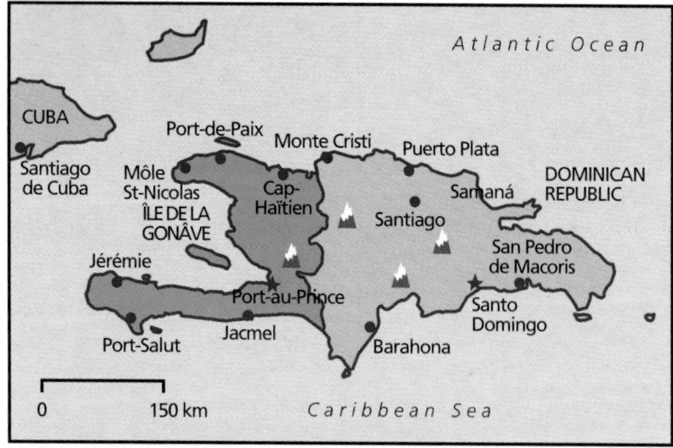

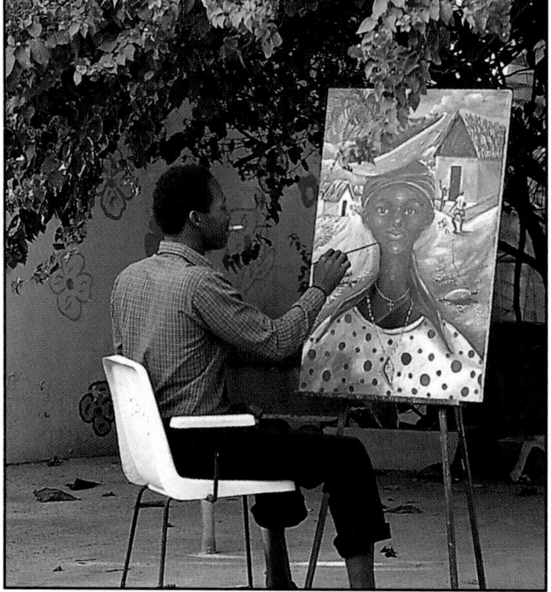

RÉFLEXION

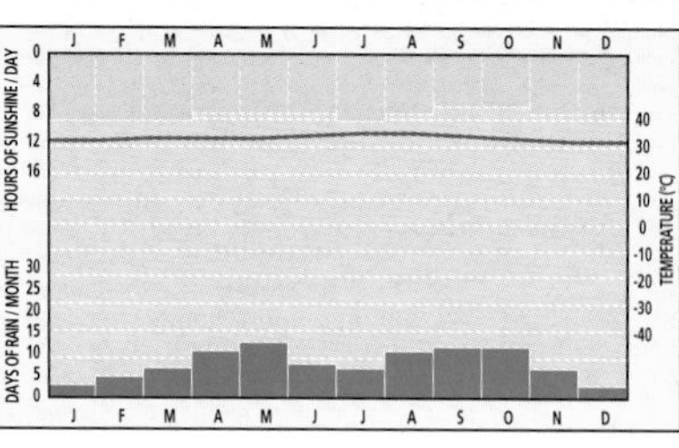

WHAT TO DO

President Aristide inherited the difficult task of putting Haiti back on its feet: he must restore the devastated economy and improve living conditions. Fortunately, Haitians are a proud and courageous people. Given time, they will surely rebuild their colourful towns and open their sunny beaches to tourists. The name Haiti comes from *Ayti*, meaning "mountain in the sea", an apt description of the island's mountainous topography, the highest point of which is Pic de la Selle, with an altitude of 2,640 m. There is not much wildlife left in Haiti, but there are still beautiful and unusual plants. Port-au-Prince and the smaller towns, like Cap-Haïtien, in the north part of the island, and Jacmel, in the south, are known not only for their interesting historical sites but also for their luxuriant forests and sandy beaches. Haiti is not in a position to welcome tourists at this time; let us hope that the situation will change soon.

WHAT TO BUY

To encourage Haiti's economic recovery, one can purchase the superb paintings by Haitian naive artists, which express all the colour and passion of the Haitian soul. To get into the mood of the hot Haitian nights, read Jacques Roumain's *Gouverneurs de la rosée*.

DOMINICAN REPUBLIC

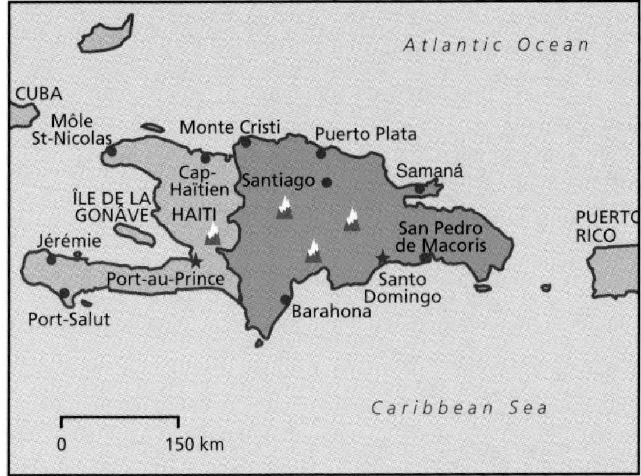

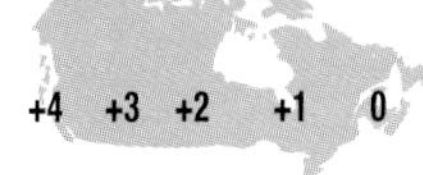

DOMINICAN REPUBLIC

Region: West Indies
Area: 48,730 km²
Capital: Santo Domingo
Airport: Santo Domingo 30 km
Population: 7,826,100
Languages: Spanish, English
Religion: Catholic
Government: presidential democracy
Voltage: 110 - 60
Vaccinations required: –
Vaccinations recommended: Ty, Po, Mal
Passport: required
Visa: not required
Currency: Dominican Republic peso
$1Cdn: 9.27 pesos
Driving: right hand
International permit: recommended
Area code: 011-809
✆ from Canada: 1-800-463-3958
✆ to Canada: 1-800-333-0111
Accommodation: ★★★★
Restaurants: ★★★
Transportation: ★★★
Cost of living: ○○
UN rank: 96
Best months: Dec to Apr
Holidays: 1, 2, 23, 26 Jan; 27 Feb; 14, 16, 17 Apr; 1 May; 15 June; 16 Aug; 25 Sept; 12 Oct; 25 Dec

DOMINICAN REPUBLIC TOURIST OFFICE

WHAT TO DO

More than 60 per cent of Dominicans still live below the poverty line. Travellers to the Dominican Republic who venture beyond the tourism centres will discover not only the evidence of this poverty, but also a land full of mountains, plains, and hills where sparkling rivers flow. The small towns, such as Higüey, Samaná, and Azua, exude West Indian charm, notably for their uncrowded beaches and friendly inhabitants, but the more popular vacation resorts, such as Puerto Plata, Cayo Levantado, and Playa Dorada are still very pleasant. La Romana is a larger town with a very lively artists' quarter. Of course, the capital, Santo Domingo, offers many attractions: Santa Maria La Menor Cathedral, Alcazar Fortress, and several museums devoted to the history of one of the oldest cities in the Americas. The mountainous region around Pico Duarte, with an altitude of 3,090 m, is heaven for climbers and hikers. Rolling hills surround these mountains, and ever-changing flora carpet the countryside.

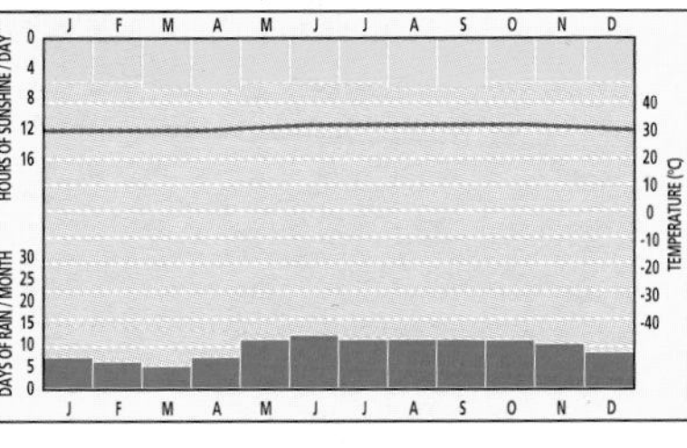

WHAT TO BUY

Pork and chicken are served with rice or black beans: the national dish is *chicharrones de pollo* (fried chicken) served with *moro de habicuelas* (rice and beans). Dominican coffee, cacao, and rum are of the highest quality. The north side of the island is rich in amber, with which jewelry, everyday objects, and works of art are made.

PUERTO RICO

+4 +3 +2 +1 0

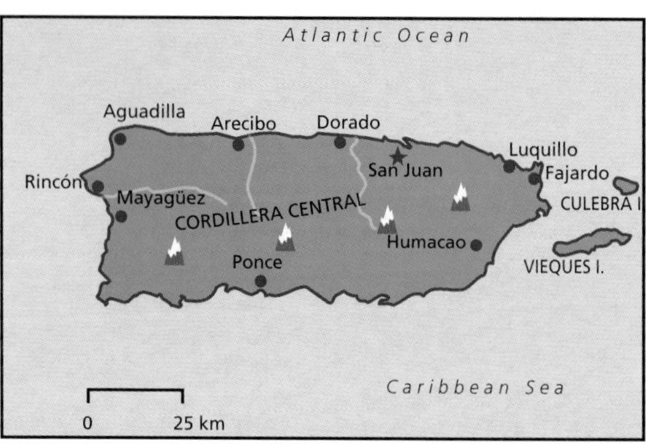

Region: West Indies
Area: 9,104 km²
Capital: San Juan
Airport: San Juan 14 km
Population: 3,802,000
Languages: Spanish, English
Religion: Catholic
Government: territory of the U.S.
Voltage: 110 - 60
Vaccinations required: –
Vaccinations recommended: Ty, Po
Passport: not required
Visa: not required
Currency: U.S. dollar
$1Cdn: .74 dollar
Driving: right hand
International permit: required
Area code: 011-809
✆ from Canada: 1-800-463-8909
✆ to Canada: 1-800-496-7123
Accommodation: ★★★★
Restaurants: ★★★★
Transportation: ★★★★
Cost of living: ○○
UN rank: –
Best months: Jan to May
Holidays: 1, 16 Jan; 12, 20 Feb; 14, 16 Apr; 29 May; 4, 25 July; 4 Sept; 9 Oct; 11 Nov; 25, 26 Dec

PUERTO RICO

WHAT TO DO

Puerto Rico, a commonwealth territory of the United States, is an ideal tourist destination. It combines the charm and casual atmosphere of the West Indies with the familiar comforts of the United States. In spite of this, Puerto Ricans have their own distinct culture, and most speak both Spanish and English. The old section of San Juan is more than 450 years old, and the El Morro and San Cristobal forts, surrounded by the city's high walls, date back to the Spanish conquest. The architecture of Old San Juan is particularly pretty, characterized by pastel-coloured houses and finely ornamented façades such as those at Plaza de San José and Plaza de Armas. San Jose Church, believed to be the oldest religious building in the New World, is an absolute must-see. The Puerto Rico Art Museum and the Pablo Casals Museum are also worth visiting. A few kilometres away from the capital, on the slopes of El Yunque, is a magnificent bird sanctuary. At night, the waters of Bahía Fosforescénte (Phosphorescent Bay) glow with an eerily beautiful light. The town of Ponce is known for its excellent art museum and the Guadalupe Cathedral, and the small town of San Germán is considered one of the most charming spots on the island. The highest mountain in the Cordillera Central is Cerro de Punta, with an altitude of 1,348 m. There's a challenge for hikers!

WHAT TO BUY

With its Spanish influence, Puerto Rican cuisine is based largely on rice, beans, and chicken: *arroz con pollo* (a chicken and rice dish) and *paella* (rice and seafood) are on all the menus. Puerto Rican rum is often served with fruit juices, like the famous piña colada, made with pineapple juice and coconut milk. Hand-rolled cigars and *santos* (statuettes representing saints and biblical characters) are unique to Puerto Rico.

J F M A M J J A S O N D
HOURS OF SUNSHINE / DAY: 0 4 8 12 16
TEMPERATURE (°C): 40 30 20 10 0 -10 -20 -30 -40
DAYS OF RAIN / MONTH: 30 25 20 15 10 5 0

A. GARDON / RÉFLEXION

AMERICAN VIRGIN ISLANDS

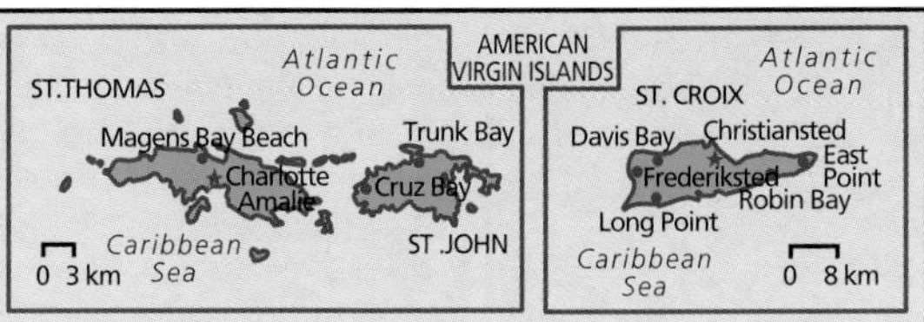

Region: West Indies
Area: 352 km^2
Capital: Charlotte Amalie
Airport: Charlotte Amalie 3 km
Population: 97,570
Languages: English, Spanish
Religions: Baptist, Catholic
Government: unincorporated U.S. territory
Voltage: 110 - 60
Vaccinations required: –
Vaccinations recommended: –
Passport: not required
Visa: not required
Currency: U.S. dollar
$1Cdn: .74 dollar
Driving: left hand
International permit: recommended
Area code: 011-809
✆ from Canada: 1-800-463-4812
✆ to Canada: ■1-800-496-0008
Accommodation: ★★★★
Restaurants: ★★★★
Transportation: ★★★
Cost of living: ○○○
UN rank: –
Best months: Feb, Mar, Apr
Holidays: 1 Jan; 12, 20 Feb; 31 Mar; 16 Apr; 29 May; 4 July; 4 Sept; 9 Oct; 25, 26 Dec

WHAT TO DO

Purchased by the United States from Denmark in 1917 for $25 million, the Virgin Islands have become a major vacation resort, especially Magens Bay, on the north coast of St. Thomas Island, one of the most beautiful bays in the West Indies. The islands of St. John and St. Croix still have a Danish flavour, notably, in the names of the towns and villages (such as Christiansted and Frederiksted). Charlotte Amalie is a unique town, with its flagstone streets, its shops, and its bay, where magnificent yachts anchor. The golf courses are drawing more and more players. St. John is the least populous island—except for the thousands of birds that nest in the National Park, and the underwater flora and fauna in Trunk Bay. Some vestiges of the Arawak Indians remain, especially at Petroglyph Falls.

WHAT TO BUY

The cuisine of the Virgin Islands uses the best the sea has to offer: the specialty is a fish soup made with whatever fresh seafood is available that day. Rum is, of course, the favourite drink, especially the rum made in the St. Thomas distilleries. The crafts are often inspired by ancient Arawak traditions. The duty-free boutiques are very popular with tourists.

BRITISH VIRGIN ISLANDS

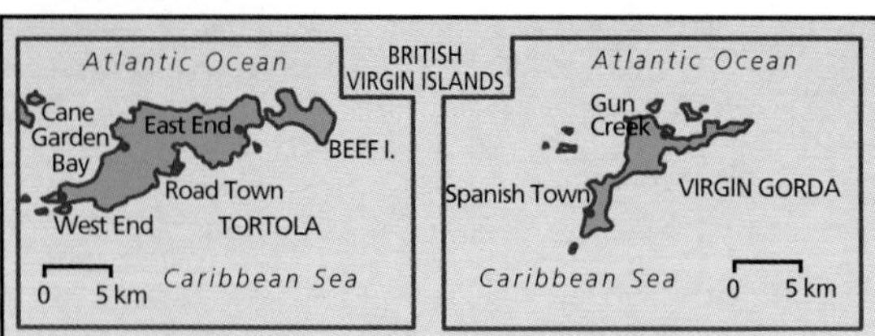

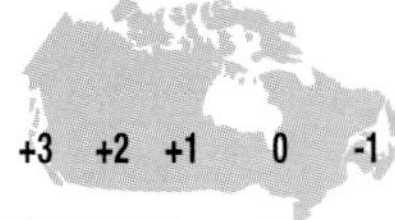

Region: West Indies
Area: 150 km²
Capital: Road Town
Airport: Road Town 14 km
Population: 12,870
Language: English
Religion: Protestant
Government: British dependent territory
Voltage: 110 - 60
Vaccinations required: –
Vaccinations recommended: Ty, Po
Passport: required
Visa: not required
Currency: U.S. dollar
$1Cdn: .74 dollar
Driving: left hand
International permit: recommended
Area code: 011-809
✆ from Canada: 1-800-387-0852
✆ to Canada: ■1-800-744-2580
Accommodation: ★★★
Restaurants: ★★★
Transportation: ★★★
Cost of living: ○○○
UN rank: –
Best months: Feb, Mar, Apr
Holidays: 1 Jan; 14, 16, 17 Apr; 1 May; 1 July; 28 Aug; 25, 26 Dec

WHAT TO DO

Cruise ships ply the waters around the British Virgin Islands, attracted by the beautiful bays, beach-lined coves, and stately groves of frangipani and mango trees overhanging the shores of the islands. The island of Tortola, and particularly Road Bay at Road Town, attracts sailors from all over the world. The north shore of the island is famous for its magnificent beaches, which are protected by an impressive coral reef. Legends of privateers and pirates who left fabulous treasures are still heard on the small island of Virgin Gorda; this is where Robert Louis Stevenson set the action of his adventure story *Treasure Island*. On Norman Island, visitors can see the "baths", fluorescent caves that have given rise to fantastic tales over the centuries.

WHAT TO BUY

Tortola rum is the main ingredient in a number of delicious, refreshing cocktails. Batiks, wooden sculptures, woven baskets, and black-coral jewelry make good souvenirs; visitors should be advised not to encourage commerce in jewelry and other objects made of tortoise shell.

ANGUILLA

+4 +3 +2 +1 0

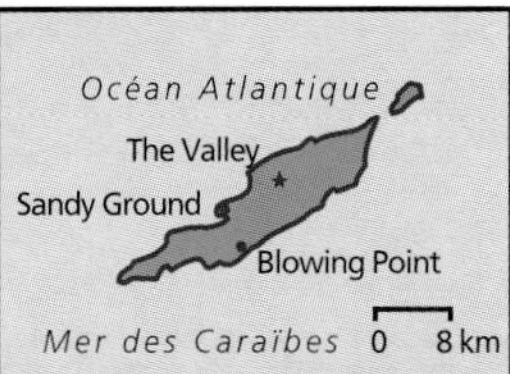

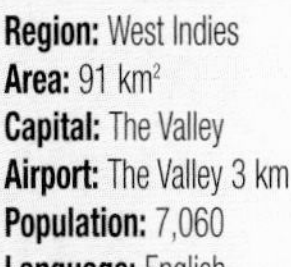

Region: West Indies
Area: 91 km²
Capital: The Valley
Airport: The Valley 3 km
Population: 7,060
Language: English
Religions: Anglican, Methodist
Government: British dependent territory
Voltage: 110/220 - 60
Vaccinations required: Yf*
Vaccinations recommended: –
Passport: required
Visa: not required
Currency: East Caribbean dollar
$1Cdn: 1.99 dollars
Driving: left hand
International permit: recommended
Area code: 011-809
✆ from Canada: 1-800-463-5831
✆ to Canada: ■1-800-744-2580
Accommodation: ★★★★
Restaurants: ★★★★
Transportation: ★★★
Cost of living: ○○○
UN rank: –
Best months: Feb, Mar, Apr
Holidays: 1 Jan; 14, 16, 17 Apr; 1, 30 May; 28 Aug; 25, 26 Dec

ANGUILLA

WHAT TO DO

The word *anguilla* means "eel"; the Spanish gave the name to this island no doubt because it is long and narrow. Some say that the beaches of Crocus Bay are the most beautiful in the world, especially the ones near the town of Sandy Ground: coral reefs protect the shores there, and the sea is always warm and calm. Several buildings of the colonial period are worth visiting, including the Dutch fort at Sandy Hill Bay and Wallblake House, the majestic estate of an old British plantation.

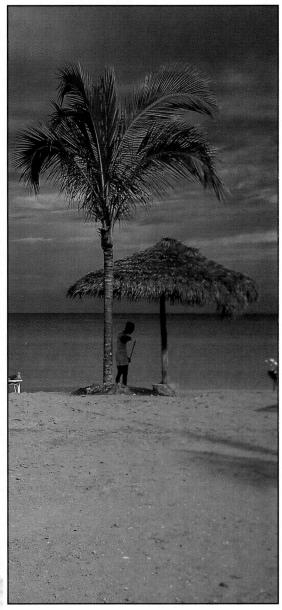

WHAT TO BUY

Lobster is the culinary specialty of Anguilla: it is served boiled or in a creamy seafood sauce. Of course, the sea is a constant theme in crafts: shell jewelry and ornaments are everywhere, as is art depicting maritime themes.

SAINT-MARTIN

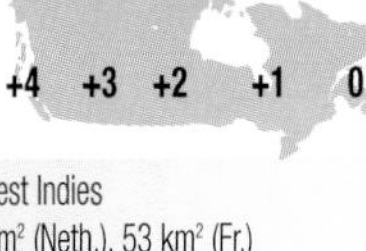

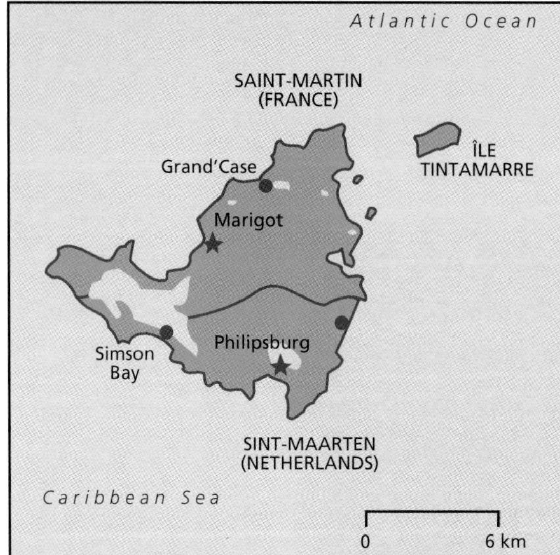

Region: West Indies
Area: 34 km² (Neth.), 53 km² (Fr.)
Capital: Philipsburg, Marigot
Airport: Juliana 15 km
Population: 32,000 (Neth.), 28,350 (Fr.)
Languages: Dutch, French, English
Religions: Catholic, Protestant
Government: Dutch and French territories
Voltage: 110/220 - 60
Vaccinations required: Yf*
Vaccinations recommended: Ty, Po
Passport: required
Visa: not required
Currency: guilder, French franc
$1Cdn: 1.32 guilders, 3.52 francs
Driving: right hand
International permit: recommended
Area codes: 011-599, 595
✆ from Canada: –
✆ to Canada: 19◆00-16
Accommodation: ★★★★
Restaurants: ★★★★
Transportation: ★★★
Cost of living: ○○○
UN rank: –
Best months: Feb, Mar, Apr
Holidays: 1 Jan; 14, 16, 17 Apr; 1 May; 14 July; 11 Nov; 25, 26 Dec

WHAT TO DO

Since 1648, this island has been governed by both France, which has the north part, and the Netherlands, which has the south part. The border is largely symbolic, even though Saint-Martin enjoys two languages, two architectural styles, two ways of life, and two distinct cultures. Going from one side of the border to the other, the name changes from Saint-Martin to Sint Maarten and vice-versa. Marigot is a charming town with beautiful beaches and some historical sites on the French side. The island of Saint-Barthélemy is another French territory ideal for a foray off the beaten path. Sint Maarten is dominated by Mount Flagstaff, an extinct volcano that stands watch over the beaches on the east coast. Philipsburg is a small town (essentially two streets) in the Dutch colonial style: its Fort Amsterdam and the monument to Queen Wilhelmina are fine examples of colonial architecture. The lagoon at Simson Bay is an incomparably beautiful natural site that attracts a variety of birds. Divers will marvel at the seabed on the south side of the island.

WHAT TO BUY

The cuisine of both sides of the island is inspired by seafood, with a place of honour given to lobster. Local specialties are objects made of woven palm leaves, sculpture, and shell jewelry.

P. LESAGE

ANTIGUA AND BARBUDA

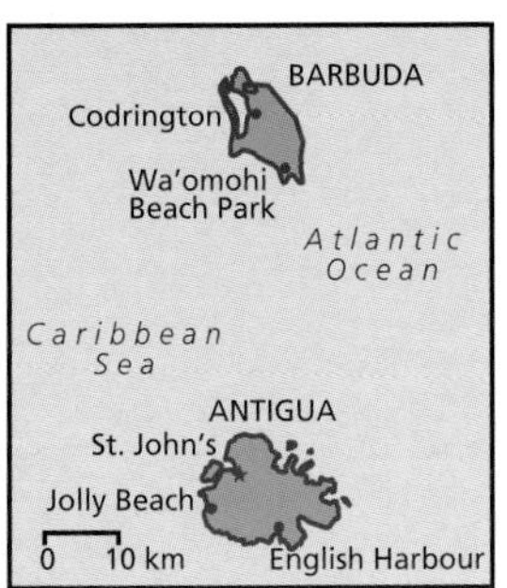

WHAT TO DO

The country of Antigua and Barbuda comprises three islands: Antigua, Barbuda, and Redonda; the last is inhabited only by herds of goats and thousands of birds that provide birdwatchers with an unending source of delight. Antigua is popular with diving aficionados because of its many bays and deep coves that attract magnificent fish. Deer and a variety of exotic birds make their home on Barbuda. Here too, the beaches are said to be among the most beautiful in the world. In St. John's, the capital of Antigua, the vestiges of the colonial era, such as St. John's Cathedral and Fort James, attest to the island's historical importance. On Greencastle Hill are megaliths placed there by the island's earliest inhabitants a number of centuries ago. The colourful and lively Antigua Carnival takes place in the last week of July.

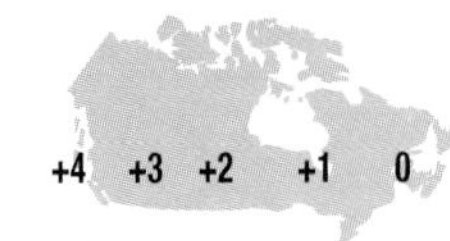

Region: West Indies
Area: 440 km²
Capital: St. John's
Airport: St. John's 10 km
Population: 64,770
Language: English
Religions: Anglican, Catholic
Government: parliamentary democracy
Voltage: 110/220 - 60
Vaccinations required: Yf*
Vaccinations recommended: –
Passport: not required
Visa: not required
Currency: Caribbean dollar
$1Cdn: 1.99 dollars
Driving: left hand
International permit: recommended
Area code: 011-809
✆ from Canada: –
✆ to Canada: ■1-800-744-2580
Accommodation: ★★★★
Restaurants: ★★★★
Transportation: ★★★
Cost of living: ○○○
UN rank: 55
Best months: Feb, Mar, Apr
Holidays: 1, 2 Jan; 14, 16, 17 Apr; 1 May; 4, 5 June; 3, 31 July; 1 Aug; 1 Nov; 25, 26 Dec

WHAT TO BUY

Antiguan white rum is excellent. The cuisine is inspired by the sea; fresh fish, shellfish, and seaweed are featured in many dishes. Dyed fabrics, colourful batiks, and shell jewelry are typical Antiguan crafts. It is not recommended to purchase bird feathers or stuffed birds.

SAINT KITTS AND NEVIS

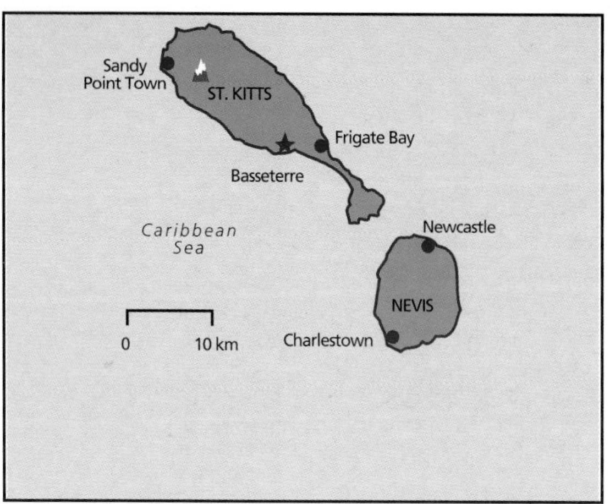

+4 +3 +2 +1 0

Region: West Indies
Area: 269 km²
Capital: Basseterre
Airport: Golden Rock 4 km
Population: 40,680
Languages: English, Créole
Religion: Anglican
Government: parliamentary democracy
Voltage: 230 - 60
Vaccinations required: Yf*
Vaccinations recommended: Ty, Po
Passport: not required
Visa: not required
Currency: East Caribbean dollar
$1Cdn: 1.99 dollars
Driving: left hand
International permit: recommended
Area code: 011-809
✆ from Canada: –
✆ to Canada: ■1-800-744-2580
Accommodation: ★★★★
Restaurants: ★★★★
Transportation: ★★★
Cost of living: ❍❍
UN rank: 70
Best months: Feb, Mar, Apr
Holidays: 1, 2 Jan; 14, 16, 17 Apr; 1 May; 4, 5 June; 7 Aug; 19 Sept; 25, 26 Dec

WHAT TO DO

Citizens of St. Kitts and Nevis live on paradisical islands. St. Kitts extends around three volcanic mountains, covered by luxuriant forest punctuated with ravines and craters. Mount Liamuiga rises more than 1,200 m; its slopes are covered with sugar-cane plantations and orchards for exotic fruits like mangoes and papayas. The island is rimmed by volcanic-sand beaches overhung by a belt of palm trees and bread trees. Nevis's name comes from "Nuestra Señora de las Nieves" (Our Lady of Snow), which is what Columbus called the island when he thought he saw eternal snow on the summit of Nevis Peak (altitude 1,090 m): in fact, the top of the mountain is often draped in clouds. The beaches are edged with coconut palms and palm trees, and a coral reef protects the north coast. Fishing and diving aficionados will enjoy the calm waters between the two islands. On St. Kitts, the capital, Basseterre, bears many signs of its English heritage, and the historical sites are worth a visit. Frigate Bay is mainly a tourist destination, with its sunny beaches and cruise ports; its golf courses are as famous as its casino. On the other side of the island is the impressive Brimstone Hill Fort, built in 1690. On Nevis, Charlestown is a lovely town, with its bougainvilleas and pastel-coloured houses. A number of old plantation estates on the island have been converted into charming hotels.

WHAT TO BUY

The cuisine in St. Kitts and Nevis features mainly seafood and pork. Mutton in a spicy sauce is a favourite dish among locals. The fresh fruits make wonderful desserts and very refreshing juices. The batiks of St. Kitts are known all over the world, and philatelists will appreciate stamps from these exotic islands. The Nevis Carnival (just after Christmas) provides an opportunity to dance to calypso music and discover the folkloric traditions of the islands.

MONTSERRAT

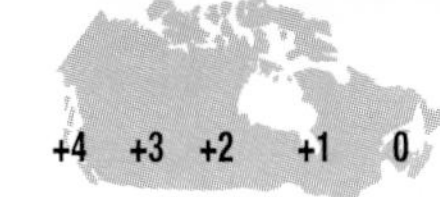

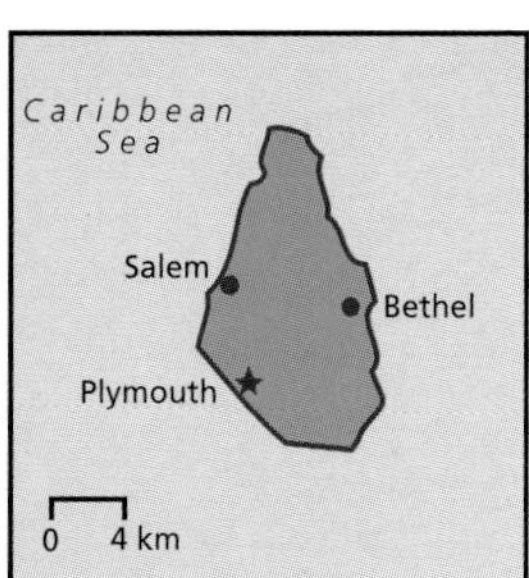

WHAT TO DO

Montserrat is a volcanic island with beautiful black-sand beaches. The moulded and mountainous countryside rises in three main peaks, the highest of which, Chances Peak, has an altitude of 915 m. The Galways Soufrière crater is at the centre of a region of spectacular sulphur springs. All paths in this region lead to Great Alps Falls. The Fox's Bay Bird Sanctuary is a paradise for observing exotic birds. The Galways Plantation, established by an Irish family in the 1660s, is now an important historical site depicting the Irish roots of the island's earliest inhabitants. In Plymouth, St. Anthony's Church and St. George Fort recall the colonial era, while the Montserrat Museum is devoted to the history of the island.

WHAT TO BUY

It is strange to see St. Patrick's Day (March 17) celebrated in a West Indian ambience: most of the ancestors of the island's European inhabitants were Irish, and their influence is still very much alive. Montserrat cuisine is thus infused with Irish flavours; goat water, for instance, is a goat stew that tastes remarkably like Irish mutton. Don't be fooled by the "mountain chicken": it's really a dish made with frogs' legs. Ceramics, batiks, and shell jewelry are among the most interesting products of local craftspeople.

Region: West Indies
Area: 100 km^2
Capital: Plymouth
Airport: Plymouth 17 km
Population: 12,710
Language: English
Religion: Anglican
Government: British dependent territory
Voltage: 220 - 60
Vaccinations required: Yf*
Vaccinations recommended: Ty, Po
Passport: not required
Visa: not required
Currency: East Caribbean dollar
$1Cdn: 1.99 dollars
Driving: left hand
International permit: recommended
Area code: 011-809
✆ from Canada: –
✆ to Canada: ■1-800-744-2580
Accommodation: ★★★
Restaurants: ★★★
Transportation: ★★★
Cost of living: ○○
UN rank: –
Best months: Feb, Mar, Apr
Holidays: 1 Jan; 14, 16, 17 Apr; 1, 29 May; 28 Aug; 23 Nov; 25, 26 Dec

GUADELOUPE

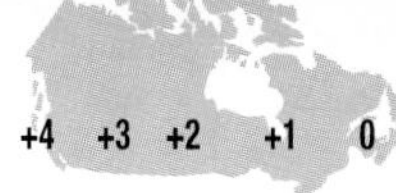

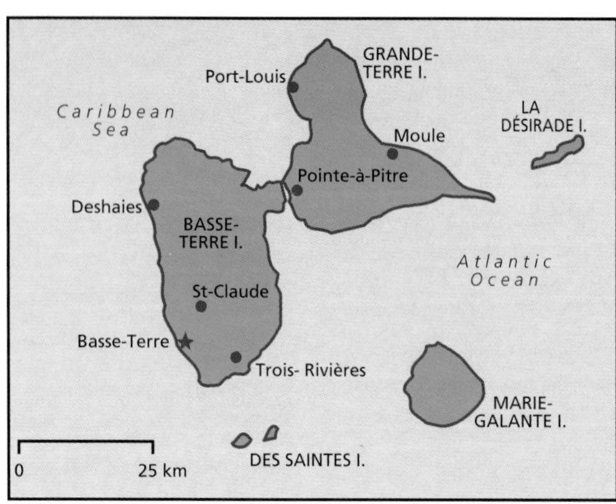

Region: West Indies
Area: 1,780 km²
Capital: Basse-Terre
Airport: Pointe-à-Pitre 3 km
Population: 428,950
Languages: French, Créole
Religion: Catholic
Government: French overseas department
Voltage: 220 - 50
Vaccinations required: Yf*
Vaccinations recommended: Ty, Po
Passport: required
Visa: not required
Currency: French franc
$1Cdn: 3.52 francs
Driving: right hand
International permit: recommended
Area code: 011-590
✆ from Canada: –
✆ to Canada: 19♦00-16
Accommodation: ★★★★
Restaurants: ★★★★
Transportation: ★★
Cost of living: ○○○
UN rank: –
Best months: Feb, Mar, Apr
Holidays: 1 Jan; 16, 17 Apr; 1, 8, 25 May; 4, 5 June; 14 July; 15 Aug; 1, 11 Nov; 25 Dec

WHAT TO DO

Before it was discovered by Columbus and colonized by the French, Guadeloupe was called Karuker by its inhabitants, the Carib Indians, who were replaced by African slaves. Today, the island group still belongs to France and remains a French Overseas Department. Because of this special connection to its parent country, Guadeloupe has a cachet unique to the West Indies. (Saint-Martin and Martinique are the other French departments in the region.) Because of the volcanic origins, Guadeloupe also has an unusual topography. Soufrière is the highest peak on the island of Basse-Terre, at an altitude of 1,467 m. Expeditions to the tropical forest around the foot of the volcano leave from the town of Saint-Claude. The town of Basse-Terre, on the coast near Soufrière, is charming with its pretty fort, cathedral, and very animated market. Point-à-Pitre, on Grande-Terre, is the liveliest town in Guadeloupe. Especially interesting is Place de la Victoire, which is surrounded by the port and the market. The Remy Naisouta Museum documents the struggle between the Caribs, the Spanish, the French, and the English. The islands of Les Saintes, Marie-Galante, and La Désirade are well known to the sailing aficionados who ply the clear waters of the West Indies. The old sugar-cane plantation on Marie-Galante is a fascinating historical site.

WHAT TO BUY

Créole cuisine makes the most of seafood: *accras*, small fried-fish patties, are a Guadeloupan specialty. Dishes are often seasoned with *colombo*, a tasty curry. Gaudeloupan rum, served with a splash of lime juice, is delightful. Colourful fabrics (*madras*), spices, *dou-dou* dolls (used in pagan rites), amulets, and roots of all types are found in the very animated markets.

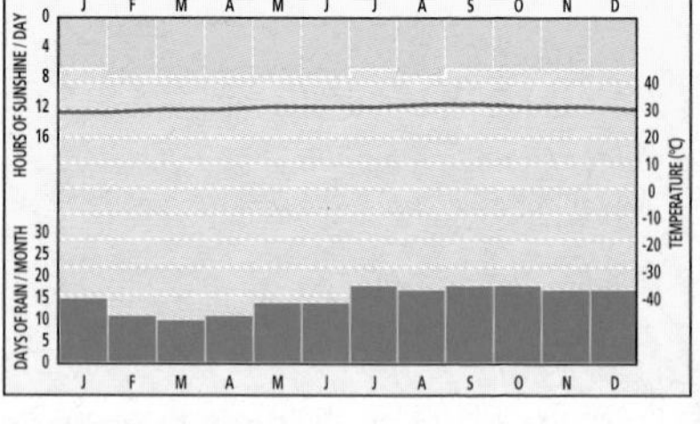

DOMINICA

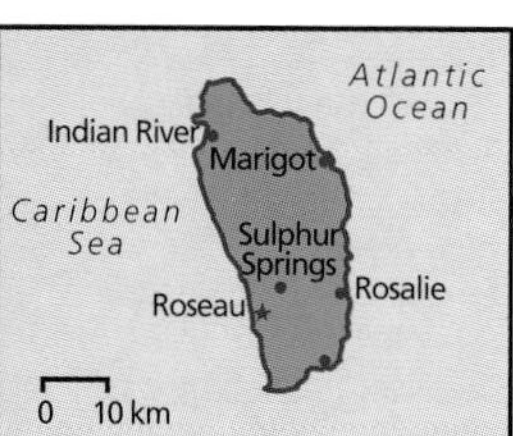

WHAT TO DO

Dominica is the most mountainous island in the West Indies, which makes it a favourite destination for hikers and trekkers. As the name indicates, Boiling Lake bubbles continuously thanks to the heat from its volcano crater: the climb up the volcano in itself makes the trip to the island worthwhile. Morne Trois Pitons National Park protects more than 17,000 acres of forest, jungle, waterfalls, and volcanoes, some of which are still active. In the Northern Forest Reserve around Morne Diablotin (the highest peak on the island at 1,447 m), one can see the famous *sisserou* and *jacquot* parrots, species threatened with extinction. The Carib Reserve in the northern part of the island belongs to the descendants of the Carib Indians who lived on the island before the arrival of the Spaniards. Trafalgar Waterfall, Desolation Valley (named for its numerous sulphurous springs and natural pools of boiling water) and Indian River, with the particularly dense vegetation on its banks, are other attractions of this magnificent island.

WHAT TO BUY

Créole dishes are usually spicy, but on Dominica they are delicately flavoured with lime juice or coconut milk. Many exotic fruits grow on these fertile lands, notably the plantain, which is eaten lightly cooked over a wood fire: delicious! Banana-tree leaves are used to make everyday items such as mats, bags, and hats.

Region: West Indies
Area: 750 km²
Capital: Roseau
Airport: Melville Hall 50 km
Population: 87,700
Languages: English, Créole
Religion: Catholic
Government: parliamentary democracy
Voltage: 220/240 - 50
Vaccinations required: Yf*
Vaccinations recommended: Ty, Po
Passport: required
Visa: not required
Currency: East Caribbean dollar
$1Cdn: 1.99 dollars
Driving: left hand
International permit: recommended
Area code: 011-809
✆ from Canada: –
✆ to Canada: ■1-800-744-2580
Accommodation: ★★★
Restaurants: ★★★
Transportation: ★★
Cost of living: ❍❍
UN rank: 64
Best months: Feb, Mar, Apr
Holidays: 1, 2 Jan; 27, 28 Feb; 14, 16, 17 Apr; 1 May; 4, 5, 18 June; 7 Aug; 3 Nov; 25, 26 Dec

J. HUARD

MARTINIQUE

+4 +3 +2 +1 0

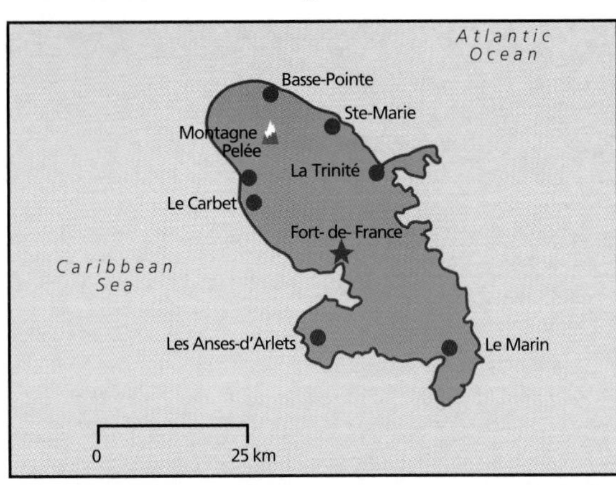

Region: West Indies
Area: 1,100 km²
Capital: Fort-de-France
Airport: Fort-de-France 15 km
Population: 392,370
Languages: French, Créole
Religion: Catholic
Government: French overseas department
Voltage: 220 - 50
Vaccinations required: Yf*
Vaccinations recommended: Ty, Po
Passport: required
Visa: not required
Currency: French franc
$1Cdn: 3.52 francs
Driving: right hand
International permit: recommended
Area code: 011-596
✆ from Canada: –
✆ to Canada: 19◆00-16
Accommodation: ★★★★
Restaurants: ★★★★
Transportation: ★★★
Cost of living: OOO
UN rank: –
Best months: Feb, Mar, Apr
Holidays: 1 Jan; 16, 17 Apr; 1, 8, 25 May; 4 June; 14 July; 15 Aug; 1, 11 Nov; 25 Dec

A. GARDON / RÉFLEXION

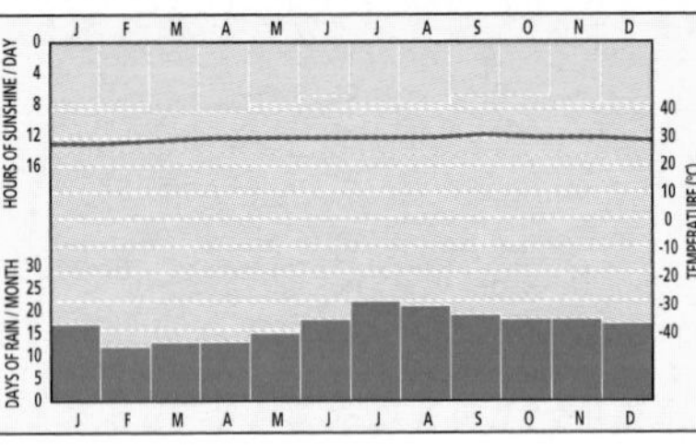

WHAT TO DO

Martinique is a French Overseas Department in the Lesser Antilles. Fort-de-France is a top-notch tourist destination, with its beautiful bay, La Savane Garden, Saint-Louis Cathedral, and fish market. The gorges and cliffs at Ajoupa-Bouillon; Diamond Rock near Le Diamant; the tomb of the Caribs; the hot springs at Le Prêcheur; and Savane des Pétrifications, at Sainte-Anne, are natural sites that draw lovers of strange geological formations, as well as amateur anthropologists. Mount Pelée, with an altitude of 1,397 m, dominates the countryside in the northern part of the island. One can watch cock fights in the *pitts*, an interesting aspect of Martinique folklore. At Basse-Pointe, the majestic estate of an old plantation, erected in 1700, sits in the middle of banana and pineapple groves, while Macouba has one of the oldest rum distilleries in Martinique.

WHAT TO BUY

Accras, cod fritters; *féroce*, an avocado dish; and stuffed cod and crab are Martinique specialties. The aged rum is particularly tasty. In Ducos, the craft centre offers coral jewelry, bamboo objects, Créole dolls, and colourful madras fabrics. The famous *colliers chou,* or *chaînes forçat,* are pieces of jewelry that come with a long history. Figurines, amulets, and voodoo ritual objects are other curiosities that reflect the mix of cultures in Martinique.

SAINT LUCIA

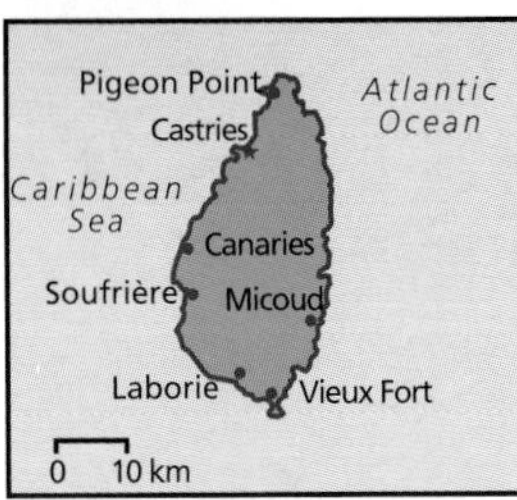

WHAT TO DO

The island of St. Lucia is dominated by Gros Piton and Petit Piton, two majestic but extinct volcanoes that stand side by side and are now thickly covered with vegetation. The town of Soufrière lies in the shadow of these twin mountains; it features a typical mix of West Indian colonial architecture and tropical luxuriance. Not far from the town, the Diamond and Sulphur Springs waterfalls testify to the geological activity of the island. The tropical forest harbours a wide variety of animals, including some parrots that are threatened with extinction. Castries, the capital, is a well-sheltered port in a lovely bay. Morne Fortune, Gros Islet, Pigeon Point, and Anse La Raye are all worth visiting for the beauty of their settings and the warm welcome of their inhabitants. Some of the historical sites on the island recall the tensions that existed between the English and the French in the seventeenth century.

WHAT TO BUY

St. Lucian cuisine features fish, lobster, crawfish, and shellfish. Locally distilled rum is excellent, as are the fruit juices. Batiks and woven items, such as rugs, baskets, and hats, are sold in all the markets. In Castries, market day provides an opportunity to pick up all sorts of crafts. Pointe Séraphine is a duty-free zone.

Region: West Indies
Area: 620 km²
Capital: Castries
Airport: Castries 3 km
Population: 145,100
Languages: English, Créole
Religion: Catholic
Government: parliamentary democracy
Voltage: 220 - 50
Vaccinations required: Yf*
Vaccinations recommended: Ty, Po
Passport: not required
Visa: not required
Currency: East Caribbean dollar
$1Cdn: 1.99 dollars
Driving: left hand
International permit: recommended
Area code: 011-809
✆ from Canada: –
✆ to Canada: ■1-800-744-2580
Accommodation: ★★★★
Restaurants: ★★★★
Transportation: ★★★
Cost of living: ○○
UN rank: 77
Best months: Feb, Mar, Apr
Holidays: 1–3 Jan; 22 Feb; 14, 16, 17 Apr; 1 May; 4, 5, 15 June; 7 Aug; 2 Oct; 13, 25, 26 Dec

SAINT VINCENT AND THE GRENADINES

+4 +3 +2 +1 0

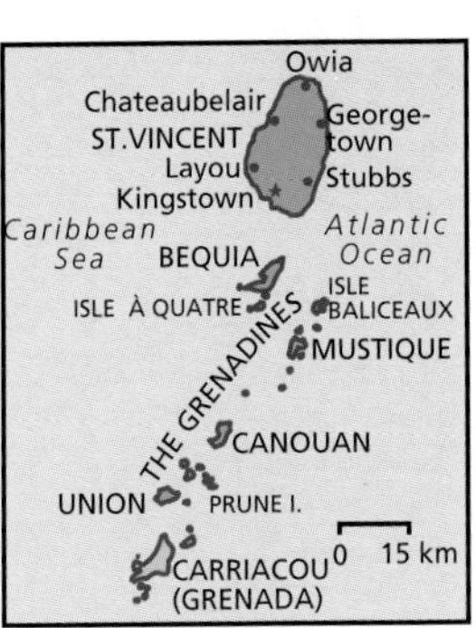

Region: West Indies
Area: 340 km²
Capital: Kingstown
Airport: Kingstown 3 km
Population: 115,440
Language: English
Religion: Anglican
Government: parliamentary democracy
Voltage: 220 - 50
Vaccinations required: Yf*
Vaccinations recommended: Ty, Po
Passport: not required
Visa: not required
Currency: East Caribbean dollar
$1Cdn: 1.99 dollars
Driving: right hand
International permit: recommended
Area code: 011-809
✆ from Canada: –
✆ to Canada: ■1-800-744-2580
Accommodation: ★★★★
Restaurants: ★★★★
Transportation: ★★★
Cost of living: ○○
UN rank: 69
Best months: Feb, Mar, Apr
Holidays: 1, 2, 23 Jan; 14, 16, 17 Apr; 1 May; 4, 5, 15 June; 7 Aug; 2, 27 Oct; 13, 25, 26 Dec

WHAT TO DO

St. Vincent is a volcanic island featuring black-sand beaches, while the Grenadines are known for their white sand. Both attract travellers seeking heavenly scenery and particularly good weather. On St. Vincent, the Soufrière Mountains rise more than 1,220 m and are dotted with waterfalls, chasms, and valleys. They are covered with dense, luxuriant vegetation. Kingstown is a pretty little town that gets very lively on market days. Of special interest are St. Mary Cathedral, Fort Charlotte, and the Botanical Gardens. The countryside surrounding Kingstown features a series of natural wonders, including Baleine Falls, in the north, and the crater at Soufrière; an expedition up the latter provides the reward of a magnificent view of the Grenadines, stretching off into the distance. These islands are favoured by sailors, who ply the waters from Bequia to Mustique to Canouan. The underwater flora and fauna are exceptionally beautiful. Fishing is forbidden at certain spots: find out where before going on a fishing trip.

J. HUARD

WHAT TO BUY

Batiks, dolls made of palm leaves, and shell jewelry are typical of the country. Fishing harpoons, similar to those made by the Arawak Indians, are sold all over the islands. Since sailing is the national sport, visitors should not miss the regattas that take place throughout the year, especially the one at Canouan in August. The carnival at the end of June is another fascinating event.

BARBADOS

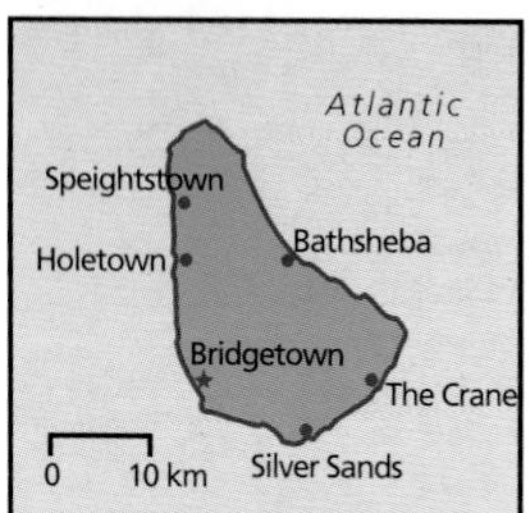

WHAT TO DO

Around 1537, a Portuguese ship heading for Brazil landed on a little island. Crew members named it "Barbados", because they thought the aboveground roots of the island's fig trees looked like hairs of a beard. Today, visitors will find long stretches of golden beaches, particularly on the west coast of the island, which is bathed by the Caribbean sea. Bridgetown is an interesting stepping-off point. Among the city's attractions are Careenage Port, where colourful boats come to dock; Trafalgar Square; and the Barbados Museum, which traces the history of the island back to the time of the Arawak Indians. Diving fans will want to head to the north and east coasts, perfect spots for underwater expeditions and exploring the caves: Animal Flower Cave, near St. Lucy, is an absolute must-see. In the interior of the island is Walchman Hall Gully, a deep ravine where lemon trees and spice trees planted 150 years ago still flourish. The estates of the sugar-cane plantations, like Villa Nova at St. John and St. Nicholas Abbey at St. Peter, recall another era.

WHAT TO BUY

The Bajans make a delicious rum: the Crop Over Festival, which takes place from mid-July to early August, celebrates the sugar-cane harvest and the ambrosial nectar drawn from it. During the festival, the warm evenings pulsate with the feverish beat of calypso. Flying fish is a typical Bajan food, well worth sampling, as are *cou-cou* (cornflour and gumbo) and pepper-pot (a spicy stew). *Mauby*, a liqueur made of fruit peels and spices, is a drink unique to Barbados. The craft shops offer *khus-khus* (straw fans), woven baskets, jewelry made of shells and coral, and objects made of coconut shell.

Region: West Indies
Area: 430 km²
Capital: Bridgetown
Airport: Bridgetown 18 km
Population: 255,830
Language: English
Religion: Protestant
Government: parliamentary democracy
Voltage: 110/220 - 50
Vaccinations required: Yf*
Vaccinations recommended: –
Passport: not required
Visa: not required
Currency: Barbados dollar
$1Cdn: 1.48 dollars
Driving: left hand
International permit: required
Area code: 011-809
✆ from Canada: –
✆ to Canada: ■1-800-744-2580
Accommodation: ★★★★
Restaurants: ★★★★
Transportation: ★★★★
Cost of living: ○○○
UN rank: 20
Best months: Feb, Mar, Apr
Holidays: 1, 2, 21 Jan; 14, 16, 17 Apr; 1 May; 4, 5 June; 7 Aug; 2 Oct; 30 Nov; 25, 26 Dec

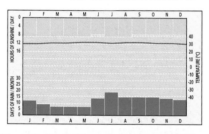

T. BOGNAR / RÉFLEXION

GRENADA

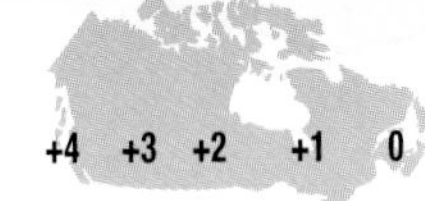

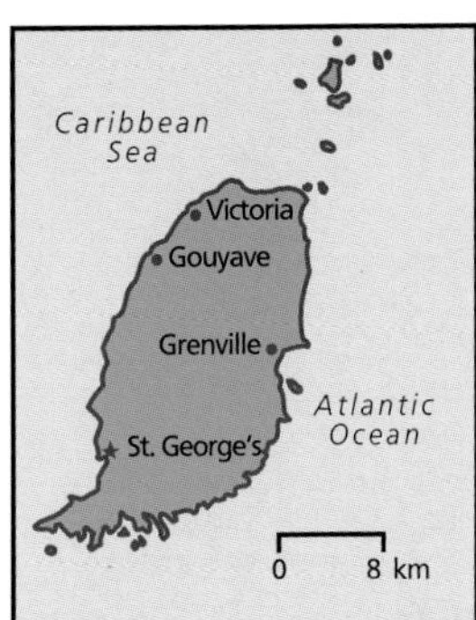

Region: West Indies
Area: 340 km²
Capital: St. George's
Airport: Pearl 25 km
Population: 94,110
Language: English
Religions: Anglican, Catholic
Government: parliamentary democracy
Voltage: 220 - 50
Vaccinations required: Yf*
Vaccinations recommended: Ty, Po
Passport: not required
Visa: not required
Currency: East Caribbean dollar
$1Cdn: 1.99 dollars
Driving: left hand
International permit: recommended
Area code: 011-809
✆ from Canada: –
✆ to Canada: ■1-800-744-2580
Accommodation: ★★★★
Restaurants: ★★★
Transportation: ★★★
Cost of living: ○○○
UN rank: 78
Best months: Feb, Mar, Apr
Holidays: 1 Jan; 7 Feb; 14, 16 Apr; 1, 22 May; 2 June; 1, 8 Aug; 25 Nov; 25, 26 Dec

WHAT TO DO

Grenada is a major producer of bananas, cacao, nutmeg, and sugar cane. These crops flank the island's mountains, including dormant volcanoes, that cover much of the island. The coasts are indented with gorges and bays that protect superb beaches, notably those at Levera Bay and Grande Anse. St. George's is a charming port town dominated by a fort built during the French regime, in 1705. The port is itself a major historical site; it was once the point of departure for spice ships. Even today, the old warehouses around it are redolent of the scent of fresh nutmeg. Annandale Falls and Morne des Sauteurs are other must-sees.

WHAT TO BUY

The Grenadian rum is excellent, and it is often served with exotic fruit juices or sprinkled with nutmeg. *Calaloo* is a fish soup typical to the island. Colourful cottons, jewelry made from shells, and, of course, fresh spices are sold in all the markets.

J. HUARD

NETHERLANDS ANTILLES

NETHERLANDS ANTILLES

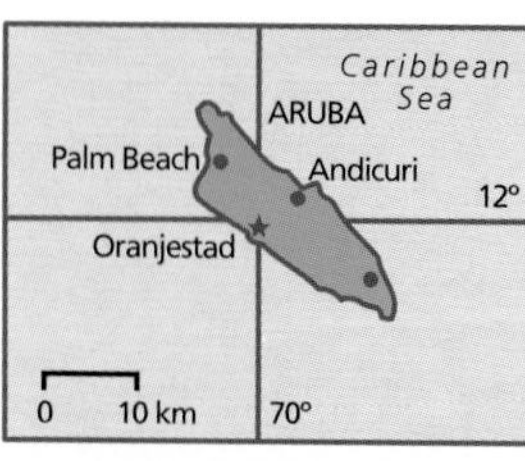

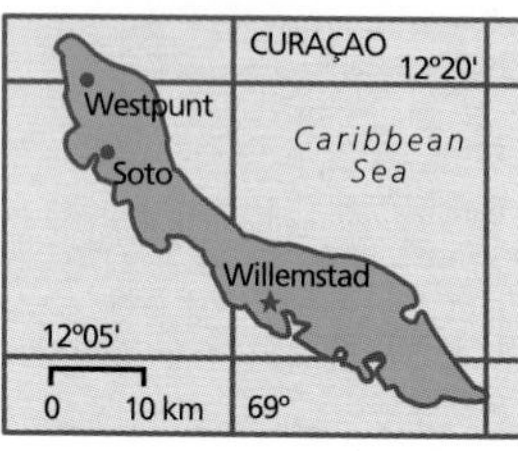

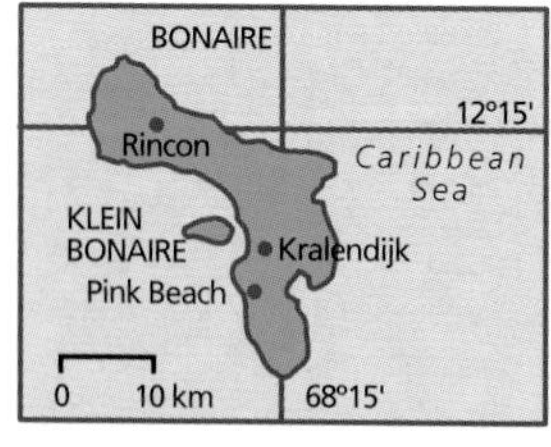

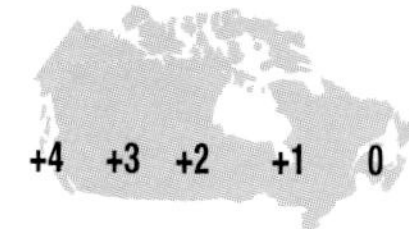

Region: West Indies
Area: 960 km²
Capital: Willemstad
Airport: Willemstad 12 km
Population: 185,800
Languages: Dutch, Papiamento, English
Religions: Catholic, Protestant
Government: dem. linked to Netherlands
Voltage: 110 - 50
Vaccinations required: Yf*
Vaccinations recommended: Ty, Po
Passport: required
Visa: not required
Currency: guilder
$1Cdn: 1.32 guilders
Driving: right hand
International permit: recommended
Area codes: 011-297, 298
✆ from Canada: 1-800-463-3127
✆ to Canada: –
Accommodation: ★★★★
Restaurants: ★★★★
Transportation: ★★★★
Cost of living: ○○○
UN rank: –
Best months: Jan to May
Holidays: 1, 2 Jan; 14, 16, 17, 30 Apr; 5, 25 May; 4, 5 June; 25, 26 Dec

WHAT TO DO

Aruba, Bonaire, and Curaçao (or ABC, as they are called) are the islands that form the Netherlands Antilles. Spanish and Dutch influences are still seen, even though the islands are separated from their colonial parents by several thousand kilometres. In Aruba, the typically Dutch windmills and pastel-coloured houses add to the charm of the town of Oranjestad. Palm Beach is well known for its magnificent beaches and for its *divi-divis* (or *watapanas*), trees that grow almost horizontally due to the wind. The Arawak Indians who once lived on the island left cave paintings in the Fontein and Arikok caverns. Bonaire draws divers who come to admire the wide range of colours of the seaweed, from deep fuchsia to pale pink. This island's Slagbaai National Park is a plant and animal sanctuary. In Curaçao visitors encounter a perfect blend of the attractions of the city and the beauties of nature: Willemstad is a lovely replica of a Dutch town full of brightly painted houses and tulip (and orchid) gardens. And Curaçao's beaches are nothing short of superb!

WHAT TO BUY

Ayacas, meat patties cooked in palm leaves, and *sopito*, a fish stew, are Aruban specialties. Curaçao's eponymous liqueur, made with orange peels and spices, is drunk at any time of day. The sea provides the raw materials—shells and coral—for most of the local crafts.

VOLVOX / RÉFLEXION

TRINIDAD AND TOBAGO

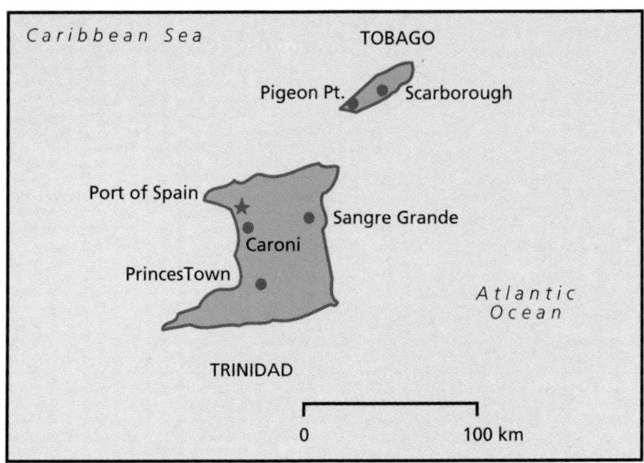

+4 +3 +2 +1 0

TRINIDAD AND TOBAGO

Region: West Indies
Area: 5,130 km²
Capital: Port-of-Spain
Airport: Port-of-Spain
Population: 1,328,290
Languages: English, Hindi, French
Religions: Catholic, Hindu
Government: parliamentary democracy
Voltage: 110/230 - 60
Vaccinations required: Yf*
Vaccinations recommended: Ty, Po
Passport: required
Visa: not required
Currency: Trinidad and Tobago dollar
$1Cdn: 4.38 dollars
Driving: left hand
International permit: required
Area code: 011-809
✆ from Canada: –
✆ to Canada: –
Accommodation: ★★★★
Restaurants: ★★★★
Transportation: ★★★
Cost of living: ○○○
UN rank: 35
Best months: Feb, Mar, Apr
Holidays: 1, 2 Jan; 4 Mar; 14, 16, 17 Apr; 4, 5 May; 15, 19 June; 1, 31 Aug; 25 Sept; 25, 26 Dec

WHAT TO DO

The carnival in Trinidad and Tobago is without doubt the prime attraction of the country. During the carnival, in February, steel bands and calypso bands wander the streets gathering groups of dancers who sway to the frantic rhythms of the music. Travellers who prefer quieter entertainment, birdwatchers in particular, flock to the lagoons around Caroni to see thousands of birds, among them ibises and pelicans. Also drawn to the area are a wide variety of butterflies, which gather nectar from the marvellous flowers, including more than 700 different types of orchids. On Tobago are found 19 varieties of hummingbirds. History-lovers will also find many attractions here. They can tour the architectural treasures of Port of Spain: a Gothic cathedral, a German castle, a Moorish parliament building, and Victorian houses! The town's museum has displays on the various colonial occupations the islands have undergone. Tobago, much smaller than its sister island, is steeped in colonial charm, particularly in Scarborough, with its fort built in 1779. The beaches are ideal for diving aficionados.

WHAT TO BUY

The cuisine of Trinidad and Tobago features a delicious mixture of Créole and West Indian flavours: seafood is the base of a soup that is often highly spiced, and the meats are frequently served with exotic fruits. The *pastelles* (meat patties served in banana-tree leaves) and *tum-tum*, a plantain purée, are tasty specialties. The carnival costumes, calypso musical instruments, and steel band drums make good souvenirs. During the carnival beware of pickpockets; they never rest!

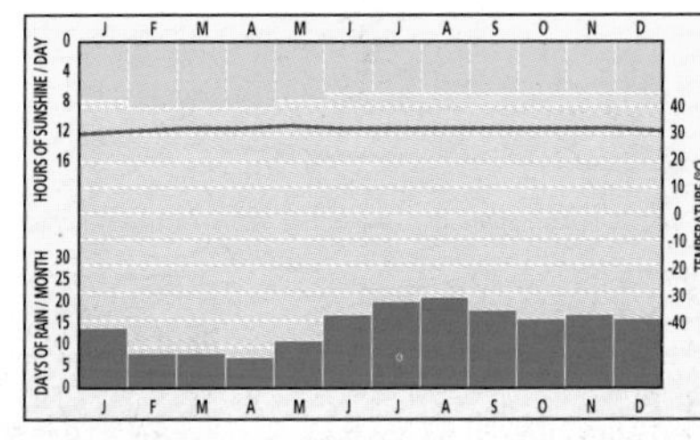

J. HUARD

LATIN AMERICA

UNITED STATES
BAHAMAS
MEXICO
CUBA
ANTILLES
Caribbean Sea
Atlantic Ocean
BELIZE
HONDURAS
GUATEMALA
EL SALVADOR
NICARAGUA
COSTA RICA
PANAMA
VENEZUELA
GUYANA
SURINAME
FRENCH GUIANA
COLOMBIA
GALAPAGOS ISLANDS
ECUADOR
PERU
BRAZIL
Pacific Ocean
BOLIVIA
PARAGUAY
EASTER ISLAND
Atlantic Ocean
CHILE
JUAN FERNANDEZ ISLANDS
ARGENTINA
URUGUAY
FALKLAND ISLANDS (U.K.)

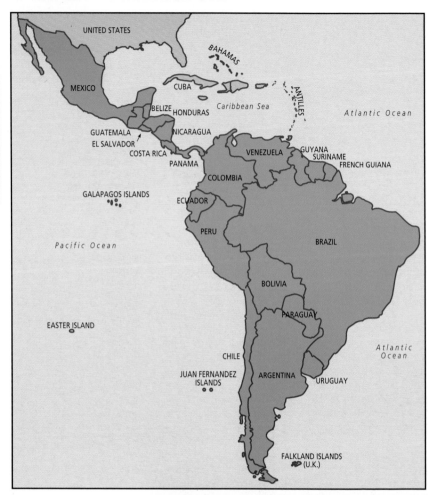

Latin America is a jigsaw puzzle of cultures most of which trace their ancestry back to Spain or Portugal. Latin Americans, whether they are Guatemalan or Bolivian, also have the broad smile and warm heart inherited from their aboriginal ancestors. Travellers to Latin America will find marvellous scenery, charming cities, friendly people, and fascinating traditions.

J. HUARD

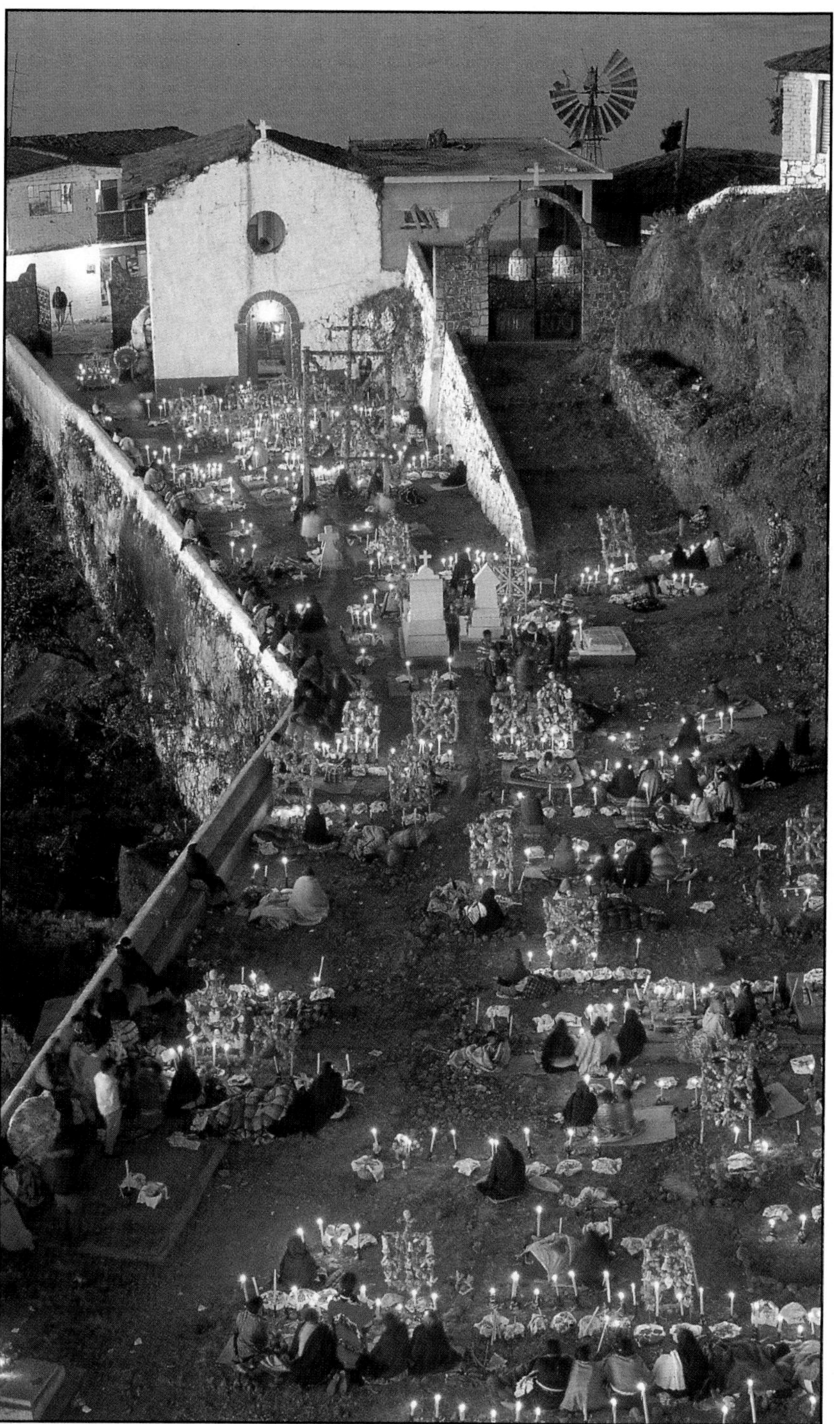

MEXICO

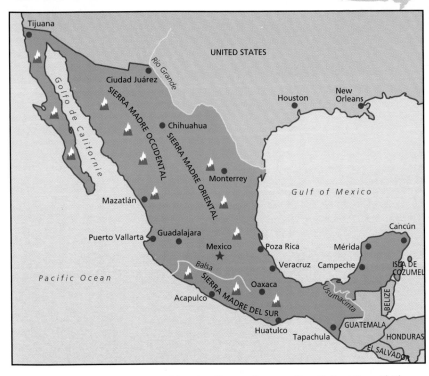

WHAT TO DO

A torrid sun pouring down on flowering cactuses in the middle of a desert is one image that one might have of Mexico. Beaches crowded with thousands of oiled bodies broiling in the sun or dusty, overpopulated cities might be others. Fortunately, Mexico has much more to offer: superb archaeological sites, verdant and snow-topped mountains, lush valleys, beautiful beaches off the beaten track, and friendly towns. The best-known resort areas in Mexico are Puerto Vallarta, Acapulco, Cancún, Manzanillo, Veracruz, and Cozumel. Travellers flock to these beach paradises to enjoy the sea (either the Pacific Ocean or the Gulf of Mexico) and the mild climate. Divers, sailboarders, and surfers will appreciate these well-equipped tourist centres. However, the country's true riches are found outside these resorts. In Yucatán is the impressive archaeological site of Chichén Itza, the old Maya-Toltec capital, with the Kukulcan pyramid, Thousand Columns Square, Temple of the Tigers, and ball courts. Other extraordinary ruins can be found in Uxmal, Mérida, and Campeche, among them Uxmal's Great Pyramid. The ruins of the pre-Hispanic cities of Téotihuacán and Palenque are also worth seeing. El Tajín, in the state of Veracruz, is famous for its majestic seven-step pyramid pierced with more than 350 niches. In Xochicalco, near Cuernavaca, are the fabulous pyramids with "Feathered Serpent" relief, a symbol dear to Mexicans. The capital, Mexico

Region: Central America
Area: 1,972,550 km²
Capital: Mexico City
Airport: Mexico City 13 km
Population: 92,202,200
Languages: Spanish, Indian languages
Religion: Catholic
Government: presidential democracy
Voltage: 110 - 60
Vaccinations required: Yf*
Vaccinations recommended: Ty, Po, Mal
Passport: required + proof of citizenship
Visa: not required
Currency: Mexican new peso
$1Cdn: 4.53 pesos
Driving: right hand
International permit: recommended
Area code: 011-52
© from Canada: –
© to Canada: 95-800-010-1990
Accommodation: ★★★★★
Restaurants: ★★★★
Transportation: ★★★★
Cost of living: ○○
UN rank: 52
Best months: Mar, Apr, Sept, Oct
Holidays: 1, 6 Jan; 5 Feb; 1, 21 Mar; 14, 16, 17, 30 Apr; 1, 5, 10 May; 16 Sept; 12 Oct; 1, 20 Nov; 12, 25, 26 Dec

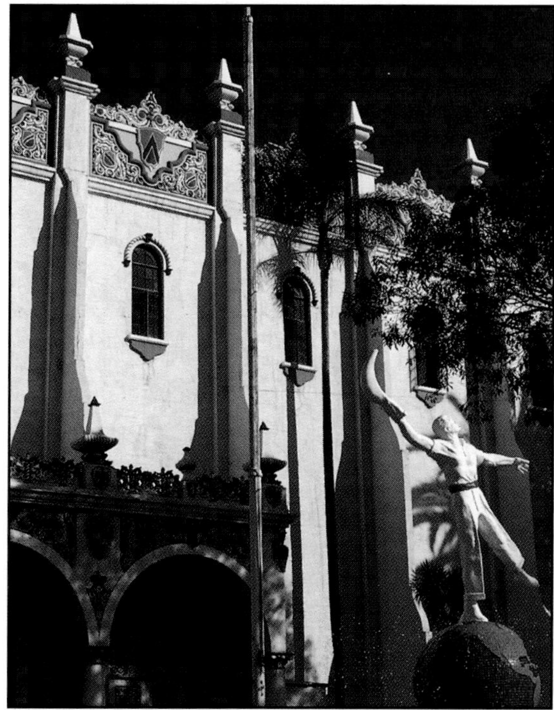

P. HALLY

MEXICO

City, remains a prime destination for travellers: the city was built on the ancient Aztec city of Tenochtitlán, protected by the slopes of mounts Popocatépetl and Ixtaccihuatl. The old district of the city has been designated a World Heritage Site by UNESCO. The very beautiful Nuestra Señora de Guadelupe Basilica, dating from 1533, and a number of Baroque churches are found there. The university district injects a good dose of youthful vitality into the city. The Anthropology and Archaeology Museum is worth visiting more than once. Like all big cities, Mexico City generates much pollution, which can cause problems for some. In contrast, to the north are the Sierra Madre and Baja California, a peninsula running parallel to the mainland: in these almost untouched regions, wildlife still reigns supreme.

WHAT TO BUY

Well-known Mexican dishes include *tacos, enchiladas*, and *tortillas*, but other dishes to sample are *mole de guajalote* (turkey in a sauce flavoured with chocolate!), *ceviche* (marinated fish), and *guacamole* (a delicately spiced avocado purée). Beware of the *picante* sauce, which can be a tongue-scorcher. For a throat-scorcher, taste the *mescal*, a fierce liquor that is not always of the best quality. A better choice might be the famous *tequila*, an agave-based liquor that is particularly refreshing served in a *margarita*. Women travellers should be careful, especially if they spend time in bars; alcohol is the pickpockets' best ally. The beaches are also places where valuables can disappear into someone else's pocket; visitors should carry with them only what they absolutely need. In the markets are pottery, *mariachi* trumpets, ceramics, colourful fabrics, leather goods, and many Mayan- and Toltec-inspired pieces of jewelry.

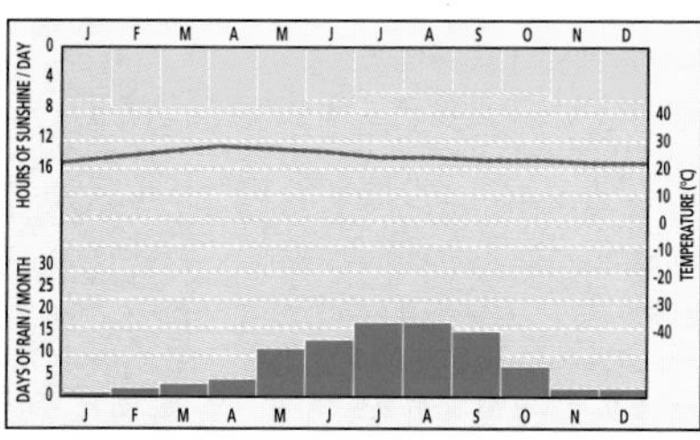

GUATEMALA

GUATEMALA

+2 +1 0 -1 -2

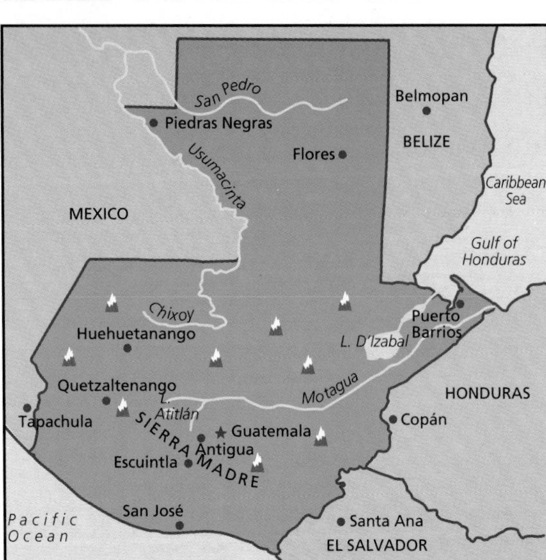

Region: Central America
Area: 108,890 km²
Capital: Guatemala City
Airport: Guatemala City 7 km
Population: 10,721,390
Languages: Spanish, Indian languages
Religion: Catholic
Government: presidential democracy
Voltage: 220 - 60
Vaccinations required: Yf*
Vaccinations recommended: Ty, Po, Mal
Passport: required
Visa: not required
Currency: quetzal
$1Cdn: 4.25 quetzals
Driving: right hand
International permit: recommended
Area code: 011-502
✆ from Canada: 1-800-463-3180
✆ to Canada: ▲198
Accommodation: ★★★
Restaurants: ★★★
Transportation: ★★
Cost of living: ○○
UN rank: 108
Best months: Nov to Apr
Holidays: 1 Jan; 14, 16, 17 Apr; 1 May; 30 June; 15 Sept; 20 Oct; 1 Nov; 25, 26 Dec

WHAT TO DO

Guatemala is a dream destination for history and archaeology buffs. The country has preserved important ruins of Mayan culture, the best known of which is Tikal. Its six majestic temples are linked by stone stairways and contain sculpted vaults and steles carved with hieroglyphic messages. Other ruins, such as Seibal, Yaxhá, and Uaxactún, are also worth visiting. For those not interested in Mayan ruins, there is lovely Lake Atitlán, which is surrounded by mountains covered in dense, lush vegetation. The larger cities, like Quetzaltenango and Guatemala City, have retained their colonial charm. Sports-minded travellers will find a challenge to their liking among the peaks of the volcanoes, which offer climbs of varying degrees of difficulty: Tajumulco, with an altitude of 4,211 m, is particularly beautiful. And beach-lovers will want to head for the coast along the Gulf of Honduras, well known for the warm waters of the Caribbean Sea, especially near the city of Puerto Barrios.

WHAT TO BUY

Guatemalan cuisine is simple and nourishing: black beans, beef, and corn are the basis of most dishes. Guatemalan coffee is very rich and is drunk boiling hot. The most beautiful fabrics in the country are found in Momostenango, while the finest pottery is found in Totonicapán. Everywhere is found beautiful silver jewelry and fine wooden statuettes. *Marimbas*, small xylophones, are the source of enchanting music.

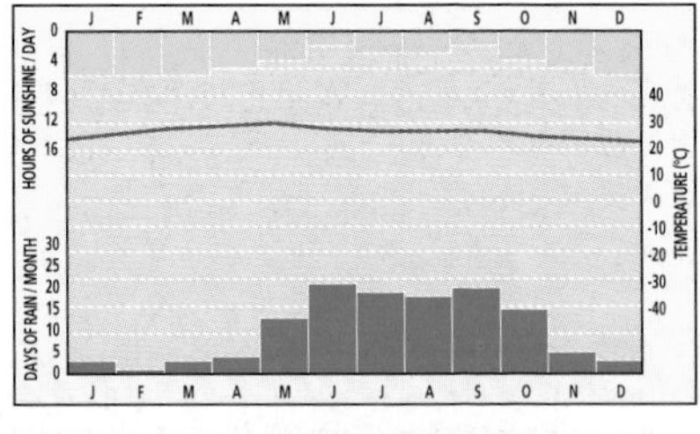

BELIZE

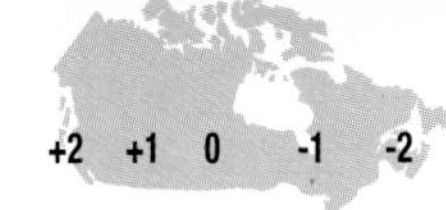

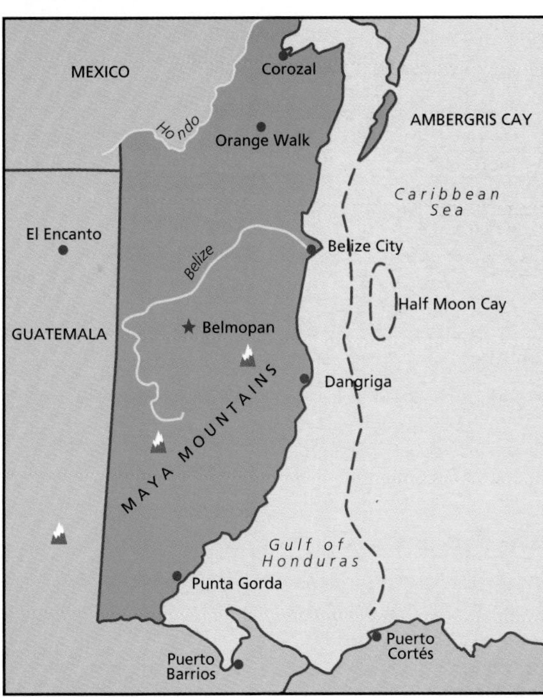

Region: Central America
Area: 22,960 km²
Capital: Belmopan
Airport: Belize City 14 km
Population: 208,950
Languages: English (off.), Spanish
Religions: Catholic, Protestant
Government: parliamentary democracy
Voltage: 220 - 60
Vaccinations required: Yf*
Vaccinations recommended: Ty, Po, Mal
Passport: required
Visa: not required
Currency: Belizean dollar
$1Cdn: 1.47 dollars
Driving: right hand
International permit: recommended
Area code: 011-501
✆ from Canada: 1-800-463-1154
✆ to Canada: 558
Accommodation: ★★★
Restaurants: ★★★
Transportation: ★★
Cost of living: ○○
UN rank: 88
Best months: Feb, Mar, Apr
Holidays: 1 Jan; 9 Mar; 14, 16, 17 Apr; 10, 21 Sept; 12 Oct; 25, 26 Dec

BELIZE

WHAT TO DO

Belize can be divided into two parts: the Atlantic coast and the interior. The coral reefs along the coast are the most important tourist attraction in the country, as much for the beauty of the coral as for the expanse of the reefs. Ambergris Cay and Half Moon Cay are highly prized for their underwater caves, extraordinary wildlife, and golden beaches. The Red Footed Booby bird sanctuary at the Half Moon Cay Natural Monument Reservation harbours species that are unique to this region. The coast, from Belize City south to Punta Gorda, features stretches of tranquil beach enveloped by coral reef. Belize City is the largest city in the country, but it has retained its colonial charm. In the interior is jungle, dotted with archaeological sites—Santa Rita, Colha, Altun Ha, Caracol, and Pusilha, to name a few. The Maya Mountains, the valleys and waterfalls of the Pine Ridge Forest Reserve, and Victoria National Park are other natural splendours worth seeing.

WHAT TO BUY

Lobster and seafood form the basis of Belizean cuisine. Wooden statuettes, Maya-inspired jewelry, and coral jewelry are sold all over the country. Fishing and gathering coral are strictly forbidden in some places.

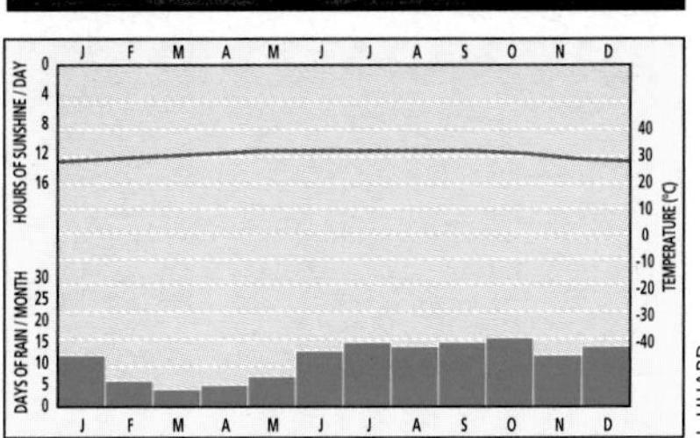

J. HUARD

EL SALVADOR

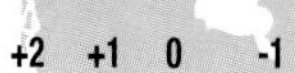

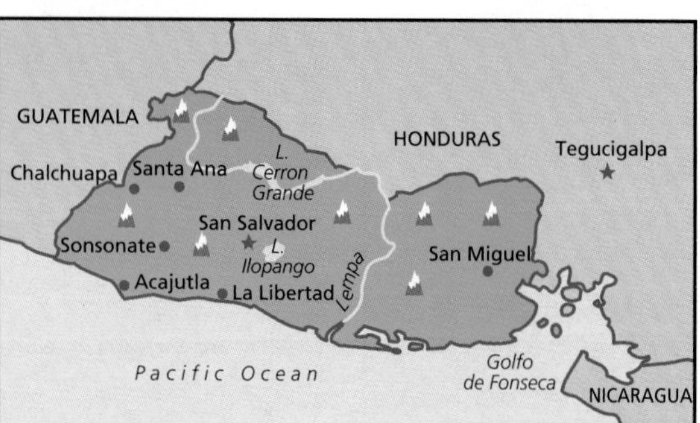

Region: Central America
Area: 21,040 km²
Capital: San Salvador
Airport: San Salvador 35 km
Population: 5,752,520
Languages: Spanish, Nahuatlpipil
Religion: Catholic
Government: presidential democracy
Voltage: 110 - 60
Vaccinations required: Yf*
Vaccinations recommended: Ty, Po, Mal
Passport: required
Visa: required
Currency: colón
$1Cdn: 6.48 colóns
Driving: right hand
International permit: recommended
Area code: 011-503
✆ from Canada: –
✆ to Canada: –
Accommodation: ★★
Restaurants: ★★
Transportation: ★★
Cost of living: ❍
UN rank: 112
Best months: Dec to May
Holidays: 1 Jan; 14, 16, 17 Apr; 1 May; 5, 6, Aug; 15 Sept; 12 Oct; 25, 26 Dec

WHAT TO DO

Many people still think of El Salvador as a country torn by civil war, even though the war was brought to a halt with the peace agreement signed between the government and the guerrillas. The tourism industry is not yet well established, but travellers who by coming encourage the economic recovery of this charming little country will not regret their decision. El Salvador's lovely Pacific beaches, some 200 volcanoes, and Mayan and pre-Colombian ruins are first-rate attractions. Amateur archaeologists will not want to miss the Tazumal ruins at Chalchuapa and the San Andres ruins. The Panchos, direct descendants of the Pilpil Indians who inhabited the country before the Spaniards arrived, live in Panchimalco. Their way of life has changed little since pre-European times. Not all of the many volcanoes that dot the country are accessible, but the peaks of the Santa Ana, San Salvador, and Izalco volcanoes are worth scaling to admire the countryside stretched out below. Of course, San Salvador, the capital, is also a prime attraction. It is a large city (the second largest in Central America) where colonial buildings blend with new constructions (built after the 1986 earthquake). Worth a visit are the St. Ignatius Church, a good example of Spanish architecture, the National Palace, and the National Theatre. Beach-lovers will want to stop awhile along the 350 km of sand on the Costa del Sol.

WHAT TO BUY

Salvadoran coffee is delicious. Corn is one of the country's main food crops, and it is found in most typically Salvadoran dishes. The crafts from the town of Ilobasco are especially fine: the leather goods, fabrics, woven baskets, pottery, and jewelry are inspired by aboriginal motifs. El Salvador's religious festivals, which can last several days and resonate with all the mysteries of the faith, are of special interest. Travellers will be surprised and delighted by the warm welcome Salvadorans extend to them.

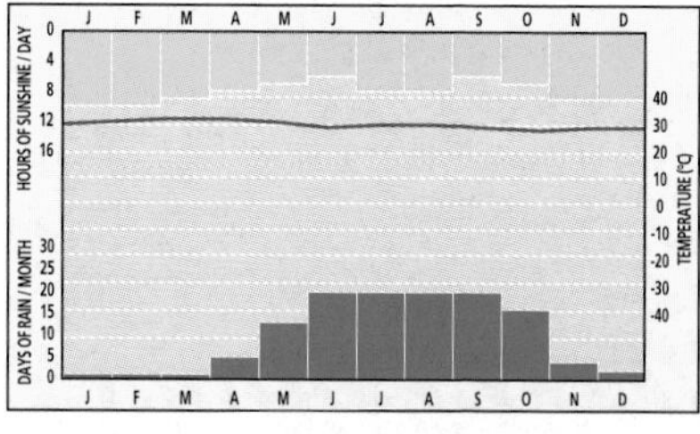

HONDURAS

+2 +1 0 -1 -2

Region: Central America
Area: 112,090 km²
Capital: Tegucigalpa
Airport: Tegucigalpa 7 km
Population: 5,314,800
Languages: Spanish (off.), Indian languages
Religion: Catholic
Government: presidential democracy
Voltage: 220 - 60
Vaccinations required: Yf*
Vaccinations recommended: Ty, Po, Mal
Passport: required
Visa: not required
Currency: lempira
$1Cdn: 6.99 lempiras
Driving: right hand
International permit: recommended
Area code: 011-504
✆ from Canada: –
✆ to Canada: –
Accommodation: ★★★
Restaurants: ★★★
Transportation: ★★★
Cost of living: ○○
UN rank: 115
Best months: Nov to Apr
Holidays: 1 Jan; 14, 16, 17 Apr; 1 May; 15 Sept; 3, 12, 21 Oct; 25, 26 Dec

HONDURAS

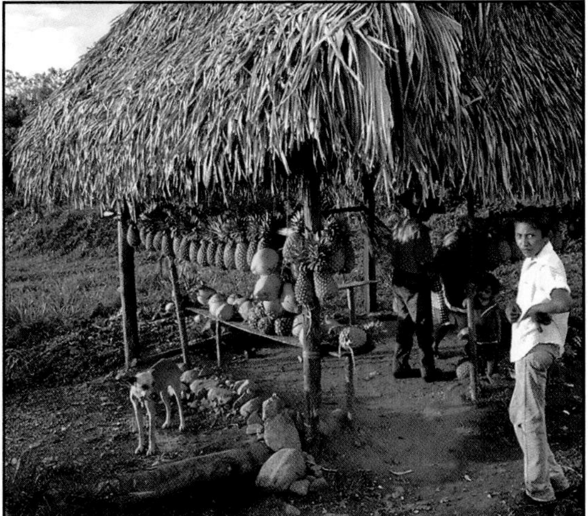

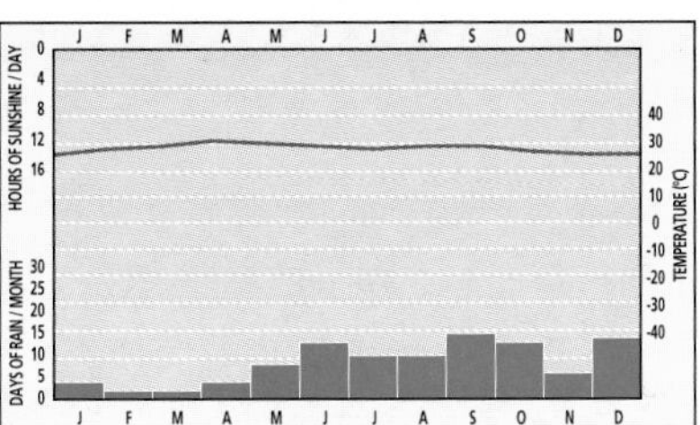

WHAT TO DO

Honduras is covered with orchards of tropical fruits (especially bananas) and large coffee and tobacco plantations—it is a true cornucopia. Although they live in one of the poorest countries in Latin America, Hondurans are proud not only of their impressive Mayan ruins but also their lovely beaches, which are bathed by the warm waters of the Caribbean Sea. In Cobán, an immense Mayan site with temples, a big amphitheatre, and an acropolis has been discovered. A visit to these archaeological treasures alone makes the trip to Honduras worthwhile. The coast from Trujillo to La Ceiba is particularly beautiful. The coral reefs that protect the Islas de la Bahia are drawing growing numbers of diving aficionados. The capital, Tegucigalpa, is a pleasant city; the cathedral, which is decorated with gold leaf and delicately carved wood, is a must-see. Some small towns have preserved their colonial charm, including Comayagua, Ojojona, and Santa Lucía.

WHAT TO BUY

Tortillas, little cornflour shells filled with meat and red beans, can be very spicy in Honduras. Bananas are the country's main resource, and they are the basis for a number of dishes, including *mondongo*, a vegetable-and-banana soup. Tobacco products, especially hand-rolled cigars, are of very high quality. Banana-tree leaves are used to make baskets, rugs, and a variety of other items. Women travelling alone will be pleasantly surprised by the politeness of Hondurans.

NICARAGUA

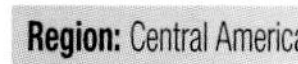

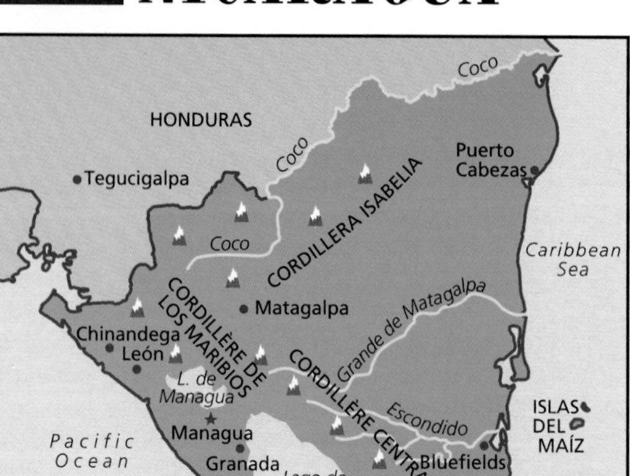

Region: Central America
Area: 129,494 km²
Capital: Managua
Airport: Managua 11 km
Population: 4,096,690
Languages: Spanish (off.), Indian languages
Religion: Catholic
Government: presidential democracy
Voltage: 110 - 60
Vaccinations required: Yf*
Vaccinations recommended: Ty, Po, Mal
Passport: required
Visa: required
Currency: new córdoba
$1Cdn: 5.6 córdobas
Driving: right hand
International permit: recommended
Area code: 011-505
✆ from Canada: 1-800-463-0729
✆ to Canada: 168
Accommodation: ★★★
Restaurants: ★★★
Transportation: ★★★
Cost of living: ○○
UN rank: 106
Best months: Dec to May
Holidays: 1 Jan; 14, 16, 17 Apr; 1 May; 15 Sept; 8, 25, 26 Dec

WHAT TO DO

After living through a period of political and economic tension, Nicaraguans want to rebuild their nation and its international image. The new government is attempting to build a tourist industry based on the country's beautiful beaches on both the Pacific and Caribbean coasts. Like Costa Rica, Nicaragua has many attractions for hikers: the Matagalpa region is particularly rich in pine forests, orchid fields, and jungles full of exotic wildlife. The Mosquito Coast and, off shore, the Islas del Maís are ideal diving territory. Managua, the Nicaraguan capital, was completely reconstructed after an earthquake almost destroyed it in 1972. Of particular interest is the district that dates back to the colonial era; it was miraculously spared during the earthquake. León has some lovely churches and a magnificent cathedral, and the pride of the town of Granada, in the shadow of the Mombacho Volcano, is the impressive San Francisco Fortress.

WHAT TO BUY

Vegetarianism was long promoted by the government to replace meat, which had become too expensive; Nicaraguans thus make an impressive variety of dishes from soybeans and other legumes. The sugar-cane plantations produce a delicious rum, and the coffee is excellent. In Matagalpa, travellers can find the pretty black pottery that Nicaragua is known for. Leather, lace, and woven goods of all sorts are sold in all the markets. Wooden sculptures as well as paintings give a glimpse into the country's past. Nicaragua is a relatively safe country for women travellers; its inhabitants will no doubt soon become familiar with the sight of tourists.

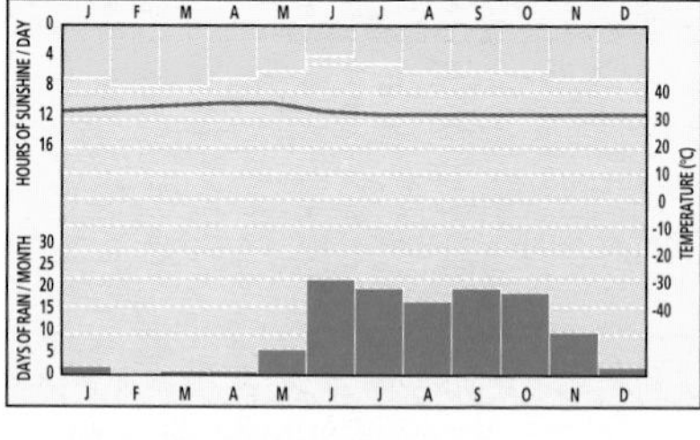

COSTA RICA

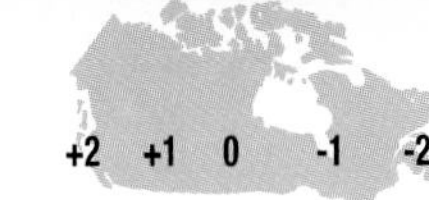

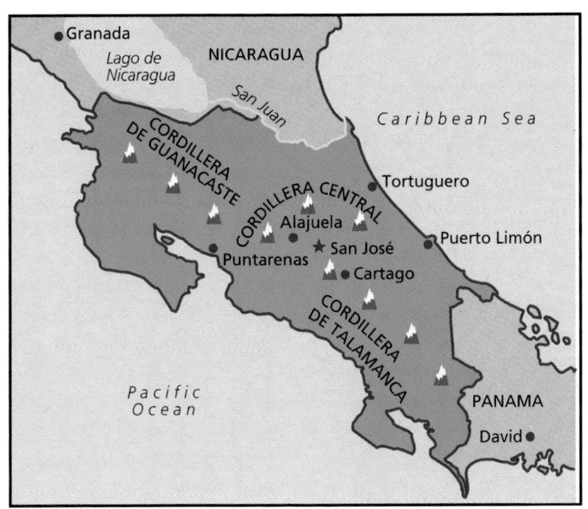

Region: Central America
Area: 51,100 km²
Capital: San José
Airport: San José
Population: 3,342,160
Languages: Spanish, English
Religion: Catholic
Government: presidential democracy
Voltage: 110/220 - 60
Vaccinations required: –
Vaccinations recommended: Ty, Po, Mal
Passport: required
Visa: not required
Currency: Costa Rican colón
$1Cdn: 134.32 colón
Driving: right hand
International permit: required
Area code: 011-506
✆ from Canada: 1-800-463-0116
✆ to Canada: 0-800-015-1161
Accommodation: ★★★★
Restaurants: ★★★★
Transportation: ★★★★
Cost of living: ○○
UN rank: 39
Best months: Dec to May
Holidays: 1 Jan; 14, 16, 17 Apr; 1, 25 May; 15 June; 25 July; 2, 15 Aug; 15 Sept; 12 Oct; 1 Nov; 8, 25, 26 Dec

COSTA RICA

WHAT TO DO

In the last few years, Costa Rica has become a favourite destination for hikers, perhaps because of its numerous ecological reserves protecting extraordinary natural sites: the Carara Biological Reserve and the Volcán Poás, Chirripón, Volcán Irazú, Braulio Carrillo, Barra Honda, Palo Verde, Rincón de la Vieja, Santa Rosa, Guanacaste, Cahuita, and Tortuguero national parks, along with the magnificent Manuel Antonio National Park—to name just a few. The coastlines along the Caribbean Sea and the Pacific Ocean are well known to divers, who come to admire the splendid underwater scenery. The sea turtles, the coral along the Caribbean coast, and the many species of fish and birds add to this country's natural wealth. In San José, the National Museum, the Gold Museum, and the Jade Museum exhibit many artifacts dating from pre-Colombian times. The excellent Museum of Natural Science has numerous specimens, and some of the animals shown are now extinct. On the Península de Nicoya are found remains of aboriginal occupation, among them the El Hacha ruins.

WHAT TO BUY

Costa Rican cuisine is quite simple: shellfish, fish, and meat (*carne*) form the basis of everyday dishes. Try the *tamales*, a mixture of meat and rice rolled in a banana-tree leaf. Beer and fruit juices are the most frequent accompaniments with meals. Sculptures, wooden figurines, leather goods (especially from the town of Moravia), hand-painted panels of wood, and woven baskets are sold in Sarchi, the capital of Costa Rican crafts.

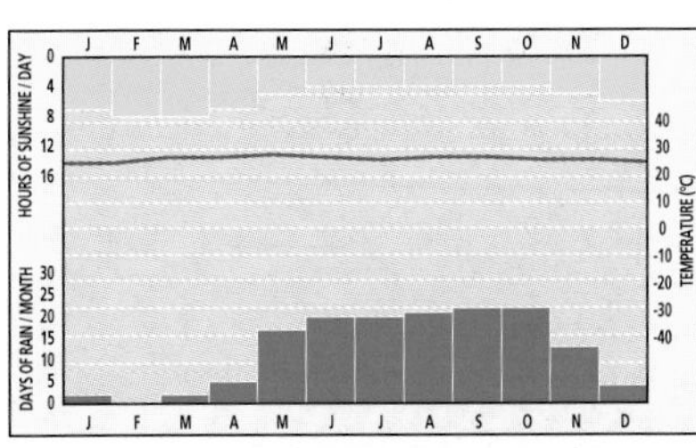

RÉFLEXION

PANAMA

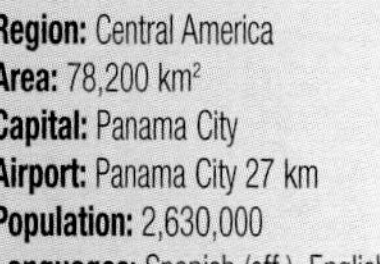

Region: Central America
Area: 78,200 km²
Capital: Panama City
Airport: Panama City 27 km
Population: 2,630,000
Languages: Spanish (off.), English
Religion: Catholic
Government: presidential democracy
Voltage: 110 - 60
Vaccinations required: Yf*
Vaccinations recommended: Ty, Po, Mal
Passport: required
Visa: not required
Currency: balboa (and U.S. dollar)
$1Cdn: .74 dollar
Driving: right hand
International permit: recommended
Area code: 011-507
✆ from Canada: –
✆ to Canada: –
Accommodation: ★★★
Restaurants: ★★★
Transportation: ★★★
Cost of living: ❍
UN rank: 47
Best months: Jan to May
Holidays: 1, 9 Jan; 28 Feb; 14, 16, 17 Apr; 1 May; 15 Aug; 12 Oct; 3, 10, 28 Nov; 8, 25, 26 Dec

J. HUARD

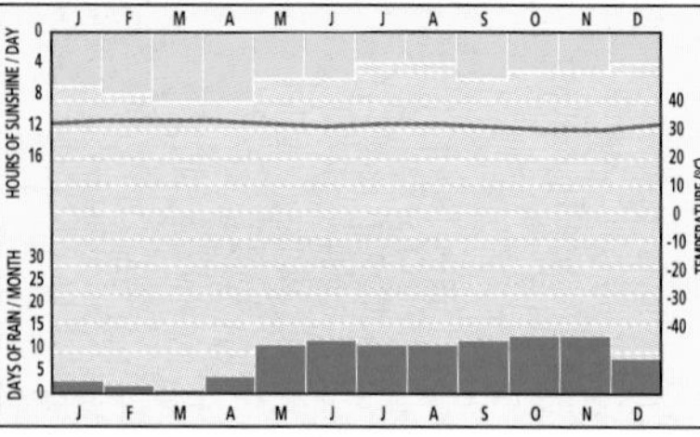

WHAT TO DO

A veritable causeway between South and Central America, Panama is bordered by two great bodies of water. The Caribbean Sea offers marvellous beaches and gorgeous islands like the Archipelago de San Blas, inhabited by the Cuña Indians. Portobelo Park, an old Spanish garrison, and Colón, more widely known for its duty-free shops than for its beautiful cathedral, are the main attractions in the northern part of the country. Darién National Park offers a glimpse of the tribal life of the Choco Indians. On the Pacific coast, there is, of course, Panama City, which blends vestiges of the Spanish colonial era with American-style modernity. Panama Viejo, or Old Panama City, has ruins that are worth a visit. The Panama Canal is an impressive construction. The Archipelago de las Perlas, in the sheltered waters of the Gulf of Panama, has seen a resurgence of tourism thanks to the beauty of its beaches. Some of the country's archaeological sites are difficult to travel to, though the Panamerican Highway provides some ease of movement. Visitors should make a point of seeing the ruins at La Pita, near Santiago, as well as the ruins at Sitio Conte, near Aguadulce.

WHAT TO BUY

Panamans love *carimanolas* (small patties filled with meat or shrimp) and *ceviche* (fish marinated in lime juice). The local beer is very refreshing. The Cuña Indians make *molas*, colourful fabric appliqués used to decorate clothes. Jewelry made of coloured pearls, macramé, and ceramics is the main craft in this duty-free country.

COLOMBIA

+3 +2 +1 0 -1

Region: South America
Area: 1,138,910 km²
Capital: Bogotá
Airport: Bogotá 12 km
Population: 35,577,560
Language: Spanish
Religion: Catholic
Government: presidential democracy
Voltage: 110 - 60
Vaccinations required: –
Vaccinations recommended: Ty, Po, Mal
Passport: required
Visa: not required
Currency: Colombian peso
$1Cdn: 667.64 pesos
Driving: right hand
International permit: recommended
Area code: 011-57
✆ from Canada: 1-800-463-9587
✆ to Canada: 980-19-0057
Accommodation: ★★★★
Restaurants: ★★★
Transportation: ★★★
Cost of living: ○○
UN rank: 50
Best months: Dec to Apr
Holidays: 1, 9 Jan; 20 Mar; 14, 16, 17 Apr; 1, 25 May; 19 Jun; 3, 20 July; 7, 21 Aug; 16 Oct; 6, 13 Nov; 8, 25, 26 Dec

COLOMBIA

WHAT TO DO

The "war on drugs" has not yet rid Colombia of its reputation as a dangerous country. Although the drug cartels never attack tourists, the tension among them is nevertheless palpable in most cities and towns. Informed and vigilant travellers, however, will find Columbia a wonderful country, where the beauty of the beaches on the Caribbean Sea and Pacific Ocean and the peaks of the Andes are rivalled only by the splendour of the Amazonian rainforest. Expeditions for the rainforest leave from Villavicencio, in the centre of the country. The state of Meta is also becoming popular for its beautiful scenery and mild climate. The huge coffee plantations on the majestic slopes of the valley between the Cordillera Central and the Cordillera Oriental are worth a visit. As well as its wealth of natural sites, Colombia has incomparable historical treasure. The San Agustín Archaeological Park, with its sculpted steles, is definitely worth the trip. The ruins at Tierradentro and buildings at Cartagena, in particular the San Sebastián Fort, are also prime attractions. In Bogotá, the Gold Museum has on display an impressive collection of pre-Colombian artifacts (more than 100,000 different items!) and the Colonial Art Museum offers exhibits on the history of the country. Medellín is a city to be avoided because of the high level of violence related to drug trafficking. Those who love sunny beaches will head for the north coast of Colombia, from Santa Marta to Barranquilla.

WHAT TO BUY

Ajiaco, a chicken-and-potato dish, is a Colombian specialty. Colombian cuisine is strongly influenced by Spanish culinary tradition, as evidenced in the *paellas* and shrimp dishes. Pre-Colombian themes are often transformed into beautiful jewelry, and the woollen and leather goods are also works of art. Anyone planning to visit Colombia should read Gabriel Garcia Marquez's masterpiece *One Hundred Years of Solitude.*

OFF. DE TOURISME DE COLOMBIE

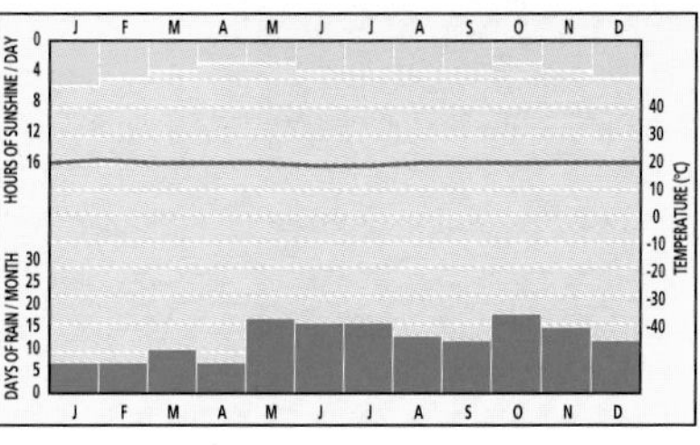

VENEZUELA

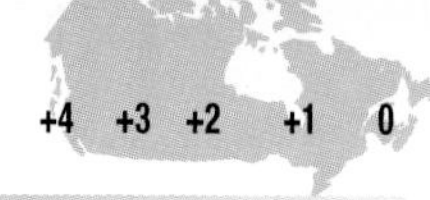

Region: South America
Area: 912,050 km²
Capital: Caracas
Airport: Caracas 27 km
Population: 20,562,410
Language: Spanish
Religion: Catholic
Government: presidential democracy
Voltage: 110 - 60
Vaccinations required: Yf*
Vaccinations recommended: Ty, Po, Mal
Passport: required
Visa: not required
Currency: bolivár
$1Cdn: 125.13 bolivárs
Driving: right hand
International permit: recommended
Area code: 011-58
✆ from Canada: 1-800-463-6564
✆ to Canada: ▲800-11100
Accommodation: ★★★★
Restaurants: ★★★★
Transportation: ★★★
Cost of living: ❍
UN rank: 46
Best months: Dec to May
Holidays: 1 Jan; 27, 28 Feb; 14, 16, 17 Apr; 1 May; 26 June; 5, 24 July; 12 Oct; 25, 26 Dec

WHAT TO DO

The name Venezuela (Little Venice) was given to this country by the first Spaniards to arrive in the region, who found houses on pilings belonging to Carib Indians. Today, most of Venezuela's cities are situated on the coast. The Caribbean Sea laps at more than 4,000 km of beaches, the best known of which are at Maiquetía, Macuto, Marbella, and Oriaco. In recent years, the Islas Los Roques and Isla de Margarita have become the most popular tourist areas. The coral reefs that shelter most of the coast are refuges for tropical fish and exotic birds, including flamboyant ibises and flamingos. On the other side of the Cordillera de Mérida is Maracaibo. The city and its lake of the same name serve as a gateway to a region peopled by Guajiro Indians, who still live in houses on pilings. At the foot of the cordillera are found the splendours Venezuela is famous for: on one side are magnificent beaches; on the other, the high snowy peaks of the Andes. The Sierra Nevada National Park offers challenging ski runs, notably, at Pico Bolivar, which has an altitude of 5,007 m. Farther east is Angel Falls, the highest falls in the world, cascading noisily from its height of 979 m. The national parks in the Llanos region protect rare species such as macaw parrots, red monkeys, and alligators. Some parks have been designated flower preserves; at Canaima, there are more than 500 varieties of orchids. One cannot go to Venezuela without visiting its capital, Caracas. Founded in 1567, the city has preserved buildings from various periods of its history: the cathedral, the old districts of San José and Las Pastora, Plaza Bolívar, and Casa Amarilla, among others. The city is very active culturally, and its many museums hold fabulous treasures.

WHAT TO BUY

The national dish of Venezuela is *pabellon criollo*, a tasty mixture of meat, black beans, rice, and plantain. Rather than bread, Venezuelans eat *arepa*, very tasty little corn-flour patties. *Guarapos* are tropical fruits fermented to make a delicious liquor, but beware: the quality of the products varies. Venezuelan coffee is excellent. Among the popular souvenirs from Venezuela are pearls from Isla de Margarita, gold jewelry, charms, ceramics, and hammocks. Crafts based on Carib Indian designs are also popular. For those who enjoy the sport, the *corridas* (bull fights) in Caracas and San Cristobal (usually held from November to March) are not to be missed.

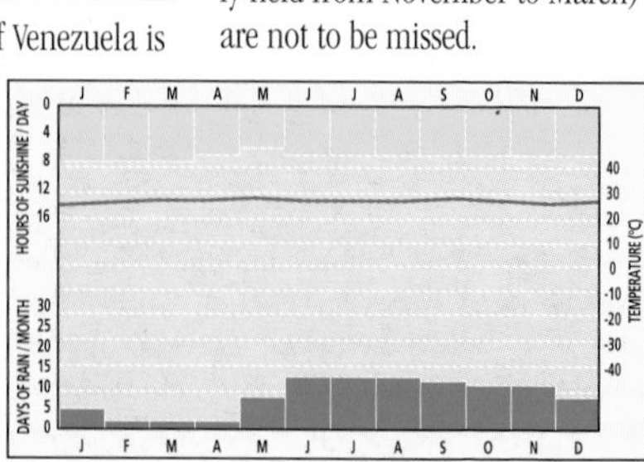

GREENBERG / CAMERIQUE / RÉFLEXION

GUYANA

+5 +4 +3 +2 +1

GUYANA

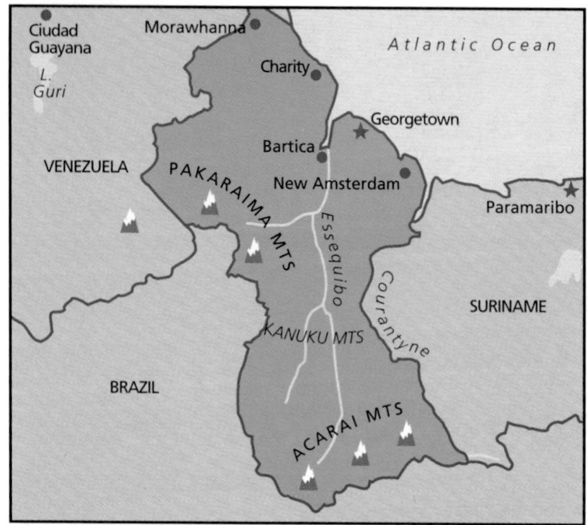

Region: South America
Area: 214,970 km²
Capital: Georgetown
Airport: Georgetown 40 km
Population: 729,430
Language: English
Religions: Catholic, Hindu
Government: presidential democracy
Voltage: 110 - 60
Vaccinations required: Yf*
Vaccinations recommended: Ty, Po, Mal
Passport: required
Visa: required
Currency: Guyana dollar
$1Cdn: 105.85 dollars
Driving: right hand
International permit: recommended
Area code: 011-592
✆ from Canada: –
✆ to Canada: 0161
Accommodation: ★★
Restaurants: ★★
Transportation: ★★
Cost of living: ○○○
UN rank: 107
Best months: Aug to Oct
Holidays: 1 Jan; 23 Feb; 14, 16, 17 Apr; 1 May; 3 July; 7 Aug; 25, 26 Dec

WHAT TO DO

Guiana, or "land of water," is what the aboriginals once called this region, where are found more than 1,600 kilometres of rivers, waterfalls, and rapids. The spectacular Kaieteur Falls (five times higher than Niagara Falls) are right in the heart of the country. Most of Guyana is covered with dense, lush jungle, much of which has not yet been explored. The cave paintings at Timehri, near the banks of the magnificent Mazaruni River, the Tramen ravines, and the Mazpuri Falls are other attractions that are worth seeing, even though travellers may have to fly into some of these sites. On the Venezuelan border, the lakes of the Rupununi River plain, are renowned for their impressively large fish, the joy of angling aficionados. In the cities, vestiges of the Dutch colonial era are still much in evidence, particularly in Georgetown, with its wooden houses and winding canals. St. George Cathedral, made entirely of wood, is a must-see, as is the famous Botanical Garden, which contains little-known varieties of palm trees and native flowers.

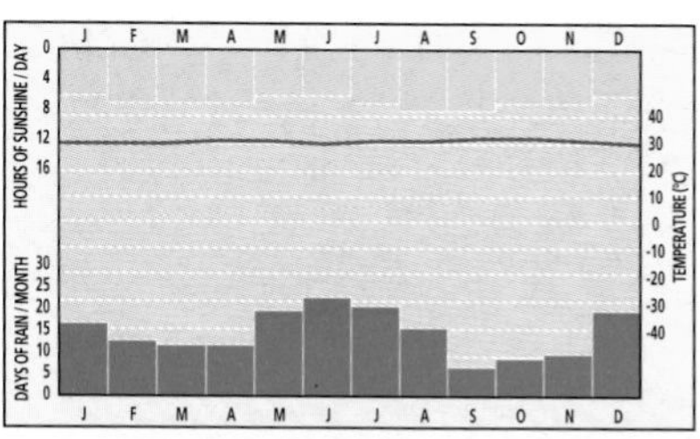

J. HUARD

WHAT TO BUY

Guyanese traditional cuisine offers shrimp cooked in coconut milk (*metamgee*), pepperpot (a meat stew), and *foo-foo* (plantain purée), a food inherited from Africa. In the markets of Georgetown are found woven baskets, rugs made of banana-tree leaves, hammocks, and terra cotta items. The sale of precious and semi-precious stones is regulated by the government.

SURINAME

+5 +4 +3 +2 +1

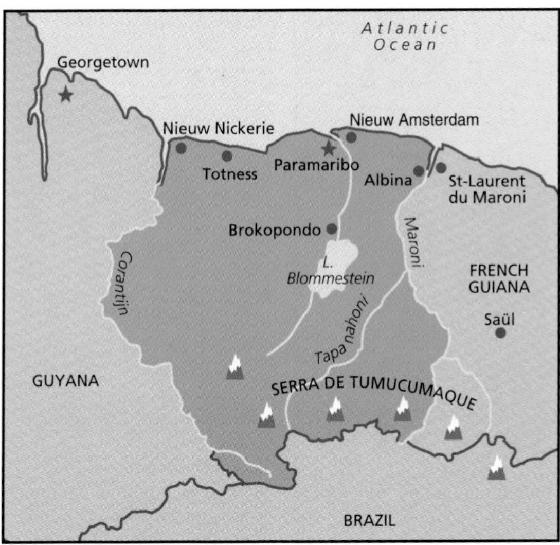

Region: South America
Area: 163,270 km²
Capital: Paramaribo
Airport: Paramaribo 45 km
Population: 422,840
Languages: Dutch (off.), Sranan, Tongo
Religions: Hindu, Christian
Government: presidential
Voltage: 110 - 60
Vaccinations required: Yf*
Vaccinations recommended: Ty, Po, Mal
Passport: required
Visa: not required
Currency: Suriname guilder
$1Cdn: 362.16 guilders
Driving: right hand
International permit: recommended
Area code: 011-597
✆ from Canada: –
✆ to Canada: –
Accommodation: ★★
Restaurants: ★★
Transportation: ★★
Cost of living: ❍❍
UN rank: 85
Best months: Aug to Dec
Holidays: 1 Jan; 4 Mar; 1 May; 1 July; 25 Nov; 25, 26 Dec

SURINAME

WHAT TO DO

Suriname was colonized by the Dutch. Today, the country is independent, but vestiges of Dutch influence are still very much in evidence, especially in the city of Paramaribo and the town of Nieuw Amsterdam. The best reason to visit Suriname is to see its natural sites: lush jungle, irrigated by long, fish-filled rivers, is home to extraordinary wildlife including plants that have not yet been named. The mangroves, rivers, jungle, and mountains are protected by the government, which has established reserves and national parks, the most interesting of which are the Raleighvallen and Noltzberg reserves and Brownsberg Park. Rare animal species, such as the tapir, live in the reserves. Paramaribo is a charming capital, where life flows at a tranquil pace in a setting redolent of the Netherlands, though a wide variety of influences are visible in the city's mosques, synagogues, temples, and churches. Boat rides on the long Suriname River leave from Nieuw Amsterdam and sail to Lake Blommestein, in the heart of the country.

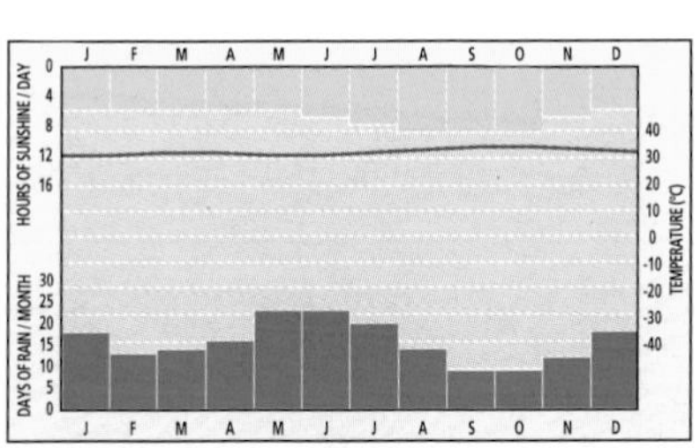

P. LESAGE

WHAT TO BUY

The ethnic diversity of Paramaribo has ensured the availability of European, Indonesian, Créole, Indian, and Chinese food. *Mocksie metie*, an assortment of meats served on a bed of rice, seems, however, to be the most popular local dish. The many varieties of wood available are an inspiration for Suriname's sculptors. In the markets of the towns and villages, travellers can buy hand-painted fabrics, silver jewelry, ceramics, and pottery.

FRENCH GUIANA

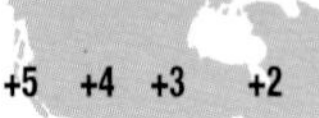

FRENCH GUIANA

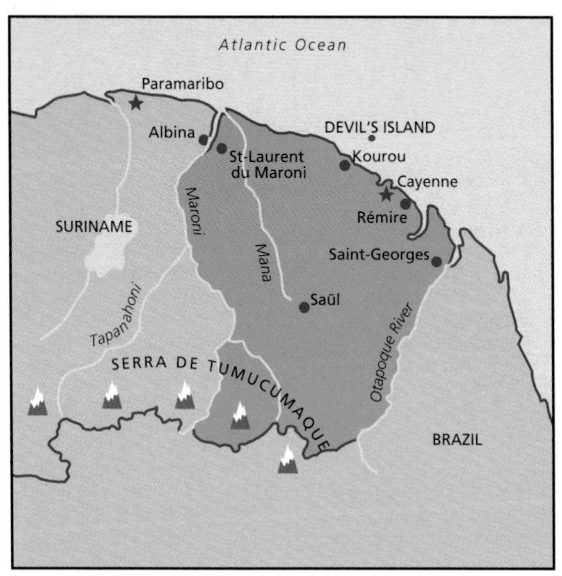

Region: South America
Area: 91,000 km²
Capital: Cayenne
Airport: Cayenne 17 km
Population: 139,300
Language: French
Religion: Catholic
Government: French overseas department
Voltage: 220 - 50
Vaccinations required: Yf*
Vaccinations recommended: Ty, Po, Mal
Passport: required
Visa: not required
Currency: French franc
$1Cdn: 3.52 francs
Driving: right hand
International permit: recommended
Area code: 011-594
✆ from Canada: –
✆ to Canada: –
Accommodation: ★★★
Restaurants: ★★★
Transportation: ★★★
Cost of living: ○○○
UN rank: –
Best months: Aug to Dec
Holidays: 1 Jan; 14, 16, 17 Apr; 1, 8, 25 May; 4, 5 June; 14 July; 15 Aug; 1, 11 Nov; 25, 26 Dec

WHAT TO DO

French Guiana is a French overseas department, with a population made up of French people, blacks, and aboriginals. This colony is having a hard time overcoming its unfortunate reputation as a country of "outlaws," based on the fact that Devil's Island was a penal colony until 1945. Today, visitors come and go completely freely, of course; some even sleep in the old prison building. Cayenne is the largest and liveliest town on the coast. The eighteenth-century buildings, fine beaches (especially at Montjoly), and the beautiful Botanical Gardens are prime attractions. The rocket-launch facility at Kourou is definitely worth seeing, as are, for different reasons, the mangroves that grow along the nearby coast, carving the scenery into strange shapes. French Guiana is also known for its abundant wildlife: the tropical forest harbours many rare species, including tapirs, ocelots, and anacondas.

WHAT TO BUY

French Guianese cuisine is mostly French and Créole: *bouillon d'Awaras* is a specialty that can be very spicy. The local craftspeople produce items woven from banana-tree leaves, wooden sculptures inspired by aboriginal traditions, and jewelry.

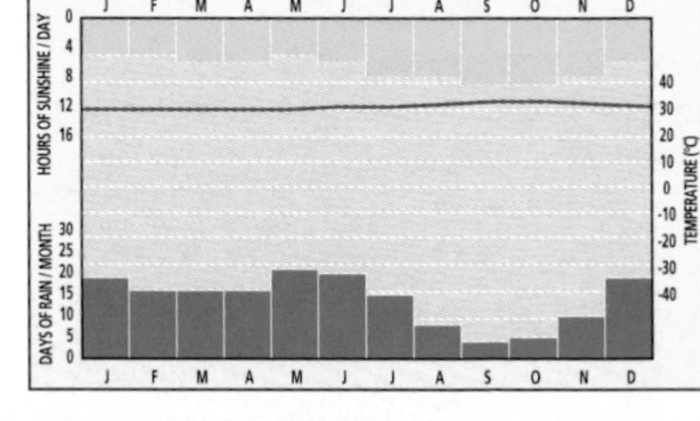

P. LESAGE

GALÁPAGOS

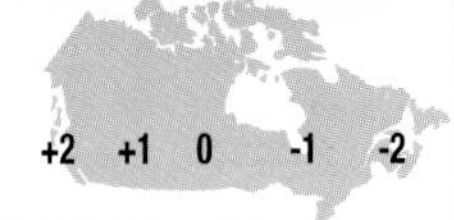

Region: Pacific Ocean
Area: 7,800 km²
Capital: Quito (Ecuador)
Airport: –
Population: approx. 9,000
Language: Spanish (off.)
Religion: Catholic
Government: province of Ecuador
Voltage: 110 - 60
Vaccinations required: Yf*
Vaccinations recommended: Ty, Po, Mal
Passport: required
Visa: required
Currency: sucre
$1Cdn: 1896.19 sucres
Driving: right hand
International permit: required
Area code: 011-593
✆ from Canada: –
✆ to Canada: –
Accommodation: ★
Restaurants: ★
Transportation: ★
Cost of living: ○○○
UN rank: –
Best months: June to Nov
Holidays: 1 Jan; 14, 16, 17 Apr; 1, 24 May; 24 July; 10 Aug; 9, 12 Oct; 2, 3 Nov; 25, 26 Dec

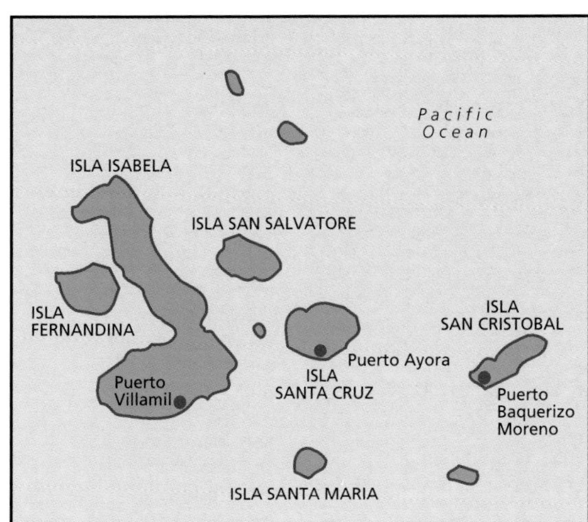

WHAT TO DO

UNESCO has named the Galápagos a World Heritage Site. These islands, which belong to Ecuador, are located almost 1,000 km to the west, in the middle of the Pacific Ocean. Organized group tours (the only way to visit) leave from Guayaquil, Ecuador. The Galápagos are exceptionally well protected, and visitors will understand why when they see the fantastic iguanas, turtles, and other colourful lizards sunning themselves by the thousands on their rocky shores. Sea lions and penguins also ply the waters of the national park. Only Puerto Ayora and Puerto Baquerizo offer tourist accommodations. The Darwin Research Centre conducts studies along the lines pioneered by Charles Darwin, who spent time on the islands in the nineteenth century.

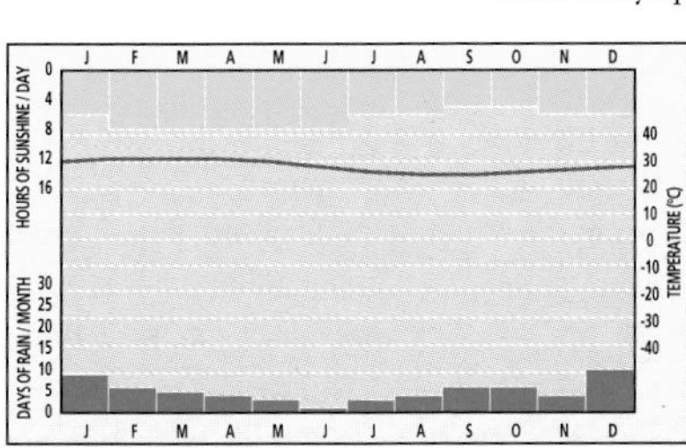

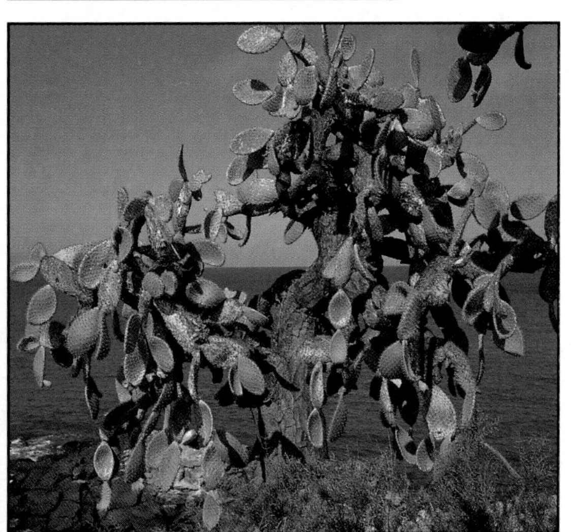

J. KROENER / REFLEXION

WHAT TO BUY

The photographs one takes on the Galápagos Islands are the best souvenirs of time spent there. A number of travel agencies offer tours to the islands, but the tours vary in quality: do a little research and comparison shopping before buying a ticket. A trip to the Galápagos costs a fair amount of money—but it is worth every cent!

ECUADOR

+3 +2 +1 0 -1

ECUADOR

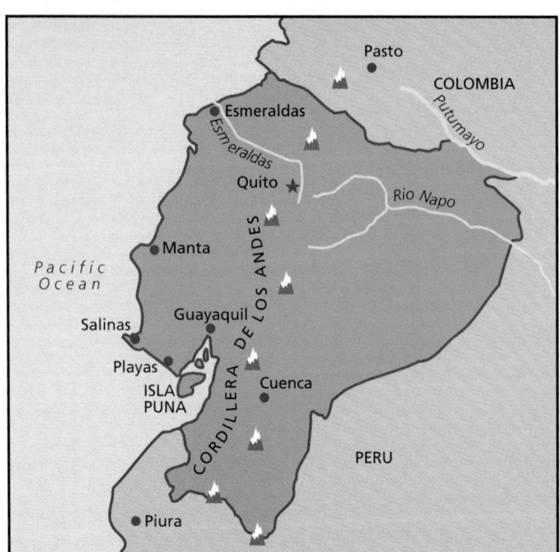

Region: South America
Area: 283,560 km² (inc. Galápagos)
Capital: Quito
Airport: Quito 8 km
Population: 10,677,100
Languages: Spanish (off.), Quechuan
Religion: Catholic
Government: presidential democracy
Voltage: 110 - 60
Vaccinations required: Yf*
Vaccinations recommended: Ty, Po, Mal
Passport: required
Visa: required
Currency: sucre
$1Cdn: 1896.19 sucres
Driving: right hand
International permit: required
Area code: 011-593
✆ from Canada: –
✆ to Canada: 999-175
Accommodation: ★★★
Restaurants: ★★★
Transportation: ★★★
Cost of living: ○○
UN rank: 74
Best months: June to Nov
Holidays: 1 Jan; 14, 16, 17 Apr; 1, 24 May; 24 July; 10 Aug; 9, 12 Oct; 2, 3 Nov; 25, 26 Dec

WHAT TO DO

As its name indicates, Ecuador straddles the equator. It is divided into three regions: La Sierra, in the Andes Cordillera, La Costa, along the Pacific coast, and El Oriente, which extends into the Amazonian forest. Almost half of the country's population lives in La Sierra. The majority of the rest live in Quito (the capital) and Guayaquil. Quito is a very beautiful city that UNESCO has named a World Heritage Site. Situated at the foot of the Pichincha Volcano, it has preserved many vestiges of the colonial era, such as sixteenth- and eighteenth-century churches and convents, as well as typical Ecuadoran houses. The San Francisco Convent and the church of the Jesuits are absolute must-sees. La Costa is washed by the Pacific, and some of its beaches are considered to be the most beautiful in South America, notably, those near the towns of Esmeraldas and Salinas. The eastern part of the country, El Oriente, is less accessible to tourists; they can, however, take organized excursions into the Amazonian forest to view wildlife in unspoiled settings. The Napo and Esmeraldas rivers are the main routes to travel to these remote regions. Experienced mountaineers will want to rise to the challenge of Cotopaxi Volcano, with an altitude of almost 5,900 m, or take on Chimborazo, rising 6,267 m.

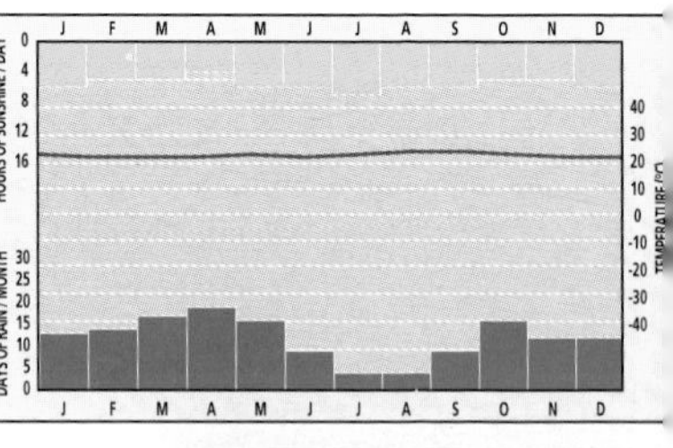

WHAT TO BUY

The cuisine is simple in Ecuador: the national dish is made of potatoes, cheese, and an avocado purée called *lorco*. Ecuadoran beer is among the best in South America. The markets in small towns like Otavalo, Ambato, and Riobamba offer crafts from all over the country: wooden sculptures, colourful figurines made of salt clay, woollen goods, rugs, printed cloth featuring aboriginal motifs, and silver jewelry. The market days (*ferias*) are particularly interesting. Women travellers are advised to dress discreetly.

J. KROENER / RÉFLEXION

PERU

+3 +2 +1 0 -1

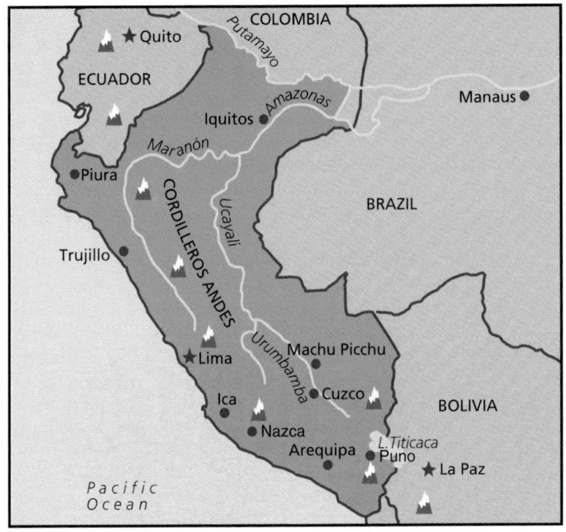

Region: South America
Area: 1,285,220 km²
Capital: Lima
Airport: Lima 16 km
Population: 23,650,680
Languages: Spanish, Quechuan, Aymara
Religion: Catholic
Government: presidential democracy
Voltage: 220 - 60
Vaccinations required: Yf*
Vaccinations recommended: Ty, Po, Mal
Passport: required
Visa: not required
Currency: new sol
$1Cdn: 1.66 sols
Driving: right hand
International permit: required
Area code: 011-51
✆ from Canada: 1-800-803-8480
✆ to Canada: 189
Accommodation: ★★★
Restaurants: ★★★
Transportation: ★★
Cost of living: ❍
UN rank: 95
Best months: May to Sept, Dec to Mar
Holidays: 1 Jan; 14, 16, 17 Apr; 1 May; 24, 29 June; 28 July; 30 Aug; 8 Oct; 1 Nov; 8, 25, 26 Dec

PERU

WHAT TO DO

Peru has four geographic regions: the coast (*costa*), the Andes (*sierra*), the tablelands (*montana*), and the Amazonian plain (*selva*). These different topographies give the country a colourful palette of landscapes, from deserts to fertile valleys, from high peaks to unexplored jungles. It is against this fabulous backdrop that visitors will find the largest archaeological sites in South America: Cuzco, the ancient capital of the Inca empire, is a World Heritage Site, with its Sacsahuaman Fortress; north of Cozco is the extraordinary Machu Picchu, with its 200 buildings, including the Torréon, considered the eighth wonder of the world. Ica and Nazca are veritable puzzles for archaeologists, who are still trying to discover the significance of the networks of lines dug into the ground in incredibly precise geometrical motifs at these sites. To appreciate its full effect, this region should be viewed from an airplane. Lake

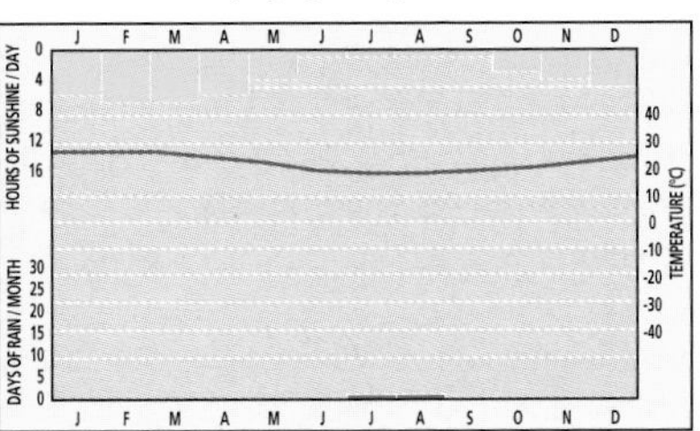

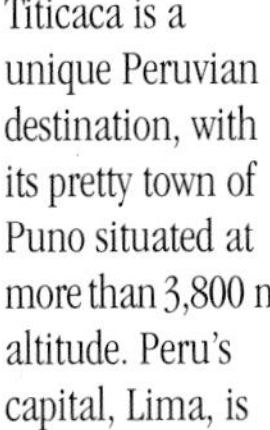

Titicaca is a unique Peruvian destination, with its pretty town of Puno situated at more than 3,800 m altitude. Peru's capital, Lima, is an old Spanish city that has preserved many monuments dating from the sixteenth, seventeenth, and eighteenth centuries, including a superb cathedral, churches (San Pedro is a fine example), and the buildings of San Marco University. The city has many museums, the largest of which are the Museum of Anthropology and Archaeology and the fascinating Museum of Gold. Trujillo is a charming seaside city with a mild climate.

WHAT TO BUY

The market in Ayacucho is well known for its pottery, leather goods, colourful fabrics, and jewelry. Peruvian alpaca knit goods are particularly handsome. Recordings of the enchanting music of the Andes flute make excellent souvenirs.

BRAZIL

WHAT TO DO

From Porto Alegre to Manaus, from Rio de Janeiro to Salvador in the state of Bahia, Brazil is as fascinating for its size (the fifth-largest country in the world) as for its natural riches, ranging from the Amazonian jungle to the plains of Pantanal. Brazilian culture is another great treasure of this country, in spite of the economic disparities between the rich and the poor. In fact, one would have to wear blinkers to avoid seeing the hordes of children begging for a few *cruzeiros* to escape the hell of the *favelas* (extremely poor slums) of Rio and São Paulo. Travellers usually begin their visit to this huge country in the legendary city of Rio de Janeiro. Its Sugar Loaf Mountain, Corcovado, Ipanema and Copacabana beaches, magnificent Jardim Botanico (botanical gardens), and famous Mardi Gras carnival are matched only by the joie de vivre of the Cariocas (inhabitants of Rio). To avoid extreme culture shock, travellers might do better to arrive at São Paulo, which is also a megalopolis, but a little less unsettling than is Rio. From there, they can travel north: Ouro Preto is a charming town full of history; Pirapora is a point of departure for boat trips on the beautiful São Francisco River; and Brasília, the capital, is a large city well known for its modern architecture. Farther into the interior, Pantanal de São Lourénço, a marshy region that has been recognized as a unique ecological site, is accessed via the town of Goiás. This part of the country, in the state of Mato Grosso, is one of the least accessible: travellers are advised to take organized excursions to the area and organized boat trips on the

Region: South America
Area: 8,511,965 km^2
Capital: Brasília
Airport: Rio de Janeiro 20 km
Population: 158,739,260
Language: Portuguese
Religion: Catholic
Government: presidential democracy
Voltage: 110/220 - 60
Vaccinations required: Yf*
Vaccinations recommended: Ty, Po, Mal
Passport: required
Visa: required
Currency: real
$1Cdn: .69 reals
Driving: right hand
International permit: required
Area code: 011-55
✆ from Canada: 1-800-463-6656
✆ to Canada: 000-8014
Accommodation: ★★★★
Restaurants: ★★★★
Transportation: ★★★
Cost of living: ○○
UN rank: 63
Best months: May to Dec
Holidays: 1 Jan; 25–28 Feb; 14, 16, 17, 21 Apr; 1, 25 May; 15 June; 7 Sept; 12 Oct; 2, 15 Nov; 25, 26 Dec

BRAZIL

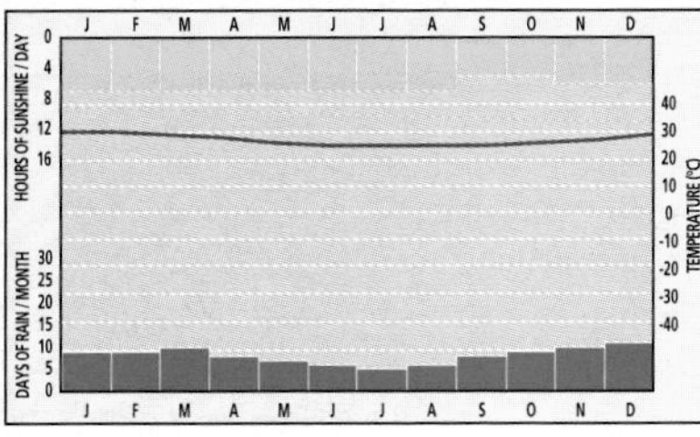

Amazon River. This river is navigable over more than 3,000 km, and most tours journey from Belém inland to Manaus, right through the heart of the Amazon rainforest, where there are still some little-known aboriginal tribes. The Cataratas Iguazú (Iguaçu Falls), on the border with Argentina and Paraguay, is worth a detour into these distant regions. But most travellers to Brazil come for its magnificent beaches, especially those between Pôrto Seguro and Ilhéus. A little farther north, the pretty town of Salvador is a special place. Its old town is now considered a World Heritage Site, worth preserving for its churches and Portuguese-style buildings (nevertheless, don't go there alone). The entire town exudes the Bahian soul, a subtle mixture of traditions inherited from Africa and Portugal. A *candomble* (half-Christian, half-pagan) ceremony is in itself worth the trip to Brazil. The works of the great Brazilian writer Jorge Amado provide a good introduction to Brazil.

WHAT TO BUY

Bahian cuisine is different from that in the rest of the country: *vatapa* (shrimp cooked in coconut milk) and *caruru*, another shrimp dish, are typical of the region. Elsewhere, *churrascos* (grilled meats, mainly beef) and *feijoadas* (a black-bean dish) are the staples. The exotic-fruit juices, served icy cold, are exceptional; the coffee and cocoa are also very tasty. *Capirina* is a very sweet mixture of *cachaça* (cane-sugar liquor) and lime juice; it's delicious—if you don't overdo it! It can never be said too often: Brazil is a dangerous country for tourists who show off their wealth. Watches, earrings, handbags, and cameras should be left at home. Women travellers should be especially careful and not follow people who come up to them claiming to be tourist guides; neither should they move around alone. By following these basic rules, visitors to this superb country will be absolutely safe. They might want to encourage the craftspeople by buying their hammocks, shell jewelry, stones from the state of Minas Gerais, and the famous *figas*, or good-luck charms.

BOLIVIA

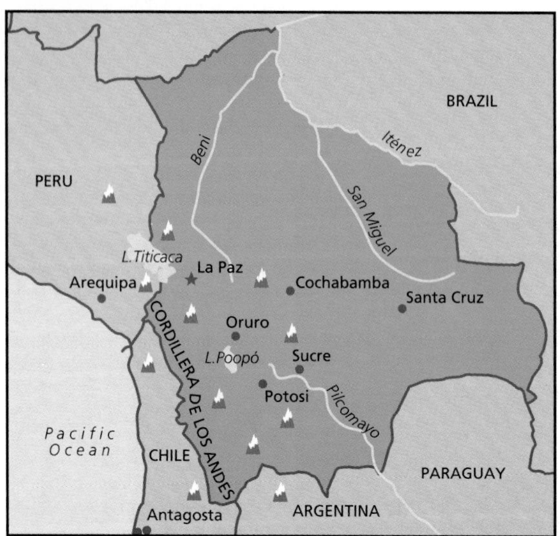

Region: South America
Area: 1,098,580 km²
Capital: La Paz, Sucre
Airport: La Paz 14 km
Population: 7,719,450
Languages: Spanish, Quechuan, Aymara
Religion: Catholic
Government: presidential democracy
Voltage: 110/220 - 50
Vaccinations required: Yf*
Vaccinations recommended: Ty, Po, Mal
Passport: required
Visa: required
Currency: boliviano
$1Cdn: 3.54 bolivianos
Driving: right hand
International permit: recommended
Area code: 011-591
✆ from Canada: 1-800-463-0228
✆ to Canada: ▲0-800-0101
Accommodation: ★★★
Restaurants: ★★★
Transportation: ★★★
Cost of living: ❍
UN rank: 113
Best months: Apr to Sept
Holidays: 1 Jan; 27 Feb; 14, 16, 17 Apr; 1 May; 15 June; 6 Aug; 2 Nov; 25, 26 Dec

WHAT TO DO

Bolivia is divided into three geographical regions—the Cordillera Occidental in the Andes, the eastern plains, and the Altiplano—and each is as stunning as the other. It is in the Altiplano that travellers can find Lake Titicaca, the largest mountain lake in the world, and vestiges of the Inca civilization at nearby Tiwanacu. The city of La Paz sits at 3,632 m altitude, making it the highest national capital in the world (some visitors even have trouble breathing when they arrive). In fact, the constitutional capital of the country is in Sucre, and the seat of the government is in La Paz. This interesting city is set against the backdrop of magnificent Mount Illimani, which rises to more than 6,880 m altitude. More courageous travellers will want to venture into the Bolivian jungle, which is rich in wildlife.

WHAT TO BUY

Empañadas, cornflour shells filled with meat and vegetables, are sold at food counters all over the country. Beware of foods that are *picante*; the Bolivian chili sauce is particularly hot! The carnival in Oruro, which takes place in February and March, is among the most colourful in South America; craftspeople take this opportunity to display their many wares, including alpaca knits, shawls, ponchos, caps, and colourful blankets. The melodies produced by the musical instruments, especially the Andean flute, are representative of the joyous Bolivian soul. Tourists, and particularly women, should be vigilant especially in the cities, where poverty is endemic.

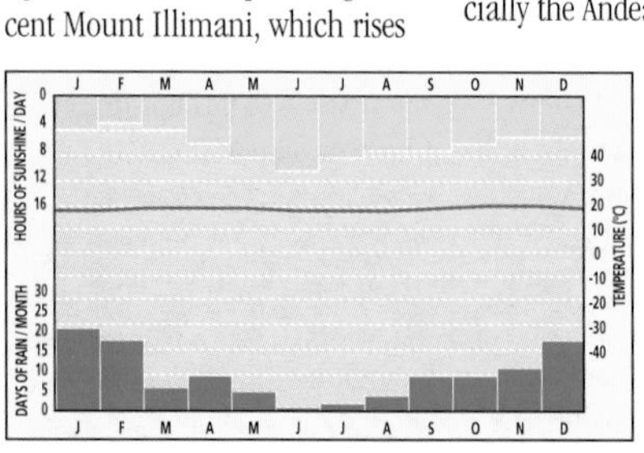

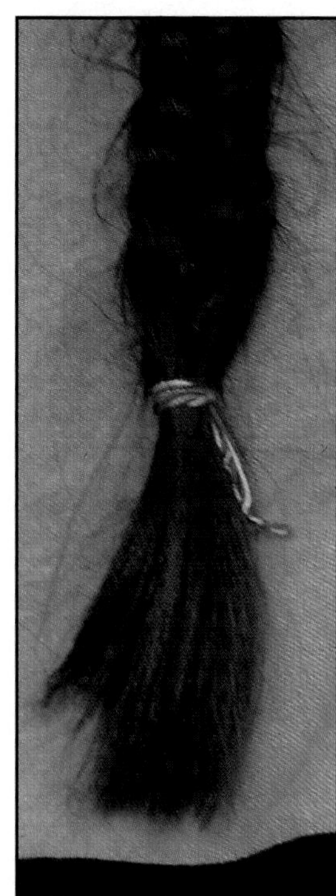

PARAGUAY

+4 +3 +2 +1 0

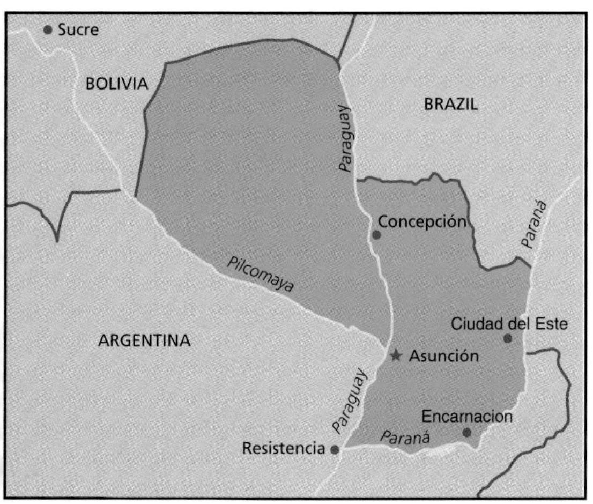

Region: South America
Area: 406,750 km²
Capital: Asunción
Airport: Asuncíon 15 km
Population: 5,213,772
Languages: Spanish (off.), Guarani
Religion: Catholic
Government: presidential democracy
Voltage: 220 - 50
Vaccinations required: Yf*
Vaccinations recommended: Ty, Po, Mal
Passport: required
Visa: not required
Currency: guaraní
$1Cdn: 1450.12 guaranís
Driving: right hand
International permit: recommended
Area code: 011-595
✆ from Canada: 1-800-463-3570
✆ to Canada: 008-13-800
Accommodation: ★★★
Restaurants: ★★★
Transportation: ★★★
Cost of living: ❍
UN rank: 84
Best months: Feb to May, Aug to Nov
Holidays: 1 Jan; 3 Feb; 1 Mar; 14, 16, 17 Apr; 1, 14, 15 May; 12, 15 June; 15 Aug; 20 Sept; 1 Nov; 8, 25, 26 Dec

WHAT TO DO

Before the Spaniards arrived, Paraguay was inhabited by Tupi-Guarani Indians. Of all South American countries, Paraguay has best preserved its Guarani identity, even though people of mixed blood are numerous today. Amateur anthropologists will want to visit the typical villages east of the Paraná River, while history lovers will be charmed by old colonial towns like San Lorenzo, founded in 1775; Yaguarón, the old Franciscan stronghold; Encarnación, cooled by breezes coming off the Paraná; and Itá, founded in 1539, with its colourful market. One must also visit the capital, Asunción, which is a real history book. The Iguaçu Falls, on the border with Argentina and Brazil, attract thousands of visitors. To make sure that they see all the beauties of the country, travellers should try to follow the Central Circuit, a road about 200 km long that leads to many of Paraguay's most interesting sites.

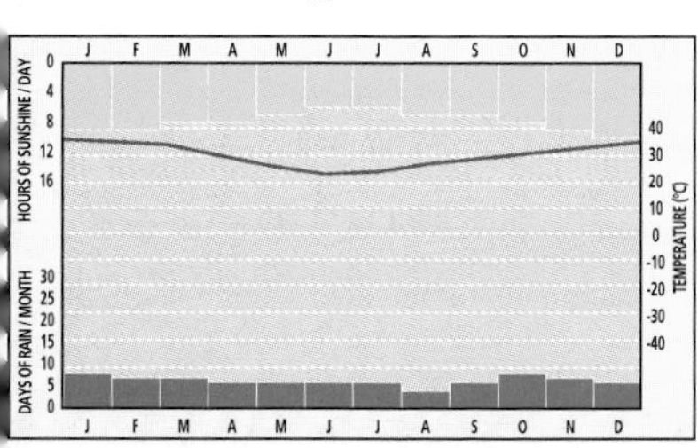

WHAT TO BUY

Paraguay's national dish is *soo-yosopy*, a delicious corn-and-meat soup. Visitors must sample *surubi*, a delicate fish from the Paraná River. *Maté*, a typically South American bitter herbal tea, and *cana*, a sugar-cane liquor, are often served with meals. *Aho-poi* fabrics, woven by Guarani villagers, *nanduti* lace from Itagua, leather goods, and carved-wood items are available throughout the country. *Bombillas*, straws for drinking *maté*, make good souvenirs.

CHILE

+4 +3 +2 +1 0

Region: South America
Area: 756,950 km²
Capital: Santiago
Airport: Santiago 16 km
Population: 13,950,560
Language: Spanish
Religion: Catholic
Government: presidential democracy
Voltage: 220 - 50
Vaccinations required: –
Vaccinations recommended: Cho, Ty
Passport: required
Visa: not required
Currency: Chilean peso
$1Cdn: 283.4 pesos
Driving: right hand
International permit: required
Area code: 011-56
✆ from Canada: 1-800-463-2492
✆ to Canada: 123-00-318
Accommodation: ★★★★
Restaurants: ★★★★
Transportation: ★★★
Cost of living: ○○
UN rank: 38
Best months: Mar, Apr, May, Oct
Holidays: 1 Jan; 14, 16, 17 Apr; 1, 21 May; 15, 29 June; 15 Aug; 18 Sept; 12 Oct; 1 Nov; 8, 25, 26 Dec

WHAT TO DO

The word "Chile" comes from *chilemapu*, a Quechuan word that means "cold country," no doubt a reference to the snowy peaks of the Andes, which cover more than half of Chile's surface. The country stretches almost 4,200 km from north to south but is never more than 180 km wide. In terms of latitude, Chile goes from the 17th to the 56th parallel, so it covers a wide range of climatic and geographic conditions, from arctic desert—one of the most arid regions on the planet—to the magnificent fjords in the south, to fertile valleys in the central region. Valparaíso and Santiago both offer all the conveniences of modern cities, while preserving the charm inherited from the colonial era. The ski centres of Porhillo and Farellones are becoming increasingly popular, and the parks at lake Todos los Santos and Desierto de Atacama are considered exceptionally beautiful. The coast between Arica and Iquique, in the north, is known for its splendid beaches. At the southern tip of the country, the Magellan Strait and Cape Horn offer otherworldly scenery. The Torres des Paine and Fitz Roy national parks are good stepping-off points for visiting this region, which is still relatively inaccessible. The more adventurous may escape to the isolated Juan Fernández Islands, some 650 km off Valparaíso, still haunted by the ghost of Daniel Defoe's legendary hero, Robinson Crusoe. Even farther into the Pacific Ocean, Easter Island's mysterious monolithic statues, erected more than a thousand years ago, still greet visitors.

WHAT TO BUY

Chileans love both seafood and red meat: *chupe de mariscos*, a fish dish, and *empañadas*, cornflour shells filled with meat, appear on every menu. *Aguardiente* is a typically South American liquor. Beware of adulterated liquors and demand that your bottle arrive unopened. Alpaca knitwear, glazed pottery, reproductions of sculptures from Easter Island, and leather items are available in markets in all the villages and towns. Lapis lazuli is very popular in Chile, and jewelers make wonderful ornaments from it. The markets in Pomaire and Santiago have the greatest variety of goods. Women travellers should dress discreetly; beachwear is acceptable only at seaside.

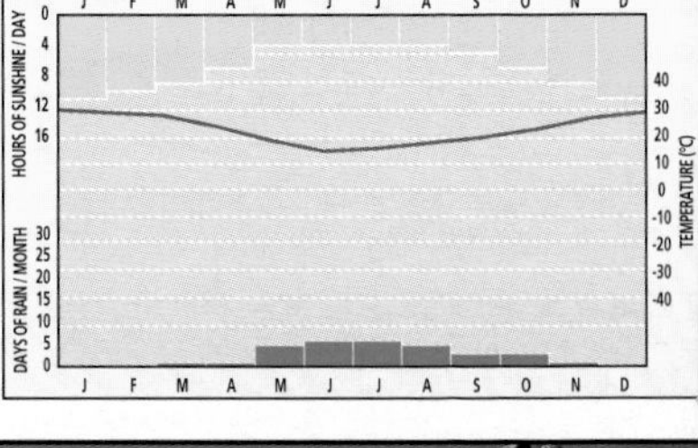

ARGENTINA

+5 +4 +3 +2 +1

WHAT TO DO

'he very large country of Argentina ; divided into four geographic egions— the Andes, Mesopotamia, .a Pampa, and Patagonia—where emperatures range from desert heat ɔ glacial cold, from hot and humid veather to the cool of gentle Atlantic reezes. Travellers will find there a vide variety of scenery; they can ravel to the peak of Cerro .concagua, with an altitude of lmost 7,000 m (the highest in the mericas) or stroll the lively streets f Buenos Aires, the city that is the erfect stepping-off point for visiting rgentina. Nicknamed the Paris of 'outh America, Buenos Aires is a ynamic national capital with a nique charm: Plaza de Mayo, Casa ?osada, the Cabildo, and the cathe- tral are superb sites in the centre of he city, which moves to the subtle hythms of the famous Argentine ango. The La Boca district produces he best shows. On the northern tip f the country, travellers should be ure to visit the famous Cataratas de guazú (Iguaçu Falls), on the bor- ler with Paraguay and Brazil. The Argentine Mesopotamia is a vast plain punctuated with *haciendas*, huge ranches where cattle graze under the watchful eyes of *gauchos.* In La Pampa, verdant farming valleys give way to desert plains, stretches of brush typically Argentinian and steppes. The triangle formed by Córdoba, San Miguel de Tucumán, and Salta is a fertile region of vineyards and orchards surrounding charming villages that seem to come straight out of another century. San Carlos de Bariloche, on the Chilean border, is well known for its lakes teeming with fish. The greatest attraction of the country is, without doubt, Patagonia. This region spreads across the entire tip of South America, including some Chilean territory: the stunningly beautiful Tierra del Fuego, the myriad of forests and lakes, the steep slopes of the Andes, and the jagged coastline dotted with little ports and lost villages seem to belong to a different planet. Especially breathtaking is the view of the convergence of the Atlantic and Pacific oceans in the Magellan Strait.

WHAT TO BUY

Argentinians love their beef: *bife de lomo, bife a caballo, churrasco*, and *puchero* are just a few of the many ways to sample beef in this country. Red meat is best accompanied by a full-bodied red wine; the wines from La Rioja are particularly good. Leather, woollen goods (ponchos, caps, and coats), *bombachas* (*gauchos'* pants), and the *bandonion* (the little accordion that gives the tango its distinctive sound) are typical of Argentina. The tango is very sensual; don't get too carried away in the arms of the professional dancers!

Region: South America
Area: 2,776,890 km²
Capital: Buenos Aires
Airport: Buenos Aires 50 km
Population: 33,913,000
Languages: Spanish (off.), English
Religion: Catholic
Government: presidential democracy
Voltage: 220 - 60
Vaccinations required: —
" recommended: Ty, Po, Mal, Yf
Passport: required
Visa: not required
Currency: peso
$1Cdn: .74 pesos
Driving: right hand
International permit: required
Area code: 011-54
✆ from Canada: 1-800-805-0477
✆ to Canada: 001-800-222-1111
Accommodation: ★★★★
Restaurants: ★★★★
Transportation: ★★★
Cost of living: ○○○
UN rank: 37
Best months: Dec to May
Holidays: 1 Jan; 14, 16, 17 Apr; 1, 25 May; 10, 19 June; 9 July; 18 Aug; 13 Oct; 8, 25, 26 Dec

ARGENTINA

VIESTI / RÉFLEXION

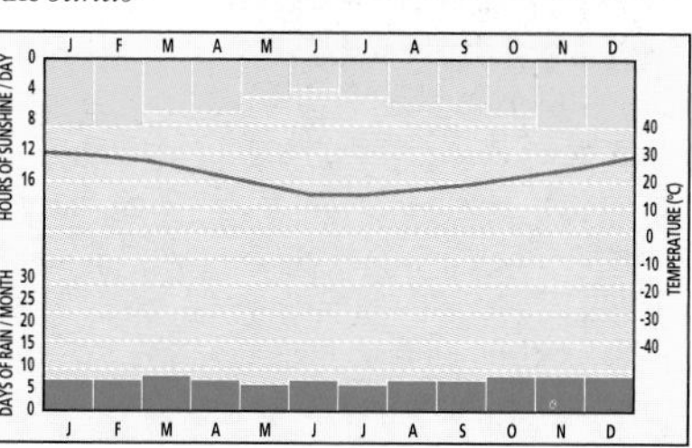

URUGUAY

+5 +4 +3 +2 +1

URUGUAY

Region: South America
Area: 176,220 km²
Capital: Montevideo
Airport: Montevideo 21 km
Population: 3,198,910
Language: Spanish
Religion: Catholic
Government: presidential democracy
Voltage: 220 - 50
Vaccinations required: –
Vaccinations recommended: Ty, Po
Passport: required
Visa: not required
Currency: new Uruguayan peso
$1Cdn: 4.78 pesos
Driving: right hand
International permit: recommended
Area code: 011-598
✆ from Canada: 1-800-463-3796
✆ to Canada: 000-149
Accommodation: ★★★
Restaurants: ★★★
Transportation: ★★★
Cost of living: ❍
UN rank: 33
Best months: Dec to Apr
Holidays: 1, 6 Jan; 14, 16, 17 Apr; 1 May; 18 July; 25 Aug; 1 Nov; 25, 26 Dec

URUGUAYAN TOURIST OFFICE

WHAT TO DO

Uruguay is a country of vast prairies. The stately *estancias*, or farm estates, are still inhabited by *gauchos*, whose work hasn't changed much over the last century. Travellers tend to visit Uruguay only for its capital, Montevideo. However, the country also offers kilometres of beaches, which have earned it the nickname "Riviera of South America". Punta del Este is one of the leading tourism centres in Uruguay, along with Atlántida, Piriápolis and Paloma. Rio de la Plata runs up to Rio Uruguay then onward into the interior. Along its shores are Mercedes and Salto, two towns that are worth a visit. Farther south is the town of Minas surrounded by lovely mountains that provide some relief to the flat countryside. Montevideo is known for its beaches, among the loveliest in the country. The cathedral and the city hall are prime attractions, as is Tablada, the cattle market, where one can see *gauchos* trading livestock.

WHAT TO BUY

The *churrascos* and *parrillas*, grilled and skewered beef, are a basic of the cuisine. *Grappa* and *cana* are the country's most famous liquors. *Boleadoras*, stones wrapped in leather pouches which are used by the *gauchos* like lassos to catch animals that get away from the herd, are unique souvenirs. Of course, all leather items made in Uruguay are top quality, and woollen goods are also very fine.

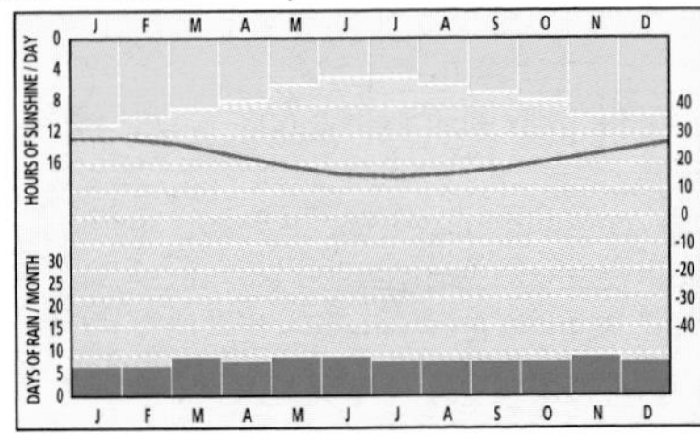

T. BOGNAR / REFLEXION

AFRICA

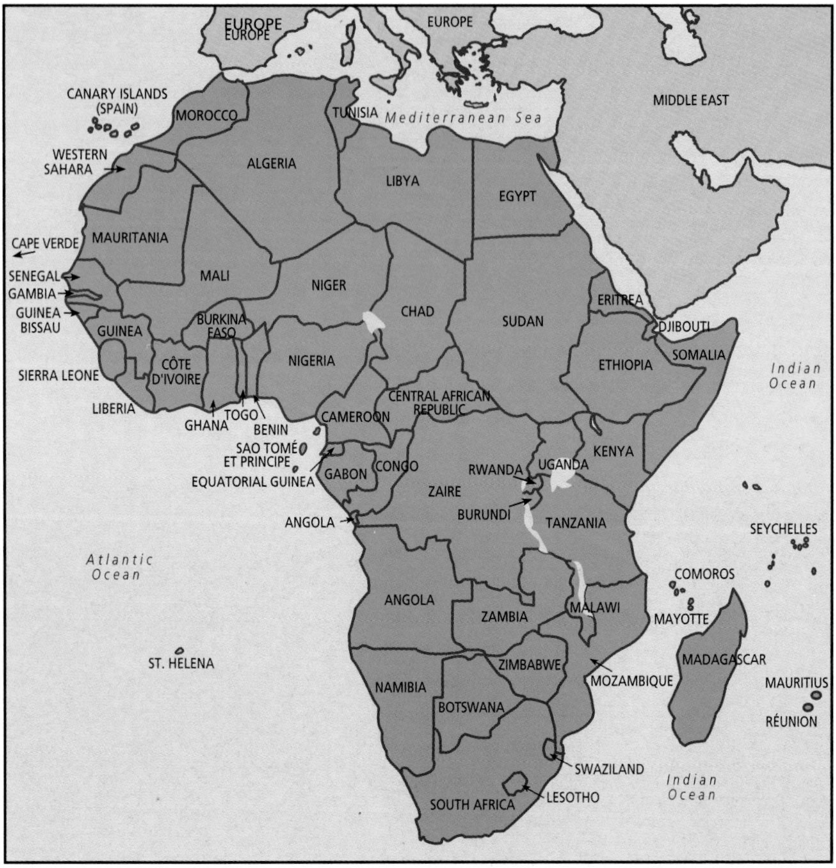

Africa's scenery takes on many faces, depending on whether one speaks of Mediterranean, Saharan, Eastern, Western, or Southern Africa or the Indian Ocean. From vast plains to virgin forests, from spectacular deserts to magnificent rivers, the African continent is full of hidden surprises and treasures. Travellers who are open to new experiences will find, against this impressive mosaic of backdrops, still unexplored regions, mysterious peoples, fabulous wildlife, and a pace of life entirely different from anything they are used to. Africa also offers visitors a culinary adventure: exotic fruits and vegetables, spicy and aromatic dishes, a variety of liquors, and a wide range of traditional cuisines —something for every palate! Some African countries are suffering the effects of war or are engaged in conflicts that are threatening the peace and stability of their countries; it is essential for tourists to inform themselves before setting out on any visit.

SDP / DUFAUX / RÉFLEXION

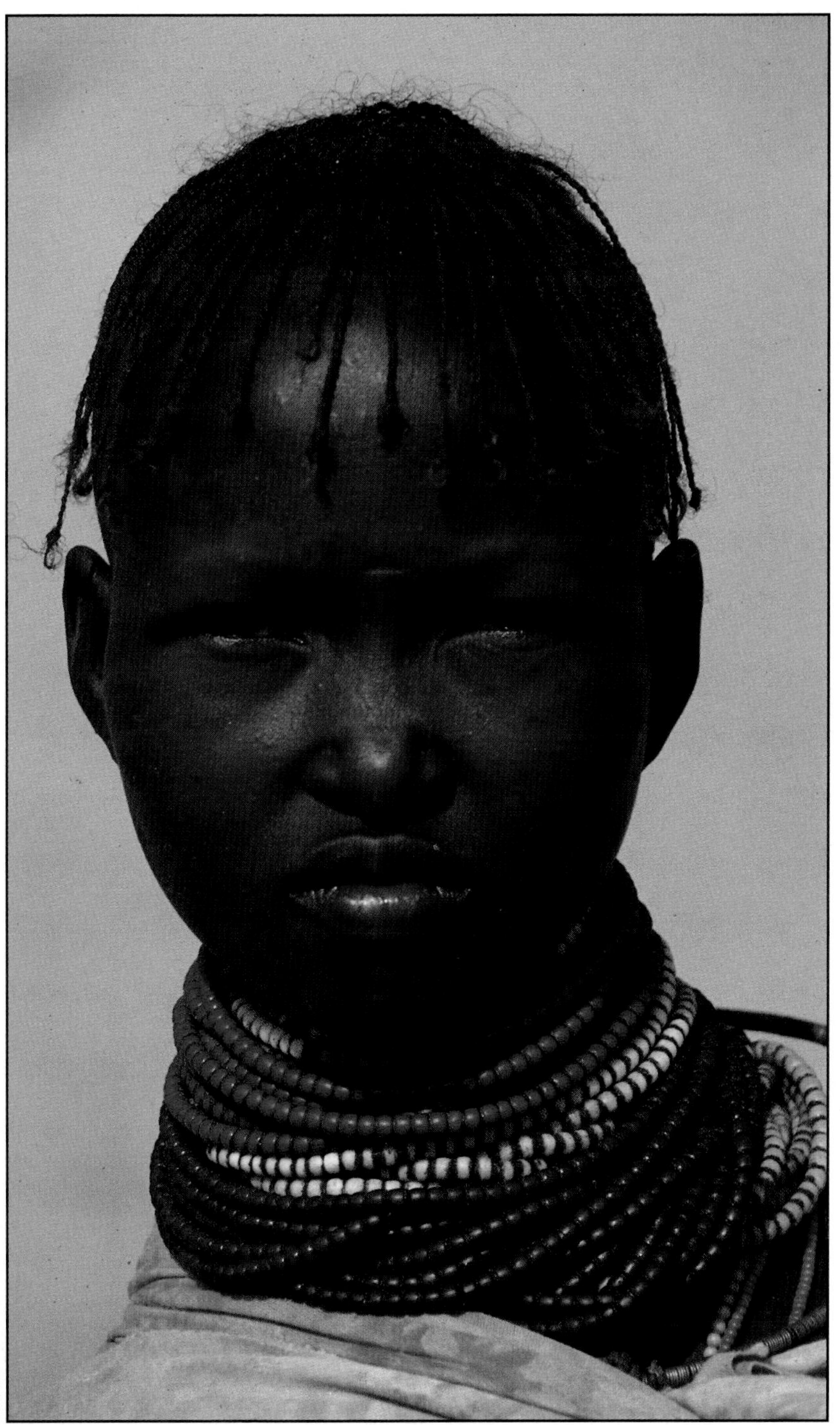

J. HUARD

AFRICA

NORTHWEST AFRICA

+8 +7 +6 +5 +4

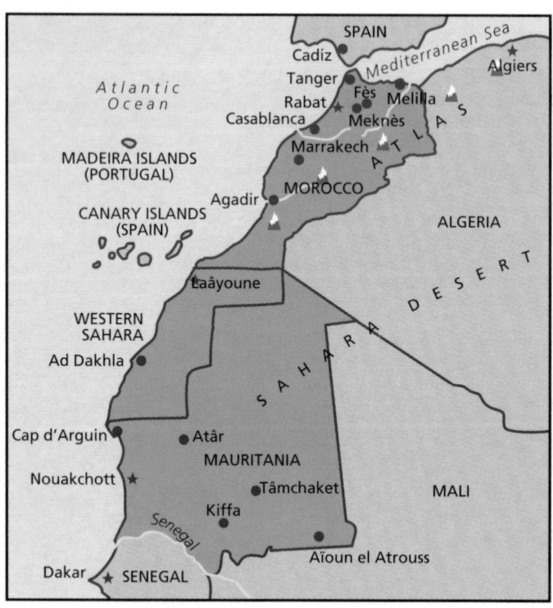

MOROCCO

Region: Africa
Area: 446,550 km²
Capital: Rabat
Airport: Rabat 10 km
Population: 28,558,640
Languages: Arabic (off.), Berber, French
Religion: Islamic
Government: constitutional monarchy
Voltage: 110/220 - 50
Vaccinations required: –
" recommended: Cho, Ty, Po, Mal
Passport: required
Visa: not required
Currency: Moroccan dirham
$1Cdn: 6.11 dirhams
Driving: right hand
International permit: recommended
Area code: 011-212
✆ from Canada: 1-800-463-1092
✆ to Canada: 00-211-0010
Accommodation: ★★★★★
Restaurants: ★★★★
Transportation: ★★★★
Cost of living: ○○
UN rank: 111
Best months: May to Oct
Holidays: 1, 11 Jan; 3, 4 Mar; 1, 11, 23, 31 May; 9 July; 8, 14, 20 Aug; 6, 18 Nov

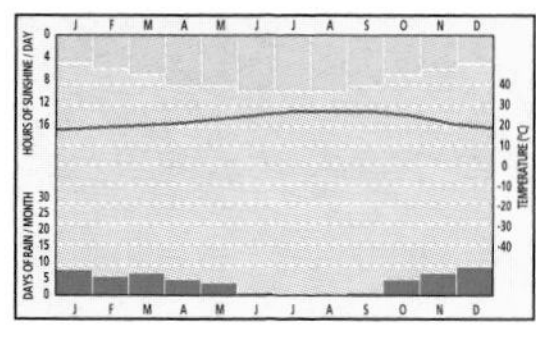

WHAT TO DO

MOROCCO is the gateway to Africa. Meknès, Marrakech, and Fès have played an important role in the country's history. Meknès is famous for having within its walls the ruins of the largest palace in the world, Dar el-Kebira, or the "Moroccan Versaille," which belonged to Sultan Mulay Ismail. The city is also known for its superb walls, mosques, souks, and medina. Marrakech is a supply depot for desert caravans and the gathering place of many nomadic peoples, especially the Saharan Maghrebs. Its Bahia Palace, open to the public, is richly adorned with cedar-wood sculptures. The tall minaret of La Koutoubia is splendid, as are the tombs of the Sa'adians, Djemaa el-Fna Square, and the Agdal and Menara gardens. Fès is famous above all for its medina, one of the most labyrinthine in Morocco, but also one of the most beautiful. One stumbles upon the tomb of Idris II, who founded the town in 809, in the bend of an alleyway! The district of the leather tanners and the Qarawiyïn Mosque are also worth visiting. Rabat is a clean, tidy capital, full of monuments as old as the city itself (it dates from the twelfth century). It is surrounded by the "Andalusian Wall" and overlooked by the Hassan Tower and the mausoleum of Muhammad V. The casbah of the Oudaïa, the Royal Palace, and the Roman site of Chella should also be seen. Tetouan, with its medina and souks, has a very different feel, for the Berbers descend the mountains from Rif to sell their products there.

Between Casablanca and Agadir, the beaches on the Atlantic Ocean are very beautiful. Some ornithologists consider MAURITANIA to be paradise for birdwatching, especially at Cap d'Arguin, on the northern tip of the Atlantic coast. Farther east, on the high plateaus in the Adrar region, the town of Atar and the villages of Ouadane and Chinguetti are fascinating for the authentic Maurish culture that still reigns there and for the vestiges of past eras found in the cave paintings and many

+9 +8 +7 +6 +5

MAURITANIA

Region: Africa
Area: 1,030,700 km²
Capital: Nouakchott
Airport: Nouakchott 4 km
Population: 2,192,780
Languages: Hassaniyah Arabic (off.), French
Religion: Islamic
Government: presidential
Voltage: 220 - 50
Vaccinations required: Yf
" recommended: Cho, Ty, Po, Mal
Passport: required
Visa: required
Currency: ouguiya
$1Cdn: 93.99 ouguiyas
Driving: right hand
International permit: recommended
Area code: 011-222
✆ from Canada: –
✆ to Canada: –
Accommodation: ★
Restaurants: ★
Transportation: ★
Cost of living: ○○
UN rank: 158
Best months: Nov, Mar
Holidays: 1 Jan; 4, 12 Mar; 1, 11, 25, 31 May; 8 Aug; 28 Nov; 25 Dec

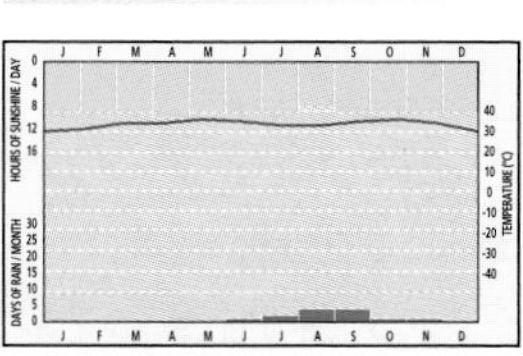

+8 +7 +6 +5 +4

W. SAHARA

Region: Africa
Area: 266,000 km²
Capital: Laâyoune
Airport: –
Population: 211,880
Language: Hassaniyah Arabic
Religion: Islamic
Government: disputed status
Voltage: 220 - 50
Vaccinations required: –
" recommended: Cho, Ty, Po, Mal
Passport: required
Visa: required
Currency: Moroccan dirham
$1Cdn: 6.11dirhams
Driving: right hand
International permit: required
Area code: 011-212
✆ from Canada: –
✆ to Canada: –
Accommodation: –
Restaurants: –
Transportation: –
Cost of living: –
UN rank: –
Best months: Oct to Mar
Holidays: 1, 11 Jan; 3, 4 Mar; 1, 11, 23, 31 May; 9 July; 8, 14, 20 Aug; 6, 18 Nov

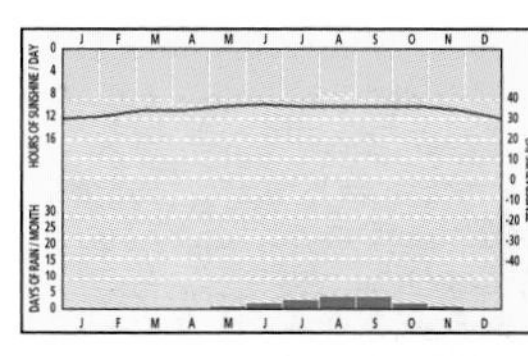

mosques. In the south, the region of the Assâba and Affollé plateaus also has much history to divulge. The WESTERN SAHARA is a large territory claimed by Morocco; the tension between the Western Saharan capital, Laâyoune, and Morocco's capital, Rabat, is such that tourism in this region has slowed. Nevertheless, the village of Ad Dakhla and the entire Atlantic coast north to Dawra are very beautiful destinations.

WHAT TO BUY

Moroccans are proud of their fine cuisine: couscous, merguez sausage, chicken, roast lamb, tahini, and kebabs are highly popular, as is mint tea. Copper is finely worked and used to make table tops, plates, teapots, vases, and a thousand other everyday objects. Leather is used for poufs, bags, shoes, and tapestries. Wool carpets and cotton fabric, caftans, and colourful fezzes abound. Avoid consuming illegal drugs: tourists are not, for instance, permitted to smoke the *kif* (hashish) that is so popular with Moroccans. Millet is the basis for many Maurish foods. Since alcoholic beverages are forbidden in Mauritana, food is washed down with mint tea or *zrig*, camel milk. Ornamented stilettos and daggers are typical local products. Copper and pewter are finely worked, and the weavers excel in the art of harmonizing colours to make extremely beautiful carpets. Camel-leather poufs are available in all sizes, shapes, and colours. The souks of the Western Sahara offer all sorts of merchandise, including leather, pottery, carpets, fabrics, and mint tea.

NORTH AFRICA

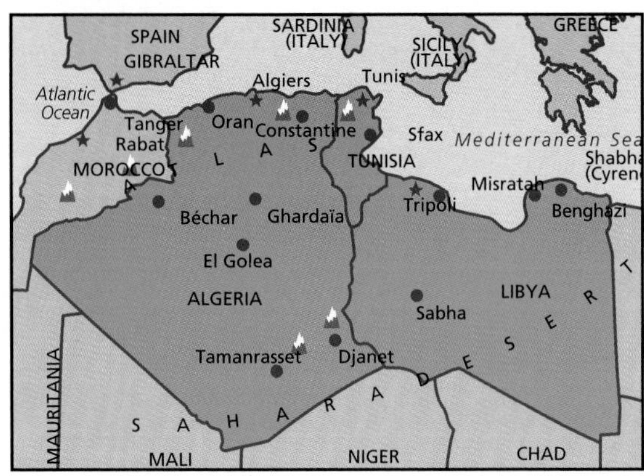

WHAT TO DO

The current tensions in ALGERIA make it a less than ideal destination for tourists. The rise of fundamentalist Islam in this country has drawn the attention of the international community because foreigners are often targets of murder attempts. Nevertheless, in Algiers, the Casbah, the old city dating back to the Turkish Empire, contains a wealth of history, revealed, notably, in its mosques and palace. The Ethnography Museum and the

+9 +8 +7 +6 +5

ALGERIA

Region: Africa
Area: 2,381,740 km²
Capital: Algiers
Airport: Algiers 19 km
Population: 27,895,100
Languages: Arabic (off.), Berber, French
Religion: Islamic
Government: presidential
Voltage: 220 - 50
Vaccinations required: Yf*
Vaccinations recommended: Ty, Po
Passport: required
Visa: required
Currency: Algerian dinar
$1Cdn: 30.43 dinars
Driving: right hand
International permit: required
Area code: 011-213
✆ from Canada: –
✆ to Canada: –
Accommodation: ★★
Restaurants: ★★
Transportation: ★
Cost of living: ❍
UN rank: 109
Best months: May to Oct
Holidays: 1 Jan; 4 Mar; 1, 11, 31 May; 10, 19 June; 5 July; 8 Aug; 1 Nov

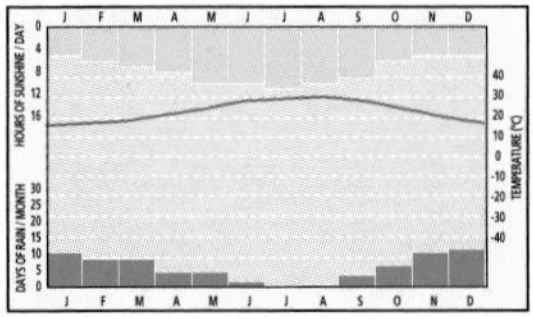

+9 +8 +7 +6 +5

LIBYA

Region: Africa
Area: 1,759,540 km²
Capital: Tripoli
Airport: Tripoli 35 km
Population: 5,057,400
Language: Arabic
Religion: Islamic
Government: military dictatorship
Voltage: 125/220 - 50
Vaccinations required: Yf
" recommended: Cho, Ty, Po, Mal
Passport: required, translated into Arabic
Visa: required
Currency: Libyan dinar
$1Cdn: .25 dinar
Driving: right hand
International permit: required
Area code: 011-218
✆ from Canada: –
✆ to Canada: –
Accommodation: ★★★
Restaurants: ★★
Transportation: ★★★
Cost of living: ❍❍❍
UN rank: 79
Best months: Apr, May, Sept, Oct
Holidays: 4, 28 Mar; 11, 31 May; 10 June; 8 Aug; 1 Sept; 7 Oct; 31 Dec

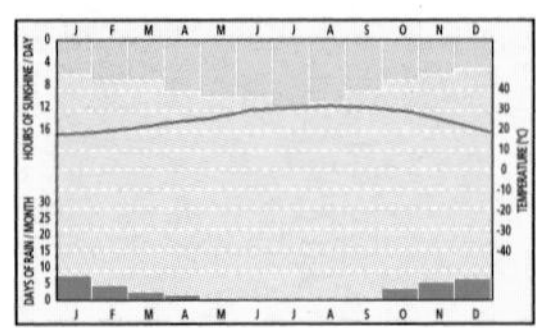

+9 +8 +7 +6 +5

TUNISIA

Region: Africa
Area: 163,610 km²
Capital: Tunis
Airport: Carthage-Tunis 7 km
Population: 8,726,570
Languages: Arabic (off.), French
Religion: Islamic
Government: presidential
Voltage: 220 - 50
Vaccinations required: Yf
Vaccinations recommended: Cho, Ty, Po
Passport: required
Visa: not required
Currency: Tunisian dinar
$1Cdn: .68 dinar
Driving: right hand
International permit: recommended
Area code: 011-216
✆ from Canada: –
✆ to Canada: –
Accommodation: ★★★★
Restaurants: ★★★★
Transportation: ★★★★
Cost of living: ❍
UN rank: 81
Best months: Mar, Apr, May, Sept, Oct
Holidays: 1 Jan; 4, 20 Mar; 9 Apr; 1, 11, 31 May; 25 July; 8, 13 Aug; 15 Oct; 7 Nov

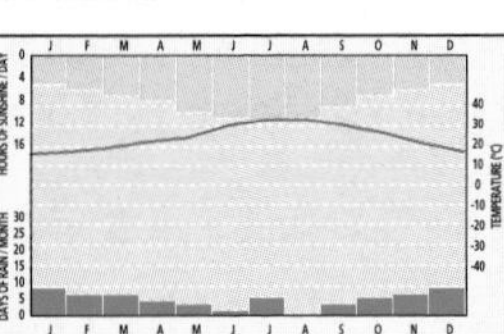

National Museum of Fine Arts are among the most opulent in Africa. East of Algiers, the Turquoise Coast is dotted with typically Mediterranean beaches and historical sites all the way to Oran. Travellers should make it a point to stop in the Mzab villages—Ghardaïa, El Ateuf, Bou Noura, Melica, and Beni Isguen—to understand what life in an oasis is like. The Grand Erg and Sahara desert regions are, in a sense, countries in themselves. Prime attractions there include the road from El Goléa to Tamanrasset, the strange Ahaggar Mountains, the cave paintings at Tassili-n-Ajjers, the resort at Dellys, Rummel's gorges at Constantine, and the oasis of Djanet, where the Tuareg caravans stop to rest. In LIBYA, the war and the political dictatorship of Colonel Kaddafi have limited the tourism industry. This country, however, is rich in history and archaeological sites: Shabhat (Cyrene) (an ancient city, founded in 631 B.C.), Lebda, and Tomeita are notable examples. Tripoli's Arch of Triumph dates from the time of Marcus Aurelius, and there are other ruins which bear witness to the city's turbulent past. Although it is very arid, the mountainous Fezzan region gave birth to the "Pearl of the Desert", Ghadamis, on the Algerian border. Gardens and palm groves grow profusely in this oasis. TUNISIA has a long and exciting history: traces of the successive conquests by Romans, Arabs, Berbers, Turks, and French can still be seen. The ancient city of Carthage is now nothing more than a suburb of Tunis, but it still comprises the baths of Antonius, Roman villas, and a garden dug up by archaeologists that is, in fact, a Punic necropolis. The ruins at Utica, near the village of Zana, are even older (about 1,000 years B.C.). Kairouan is a holy city for Muslims, and its mosques are fascinating. Sbeïtla, south of Tell, has important Roman ruins, including an aqueduct and a number of temples. At the Bardo Archaeological Museum in Tunis, one can see beautiful Carthaginian, Byzantine, Roman, and Arab treasures, while the National Museum features prehistoric and Punic artifacts. Travellers should make a point of seeing the Tunis medina. The Mediterranean coast, between Cap Blanc and Bizerte, is stunning. Tabarka, farther west, is a perfect holiday town. Hammamet is very popular for its medina, souks, and Turkish baths. Sousse and Monastir, on the east coast, combine very pretty beaches and all the conveniences of large cities. From Gabès, visitors can hop over to the very beautiful island of Jerba, or travel inland to visit the oases of Gafsa, Tozer, and Nefta, where the banana trees, date palms, and pomegranate trees attract a wide variety of wildlife. On the road linking Gabès, Matmata, Médenine, and Zarzis, entire villages have been dug into the earth to provide relief from the sun's rays and desert heat. The Berber villages of Chenini, Ksar Djouama, and Douriat are built in *ghorfas*, circular structures that resemble the inside of a beehive.

WHAT TO BUY

Algerian couscous is among the best in the world. Algeria produces a delicious, full-bodied wine that, unfortunately, is getting harder and harder to obtain. The local craftspeople produce carpets, pottery, jewelry, moroccoed leather, and finely worked gold. The *darbouka*, Arab drum, is a very beautiful musical instrument. Camel skin is used to make all sorts of things, from bags to babouches (Turkish slippers) and blankets. Be careful not to transgress the country's new laws concerning liquor and women's clothing. In Libya, the souks offer woven fabrics, goldwork, tanned leather, and jewelry. Women do not have complete freedom of movement, and female travellers must be very discreet. The cuisine of Tunisia features *tajines* (couscous) and *dorados* (mutton). Tunisian coffee is world renowned, and the wine is surprisingly full of character, as is the *vouka*, a liquor made from figs, and the *thibarine*, a liquor made from dates. Each region has its specialty: carpets from Kairouan, wire bird cages from Sidi Bouzid, perfumes mixed from the orange blossoms and jasmine of Nabeul, pottery from the island of Jerba, Bedouin jewelry from the south of the country. Ceramics, leather goods, silver, and carpets, all of them of high quality, are sold in all the souks. Note that all genuine Roman and Carthaginian antiques are now in museums.

EGYPT

+10 +9 +8 +7 +6

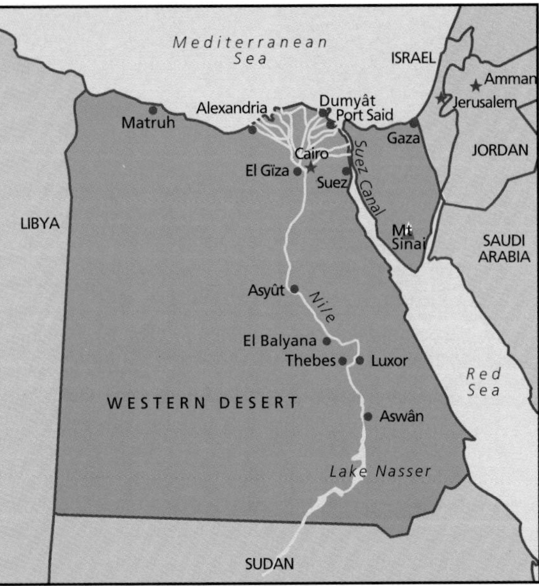

Region: Africa
Area: 1,001,450 km²
Capital: Cairo
Airport: Cairo 22 km
Population: 60,765,030
Language: Arabic (off.)
Religion: Islamic
Government: presidential
Voltage: 220/110 - 50
Vaccinations required: Yf*
Vaccinations recommended: Cho, Ty, Po
Passport: required
Visa: required
Currency: Egyptian pound
$1Cdn: 2.47 pounds
Driving: right hand
International permit: required
Area code: 011-20
✆ from Canada: –
✆ to Canada: 365-3643
Accommodation: ★★
Restaurants: ★★
Transportation: ★★
Cost of living: ❍
UN rank: 110
Best months: Nov to Mar
Holidays: 4 Mar; 24, 25 Apr; 1, 11, 31 May; 18 June; 23 July; 8 Aug; 6, 24 Oct; 23 Dec

WHAT TO DO

Again this year, radical Muslims have attacked groups of foreign tourists who came to Egypt to discover the majesty of the pyramids, the Sphinx, and the other monuments left behind by the pharaohs. Therefore, extreme caution is advised of travellers who want to visit this country. The history of Egypt reveals, however, that events have transformed the country over the centuries without altering the magnificence of its heritage. In Cairo, the Egyptian Museum has the largest collection in the world of objects from the era of the pharaohs; the Tutankhamen collection is undoubtedly the most impressive. The Museum of Islamic Art also has very extensive documentation. Al-Azhar University, founded in 973, is the oldest in the world, and the Ibn Tulun Mosque is the oldest and largest in Egypt. Many other mosques are also worth a look, especially Sultan Hasan's Mosque, dating from the fourteenth century. Coptic art is on view throughout Cairo's old city. South of Cairo, in Saqqâra, are found the country's oldest monuments. An ancient royal necropolis, this desert region is full of funerary steles and mortuary monuments. Pharaoh Zozer's Pyramid, built in 2650 B.C., is

J. HOARD

particularly breathtaking, as is the Ounas Pyramid, which contains famous hieroglyphics. In Ti's Tomb are beautiful friezes representing Egyptian life as it was at the time they were carved. The sarcophaguses of the tombs of the god Apis are truly stunning. As for Alexandria, it has ruins dating back to the time of its namesake, Alexander the Great, including the white-marble amphitheatre. The Greco-Roman Museum offers a major collection, and the catacombs of Kom El Shuqqaffa are very interesting. The sunny Mediterranean beaches of Matruh are yet another attraction of this wonderful region. Boating down the Nile is the best way to see the country from Luxor south to Aswân. In Luxor, travellers will admire Karnak Temple, the largest archaeological site in the world, with its rows of columns and impressive museum. The Valley of the Kings has the most richly decorated tombs, including those of Tutankhamen and Ramses. In the ancient city of Abydos, today called El Balyana, the temple of Sethi the First offers incredibly beautiful murals and friezes. The Sinai Desert, bounded by the Gulf of Suez, the Gulf of Aqaba, the Red Sea, and the Mediterranean Sea, is a marvel of nature. This desert has been transformed into a series of holiday resorts because of its beaches. Dumyât, on the shores of the Nile, and the resort at Râs el Barr must be seen. Mount Sinai, where Moses received the Ten Commandments, and the St. Catherine Monastery are among the most important sites in the history of humanity.

WHAT TO BUY

Egyptian cuisine is tasty and fragrant: beans (*foul*), kebabs, and chickpea dips (*humus*) are on all the menus. Mint tea and fresh dates are always served in the heat of the afternoon. The Khan al-Khalili Bazaar, in Cairo, is the largest and best supplied in Egypt; in it you'll find rolls of painted cotton vaguely resembling papyrus, fabrics printed with hieroglyphs, and gold and silver jewelry inspired by pharaonic themes, as well as copper finely worked into goblets and plates. Authentic Egyptian art is magnificent, but don't forget that the real antiques are firmly ensconced in museums. Female travellers should be very discreet: bare arms and legs are not acceptable in Egypt.

WESTERN AFRICA

CAPE VERDE

Region: Africa
Area: 4,030 km²
Capital: Praia
Airport: Sal
Population: 423,120
Languages: Portuguese, Créole
Religion: Catholic
Government: parliamentary democracy
Voltage: 220 - 50
Vaccinations required: Yf
" recommended: Cho, Ty, Po, Mal
Passport: required
Visa: required
Currency: Cape Verde escudo
$1Cdn: 61.07 escudos
Driving: right hand
International permit: recommended
Area code: 011-238
✆ from Canada: –
✆ to Canada: –
Accommodation: ★★
Restaurants: ★★
Transportation: ★★
Cost of living: ○○
UN rank: 122
Best months: Jan to May
Holidays: 1, 20 Jan; 4, 8 Mar; 16 Apr; 11 May; 5 July; 24 Sept; 14 Nov; 25 Dec

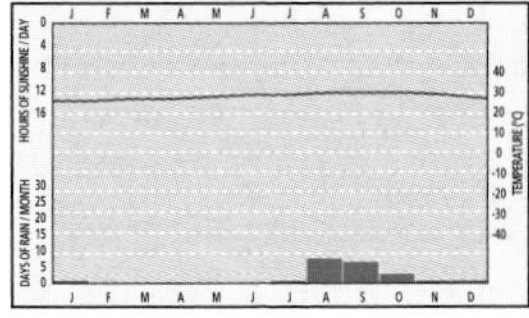

WHAT TO DO

CAPE VERDE proclaimed its independence from Portugal in 1975 and now, as a sovereign state, has a common administration with Guinea-Bissau. The capital, Praia, on the island of Santiago, is a fishing port. The beaches of Santiago are its main attraction; one of the most beautiful is found at Tarrafal. Cidade Velha (the old town) has fascinating Portuguese ruins. The town of Mindelo, on the island of São Vicente, still has its colonial charm. Mount Fogo, on the island of Fogo, is a crater that can be climbed. The airport is on Sal, another island worth a visit. THE GAMBIA is locked in by Senegal, and life there follows the rhythm of the Gambia River. Along its shores are bird sanctuaries, interspersed with cotton fields and mangrove stands. Fort James is famous for its slave ports. In Banjul, the capital, the colonial architecture dating from the nineteenth century and a fine national museum are eloquent reminders of Gambia's past. The headstones at the Wassu Cemetery and the Abuko Reserve are also must-sees. Conakry, the capital of GUINEA, moves to the beat of the country's music and dance. Tourism has become important to this country and the beaches on the Îles de Los are always crowded with vacationers. At Pita, in the Fouta-Djallon mountain range, the Kinkon

MAURITIUS / REINHARD / RÉFLEXION

+8 +7 +6 +5 +4

GAMBIA

Region: Africa
Area: 11,300 km²
Capital: Banjul
Airport: Banjul 29 km
Population: 959,300
Languages: English (off.), Diola, Mandinka
Religion: Islamic
Government: parliamentary democracy
Voltage: 220 - 50
Vaccinations required: Yf
" recommended: Cho, Ty, Po, Mal
Passport: required
Visa: not required
Currency: dalasi
$1Cdn: 7.03 dalasi
Driving: right hand
International permit: required
Area code: 011-220
✆ from Canada: –
✆ to Canada: –
Accommodation: ★★★
Restaurants: ★★★
Transportation: ★★★
Cost of living: OO
UN rank: 166
Best months: Nov, Mar, Apr, May
Holidays: 1 Jan; 18 Feb; 4 Mar; 14, 16, 17 Apr; 1, 11, 25, 31 May; 8 Aug; 25 Dec

+8 +7 +6 +5 +4

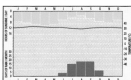

GUINEA

Region: Africa
Area: 245,860 km²
Capital: Conakry
Airport: Conakry 13 km
Population: 6,391,540
Languages: French (off.), Malinke
Religions: Islamic, animist
Government: presidential, military
Voltage: 220 - 50
Vaccinations required: Yf
" recommended: Cho, Ty, Po, Mal
Passport: required
Visa: required
Currency: Guinea franc
$1Cdn: 728.68 francs
Driving: right hand
International permit: required
Area code: 011-224
✆ from Canada: –
✆ to Canada: –
Accommodation: ★
Restaurants: ★
Transportation: ★
Cost of living: OO
UN rank: 173
Best months: Jan, Feb, Mar
Holidays: 1,2 Jan; 4 Mar; 3,16,17 Apr; 1,11,25 May; 4,5 June; 8,15 Aug; 2 Oct; 1 Nov; 25 Dec

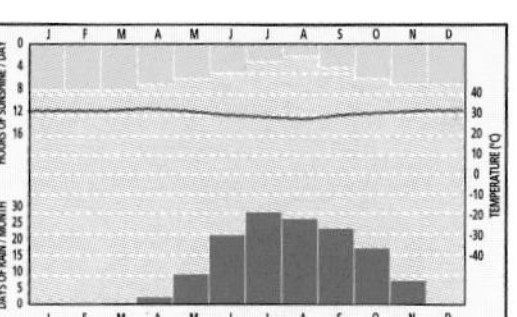

+8 +7 +6 +5 +4

GUINEA BISSAU

Region: Africa
Area: 36,120 km²
Capital: Bissau
Airport: Bissau 11 km
Population: 1,098,240
Languages: Portuguese (off.), Créole
Religion: animist
Government: Multi-party
Voltage: 220 - 50
Vaccinations required: Yf
" recommended: Cho, Ty, Po, Mal
Passport: required
Visa: required
Currency: Guinea peso
$1Cdn: 12328.20 pseos
Driving: right hand
International permit: recommended
Area code: 011-245
✆ from Canada: –
✆ to Canada: –
Accommodation: ★★
Restaurants: ★★
Transportation: ★★
Cost of living: OO
UN rank: 164
Best months: Jan to May
Holidays: 1, 20 Jan; 4, 8 Mar; 16 Apr; 11 May; 10, 24 Sept; 14 Nov; 25 Dec

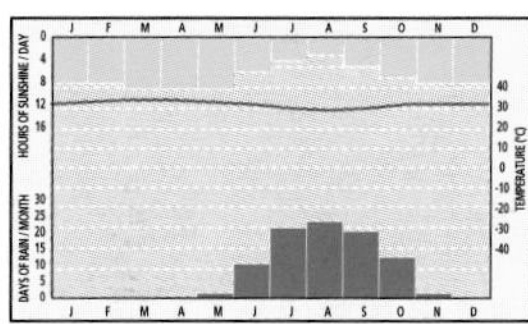

Waterfall is extremely impressive. Ðalaba, an old spa town, offers incredible scenery. GUINEA-BISSAU, until 1974 Portuguese Guinea, has retained the language of its colonizer and preserved many superb monuments built by the Portuguese between 1879 and 1974. The Bissau Museum is worth a visit for its lovely collection of African masks and artifacts, and the Presidential Palace is also interesting, but it is the islands of the Arquipélago dos Bijagós, especially Bubaque, that will most fascinate travellers. LIBERIA is famous for its Firestone rubber plantation, one of the largest in the world. This forest of trees whose trunks are lacerated to harvest sap is indeed impressive. The museum on the island of Providence recalls the tormented history of the first American-Liberians. The island's capital, Monrovia, has preserved a number of buildings in the style of plantations of the American South. The beaches around Robertsport are famous for their soft sand, while Sarp National Park is famous for its fine scenery. Unfortunately, civil war rages in Liberia; already more than 150,000 people have died as a result. SENEGAL is the best stepping-off point for travellers who are coming to Africa for the first time: its large cities feature the modernism of Europe against an exotic backdrop, while the villages in the interior are resolutely African. In the capital, Dakar, the Presidential Palace and the train station are lovely examples of colonial architecture. The cathedral, the mosque, the medina, and the residential district are just some of the city's many attractions. The Negro-African Art Museum provides a good initiation into African, and particularly Senegalese, art. On the island of Gorée, once a slave pen, one finds today tranquil colonial houses, a fort, a manor house, and very beautiful beaches. On the mainland, the beaches of the Almadies are well known. The Petite Côte, between the pleasant villages of M'Bour and Joal-Fadiout, is a prime area for beaches. To the north, travellers should make a point of going to Saint-Louis, the old capital, to sample its seventeenth-century colonial charm. Visit also Touba, for its mosque, and Djoudg National Park, for its birds. Farther south, Tambacounda opens onto the Niokolo-Koba National Park, inhabited by buffalo, gazelles, and African green monkeys. From Ziguinchor to Cap Skirring, the Casamance is a paradise for migratory birds. The wealth of SIERRA LEONE resides in its diamonds—then its beaches. Lomely, Goderich, Hamilton, Number 2, York, Black Johnson, Kent, and the ones on Banana Island are among the best in Africa. Binkongo Falls, near Sefadu, and Bumbuna Falls, near Magburaka, are spectacular natural wonders. On the border with Guinea, Outama-Kilimi National Park is a major attraction. In Freetown, the capital of Sierra Leone, many of the buildings seem to have been abandoned; however, the Parliament, the court-house, the National

+8 +7 +6 +5 +4

LIBERIA

Region: Africa
Area: 111,370 km²
Capital: Monrovia
Airport: Monrovia 60 km
Population: 2,972,780
Languages: English (off.), Mandé
Religions: animist, Islamic
Government: presidential
Voltage: 110 - 50
Vaccinations required: Yf
" recommended: Cho, Ty, Po, Mal
Passport: required
Visa: required
Currency: Liberian dollar
$1Cdn: .74 dollar
Driving: right hand
International permit: recommended
Area code: 011-231
✆ from Canada: –
✆ to Canada: –
Accommodation: ★
Restaurants: ★
Transportation: ★
Cost of living: ❍
UN rank: 144
Best months: Jan, Feb, Mar
Holidays: 1,2 Jan; 8,15 Mar; 14,16,17 Apr; 25 May; 26 July; 24 Aug; 2,29 Nov; 25 Dec

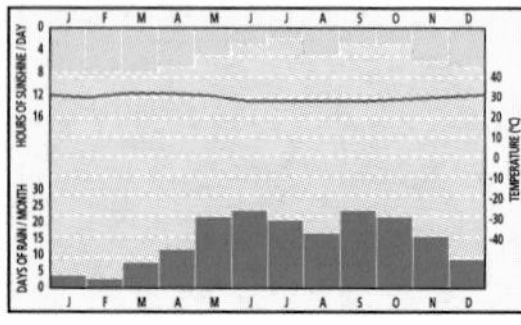

+8 +7 +6 +5 +4

SENEGAL

Region: Africa
Area: 196,190 km²
Capital: Dakar
Airport: Dakar 17 km
Population: 8,730,510
Languages: French (off.), Wolof
Religions: Islamic, Christian
Government: presidential
Voltage: 220 - 50
Vaccinations required: Yf*
" recommended: Cho, Ty, Po, Mal
Passport: required
Visa: required
Currency: CFA franc
$1Cdn: 355.95 francs
Driving: right hand
International permit: required
Area code: 011-221
✆ from Canada: –
✆ to Canada: –
Accommodation: ★★★★
Restaurants: ★★★
Transportation: ★★★
Cost of living: ❍❍
UN rank: 143
Best months: Jan to May
Holidays: 1,2 Jan; 4 Mar; 4,16,17 Apr; 1,11, 25,31 May; 4,5 June; 8, 5 Aug; 1 Nov; 25 Dec

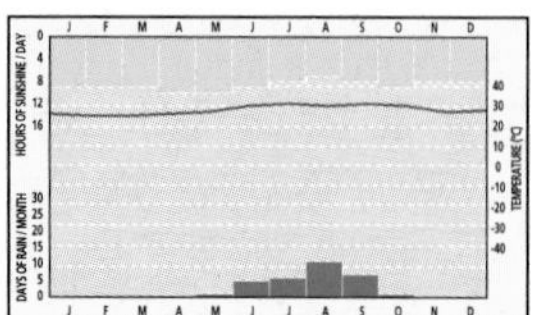

+8 +7 +6 +5 +4

SIERRA LEONE

Region: Africa
Area: 71,740 km²
Capital: Freetown
Airport: Freetown 24 km
Population: 4,630,040
Languages: English (off.), Krio
Religions: Islamic, animist
Government: presidential
Voltage: 220 - 50
Vaccinations required: Yf
" recommended: Cho, Ty, Po, Mal
Passport: required
Visa: required
Currency: leone
$1Cdn: 537.35 leones
Driving: right hand
International permit: required
Area code: 011-232
✆ from Canada: –
✆ to Canada: –
Accommodation: ★★
Restaurants: ★★
Transportation: ★
Cost of living: ❍❍
UN rank: 170
Best months: Jan, Feb, Mar
Holidays: 1 Jan; 4 Mar; 14–17, 27 Apr; 11 May; 8 Aug; 25 Dec

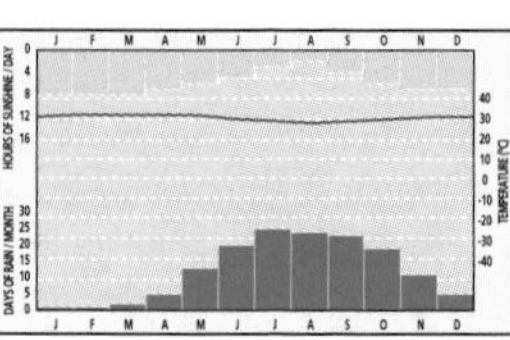

Museum, and the major artery, Siaka Stevens Road have a certain charm. Bunce Island was a stopover point for slave traders; today, the fortress contains a number of interesting hiking trails.

WHAT TO BUY

Cachupa, a delicious mixture of beans and vegetables, is the national dish of Cape Verde. Recordings by the talented singer Césaria Evora provide a taste of the melodious mixture of Portuguese and African musical cultures. The craftspeople fashion items from sea shells, coconut shells, and palm leaves. Gambian cuisine is rich and tasty: the *benachin* is particularly good. Mandingues, Ouolofs, and Peuls share the artistic and craft scenes. The batiks, printed-cotton shirts, wooden figurines, masks, pottery, woven fabrics, and gold- and silver-wire jewelry are well known and can be found at the Bakau Market, just outside Banjul. Music from the *kora*, a type of harp made of kidskin, and the *balafon*, a percussion instrument, often float gently in the evening breeze in Guinea. Carved and highly polished wooden animal sculptures make good souvenirs. *Boubous* are magnificent clothes decorated with embroidery, worn by both men and women. Masks of horned animals, bracelets and ankle bracelets, skirts of dried grass, and neck bells are characteristic of Guinea-Bissau, where the markets also offer sculptures and objects in painted terracotta. In Liberia, the markets of Monrovia offer dyed and richly coloured fabrics. Sculptors carve soapstone, making masks and amulets; others work with greenwood or hevea. Beware: true ebony-wood sculptures are very rare and very expensive. Visitors to Senegal absolutely must sample the chicken *yassa* and *tiebou dienne*, a rice-and-fish dish. The *kora*, which is played by griots, or travelling poets, is a stringed instrument typical of Senegal. In Dakar, the markets offer a wide choice of crafts. Wooden sculptures and gold and silver jewelry make very popular gifts. The purchase of anything that resembles ivory is not recommended. In Sierra Leone, the Mekani batiks are known for their quality and the woven baskets of Freetown for their variety. The jewelers frequently use diamonds to adorn their very beautiful pieces.

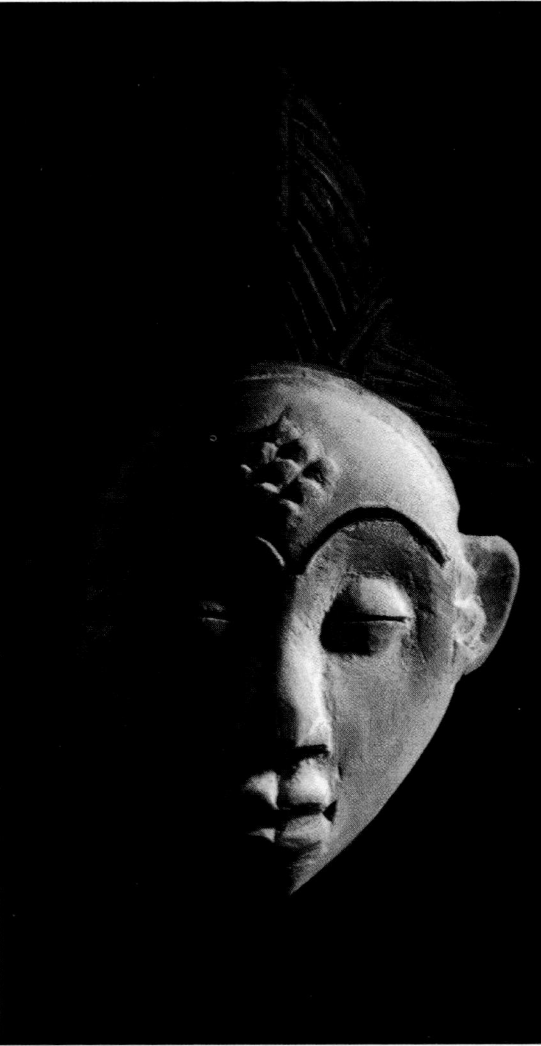
GALERIE ARTEFACT

SAHARAN AFRICA

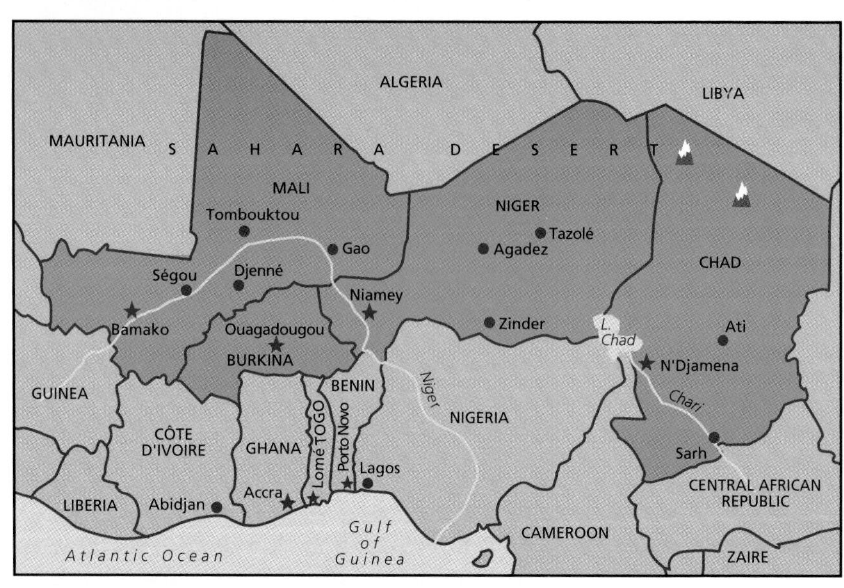

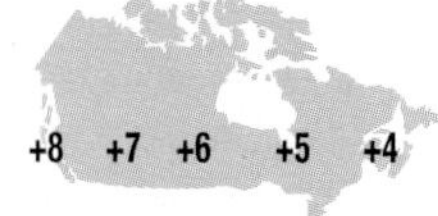

BURKINA FASO

Region: Africa
Area: 274,200 km²
Capital: Ouagadougou
Airport: Ouagadougou 8 km
Population: 10,134,670
Languages: French (off.), Mossi
Religions: animist, Islamic
Government: presidential
Voltage: 220 - 50
Vaccinations required: Yf
" recommended: Cho, Ty, Po, Mal
Passport: required
Visa: required
Currency: CFA franc
$1Cdn: 355.95 francs
Driving: right hand
International permit: recommended
Area code: 011-226
✆ from Canada: –
✆ to Canada: –
Accommodation: ★★★
Restaurants: ★★★
Transportation: ★★
Cost of living: ○○○
UN rank: 172
Best months: Dec, Jan, Feb
Holidays: 1, 3 Jan; 4, 8 Mar; 16, 17 Apr; 1, 11, 25 May; 4, 8, 15 Aug; 15 Oct; 1 Nov; 25 Dec

WHAT TO DO

The name BURKINA FASO means "Country of Honest Men." Once called Upper Volta, this country has undergone great transformations since 1983, the year of the last coup d'état. Now it is ready to greet tourists who are ready for adventure. The National Ethnology Museum has fine displays of Mossi culture. Also interesting are the large market at Bobo-Dioulasso and the waterfalls near Banfora. The Po, Arly, and "W" national parks are good places to take a safari. MALI should be worked into any African itinerary: the country is extraordinarily rich in historical sites and indigenous tribes. The most beautiful route to follow through Mali is the River Niger, which snakes from the capital, Bamako, to Gao, at the other end of the country, passing through Mopti and Tombouctou (formerly known as the legendary Timbuktu). Mopti is known primarily as the point of departure for expeditions to the Dogon villages and for Djenné, but visitors should also make a point of seeing the town's mosque and port. The Dogon region is in itself a marvel deserving of a longer description. Tombouctou, in the middle of the desert, is a transit point for the Tuareg nomads, and its old village and fourteenth-century mosque are must-sees. Also not to be missed is the mosque in Djenné, an excellent example of Sudanese architecture. NIGER is well known for the beauty of its scenery. The mountains of the Aïr Range are truly majestic. The oases of Tafadek, Tîmia, and Igoulousef, and the prehistoric sites near Iferouâne, are absolute must-sees. At Tazolé is the largest repository of dinosaur remains in the world. The Djado Plateau is known for its cave paintings of elephants and antelopes. Agadez, Niamey (the capital), and Zinder are the largest towns and the points of departure for tourist excursions. In CHAD, the Bornou kingdom reached its apogee in the sixteenth century, and N'Dja-

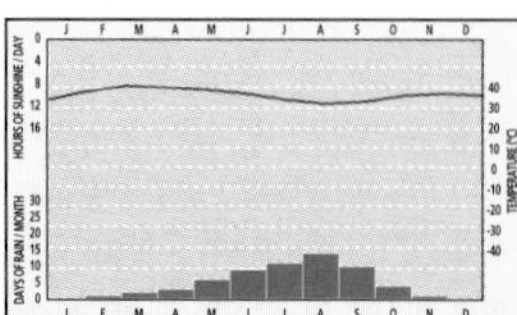

mena, the capital, has preserved some relics of this period. This city, a port on the Chari River, makes for an interesting visit: the markets are colourful and the museum offers an excellent collection of ancient art. The Zakouma National Park, in the south, is home to herds of elephants constantly on the move to find the next water hole.

WHAT TO BUY

In Burkina, the animalist sculptors of Ouagadougou are known for their finely detailed bronzes. The wooden statuettes, masks, baskets, jewelry, and fabrics are interesting, as are the famous chamois made in Ouagadougou tanneries. In Mali, *Captain Sangba* is the name of a typical and delicious dish made of highly spiced meat cooked with banana purée and rice. Beware of vendors claiming to sell ancient Dogon art: it has almost completely disappeared. The crafts, however, are accessible and very pretty. *Kora*, a game played throughout Africa, is very popular in Mali. In Niger, the prettily ornamented Agadez cross protects its wearer from the "evil eye." In the big market in Niamey are found the large and colourful cotton blankets from Jerma. The Hausas and Bedouins produce crafts well suited to their desert living conditions. The Toubous nomads in Chad have a very rich craft tradition; they produce carpets and camel-skin blankets, finely carved knives and *kandjars*, highly decorated cotton, worked leather, pottery, and copper objects.

+8 +7 +6 +5 +4

MALI

Region: Africa
Area: 1,240,000 km²
Capital: Bamako
Airport: Bamako 15 km
Population: 9,113,000
Languages: French (off.), Mandé
Religions: Islamic, animist
Government: presidential
Voltage: 220 - 50
Vaccinations required: Yf
" recommended: Cho, Ty, Po, Mal
Passport: required
Visa: required
Currency: CFA franc
$1Cdn: 355.95 francs
Driving: right hand
International permit: recommended
Area code: 011-223
✆ from Canada: –
✆ to Canada: –
Accommodation: ★★★
Restaurants: ★★★
Transportation: ★★
Cost of living: ❍❍
UN rank: 167
Best months: Dec, Jan, Feb
Holidays: 1, 20 Jan; 4, 26 Mar; 16 Apr; 1, 11, 25 May; 8 Aug; 22 Sept; 25 Dec

+9 +8 +7 +6 +5

NIGER

Region: Africa
Area: 1,267,000 km²
Capital: Niamey
Airport: Niamey 12 km
Population: 8,971,610
Languages: French (off.), Hausa
Religion: Islamic
Government: presidential
Voltage: 220 - 50
Vaccinations required: Yf
" recommended: Cho, Ty, Po, Mal
Passport: required
Visa: required
Currency: CFA franc
$1Cdn: 355.95 francs
Driving: right hand
International permit: required
Area code: 011-227
✆ from Canada: –
✆ to Canada: –
Accommodation: ★★
Restaurants: ★★
Transportation: ★★
Cost of living: ❍❍
UN rank: 169
Best months: Dec, Jan, Feb
Holidays: 1, 2 Jan; 4 Mar; 1, 11 May; 3, 8 Aug; 18, 25 Dec

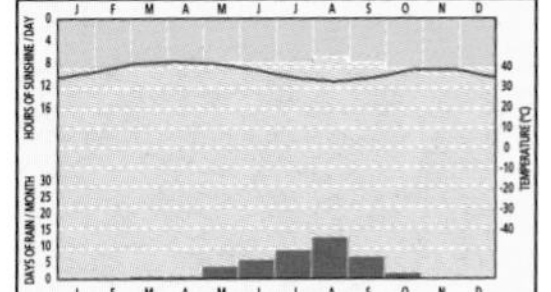

+9 +8 +7 +6 +5

CHAD

Region: Africa
Area: 1,284,000 km²
Capital: N'Djamena
Airport: N'Djamena 4 km
Population: 5,466,780
Languages: French (off.), Arabic (off.)
Religions: Islamic, Christian
Government: presidential
Voltage: 220 - 50
Vaccinations required: Yf*
" recommended: Cho, Ty, Po, Mal
Passport: required
Visa: required
Currency: CFA francs
$1Cdn: 355.95 francs
Driving: right hand
Int'l permit: required + travel pass
Area code: 011-235
✆ from Canada: –
✆ to Canada: –
Accommodation: ★★
Restaurants: ★★
Transportation: ★
Cost of living: ❍❍
UN rank: 168
Best months: Dec, Jan, Feb
Holidays: 1 Jan; 4 Mar; 16, 17 Apr; 1, 11, 25 May; 8, 11 Aug; 1, 28 Nov; 1, 25 Dec

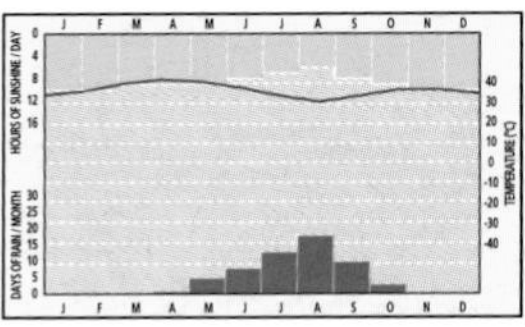

HORN OF AFRICA AND SUDAN

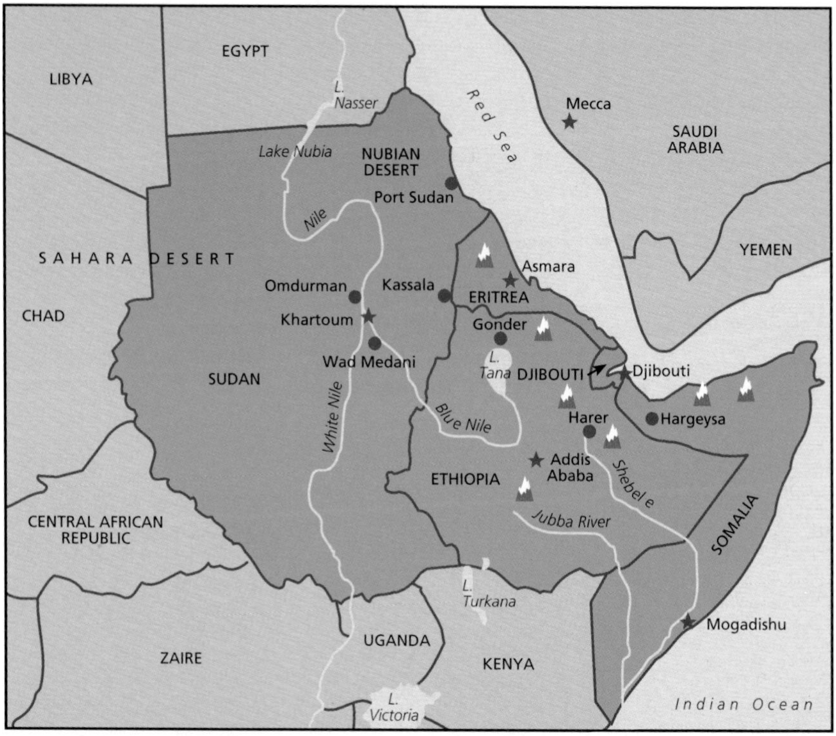

DJIBOUTI

Region: Africa
Area: 21,980 km^2
Capital: Djibouti
Airport: Djibouti 5 km
Population: 413,000
Languages: French (off.), Arabic
Religions: Islamic, Christian
Government: presidential
Voltage: 220 - 50
Vaccinations required: Yf*
" recommended: Cho, Ty, Po, Mal
Passport: required
Visa: required
Currency: Djibouti franc
$1Cdn: 130.82 francs
Driving: right hand
International permit: recommended
Area code: 011-253
✆ from Canada: –
✆ to Canada: –
Accommodation: ★★★
Restaurants: ★★★
Transportation: ★★★
Cost of living: ❍❍
UN rank: 163
Best months: Nov to Apr
Holidays: 1 Jan; 15 Mar; 16 Apr; 21, 27 June; 25 Dec

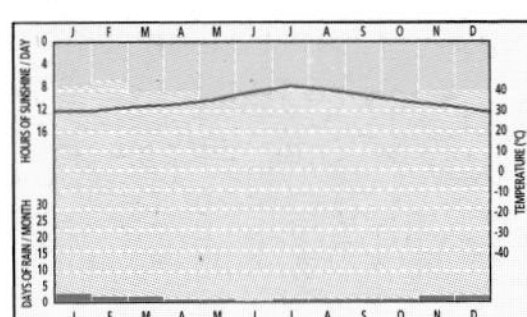

ERITREA

Region: Africa
Area: 121,320 km^2
Capital: Asmara
Airport: Asmara
Population: 3,782,550
Languages: Tigrinya, Arabic
Religions: Islamic, Christian
Government: presidential
Voltage: 220 - 50
Vaccinations required: Yf*
" recommended: Cho, Ty, Po, Mal
Passport: required
Visa: required
Currency: birr
$1Cdn: 4.66 birrs
Driving: right hand
International permit: recommended
Area code: 011-251
✆ from Canada: –
✆ to Canada: –
Accommodation: –
Restaurants: –
Transportation: –
Cost of living: –
UN rank: –
Best months: Dec, Jan, Feb
Holidays: 24 May

ETHIOPIA

Region: Africa
Area: 1,127,127 km^2
Capital: Addis Ababa
Airport: Addis Ababa
Population: 54,927,110
Languages: Amharic (off.), Tigrinya, Somali
Religions: Christian, Islamic
Government: parliamentary democracy
Voltage: 220 - 50
Vaccinations required: Yf*
" recommended: Cho, Ty, Po, Mal
Passport: required
Visa: required
Currency: Ethiopian birr
$1Cdn: 4.66 birrs
Driving: right hand
International permit: required
Area code: 011-251
✆ from Canada: –
✆ to Canada: –
Accommodation: ★
Restaurants: ★
Transportation: ★
Cost of living: ❍
UN rank: 161
Best months: Jan, Feb, Mar
Holidays: 7, 19 Jan; 2, 4 Mar; 6, 21, 23 Apr; 1, 11, 28 May; 8 Aug; 11 Sept

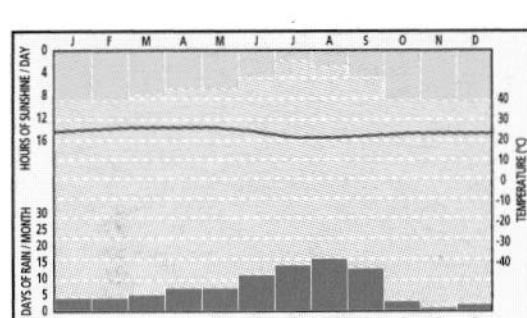

WHAT TO DO

Its common border with war-torn Somalia has not yet affected DJIBOUTI, a relatively peaceful country, in spite of the extreme poverty of the citizens and its few natural resources. Djibouti offers instead great natural beauty: Lake Abhe, on the border with Ethiopia, is home to thousands of pink flamingos and pelicans. Interestingly, it is one of the lowest under-sea-level sites in the world. In the Gulf of Tadjoura, the reefs and underwater life are superb. The main attractions in Obock and Tadjoura are the mosques and the remains of the country's colonial past. Surrounded by two warring countries, Sudan and Somalia, ERITREA is struggling to maintain its fragile economic and social balance. This young country gained independence from Ethiopia in 1993. The tourism industry is not yet in full swing, but the capital, Asmara, the towns of Akordat and Keren, the port of Massawa on the Red Sea, and the village of Algana, in the north, are tourist destinations. The Dahlak Archipelago, in the Red Sea, is unspoiled and sparsely populated: an ideal destination for adventurers! ETHIOPIA, though associated by many solely with famine, is a country with a strong identity and culture. The National Museum in the capital, Addis Ababa, recalls the tumultuous history of the country. The National Palace is very interesting, as are the mausoleum of Menelik II, the Parliament, and Saint-Georges Cathedral. The Ethnology and Archaeology Museum is fascinating. The ruins at Aksum, the ancient royal capital, are worth a trip, as is the city of Gonder, another ancient royal capital with many palaces and seventeenth-century churches. Harer seems almost untouched by modern history. Ethiopia's national parks preserve unspoiled fauna and flora. The route between the gorges of the Blue Nile and the monasteries of Bahir Dar is particularly spectacular. It is in Hadar Valley that a humanoid skeleton three million years old was discovered in 1974. Unfortunately, war is still raging in SOMALIA. Many villages and towns have been destroyed since hostilities broke out. Mogadishu, the capital, is no longer open to tourists, and violent battles have taken place at Berbera and Burco, thus extending the damage beyond the capital. War has been raging in SUDAN for almost 27 years, and with the recent deterioration of the situation, hope for a quick end to the conflict has faded. This is unfortunate because the country abounds with tourist attractions, especially archaeological sites: the National Museum in Khartoum exhibits pieces dating from 4000 B.C. The abundance and diversity of the fauna and flora is another attraction.

+11 +10 +9 +8 +7

SOMALIA

Region: Africa
Area: 637,660 km²
Capital: Mogadishu
Airport: Mogadishu
Population: 6,666,880
Languages: Somali (off.), Arabic
Religion: Islamic
Government: republic
Voltage: 220 - 50
Vaccinations required: Yf*, Cho*
Vaccinations recommended: Ty, Po, Mal
Passport: required
Visa: required
Currency: Somali shilling
$1Cdn: 4.66
Driving: left hand
International permit: required
Area code: 011-252
✆ from Canada: –
✆ to Canada: –
Accommodation: ★
Restaurants: ★
Transportation: ★
Cost of living: ○○
UN rank: 165
Best months: Dec, Jan, Feb
Holidays: 1 Jan; 4 Mar; 1, 11 May; 26 June; 1 July; 8 Aug; 21, 22 Oct

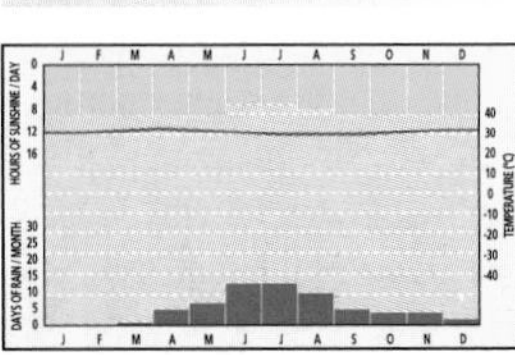

+10 +9 +8 +7 +6

SUDAN

Region: Africa
Area: 2,505,810 km²
Capital: Khartoum
Airport: Khartoum 4 km
Population: 29,419,800
Languages: Arabic (off.), Dinka
Religion: Islamic
Government: military dictatorship
Voltage: 240 - 50
Vaccinations required: Yf*, Cho*
Vaccinations recommended: Ty, Po, Mal
Passport: required
Visa: required
Currency: Sudanese dinar
$1Cdn: 36.29 dinars
Driving: left hand
Int'l permit: required + travel pass
Area code: 011-249
✆ from Canada: –
✆ to Canada: –
Accommodation: ★
Restaurants: ★
Transportation: ★
Cost of living: ○○○
UN rank: 151
Best months: Nov to Mar
Holidays: 1 Jan; 4 Mar; 11, 31 May; 30 June; 8 Aug; 25 Dec

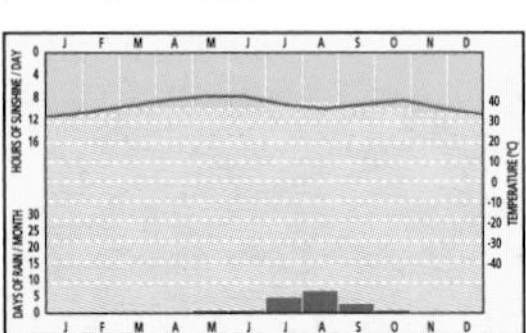

WHAT TO BUY

The art of the Afars and Issas reflects their nomadic lifestyle prior to colonization. The musical instruments, drums and stringed instruments produce very melodious sounds. The many colourful markets offer fabrics, jewelry, and everyday objects. Wooden sculptures, hand-woven carpets, musical instruments (including the wood drum), and a honey liquor called *tej* are good souvenirs to take home from Eritrea. In Ethiopia, the flourishing Addis Ababa *mercato* (market) acts as a meeting place for artisans from all over the country: the wares of potters from Falasha, jewelers from Labilea, and weavers from Makale fill the stalls. The art of the Danakils, nomads living in the steppes between the mountains and the Red Sea, is very beautiful. Magnificent wooden sculptures, woven baskets, and dyed fabrics are typical of Somalia. In Sudan, shields made of animal skin, spears, ornaments, and everyday objects of tribal life make good souvenirs. They are sold mainly in the villages. The Hamites have their own traditions, which they express through their sculptures and jewelry.

J. HUARD

GULF OF GUINEA

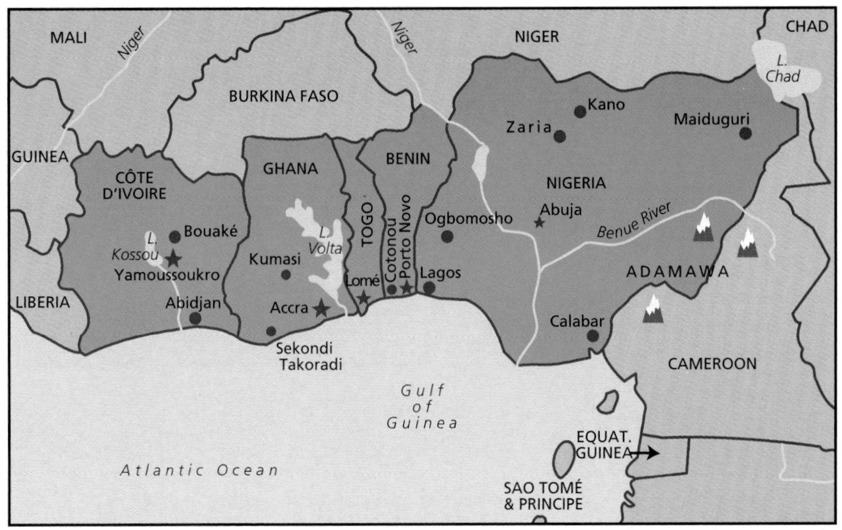

WHAT TO DO

Art-lovers will be familiar with the ancient kingdom of BENIN, well known for its superb bronzes. Today, the Republic of Benin attracts tourists largely for its natural beauty. The Pendjari and "W" national parks are wildlife reserves full of cheetahs and hippopotamuses. The huts of the village of Ganvié, near Cotonou, are built of bamboo on pilings. Abomey is a walled city where the kings of Benin rest in their tombs. CÔTE D'IVOIRE (Ivory Coast) got its name from the ivory trade that the Portuguese carried on there in the fifteenth century. Today, with no ivory to sell, the country could be called the "Cocoa Coast," because it is the world's top producer of this staple. Yamoussoukro, the capital, is a modern city that lives in the shadow of the better-known city of Abidjan, which has been dubbed Africa's "City of Light." Take note: Abidjan is one of the most expensive cities in Africa. In Yamoussoukro, the Notre-Dame-de-la-Paix Cathedral, modelled on St. Peter's Basilica in Rome, is a major attraction. Sassandra, an ancient slave port, is now a charming fishing village. In Man, crossing the vine bridge suspended over the waterfall is not recommended for the faint of heart! Zala is known for its *bacoub* dancers. In Kassoumbarga, make sure to see the mosque built entirely from dirt. The Komoé and Banco national parks are reserves for a wide variety of birds and animals. In GHANA, the slave trade on the Gold Coast left behind a number of outposts and forts, and the museum in Kumasi gives a good accounting of that era. Accra, the capital, also has a very interesting museum of history. Legon University and the Aburi Botanical Garden are other attractions of Accra. At the mouth of the Volta is the town of Ada, stretching alongside lagoons that provide a habitat for thousands of birds. The Mole Game Reserve, the three arms of Lake Volta, and the Boufom Sanctuary are fascinating natural sites. In NIGERIA, Lagos has a reputation for being a violent city, and also for having a very lively cultural life. Nigerian artists have gained worldwide renown; Wole Soyinka has received the Nobel Prize for literature. Visitors should make a point of touring the old towns of Kano, Kaduna, and Zaria to see the typical architecture; see also the emir's palace in Zaria and the cloth-dying baths in Kano . The coast, bathed by the Gulf of Guinea, is criss-crossed by the many tributaries of the huge Niger River. At Jos, on the high-altitude Bauchi Plateau, is a museum offering a survey of Nigerian art. The nearby Yankari Game Reserve is also worth a visit. TOGO's exceptional beaches stretch from Lomé, the capital, all the way to neighbouring Benin. The National Museum of Lomé offers a very beautiful exhibition of traditional Togolese artifacts, sculptures, pottery, and costumes. The Bé neighbourhood is known for its witch doctors and enchanters and their unusual merchandise. Kpalimé, near Mount Agou, is a good spot to explore the cascades and appreciate the scenery. Atakpamé is the centre of the cotton plantations. To the north, the Valley of the Tamberma, between Niamtougou and Kandé, is known for its unique fortified terracotta buildings.

GULF OF GUINEA

WHAT TO BUY

The elongated statuettes of Benin are recognized for their beauty and originality; ebony masks and wooden sculptures are other specialties of this country. The teak and bronzes of Benin are unique. These latter, however, are found only in the museums (especially those of Benin City, in Nigeria). Pottery and tapestries often represent scenes of past and present tribal life. In Côte d'Ivoire, visitors

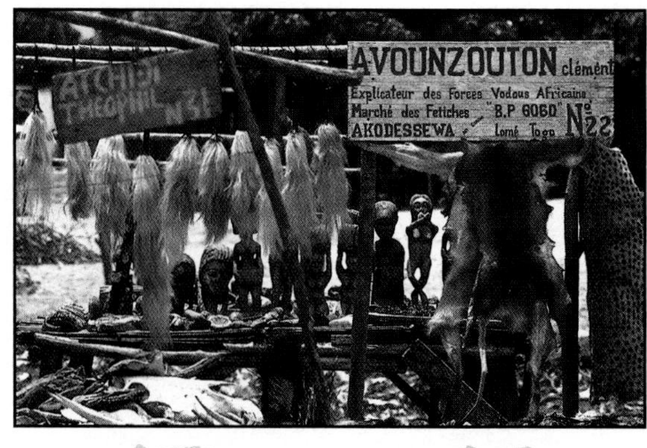

J. HUARD

+9 +8 +7 +6 +5

BENIN

Region: Africa
Area: 112,620 km²
Capital: Porto-Novo
Airport: Cotonou 5 km
Population: 5,341,710
Languages: French (off.), Fon
Religion: animist
Government: presidential
Voltage: 220 - 50
Vaccinations required: Yf
" recommended: Cho, Ty, Po, Mal
Passport: required
Visa: required
Currency: CFA franc
$1Cdn: 355.95 francs
Driving: right hand
International permit: required
Area code: 011-229
✆ from Canada: –
✆ to Canada: –
Accommodation: ★★★
Restaurants: ★★
Transportation: ★
Cost of living: ❍❍
UN rank: 156
Best months: Dec, Jan, Feb
Holidays: 1 Jan; 4 Mar; 16, 17 Apr; 1, 11, 25 May; 4, 5 June; 1, 8, 15 Aug; 1 Nov; 25 Dec

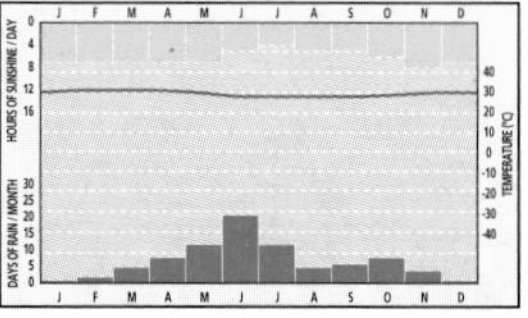

+8 +7 +6 +5 +4

CÔTE D'IVOIRE

Region: Africa
Area: 322,460 km²
Capital: Yamoussoukro
Airport: Abidjan 16 km
Population: 14,295,510
Languages: French (off.), Akan, Dioula
Religions: animist, Islamic
Government: presidential
Voltage: 220 - 50
Vaccinations required: Yf
" recommended: Cho, Ty, Po, Mal
Passport: required
Visa: required
Currency: CFA franc
$1Cdn: 355.95 francs
Driving: right hand
International permit: required
Area code: 011-225
✆ from Canada: –
✆ to Canada: –
Accommodation: ★★★
Restaurants: ★★★
Transportation: ★★★
Cost of living: ❍❍
UN rank: 136
Best months: Dec to may
Holidays: 1 Jan; 4 Mar; 16, 17 Apr; 1, 11, 25 May; 4, 5 June; 15 Aug; 1 Nov; 7, 25 Dec

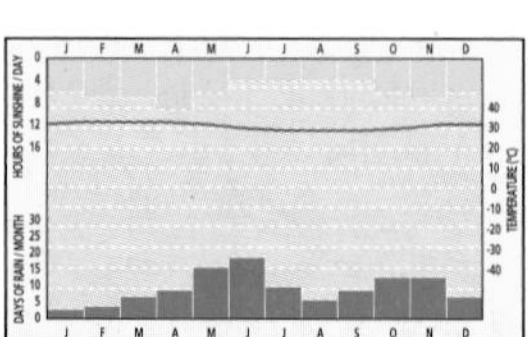

+8 +7 +6 +5 +4

GHANA

Region: Africa
Area: 238,540 km²
Capital: Accra
Airport: Accra 10 km
Population: 17,225,190
Languages: English (off.), Akan, Ewe
Religions: animist, Islamic, Christian
Government: presidential
Voltage: 250 - 50
Vaccinations required: Yf*
" recommended: Cho, Ty, Po, Mal
Passport: required
Visa: required
Currency: cedi
$1Cdn: 868.74 cedis
Driving: right hand
International permit: recommended
Area code: 011-233
✆ from Canada: –
✆ to Canada: –
Accommodation: ★★
Restaurants: ★★
Transportation: ★★
Cost of living: ❍❍
UN rank: 134
Best months: Nov, Dec, Jan
Holidays: 1, 2 Jan; 6 Mar; 14, 16, 17 Apr; 1 May; 5 June; 3 July; 4, 25, 26, 31 Dec

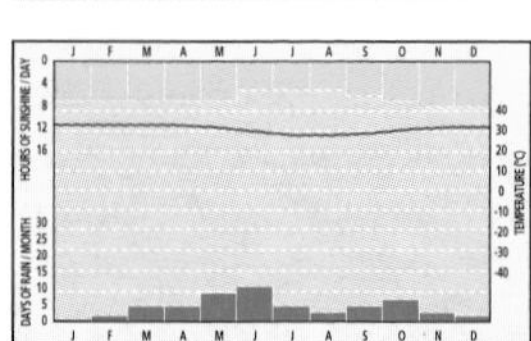

J. HUARD

+9 +8 +7 +6 +5

NIGERIA

Region: Africa
Area: 923,770 km²
Capital: Abuja
Airport: Lagos 22 km
Population: 98,092,000
Languages: English (off.), Hausa
Religions: Islamic, Christian
Government: military regime
Voltage: 220 - 50
Vaccinations required: Yf*
" recommended: Cho, Ty, Po, Mal
Passport: required
Visa: required
Currency: naira
$1Cdn: 62.57 nairas
Driving: right hand
International permit: required
Area code: 011-234
✆ from Canada: –
✆ to Canada: –
Accommodation: ★★
Restaurants: ★★
Transportation: ★★
Cost of living: ○○○
UN rank: 139
Best months: Nov to Mar
Holidays: 1 Jan; 4 Mar; 14, 16, 17 Apr; 1, 11 May; 8 Aug; 1 Oct; 25, 26 Dec

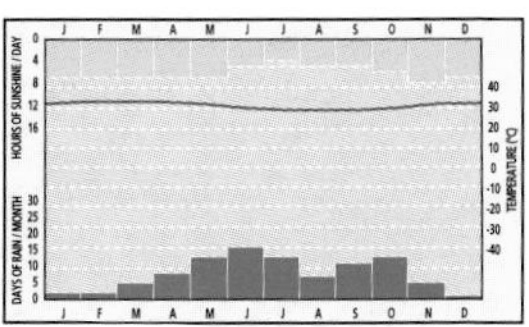

+8 +7 +6 +5 +4

TOGO

Region: Africa
Area: 56,790 km²
Capital: Lomé
Airport: Lomé 4 km
Population: 4,256,000
Languages: French (off.), Ewe
Religions: animist, Catholic
Government: presidential
Voltage: 220 - 50
Vaccinations required: Yf
" recommended: Cho, Ty, Po, Mal
Passport: required
Visa: not required
Currency: CFA franc
$1Cdn: 355.95 francs
Driving: right hand
International permit: required
Area code: 011-228
✆ from Canada:
✆ to Canada:
Accommodation: ★★★
Restaurants: ★★★
Transportation: ★★★
Cost of living: ○○○
UN rank: 145
Best months: Nov, Dec, Jan
Holidays: 1, 13, 24 Jan; 4 Mar; 16, 17, 27 Apr; 1, 11, 25 May; 4, 5, 21 June; 15 Aug; 1 Nov; 25 Dec

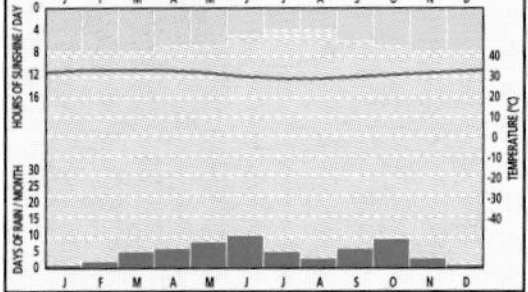

must sample *attiéké* (a vegetable dish) and *foutou* (banana and peanut sauce) in a *maquis*, an open-air restaurant. African masks are not just works of art; they are indissociable from the sacred rituals that all visitors to Africa must respect. Malachite objects, natural-cotton tapestries painted with the black mud of Fakaha, pottery from the village of Katiola, and traditional Senoufo and Malinké dance masks are good purchases. The traditional dishes of Ghana are *kontomere*, a nut-based stew, and *banku*, a corn soup, with a base of peanuts and nuts. The country even produces its own whisky. The Accra Art Centre is always crowded with shoppers and craftspeople, who come to sell the famous *kente* fabric made by the Ashanti of Bonyeri, worked gold jewelry, terracotta pots and vases, and the well-known fertility statuettes, with a flat, round head topping a neck circled with rings. The typically Ghanaian wooden stools are found everywhere and in a variety of styles. Nigerians like spicy dishes: watch out for *kilishi*, very hot dried meat. They prepare their fish in a very delicate manner, however. Yoruba masks, which often cover the entire body, are typical of Nigeria. Ceremonies of all sorts are brightened up by jewelry, notably, bracelets for biceps, calves, ankles, and wrists, often made of leather decorated with multicoloured beads. The sculptors make wooden gates that are true works of art. The dyers create batiks that are almost magical. The leathers of Sokoto are known all over the world: your favourite bag may even be made with Nigerian leather! Togolese cuisine is elegant, as is Senegal's. Take home leather sandals from Lomé, as well as batiks, statuettes, and talismans. Refrain from purchasing stuffed animals and ivory objects.

EQUATORIAL AFRICA

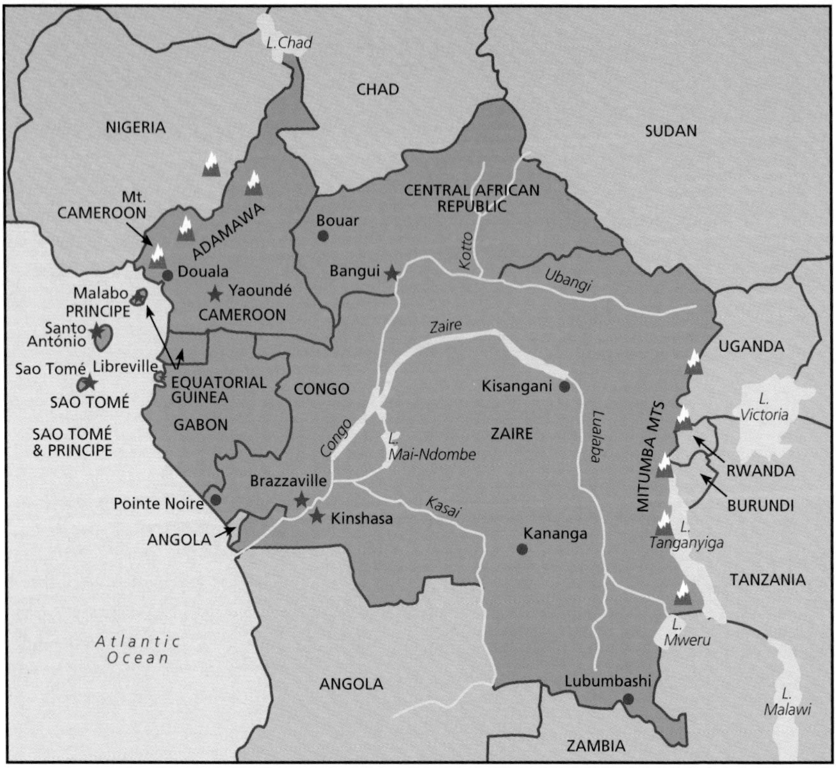

L. Chad
CHAD
NIGERIA
SUDAN
CENTRAL AFRICAN REPUBLIC
Mt. CAMEROON
ADAMAWA
Bouar
Douala
Bangui
Kotto
Ubangi
Malabo
PRINCIPE
Yaoundé
CAMEROON
Santo António
Zaire
UGANDA
Sao Tomé
Libreville
EQUATORIAL GUINEA
CONGO
Kisangani
SAO TOMÉ
L. Victoria
GABON
ZAIRE
Lualaba
MITUMBA MTS
SAO TOMÉ & PRINCIPE
Congo
L. Mai-Ndombe
RWANDA
Brazzaville
BURUNDI
Pointe Noire
Kasai
Kinshasa
ANGOLA
Kananga
L. Tanganyiga
TANZANIA
L. Mweru
Atlantic Ocean
ANGOLA
Lubumbashi
L. Malawi
ZAMBIA

WHAT TO DO

CAMEROON, with its savannahs, forests, volcanoes, rivers, and exceptionally pleasant climate, has a very special charm. Mount Fédé, which overlooks the capital, Yaoundé, moderates this city's clement temperatures. In Douala, which is dominated by Cameroon Mountain, the cathedral and national crafts market are must-sees, as are the museum and the port in the Gulf of Guinea. To the north, at the foot of the Mandara Mountains, is Maroua, the point of departure for expeditions to Waza National Park, where the luckiest travellers will catch a glimpse of rare birds such as storks and tufted cranes. In the CENTRAL AFRICAN REPUBLIC, the capital, Bangui is a tropical city built on the shores of the Ubangi River. Pygmy tribes live in the region around Mbaïki and on the shores of the Lobaye River. In the western part of the country, in Bouar, is a sacred burial ground surrounded by megalithic monuments. Visit CONGO via its main artery, the Congo River, once called the Zaire River. Foulakari Falls, the many rapids, and the cliff dubbed "God's Hole" are magnificent sights along the river's route. The capital, Brazzaville, boasts a beautiful museum of African art. Libreville, the capital of GABON, is a pleasant coastal city. Its lush vegetation and pleasant climate make it a true paradise. The Saint-Michel Cathedral is a work of art in itself, and the Museum presents masks and sculptures

J. HUARD

by the Bakélé and Fang tribes. The densest region of the eastern plateau has many suspended liana-vine bridges, and the country's parks and reserves are home to crocodiles, monkeys, panthers, and elephants. The two territories of EQUATORIAL GUINEA, the island of Bioko and the territory of Río Muni on the mainland, are tucked in between Cameroon and Gabon and separated by the Gulf of Guinea. Tourism is almost nonexistent in this small country. ZAIRE, which straddles the equator, has a very favourable climate. The capital, Kinshasa, on the shores of the Congo River, is the intellectual centre of the country. Kinshasa University and the National Museum, which features Zairian art, are worth seeing. In the region around the town of Mbanza-Ngungu are found waterfalls, caves, and forests. The road to Moanda and the beaches on Zaire's short stretch of Atlantic coastline are prime attractions. The road from Beni to Goma through the mountains is one of the most beautiful in the country. The national parks are home to a wide variety of jungle animals.

WHAT TO BUY

In Cameroon, the potters produce all sorts of bowls, vases, and goblets in painted and decorated terracotta. Camelhair carpets are popular as are the garments heavily ornamented with dried beans. The animalist sculptors of the Central African Republic make magnificent

+9 +8 +7 +6 +5

CAMEROON

Region: Africa
Area: 475,440 km²
Capital: Yaoundé
Airport: Douala 10 km
Population: 13,132,200
Languages: English (off.), French (off.), Bantu
Religions: Catholic, Islamic
Government: presidential
Voltage: 220 - 50
Vaccinations required: Yf
" recommended: Cho, Ty, Po, Mal
Passport: required
Visa: required
Currency: CFA franc
$1Cdn: 355.95 francs
Driving: right hand
International permit: recommended
Area code: 011-237
✆ from Canada:
✆ to Canada: –
Accommodation: ★★★
Restaurants: ★★★
Transportation: ★★
Cost of living: ○○
UN rank: 124
Best months: Jan, Feb
Holidays: 1, 2 Jan; 13 Feb; 4 Mar; 14–16 Apr; 1, 20, 25 May; 8, 15 Aug; 25 Dec

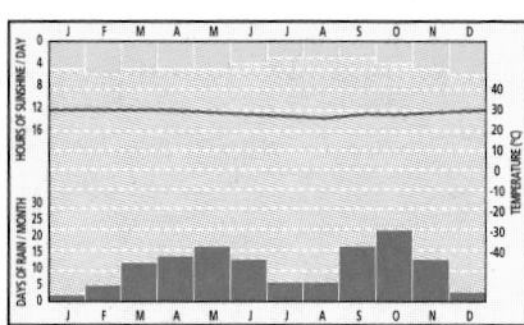

+9 +8 +7 +6 +5

C.A.R.

Region: Africa
Area: 622,980 km²
Capital: Bangui
Airport: Bangui 10 km
Population: 3,142,190
Languages: French (off.), Sango
Religions: animist, Catholic
Government: presidential
Voltage: 220 - 50
Vaccinations required: Yf
" recommended: Cho, Ty, Po, Mal
Passport: required
Visa: required
Currency: CFA franc
$1Cdn: 355.95 francs
Driving: right hand
International permit: required
Area code: 011-236
✆ from Canada: –
✆ to Canada: –
Accommodation: ★★★
Restaurants: ★★★
Transportation: ★★
Cost of living: ○○
UN rank: 160
Best months: Dec, Jan, Feb
Holidays: 1 Jan; 29 Mar; 16,17 Apr; 1,25 May; 4,5 June; 13,15 Aug; 1 Sept; 1 Nov; 1,25 Dec

+9 +8 +7 +6 +5

CONGO

Region: Africa
Area: 342,000 km²
Capital: Brazzaville
Airport: Brazzaville 4 km
Population: 2,446,910
Languages: French (off.), Kongo
Religions: Catholic, animist
Government: presidential
Voltage: 220 - 50
Vaccinations required: Yf
" recommended: Cho, Ty, Po, Mal
Passport: required
Visa: required
Currency: CFA franc
$1Cdn: 355.95 francs
Driving: right hand
International permit: required
Area code: 011-242
✆ from Canada: –
✆ to Canada: –
Accommodation: ★★
Restaurants: ★★
Transportation: ★★
Cost of living: ○○
UN rank: 123
Best months: June to Oct
Holidays: 1 Jan; 16, 17 Apr; 1 May; 15 Aug; 1 Nov; 25 Dec

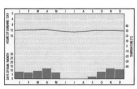

pieces from ebony, and the goldsmiths work their chosen metal with great elegance. Traditional art objects are always very colourful. In Congo, mahogany and ebony are used to make round, flat Batéké painted masks and figurines, as well as domestic objects. Gabon's dances and music are very sophisticated: the kidskin drums, *balafon*, and flutes are typical. The Bantu art of Gabon is highly prized. Equatorial Guinea offers plaited items and wooden sculptures. Zairian painters are becoming better and better known in the art world. Craftspeople use cotton to make magnificent printed fabrics, used in handbags, dresses, shawls, and tablecloths.

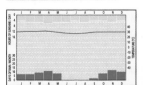

J. HUARD

+9 +8 +7 +6 +5

GABON

Region: Africa
Area: 267,670 km²
Capital: Libreville
Airport: Libreville
Population: 1,139,010
Languages: French (off.), Bantu
Religions: Christian, animist
Government: presidential
Voltage: 220 - 50
Vaccinations required: Yf*
" recommended: Cho, Ty, Po, Mal
Passport: required
Visa: required
Currency: CFA franc
$1Cdn: 355.95 francs
Driving: right hand
International permit: recommended
Area code: 011-241
✆ from Canada: –
✆ to Canada: –
Accommodation: ★★★
Restaurants: ★★★
Transportation: ★★
Cost of living: ❍❍❍
UN rank: 114
Best months: Aug, Sept
Holidays: 1 Jan; 4,12 Mar; 16,17 Apr; 1,11, 25 May; 4,5 June; 8,15, 17 Aug; 1 Nov; 25 Dec

+9 +8 +7 +6 +5

EQ. GUINEA

Region: Africa
Area: 28,050 km²
Capital: Malabo
Airport: Malabo
Population: 409,550
Languages: Spanish (off.), Créole
Religions: Christian, animist
Government: presidential
Voltage: 220 - 50
Vaccinations required: Yf*
" recommended: Cho, Ty, Po, Mal
Passport: required
Visa: required
Currency: CFA franc
$1Cdn: 355.95 francs
Driving: right hand
International permit: recommended
Area code: 011-240
✆ from Canada: –
✆ to Canada: –
Accommodation: ★★
Restaurants: ★★
Transportation: ★
Cost of living: ❍
UN rank: 150
Best months: June to Oct
Holidays: 1 Jan; 5 Mar; 16, 17 Apr; 1, 25 May; 12 Oct; 10, 25 Dec

+9 +8 +7 +6 +5

ZAIRE

Region: Africa
Area: 2,345,410 km²
Capital: Kinshasa
Airport: Kinshasa 25 km
Population: 42,685,000
Languages: French, Kiswahili, Lingali
Religion: Christian
Government: presidential
Voltage: 220 - 50
Vaccinations required: Yf*
" recommended: Cho, Ty, Po, Mal
Passport: required
Visa: required
Currency: zaire
$1Cdn: 3885.42 zaires
Driving: right hand
International permit: required
Area code: 011-243
✆ from Canada: –
✆ to Canada: –
Accommodation: ★★
Restaurants: ★★
Transportation: ★
Cost of living: ❍❍❍
UN rank: 140
Best months: June, July, Aug
Holidays: 1, 4 Jan; 30 Apr; 1 May; 24, 30 June; 1 Aug; 14, 27 Oct; 17, 24 Nov; 25 Dec

EAST AFRICA

+10 +9 +8 +7 +6

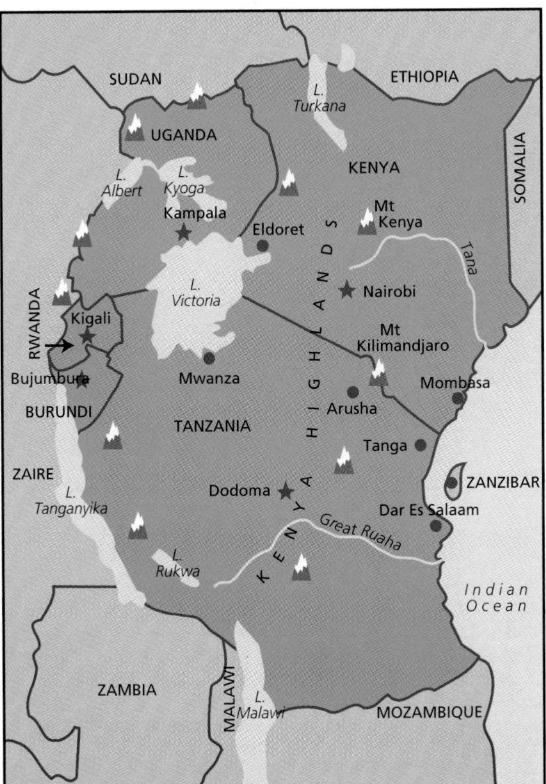

BURUNDI

Region: Africa
Area: 27,830 km²
Capital: Bujumbura
Airport: Bujumbura 11 km
Population: 6,124,750
Languages: Kirundi (off.), French (off.)
Religion: Christian
Government: presidential
Voltage: 220 - 50
Vaccinations required: Yf*
" recommended: Cho, Ty, Po, Mal
Passport: required
Visa: required
Currency: Burundi franc
$1Cdn: 169.51 francs
Driving: right hand
International permit: required
Area code: 011-257
✆ from Canada: –
✆ to Canada: –
Accommodation: ★★
Restaurants: ★★
Transportation: ★★
Cost of living: ❍❍❍
UN rank: 152
Best months: June to Oct
Holidays: 1 Jan; 5 Feb; 16 Apr; 1, 25 May; 4 June; 1 July; 15 Aug; 1 Nov; 25 Dec

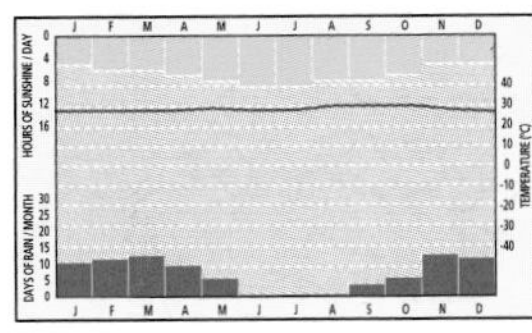

WHAT TO DO

BURUNDI has not been immune to the atrocities that have plagued Rwanda. The Tutsi minority and Hutu majority maintain a precarious peace that could shatter at any time. However, Burundi still has the feel of a resort thanks to Lake Tanganyika and the beaches near the capital, Bujumbura, which are perfect for water sports. From Rutana flows one of the sources of the Nile. KENYA is an increasingly popular destination for travellers seeking the exoticism of Africa and unspoiled yet accessible natural wonders. The Kenyan tourist industry specializes in organizing excursions to game sanctuaries to observe giraffes, elephants, gazelles, lions, antelopes, gnus, baboons, pink flamingos, and vultures. The best known national parks and reserves are the Tsavo, Meru, Marsabit, Mount Kenya, Aberdare, and Sibiloi national parks, and the Masai Mara Reserve (on the Tanzanian border). Mountains, savannah, desert, forest, and sea provide the setting for these parks, each of which is more interesting than the next. It is essential to have good field glasses when visiting these parks. The capital, Nairobi, is the departure point for most safaris, and its museum offers an impressive collection of African art objects, as well as an ethnographic portrait of the country. Eldoret is a good midway point between Nairobi and Lake Turkana (or Lake Rudolf). Squeezed between Rwanda and Sudan, two countries at war, UGANDA has been able to maintain its political stability despite the 150,000 refugees that have flooded into it from the north and south. The capital, Kampala, is a pleasant, modern city that has kept its African charm. Lake Victoria has some nice beaches, especially the one at Entebbe. The Sese Islands are scenic and

+11 +10 +9 +8 +7

KENYA

Region: Africa
Area: 582,650 km²
Capital: Nairobi
Airport: Nairobi
Population: 28,240,660
Languages: English (off.), Swahili
Religions: Christian, animist
Government: presidential
Voltage: 220 - 50
Vaccinations required: Yf*
" recommended: Cho, Ty, Po, Mal
Passport: required
Visa: not required
Currency: Kenya shilling
$1Cdn: 42.46 shillings
Driving: left hand
International permit: recommended
Area code: 011-254
✆ from Canada: –
✆ to Canada: –
Accommodation: ★★★
Restaurants: ★★★
Transportation: ★★★
Cost of living: ○○○
UN rank: 125
Best months: Jan, Feb, July, Aug, Sept
Holidays: 1, 2 Jan; 4 Mar; 14, 16, 17 Apr; 1, 11 May; 1 June; 10, 20 Oct; 12, 25 Dec

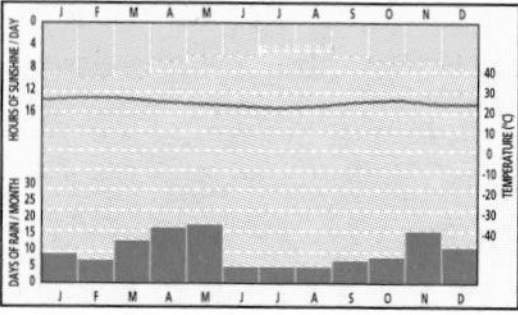

+11 +10 +9 +8 +7

UGANDA

Region: Africa
Area: 236,040 km²
Capital: Kampala
Airport: Entebbe 35 km
Population: 19,121,940
Languages: English (off.), Bantu
Religion: Christian
Government: presidential
Voltage: 220 - 50
Vaccinations required: Yf*
" recommended: Cho, Ty, Po, Mal
Passport: required
Visa: required
Currency: new Uganda shilling
$1Cdn: 705.18 shillings
Driving: left hand
International permit: required
Area code: 011-256
✆ from Canada: –
✆ to Canada: –
Accommodation: ★★
Restaurants: ★★
Transportation: ★★
Cost of living: ○○
UN rank: 154
Best months: Jan, Feb
Holidays: 1, 26 Jan; 4, 8 Mar; 14, 16, 17 Apr; 1 May; 3, 9 June; 9 Oct; 25, 26 Dec

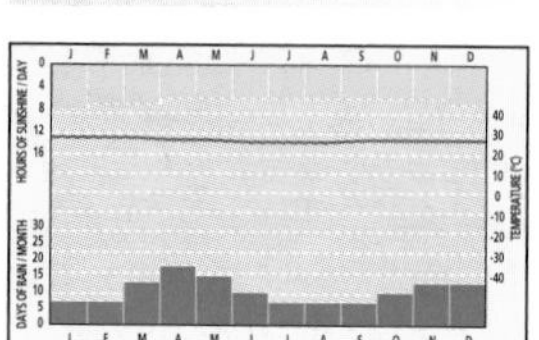

+10 +9 +8 +7 +6

RWANDA

Region: Africa
Area: 26,340 km²
Capital: Kigali
Airport: Kigali 12 km
Population: 8,373,970
Languages: French (off.), Kinyarwanda (off.)
Religions: Christian, animist
Government: presidential
Voltage: 220 - 50
Vaccinations required: Yf
" recommended: Cho, Ty, Po, Mal
Passport: required
Visa: required
Currency: Rwanda franc
$1Cdn: 161.94 francs
Driving: right hand
International permit: required
Area code: 011-250
✆ from Canada: –
✆ to Canada: –
Accommodation: ★★
Restaurants: ★★
Transportation: ★
Cost of living: ○○○
UN rank: 153
Best months: June, July
Holidays: 1,28 Jan; 16,17 Apr; 1,25 May; 4,5 June; 1,5 July; 1,15 Aug; 8,25 Sept; 26 Oct; 1 Nov; 25 Dec

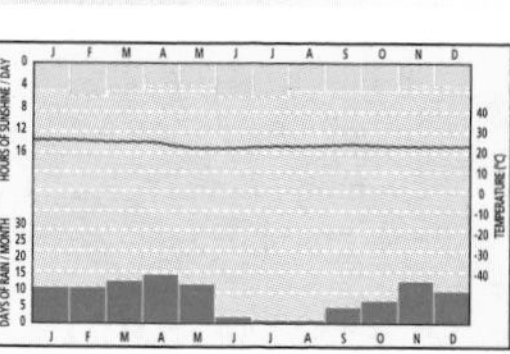

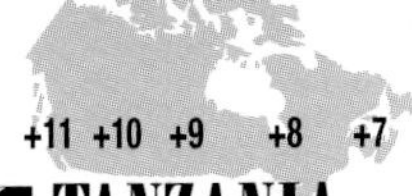

TANZANIA

Region: Africa
Area: 945,090 km2
Capital: Dodoma
Airport: Dar es Salaam 13 km
Population: 27,985,660
Languages: English (off.), Swahili (off.)
Religions: Islamic, Christian
Government: presidential
Voltage: 220 - 50
Vaccinations required: Yf*
" recommended: Cho, Ty, Po, Mal
Passport: required
Visa: required
Currency: Tanzanian shilling
$1Cdn: 428.56 shillings
Driving: left hand
International permit: recommended
Area code: 011-255
✆ from Canada: –
✆ to Canada: –
Accommodation: ★★★
Restaurants: ★★★
Transportation: ★★★
Cost of living: ◯◯◯
UN rank: 148
Best months: July, Aug, Sept
Holidays: 1, 12 Jan; 5 Feb; 4 Mar; 14, 16, 17, 26 Apr; 1, 11 May; 7 July; 8 Aug; 9, 25 Dec

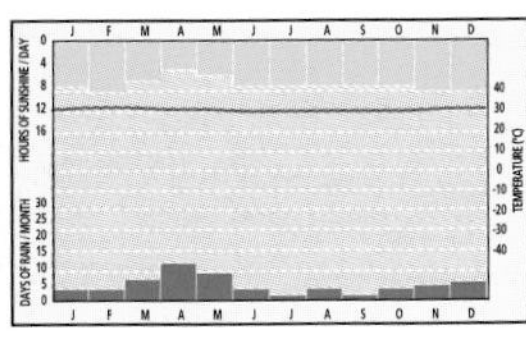

J. HUARD

pristine, as is Ruwenzori National Park, which some say is the most beautiful in Africa. The terrible tragedy of RWANDA will haunt humanity for years to come: hundreds of thousands dead, two million refugees, and millions of deportees. The images of horror broadcasted to the world have obscured the natural beauty of the country, especially of its fauna and flora. Tourism, of course, is unthinkable at this time. TANZANIA's many parks and reserves, have preserved an impressive amount and variety of wildlife: Ruaha, Serengeti, and Selous national parks are among the most interesting. The latter, the largest game reserve in the world, has the highest concentration of elephants in Africa. Climbers will be familiar with Mount Kilimandjaro, the highest peak in Tanzania—and in Africa—at an altitude of 5,963 m. Dar es Salaam and Dodoma, the capital, are major cities that offer all the usual amenities and attractions: museums, markets, churches, mosques, gardens, and numerous examples of local architecture. The coast of Tanzania is washed by the Indian Ocean and abounds with coral. The island of Zanzibar is a famed spice-growing centre; cloves, cinnamon, nutmeg, and pepper grow there against a backdrop of sumptuous mansions and rock gardens.

WHAT TO BUY

The two major ethnic groups of Burundi are skillful at using the natural resources of the country in their art. The wooden statues and items made of woven banana leaves are well known. In Nairobi you'll find statuettes, glass-bead jewelry, and woven goods from all over the country. The *kanga*, a delicately woven fabric that Kenyans, both men and women, wear draped makes a fine souvenir or gift. Kenya also offers nicely decorated soapstone bowls, plates, and vases. Avoid purchasing objects made of ivory or any other animal horn. It is strictly forbidden to take pictures of tribespeople in Kenya, which is too bad, since the Masai are among the most handsome people in the world. The national drinks of Uganda are very strong tea and *waragi*, a banana liquor. Cotton and other fibres are woven into fine products. The most typical item from Rwanda is the *panga,* a cutlass with a curved blade. In Tanzania, the markets of Dodoma offer a wide range of African crafts, but it is the everyday objects, especially those made of teak, that stand out.

TROPICAL AFRICA

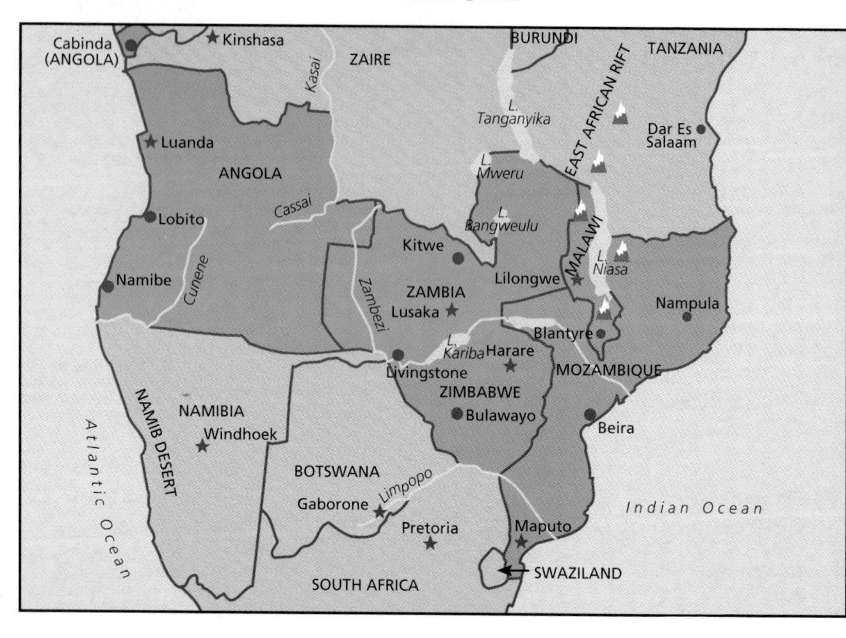

WHAT TO DO

According to the United Nations, the civil war in ANGOLA has left tens of thousands of dead in two years. This often forgotten war has destroyed almost the entire country, leaving Luanda, the capital, and Huambo, the main centre of the conflict, in total chaos. Signs of Angola's past as a Portuguese colony have all but disappeared. Aside from the capital, the main areas of interest are the parks and wildlife reserves. The Quicama National Park, the Luando Reserve, Cameia National Park, and Calandula Falls, near Malanje, are oases of untouched nature. MALAWI's Lake Niasa (once called Lake Malawi), is one of the largest lakes in Africa, comprising much of the country's eastern border. Its shores are sandy and its waters are home to more than 300 species of fish, some of which are found nowhere else in the world. The region also draws a wide variety of water birds. A boat will take you the length of the lake from Monkey Bay north to Karonga, via Nikhotakota and the island of Likoma. The mountains, especially Mount Nyika in the north, shelter birds and butterflies that gather nectar from the region's rare flowers. Each of Malawi's numerous reserves and parks has its own attractions, but they all have in common a wealth and diversity of wildlife. The city of Blantyre, the towns of Limbe, Zomba, and Mzuzu, and the capital, Lilongwe, combine colonial charm and African heritage. The civil war in MOZAMBIQUE started in 1977, and it is only this year that the end of the hostilities seems to be in sight. Reconstruction promises to be a long-term project. For tourists, the situation is still somewhat precarious; they should stay away, as yet, from the Sofala district, discovered by Vasco da Gama in 1498 and still imbued with Portuguese influence. Maputo, the capital, is a modern city that has an interesting market and a good museum of art. The elephant park is a must-see. Gorongosa National Park is in Sofala Province; Marromeu National Park is situated at the mouth of the Zambezi River. ZAMBIA is well known to paleontologists. Here, north of the capital, Lusaka, were found the cranium of "Rhodesia Man," more than 110,000 years old, and artifacts more than 40,000 years old. Most travellers, however, come to see the country's flora and fauna. The many parks and reserves—19 of them—invite visitors to observe the animals from as close as possible without endangering them or interfering with their environment. Kafue National Park, near Lusaka, is one of the largest in Africa; thousands of birds come to drink at the Kafue River, as do rhinoceroses, elephants, antelopes, lions, zebras, monkeys, and many other species. Living-

+9 +8 +7 +6 +5

ANGOLA

Region: Africa
Area: 1,246,700 km²
Capital: Luanda
Airport: Luanda 4 km
Population: 9,803,580
Languages: Portuguese (off.), Bantu
Religions: Christian, animist
Government: in transition
Voltage: 220 - 50
Vaccinations required: Yf*
" recommended: Cho, Ty, Po, Mal
Passport: required
Visa: required
Currency: kwanza
$1Cdn: 892.58 kwanzas
Driving: right hand
International permit: required
Area code: 011-244
✆ from Canada: –
✆ to Canada: –
Accommodation: ★
Restaurants: ★
Transportation: ★
Cost of living: OO
UN rank: 155
Best months: Dec, Jan, Feb
Holidays: 1 Jan; 4 Feb; 27 Mar; 14 Apr; 1 May; 1 Aug; 17 Sept; 11 Nov; 1, 25 Dec

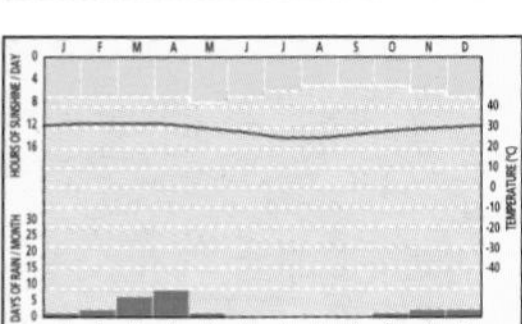

+10 +9 +8 +7 +6

MALAWI

Region: Africa
Area: 118,480 km²
Capital: Lilongwe
Airport: Lilongwe 35 km
Population: 9,732,410
Languages: Chewa (off.), English (off.)
Religions: Christian, animist, Islamic
Government: multi-party
Voltage: 240 - 50
Vaccinations required: Yf*
" recommended: Cho, Ty, Po, Mal
Passport: required
Visa: not required
Currency: kwacha
$1Cdn: 11.14 kwachas
Driving: left hand
International permit: recommended
Area code: 011-265
✆ from Canada: –
✆ to Canada: –
Accommodation: ★★★
Restaurants: ★★★
Transportation: ★★★
Cost of living: OOO
UN rank: 157
Best months: May to Sept
Holidays: 1 Jan; 3 Mar; 14–17 Apr; 14 May; 6 July; 17 Oct; 21, 25, 26 Dec

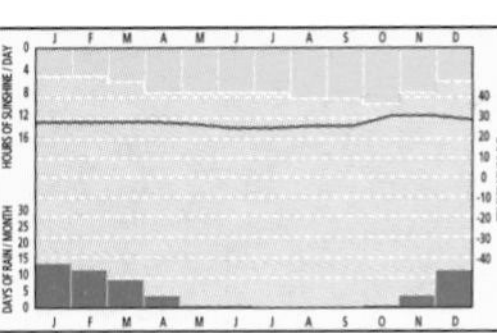

+10 +9 +8 +7 +6

MOZAMBIQUE

Region: Africa
Area: 801,600 km²
Capital: Maputo
Airport: Maputo
Population: 17,346,280
Languages: Portuguese (off.), Bantu
Religions: animist, Christian
Government: presidential
Voltage: 220 - 50
Vaccinations required: Yf*, Cho
" recommended: Ty, Po, Mal
Passport: required
Visa: required
Currency: metical
$1Cdn: 6964.98 meticals
Driving: left hand
International permit: required
Area code: 011-258
✆ from Canada: –
✆ to Canada: –
Accommodation: ★
Restaurants: ★
Transportation: ★
Cost of living: OO
UN rank: 159
Best months: May to Oct
Holidays: 1 Jan; 3 Feb; 4 Mar; 7, 16 Apr; 1, 11 May; 25 June; 7, 25 Sept; 25 Dec

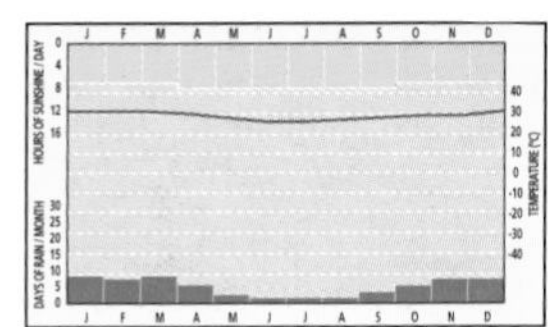

stone (or Maramba), like Lusaka, is a pleasant town for tourists thanks especially to its Anthropology Museum, dedicated to the English explorer David Livingstone, and to its large hotels. But most visitors come to see the celebrated Victoria Falls, on the border with Zimbabwe: this waterfall, 108 m high, churns down a gorge only 75 m wide! The site is in a national park, which is in itself very beautiful. ZIMBABWE is a region of Africa full of remarkable prehistoric remains that attract not just amateur archaeologists but also history buffs. In Rhodes Matopos National Park, are mysterious granite monoliths that still guard the secret of their origin, and caves full of prehistoric paintings. The Great Zimbabwe National Monument preserves the impressive ruins of a city dating perhaps as far back as the Stone Age. Nature-lovers will want to visit Hwange National Park, the largest elephant sanctuary in Africa. The country's mountain ranges have lots of facilities for

J. HUARD

+10 +9 +8 +7 +6

ZAMBIA

Region: Africa
Area: 752,610 km²
Capital: Lusaka
Airport: Lusaka 26 km
Population: 9,188,200
Languages: English (off.), Swahili
Religions: Islamic, Christian
Government: presidential
Voltage: 220 - 50
Vaccinations required: Yf*
" recommended: Cho, Ty, Po, Mal
Passport: required
Visa: not required
Currency: Zambian kwacha
$1Cdn: 692.22 kwachas
Driving: left hand
International permit: required
Area code: 011-260
✆ from Canada: –
✆ to Canada: 00883
Accommodation: ★★★
Restaurants: ★★★
Transportation: ★★★
Cost of living: ○○○
UN rank: 138
Best months: May to Sept
Holidays: 1, 2 Jan; 13 Mar; 14–17 Apr; 1, 25 May; 3, 4 July; 7 Aug; 24 Oct; 25 Dec

+10 +9 +8 +7 +6

ZIMBABWE

Region: Africa
Area: 390,580 km²
Capital: Harare
Airport: Harare 12 km
Population: 10,975,080
Languages: English (off.), Shona
Religions: Islamic, Christian
Government: presidential
Voltage: 220 - 50
Vaccinations required: Yf*
" recommended: Cho, Ty, Po, Mal
Passport: required
Visa: not required
Currency: Zimbabwe dollar
$1Cdn: 6.29 dollars
Driving: left hand
International permit: required
Area code: 011-263
✆ from Canada: –
✆ to Canada: 110897
Accommodation: ★★★★
Restaurants: ★★★★
Transportation: ★★★★
Cost of living: ○○○
UN rank: 121
Best months: May to Oct
Holidays: 1, 2 Jan; 14, 16-18 Mar; 18 Apr; 1, 25 May; 11, 12 Aug; 25, 26 Dec

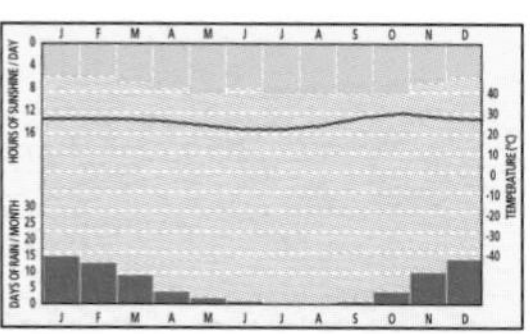

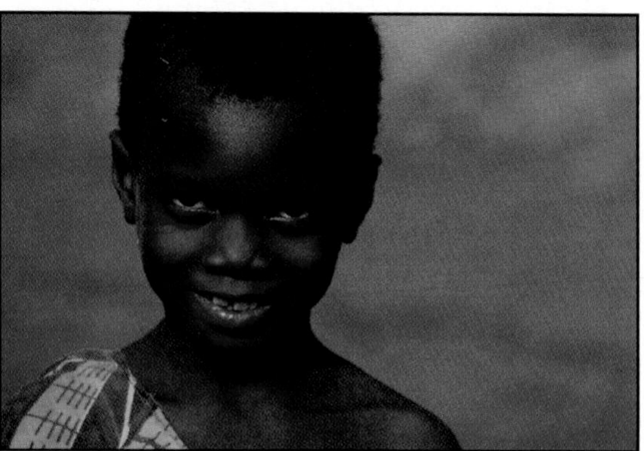

J. HUARD

those who appreciate fresh and spectacular scenery. Mount Inyangani, 2,590 m high, is a paradise of gorges, cliffs, forests, and valleys. Harare, the capital, is a modern city set in lush surroundings. The city has a museum of modern art and many art galleries, reflecting its cosmopolitanism. Nature has a place of honour at both the Botanical Garden and the Harare Game Park.

WHAT TO BUY

Along with diamonds and oil, coffee is Angola's major export. The Bochimans and Bantus make beautiful crafts. Angolan women often wear very colourful draped fabrics and unusual hair ornaments. Malawi's animalist sculptors are experts at working ebony, other carvers use soapstone to make platters, bowls, and sculptures. The country has grown aromatic tobacco and delicious tea for over a century. The Chewas have a rich musical tradition: they still stretch kidskin over hollowed-out tree trunks to make drums. In Mozambique, leather, colourful printed cottons, and objects woven from grasses and reeds are interesting purchases, as are the sculpted wooden masks. In Zambia, the Kabwata Cultural Village in Lusaka offers samples of the wares of the country's craftspeople, as well as information on Zambian artistic and cultural traditions. Jewelry made from copper, precious stones, and gold is available here. Corn beer is a specialty of Zimbabwe. Copper is used to make jewelry, everyday items, and engravings; soapstone is carved to make bowls and plates, and wood is used to make masks, statuettes, and musical instruments. The leather is finely worked, and the cottons are colourful. Zimbabwe is one African country where tourists can travel in safety.

SOUTHERN AFRICA

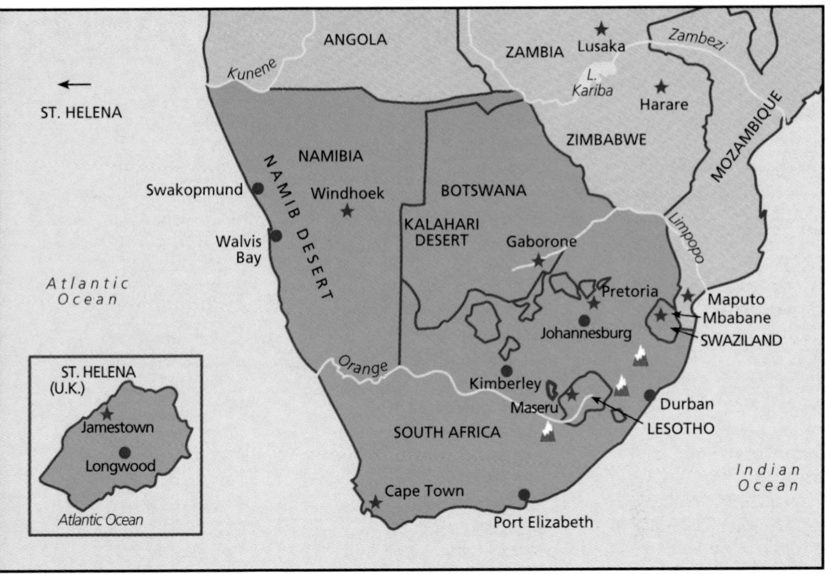

WHAT TO DO

SOUTH AFRICA is a very rich country. Its richness comes from its heavenly climate, beaches, wildlife reserves, and scenery, and from its diversity of cultures, including Afrikaans, Hottentot, Bantu, Bochiman, Zulu, and Swazi. Thanks largely to the gold-mining industry, Johannesburg has become a major city. Its bird sanctuary and wild-flower reserve are major attractions, as are its Zoological Park and Botanical Garden. The city has many museums: the Adler Museum of Medicine, the Africana Museum, and the Mining Museum are of particular interest. The Austin Robert Bird Sanctuary and the many wildlife reserves, like Derdepoort Regional Park and Wonderboom Reserve, make the region around Pretoria, the capital, a paradise for lovers of plants and animals. Kruger National Park is home to some of the most majestic animals on the planet. In Nelspruit, visitors should visit the huge caves and Dinosaur Park. The magnificent waterfall in Augrabies Falls National Park is an island of coolness and the habitat of a multitude of monkeys and rhinoceroses. Kalahari Gemsbok National Park is one of the few virtually untouched spots left in the world. In the south, near Port Elizabeth, is the Addo Elephant National Park, gateway to another vast region of parks and reserves. The country also has numerous pleasant beaches, especially those on the Romantic Coast, which stretches to East London. Cape Town and the surrounding region are dedicated to agriculture and vineyards. BOTSWANA is a little-known country: the Kalahari Desert covers more than three quarters of its territory, and much of the remaining land is devoted to parks and wildlife reserves. Travellers should make a point of going to the Okavango Delta, in the Moremi Wildlife Reserve; in the Okavango region are also the spectacular Chobe National Park and Nxai Pan Park. The Central Kalahari Game Reserve, in the middle of Botswana, is nothing short of fabulous. The capital, Gaborone, is a university town, and it has carefully preserved the customs and traditions of the country's tribes. Encircled by South Africa is LESOTHO, a mountainous country with an average altitude of 1,500 m. The Drakensberg Mountains attract hikers and birdwatchers (more than 280 species come there to nest). This is also where is found the source of the very beautiful Orange River. The capital, Maseru, is a good point of departure for anthropological, biological, and botanical excursions. Tourism is almost nonexistent in Lesotho, but if you're visiting South Africa, you shouldn't pass this little paradise by. NAMIBIA is without a doubt one of the most beautiful countries in Africa: the Namib Desert stretches along the Atlantic coast, the central

+10 +9 +8 +7 +6

SOUTH AFRICA

Region: Africa
Area: 1,219,912 km²
Capitals: Pretoria, Cape Town
Airport: Cape Town 25 km, Johannesburg
Population: 43,930,640
Languages: Afrikaans (off.), English (off.), Bantu
Religions: Islamic, Christian, Hindu
Government: presidential democracy
Voltage: 250 - 50
Vaccinations required: Yf*
" recommended: Cho, Ty, Po, Mal
Passport: required
Visa: required
Currency: rand
$1Cdn: 2.66 rands
Driving: left hand
International permit: required
Area code: 011-27
✆ from Canada: 1-800-463-2838
✆ to Canada: 0-800-99-0014
Accommodation: ★★★★★
Restaurants: ★★★★★
Transportation: ★★★★
Cost of living: ○○○
UN rank: 93
Best months: Dec, Jan, Feb
Holidays: 1 Jan; 6, 14, 16 Apr; 1, 25, 31 May; 10 Oct; 16, 25, 26 Dec

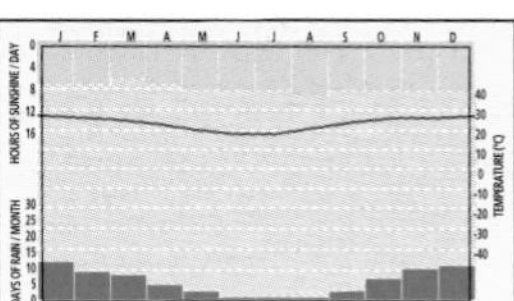

+10 +9 +8 +7 +6

BOTSWANA

Region: Africa
Area: 600,370 km²
Capital: Gaborone
Airport: Gaborone 15 km
Population: 1,359,360
Languages: English (off.), Tswana
Religions: Islamic, Christian, Hindu
Government: presidential
Voltage: 220 - 50
Vaccinations required: Yf*
" recommended: Cho, Ty, Po, Mal
Passport: required
Visa: not required
Currency: pula
$1Cdn: 2.04 pulas
Driving: left hand
International permit: recommended
Area code: 011-267
✆ from Canada: –
✆ to Canada: –
Accommodation: ★★★
Restaurants: ★★★
Transportation: ★★★
Cost of living: ○○○
UN rank: 87
Best months: Aug, Sept
Holidays: 1, 2 Jan; 14, 16,17 Apr; 25 May; 17, 18 July; 30 Sept; 1 Oct; 25, 26 Dec

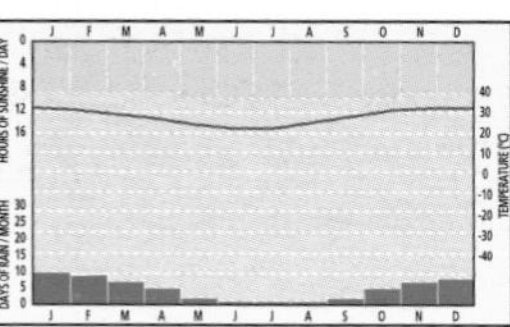

LESOTHO

Region: Africa
Area: 30,350 km²
Capital: Maseru
Airport: –
Population: 1,944,500
Languages: English (off.), Sesotho (off.)
Religion: Christian
Government: constitutional monarchy
Voltage: 220 - 50
Vaccinations required: Yf*
" recommended: Cho, Ty, Po, Mal
Passport: required
Visa: required
Currency: loti
$1Cdn: 2.66 lotis
Driving: left hand
International permit: required
Area code: 011-266
✆ from Canada: –
✆ to Canada: –
Accommodation: ★★
Restaurants: ★★
Transportation: ★
Cost of living: ○○○
UN rank: 120
Best months: Nov to Mar
Holidays: 1 Jan; 13, 21 Mar; 14, 16, 17 Apr; 25 May; 6, 17 July; 4, 5 Oct; 25, 26 Dec

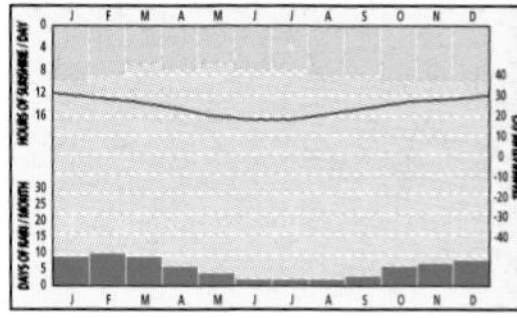

plateaus rise up to 2,000 m in altitude, and the Caprivi region offers fabulous scenery and wildly contrasting climates. Some consider the Etosha National Park, containing the dry lake basin of the same name, to be one of the most beautiful and unspoiled in Africa, perhaps in the world. An amazing diversity of wildlife species coexist in peace in this paradise. The Waterberg plateau is a sanctuary for species threatened with extinction. The town of Swakopmund is an oasis of life in a stunning lunar-like landscape of dunes on the edge of the Namib Desert. Fish River Canyon features high cliffs and dramatic waterfalls. The cave paintings of Twyfelfontein, near the peak of Mount Brandberg, testify to the long human habitation of the region. The architecture in Windhoek, the capital, recalls the city's German colonial past. SWAZILAND is a small country with a wealth of tourist attractions. Casinos, golf courses, spas, equestrian centres, great hotels, and sports complexes have sprouted like mushrooms in the lush Ezulwini

+10 +9 +8 +7 +6

NAMIBIA

Region: Africa
Area: 825,418 km²
Capital: Windhoek
Airport: Windhoek 40 km
Population: 1,595,570
Languages: English (off.), Afrikaans, German
Religion: Christian
Government: presidential
Voltage: 240 - 50
Vaccinations required: Yf*
" recommended: Cho, Ty, Po, Mal
Passport: required
Visa: required
Currency: Namibian dollar
$1Cdn: 2.66 dollars
Driving: left hand
International permit: required + 23 yrs
Area code: 011-264
✆ from Canada: –
✆ to Canada: –
Accommodation: ★★★
Restaurants: ★★★
Transportation: ★★★
Cost of living: ○○○
UN rank: 127
Best months: Apr, May, Aug, Sept, Oct
Holidays: 1 Jan; 21 Mar; 14, 16, 17 Apr; 1, 4, 25 May; 26 Aug; 10, 25, 26 Dec

+10 +9 +8 +7 +6

SWAZILAND

Region: Africa
Area: 17,360 km²
Capital: Mbabane
Airport: Manzini 8 km
Population: 936,370
Languages: English (off.), Siswati (off.)
Religions: Christian, traditional
Government: monarchy
Voltage: 220 - 50
Vaccinations required: Yf*
" recommended: Cho, Ty, Po, Mal
Passport: required
Visa: not required
Currency: lilangeni
$1Cdn: 2.66 lilangenis
Driving: left hand
International permit: required
Area code: 011-268
✆ from Canada: –
✆ to Canada: –
Accommodation: ★★★
Restaurants: ★★★
Transportation: ★
Cost of living: ○○○
UN rank: 117
Best months: Apr, Oct
Holidays: 1 Jan; 14, 16–19, 25 Apr; 25 May; 22 July; 6 Sept; 25, 26 Dec

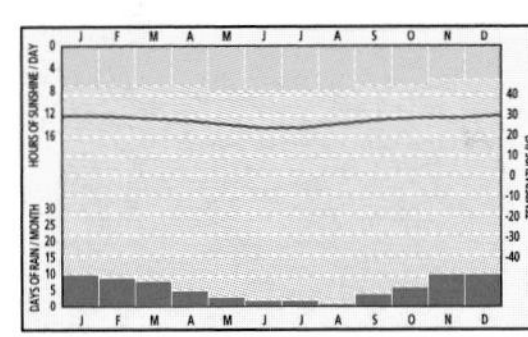

J. HUARD

Valley. At the Mantenga Falls and Mlilwane Sanctuary are preserved the extraordinary paintings by the Bochimans of the Nhlangano region. Climbers will appreciate Mount Emblemble, rising some 1,800 m in altitude, and white-water adventurers will love the Mkondo River.

WHAT TO BUY

People eat well in South Africa, and the locally produced wines are becoming better known throughout the world. The art of the Bantus and Zulus is rich in symbols, and the masks, figurines, musical instruments, and various cult objects make fine souvenirs. Their flat stones painted with hunting scenes are also very beautiful. The raw materials of choice for jewelers are obviously gold and diamonds. Elephants are protected by very strict laws: it is thus not recommended to purchase objects made of ivory. Botswana's primary crafts are wooden sculptures and weaving; the art of the Kalahari Desert tribes is unlike anything else in the world. Wool, skins, and leather are important commodities in Lesotho. Diamonds are, however, at the heart of the economy. Sources of inspiration are not lacking for the animalist sculptors of Namibia, who make magnificent statuettes out of a wide assortment of woods. The Hottentots, Bochimans, and Bantus had contact with white South Africans, but, fortunately, they've kept their own cultures intact and express them in their art and crafts. In Mantenga, the art centre offers a wide range of Swaziland's arts and crafts. The markets of Mbabane and Manzini offer woven goods, prettily dyed cotton, baskets, jewelry, precious stones, and musical instruments.

INDIAN OCEAN

+11 +10 +9 +8 +7

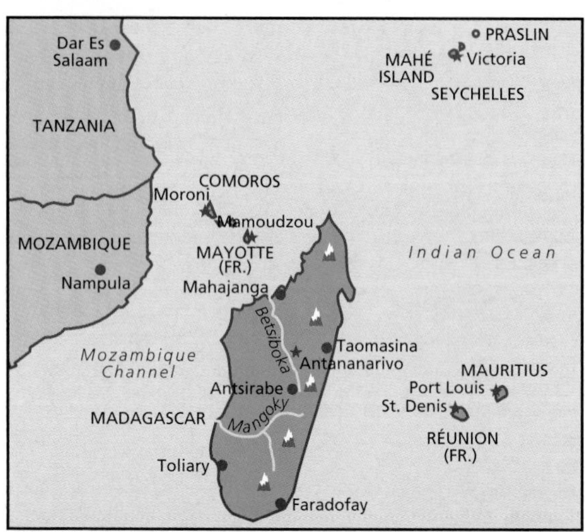

RÉFLEXION

COMOROS

Region: Indian Ocean
Area: 2,170 km²
Capital: Moroni
Airport: Moroni 20 km
Population: 530,140
Languages: Arabic (off.), French (off.)
Religions: Islamic, Christian
Government: presidential
Voltage: 220 - 50
Vaccinations required: Yf
Vaccinations recommended: Cho, Ty, Po
Passport: required
Visa: required
Currency: Comoros franc
$1Cdn: 266.96 francs
Driving: right hand
International permit: required
Area code: 011-269
✆ from Canada: –
✆ to Canada: –
Accommodation: ★★★
Restaurants: ★★★
Transportation: ★
Cost of living: ○○○
UN rank: 141
Best months: Aug, Sept
Holidays: 11 Jan; 15 Mar; 13, 21 May; 11, 20 June; 6 July; 19 Aug

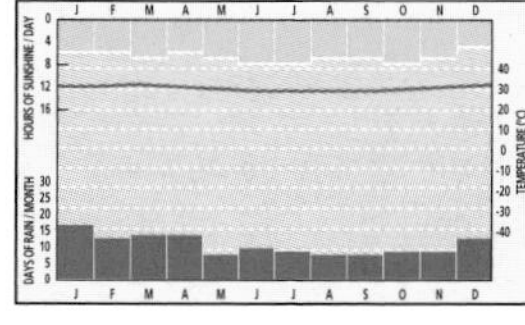

WHAT TO DO

Moroni is the capital of the island nation COMOROS, as the royal mausoleums and fortress testify. The butterflies on the island of Grande Comore (or Njazidja) draw scores of amateur entomologists, but these magnificent insects, some varieties of which live only in the marshes of these islands, are protected by very strict laws. On Grande Comore, visitors can also climb into the crater of the volcano of Mount Kartala, the largest in the world. The island of Mohéli is home to giant turtles, and the island of Anjouan is known for its perfume distilleries. The wildlife of MADAGASCAR is unique: more than 3,000 butterfly varieties and lemurians live there. The country's isolation has also helped preserve hundreds of unique plants and flowers. Tourism has increased over the last few years with the introduction of organized excursions highlighting the country's natural wonders. The city of Antsirabé is sur-

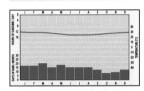

+11 +10 +9 +8 +7

MADAGASCAR

Region: Indian Ocean
Area: 587,040 km²
Capital: Antananarivo
Airport: Antananarivo
Population: 13,427,760
Languages: Malagasy (off.), French (off.)
Religions: traditional, Christian
Government: presidential
Voltage: 220 - 50
Vaccinations required: Yf
" recommended: Cho, Ty, Po, Mal
Passport: required
Visa: required
Currency: Malagasy franc
$1Cdn: 3290.14 francs
Driving: right hand
International permit: required
Area code: 011-261
✆ from Canada: –
✆ to Canada: –
Accommodation: ★★★
Restaurants: ★★★
Transportation: ★★
Cost of living: ❍
UN rank: 131
Best months: Sept, Oct
Holidays: 1 Jan; 29 Mar; 16, 17 Apr; 1, 4, 5, 25 May; 26 June; 15 Aug; 1 Nov; 25 Dec

+12 +11 +10 +9 +8

MAURITIUS

Region: Indian Ocean
Area: 1,860 km²
Capital: Port Louis
Airport: Ramgoulam 43 km
Population: 1,116,930
Languages: English (off.), French, Créole
Religions: Catholic, Protestant, Hindu
Government: parliamentary
Voltage: 220 - 50
Vaccinations required: Yf*
Vaccinations recommended: Cho, Ty, Po
Passport: required
Visa: not required
Currency: Mauritian rupee
$1Cdn: 12.9 rupees
Driving: left hand
International permit: recommended
Area code: 011-230
✆ from Canada: –
✆ to Canada: 73110
Accommodation: ★★★★
Restaurants: ★★★
Transportation: ★★
Cost of living: ❍❍❍
UN rank: 60
Best months: May to Oct
Holidays: 1, 2, 30, 31 Jan; 12 Feb; 4, 12, 17 Mar; 1 May; 12 Sept; 1 Nov; 25 Dec

+11 +10 +9 +8 +7

MAYOTTE

Region: Indian Ocean
Area: 375 km²
Capital: Mamoudzou
Airport: Pamandzi
Population: 93,470
Languages: French, Mahori
Religions: Islamic, Christian
Government: French territorial collectivity
Voltage: 220 - 50
Vaccinations required: –
Vaccinations recommended: Mal
Passport: required
Visa: required
Currency: French franc
$1Cdn: 3.52 francs
Driving: right hand
International permit: required
Area code: 011-269
✆ from Canada: –
✆ to Canada: –
Accommodation: ★★★
Restaurants: ★★★
Transportation: –
Cost of living: ❍❍❍
UN rank: –
Best months: Aug, Sept
Holidays: 1 Jan; 16, 17 Apr; 1, 8, 25 May; 4, 5 June; 14 July; 15 Aug; 1, 11 Nov; 25 Dec

J. HUARD

rounded by volcanoes and their beautiful lakes. The southern region is particularly interesting for its cactuses and carnivorous plants, spas, and beaches, but the main attraction is Isalo National Park. To the north, Nosy Bé is also very interesting: this island surrounded by islands, is a paradise of aromatic plants. As for the cities, the capital, Antananarivo, has preserved the very handsome Palace of the Queen and several buildings dating from the dynasty of the Merinas. Not so long ago, the main industry of MAURITIUS was sugar cane. Today, it might be tourism. The country's very beautiful beaches, clear, clean ocean, and gardens of exotic flowers make it a very popular destination. In Port-Louis, the capital, are many charming buildings dating from the colonial era. The National Museum of Natural History offers a

+12 +11 +10 +9 +8

RÉUNION

Region: Indian Ocean
Area: 2,510 km²
Capital: Saint-Denis
Airport: Gillot 5 km
Population: 652,860
Languages: French (off.), Créole
Religion: Catholic
Government: French overseas department
Voltage: 220 - 50
Vaccinations required: Yf*
Vaccinations recommended: Cho, Ty, Po
Passport: required
Visa: not required
Currency: French franc
$1Cdn: 3.52 francs
Driving: right hand
International permit: recommended
Area code: 011-262
✆ from Canada: –
✆ to Canada: –
Accommodation: ★★★★
Restaurants: ★★★★
Transportation: ★★
Cost of living: ○○
UN rank: –
Best months: Dec, Jan, Feb
Holidays: 1 Jan; 16,17 Apr; 1 8,25 May; 4,5 June; 14 July; 15 Aug; 1,11 Nov; 25 Dec

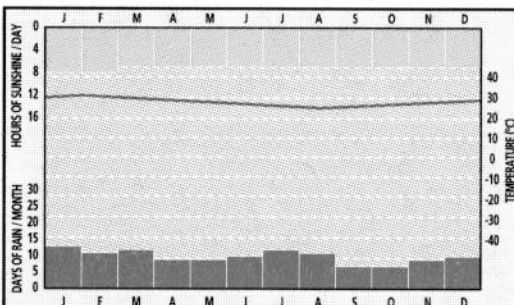

+12 +11 +10 +9 +8

SEYCHELLES

Region: Indian Ocean
Area: 455 km²
Capital: Victoria
Airport: Mahé
Population: 72,120
Languages: English (off.), French (off.), Créole
Religion: Catholic
Government: presidential
Voltage: 220 - 50
Vaccinations required: Yf*
Vaccinations recommended: Ty
Passport: required
Visa: not required
Currency: Seychelles rupee
$1Cdn: 3.43 rupees
Driving: right hand
International permit: recommended
Area code: 011-248
✆ from Canada: –
✆ to Canada: –
Accommodation: ★★★★
Restaurants: ★★★★
Transportation: ★★
Cost of living: ○○○
UN rank: 83
Best months: May to Oct
Holidays: 1 Jan; 14–16 Apr; 1 May; 5, 15,18,29 June; 15 Aug; 1 Nov; 8,25 Dec

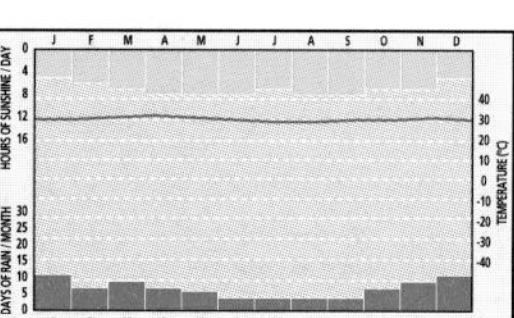

permanent exhibition on the dodo, an extinct bird. MAYOTTE (or Mahore) is a French territory once associated with neighbouring Comoros. Its tourism industry is concentrated around the superb beaches, which feature lovely coral as well as lagoons tailor-made for diving. Mamoudzo, the capital, and Dzaoudzi are the island's main towns. Many of their buildings bear witness to the colonial history of Comoros. The Arabs that lived on the territory in the fifteenth century left a mosque in Chingoni. RÉUNION is an island of volcanic origin. This accounts for the diversity of its features, from high mountain ranges to deep valleys. The Cilaos, Salazie, and Mafate cirques are natural amphitheatres that are very popular with hikers. The Natural History Museum in the capital, Saint-Denis, provides a good introduction to those planning to visit the island's verdant valleys and volcanoes. In the SEYCHELLES, a paradise for birdwatchers, the islands of Praslin, Frégate, Curieuse, and La Digue are home to many varieties of sea birds, especially sterns. The islands of Denis and Aride are more remote, but nature-lovers will find them magnificent. The island of Mahé is rimmed with fine-sand beaches over which float the aromas of cinnamon and vanilla from nearby plantations. Victoria, the capital, has retained the charm of its colonial era. Its Botanical Garden boasts orchids and patchouli flowers, and its National Museum provides a good account of the history and life of the country.

WHAT TO BUY

In Comoros are grown many essences for perfumes, including ylang-ylang, jasmine, and orange blossom. The markets are also redolent with the scent of spices such as vanilla and cloves. Pearls, mother-of-pearl, and shells are used to make beautiful jewelry. The pottery, sculptures, and fabrics of the islands are also stunning. In Madagascar, the Zuma d'Antananarivo Market offers all sorts of products, from cloves, vanilla, tobacco, sugar cane, patchouli, and ylang-ylang to furniture and inlaid wooden items. The funerary art is surprising, but it is rich in symbols and beautifully turned. Visitors should not encourage the trade in zebu skins and dried flowers from species threatened with extinction. Some of the turtles in Mauritius may have reached the ripe old age of a hundred years! It is not recommended to buy objects made of tortoise shell. Mayotte's jewelry, made with coral, pearls, and shells is very popular. The potters and weavers decorate their work with pretty figurative images inspired by island life. Créole cuisine gives Réunion its unique aroma. White rum is often flavoured there with vanilla, cinnamon, and anise, and then it is called *rhum arrangé*. Multicoloured batiks, printed fabrics, and paintings are the specialties of the Seychelles. Pottery, sculpture, and coral and sea-coco jewelry are also readily available.

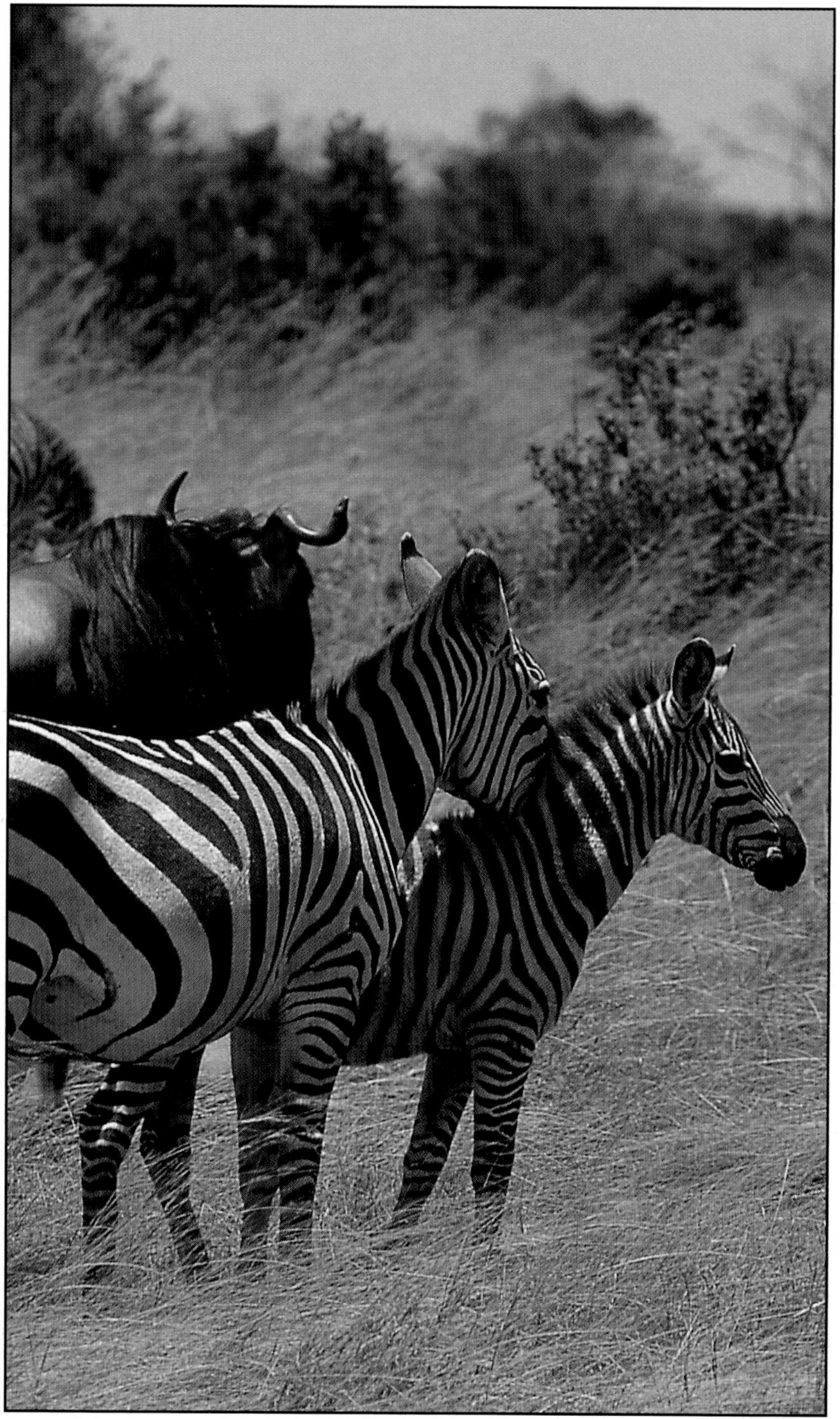

Canadian representatives abroad

ALBANIA
Embassy
Budakeszi ut. 32
1121 Budapest, Hungary

ALGERIA
Embassy
27 bis, rue des Frères Benhafid
Hydra, Algeria
or
P.O. Box 225, Alger-Gare
1600 Alger, Algeria
Tel.: (011-213-2) 69-16-11
Telex: Canad Alger
Fax: (011-213-2) 69-39-20

ANGOLA
High Commission
C.P. 1430
Harare, Zimbabwe
Consulate
Rua Rei Katyavala 113
Luanda, Angola
Tel.: (011-244-2) 330-243
Fax: (011-244-2) 343-754, 393-4455
(from 9 p.m. to 8 a.m. Angola time)

ANTIGUA AND BARBUDA
High Commission
P.O. Box 404, Bridgetown
Barbados

ARGENTINA
Embassy
2828 Tagle
1425 Buenos Aires, Argentina
or
Casilla de Correo 1598
Buenos Aires, Argentina
Tel.: (011-54-1) 805-3032
Telex: Domcan Buenos Aires
Fax: (011-54-1) 806-1209

ARMENIA
Embassy
23 Starokonyushenny Pereulok
Moscow, 121002 Russia

AUSTRALIA
High Commission
Commonwealth Ave.
Canberra ACT 2600, Australia
Tel.: (011-61-6) 273-3844
Fax: (011-61-6) 273-3285
Consulate
Level 5, Quay West Building
111 Harrington Street
Sydney, N.S.W. 2000, Australia
Tel.: (011-61-2) 364-3000
Telex: Canadian Sydney
Fax: (011-61-2) 364-3098
Consulate
11th Floor, National Mutual Centre,
111 St. George's Terrace
Perth, Western Australia 6000
Tel.: (011-61-9) 321-1156
Fax: (011-61-9) 321-1151

AUSTRIA
Embassy
Laurenzerber 2, A-1010, Vienna
Austria
Tel.: (011-43-1) 531-38-3000
Telex: Domcan Vienna
Fax: (011-43-1) 531-38-3321

AZERBAIDJAN
Embassy
Nenehatun Caddesi no. 75
Gaziosmanpasa 06700
Ankara, Turkey

BAHAMAS
High Commission
P.O. Box 1500, Kingston 10
Jamaica
Consulate
No. 21 Out Island Traders Building
Ernest Street, Nassau, Bahamas
or
P.O. Box SS-6371, Nassau, Bahamas
Tel.: (1-809) 393-2123, 393-2124
Fax: (1-809) 393-1305

BAHRAIN
Embassy
P.O. Box 25281
13113 (Safat), Kuwait City, Kuwait

BANGLADESH
High Commission
House CWN 16/A
Road 48, Gulshan, Bangladesh
or
P.O. Box 569, Dhaka, Bangladesh
Tel.: (011-880-2) 88-36-39, 60-70-71
Telex: Domcan Dhaka
Fax: (011-880-2) 88-30-43

BARBADOS
High Commission
Bishop's Court Hill
St. Michael, Barbade
or
P.O. Box 404, Bridgetown, Barbados
Tel.: (809) 429-3550
Telex: Domcan Bridgetown
Fax: (809) 429-3780

BELGIUM
Embassy
2, avenue de Tervuren
1040 Brussels, Belgium
Tel.: (011-32-2) 741-0611
Telex: Domcan Brussels
Fax: (011-32-2) 741-0613

BELIZE
Consulate
85 North Front Street
Belize City, Belize
Tel.: (011-501-02) 33-722
Fax: (011-501-02) 30-060

BELORUSSIA
Embassy
23 Starokonyushenny Pereulok,
Moscow, 121002 Russia

BENIN
Embassy
P.O. Box 54506, Ikoyi Station
Lagos, Nigeria

BERMUDA
Consulate
1251 Ave. of the Americas
New York, N.Y. 10020, USA

BOLIVIA
Embassy
Casilla 18-1126
Correo Miraflores, Lima, Peru
Consulate
Avenida 20 de Octubre 2475
Plaza Avaroa, Sopocachi, La Paz
Bolivia
or
Casilla Postal 13045, La Paz, Bolivia
Tel.: (011-591-2) 37-52-24
Fax: (011-591-2) 32-94-35

BOTSWANA
High Commission
P.O. Box 1430
Harare, Zimbabwe
Consulate
P.O. Box 1009, Gaborone, Botswana
Tel.: (011-267) 371-659

BRAZIL
Embassy
Setor de Embaixadas Sul,
Avenida das Nacoes, lote 16,
70410-900 Brasilia D.F., Brazil
or
Caixa Postal 00961, 70359-900
Brasilia D.F., Brazil
Tel.: (011-55-61) 321-2171
Telex: Canada Brasilia
Fax: (011-55-61) 321-4529
Consulate
Edificio Top Center
Avenida Paulista 854, 5th Floor
01310-913 Sao Paulo, Brazil
or
Caixa Postal 22002, 01410 Sao Paulo
Brazil
Tel.: (011-55-11) 287-2122, -2234
Fax: (011-55-11) 251-5057
Consulate
Rua Lauro Muller, 116, Sala 1104
Torre Rio Sul-Botafogo
22290 Rio de Janeiro, Brazil
Tel.: (011-55-21) 275-2137
Fax: (011-55-21) 541-3898

BRITAIN
High Commission
Macdonald House, 1 Grosvenor Sq.

London, W1X OAB,
England, U.K.
Tel.: (011-44-171) 258-6600
Fax: (011-44-171) 258-6333
Consular and Passport Services:
38 Grosvenor Street,
London, W1X OAA
England, U.K.
Tel.: (011-44-171) 258-6356, 258-6316
Fax: (011-44-171) 258-6506
Canada House:
Trafalgar Sq., rue Cockspur,
London, SW1Y 5BJ.
Tel.: (011-44-171) 629-9492
Fax: (011-44-171) 258-6322
Consulate
3 George Street
Edinburgh
Tel.: (011-32) 220-4333

BRUNEI
High Commission
Robinson Road, P.O. Box 845
Singapore 9016
Republic of Singapore

BULGARIA
Embassy
Budakeszi ut. 32,
1121 Budapest, Hungary

BURKINA-FASO
Embassy
Canadian Development Centre
Ouagadougou, Burkina-Faso
or
P.O.Box 548, Ouagadougou 01
Province du Kadiogo, Burkina-Faso
Tel.: (011-226) 31-18-94, 31-18-95
Fax: (011-226) 31-19-00

BURUNDI
Consulate
Boulevard 28 novembre,
Bujumbura, Burundi
or
C.P. 5, Bujumbura, Burundi
Tel.: (011-257) 22-16-32
Fax: (011-257) 22-28-16

CAMBODIA
Embassy
c/o The Australian Embassy
Villa 11, Street 254, Chartaumuk
Daun Penh District, Phnom Penh
Tel.: (011-855-23) 26 000, 26 001
Fax: (011-855-23) 26 003

CAMEROON
Embassy
Immeuble Stamatiades,
Place de l'Hôtel de Ville
Yaoundé Cameroon
or
P.O. Box 572, Yaoundé, Cameroon
Tel.: (011-237) 23-02-03, 22-19-36
Fax: (011-237) 22-10-90

CAPE-VERDE
Embassy
P.O. Box 3373, Dakar, Senegal

CENTRAL AFRICAN REPUBLIC
Embassy
P.O. Box 572, Yaoundé, Cameroon

CHAD
Embassy
P.O. Box 572, Yaoundé, Cameroon

CHILE
Embassy
Ahumada 11, 10th Floor, Santiago, Chile
or
Casilla 427, Santiago, Chile
Tel.: (011-56-2) 696-2256, -2257
Telex: Domcan Santiago de Chile
Fax: (011-56-2) 696-2424

CHINA
Embassy
19 Dong Zhi Men Wai Street,
Chao Yang District
Beijing, People's Republic of China
100600
Tel.: (011-86-1) 532-3536
Telex: Domcan Peking
Fax: (011-86-1) 532-4311
Consulate
American International Centre,
at Shanghai Centre, West Tower, Suite 604
1376 Nanjing Xi Lu
Shanghai 200040,
People's Republic of China
Tel.: (011-86-21) 279-8400
Fax: (011-86-21) 279-8401
Consulate
China Hotel Office Tower,
Suite 1563-4, Liu Hua Lu,
Guangzhou 510015,
People's Republic of China
Tel.: (011-86-20) 666-0569
Fax: (011-86-20) 667-2401

COLOMBIA
Embassy
Calle 76, no. 11-52
Bogota, Colombia
or
Apartado Aereo 53531
Bogota 2, Colombia
Tel.: (011-57-1) 313-1355
Télec.: (011-57-1) 313-3071

COMOROS
High Commission
P.O. Box 1022, Dar es-Salaam, Tanzania

CONGO
Embassy
c/o The Embassy of the United
States of America (Canadian Office),
310 avenue des Aviateurs
Kinshasa, Zaïre

COSTA RICA
Embassy
Cronos Building, Calle 3 y Avenida Central,
San José, Costa Rica
or
Apartado Postal 10303
San José, Costa Rica
Tel.: (011-506) 255-3522
Fax: (011-506) 223-2395

CÔTE D'IVOIRE
Embassy
Immeuble Trade Center
23 Nogues Avenue
Le Plateau, Abidjan
Côte d'Ivoire
or
P.O. Box 4104
Abidjan 01, Côte d'Ivoire
Tel.: (011-225) 21-20-09
Fax: (011-225) 21-77-28

CROATIA
Embassy
Hotel Esplanade
Mihanoviceva 1
41000 Zagreb, Croatia
Tel.: (011-385-1) 477-885, 477-754
Télec.: (011-385-1) 477-913

CUBA
Embassy
Calle 30, No. 518 Esquina a7a, Miramar
Havana, Cuba
Tel.: (011-53-7) 33-25-16, 33-25-27
Telex: Domcan Havana
Fax: (011-53-7) 33-20-44

CYPRUS
High Commission
The Canadian Ambassy
P.O. Box 6410
Tel Aviv 61063, Israel
Consulate
15 Themistocles Dervis Street,
Margarita House, Suite 403,
Nicosia, Cyprus
or
P.O. Box 2125, Nicosia, Cyprus
Tel.: (011-357-2) 45-16-30
Telex.: (011-357-2) 45-90-96

CZECH REPUBLIC
Embassy
Mickiewiczova 6, 125 33 Prague 6,
Czech Republic
Tel.: (011-42-2) 2431-1108, -1109
Telex: Domcan Prague
Fax: (011-42-2) 2431-0294

DENMARK
Embassy
Kr. Bernikowsgade 1,
1105 Copenhagen K, Denmark
Tel.: (011-45-33) 12-22-99
Fax: (011-45-33) 14-05-85

DJIBOUTI
Embassy
P.O. Box 1130
Addis Ababa, Ethiopia

DOMINICA
High Commission
P.O. Box 404
Bridgetown, Barbados

DOMINICAN REPUBLIC
Embassy
Maximo Gomez 30
Sainto Domingo
Dominican Republic
Tel.: (809) 689-0002
Fax: (809) 682-2691
Consulate
Beller 51, Suite 3
Puerto Plata, Dominican Republic
Tel.: (809) 586-5761, 586-3305
Fax: (809) 586-5762

ECUADOR
Embassy
Apartado Aereo 53531,
Bogota 2, Colombia
Consulate
General Cordova 800
y Victor Manuel Rendon,
Edificio Torres de la Merced, Piso 21,
Oficina 6, Guayaquil, Ecuador
Tel.: (011-593-4) 566-747
Fax: (011-593-4) 314-562

EGYPT
Embassy
6 Mohamed Fahmi El Sayed Street,
Garden City, Cairo, Egypt
or
P.O. Box 1667, Cairo, Egypt
Tel.: (011-20-2) 354-3110
Telex: Domcan Cairo
Fax: (011-20-2) 356-3548

EL SALVADOR
Embassy
P.O. Box 400, Guatemala,
C.A., Guatemala
Consulate
111 Avenida Las Palmas, Colonia
San Benito
San Salvador, El Salvador
or
Apartado Postal 3078,
Centro de Gobierno
San Salvador, El Salvador
Tel.: (011-503) 241-648, 983-292
Fax: (011-503) 790-765

EQUATORIAL GUINEA
Embassy
P.O. Box 4037
Libreville, Gabon

ERITREA
Embassy
P.O. Box 1130
Addis Ababa, Ethiopia

ESTONIA
Embassy
Toom Kooli 13, 2nd Floor
0100 Tallinn, Estonia
Tel.: (011-371) 631-3570
Fax: (011-371) 631-3573

ETHIOPIA
Embassy
Old Airport Area, Higher 23,
Kebele 12, House Number 122,
Addis Ababa, Ethiopia
or
P.O. Box 1130, Addis Ababa, Ethiopia
Tel.: (011-251) 71-30-22
Telex: Domcan Addis Ababa
Fax: (011-251) 71-30-33

EUROPEAN UNION
The Mission of Canada
Avenue de Tervuren 2
1040 Brussels, Belgium
Tel.: (011-32-2) 741-0660,
735-6193 (Night line)
Fax: (011-32-2) 741-0629

FIJI
High Commission
P.O. Box 12049, Thorndon,
Wellington, New Zealand
Consulate
L.I.C.I. Building, 7th Floor
Butt Street, Suva, Fiji

FINLAND
Embassy
P. Esplanadi 25B
00100 Helsinki, Finland
or
P.O. Box 779,
00101 Helsinki, Finland
Tel.: (011-358-0) 17-11-41
Téléc. (011-358-0) 60-10-60

FRANCE
Embassy
35, avenue Montaigne
75008 Paris, France
Tel.: (011-33-1) 44-43-29-00
Fax: (011-331-) 44-43-29-99
Telex: Stadacona Paris
Consulate
Bonnel Building, Part-Dieu,
Corner Bonnel and Garibaldi
74 de Bonnel Street, 3rd Floor
69003 Lyon, France
Tel.: (011-33) 72-61-15-25
Fax: (011-33) 78-62-09-36
Consulate
Polysar France, rue du Ried
La Wantzenau, France
or
Polysar France, C.P. 7
67610 La Wantzenau, France
Tel.: (011-33) 88-96-65-02
Fax: (011-33) 88-96-64-54
Consulate
30, boul. de Strasbourg
31014 Toulouse, France
Tel.: (011-33) 61-99-30-16
Fax: (011-33) 61-63-43-37
Consulate
Institut Frecher
C.P. 903, St. Pierre
Saint-Pierre et Miquelon, F-97500
Tel.: (508) 41-55-10
Fax: (508) 41-55-01

GABON
Embassy
P.O. Box 4037, Libreville, Gabon
Tel.: (011-241) 74-34-64, 74-34-65
Fax: (011-241) 74-34-66

GAMBIA
Embassy
P.O. Box 3373, Dakar, Senegal

GEORGIA
Embassy
Nenehatun Caddesi no. 75
Gaziosmanpasa 06700
Ankara, Turkey

GERMANY
Chancery
Friedrich-Wilhelm-Strasse 18
53113 Bonn, Germany
Tel.: (011-49-228) 968-0
Telex: Domcan Bonn
Fax: (011-49-228) 968-3904
Embassy
Friedrichstrasse, 95, 10117 Berlin
Tel.: (011-49-30) 261-1161
Fax: (011-49-30) 262-9206
Consulate
Prinz-Georg Strasse 126
D-40479
Düsseldorf
Tel.: (011-49-211) 17-21-70
Telex: Canadian Düsseldorf
Fax: (011-49-211) 35-91-65
Consulate
Tal 29, 80331 Munich
Tel.: (011-49-89) 29-06-50
Fax: (011-49-89) 228-5987

GHANA
High Commission
42 Independence Ave
Accra, Ghana
or
P.O. Box 1639, Accra, Ghana
Tel.: (011-233-21) 77-37-91
Fax: (011-233-21) 77-37-92

GREECE
Embassy
4 Ioannou Gennadiou Street
Athens 115 21, Greece
Tel.: (011-30-1) 725-4011
Fax: (011-30-1) 725-3994

GREENLAND
Consulate
Groenlandsfly A/S
3900 Nuuk, Greenland
Tel.: (011-299) 28888
Fax: (011-299) 27288

GRENADA
High Commission
P.O. Box 404 Bridgetown, Barbados

GUATEMALA
Embassy
13 Calle 8-44, Zone 10,
Guatemala City, Guatemala
or
P.O. Box 400, Guatemala, C.A.
Tel.: (011-502-2) 33-61-04
Telex: Canadian Guatemala City
Fax: (011-502-2) 33-61-61

GUINEA
Embassy
P.O. Box 99
Conakry, Guinea
Tel.: (011-224) 41-23-95, 41-44-48
Fax: (011-224) 41-42-36

GUINEA-BISSAU
Embassy
P.O. Box 3373, Dakar, Senegal

GUYANA
High Commission
High et Young Streets,
Georgetown, Guyana
or
P.O. Box 10880, Georgetown, Guyana
Tel.: (011-592-2) 72081, -5
Telex: Domcan Georgetown
Fax: (011-592-2) 58380

HAITI
Embassy
Édifice Banque Nova Scotia
route de Delmas
Port-au-Prince, Haiti
or
C.P. 826, Port-au-Prince, Haiti
Tel.: (011-509) 23-2358
Telex: Domcan Port-au-Prince
Fax: (011-509) 23-8720

HONDURAS
Embassy
Edificio Comercial Los Castanos, 60 Piso,
boulevard Morazan, Tegucigalpa,
Honduras
or
Apartado Postal 3552
Tegucigalpa, Honduras
Tel.: (011-504) 31-45-45, 31-45-51
Fax: (011-504) 31-57-93

HONG KONG
Commission
11-14th Floors, One Exchange Square,
8 Connaught Place
Hong Kong
or
GPO Box 11142
Hong Kong
Tel.: (011-852) 810-4321
Telex: Domcan Hong-Kong
Fax: (011-852) 2810-6736

HUNGARY
Embassy
Budakeszi ut. 32
1121 Budapest, Hungary
Tel.: (011-36-1) 275-1200
Fax: (011-36-1) 275-1210

ICELAND
Embassy
Oscar's Gate 20, 0244 Oslo, Norway
Consulate
Sudurlandsbraut 10,
108 Reykjavik, Iceland
or
P.O. Box 8094, 128 Reykjavik, Iceland
Tel.: (011-354-5) 680-820
Fax: (011-354-5) 680-899

INDIA
High Commission
7/8 Shantipath, Chanakyapuri
New Delhi 110021, India
or
P.O. Box 5207, New Delhi, Inda
Tel.: (011-91-11) 687-6500
Fax.: (011-91-11) 687-6579
Consulate
41/42 Maker Chambers VI,
Jamnalal Bajaj Marg, Nariman Point
Bombay 400 021, India
Tel.: (011-91-22) 287-6027, 287-5479
Fax: (011-91-22) 287-5514

INDONESIA
Embassy
5th Floor, WISMA Metropolitan,
Jalan Jendral Sudirman, Jakarta,
Indonesia
or
P.O. Box 1052
Jakarta 10010, Indonesia
Tel.: (011-62-21) 525-0709
Telex: Domcan Jakarta
Fax: (011-62-21) 571-2251

IRAN
Embassy
57 Shahid Javah-e-Sarfaraz (Daryaye-Noor)
Ostad-Motahari Avenue,
Tehran, Iran
or
P.O. Box 11365-4647,
Tehran, Iran
Tel.: (011-98-21) 873-2623, -24, -25
Fax: (011-98-21) 873-3202

IRAQ
Embassy
P.O. Box 815403
Amman, Jordan 11180

IRELAND
Embassy
65 St. Stephen's Green
Dublin 2, Ireland
Tel.: (011-353-1) 478-1988
Telex: Domcan Dublin
Fax: (011-353-1) 478-1285

ISRAEL
Embassy
220, Rehov Hayarkon
Tel Aviv 63405, Israel
or
P.O. Box 6410, Tel Aviv 61063, Israel
Tel.: (011-972-3) 527-2929
Telex: Domcan Tel-Aviv
Fax: (011-972-3) 527-2333

ITALY
Embassy
Via G.B. de Rossi 27
00161 Rome, Italy
Tel.: (011-39-6) 44598.1
Telex: Domcan Rome
Fax: (011-39-6) 44598.750
Consulate
Via Vittor Pisani 19
20124 Milan, Italy
Tel.: (011-39-2) 6758.1, 669-80600
Telex: Cantracom Milan
Fax: (011-39-2) 6758-3900

JAMAICA
High Commission
Mutual Security Bank Building
30-36 Knutsford Blvd.
Kingston 5, Jamaica
or
P.O. Box 1500, Kingston 10, Jamaica
Tel.: (1-809) 926-1500, -1, -2, -3
Telex: Beaver Kingstonja
Fax: (1-809) 926-1702
Consulate
29 Gloucester St.
Montego Bay, Jamaica
Tel.: (1-809) 952-6198
Fax: (1-809) 979-1086

JAPAN
Embassy
3-38 Akasaka 7-chome,
Minato-ku, Tokyo, Japan 107
Tel.: (011-81-3) 3408-2101
Telex: Domcan Tokyo
Fax: (011-81-3) 3479-5320
Consulate
FT Building, 9F, 4-8-28 Watanabe-Dori,
Chuo-Ku, Fukuoka-Shi, Fukuoka Préf.,
Japan 810
Tel.: (011-81-92) 752-6055
Fax: (011-81-92) 752-6077
Consulate
Nakato Marunouchi Building, 6F,
3-17-6 Marunouchi, Naka-Ku,
Nagoya-Shi, Aichi Préf., Japan
Tel.: (011-81-52) 972-0450
Fax: (011-81-52) 972-0453
Consulate
Daisan Shoho Building, 12th Floor, 2-2-3
Nishi Shinsaibashi
Chuo-Ku, Osaka 542, Japan
or
P.O. Box 150
Osaka, Minami 542-91, Japan
Tel.: (011-81-6) 21-4910
Fax: (011-81-6) 212-4914

JORDAN
Embassy
Pearl of Shmeisani Building, Shmeisani,
Amman, Jordan 11180
or

P.O. Box 815403, Amman, Jordan 11180
Tel.: (011-962-6) 66-61-24
Fax: (011-962-6) 68-92-27

KAZAKHSTAN
Embassy
157 Prospekt Abaya, 6th Floor
480009,
Almaty, Kazakhstan
Tel.: (011-7-3272) 50-93-81
Fax: (011-7-3272) 50-93-80

KENYA
High Commission
Comcraft House, Hailé Sélassié Avenue
Nairobi, Kenya
or
P.O. BOX 30481, Nairobi, Kenya
Tel.: (011-254-2) 21-48-04
Fax: (011-254-2) 22-69-87

KIRIBATI
High Commission
P.O. Box 12-049, Thorndon
Wellington, New Zealand

KOREA
Embassy
10th and 11th Floors, Kolon Building,
45 Mugyo-Dong, Jung-Ku
Seoul 100-170, Korea
or
P.O. Box 6299, Seoul 100-662, Korea
Tel.: (011-82-2) 753-2605, -2606
Télec.: (011-82-2) 755-0686
Consulate
c/o Bumin Mutual Savings and Finance Corporation
No. 32-1, 2-GA,
Daecheung-Dong, Chung-Ku, Pusan, Korea
Tel.: (011-8251) 246-7024, 246-3205
Fax: (011-8251) 247-8443, 246-5658

KUWAIT
Embassy
Block 4, House No. 24, Al-Mutawakel,
Da Aiyah, Kuwait
P.O. Box 25281, 13113 (Safat) Kuwait
Tel.: (011-965) 256-3025
Fax: (011-965) 256-4167

KYRGYZSTAN
Embassy
157 Prospekt Abaya, 6th Floor
480009, Almaty, Kazakhstan
Tel.: (011-7-3272) 50-93-81
Fax: (011-7-3272) 50-93-80

LAOS
Embassy
P.O. Box 2090, Bangkok 10500, Thailand

LATVIA
Embassy
Doma laukums 4, 4th Floor
Riga LV-1977
Tel.: (011-371) 783-0141
Fax: (011-371) 783-1040

LEBANON
Embassy
Coolrite Building
434 Autostrade Jall-ed-Dib
Kaza Metin, Mount Lebanon

LESOTHO
High Commission
P.O. Box 26006,
Arcadia,
Pretoria 0007, South Africa
Consulate
1st Floor, Maseru Book Centre Kingsway
Box 1165, Maseru, Lesotho
Tel.: (011-266) 325-632
Fax: (011-266) 316-462

LIBERIA
High Commission
P.O. Box 1639, Accra, Ghana

LIBYA
Embassy
P.O. Box 31, Belvédère,
1002 Tunis, Tunisia

LITHUANIA
Embassy
Didzioji 8-5, 2001 Vilnius, Lithuania
Tel.: (011-370-2) 220-898, 220-865
Fax: (011-370-2) 220-884

LUXEMBOURG
Embassy
Avenue de Tervuren 2,
1040 Brussels, Belgium
Consulate
c/o Price Waterhouse and Co,
24-26 avenue de la Liberté
Luxembourg L-1930
or
P.O. Box 1443, Luxembourg, Luxembourg
Tel.: (011-352) 40-24-20
Fax: (011-352) 4-24-55 poste 600

MACAO
Commission
P.O. Box 20264, Hennessy Road Post Office,
Hong Kong

MADAGASCAR
High Commission
P.O. Box 1022, Dar es-Salaam, Tanzania
Consulate
QIT-Madagascar Minerals,
Villa Paula Androhibe, Lot II-J-169
Villa 3H Ivandry,
Antananarivo, Madagascar
or
C.P. 4003
Antananarivo 101, Madagascar
Tel.: (011-261-2) 425-59
Fax: (011-261-2) 425-06

MALAWI
High Commission
P.O. Box 31313, Lusaka, Zambia
Consulate
c/o Comet Ltd.
Box 51146, Blantyre-Limbe, Malawi
Tel.: (011-265) 643-277
Fax: (011-265) 643-446

MALAYSIA
High Commission
7th Floor, Place MBF,
172 Jalan Ampang,
50450 Kuala Lumpur, Malaysia
or
P.O. Box 10990
50732 Kuala Lumpur, Malaysia
Tel.: (011-60-3) 261-2000
Night line: 261-2031
Fax: (011-60-3) 261-3248

MALDIVES
High Commission
P.O. Box 1006, Colombo, Sri Lanka

MALI
Embassy
P.O. Box 198, Bamako, Mali
Tel.: (011-223) 22-22-36
Fax: (011-223) 22-43-62

MALTA
Embassy
Via G.B. de Rossi 27,
00161 Rome, Italy
Consulate
Demajo House, 103, Archbishop Street,
Valletta, Malta
Tel.: (011-356) 233-121, 233-126
Fax: (011-356) 235-145

MAURITANIA
Embassy
P.O. Box 3373, Dakar, Senegal

MAURITIUS
High Commission
P.O. Box 26006, Arcadia
Pretoria 0007,
South Africa

MEXICO
Embassy
Calle Schiller no. 529
(Rincon del Bosque),
Colonia Polanco,
11560 Mexico, D.F. Mexico
or
Apartado Postal 105-05
11580 Mexico, D.F. Mexico
Tel.: (011-52-5) 724-7900
Fax: (011-52-5) 724-7980
Consulate
Hotel Club del Sol, Costera Miguel Aleman, esq. Reyes Catolicos,
Acapulco, Guerrero, Mexico
or
Apartado Postal 94-C
39300 Acapulco, Guerrero, Mexico
Tel.: (011-52-74) 85-66-21, 85-66-00 ext. 7347
Fax: (011-52-74) 85-65-95, 85-66-21
Consulate
Centro Comercial Plaza Mexico,
Local 312,Avenida Tulum 200, esq. Agua

77500 Cancun, Quintana Roo, Mexico
Tel.: (011-52-98) 84-37-16
Fax: (011-52-98) 84-61-25
Consulate
Hotel Fiesta Americana, Local 30-A
Aurelio Aceves 225
44100 Guadalajara, Jalisco, Mexico
Tel.: (011-52-36) 15-86-65, 25-34-34
ext. 3005
Fax: (011-52-36) 30-37-25
Consulate
Hotel Playa Mazatlan
Zona Dorada Rodolfo, Loaiza 202,
82110 Mazatlan, Sinaloa, Mexico
or
Apartado Postal 614
82110 Mazatlan, Sinaloa, Mexico
Tel.: (011-52-69) 13-73-20, 13-44-44
ext. 370
Fax: (011-52-69) 14-66-55, 14-03-66
Consulate
Calle Hidalgo 226, Colonia Centro
48300 Puerto Vallarta, Jalisco, Mexico
Tel.: (011-52-322) 253-98
Fax: (011-52-322) 235-17
Consulate
German Gedovius 5-201, Condominio del Parque
Desarrollo Urbano Rio Tijuana
22320 Tijuana, Baja California Norte, Mexico
Tel.: (011-52-66) 84-04-61
Fax: (011-52-66) 84-04-61
ask for facsimile

MOLDAVA
Embassy
P.O. Box 2966, Post Office No. 22
Bucharest, Romania

MONACO
Embassy
35, avenue Montaigne,
75008 Paris, France

MONGOLIA
Embassy
19 Dong Zhi Men Wai Street,
Chao Yang District, Beijing
People's Republic of China,
100600

MOROCCO
Embassy
13 bis, rue Jaafar As-Sadik
Rabat-Agdal, Morocco
or
C.P. 709, Rabat-Agdal, Morocco
Tel.: (011-212-7) 67-28-80
Fax: (011-212-7) 67-21-87

MOZAMBIQUE
Embassy
Rue Thomas Nduda, 1345,
Maputo, Mozambique
or
P.O. Box 1578, Maputo, Mozambique
Tel.: (011-258-1) 492-623
Fax: (011-258-1) 492-667

MYANMAR (Burma)
Embassy
P.O. Box 2090
Bangkok 10500, Thailand

NAMIBIA
High Commission
P.O. Box 26006
Arcadia,
Pretoria 0007, South Africa

NEPAL
High Commission
P.O. Box 5207, New Delhi, India

NETHERLANDS
Embassy
Sophialaan 2514 JP, The Hague,
Netherlands
Tel.: (011-31-70) 361-4111
Telex: Domcan The Hague
Fax: (011-31-70) 356-1111
Consulate
Maduro and Curiels Bank, N.V.
Plaza JoJo Correa 2-4, Willemstad,
Curaçao, Netherlands Antilles
or
P.O. Box 305
Curaçao, Netherlands Antilles
Tel.: (011-599-9) 66-11-15
Telex: Madurobank
Fax: (011-599-9) 66-11-22, 66-11-30

NEW ZEALAND
High Commission
61 Molesworth Street Thorndon,
Wellington, New-Zealand
or
P.O. Box 12-049, Thorndon
Wellington, New-Zealand
Tel.: (011-64-4) 473-9577
Fax: (011-64-4) 471-2082
Telex: Domcan Wellington
Consulate
Level 9, Centre Jetset 44-48, Emily Place
Auckland, New-Zealand
or
P.O. Box 6186, Wellesley Street,
Auckland, New-Zealand
Tel.: (011-64-9) 309-3690
Fax: (011-64-9) 307-3111

NICARAGUA
Embassy
Apartado Postal 10303, San José
Costa Rica
Consulate
208 Calle del Triunfo
Frente Plazoleta Telcor Central
Managua, Nicaragua
or
Apartado 514
Managua, Nicaragua
Tel.: (011-505-2) 28-75-74, 28-13-04
Fax: (011-505-2) 28-48-21

NIGER
Embassy
Sonara II Building, av. du Premier Pont,
Niamey, Niger
or
P.O. Box 362, Niamey, Niger
Tel.: (011-227) 73-36-86, 73-36-87
Fax: (011-227) 73-50-64

NIGERIA
High Commission
Committee of Vice-Chancellors Building,
Plot 8A
4 Idowu Taylor Street,
Victoria Island, Lagos, Nigeria
or
P.O. Box 54506, Ikoyi Station
Lagos, Nigeria
Tel.: (011-234-1) 262-2512, 262-2515
(night line)
Telex: Domcan Lagos
Fax: (011-234-1) 262-2517
or
Canadian High Commission Liaison Office
Plot no. 622, Gana Street, Zone A5
Maitama, Abuja, FCT, Nigeria
or
Canadian High Commission Liaison Office
P.O. Box 6924 Wuse, Abuja,
FCT, Nigeria
Tél. and Fax: (011-234-090) 803-249

NORWAY
Embassy
Oscar's Gate 20, Oslo 0244, Norway
Tel.: (011-47) 22-46-69-55,
Night line: 22-46-69-59
Fax: (011-47) 22-69-34-67

OMAN
Embassy
P.O. Box 25281, 13113 (Safat)
Kuwait, Kuwait
Consulate
Moosa Abdul Rahman Hassan Building,
Flat No. 310, Bldg 477, Way 2907
A'Noor Street, Ruwi
Muscat, Sultanate of Oman
Tel.: (011-968) 791-738
Fax: (011-968) 791-740
or

PAKISTAN
High Commission
Diplomatic Enclave, Sector G-5
Islamabad, Pakistan
or
G.P.O. Box 1042, Islamabad, Pakistan
Tel.: (011-92-51) 21-11-01, 21-11-07
Night line
Telex: Domcan Islamabad
Fax: (011-92-51) 21-15-40
Consulate
Beach Luxury Hotel, Room 120, Moulvi
Tamiz Uddin Khan Road, Karachi 0227,
Pakistan
Tel.: (011-92-21) 55-11-00
Fax: (011-92-21) 55-12-22

PANAMA
Embassy
Apartado Postal 10303, San José, Costa Rica
Consulate
Edificio Proconsa
Aero Peru, Piso 5B, Calle Manuel Maria y Caza,
Campo Alegre, Panama City
or
Apartado Postal 3658
Balboa, Panama
Tel.: (011-507) 64-70-14
Fax: (011-507) 23-54-70

PAPUA NEW GUINEA
High Commission
Commonwealth Avenue
Canberra A.C.T. 2600, Australia
Consulate
Second Floor-The Lodge
Brampton Street, Port Moresby
Papua New Guinea
or
P.O. Box 851, Port Moresby
Papua New Guinea
Tel.: (011-675) 21-35-99
Fax: (011-675) 21-36-12

PARAGUAY
Embassy
Casilla 27
Santiago, Chile
Consulate
El Paraguayo Independiente 995,
Entrepiso, Oficinas 1 y 2,
Asunción, Paraguay
or
Casilla 2577, Asunción, Paraguay
Tel.: (011-595-21) 44-95-05, 49-17-30
Fax: (011-595-21) 44-95-06

PERU
Embassy
Calla Libertad 130,
Miraflores, Lima, Peru
or
Casilla 18-1126, Correo Miraflores
Lima, Peru
Tel.: (011-51-14) 44-40-15, 44-38-41, 44-38-93
Telex: Domcan Lima
Fax: (011-51-14) 44-43-47

PHILIPPINES
Embassy
9th and 11th Floors, Allied Bank Centre, 6754 Ayala Avenue, Makati
Metro Manila, Philippines
or
P.O. Box 2168, Makati Central Post Office
1299 Makati, Metro Manila, Philippines
Tel.: (011-63-2) 810-8861
Telex: Domcan Manila
Fax: (011-63-2) 810-8839

POLAND
Embassy
Ulica Matejki 1/5
Warsaw 00-481, Poland
Tel.: (011-48-22) 29-80-51, 29-80-54 (Night line)
Fax: (011-48-22) 29-64-57

PORTUGAL
Embassy
Avenida da Liberdade 144/56,
4th Floor, 1200 Lisbon, Portugal
Tel.: (011-351-1) 347-4892
Telex: Domcan Lisbon
Fax: (011-351-1) 347-6466
Consulate
Rua Frei Lourenço de Sta Maria No. 1,
1st Floor, # 79,
8001 Faro, Portugal
Tel.: (011-351-89) 80-37-57, 80-30-00
Fax: (011-351-89) 80-47-77

QATAR
Embassy
P.O. Box 25281
13113 (Safat) Kuwait City, Kuwait

ROMANIA
Embassy
36 Nicolae Iorga
71118 Bucharest, Romania
or
P.O. Box 117, Post Office no. 22
Bucharest, Romania
Tel.: (011-40-1) 312-8345, 312-0365
Fax: (011-40-1) 312-9680

RUSSIA
Embassy
23 Starokonyushenny Pereulok,
Moscow, 121002 Russia
Tel.: (011-7-095) 956-6666
Telex: Canada Moscow
Fax: (011-7-095) 241-4400
Consulate
Grand Hotel Europe
St-Petersburg, Russia
Tel.: (011-7-812) 119-6000
Fax: (011-7-812) 375-3000

RWANDA
Embassy
rue Akagera, Kigali, Rwanda
Tel.: (011-250) 73210, 73278
Fax: (011-250) 72719
or
P.O. Box 1177
Kigali, Rwanda

SAINT KITTS AND NEVIS
High Commission
P.O. Box 404
Bridgetown, Barbados

SAINT LUCIA
High Commission
P.O. Box 404, Bridgetown, Barbados

SAINT VINCENT AND THE GRENADINES
High Commission
P.O. Box 404, Bridgetown, Barbados

SAN MARINO
Embassy
Via G.B. de Rossi 27, 00161 Rome, Italy

SAO TOME AND PRINCIPE
Embassy
P.O. Box 4037, Libreville, Gabon

SAUDI ARABIA
Embassy
Diplomatic Quarter
Riyadh
or
P.O. Box 94321
Riyadh 11693, Saudi Arabia
Tel.: (011-966-1) 488-2288
Telex: Domcan Riyadh
Fax: (011-966-1) 488-1997
Consulate
Headquarters Building
Zahid Corporate Group,
Jeddah, Saudi Arabia
or
P.O. Box 8928, Jeddah 21492
Saudi Arabia
Tel.: (011-966-2) 667-1156
Fax: (011-966-2) 669-0727

SENEGAL
Embassy
45, av. de la République, Dakar, Senegal
or
P.O. Box 3373, Dakar, Senegal
Tel.: (011-221) 23-92-90
Telex: Domcan Dakar
Fax: (011-221) 23-87-49

SEYCHELLES
High Commission
P.O. Box 1022, Dar es-Salaam, Tanzania

SIERRA LEONE
High Commission
P.O. Box 1639, Accra, Ghana

SINGAPORE
High Commission
80 Anson Road, 14th and 15th Floors
IBM Towers
Singapore 0207 Singapore
or
Robinson Road, P.O. Box 845
Singapore 9016, Singapore
Tel.: (011-65) 225-6363
Telex: Canadian Singapore
Fax: (011-65) 225-2450

SLOVAKIA
Embassy
Mickiewiczova 6,125 33 Prague 6,
Czech Republic
Consulate
c/o Blaha & Erben & Novak & Werner
Advokatska Kancelaria
Stefanikova 47,811 04
Bratislava, Czech Republic

SLOVENIA
Embassy
Budakeszi ut. 32
1121 Budapest, Hungary

SOLOMON (ISLANDS)
High Commission
Commonwealth Ave.
Canberra A.C.T. 2600, Australia

SOMALIA
High Commission
P.O. Box 30481, Nairobi, Kenya

SOUTH AFRICA
High Commission
1103 Arcadia
Hatfield 0083, Pretoria
South Africa
or
P.O. Box 26006, Arcadia
Pretoria 0007, South Africa
Tel.: (011-27-12) 342-6923
Telex: Candom Pretoria
Fax.: (011-27-12) 342-3837
High Commission
19th Floor, Reserve Bank Building
30 Hout Street
Capetown 8001, South Africa
or
P.O. Box 683
Capetown 8000, South Africa
Tel.: (011-27-21) 23-5240.
Night line: 23-5242
Telex: Candom Capetown
Fax: (011-27-21) 23-4893

SPAIN
Embassy
Edificio Goya
Calle Nunez de Balboa 35
28001 Madrid, Spain
or
Apartado 587,
28080 Madrid, Spain
Tel.: (011-34-1) 431-4300
Fax: (011-34-1) 431-2367
Consulate
Via Augusta 125, Atico 3A
Barcelona 08006, Spain
Tel.: (011-34-3) 209-0634
Fax: (011-34-3) 410-7755
Consulate
Edificio Horizonte, Plaza de la
Malagueta 3, First Floor
29016 Malaga, Spain
or
Apartado Postal 99
29080 Malga, Spain
Tel.: (011-34-52) 22-33-46
Fax: (011-34-52) 22-40-23
Consulate
Avenida de la Constitución 30, Second
Floor
41001, Seville, Spain
Tel.: (011-34-54) 422-9413

SRI LANKA
High Commission
6 Gregory's Road, Cinnamon Gardens,
Colombo 7, Sri Lanka
or
P.O. Box 1006, Colombo, Sri Lanka
Tel.: (011-94-1) 69-58-41, 69-58-42
Telex: Domcanada Colombo
Fax: (011-94-1) 68-70-49

SUDAN
Embassy
P.O. Box 1130, Addis Ababa, Ethiopia

SURINAME
High Commission
P.O. Box 10880, Georgetown, Guyana
Consulate
Waterkant 90-94
P.O. Box 1849-1850
Paramaribo, Suriname
Tel.: (011-597) 471-222
Fax: (011-597) 475-718

SWAZILAND
Embassy
P.O. Box 26006, Arcadia
Pretoria 0007, South Africa

SWEDEN
Embassy
Tegelbacken 4 (Seventh Floor),
Stockholm, Sweden
or
P.O. Box 16129
S-10323 Stockholm, Sweden
Tel.: (011-46-8) 453-3000
Fax: (011-46-8) 24-24-91

SWITZERLAND
Embassy
Kirchenfeldstrasse 88
3005 Berne, Switzerland
or
P.O. Box 3000, Berne 6, Switzerland
Tel.: (011-41-31) 352-63-81
Telex: Domcan Berne
Fax: (011-41-31) 352-73-15

SYRIA
Embassy
Lot 12, Mezzeh Autostrade, Damascus,
Syria
or
P.O. Box 3394, Damascus, Syria
Tel.: (011-963-11) 2236-851, 2236-892
Fax: (011-963-11) 2228-034

TAJIKISTAN
Embassy
157, Prospekt Abaya, 6th Floor
480009, Almaty, Kazakhstan
Tel.: (011-7-3272) 50-93-81
Fax: (011-7-3272) 50-93-80

TANZANIA
High Commission
38 Mirambo Street
Dar es-Salaam, Tanzania
or
P.O. Box 1022
Dar es-Salaam, Tanzania
Tel.: (011-255-51) 46000, 46011
Fax: (011-255-51) 46000, 46005, 46009
(Night line)

THAILAND
Embassy
Boonmitr Building, 11th Floor
138 Silom Road
Bangkok 10500 Thailand
or
P.O. Box 2090, Bangkok 10500, Thailand
Tel.: (011-66-2) 237-4125
Fax: (011-66-2) 236-6463
Consulate
c/o Raming Tea Co. Ltd.
151 Super Highway
Tasala, Chiang Mai 50000
Thailand
Tel.: (011-66-53) 24-22-92
Fax: (011-66-53) 24-26-16

TOGO
High Commission
P.O. Box 1639, Accra, Ghana

TONGA
High Commission
P.O. Box 12-049, Thorndon
Wellington, New Zeland

TRINIDAD AND TOBAGO
High Commission
Huggins Building, 72 South Quay
Port of Spain, Trinidad and Tobago
or
P.O. Box 1246
Port of Spain, Trinidad and Tobago
Tel.: (1-809) 623-7254
Telex: Domcan Port of Spain
Fax: (1-809) 624-4016

TUNISIA
Embassy
3 du Sénégal Street, Place d'Afrique
Tunis, Tunisia
or
P.O. Box 31, Belvédère
1002 Tunis, Tunisia
Tel.: (011-216-1) 798-004, 796-577
Telex: Domcan Tunis
Fax: (011-216-1) 792-371

TURKEY
Embassy
Nenehatun Caddesi No. 75
Gaziosmanpasa
06700, Turkey
Tel.: (011-90-312) 436-1275
Telex: Domcan Ankara
Fax: (011-90-312) 446-4437
Consulate
Büyükdere Cad. 107/3, Begün Han, 80300
Gayrettepe, Istanbul, Turkey
Tel.: (011-90-1) 271-5174, 275-0780
Fax: (011-90-1) 272-3427

TURKMENISTAN
Embassy
157 Prospekt Abaya
6th Floor
480009 Almaty, Kazakhstan
Tel.: (011-7-3272) 50-93-81
Fax: (011-7-3272) 50-93-80

TUVALU
High Commission
P.O. Box 12-049, Thorndon
Wellington, New Zeland

UGANDA
High Commission
P.O. Box 30481, Nairobi, Kenya
Consulate
92/94, Fifth Street, Industrial Area,
Kampala, Uganda
or
Uganda Bata, P.O. Box 422
Kampala, Uganda
Tel.: (011-256-41) 25-81-41
Fax: (011-256-41) 24-13-80

UKRAINE
Embassy
31 rue Yaroslaviv Val Street
Kiev 252034, Ukraine
Tel.: (011-7-044) 212-2112-, 212-2263
Fax: (011-7-044) 291-2339, 225-1305

UNITED ARAB EMIRATES
Embassy
P.O. Box 25281, 13113 (SAFAT)
Kuwait City, Kuwait
Consulate
Juma Al Majid Building, Suite 708
Khalid Ibn Al Waleed Street,
Bur Durbai, United Arab Emirates
Tel.: (011-971-4) 52-17-17
Fax: (011-971-4) 51-77-22

UNITED STATES OF AMERICA
Embassy
501 Pennsylvania Ave. N. W.,
Washington, D.C. 20001
Tel.: (202) 682-1740
Telex: Beaver Washington
Fax: (202) 682-7726
Consulate
One CNN Center, South Tower, Suite 400
Atlanta, GA, 30303-2705 U.S.A.
Tel.: (404) 577-6810
Tel. Nightline: 577-6812
Fax: (404) 524-5046
Consulate
3 Copley Place, Suite 400
Boston Mass., 02116 U.S.A.
Tel.: (617) 262-3760
Fax: (617) 262-3415
Consulate
1 Marine Midland Center, Suite 3000
Buffalo, N. Y., 14203-2884
Tel.: (716) 858-9500
Fax: (716) 852-4340
Consulate
Two Prudential Plaza,
180 N. Stetson Avenue, Suite 2400
Chicago, Illinois 60601
Tel.: (312) 616-1860
Fax: (312) 616-1877
Consulate
St. Paul Place, 750 North St. Paul Street,
Suite 1700,
Dallas, Texas 75201-3247
Tel.: (214) 922-9806
Telex: Canadian Dallas
Fax: (214) 922-9815
Consulate
600 Renaissance Center, Suite 1100
Detroit, Michigan 48243-1798
Tel.: (313) 567-2340
Fax: (313) 567-2164
Consulate
300 South Grand Avenue, 10th floor
Los Angeles, Calif. 90071
Tel.: (213) 687-7432
Fax: (213) 620-8827
Consulate
200 South Biscayne Boulevard, Suite 1600
Miami, Florida 33131 U.S.A.
Tel.: (305) 579-1600
Consulate
701-4th Avenue South,
Minneapolis, Minn. 55415 U.S.A.
Tel.: (612) 333-4641
Fax: (612) 332-4061
Consulate
1251 Ave. of the Americas, 16th floor
New York, N.Y. 10020-1175
Tel.: (212) 768-2400, (212) 596-1600
Fax: (212) 596-1790
Consulate
412 Plaza 600, Sixth and Stewart
Seattle, Wash. 98101-1286
Tel.: (206) 443-1777
Fax: (206) 443-1782

URUGUAY
Embassy
Casilla de Correo 1598
Buenos Aires, Argentina
Consulate
Edificio Torre Libertad
Plaza Cagancha 1335, Piso 10
11100 Montevideo, Uruguay
Tel.: (011-598-2) 92-20-29, 92-20-30
Fax: (011-598-2) 92-02-23

UZBEKISTAN
Embassy
157 Prospekt Abaya, 6th Floor
480009 Almaty, Kazakhstan
Tel.: (011-7-3272) 50-93-81
Fax: (011-7-3272) 50-93-80

VANUATU
High Commission
Commonwealth Avenue
Canberra A.C.T. 2600
Australia

VATICAN
Embassy
Via della Conciliazione 4/D -
00193 Rome, Italy
Tel.: (011-39-6) 6830-7316, 7386
Fax: (011-39-6) 6880-6283

VENEZUELA
Embassy
Edificio Torre Europa, 7th Floor
Avenida Francisco de Miranda
Campo Alegre, Caracas
or
Apartado 62302, Caracas 1060A
Venezuela
Tel.: (011-58-2) 951-6166
Fax: (011-58-2) 951-4950

VIET NAM
Embassy
31 Hong Vuong Street
Hanoi
Viet Nam
Tel.: (011-84-4) 23-55-00
Fax: (011-84-4) 23-53-51

WESTERN SAMOA
High Commission
P.O. Box 12049, Thorndon
Wellington, New Zeland

YEMEN
Embassy
P.O. Box 94321
Riyad 11693, Saudi Arabia

EX-YUGOSLAVIA
Embassy
Kneza Milosa 75
11000 Belgrade, Yugoslavia
Tel.: (011-381-11) 64-46-66, 64-45-47
(Night line)
Telex: Domcan Belgrade
Fax: (011-381-11) 64-14-80

ZAIRE
Canadian Office
c/o Embassy of the United
States of America
310 avenue des Aviateurs
Kinshasa, Zaire
Tel.: (011-243-12) 21-532, 21-913
Telex: Amembassy Kinshasa
Fax: (011-243-88) 43-805

ZAMBIA
High Commission
5199 United Nation Avenue
Lusaka, Zambia
or
P.O. Box 31313
Lusaka, Zambia
Tel.: (011-260-1) 25-08-33
Telex: Domcan Lusaka
Fax: (011-260-1) 25-41-76

ZIMBABWE
High Commission
45 Baines Avenue, Harare, Zimbabwe
or
P.O. Box 1430, Harare, Zimbabwe
Tel.: (011-263-4) 25-08-33
Telex: Canad Harare
Fax: (011-263-4) 25-41-76

Diplomatic, consular and tourism representatives in Canada

ALBANIA
Embassy
1511 K Street, N.W. Suite 1000
Washington, D.C., 20005, USA
Tel.: (202) 223-4942
Fax: (202) 628-7342

ALGERIA
Embassy
435 Daly Avenue
Ottawa, Ontario K1N 6H3
Tel.: (613) 789-8505, -0282
Fax: (613) 789-1406

ANTIGUA AND BARBUDA
High Commission
112 Kent Street, Suite 1610
Place de la Ville, Tower B
Ottawa, Ontario K1P 5P2
Tel.: (613) 236-8952
Fax: (613) 236-3042
Consulate
60 St.Clair Avenue East, Suite 304
Toronto, Ontario M4T 1N5
Tel.: (416) 961-3085
Fax: (416) 961-7218

ARGENTINA
Embassy
Royal Bank Center
90 Sparks Street, Suite 620
Ottawa, Ontario K1P 5B4
Tel.: (613) 236-2351, -2354
Fax: (613) 235-2659
Consulate
2000 Peel Street, Suite 710
Montréal, Québec H3A 2W5
Tel.: (514) 842-6582
Fax: (514) 842-5797
Consulate
1 First Canada Place, Suite 5840
Toronto, Ontario M5X 1K2
Tel.: (416) 603-0232
Fax: (416) 603-0868

ARUBA
Tourist Office
86 Bloor Street West, Suite 204
Toronto, Ontario M5S 1M5
Tel.: (416) 975-1950
1-800-268-3042
Fax: (416) 975-1947

AUSTRALIA
High Commission
50 O'Connor Street, Suite 710
Ottawa, Ontario K1P 6L2
Tel.: (613) 236-0841
Fax: (613) 236-4376
Tourist Office
Distribution Centre
2 Bloor Street West, Suite 1730
Toronto, Ontario M4W 3E2
Tel.: (416) 925-9575
Fax: (416) 925-9312
Consulate
175 Bloor Street East,
Suite 314, 3rd Floor
Toronto, Ontario M4W 3R8
Tel.: (416) 323-1155
Fax: (416) 323-3910
Consulate
World Trade Centre Office
Complex
999 Canada Place, Suite 602
Vancouver, BC V6C 3E1
Tel.: (604) 684-1177
Fax: (604) 684-1856

AUSTRIA
Embassy
445 Wilbrod Street
Ottawa, Ontario K1N 6M7
Tel.: (613) 789-1444, -3429, -3430
Fax: (613) 789-3431
Consulate
1131 Kensington Road N.W.
Calgary, AB T2N 3P4
Tel.: (403) 283-6526
Fax: (403) 283-4909
Consulate
1718 Argyle Street, Suite 710
Halifax, NS B3J 3N6
Tel.: (902) 429-8200
Fax: (902) 425-0581
Consulate
2401 Saskatchewan Drive Plaza, Suite 100
Regina, SK S4P 4H9
Tel.: (306) 359-7777
Fax: (306) 522-3299
Consulate
360 Bay Street, Suite 1010
Toronto, Ontario M5H 2Y6
Tel.: (416) 863-0649
Fax: (416) 869-7851
Consulate
1810 Alberni Street, Suite 206
Vancouver, BC V6G 1B3
Tel.: (604) 687-3338
Fax: (604) 681-3578
Consulate
1350 Sherbrooke Street West, Suite 1030
Montréal, Québec H3G 1J1
Tel.: (514) 845-8661
Fax: (514) 284-3503
Tourist Office
1010 Sherbrooke Street West, Suite 1410
Montréal, Québec H3A 2R7
Tel.: (514) 849-3709
Fax: (514) 849-9577
or
2 Bloor St. East, Suite 3330
Toronto, Ontario M4W 1A8
Tel.: (416) 967-3348
Fax: (416) 967-4101

AZERBAIJAN
Embassy
927 15th Street NW, Suite 700
Washington, D.C., 20005, USA
Tel.: (202) 842-0001
Fax: (202) 842-0004

BAHAMAS
High Commission
360 Albert Street, Suite 1020
Ottawa, Ontario K1R 7X7
Tel.: (613) 232-1724
Fax: (613) 232-0097
Tourist Office
121 Bloor St. East, Suite 1101
Toronto, Ontario M4W 3M5
Tel.: (416) 968-2999
1-800-667-3777
Fax: (416) 968-6711

BAHRAIN
Embassy
3502 International Drive North West
Washington, D.C., 20008, USA
Tel.: (202) 342-0741
Fax: (202) 362-2192
Consulate
1869 René Lévesque West
Montréal, Québec H3H 1R4
Tel.: (514) 931-7444
Fax: (514) 931-5988

BANGLADESH
High Commission
85 Range Road, Suite 402
Ottawa, Ontario K1N 8J6
Tel.: (613) 236-0138, -0139
Fax: (613) 567-3213

BARBADOS
High Commission
130 Albert Street, Suite 600
Ottawa, Ontario K1P 5G4
Tel.: (613) 236-9517, -9518
Fax: (613) 230-4362
Consulate
5160 Yonge Street, Suite 1800
North York, Ontario M2N 6L9
Tel.: (416) 512-6565, -6566, -6567, -6568
Fax: (416) 512-6580
Consulate
4800 De Maisonneuve West, Suite 523
Westmount, Québec H3Z 1M2
Tel.: (514) 932-3206
Fax: (514) 932-3775

Consular Representatives
2020 Haro Street, Suite 401
Vancouver, BC V6G 1J3
Tel.: (604) 872-4444

BELGIUM
Embassy
80 Elgin Street, 4th Floor
Ottawa, Ontario K1P 1B7
Tel.: (613) 236-7267
Fax: (613) 236-7882
Télex: 053-3568
Tourism Office
P.O. Box 760, succursale N.D.G.
Montréal, Québec H4A 3S2
Tel.: (514) 484-3594
Fax: (514) 489-8965
Consulate
908 18th Avenue S.W.
Calgary , AB T2P 0H1
Tel.: (403) 265-5777
Fax: (403) 244-2094
Consulate
155-10250, 101st Street
Edmonton, AB T5J 3P4
Tel.: (403) 425-0184
Fax: (403) 466-2832
Consulate
1050 Bellevue ave.
Halifax, NS B3H 3L9
Tel.: (902) 423-6323
Consulate
999 de Maisonneuve Boulevard West, Suite 850
Montréal, Québec H3A 3L4
Tel.: (514) 849-7394
Fax: (514) 844-3170
Telex: (514) 052-6891
Consulate
2 Bloor Street West, Suite 2006
Toronto, Ontario M4W 3E2
Tel.: (416) 944-1422
Fax: (416) 944-1421
Telex: 06-23564
Consulate
Birks Place, Suite 570
688 West Hastings Street
Vancouver, BC V6B 1P1
Tel.: (604) 684-6838
Fax: (604) 684-0371
Consulate
15 Acadia Bay
Winnipeg, MB R3T 3J1
Tel.: (204) 261-1415

BELIZE
High Commission
2535 Massachusetts Avenue, N.W.
Washington, D.C., 20008, USA
Tel.: (202) 332-9636
Fax: (202) 332-6888
Consulate
1080 Beaver Hall Hill, Suite 1720
Montréal, Québec H2Z 1S8
Tel.: (514) 871-4741
Fax: (514) 397-0816
Consulate
1112 West Pender Street, Suite 904
Vancouver, BC V6E 2S1
Tel.: (604) 683-4517
Fax: (604) 683-4518

BENIN
Embassy
58 Glebe Avenue
Ottawa, Ontario K1S 2C3
Tel.: (613) 233-4429, -4868, -5273
Fax: (613) 233-8952
Consulate
429 Viger Avenue East
Montréal, Québec H2L 2N9
Tel.: (514) 769-6088, 849-3965
and
1207 11th Avenue South West, Suite 700
Calgary, AB T3C 0M5
Tel.: (403) 245-8405

BERMUDA
Tourism Office
1200 Bay Street, Suite 1004
Toronto, Ontario M5R 2A5
Tel.: 1-800-387-1304
Fax: (416) 923-9600

BOLIVIA
Embassy
130 Albert Street, Suite 504
Ottawa, Ontario K1P 5G4
Tel.: (613) 236-5730
Fax: (613) 236-8237
Consulate
11231 Jasper Avenue
Edmonton, AB T5K 0L5
Tel.: (403) 488-1525
Fax: (403) 488-0350
Consulate
18 Severn Avenue
Westmount, Québec H3Y 2C7
Tel.: (514) 989-5132
Fax: (514) 989-5132
Consulate
1040 West Georgia Street, Suite 1130
Vancouver, BC V6E 4H1
Tel.: (604) 685-8121, -8124
Fax: (604) 685-8120

BOTSWANA
High Commission
Intelsat Blv.
3400 International Drive, N.W., Suite 7M
Washington, D.C., 20008, USA
Tel.: (202) 244-4990
Fax: (202) 244-4164
Consulate
14 South Drive
Toronto, Ontario M4W 1R1
Tel.: (416) 978-2495
Fax: (416) 324-8239

BRAZIL
Embassy
450 Wilbrod Street
Ottawa, Ontario K1N 6M8
Tel.: (613) 237-1090
Fax: (613) 237-6144
Telex: 053-3176 Brasembott
Consulate
2000 Mansfield Street, Suite 1700
Montréal, Québec H3A 3A5
Tel.: (514) 499-0968
Fax: (514) 499-3963
Consulate
77 Bloor Street West, Suite 1109
Toronto, Ontario M5S 1M2
Tel.: (416) 922-2503
Fax: (416) 922-1832
Consulate
1140 Pender Street West, Suite 1300
Vancouver, BC V6E 4G1
Tel.: (604) 687-4589
Fax: (604) 681-6534
Consulate
8619 Strathearn Drive
Edmonton, AB T6C 4C6
Tel.: (403) 466-3130
Fax: (403) 465-0247

BRITAIN (United Kingdom of)
High Commission
80 Elgin Street
Ottawa, Ontario K1P 5K7
Tel.: (613) 237-1530
Fax: (613) 237-7980
Consulate
1000 de la Gauchetière West, Suite 4200
Montréal, Québec H3H 4W5
Tel.: (514) 866-5863
Fax: (514) 866-0202
Consulate
777 Bay Street, Suite 2800, College Park
Toronto, Ontario M5G 2G2
Tel.: (416) 593-1290
Fax: (416) 593-1229
Tourist Office
111 Road Avenue, Suite 450
Toronto, Ontario M5R 3J8
Tel.: (416) 925-6328

BRUNEI
High Commission
866 United Nations Plaza, Suite 248
New York, NY, 10017, USA
Tel.: (212) 838-1600
Fax: (212) 980-6478
BULGARIA
Embassy
325 Stewart Street
Ottawa, Ontario K1N 6K5
Tel.: (613) 789-3215
Fax: (613) 789-3524
Consulate
65 Overlea Boulevard, Suite 406
Toronto, Ontario M4H 1P1

Tel.: (416) 696-2420, -2778
Fax: (416) 696-8019

BURKINA FASO
Embassy
48 Range Road
Ottawa, Ontario K1N 8J4
Tel.: (613) 238-4796, -4797
Fax: (613) 238-3812
Telex: 053-4413
Consulate
372 Bay Street, Suite 610
Toronto, Ontario M5H 2W9
Tel.: (416) 867-8669

BURMA
(see Myanmar)

BURUNDI
Embassy
50 Kaymar Street, Rothwell Heights
Ottawa, Ontario K1G 7C9
Tel.: (613) 741-8828, -7458
Fax: (613) 741-2424
Consular Représentatives
4017 Lacombe Street
Montréal, Québec H3T 1M7
Tel.: (514) 739-5204
and
5 Dewbourne Avenue
Toronto, Ontario M5P 1Z1
Tel.: (416) 932-8212
Fax: (416) 922-3667

CAMEROON
Embassy
170 Clemow Avenue
Ottawa, Ontario K1S 2B4
Tel.: (613) 236-1522, -1524, -1569
Fax: (613) 236-3885

CAPE VERDE
Embassy
3415 Massachusetts Avenue North West
Washington, D.C., 20007, USA
Tel.: (202) 965-6820
Fax: (202) 965-1207
Telex: 440294

CAYMAN (Islands)
Tourist Office
234 Eglinton East, Suite 306
Toronto, Ontario M4P 1K5
Tel.: (416) 485-1550
1-800-263-5805

CENTRAL AFRICAN REPUBLIC
Embassy
1618 22nd Street North West
Washington, D.C., 20008 USA
Tel.: (202) 483-7800
Consulate
225 St-Jacques Street West, 3rd Floor
Montréal, Québec H2Y 1M6
Tel.: (514) 849-8381
Fax: (514) 849-8383

CHAD
Embassy
2002 R Street North West
Washington, D.C., 20009, USA
Tel.: (202) 462-4009

CHILE
Embassy
151 Slater Street, Suite 605
Ottawa, Ontario K1P 5H3
Tel.: (613) 235-4402, -9940
Fax: (613) 235-1176
Consulate
1010 Sherbrooke West, Suite 710
Montréal, Québec H3A 2R7
Tel.: (514) 499-0405
Fax: (514) 499-8914
Consulate
170 Bloor Street West, Suite 800
Toronto, Ontario M5S 1T9
Tel.: (416) 924-0112, -0106
Fax: (416) 924-9563
Consulate
1185 West Georgia Street, Suite 1250
Vancouver, BC V6E 4E6
Tel.: (604) 681-9162
Fax: (604) 682-2445

CHINA
Embassy
515 St Patrick Street
Ottawa, Ontario K1N 5H3
Tel.: (613) 789-3434
Fax: (613) 789-1911
Consulate
240 St.George Street
Toronto, Ontario M5R 2P4
Tel.: (416) 964-7260
Fax: (416) 324-6468
Consulate
3380 Granville Street
Vancouver, BC V6H 3K3
Tel.: (604) 734-7492
Fax: (604) 734-0154

COLOMBIA
Embassy
360 Albert Street, Suite 1002
Ottawa, Ontario K1R 7X7
Tel.: (613) 230-3761
Fax: (613) 230-4416
Consulate
1010 Sherbrooke Street West, Suite 420
Montréal, Québec H3A 2R7
Tel.: (514) 849-4852
Fax: (514) 849-4324
Consulate
1 Dundas Street W., suite 2108
Toronto, Ontario M5G 1Z3
Tél: (416) 977-0098
Fax: (416) 977-1725
Consulate
789 West Pender, Suite 890
Vancouver, BC V6C 1H2
Tel.: (604) 685-6435
Fax: (604) 685-6485

COMOROS
Embassy
336 East 45th Street, 2nd Floor
New York, NY, 10021, USA
Tel.: (212) 972-8010, -8042
Fax: (212) 983-4712

CONGO
Embassy
4891 Colorado Avenue North West
Washington, D.C., 20011, USA
Tel.: (202) 726-5500
Fax: (202) 726-1860
Telex: 197370
Consular Representative
2 Cedar Avenue
Pointe-Claire, Québec H9S 4Y1
Tel.: (514) 697-3781
Permament Mission at the United Nations
14 East, 65th Street
New York, NY, 1002, USA
Tel.: (212) 744-7840

COSTA RICA
Embassy
135 York Street, Suite 208
Ottawa, Ontario K1N 5T4
Tel.: (613) 562-2855
Fax: (613) 562-2582
Consulate
1425 René Lévesque West, Suite 602
Montréal, Québec H3G 1T7
Tel.: (514) 393-1057
Fax: (514) 393-1624
Consulate
164 Avenue Road
Toronto, Ontario M5R 2H9
Tel.: (416) 961-6773
Fax: (416) 961-6771
Consulate
1550 Alberni Street, Suite 804
Vancouver, BC V6G 1A5
Tel.: (604) 669-0797
Fax: (604) 669-4659

CÔTE-D'IVOIRE
Embassy
9 Marlborough Avenue
Ottawa, Ontario K1N 8E6
Tel.: (613) 236-9919
Fax: (613-563-8287
Consulate
260 Adelaide Street East, Box 110
Toronto, Ontario M5A 1N1
Tel.: (416) 366-8490
Fax: (416) 947-1534
Consulate
417 St.Pierre Street, Suite 602
Montréal, Québec H2Y 2N4
Tel.: (514) 845-8121
Fax: (514) 845-1271

CROATIA
Embassy
130 Albert Street, Suite 1700
Ottawa, Ontario K1P 5G4
Tel.: (613) 230-7351
Fax: (613) 230-7388
Consulate
918 Dundas Street East, Suite 302
Mississauga, Ontario L4Y 2B8
Tel.: (905) 277-9051
Fax.: (905) 277-5432

CUBA
Embassy
388 Main Street
Ottawa, Ontario K1S 1E3
Tel.: (613) 563-0141
Fax: (613) 563-0068
Consulate
1415 Pine Avenue West
Montréal, Québec H3G 2B2
Tel.: (514) 843-8897
Fax: (514) 982-9034
Telex: 052-5228
Consulate
5353 Dundas Street West
Square Kipling, Suite 401
Toronto, Ontario M9B 6H8
Tel.: (416) 234-8181
Fax: (416) 234-2754
Telex: 0622226
Tourist Office
440 René Lévesque West, Suite 1105
Montréal, Québec H2Z 1V7
Tel.: (514) 875-8004
Fax: (514) 875-8005

CURAÇAO
Tourist Office
475 Park Ave. S., Suite 2000
New York, NY, 1006, USA
Tel.: (212) 683-7660
Fax: (212) 683-2937
1-800-270-3350

CYPRUS
High Commission
2211 R Street North West
Washington, D.C., 20008, USA
Tel.: (202) 462-5772
Fax: (202) 483-6710
Consular Representative
2930 Édouard Montpetit Street, Suite PH2
Montréal, Québec H3T 1J7
Tel.: (514) 735-7233

CZECH REPUBLIC
Embassy
541 Sussex Drive
Ottawa, Ontario K1N 6Z6
Tel.: (613) 562-3875
Fax: (613) 562-3878
Consulate
1305 Pins Avenue West
Montréal, Québec H3G 1B2
Tel.: (514) 849-8983
Fax: (514) 849-4117

DENMARK
Embassy
47 Clarence Street, Suite 450
Ottawa, Ontario K1N 9K1
Tel.: (613) 234-0704
Fax: (613) 234-7368
Consulate
1 Place Ville-Marie, 35th Floor
Montréal, Québec H3B 4M4
Tel.: (514) 877-3060
Fax: (514) 871-8977
Consulate
151 Bloor Street West, Suite 310
Toronto, Ontario M5S 1S4
Tel.: (416) 962-5661
Fax: (416) 962-3668
Consulate
1235-11th Avenue South West
Calgary, AB T3C 0M5
Tel.: (403) 245-5755
Tourist Office
P.O. Box 636
Mississauga, Ontario L5M 2C2
Tel.: (905) 820-8984

DJIBOUTI
Embassy
1156-15th Street North West, Suite 515
Washington, D.C., 20005, USA
Tel.: (202) 331-0270
Fax: (202) 331-0302
Telex: 4490085 AMDJUS

DOMINICA
(See Eastern Caribbean States)

DOMINICAN REPUBLIC
Consulate
1055 St.Mathieu, Suite 241
Montréal, Québec H3H 2S3
Tel.: (514) 933-9008
Fax: (514) 933-2070
Tourist Office
2080 Crescent Street
Montréal, Québec H3G 2B8
Tel.: 1-800-563-1611
Fax: (514) 499-1918

EASTERN CARIBBEAN STATES
(Dominica, Grenada, Montserrat, Saint Kitts and Nevis, Saint Lucia and Saint Vincent and Grenadines)
112 Kent Street, Suite 1610
Place de Ville, Tower B
Ottawa, Ontario K1P 5P2
Tel.: (613) 236-8952
Fax: (613) 236-3042

ECUADOR
Embassy
50 O'Connor Street, Suite 1311
Ottawa, Ontario K1P 6L2
Tel.: (613) 563-8206
Fax: (613) 235-5776
Consulate
1010 St.Catherine Street West, Suite 440
Montréal, Québec H3B 3R3
Tel.: (514) 874-4071
Fax: (514) 874-4071
Consulate
151 Bloor Street West, Suite 470
Toronto, Ontario M5S 1S4
Tel.: (416) 968-2077
Fax: (416) 968-3348
Consulate
7100 Gilbert Road, Suite 802
Richmond, BC V7C 5C3
Tel.: (604) 273-8577
Fax: (604) 273-8576
Consulate
P.O. Box 29, RR#1, Suite 6
Okotoks, AB T0L 1T0
Tel.: (403) 221-8822
Fax: (403) 221-8821

EGYPT
Embassy
454 Laurier Avenue East
Ottawa, Ontario K1N 6R3
Tel.: (613) 234-4931, -4935, -4958
Fax: (613) 234-9347
Consulate
1 Place Ville-Marie, Suite 2617
Montréal, Québec H3B 4S3
Tel.: (514) 866-8455
Fax: (514) 866-0835
Tourist Office
1253 McGill College Avenue, Suite 250
Montréal, Québec H3B 2Y5
Tel.: (514) 861-4420

EL SALVADOR
Embassy
209 Kent Street, Suite 504
Ottawa, Ontario K2P 1Z8
Tel.: (613) 238-2939
Fax: (613) 238-6940
Consulate
4330 Sherbrooke West
Westmount, Québec H3Z 1E1
Tel.: (514) 934-3678
Fax: (514) 934-3707
Consulate
1166 Alberni Street, Suite 1406
Vancouver, BC V6E 3Z3
Tel.: (604) 732-8142
Consulate
292 Sheppard Avenue West, Suite 200
Willowdale, Ontario M2N 1N5
Tel.: (416) 512-8196
Fax: (416) 512-8139

ERITREA
Embassy
910 17th Street N.W., Suite 400
Washington, D.C., 20006, USA
Tel.: (202) 429-1991
Fax: (202) 429-9004

ESTONIA
Embassy
1030 15th Street NW, suite 1000

Washington, D.C., 20005, USA
Tel.: (202) 789-0320
Fax: (202) 789-0471
Consulate
958 Broadview Avenue, Suite 202
Toronto, Ontario M4K 2R6
Tel.: (416) 461-0764
Fax: (416) 461-0448

ETHIOPIA
Embassy
151 Slater Street, Suite 210
Ottawa, Ontario K1P 5H3
Tel.: (613) 235-6637, -6790
Fax: (613) 235-4638

EUROPEAN UNION
Delegation
350 Sparks Street, Suite 1110
Ottawa, Ontario K1R 7S8
Tel.: (613) 238-6464
Fax: (613) 238-5191
Tourist Office
Constitution Square
360 Albert Street, Suite 801
Ottawa, Ontario K1R 7X7
Tel.: (613) 230-8654
Fax: (613) 230-3683

FIDJI (Island)
Embassy
1 United Nation Plaza, 26th Floor
New York, NY, 10017, USA
Tel.: (212) 355-7316
Fax: (212) 319-1896
Consulate
130 Slater Street, Suite 750
Ottawa, Ontario K1P 6E2
Tel.: (613) 233-9252
Fax: (613) 594-8705
Consulate
1840 Clark Drive
Vancouver, BC V5N 3G4
Tel.: (604) 254-5544

FINLAND
Embassy
55 Metcalfe Street, Suite 850
Ottawa, Ontario K1P 6L5
Tel.: (613) 236-2389
Fax: (613) 238-1474
Tourist Office
1200 Bay Street, Suite 604
Toronto, Ontario M5R 2A5
Tel.: 1-800-346-4636
or (416) 964-9159
Consulate
Stock Exchange Tower, Suite 3400
P.O. Box 242
800 Place Victoria
Montréal, Québec H4Z 1E9
Tel.: (514) 397-7437
Fax: (514) 397-7600

FRANCE
Embassy
42 Sussex Drive
Ottawa, Ontario K1M 2C9
Tel.: (613) 789-1795
Fax: (613) 789-0279
Consulate
1 Place Ville-Marie, Suite 2601
Montréal, Québec H3B 4S3
Tel.: (514) 878-4385
Fax: (514) 878-3981
Telex: 052-4890
Consulate
130 Bloor St West, Suite 400
Toronto, Ontario M5S 1N5
Tel.: (416) 925-8041
Fax: (416) 925-3076
Consulate
The Vancouver Building
736 Granville Street, Suite 1201
Vancouver, BC V6Z 1H9
Tel.: (604) 681-4345
Fax: (604) 681-4287
Tourist Office
Esso Tower
1981 McGill College Avenue
Suite 490
Montréal, Québec H3A 2W9
Tel.: (514) 288-4264
30 St.Patrick Street, Suite 700
Toronto, Ontario M5T 3A3
Tel.: (416) 593-4723
Fax: (416) 979-7587
Vendanges
429 Viger Street East
Montréal, Québec H2L 2N9
Tel.: (514) 844-1600
Vendanges
France-Quebec Association
9 Place Royale
Québec, Québec G1K 4G2
Tel.: (418) 643-1616
1-800-1661-9965

GABON
Embassy
4 Range Road
Ottawa, Ontario K1N 8J5
Tel.: (613) 232-5301, -5302
Fax: (613) 232-6916
Telex: 053-4295
Consulate
85 St.Catherine Street West
Montréal, Québec H2X 3P4
Tel.: (514) 287-8500
Fax: (514) 287-8643
Telex: 055-60122

GAMBIA
High Commission
1155-15th Street North West
Suite 1000
Washington, D.C., 20005, USA
Tel.: (202) 785-1399
Fax: (202) 785-1430
Consulate
102 Bloor Street West, Suite 510
Toronto, Ontario M5S 1M8
Tel.: (416) 923-2935

GERMANY
Embassy
275 Slater Street, 14th Floor
Ottawa, Ontario K1P 5H9
Tel.: (613) 232-1101
Fax: (613) 594-9330
Consulate
1250 René Lévesque Avenue, Suite 4315
Montréal, Québec H3B 4X8
Tel.: (514) 931-2277
Fax: (514) 931-2739
Consulate
77 Admiral Road
Toronto, Ontario M5R 2L4
Tel.: (416) 925-2813
Fax: (416) 925-2818
Consulate
World Trade Centre
999 Canada Place, Suite 704
Vancouver, BC V6C 3E1
Tel.: (604) 684-8377
Fax: (604) 684-8334
Tourist Office
175 Bloor Street East
North Tower, Suite 604
Toronto, Ontario M4W 3R8
Tel.: (416) 968-1570
Fax: (416) 968-1986

GHANA
High Commission
1 Clemow Avenue
Ottawa, Ontario K1S 2A9
Tel.: (613) 236-0871, -0872, -0873
Fax: (613) 236-0874
Consulate
1420 Sherbrooke Street West, Suite 900
Montréal, Québec H3G 1K3
Tel.: (514) 849-1417
Fax: (514) 849-2643

GREECE
Embassy
76-80 MacLaren Street
Ottawa, Ontario K2P 0K6
Tel.: (613) 238-6271, -6272, -6273
Fax: (613) 238-5676
Consulate
1170 Place du Frère André, 3rd Floor
Montréal, Québec H3B 3C6
Tel.: (514) 875-2119
Fax: (514) 875-8781
Consulate
365 Bloor Street East, Suite 1800
Toronto, Ontario M4W 3L4
Tel.: (416) 515-0133, -0134
Fax: (416) 515-0209
Consulate
1200 Burrard Street, Suite 501
Vancouver, BC V6Z 2C7
Tel.: (604) 681-1381
Fax: (604) 681-6656
National Tourist Offices
1233 de la Montagne Avenue, Bureau 101
Montréal, Québec H3G 1Z2
Tel.: (514) 871-1535

or
1300 Bay St, Main Level
Toronto, Ontario M5R 3L8
Tel.: (416) 968-2220
Fax: (416) 968-6533

GRENADA
Tourist Office
439 University Avenue, Suite 820
Toronto, Ontario M5G 1Y8
Tel.: (416) 595-1339
Fax: (416) 595-8278
(See West Indies)

GUATEMALA
Embassy
130 Albert Street, Suite 1010
Ottawa, Ontario K1P 5G4
Tel.: (613) 233-7237
Fax: (613) 233-0135
Consulate
50 Aberdeen Street
Québec, Québec G1R 2C7
Tel.: (418) 523-0426
Consulate
P.O. Box 319, Norval
Toronto, Ontario L0P 1K0
Tel.: (416) 873-9167

GUINEA
Embassy
483 Wilbrod Street
Ottawa, Ontario K1N 6N1
Tel.: (613) 789-8444, -3418, -3428
Fax: (613) 789-7560
Consular Representative
1st John's Road
Toronto, Ontario M6P 4C7
Tel.: (416) 656-4812
Fax: (416) 767-6070

GUINEA-BISSAU
Embassy
918 16th Street N.W.
Mezzanine Suite
Washington, D.C., 20006, USA
Tel.: (202) 872-4222
Consulate
Place Mercantile
770, rue Sherbrooke West, 13th Floor
Montréal, Québec H3A 1G1
Tel.: (514) 842-9831
Fax: (514) 288-7389

GUYANA
High Commission
Burnside Building, 151 Slater Street,
Suite 309
Ottawa, Ontario K1P 5H3
Tel.: (613) 235-7249, -7240
Fax: (613) 235-1447
Consulate
505 Consumers Road, Suite 206
Willowdale, Ontario M2J 4V8
Tel.: (416) 694-6040, -6059
Fax: (416) 494-1530

HAITI
Embassy
112 Kent Street
Place de Ville, Tower B, Suite 212
Ottawa, Ontario K1P 5P2
Tel.: (613) 238-1628, -1629
Fax: (613) 238-2986
Consulate and Tourist Office
1801 McGill College Avenue
10th Floor, Suite 1050
Montréal, Québec H3A 2N4
Tel.: (514) 499-1919, -1934
Fax: (514) 499-1818

HONDURAS
Embassy
151 Slater Street, Suite 908
Ottawa, Ontario K1P 5H3
Tel.: (613) 233-8900
Fax: (613) 232-0193
Consulate
1650 de Maisonneuve Ave West, Suite 306
Montréal, Québec H3H 2P3
Tel.: (514) 937-1138
Consulate
22 Front St. West, Suite 1401
Toronto, Ontario M5J 1C4
Tel.: (416) 867-9087
Fax: (416) 867-9320
Consulate
510 West Hastings Street, Suite 1026
Vancouver, BC V6B 1L8
Tel.: (604) 685-7711

HONG-KONG
High Commission
80 Elgin Street
Ottawa, Ontario K1P 5K7
Tel.: (613) 237-1530
Fax: (613) 237-7980

HUNGARY
Embassy
299 Waverley Street
Ottawa, Ontario K2P 0V9
Tel.: (613) 230-2717
Fax: (613) 230-7560
Consulate
1200 McGill College Avenue, Suite 2030
Montréal, Québec H3G 4G7
Tel.: (514) 393-1555
Consulate
102 Bloor West, Suite 450
Toronto, Ontario M5S 1M8
Tel.: (416) 923-3596, -3597, -3598
Consulate
1650 West 2nd Avenue
Vancouver, BC V6J 4R2
Tel.: (604) 734-6698

ICELAND
Embassy
1156-15th North West St., Suite 1200
Washington, D.C., 20005, USA
Tel.: (202) 265-6653
Fax: (202) 265-6656

INDIA
High Commission
10 Springfield Road
Ottawa, Ontario K1M 1C9
Tel.: (613) 744-3751, -3752, -3753
Fax: (613) 744-0913
Tourist Office
60 Bloor Street West, Suite 1003
Toronto, Ontario M4W 3B8
Tel.: (416) 962-3787
Fax: (416) 962-6279
Consulate
2 Bloor Street West, Suite 500
Toronto, Ontario M4W 3E2
Tel.: (416) 960-0751, - 0752
Fax: (416) 906-9812
Consulate
325 Howe Street, 2nd Floor
Vancouver, BC V6C 1Z7
Tel.: (604) 662-8811
Fax: (604) 682-2471

INDONESIA
Embassy
287 MacLaren Street
Ottawa, Ontario K2P 0L9
Tel.: (613) 236-7403
Fax: (613) 563-2858, 230-7361
Consulate
425 University Avenue, 9th Floor
Toronto, Ontario M5G 1T6
Tel.: (416) 591-6461
Fax: (416) 591-6613

IRAN
Embassy
245 Metcalfe Street
Ottawa, Ontario K2P 2K2
Tel.: (613) 235-4726
Fax: (613) 232-5712
Consular Section: (613) 233-4726

IRAQ
Embassy
215 McLeod Street
Ottawa, Ontario K2P 0Z8
Tel.: (613) 236-9177
Fax: (613) 567-1101

IRELAND
Embassy
170 Metcalfe Street
Ottawa, Ontario K2P 1P3
Tel.: (613) 233-6281
Fax: (613) 233-5835
Tourist Office
160 Bloor Street East, Suite 1150
Toronto, Ontario M4W 1B9
Tel.: (416) 929-2777
Tourist Office
111 Road Avenue, Suite 450
Toronto, Ontario M5R 3J8
Tel.: (416) 925-6368

ISRAEL
Embassy
50 O'Connor Street, Suite 1005

Ottawa, Ontario K1P 6L2
Tel.: (613) 567-6450
Fax: (613) 237-8865
Consulate
1155 René Lévesque Boulevard West, Suite 2620
Montréal, Québec H3B 4S5
Tel.: (514) 393-9372
Fax: (514) 393-8795
Tourist Office
160 Bloor Street West, Suite 700
Toronto, Ontario M5S 2V6
Tel.: (416) 964-3784

ITALY
Embassy
275 Slater Street, 21st Floor
Ottawa, Ontario K1P 5H9
Tel.: (613) 232-2401, -2402, -2403
Telec: (613) 233-1484
Consulate
3489 Drummond Avenue
Montréal, Québec H3G 1X6
Tel.: (514) 849-8351
Fax: (514) 499-9471
Consulate
136 Beverley Street
Toronto, Ontario M5T 1Y5
Tel.: (416) 977-1566
Fax: (416) 977-1119
Consulate
1200 Burrard Street, Suite 705
Vancouver, BC V6Z 2C7
Tel.: (604) 684-7288
Fax: (604) 685-4263
Tourist Office
1 Place Ville-Marie, Suite 1914
Montréal, Québec H3B 2C3
Tel.: (514) 866-7667

JAMAICA
High Commission
275 Slater Street, Suite 800
Ottawa, Ontario K1P 5H9
Tel.: (613) 233-9311, -9314
Fax: (613) 233-0611
Consulate
214 King Street West, Suite 400
Toronto, Ontario M5H 1K4
Tel.: (416) 598-3008
Fax: (416) 598-4928

JAPAN
Embassy
255 Sussex Drive
Ottawa, Ontario K1N 9E6
Tel.: (613) 241-8541
Fax: (613) 241-2232
Consulate
600 de la Gauchetière Street West, Suite 2120
Montréal, Québec H3B 4L8
Tel.: (514) 866-3429
Fax: (514) 395-6000
Consulate
1177 Hastings West, Suite 900
Vancouver, BC V6E 2K9
Tel.: (604) 684-5868
Fax: (604) 684-6939
Consulate
Toronto-Dominion Bank Tower, Suite 2702
P.O. Box 10, Toronto-Dominion Centre
Toronto, Ontario M5K 1A1
Tel.: (416) 363-7038
Fax: (416) 367-9392
Tourist Office
165 University Avenue, Suite 1112
Toronto, Ontario M5H 3B8
Tel.: (416) 366-7140
Fax: (416) 366-4530

JORDAN
Embassy
100 Bronson Avenue, Suite 701
Ottawa, Ontario K1R 6G8
Tel.: (613) 238-8090
Fax: (613) 232-3341

KENYA
High Commission
415 Laurier Avenue East
Ottawa, Ontario K1N 6R4
Tel.: (613) 563-1773, -1774, -1775, -1776
Fax: (613) 233-6599

KOREA (SOUTH)
Embassy
151 Slater Street, 5th Floor
Ottawa, Ontario K1P 5H3
Tel.: (613) 232-1715
Fax: (613) 232-0928
Consulate
1000 Sherbrooke Street West, Suite 1710
Montréal, Québec H3A 3G4
Tel.: (514) 845-3243
Fax: (514) 845-8517
Consulate
555 Avenue Road
Toronto, Ontario M4V 2J7
Tel.: (416) 920-3809
Telec: (416) 924-7305
Consulate
1066 Hastings Street West, Suite 830
Vancouver, BC V6E 3X1
Tel.: (604) 681-9581
Fax: (604) 681-4864
Tourist Office
480 University Street, Suite 406
Toronto, Ontario M5G 1V2
Tel.: (416) 348-9056
Fax: (416) 349-9058

KUWAIT
Embassy
80 Elgin Street
Ottawa, Ontario K1P 1C6
Tel.: (613) 780-9999
Fax: (613) 780-9905

KYRGYZSTAN
Embassy
1511 K. Street N.W., Suite 705
Washington, D.C., USA, 20005
Tel.: (202) 347-3732
Fax: (202) 347-3718

LAOS
Embassy
2222 S Street North West
Washington, D.C., 20008, USA
Tel.: (202) 332-6416
Fax: (202) 332-4923

LATVIA
Embassy
112 Kent Street, Suite 2007
Place de Ville, Tower B
Ottawa, Ontario K1P 5P2
Tel.: (613) 238-6868
Fax: (613) 238-7044
Consulate
230 Clemow Avenue
Ottawa, Ontario K1P 2B6
Tel.: (613) 238-6868
Fax: (613) 238-7044

LEBANON
Embassy
640 Lyon Street
Ottawa, Ontario K1S 3Z5
Tel.: (613) 236-5825, -5855
Fax: (613) 232-1609
Consulate
40 Côte Sainte-Catherine
Montréal, Québec H2V 2A2
Tel.: (514) 276-2638
Fax: (514) 276-0090

LESOTHO
High Commission
202 Clemow Avenue
Ottawa, Ontario K1S 2B4
Tel.: (613) 236-9449, -0960
Fax: (613) 238-3341
Consulate
4750 The Boulevard
Westmount, Québec H3Y 1V3
Tel.: (514) 482-6568
Fax: (514) 483-6595

LIBERIA
Consulate
1080 Beaver Hall Hill, Suite 1720
Montréal, Québec H2Z 1S8
Tel.: (514) 871-9571
Fax: (514) 397-0816

LIBYA
Embassy to the United Nations
309-315 East 48th Street
New York, NY, 10017, USA
Tel.: (212) 752-5775
Fax: (212) 593-4787

LICHTENSTEIN
(see Switzerland)

LITHUANIA
Embassy
2622 16th Street, N.W.
Washington, D.C., 20009, USA
Tel.: (202) 234-5860
Fax: (202) 328-0466

LUXEMBOURG
Embassy
2200 Massachusetts Avenue North West
Washington, D.C., 20008, USA
Tel.: (202) 265-4171
Fax: (202) 328-8270
Consulate
3877 Draper Avenue
Montréal, Québec H4A 2N9
Tel.: (514) 489-6052

MADAGASCAR
Embassy
282 Somerset Street West
Ottawa, Ontario K2P 0J6
Tel.: (613) 563-2506, -2438
Fax: (613) 231-3261
Consulates
8530 Saguenay Street
Brossard, Québec J4X 1M6
Tel.: (514) 672-0353
Fax: (514) 672-0353
or
396 Claremont Crescent
Oakville, Ontario L6J 6K1
Tel.: (416) 845-8914

MALAWI
High Commission
7 Clemow Avenue
Ottawa, Ontario K1S 2A9
Tel.: (613) 236-8931
Fax: (613) 236-1054
Consulate
5437 Plamondon Crescent
St. Lambert, Québec J4S 1W4
Tel.: (514) 466-9543
or
21 Dale Avenue, Suite 544
Toronto, Ontario M4W 1K3
Tel.: (416) 234-9333

MALAYSIA
High Commission
60 Boteler Street
Ottawa, Ontario K1N 8Y7
Tel.: (613) 241-5182
Fax: (613) 241-5214
Telex: 053-3520
Consulate
150 York Street, Suite 1110
Toronto, Ontario M5H 3S5
Tel.: (416) 947-0004
Fax: (416) 947-0006
Consulate
925 West Georgia, Suite 1900
Vancouver, BC V6C 3L2
Tel.: (604) 689-9550
Fax: (604) 685-9520

MALI
Embassy
50 Goulburn Avenue
Ottawa, Ontario K1N 8C8
Tel.: (613) 232-1501, -3264
Fax: (613) 232-7429
Consulate
1 Westmount Square, Suite 1810
Westmount, Québec H3Z 2P9
Tel.: (514) 939-1267
Fax: (514) 939-1296

MALTA
High Commission
2017 Connecticut Avenue North West
Washington, D.C., USA, 20008
Tel.: (202) 462-3611
Fax: (202) 387-5470
Telex: 64231
Consulate
1 St. John's Road, Suite 305
Toronto, Ontario M6P 4C7
Tel.: (416) 767-4902, -2901
Fax: (416) 767-0563
Consulate
3461 Northcliffe
Montréal, Québec H4A 3K8
Tel.: (514) 284-3627
Fax: (514) 284-1860
Tourist Office
Malta National Tourism Office
Empire State Building
350 5th ave, Suite 4412
New York, NY
Tel.: (212) 695-9520

MARTINIQUE
Tourist Board
1981 McGill College Avenue, Suite 480
Montréal, Québec H3A 2W9
Tel.: (514) 844-8566
1-800-361-9099
Fax: (514) 844-8901

MAURITANIA
Embassy
249 McLeod Street
Ottawa, Ontario K2P 1A1
Tel.: (613) 237-3283
Fax: (613) 237-3287

MAURITIUS
High Commission
Van Ness Centre
4301 Connecticut Avenue North West,
Suite 441
Washington, D.C., 20008, USA
Tel.: (202) 244-1491
Fax: (202) 966-0983
Consulate
606 Cathart Street, Suite 200
Montréal, Québec H3B 1K9
Tel.: (514) 393-9500
Fax: (514) 393-9324

MEXICO
Embassy
45 O'Connor Street, Suite 1500
Ottawa, Ontario K1P 1A4
Tel.: (613) 233-8988, -9272, -9917
Fax: (613) 235-9123
Tourist Offices
1 Place Ville-Marie, Suite 1526
Montréal, Québec H3B 2B5
Tel.: (514) 871-1052
Fax: (514) 871-3825
or
2 Bloor St. West, # 1801
Toronto, Ontario M4W 3E2
Tel.: (416) 925-0704, -1876
Fax: (416) 925-6061
Consulate
2000 Mansfield Street, Suite 1015
Montréal, Québec H3A 2Z7
Tel.: (514) 288-2502, -4917, -2707
Fax: (514) 288-8287

MONACO
Tourist Office
845 Third Avenue
New York, NY, 10022, USA
Tel.: 1-800-753-9696
(Service in French)
Consulate
1155 Sherbrooke West, Suite 1500
Montréal, Québec H3A 2W1
Tel.: (514) 849-0589
Fax: (514) 631-2771
Consulate
1111 Melville Street, Suite 500
Vancouver, BC V6E 4H7
Tel.: (604) 682-4633
Fax: (604) 684-0015

MONGOLIA
Embassy
2833 M Street North West
Washington, D.C., 20007, USA
Tel.: (202) 333-7117
Fax: (202) 298-9227

MONTSERRAT
(See Eastern Caribbean States)

MOROCCO
Embassy
38 Range Road
Ottawa, Ontario K1N 8J4
Tel.: (613) 236-7391, -7392, -7393
Fax: (613) 236-6164
Consulate
1010 Sherbrooke Street West, Suite 1510
Montréal, Québec H3A 2R7
Tel.: (514) 288-8750, -6951
Fax: (514) 288-4859
Tourist Office
2001 University Street, Suite 1460
Montréal, Québec H3A 2A6

Tel.: (514) 842-8111
Fax: (514) 842-8111
Fax: (514) 842-5316

MOZAMBIQUE
Embassy
1990 M Street North West, suite 570
Washington, D.C., 20036, USA
Tel.: (202) 293-7146

MYANMAR
Embassy
85 Range Road, Suite 902
Ottawa, Ontario K1N 8J6
Tel.: (613) 232-6434, -6446
Fax: (613) 232-6435

NAMIBIA
High Commission
1605 New Hampshire Avenue N.W.
Washington, D.C., 20009, USA
Tel.: (202) 986-0540
Fax: (202) 986-0443
Consulate
122 Avondale Avenue South
Waterloo, Ontario N2L 2G3
Tel.: (519) 578-5932
Fax: (519) 578-7799

NEPAL
Embassy
2131 Leroy Place North West
Washington, D.C., 20008, USA
Tel.: (202) 667-4550
Fax: (202) 667-5534
Telex: 440085 EVER UI
Tourist Office
BDO Dunwoody Ward Mallette
Royal Bank Plaza
P.O. Box 33
Toronto, Ontario M5J 2J9
Tel.: (416) 865-0210
Fax: (416) 865-0904

NETHERLANDS
Embassy
350 Albert Street, Suite 2020
Ottawa, Ontario K1R 1A4
Tel.: (613) 237-5030
Fax: (613) 237-6471
Consulate
1245 Sherbrooke Street West, Suite 2201
Montréal, Québec H3A 3L6
Tel.: (514) 849-4247, -4248
Fax: (514) 849-8260
Consulate
1 Dundas Street West, Suite 2106
Toronto, Ontario M5G 1Z3
Tel.: (416) 598-2520
Fax: (416) 598-8064
Consulate
Crown Trust Building
475 Howe Street, Suite 821
Vancouver, BC V6C 2B3
Tel.: (604) 684-6448, -6449
Fax: (604) 684-3549

Tourist Office
25 Adelaide Street East, Suite 710
Toronto, Ontario M5C 1Y2
Tel.: (416) 363-1577
Fax: (416) 363-1470

NEW ZEALAND
High Commission
Metropolitain House
99 Bank Street, Suite 727
Ottawa, Ontario K1P 6G3
Tel.: (613) 238-5991
Fax: (613) 238-5707
Consulate
888 Dunsmuir Street, Suite 1200
Vancouver, BC V6C 3K4
Tel.: (604) 684-7388
Fax: (604) 684-7333

NICARAGUA
Embassy
130 Albert Street, Suite 407
Ottawa, Ontario K1P 5G4
Tel.: (613) 234-9361, -9362
Fax: (613) 238-7666

NIGER
Embassy
38 Blackburn Avenue
Ottawa, Ontario K1N 8A2
Tel.: (613) 232-4291, -4292, -4293
Fax: (613) 230-9808
Consulate
245 St-Jacques Street West, Suite 420
Montréal, Québec H2Y 1M6
Tel.: (514) 849-4222

NIGERIA
High Commission
295 Metcalfe Street
Ottawa, Ontario K2P 1R9
Tel.: (613) 236-0521
Fax: (613) 236-0529

NORWAY
Embassy
Royal Bank Centre
90 Sparks Street, Suite 532
Ottawa, Ontario K1P 5B4
Tel.: (613) 2238-6571
Fax: (613) 238-2765
Consulate
1155 René Lévesque Blvd West, Suite 3900
Montréal, Québec H3B 3V2
Tel.: (514) 874-9087
Fax: (514) 397-3063
Consulate
2600 South Sheridan Way
Mississauga, Ontario L5J 2M4
Tel.: (905) 822-2339
Fax: (905) 855-1450
Tourist Office
655 Third Avenue
New York, NY, 10017, USA
Tel.: (212) 949-2333

OMAN
Embassy
2342 Massachusetts Avenue North West
Washington, D.C., 20008, USA
Tel.: (202) 387-1980
Fax: (202) 745-4933

PAKISTAN
High Commission
Burnside Building
151 Slater Street, Suite 608
Ottawa, Ontario K1P 5H3
Tel.: (613) 238-7881
Fax: (613) 238-7296
Consulate
3421 Peel Street
Montréal, Québec H3A 1W7
Tel.: (514) 845-2297
Fax: (514) 845-1354
Consulate
4881 Yonge Street, Suite 810
Willowdale, Ontario M2N 5X3
Tel.: (416) 250-1255
Fax: (416) 250-1321

PANAMA
Embassy
2862 McGill Terrace North West
Washington, D.C., 20008, USA
Tel.: (202) 483-1407
Fax: (202) 483-8413
Consulate
1425 René Lévesque Blvd West, Suite 904
Montréal, Québec H3G 1T7
Tel.: (514) 874-1929
Fax: (514) 874-1929

PAPUA NEW GUINEA
High Commission
1615 New Hampshire Avenue, Suite 300
Washington, D.C., 20009, USA
Tel.: (202) 745-3680
Fax: (202) 745-3679
Consulate
22 St.Clair Avenue East, Suite 501
Toronto, Ontario M4T 2S3
Tel.: (416) 926-1400

PARAGUAY
Embassy
151 Slater Street, Suite 401
Ottawa, Ontario K1P 5H3
Tel.: (613) 567-1283
Fax: (613) 567-1679
Consulate
1 Place Ville-Marie, Suite 2820
Montréal, Québec H3B 4R4
Tel.: (514) 398-0465
Fax: (514) 487-0188

PERU
Embassy
130 Albert Street, Suite 1901
Ottawa, Ontario K1P 5G4
Tel.: (613) 238-1777
Fax: (613) 232-3062
Telex: 053-3754

Consulate
(+ Tourist information)
550 Sherbrooke West, Suite 376
West Tower
Montréal, Québec H3A 1B9
Tel.: (514) 844-5123
Fax: (514) 843-8425
Consulate
10 Saint Mary Street, Suite 301
Toronto, Ontario M4V 1P9
Tel.: (416) 963-9696
Fax: (416) 963-9074

PHILIPPINES
Embassy
130 Albert Street, Suite 606-608
Ottawa, Ontario K1P 5G4
Tel.: (613) 233-1121, -1122, -1123
Fax: (613) 233-4165
Consulate
3300 Cote Vertu, Suite 202
Saint-Laurent, Québec H4R 2B7
Tel.: (514) 335-0478
Fax: (514) 335-2786
Consulate
151 Bloor Street West, Suite 365
Toronto, Ontario M5S 1S4
Tel.: (416) 922-7181
Fax: (416) 922-3638
Consulate
470 Granville Street, Suite 301-308
Vancouver, BC V6C 1V5
Tel.: (604) 685-7645
Fax: (604) 685-9945

POLAND
Embassy
443 Daly Avenue
Ottawa, Ontario K1N 6H3
Tel.: (613) 789-0468, -3376
Fax: (613) 789-1218
Consulate
1500 Pine Avenue West
Montréal, Québec H3G 1B4
Tel.: (514) 937-9481
Fax: (514) 937-7272
Consulate
2603 Lakeshore Blvd West
Toronto, Ontario M8V 1G5
Tel.: (416) 252-5471
Fax: (416) 252-0509

PORTUGAL
Embassy
645 Island Park Drive
Ottawa, Ontario K1Y 0B8
Tel.: (613) 729-0883, -2922
Fax: (613) 729-4236
Consulate
2020 University Street, Suite 1725
Montréal, Québec H3A 2A5
Tel.: (514) 499-0359
Fax: (514) 499-0366
Consulate
121 Richmond Street West, 7th floor
Toronto, Ontario M5H 2K1
Tel.: (416) 360-8260
Fax: (416) 360-0350
Tourist Office
60 Bloor Street West, Suite 1005
Toronto, Ontario M4W 3B8
Tel.: (416) 921-7376
Fax: (416) 921-1353

PUERTO RICO
Tourist Offices
43 Colburn Street, Suite 301
Toronto, Ontario M5J 1E3
Tel.: (416) 368-2680

QATAR
Embassy to the United Nations
747 Third Avenue, 22nd Floor
New York, NY 10017 USA
Tel.: (212) 486-9335, -9336
Fax: (212) 458-4952, 308-5630

ROMANIA
Embassy
655 Rideau Street
Ottawa, Ontario K1N 6A3
Tel.: (613) 789-3709, -5345
Fax: (613) 789-4365
Consulate
1111 St-Urbain Street, Suite M01-04
Montréal, Québec H2Z 1X6
Tel.: (514) 876-1792, -1793
Fax: (514) 876-1797
Consulate
111 Peter Street, Suite 530
Toronto, Ontario M5V 2H1
Tel.: (416) 585-5802, -9177
Fax: (416) 585-4798

RUSSIA
Embassy
285 Charlotte Street
Ottawa, Ontario K1N 8L5
Tel.: (613) 235-4341
Fax: (613) 236-6342
Consulate
3685 Musée Avenue
Montréal, Québec H3G 2E1
Tel.: (514) 843-5901, 982-9041
Fax: (514) 842-2012
Tourist information
1801 McGill College, Suite 630
Montréal, Québec H3A 2N4
Tel.: (514) 849-6394
Fax: (514) 849-6743

RWANDA
Embassy
121 Sherwood Drive
Ottawa, Ontario K1Y 3V1
Tel.: (613) 722-5835, -7921
Fax: (613) 729-3291
Consulate
1600 Delorimier Street
Montréal, Québec H2K 3W5
Tel.: (514) 526-1392
Fax: (514) 521-7081
Consulate
211 Consumers Rd. Suite 102
Willowdale, Ontario M2J 4G8
Tel.: (416) 493-5474
Fax: (416) 493-8171

SAINT KITTS AND NEVIS
Tourist Office
11 Yorkville Avenue, Suite 508
Toronto, Ontario M4W 1L3
Tel.: (416) 921-7717
Fax: (416) 921-7997
(see Eastern Caribbean States)

SAINT LUCIA
Consulate
3 Dewberry Drive
Markham, Ontario L3S 2R7
Tel.: (416) 472-1423
Fax: (416) 472-6379
Tourist Office
4975 Dundas Street West, Suite 457
Islington, Etobicoke, Ontario M9A 4X4
Tel.: 1-800-456-3984 et (416) 236-0936

SAINT VINCENT AND THE GRENADINES
Consulate
210 Sheppard Street East,
Ground Floor
Willowdale, Ontario M2N 3A9
Tel.: (416) 222-0745
Fax: (416) 222-3830
Tourist Office
32 Park Road
Toronto, Ontario M4W 2N4
Tel.: (416) 924-5796
(see Eastern Caribbean States)

SAMOA (AMERICAN)
High Commission
820-2nd Avenue, Suite 800B
New York, NY, 10017 USA
Tel.: (212) 599-6196

SAO TOMÉ AND PRÍNCIPE
Mission to the United Nations
801 Second Avenue, Room 1504
New York, NY, 10017 USA
Tel.: (212) 697-4212
Consulare Representation
4068 Beaconsfield Avenue
Montréal, Québec H4A 2H3
Tel.: (514) 484-2706

SAUDI ARABIA
Embassy
99 Bank Street, Suite 901
Ottawa, Ontario K1P 6B9
Tel.: (613) 237-4100, -4101, -4102, -4103
Fax: (613) 237-0567

SENEGAL
Embassy
57 Malborough Avenue

Ottawa, Ontario K1N 8E8
Tel.: (613) 238-6392
Fax: (613) 238-2695
Consulate
97 Old Forest Mille Road
Toronto, Ontario M5P 2R8
Tel.: (416) 923-7492
Consulate
244 rue Sherbrooke Est, Suite 313
Montréal, Québec H2X 1G1
Tel.: (514) 526-8183

SEYCHELLES
High Commission
820 Second Avenue, Suite 900F
New York, NY, 10017 USA
Tel.: (212) 687-9766
Fax: (212) 922-9177
Consulate
417 Saint-Pierre Street, Suite 403
Montréal, Québec H2Y 2M4
Tel.: (514) 284-2199
Fax: (514) 845-0631
Tourist Office
820 Second Avenue, Suite 900F
New York, NY, 10017 USA
Tel.: (212) 687-9766
Fax: (212) 922-9177

SIERRA LEONE
High Commission
1701-19th Street North West
Washington, D.C., 20009, USA
Tel.: (202) 939-9261

SINGAPORE
High Commission
231 East 51st Street
New York, NY, 10022, USA
Tel.: (212) 826-0840, -0841
Fax: (212) 826-2964
Consulate
999 West Hastings Street, Suite 1305
Vancouver, BC V6C 2W2
Tel.: (604) 669-5115
Fax: (604) 669-5153

SLOVAKIA
Embassy
50 Rideau Terrace
Ottawa, Ontario K1M 2A1
Tel.: (613) 749-4442
Fax.: (613) 749-4989
Consulate
999 de Maisonneuve Blvd West, 18th Floor
Montréal, Québec H3A 3L4
Tel.: (514) 288-9797
Fax: (514) 288-2697

SLOVENIA
Embassy
150 Metcalfe Street, Suite 2101
Ottawa, Ontario K2P 1P1
Tel.: (613) 565-5781, -5782
Fax: (613) 565-5783

SOLOMON ISLANDS
High Commission
820-2nd Avenue, suite 800B
New York, N.Y., 10017 U.S.A.
Tel.: (212) 599-6194

SOUTH AFRICA
High Commission
15 Sussex Drive
Ottawa, Ontario K1M 1M8
Tél.: (613) 744-0330
Fax: (613) 741-1639
Consulate
1 Place Ville-Marie, Suite 2615
Montréal, Québec H3B 4S3
Tél.: (514) 878-9217
Fax: (514) 878-4751
Consulate
Stock Exchange Tower
2 First Canadian Place, Suite 2300
P.O. Box 424
Toronto, Ontario M5X 1E3
Tél.: (416) 364-0314
Fax: (416) 364-1737
Tourist Office
4119 Lawrence Avenue East Suite 205
Scarborough, Ontario M1E 2S2
Tél.: (416) 283-0563
Fax: (416) 283-5465

SPAIN
Embassy
350 Sparks Street, Suite 802
Ottawa, Ontario K1R 7S8
Tel.: (613) 237-2193, -2194
Fax: (613) 236-9246
Consulate
1 Westmount Square, Suite 1456,
Wood Avenue
Westmount, Québec H3Z 2P9
Tel.: (514) 935-5235
Fax: (514) 935-4655
Consulate
1200 Bay Street, Suite 400
Toronto, Ontario M5R 2A5
Tel.: (416) 967-4949
Fax: (416) 925-4949
Tourist Office
102 Bloor Street West, Suite 1400
Toronto, Ontario M4W 2B8
Tel.: (416) 961-3131
Fax: (416) 961-1992

SRI LANKA
High Commission
333 Laurier Avenue West, Suite 1204
Ottawa, Ontario K1P 1C1
Tel.: (613) 233-8440, -8449
Fax: (613) 238-8448
Consulate
890 West Pender Street, Suite 602
Vancouver, BC V6C 1K4
Tel.: (604) 662-8668
Fax: (604) 662-8668

SUDAN
Embassy
85 Range Road, Suite 507-510
Ottawa, Ontario K1N 8J6
Tel.: (613) 235-4999, -4000
Fax: (613) 235-6880

SURINAME
Embassy
Van Ness Center
4301 Connecticut Avenue North West,
Suite 108
Washington, D.C., USA, 20008
Tel.: (202) 244-7488, -7590
Fax: (202) 244-5878

SWAZILAND
High Commission
130 Albert Street, Suite 104
Ottawa, Ontario K1P 5G4
Tel.: (613) 567-1480
Fax: (613) 567-1058
Télex: 053-3185

SWEDEN
Embassy
Mercury Court
377 Dalhousie Street
Ottawa, Ontario K1N 9N8
Tel.: (613) 241-8553
Fax: (613) 241-2277
Consulate
Tour de la Bourse
800 Place Victoria, # 3400
Montréal, Québec H4Z 1E9
Tel.: (514) 866-4019
Fax: (514) 397-7600
Consulate
2 Bloor Street West, Suite 1504
Toronto, Ontario M4W 3E2
Tel.: (416) 963-8768
Fax: (416) 923-8809

SWITZERLAND
Embassy
5 Malborough Avenue
Ottawa, Ontario K1N 8E6
Tel.: (613) 235-1837
Fax: (613) 563-1394
Consulate
1572 Dr. Penfield Avenue
Montréal, Québec H3G 1C4
Tel.: (514) 932-7181
Fax: (514) 932-9028
Consulate
154 University Avenue, Suite 601
Toronto, Ontario M5H 3Y9
Tel.: (416) 593-5371
Fax: (416) 593-5083
Consulate
999 Canada Place, Suite 790
Vancouver, BC V6C 3E1
Tel.: (604) 684-2231
Fax: (604) 684-2806
National Tourist Office
926 The East Mall

Etobicoke, Ontario M9B 6K1
Tel.: (416) 695-2090

SYRIA
Embassy
2215 Wyoming Avenue North West
Washington, D.C., 20008, USA
Tel.: (202) 232-6313
Fax: (202) 232-5184
Consulate
1111 St.Urbain, Suite 109
Montréal, Québec H2Z 1Y6
Tel.: (514) 397-9595
Fax: (514) 397-6801

TANZANIA
High Commission
50 Range Road
Ottawa, Ontario K1N 8J4
Tel.: (613) 232-1500, -1509
Fax: (613) 232-5184

THAILAND
Embassy
180 Island Park Drive
Ottawa, Ontario K1Y 0A2
Tel.: (613) 722-4444
Fax: (613) 722-6624
Consulate
1155 boul. René-Lévesque West, Suite 2500
Montréal, Québec H3B 2K4
Tel.: (514) 871-1271
Fax: (514) 875-8967
Consulate
40 King Street West
44th Floor
Toronto, Ontario M5H 3Y4
Tel.: (416) 367-6750
Fax: (416) 367-6749
Consulate
736 Granville Street, Suite 106
Vancouver, BC V6Z 1G3
Tel.: (604) 687-1143
Fax: (604) 687-4434

TOGO
Embassy
12 Range Road
Ottawa, Ontario K1N 8J3
Tel.: (613) 238-5916, -5917
Fax: (613) 235-6425

TRINIDAD AND TOBAGO
High Commission
75 Albert Street, Suite 508
Ottawa, Ontario K1P 5E7
Tel.: (613) 232-2418, -2419
Fax: (613) 232-4349

TUNISIA
Embassy
515 O'Connor Street
Ottawa, Ontario K1S 3P8
Tel.: (613) 237-0330, -0332
Fax: (613) 237-7939
Consulate
511 Place d'Armes, Suite 501
Montréal, Québec H2Y 2W7
Tel.: (514) 844-6909
Fax: (514) 844-5895

TURKEY
Embassy
197 Wurtemburg Street
Ottawa, Ontario K1N 8L9
Tel.: (613) 789-4044, -3440
Fax: (613) 789-3442
Tourist Office
Consitution Square
360 Albert Street, Suite 801
Ottawa, Ontario K1R 7X7
Tel.: (613) 230-8654
Telec.: (613) 230-3683

TURKS AND CAICOS ISLANDS
Tourist Office
57 36th Street
Toronto, Ontario M8W 3L1
Tel.: (416) 253-6863

UGANDA
High Commission
231 Cobourg Street
Ottawa, Ontario K1N 8J2
Tel.: (613) 789-7797, -0110, -0133
Fax: (613) 789-8909
Telex: 053-4469

UKRAINE
Embassy
331 Metcalfe Street
Ottawa, Ontario K2P 1S3
Tel.: (613) 230-2961
Fax: (613) 230-2400
Consulate
2120 Bloor Street West
Toronto, Ontario M6S 1M8
Tel.: (416) 763-3114
Fax: (416) 763-2323

UNITED ARAB EMIRATES
Embassy
747 Third Avenue, 36th Floor
New York, NY, 10017, USA
Tel.: (212) 371-0480
Fax: (212) 371-4923

UNITED STATES OF AMERICA
Embassy
100 Wellington Street
Post Office Box 866, Station B
Ottawa, Ontario K1P 5T1
Tel.: (613) 238-5335
Fax: (613) 238-8750
Consulate
455 René Lévesque Boulevard
P.O. Box 65, Postal Station Desjardins
Montréal, Québec H2Z 1Z2
Tel.: (514) 398-9695
Consulate
360 University Avenue
Toronto, Ontario M5G 1S4
Tel.: (416) 595-1700
Consulate
615 Macleod Trail S.E., Suite 1050
Calgary, AB T3G 4T8
Tel.: (403) 266-8962
Consulate
1 Ste. Geneviève Street
2 Place Terrasse Dufferin
P.O. Box 939
Québec, Québec G1R 4T9
Tel.: (418) 692-2095
Consulate
1075 West Pender Street
Vancouver. BC V6E 4E9
Tel.: (604) 685-1930
Fax: (604) 688-8087

URUGUAY
Embassy
130 Albert Street, Suite 1905
Ottawa, Ontario K1P 5G4
Tel.: (613) 234-2727
Fax: (613) 233-4670
Consulate
5000 Dufferin Street, Suite 202
Toronto, Ontario M3H 5T5
Tel.: (416) 736-9022
Fax: (416) 736-9422

VATICAN CITY
Apostolic Nunciature
724 Manor Avenue, Rockcliffe Park
Ottawa, Ontario K1M 0E3
Tel.: (613) 746-4914
Fax: (613) 746-4786

VENEZUELA
Embassy
32 Range Road
Ottawa, Ontario K1N 8J4
Tel.: (613) 235-5151
Fax: (613) 235-3205
Consulate
2055 Peel Street, Suite 400
Montréal, Québec H3A 1V4
Tel.: (514) 842-3417, -3418
Fax: (514) 287-7101
Consulate
365 Bloor Street East, Suite 1904
Toronto, Ontario M4W 3L4
Tel.: (416) 960-6070, -6071
Fax: (416) 960-6077

VIETNAM
Embassy
25B Davidson Drive
Gloucester, Ontario K1J 6L7
Tel.: (613) 744-4963
Fax: (613) 744-1709
Telex: 053-3205
Tourist Information
Voyages Express
1481 Amherst Street
Montréal (Québec) H2L 3L2
Tel.: (514) 526-2877
Fax: (514) 526-7355

VIRGIN ISLANDS (AMERICAN)
Tourist Office
3300 Bloor Street West, Suite 3210
Center Tower
Toronto, Ontario M8X 2X3
Tel.: (416) 233-4348
1-800-465-8784

VIRGIN ISLANDS (BRITISH)
Tourist Office
370 Lexington Avenue, Suite 313
New York, NY, 10017, USA
Tel.: 1-800-835-8530
Fax: (212) 949-8254

YEMEN
Embassy
350 Sparks Street, Suite 1100
Ottawa, Ontario K1R 7S8
Tel.: (613) 232-8525, -8582
Fax: (613) 232-8276

YUGOSLAVIA
Embassy
17 Blackburn Street
Ottawa, Ontario K1N 8A2
Tel.: (613) 233-6289
Fax: (613) 233-7850
Consulate
1200 du Fort Street
Montréal, Québec H3H 2B3
Tel.: (514) 939-1200

ZAIRE
Embassy
18 Range Road
Ottawa, Ontario K1N 8J3
Tel.: (613) 797-3711
Fax: (613) 747-9152
Consulate
417 St. Pierre Street, Suite 602
Montréal, Québec H2Y 2M4
Tel.: (514) 845-8121

ZAMBIA
High Commission
130 Albert Street, Suite 1610
Ottawa, Ontario K1P 5G4
Tel.: (613) 563-1513
Fax: (613) 235-0430
Telex: 053-4418

ZIMBABWE
High Commission
332 Somerset Street West
Ottawa, Ontario K2P 0J9
Tel.: (613) 237-4388
Fax: (613) 563-8269

Bibliography

FOREIGN AFFAIRS AND INTERNATIONAL TRADE CANADA
Canadian Representatives Abroad, Supply and Services Canada, Ottawa, December 1994
FOREIGN AFFAIRS AND INTERNATIONAL TRADE CANADA
Diplomatic, Consular, and other representatives in Canada, Supply and Services Canada, Ottawa, December 1994
TIM, Travel Information Manual, TIM Editor, Netherlands, January 1994
WORLD HEALTH ORGANIZATION
"Les carnets" from the CLINIQUE-VOYAGE, Maisonneuve-Rosemont Hospital, Montréal
Various Tourism and Statistics sources

Printed in Canada

Index of countries and destinations

Notes

Notes

Bon Voyage!